P9-DDX-422

HGS

The official motto
of the Province of Ontario
may be translated
"As Ontario Began Loyal,
Loyal She Remains"

LOYAL SHE REMAINS

A pictorial history of Ontario

LOYAL SHE REMAINS

Published by:
The United Empire Loyalists' Association of Canada
38 Prince Arthur Avenue
Toronto, Ontario, Canada M5R 1A9

Canadian Cataloguing in Publication Data
Main entry under title:
Loyal she remains: a pictorial history of Ontario

Includes index.
ISBN 0-9691566-0-X (trade) – ISBN 0-9691566-1-8 (deluxe)

Limited ed. of 500 copies.
Includes index.
ISBN 0-9691566-2-6

1. Ontario – History. I. United Empire Loyalists' Association of Canada.

FC3061.L69 1984 971.3 C84-098608-4
F1058.L69 1984

Printed and bound in Canada

Printer: Southam Murray Printing
Binder: The Bryant Press Ltd.
Typographer: Mono Lino Typesetting Co. Ltd.

DEDICATION

The Honourable William G. Davis
Premier of Ontario

Beginning with the U.E. Loyalists during and immediately following the American Revolution *and* continuing to the present with the arrival of the "boat people" from Viet Nam, Ontario recognizes the immense contribution these diverse exiles of multicultural background have made to the evolutionary growth of this province. Thus it is that this book is dedicated to the tens of thousands of refugees who have fled fratricidal wars and political persecution over a two hundred year period beginning in 1784 and have planted new roots in a new land.

William Davis

STAFF

Staff for *LOYAL SHE REMAINS*

Publication Co-ordinator
William Koene

Co-editors
Mary Beacock Fryer
Charles J. Humber

Picture Editor
Geoffrey R. D. Fryer

Business Biography Writer
George Hancocks

Proofreaders
Eileen Edwards Roberts
E. J. Chard
Kenneth Weir

Production and Design
George Perkins
Norman Melchior
Tony Miggiani
Howard Pain
Randy Davis

Promotion and Sales
Angela Dea Cappelli Clark
R. J. (Reg) Dawe
Terry O'Neil

Direct Mail Co-ordinator
Hugh J. Bartley

Office Administration
Joan I. Aggiss

CONTENTS

CONTRIBUTORS

Co-ordinating Editors
MARY BEACOCK FRYER was born in Brockville, Ontario; M.A. in historical geography, Edinburgh University; author of three chapters in *LOYAL SHE REMAINS*, four recent books on Ontario Loyalists – *Loyalist Spy, Escape, King's Men, Buckskin Pimpernel* – as well as the narratives for two pictorial histories, one on the Thousand Islands, the other on the Rideau Waterway, and part of *The Lives of the Princesses of Wales*.

CHARLES J. HUMBER was born in Montreal; B.A. Temple University, M.A. University of Wisconsin; National President, The United Empire Loyalists' Association of Canada (1982-84); Vice-President, Toronto Postcard Club; antiquarian and noted collector of Upper Canadian furniture and antiques; Vice Chairman, John Graves Simcoe Association; public speaker; author of two chapters in *LOYAL SHE REMAINS*; high school teacher of English with The Toronto Board of Education.

Picture Editor
GEOFFREY R.D. FRYER was born in England and educated there and at the University of Toronto. An architect and town planner, he is a keen amateur photographer, who as well as selecting and arranging many of the illustrations in *LOYAL SHE REMAINS*, contributed some of his own photographs on Ontario landmarks.

Foreword
THE RIGHT HONOURABLE ROLAND MICHENER. P.C. (1962), C.C., C.M.M., C.D., Q.C., M.A., D.C.L., LL.D., U.E., Governor General of Canada, 1967-1974.

Preface
THE HONOURABLE EUGENE A. FORSEY, O.C., PH.D., U.E. Summoned to the Senate of Canada 1970, retired 1979. Author of *The Royal Power of Dissolution of Parliament in the British Commonwealth* and *Trade Unions in Canada 1812-1902*.

The Authors
REV. JOHN F. ALLAN was born in St. Catharines, Ontario; the minister of Trinity Presbyterian Church, York Mills, Toronto; he was educated at the University of Western Ontario and the Presbyterian College, Montreal.

PAUL AXELROD was born in London, Ontario; M.A. University of Toronto; PH.D. York University; Professor of History, York University; author of *Scholars and Dollars: Politics, Economics and the Universities of Ontario, 1945-1980*.

MICHAEL BLISS was born in Kingsville, Ontario; PH.D. University of Toronto; Professor of History, University of Toronto; prolific author among whose recent works are *A Canadian Millionaire: The Life and Business Times of Sir Joseph Flavelle, 1858-1939*, and *The Discovery of Insulin*.

ARTHUR BOUSFIELD was born in Peterborough, Ontario; M.A. in history, Editor of *Monarchy Canada*, and contributor to *The Lives of the Princesses of Wales*.

DEBORAH FORMAN was born in Toronto; M.L.S.; M.A. in history, Concordia University; Librarian, Ontario Legislative Library.

BARBARA FRYER was born in Toronto; B.A. in Spanish and German, McGill University; graduate of the School of Journalism, Carleton University; she has worked for Dundurn Press, Toronto, and is now a technical writer for IBM.

STROME GALLOWAY was born in Saskatchewan and moved to Ontario at age seven. After working as a newspaperman, he served overseas as a lieutenant in 1939; he retired from the armed forces as a full colonel in 1969; Fellow of the Heraldry Society of Canada; author of *A Regiment at War, The General Who Never Was*, a revised edition of *Beddoe's Canadian Heraldry*, and *The White Cross in Canada*.

ELIZABETH HANCOCKS was born in Toronto, A.O.C.A. Ontario College of Art; first Canadian to be certified by the Board of Certification of Genealogists, Washington, D.C.; Dominion Genealogist, U.E.L. Association of Canada; awarded the Queen Elizabeth Silver Medal for work on Loyalist lineages; author of seven books on genealogy.

GEORGE HANCOCKS was born in Hamilton, Ontario; B.A. in philosophy, University of Western Ontario; former editor of *Canadian Homes*; involved in writing, editing and public relations since 1956; editor of *Families*; founder and publisher of the *Canadian Genealogist*.

MICHIEL HORN was born in the Netherlands and came to Canada after World War II with his parents; PH.D. in history, University of Toronto; Chairman of the History Department, Glendon College, York University.

SARA KEITH was born in Texas; as a daughter of a career officer in the United States army, she lived in many countries before deciding on Canada; PH.D. in English, University of London, England; taught English at Acadia and Laurentian Universities.

BRIAN LAND was born in Niagara Falls, Ontario; M.L.S.; M.A. in political science, University of Toronto; Director of Research and Information Services, the Ontario Legislative Library.

LAUREL SEFTON MACDOWELL was born in Hamilton, Ontario; PH.D. University of Toronto; Professor of History at McMaster University; daughter of the late Larry Sefton, Ontario President of the United Steel Workers of America; author of *Remember Kirkland Lake: The Gold Miners' Strike 1941-42*.

ROBERT NIXON, M.P.P. for Brant-Oxford-Norfolk, was born in St. George, Ontario, in the riding he represents; B.SC. McMaster University which also made him an Honorary Doctor of Laws; former head of the science department of North Park Collegiate, Brantford; son of former premier, Harry Nixon, and onetime leader of the Liberal Party in the Ontario Legislature.

JAN NOEL was born in Toronto; M.A. University of Ottawa; presently engaged in PH.D. work, University of Toronto, where her area of study is the Pre-Confederation temperance movement in British North America.

MARGARET PENMAN was born in Toronto; PH.D. in English, University of London, England; former Dean of Women, Victoria University, University of Toronto; Fellow of New College, University of Toronto; has made a study of problems faced by immigrants of many backgrounds; author of a new book on the Toronto Public Library System, 1883-1983.

COLIN READ was born in England, came to Canada as a child with his parents and was educated in Peterborough; PH.D. in history, University of Toronto; author of *The Rising in Western Upper Canada 1837*.

GARRY TOFFOLI was born in Toronto; B.A. in political science, York University; Toronto Chairman of The Monarchist League of Canada, contributor to *The Lives of the Princesses of Wales*.

DONALD BLAKE WEBSTER was born in Rochester, New York; M.A. in history and economics, University of Rhode Island; Curator of the Canadiana Gallery, Royal Ontario Museum; Professor, History of Art, University of Toronto; author of several books, including *English-Canadian Furniture of the Georgian Period, Early Canadian Pottery*, and *Decorated Stoneware Pottery of North America*; organizer of "Georgian Canada: Conflict and Culture (1745-1820)," a 1984 ROM Bicentennial Exhibition.

PATRICK C.T. WHITE was born in British Columbia; PH.D. University of Minnesota; Professor of History, University of Toronto; specialist in Canadian American relations; author of *A Nation on Trial: America and the War of 1812*.

FOREWORD

The Right Honourable Roland Michener, P.C., C.C.
Governor General of Canada (1967-1974)

In this book we now have a well-rounded, illustrated account of how Ontario emerged from a land of native peoples to become the most populous province in the Canadian Confederation, which, in territory and potential, is among the great nations of the world.

The first to come *en masse* to this almost empty land were refugees from the rebellious colonies to the south who came to settle in the Niagara district and the upper St. Lawrence two hundred years ago.

These Loyalists brought with them to future Ontario their inheritance of freedom and order under British institutions, including the British Crown and parliamentary and judicial institutions, for which they had fought, suffered and would not abandon.

Subsequently, the 1791 separate constitution for Upper Canada provided for government in the name of the British constitutional Monarch, an elected legislature, judiciary independence and the rule of law, as Dr. Forsey explains so well in the following page.

Without these same Loyalists and similar folk who came after them, it is doubtful that much of Canada could have resisted the vigorous expansion of the United States.

As a beacon of freedom, these institutions all survive today with some modification. Here we continue a free and successful monarchy, a vivid example of responsible parliamentary government.

Some might think that this history and the bicentennial celebration which it reinforces are significant only to the descendants of the Loyalists of British origin. In my view, that is not the case at all. For one reason they were varied ethnically as are the Canadians of today, comprising many nationalities from Europe, some Black escaping slaves from the Southern colonies, and about 1000 Indians who were loyal allies of the British and settled in the Six Nations Reserves near Brantford and Deseronto. In effect, they began our oft-mentioned mosiac.

The foundation which they laid, although not perfect, does basically support our free, orderly and stable, democratic and law-abiding society, a heritage for all Canadians of today.

The whole story is told and illustrated in this volume by knowledgeable and devoted Canadian authors, brought together under the auspices of The United Empire Loyalists' Association of Canada.

This heirloom should be read with pleasure and interest by all those who live in Ontario and are happy to be Canadians.

Ut Incepit Fidelis Sic Permanet

Roland Michener

PREFACE

The Honourable Eugene A. Forsey
Honorary President, The United Empire Loyalists' Association of Canada

It is fitting that The United Empire Loyalists' Association of Canada should sponsor this history of Ontario. For Ontario owes its creation to the Loyalists. There were, of course, people in what is now Ontario before the Loyalists came, notably the Indians and the French. But they were few and scattered. Without the Loyalists, there would have been no Ontario. There would, indeed, have been no Canada: just a few feeble, sparsely settled colonies which would soon, inevitably, have succumbed to the overwhelming pressure of the United States. It was the fact that our first great wave of post-Conquest immigrants came here with a determination to resist absorption by the United States that gave the English-speaking colonies the will, and all the colonies the strength, to maintain a distinct identity.

The Empire the Loyalists fought for is gone. But the values it stood for are not. They are enshrined in our present Canadian Constitution: "peace, order and good government"; constitutional monarchy ("a Constitution similar in principle to that of the United Kingdom"); freedom by orderly development, as in that "land of just and old renown/Where freedom slowly broadens down/From precedent to precedent"; that land to which we owe our parliamentary institutions and the rule of law.

The Fathers of Confederation were the heirs and beneficiaries of the Loyalists. The Fathers started us on the road to full nationhood. But without the Loyalists there would have been no Fathers even to contemplate that road. The legacy of the Loyalist founders of Ontario, and of those who built on the foundations they laid, is ours. This book, we hope, will give Ontarians of today, young and old, natives and newcomers, of every national origin, every mother tongue, every race, creed and colour, a fuller knowledge, a deeper understanding of their heritage and what it means; a firmer resolve to preserve, develop and enrich it.

Eugene Forsey

PROLOGUE

Charles J. Humber
National President (1982-1984)
The United Empire Loyalists' Association of Canada

In 1982, the government of Ontario invited all Ontarians to celebrate their province's 1984 bicentennial. Less than eighteen months later, a vast majority of Ontario municipalities had responded by forming more than 750 bicentennial committees.

Such enthusiasm assured the 1984 celebration would encourage citizens of Ontario to examine their province's cultural roots as well as their provincial identity. Needless to say, 1984 would generate unprecedented "heritage awareness" throughout the province.

This interest in the significant happenings of 1784 was an affirmation that the Loyalist settlements along the upper St. Lawrence and in the Niagara region were the origins, the very nuclei of future Ontario as we know it today.

By observing the importance of 1784 to Ontario, the government was reinforcing a tradition begun in 1884. At that time, Ontario's Lieutenant Governor, The Honourable John Beverley Robinson, attended ceremonies near Adolphustown at which time citizens of Ontario celebrated their one hundredth birthday. The same year, in Toronto, prominent citizens such as Mayor Boswell, Senator Allan, Rev. Scadding, Chiefs Green and Hill of the Six Nations, W. Kirby, D.B. Read, George T. Denison, William Hamilton Merritt, Secords, Ryersons, and Playters, celebrated the province's centennial in addition to Toronto's semicentennial. Similar festivities took place at Niagara-on-the-Lake. The 1884 centennial jubilee began a tradition, and when Belleville observed the 140th anniversary of the province in 1924, it sustained that tradition by dedicating a memorial to the Loyalists in that city's downtown. Five years later, in Hamilton, another celebration took place when a Vernon March bronze statue was unveiled to honour the 145th anniversary of the arrival of the Loyalists. Five years later, the Canadian government commemorated Ontario's sesquicentennial by issuing a Loyalist stamp, the subject of which was March's Hamilton statue. The Canada Post Corporation maintained this tradition in 1983 when announcing it would recognize Ontario's bicentennial, in 1984, with still another stamp, thereby re-emphasizing the importance of the Loyalists to Ontario.

As a consequence of Ontario's invitation to celebrate 1984, one of the events that Cornwall is commemorating is the 25th anniversary of the opening of the St. Lawrence Seaway; the city of Toronto is currently celebrating its sesquicentennial; the Black community is celebrating 150 years of emancipation throughout the British Empire. Other communities are celebrating their heritage with homecomings, huge barbecues, contests of all sorts, such as a marathon relay run in Prince

United Empire Loyalist Monument in Adolphustown, Ontario, erected in 1884, the 100th anniversary of the arrival of Loyalist refugees to future Ontario. Sketch by Ruth Brooks, 1983.

Monument erected by citizens of Belleville, Ontario in 1924 to honour the 140th anniversary of the arrival of the U.E. Loyalists to future Ontario.

Edward County and Queen Victoria look-alike contests and much more, including visits by Her Majesty The Queen and His Holiness Pope John Paul II.

The United Empire Loyalists' Association, caught up in the spirit of bicentennial celebration, decided to commemorate 1984 by publishing a history of Ontario. Little did it realize that its first major publication venture would grow into such a large, popular history of the province, highly illustrative, the first volume of its kind ever published in Canada. This 696 page volume with over 1000 illustrations not only explores the past 200 years but examines, as well, the land which has been attracting Europeans to it since the 17th century and which at one time was inhabited only by the native peoples.

In the process of publishing *LOYAL SHE REMAINS*, we have truly discovered the great diversity of the province and hope to share our findings during the 1984 bicentennial year of celebration, trusting at the same time that this publication will inspire future generations to re-examine, in a similar manner, the history of the province. Our history, we have unquestionably found, is not prosaic as some would claim. In fact, the opposite is true! This is particularly confirmed when examining the early history of the province, especially the story of the natives before the coming of the Europeans as well as their interrelationship with the Jesuits of the 17th century. Further, the story of the fur traders, the romantic escapades of the explorers, the persistent survival of a French culture in the southwestern part of the province as well as the dramatic influx of over 6,000 exiled war refugees in 1784, following the American Revolution, are all testimony that our early history is an epic story. Not to teach these stories systematically and yearly is a travesty depriving still one more generation of Ontarians from grasping their provincial identity. It is much like going to the theatre only to discover that the curtain doesn't rise until the third act.

As important as are the early critical years of our history, it surely would be incorrect to suggest they supersede in importance the two hundred years of evolutionary growth that the province has experienced since the 1784 influx of Loyalists. Certainly, some periods or historical events over these years have been over-emphasized, still others de-emphasized, even slighted. Nevertheless, the historical panorama of the province, as it comes into clearer focus during the bicentennial period, will, undoubtedly, encourage those who are inclined to explore our history to recognize unequivocally that the Ontario story is a series of heroic episodes interlinked by a common denominator that undeniably claims loyalty to the British parliamentary system, a tradition that has kept us all united and free. *LOYAL SHE REMAINS* commemorates the Ontario story during the 1984 bicentennial year of celebrations.

Charles J. Humber
Co-editor, *LOYAL SHE REMAINS*

As part of the Ontario Bicentennial in 1984, the Ontario Ministry of Transportation and Communication is renaming Highway 33, the highway between Kingston and Trenton. It is to be opened by Queen Elizabeth II and henceforth designated the Loyalist Parkway. *The sign shown here will, at intervals, mark this 90 kilometre thoroughfare.*

This logo, commissioned by the Ontario government for the 1984 bicentennial, has been made evident throughout the province by the more than 750 municipalities that have incorporated it visually on letterheads, posters, banners, flags....

INTRODUCTION

By Mary Beacock Fryer

Ontario means "Shining Waters." Anyone pondering past events must surely regret that this name has not been used in the interest of continuity since the early days, instead of the various name changes.

The French claim brought the southern part of the province under the umbrella of New France. Then, after the Quebec Act of 1774, British administrators regarded the wilderness west of the French seigneuries as "beyond the pale." Under the Quebec Act, Ontario was part of the vast, unorganized territory that was reserved for the native peoples, where, except for French farmers already settled around Windsor, white settlement was prohibited.

The year 1984 was chosen for the Ontario Bicentennial because 1784 was a watershed – the year when an important change in British policy on interior lands was implemented. In the autumn of 1783, the British government permitted the governor of Quebec, General Frederick Haldimand, to open the western lands to white settlers, to accommodate displaced American Loyalists who had come seeking his protection. As a result, in 1784, over 6,000 Loyalists were resettled in Ontario.

The Loyalists had an importance out of all proportion to their numbers, even after later arrivals brought their numbers to about 10,000. Without them and their appeals to be freed from the provisions of the Quebec Act, there never would have been a province of Ontario. To satisfy the Loyalists, Quebec was partitioned in 1791 to form two new British provinces – Upper and Lower Canada.

Without the Constitutional Act of 1791, Ontario would have remained unorganized Indian territory – a kind of vacuum irresistible to Americans from the south. By the 1790s, land-hungry Americans were flocking north, but, unlike their earlier migrations into Kentucky and Ohio, they could not make the rules. They came, not to Indian land, but to a British province with an established government and a set of laws. By opening the western lands in 1784, Britain took the first step towards giving Canada an east-west axis, opposing what has been called the natural north-south grain of the continent.

Without the resettlement of the Loyalists, and the British province that followed, the fine agricultural lands of Southern Ontario would have been overrun by Americans. Once enough of them had arrived, their appeals to the Congress would have led to annexation, a process that already had precedents. Furthermore, under similar circumstances, Canada averted annexation in 1870 with the establishment of Manitoba. At that time, the half million residents of Minnesota were arguing that the Precambrian Shield was a natural

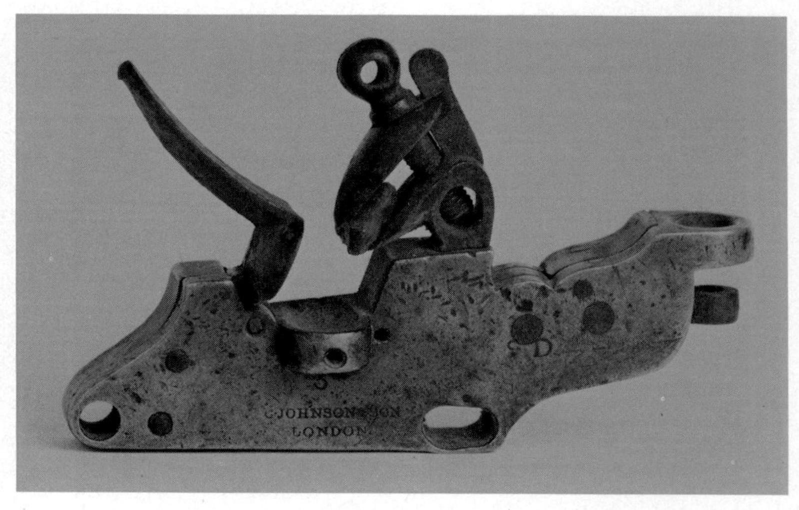

This flintlock was used on a small cannon by Nicolas Emigh (Amey) at The Battle of Saratoga, Oct. 17, 1777. As a Loyalist refugee, this Ensign settled near Millhaven in Ernestown Township, Lennox and Addington County, June 1784, bringing with him a rare Loyalist artifact from The American Revolutionary war period.

western boundary for Canada. By about 1800, the same rationalization might have decreed that the Ottawa River was Canada's natural western limit.

In the 1790s, Britain was in no position to worry over American expansionism. She was embroiled in a twenty-year struggle with France and not able to expend many troops to save Southern Ontario from an American take-over. Nor until after the War of 1812 did the mother country place much value on central Canada. Her vital interests – the fur trade and naval supremacy – were served through Hudson Bay and Halifax. A more positive policy towards Upper Canada did not emerge until after the defeat of Napoleon, when an economic depression swept Britain. By 1816 Upper Canada had become an asset, a haven for people facing a bleak future in the mother country.

Over the next few decades, thousands of immigrants from the British Isles flowed into the province. The original Loyalist stock was heavily diluted by people of British birth. With the change in ethnic composition grew the notion that the Loyalists, who had stood up for the Empire, were also people exclusively of British origin. Yet the Bibles of families with names like Miller, Ball, Meyers and Dafoe were in German.

In 1841, as the dust was settling after the rebellions, Upper and Lower Canada were united as Canada West and Canada East – names that never caught on. Upper Canadians continued to call their half Upper Canada, a name still preserved in the province's law society and its oldest independent school.

Ontario, the name settled on at Confederation, caught on but only gradually. By contrast, a francophone resident of Quebec tends to be first a Quebecker and second a Canadian. The opposite applies to Ontario where anglophones are more likely to say they are Canadians and to identify with the national scene. This lack of provincial feeling may be a consequence of Ontario's position in the provincial hierarchy, based on innate wealth – the legacy of good agricultural land in the South and natural resources in the North. Inevitably a financial heartland grew in Ontario that soon dominated the entire country. Bay Street, with the Toronto Stock Exchange, came to symbolize Ontario's strong position.

The Ontario preoccupation with the country as a whole may have impeded the evolution of a provincial identity. Upper Canadians did have a distinct sense of identity, but later, rather than switch to a new provincial awareness, they appeared content to drop the "Upper."

Yet one pervading theme threads through the Ontario story – loyalty – from the founders to the Ontario motto, which in essence means "Loyal she began, loyal she remains." Some devil's advocates may say loyal, but to what? Do they overlook the protests that greet suggestions that the Crown is outmoded? Would the Ontario government have retained the Union Jack on the provincial flag, after it ceased to be on the national flag, if the people that government represents wanted to cut ties with the past?

Mary Beacock Fryer

Mary Beacock Fryer
Co-editor, *LOYAL SHE REMAINS*

Fenian Raid Medal, Reverse. This Canada General Service Medal was presented to Mary Beacock Fryer's grandfather in 1897. The rim is inscribed, Pte. T.E. Seaman, 1st Company, Brockville Rifles.

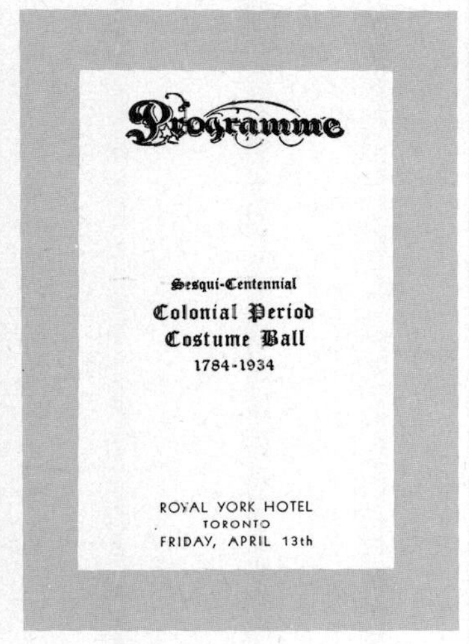

Loyalist descendants celebrated the provincial sesquicentennial in 1934.

BEGIN

NINGS

CHAPTER 1

THE LAND

by John Warkentin

Ontario is vast. Its northern coast reaches a higher latitude than the southern tip of the Alaskan Panhandle and is inhabited by polar bears and walrus. Its southern extremity is in the same latitude as northern California and Rome. From east to west it reaches from the longitude of New York to that of Kansas City, or almost half way across the United States. Ontario is a very big land indeed.

J. TUZO WILSON C.C.

Ontario comprises over one tenth of the total area of Canada. From Toronto to Kenora is farther than from Toronto to Halifax. Yet it is difficult to comprehend the great size of the province because it is not neatly laid out in one compact block. The great jutting peninsulas and linked arcs of the lake shores and rivers along the southern boundary and the immense sweeping curves of the sea coasts of Hudson and James Bays far to the north have produced a complicated configuration. Complex though Ontario may be in its boundaries, and over 400,000 sq. miles (1,036,000 km^2) in size, it is relatively low in elevation compared to other parts of Canada. The highest point in Ontario, to the west of Lake Temiskaming, 2,275 feet (694 m) above sea level, is so inconspicuous that it was found only a few years ago. Occasionally the surface of the province rises gradually into broad plateaus and domes and may even drop sharply in escarpments from these heights, but the higher areas tend to range only from 1,500 feet (457 m) to 2,000 feet (610 m) in elevation.

Low though Ontario may be compared to the Appalachians and the Western Cordilleran Mountains, or even the High Plains of Alberta, it does not lack for variety in land and water. Contrasts in bedrock, differences produced by glaciation, and the presence of many lakes result in a number of distinctive natural regions in Ontario. In looking at them we will start with the Great Lakes and move northward.

Ontarians are not a maritime folk. That does not diminish the tremendous importance of the Great Lakes in affecting the growth and present life of the province. In the 18th and 19th centuries, Lake Ontario and the St. Lawrence River comprised the "front" of Ontarian settlement, particularly for the Loyalists. Later, towns developed on their shores. Today, the lakes are vital as industrial sites, for supplying water to our cities, and in conveying bulk commodities cheaply. And every lake-side city and town is working hard to reclaim its waterfront from industrial activities and thus enrich the lives of its citizens.

The agricultural wealth of Ontario is concentrated in the peninsulas between Lakes Huron and Erie and Ontario and in the "mesopotamia" between the Ottawa and St. Lawrence rivers in extreme eastern Ontar-

Right: *Orientation Map. Ontario's major land types are delimited on this map of the province. The most habitable areas, with the prime agricultural land, are in the Great Lakes-St. Lawrence Lowland.*
Left: *Layered Rocks. In Ontario, igneous rocks, mainly granites, are the oldest and hardest of rock formations. Younger formations, created by the cementing of sediments under ancient seas, are known as sedimentary rocks — sandstone, limestone and shale. These are identified by their horizontal layers, as shown along the Niagara Escarpment on the Bruce Peninsula.*

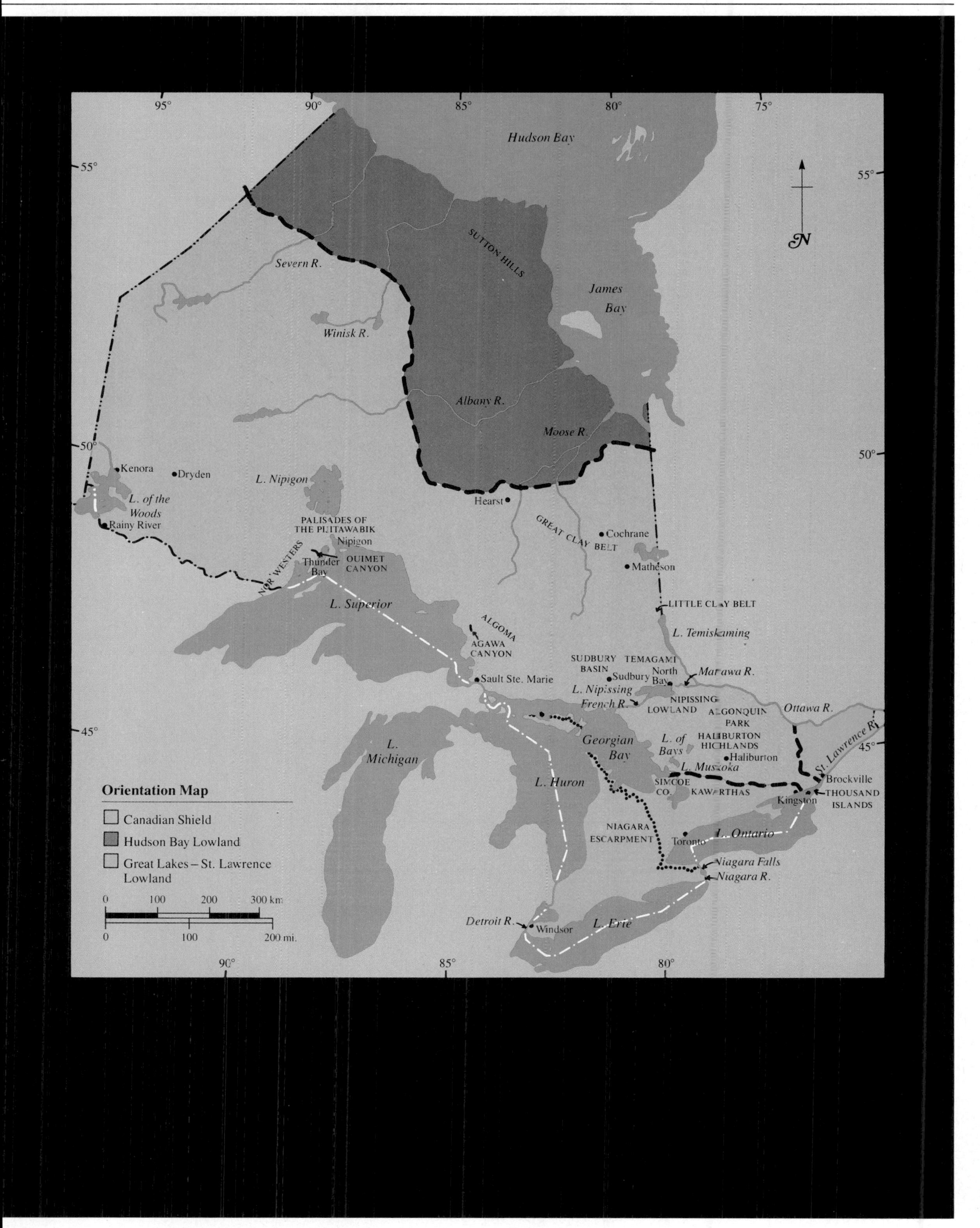

Hudson Bay
James Bay
Severn R.
Winisk R.
Albany R.
Moose R.
SUTTON HILLS
Kenora
Dryden
L. Nipigon
L. of the Woods
Rainy River
Hearst
GREAT CLAY BELT
Cochrane
Matheson
PALISADES OF THE PUITAWABIK
Nipigon
Thunder Bay
OUIMET CANYON
NOR'WESTERS
L. Superior
LITTLE CLAY BELT
L. Temiskaming
ALGOMA
AGAWA CANYON
SUDBURY BASIN
Sudbury
TEMAGAMI
North Bay
Mattawa R.
Sault Ste. Marie
L. Nipissing
French R.
NIPISSING LOWLAND
ALGONQUIN PARK
Ottawa R.
L. Michigan
Georgian Bay
L. of Bays
HALIBURTON HIGHLANDS
Haliburton
St. Lawrence R.
L. Muskoka
L. Huron
SIMCOE CO.
KAWARTHAS
Brockville
Kingston
THOUSAND ISLANDS
NIAGARA ESCARPMENT
Toronto
L. Ontario
Niagara Falls
Niagara R.
Detroit R.
Windsor
L. Erie
Orientation Map
Canadian Shield
Hudson Bay Lowland
Great Lakes – St. Lawrence Lowland
0 100 200 300 km
0 100 200 mi.

io. This region, called the Great Lakes-St. Lawrence Lowland, consists of layers of limestone, sandstone and shale which overlap the igneous and metamorphic rocks of the Canadian Shield, the ancient nucleus of the North American continent. From Kingston to Brockville, a rib of the Shield, of which the Thousand Islands is a part, rises through the sedimentary rocks cutting off the eastern part of the lowland from the western. The latter much larger section is divided into two levels by the Niagara Escarpment, a steep wall of rock notched by many spectacular valleys including the Niagara Gorge. West of the Escarpment, a plateau surface up to 1,790 feet (546 m) above sea level, slopes gently downward to Lake Erie, 1,200 feet (366 m) lower in elevation. Level or gently inclined surfaces characterize the sedimentary beds which underlie the Great Lakes-St. Lawrence Lowland, but a thick mantle of glacial deposits masks much of the bedrock, producing undulating plains, smooth flowing hills, and rough stony ridges. In places the mantle and soil is thin, for example on the limestone plains near Kingston, which caused great difficulty for Loyalist settlers in the 1780s. By and large, however, the glaciers provided a fine parent material in the lowland soil which is rich and has become the most productive agricultural land in Canada.

Two thirds of Ontario is Canadian Shield, rocks four and five times as old as the sedimentary beds which overlap its margins. The Shield has been subjected to many geological evolutions. Here are granites solidified from molten intrusions, gneisses contorted by heat and pressure, ancient lava flows, and numerous formations containing metals. Igneous and metamorphic rocks tend to be resistant to erosion. Here is none of the evenness of surface of the sedimentary lowland; rock knobs, low hills and broken cliffs are characteristic, and deep valleys and even canyons are found where rock was fractured and erosion thus made easier. Extensive uplands and plateaus, contrasting with lower areas, make it possible to identify major sub-regions.

From an arc extending from Georgian Bay, through the Kawarthas to the Ottawa River, the surface rises to a broad dome reaching 1,925 feet (585 m) in Algonquin Park, and then drops towards Lake Nipiss-

Left: *A Group of Seven Vision of Algoma.* The Solemn Land *reflects the striking beauty of the Algoma landscape in Northern Ontario and the genius of J.E.H. MacDonald. He produced, in the words of G. Blair Laing, "the most elegant work of any Canadian painter."*
Right below: *Farm Land Near Uxbridge. The gently rolling landscape shown in this aerial oblique is typical of the land which makes Ontario the most productive agricultural province in Canada.*

Left: *Niagara Falls in Winter. Most visitors see the falls in summer but they are hauntingly spectacular when the waters of Lake Erie, that feed great hydro-electric generators, flow between borders of glistening ice. Father Louis Hennepin, thought to be the first European to view the falls, marvelled at the sight, but to early travellers they were a barrier that required wearisome portages.*
Right top: *Northern Ontario Portage. The French River, with its swift rapids and difficult portages was a challenge to such explorers as Brûlé, Champlain, La Vérendrye, Mackenzie and Thompson, as well as the North West Company fur traders whose persevering paddles were either aimed at Fort William or Montreal.*
Right below: *Sketch on Birch Bark, 1792 by Mrs. Simcoe. When passing through the Thousand Islands, Elizabeth Simcoe recorded in her diary "these innumerable isles have a pretty appearance."*

ing. Patches of glacial sands, gravels, and clays occur, but there is not nearly the continuous mantle of glacial deposits that overlies the Great Lakes-St. Lawrence Lowland. Glaciation completely disrupted the pre-existing river system and produced numerous basins in the scoured bed-rock now occupied by lakes with intricate inlets and islands. In the late 19th century, the rugged higher areas north of Haliburton became known as the Haliburton Highlands, or the Highlands of Ontario.

The Nipissing Lowland, a gap in the Shield occupied by the Mattawa River, Lake Nipissing, and the French River, permits easy access by canoe between the Ottawa River and Georgian Bay. Scattered pockets of clay and sand are found from Mattawa to the Sudbury Basin and then along the north shore of Lake Huron to Sault Ste. Marie and they make farming possible over a long narrow east-west belt.

Northward, the land rises again as a barrier wall all the way from the Ottawa River to Sault Ste. Marie, and this wall continues all along the north shore of Lake Superior, where it springs sharply out of the water, to and beyond Thunder Bay. This is the southward-facing front of a gigantic plateau area, 1,800 feet (550 m) to 2,000 feet (610 m) in elevation, which slopes consistently downward over a distance of about 400 miles (650 km) to sea level at Hudson Bay. Regional names, some widely known and others less familiar, are given to different parts of the plateau: Temagami, Algoma, the Palisades of the Pijitawabik, and the Nor' Westers are examples. Deep valleys were eroded in the plateau surface, forming spectacular chasms such as Agawa and Ouimet Canyons. Along the north shore of Lake Superior is the most spectacular scenery in Ontario, especially in the stretch from Nipigon to the U.S. border. South of Thunder Bay, for example, resistant igneous cap rocks have protected the flat-topped mountains called the Nor' Westers, from erosion.

On the Ontario-Quebec border, the southern wall of the plateau is broken by valleys in zones where the bedrock is weakened by joints called faults, along which blocks of land have moved downwards forming long linear valleys and wide basins. The Upper Ottawa River and Lake Temiskaming occupy such depressions. Clays were laid down in a form-

Left top: **North Shore, Georgian Bay.** *The smooth granite, left by glaciation, combines with its sparse tree cover and abundant lakes to create the familiar Northern Ontario landscape. The Group of Seven painters communicated their fresh vision of this land to an appreciative public.*

Far left below: *The Bancroft Area. Bancroft lies in the northern part of Hastings County. Its surrounding region provides lakes for recreation and a rich harvest of lumber. It is also noted for a wide variety of minerals which include uranium, gold, gemstones and, at Madoc, seventy kilometres south of Bancroft, talc.*

Left below: *Ouimet Canyon. Situated sixty-five kilometres northeast of Thunder Bay, this canyon is three kilometres long. It is about 150 metres wide and over 120 metres deep.*

Right below: *Sand Dunes, Prince Edward County. The southwest shores of Prince Edward County boast extensive sand dunes up to twenty-five metres in height, which form barriers separating East and West Lakes from Lake Ontario. There are three provincial parks on the dunes, Sand Banks, Outlet Beach and North Beach.*

er glacial lake in the basin north of Lake Temiskaming, and this area is now known as the Little Clay Belt.

Glacial deposits mantle much of the surface of the plateau. North of Temagami, Algoma, and Lake Superior, these deposits include great belts of sand, gravel and clay. North of Matheson, reaching beyond Cochrane and far into Quebec on the east and to Hearst on the west, are the extensive deposits of clay and silt called the Great Clay Belt. Outcrops of bedrock occasionally rise above the surface, or are seen in river beds, but the dominant surface is a generally flat plain, far removed from the common conception of the Shield as a rough, rocky, rugged land. Drainage is so poor that muskeg and peat are common.

Overlapping the Shield to the north, and continuing the gentle downward slope all the way to the sea, is another zone of younger sedimentary rocks, the Hudson Bay Lowland, similar in geology to the Great Lakes-St. Lawrence Lowland. It is a much larger lowland, comprising over a quarter of Ontario, but it does not have sharp linear ridges such as the Niagara Escarpment. However, the igneous and metamorphic rocks of the Shield do poke through the sedimentary rock in one small area to form the Sutton Hills. The great weight of the continental ice sheets so depressed the land that much of this northern lowland was covered by the ocean after the glaciers melted. The land rebounded gradually once the great glacial load was gone and it is still rising, but it remains very poorly drained and comprises what probably is the largest muskeg in the world. Only the St. Lawrence and Ottawa Rivers in Ontario can compare with the great northern rivers, the Severn, Winisk, Albany, Moose and others, which cross the lowland carrying water from the plateau to the sea. Along these streams the drainage is better, and belts of trees trace the river courses. The Hudson Bay shore is no scenic match for the coast of Lake Superior. On this gentle slope even the exact location of the shoreline is difficult to establish, since between high and low tide the water line moves back and forth over a long distance, though the vertical tidal movement averages only seven feet.

The land surfaces just described could hardly be seen by early European travellers because great, dense forests covered almost all of pre-

sent-day Ontario. In the deciduous and mixed forest areas of the southern lowland the few small, brightly sunlit grass and scrub openings in sandy areas, vividly impressed visitors because they were so exceptional. Other forest openings were produced by Huron Indians while clearing small patches for agricultural use in present Simcoe County. Farther north boreal forests dominated, and in the Shield, cliff faces were largely bare though trees did manage to anchor themselves in the merest crevices. It was the wetlands, the swamps and muskegs, which produced the largest gaps in the tree cover, and completely dominated the landscape in the Hudson Bay Lowland. The cool immediate shores of the Bay were tundra, the vegetation of the Arctic.

The broad transition from mainly deciduous, to mixed, and finally to boreal trees, is a reflection of the climatic differences found in a province which extends from 41°41′ N to 56°51′ N, a distance of over 1,000 miles. Precipitation is adequate for agriculture in all parts of Ontario, but not until agricultural settlers, over the course of several generations, had moved into various parts of the province, including the northern clay belts, were the full extremes of climate associated with different latitudes, the niceties of the varying lengths of the frost-free and growing seasons, and the differences introduced by lake shores and higher elevations, fully appreciated.

Experience often showed that errors had been made in the initial evaluation of soil and climate. Yet some early guesses and generalizations on resources did correspond roughly to what we know today. Robert Gourlay, that gadfly to the provincial establishment, was just as audacious in his resource appraisals as in his social criticisms. On a map included in his famous *Statistical Account of Upper Canada* (probably based on a little knowledge and much inspired guesswork) he divided North America into agricultural zones which reveal a bias against the warmer parts of the United States, but also represent a remarkably prescient classification of the resource zones of Ontario as they were to develop. Gourlay left Upper Canada in 1818, and published his *Statistical Account* in 1822. In identifying the best agricultural land, he produced what was, in effect, the first resource map of the province.

Right: *Georgian Bay Landscape. A contemporary etching in aquatint by Ed Bartram,* Spring Sans Souci, *hand-painted in an edition of thirty-five in 1978, captures the essence of Georgian Bay's rugged beauty — water, sky and the Pre-Cambrian Shield.*
Left below: *The Great Elm on the Guild Estate. Destroyed by lightning in the early 1940s, this elm was said to be the tallest tree east of the Rockies. The landmark, which stood sixty metres high on the Scarborough Bluffs, was a veteran of 125 years when Jacques Cartier explored the St. Lawrence River, and was approximately 430 years old when John Graves Simcoe first came to Toronto Harbour in 1793.*

7/35
Spring Sans Souci
Northern Image Series
Bartram /78

Left top: ***Kakabeka Falls.*** *Thirty kilometres west of Thunder Bay the Kaministikwia River tumbles thirty-three metres down the Kakabeka Falls. Its 100-metre width is about one third that of the American Falls at Niagara, but the height is two thirds. The brown colour of the water indicates a high iron content. Fur traders portaged around the falls, going from and to Fort William.*

Far left below: *Autumn Colours. This familiar autumn woodland scene was photographed on the Niagara Peninsula.*

Left below: *Mushrooms. Many species of mushrooms may be found growing wild in Ontario woodlands and collected by those who know which species are edible.*

Right below: *Gourlay's Map. Robert Gourlay, the Scottish "gadfly of the provincial establishment" in the early 1800s, prepared the first resource map of Eastern North America. In showing Southern Ontario as the best land for agriculture, Gourlay was astonishingly astute. His anti-American prejudice surfaced when he decided that a belt of land west of Washington was "Bad."*

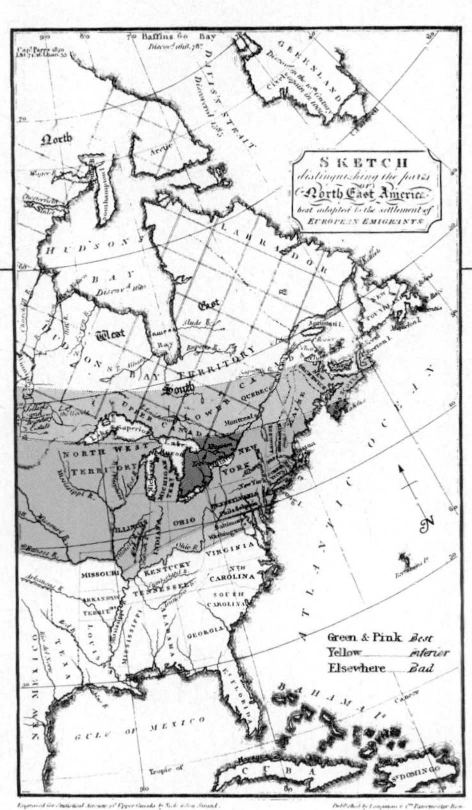

Responses to a new land are coloured by the attitudes to nature, scenery and wilderness to which an observer has been conditioned in his or her homeland. Perceptions will also be affected by whether the person is searching for resources and evaluating the possibilities for permanent agricultural settlement or exploring for purely scientific purposes. Often, of course, these objectives are combined in any single individual.

The earliest written records of both Southern and Northern Ontario date from the first third of the 17th century. Already in 1615, Champlain reported that the "ill-favoured" country of the Canadian Shield between the Ottawa River and Lake Huron was not suited for agriculture, while present-day Simcoe County, a part of the southern lowland where Hurons cultivated the land, was "of pleasing character." Sixteen years later, while exploring Hudson Bay, Thomas James referred to the desolate southwestern shore in present Ontario as "a most shallow and perilous coast" and to an island in James Bay as "utterly barren of all Goodness."

Great natural features stir human emotions and Louis Hennepin, one of the first Europeans to see Niagara Falls, in 1678, expressed feelings which have been repeated countless times. He wished that someone had been with them "who could have descry'd the Wonders of this prodigious frightful Fall, so as to give the Reader a just and natural Idea of it," and he described it as "the most Beautiful, and at the same time most frightful Cascade in the World." By contrast, most of Ontario was regarded as a gloomy land under its dark canopy of trees, and as a forbidding wilderness. Farming was to change that view of the Great Lakes-St. Lawrence Lowland, and after a time even the wilderness of the Shield became looked upon as attractive.

Agricultural colonization by Europeans in the southern Lowland was begun near present day Windsor by the French in the mid-18th century, followed a generation later by the Loyalists in their settlements on the St. Lawrence River, in the area near Kingston, including Prince Edward County, and in the Niagara Peninsula. Most travellers in the early 19th century thought this region flat and uninteresting and depressingly monotonous. Such negative reactions partly stemmed from the overwhelming forests which obscured the land so much that even such a prominent landform as the Niagara Escarpment was not identified as a continuous feature along its entire length for many decades.

During the first half of the 19th century, through heartbreaking toil by farmers, this overwhelming forest was destroyed and cleared. This process was looked at with horror by a few observers, with grim satisfaction by most inhabitants. A new landscape of fields, farmsteads, roads and fences gradually took shape. Visitors from Great Britain, looking for the familiar gentle contours of home, recoiled when they saw this raw stump-filled land, and were particularly aghast at the log fences which in their eyes disfigured the land. They rarely found the planted flowers and shrubs they longed to see, but they soon reported a satisfying substitute in the farm orchards. These added a much needed graciousness to individual farmsteads and the remnants of these old orchards are still occasionally visible today.

By the 1850s a mature and fairly attractive landscape was in place in the longer-settled areas along the Detroit and Niagara Rivers and on the Lake Ontario front, and elsewhere in the lowland, settlement was well under way. Over the next 40 years, farming generally prospered and much of the rural Ontario landscape we see today was created. Rather open farmsteads, with commodious barns and a few planted trees emerged. Sometimes these were formal layouts, but nothing like the severe rectangular order which appeared on the western prairie was imposed on the land. In contrast to the adjacent United States, where wooden homes were typical, in Ontario, brick and native stone, and even fieldstone were frequently used in building farm homes.

Soil erosion was a danger on steeper slopes no longer protected by tree cover and on sandy tracts when grain was grown year after year, so that after only a few decades of farming a damaged land was visible in such areas of hazard. On the whole, however, a pleasant, comfortable, serene landscape of substantial farms was created in the 19th century after several generations of settlement, very attractive in its own right, even though little was said in its praise in taciturn Ontario.

Today, Southern Ontario is recognized as one of the best farming

Right: *Bird's Foot Clover North of Kingston. This field was probably cleared of trees by an early settler. However, patches of natural meadowland bright with wild flowers — gaps in the impenetrable forests — delighted the pioneers.*

Left below: *Relief Map. This map shows the main areas that lie above 300 metres approximately. The extent of the territory below that level indicates that much of Ontario is lowland.*

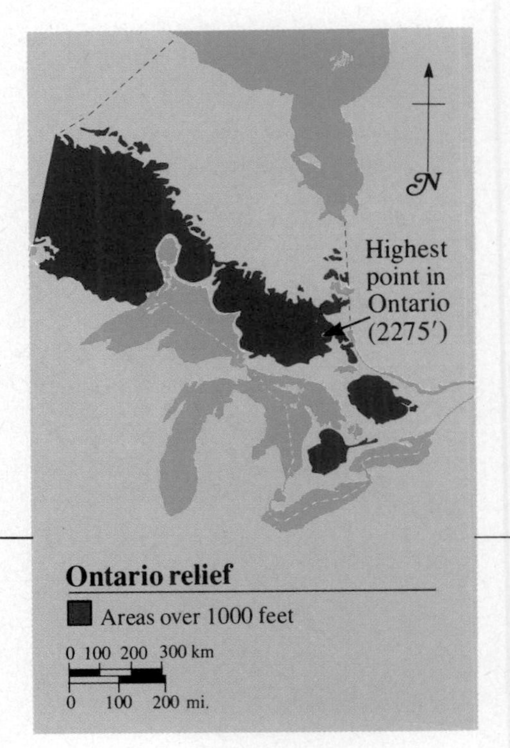

areas in Canada, with over one half of what is rated as the country's highest quality agricultural land by the Canada Land Inventory. Average temperatures are sufficiently high in the summer and the growing season long enough that highly productive field crops, such as corn (which requires much heat and a long time to mature), can be grown. In special areas close to the lakes, fruit is spared from early and late frosts and specialized fruit growing belts have emerged since the late 19th century.

One of the great shifts in response to the Ontario landscape occurred in the 19th century and involved the Shield. Until the 1850s it was viewed as a dangerous, frightening area, sterile, desolate and a truly appalling land much as mountain areas were regarded in Europe. Such reactions confirmed the impressions of Champlain. However, resource development began in the early 19th century, as the southern Shield became a great timber producing area. Lumbermen moved northward in a great pincers movement, up the Ottawa River and along Georgian Bay, and later along the north shore of Lake Huron, always following rivers into higher country. The destruction of trees for timber was augmented by destruction from fire. Though lumbermen in their strenuous activities might give but little attention to scenery, others began to do so.

In the 1850s and 60s a revolutionary change in attitude to the face of the Shield took place, a change from abhorrence to appreciation. Ontario's population stood at just over one million, with a small but increasing urban component. New railroads in the 1870s made the southern margins of the Shield accessible to sportsmen from the towns. The lakes with beaches and shore cliffs backed by high rock knobs, and the numerous rivers with picturesque rapids were quickly adopted as a delightful recreational land for hunters, anglers, canoeists and campers. It became a playground, a tamed wilderness. Tourist brochures were produced, tourist camps and lodges established. A new landscape had been discovered and names such as Muskoka and Lake of Bays became famous. In the 1880s a few far-sighted persons saw a need for preserving the forest for timber, and the woods, lakes and rivers for recreational purposes, and by 1893 Algonquin Park was established by the provin-

Left: *Ploughed Field, Leslie Street. Metropolitan Toronto's Leslie Street extends north into the Towns of Markham and Richmond Hill, where many farmers of German origin have cultivated the land for several generations.*
Far left below: *Rail Fence. The clearing of the farm lands of Southern Ontario provided the settlers with large quantities of cedar timber, which could be employed to enclose fields in numerous ways, such as this zig-zag "snake" fence.*
Left below: *Root or Stump Fence. When the forest trees had been cut down, there remained the backbreaking job of clearing the stumps and roots from the land. These materials were then pressed into service for fencing and were effective for containing livestock.*

cial government. A decade later when the Temiskaming and Northern Ontario Railroad reached Temagami, that region became a highly publicized vacation ground, and the process was later repeated in the Algoma, Thunder Bay and Lake of the Woods areas.

The scanty mantle of glacial deposits which covers much of the Shield proved a tempting resource both to governments anxious to encourage further agricultural expansion and would-be farmers seeking land. In the 1850s colonization roads were driven into the Huron-Ottawa tract, the area between Lake Huron and the Ottawa River, and farmers followed. When the CPR main line was built in the 1880s, farmers took up land in the small clay pockets adjacent to the line at North Bay and Sudbury, and even went up to the Ottawa River to the clay plains north of Lake Temiskaming. The T. and N.O. reached the latter outpost of farming in 1904, and then carried northward to reach the clay deposits about Cochrane in 1908. Farmers flowed into both areas, soon widely known respectively as the Little and Great Clay Belts. To the west, patches of farm land were occupied near the north shore of Lake Huron, at Thunder Bay, Rainy River, and Dryden. Farming has not been easy in this northern country, which became known as New Ontario. Growing seasons are shorter than in Southern Ontario restricting the range of crops which can be grown, crops are in danger of being damaged by frost, and soils are less fertile. On sandy patches virtual deserts were created by farmers, and there has been a gradual abandonment of farms in the Huron-Ottawa tract, an area called "the Unheroic North" by Merrill Denison because of the harsh, debilitating economic and social conditions for farming. However, on well drained clay soils in the Little Clay Belt, at Rainy River, and parts of the Great Clay Belt, agriculture prospered. Indians continue to live in the Shield, often on remote reservations, and mining and pulp and paper enterprises are extremely important nodes of economic activity and settlement in specific localities.

Besides being the scene of a wide range of human activities, the Ontario part of the Canadian Shield entered the Canadian imagination in a special and powerful way in the 20th century. It was the Group of

Right top: *A Leeds County Farmstead in 1850. By the middle of the 19th century, farms in areas settled the earliest had begun to "wear a neat appearance." Rotting stumps and cabins had given way to tidy, fenced fields, houses often of stone, and substantial farm buildings.*
Right below: *Logs on Lake Nipissing. Logs floating along Ontario's waterways were once a familiar sight. Now, such scenes are to be found mainly in Northwestern Ontario. Most accessible areas have been logged out. Elsewhere, logs are moved by road.*
Far right below: *Typical Stone Mill. Ontario is blessed with waterfalls, invaluable as millsites for the pioneers and throughout the 19th century. The first mills produced sawn lumber and flour. Later, they became more specialized. Many Scottish stone masons came to Ontario to work on the Rideau Canal. Afterwards, they built fine stone structures, including mills, which are scattered all over Southern Ontario. Some are in ruins, but a few have been restored.*
Left below: *Grapes in Vineyard, Niagara Peninsula. The Niagara fruit belt is the best fruit-growing land in North America. Lying between the south shore of Lake Ontario and the escarpment, it has a near-perfect blend of soil and climate for peaches, cherries and other fruit crops. From grapes come excellent local wines.*

Seven painters who taught Canadians how to perceive this land. They stressed those lineaments which showed the fundamental physical form of a particular district, contrasted the basic elements of water, rock and trees to show the inherent force and tension in the landscape, and used vivid impressionistic colours. This revealed and displayed the essential Shield in such a straightforward, powerful, appealing way that this wilderness became a symbolic national landscape. A much larger public can now afford to travel and vacation in the Shield than in the 1920s, and richer, more complex attitudes to the natural environment prevail today. These include a broader concern for conservation and a deeper wilderness ethic for which the earlier artists' responses provided both a foundation, and vital stimulation.

North of the Shield, the remote Hudson Bay Lowland lies waterlogged in its great muskegs, crossed by a few wide placid master streams, with only a few sparse settlements. With its severe winters and poor drainage, the vast Lowland, this difficult-to-spoil wilderness whose northern limit is the treeline, it is likely to remain the realm of the trapper and the preserve of wildlife. To south and north lie landscapes that have appealed to the imagination of the public – the rugged Shield and the treeless Arctic. The beloved Canadian poet, E.J. Pratt, saw the Shield as a "sleeping giant." His symbolism could also be used to portray the boundless Lowland. The spirit of this land is becoming better known through the books of the naturalist and novelist Fred Bodsworth, but it remains an unknown and uninterpreted land to most Ontarians.

Modern Attitudes to the Land

Contrasting ways of making a living characterize resource development in Southern and Northern Ontario. In the South, highly specialized farm regions have developed in the midst of general mixed farming. In the North the multiple uses to which land can be put often conflict, and there is competition amongst Indians, mining companies, forest industries, farmers, and recreational users. In the South much land was being ruined by farmers after a few generations on the land, but fundamental improvements have resulted from reforestation beginning in the

Left: *Road Near Mount St. Patrick. To open up the interior, the government financed colonization roads which reduced the people's dependence on waterways. This road facilitated the settlement of Renfrew County.*
Far left below: *Hunting Party, Rosseau Lake, Muskoka. Late in the 19th century, Southern Ontarians began visiting the Canadian Shield. The first were hunters and fishermen. While deer are a renewable resource, the numbers taken soon alarmed conservationists, who cautioned others to worry over the ability of the land to replenish its natural resources.*
Left below: *Bigwin Inn, Lake of Bays, Muskoka. This 1929 view, taken from the Bigwin tower, shows a typical Shield landscape of lake and woods towards the close of the passenger steamboat era.*
Right below: *Louis Hémon Tablet, Chapleau. The grave of the author of the novel* Maria Chapdelaine *is at Chapleau, on the Clay Belt. Hémon wrote of a family on the Quebec part of the Clay Belt, but much of what he said about the hard life applied equally to Ontario.*

1920s, from the water control efforts of the Conservation Authorities after 1940, and from education campaigns for more careful farming. In the North there was a need for forest protection, both from fire and short-sighted exploiters, and in the late 1920s, Grey Owl was calling for a change in attitude towards our resources, pleading strongly for conservation. But conservation problems remain in all parts of the province, heightened by the serious environmental hazards and pollution created by modern industrial technology, which range from the problem of storing harmful solid and liquid wastes to the degradation produced by acid rain.

Today, government institutions, private organizations, and individuals work to promote a sense of stewardship for the land. It is recognized that the land has great aesthetic and emotional value, which, besides providing man with essential food and material requirements, fulfills other human needs as well. Paradoxically, in most Ontarians there is a deeper appreciation for the distant North (the terrain of the Shield) than for the rural landscapes of the South, apart from the Niagara Escarpment and its associated features. This is where the voice and hand of the artist is essential; to portray, to interpret and to help us understand the special qualities of all parts of Ontario.

Right: *Reforestation by Machine. The regeneration of Ontario's forests is essential for the lumber and pulp and paper industries, to maintain their importance in the economy. Planting seedlings by machine is the newest method.*

Left below: *Original Stand of White Pine, Algonquin Park. The beautiful eastern white pine* (Pinus Strobus) *with its soft needles is native to most of Ontario south of the 50th parallel. Specimens like those shown are now rare. They could reach heights of fifty-five metres with trunk diameters of one and one-half metres, although many of half these dimensions were harvested. White pines made the best masts for the Royal Navy, and were also cut for the square-timber trade, because the trunks were so straight.*

CHAPTER 2

NATIVE PEOPLES IN THE YEAR 1600

by Robert Nixon

They but forget we Indians owned the land
From ocean unto ocean; that they stand
Upon a soil that centuries agone
Was our sole kingdom and our right alone.
from "A Cry From An Indian Wife"

FROM "A CRY FROM AN INDIAN WIFE"
PAULINE JOHNSON (TEKAHIONWAKE)

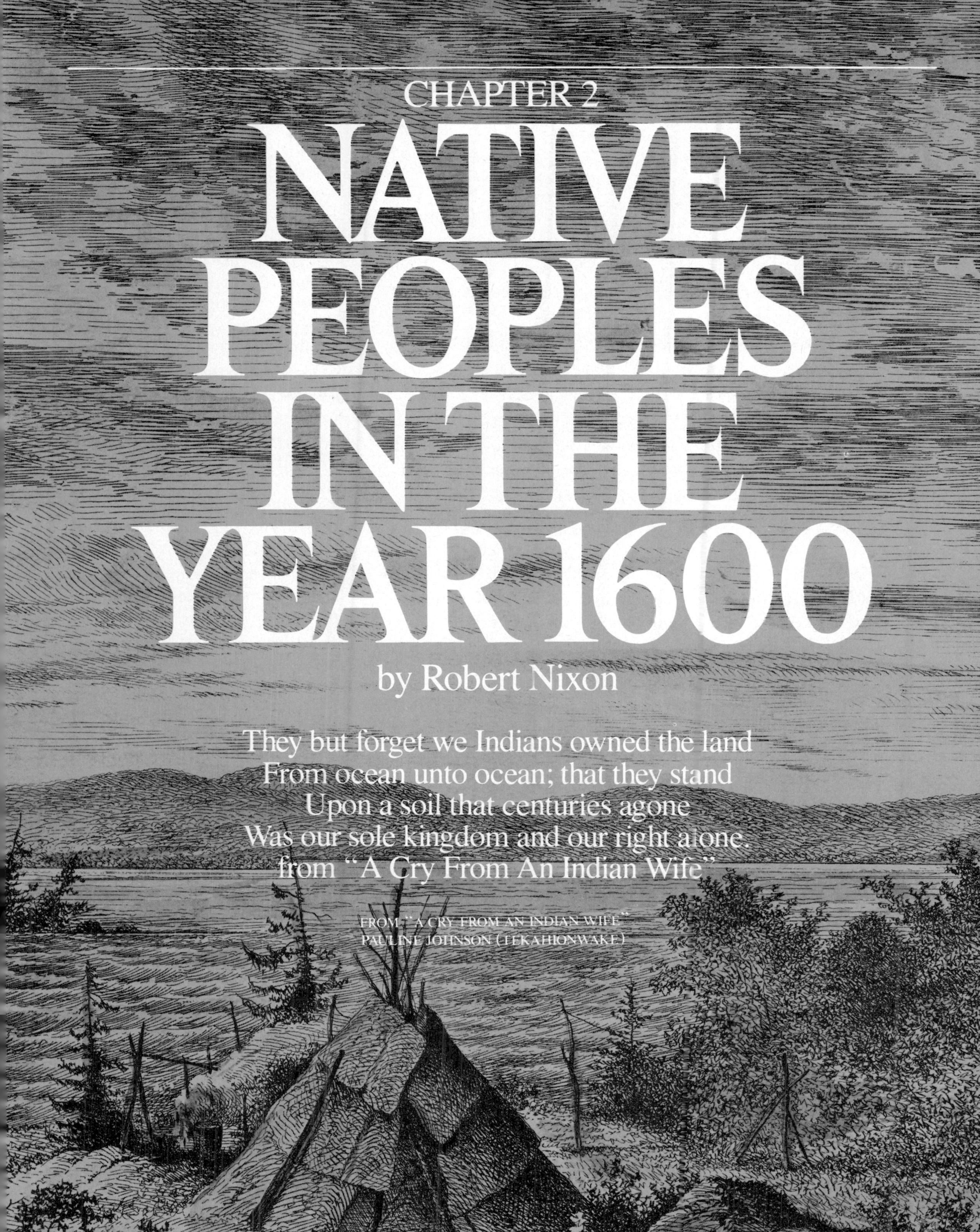

Before any European ever saw Ontario, the land was lived in by people thought to have originated in Asia, who crossed a land bridge that no longer exists into Alaska. They spread out all over North and South America and the islands of the Caribbean. When Christopher Columbus made his historic voyage across the Atlantic in 1492, he was convinced he had reached India, his hoped-for objective, and he called the bronze-skinned, black-haired people he found "Indians." Although other names are in use — natives or Amerindians — the name "Indian" remains the one best understood for Canada's native peoples who are not Inuits of the north.

When the first Europeans penetrated as far inland as Ontario, they encountered Indians who belonged to two main language groups, both of which extended far beyond the present boundaries of the province, Indians whose ways of life differed somewhat. One language group was the Algonkian, subdivided into a number of dialects which were sufficiently similar for guides from Quebec to act as interpreters as far west as Lake Winnipeg. The other language group was the Iroquoian, and in a similar fashion dialects spread from Southern Ontario as far as South Carolina.

The Algonkians were people of the northern woodlands who lived by hunting and by gathering wild fruits and rice. They practised no agriculture, mainly because their territory had little good soil and a short growing season. These tribes were not highly organized. Their religious leaders were their medicine men who devised rituals to protect their people from evil spirits, although they worshipped in common their god Manitou, the Great Spirit. They went to war occasionally, but for the most part their lives were spent in their quest for food, and in making their clothing from the furs of the animals they hunted. They were skilled in working with skins and with birch bark, and they made the best canoes of any tribe. Their houses were small with a frame of poles, usually covered with large slabs of bark — simple structures characteristic of a nomadic people constantly on the move.

In Ontario the Algonkians divided into three main groups: the Cree of the James Bay and Hudson Bay lowlands, the Algonquins along the

Right top: *Manitoulin Island. The island is home to many of Ontario's native peoples. In 1600 it was part of the territory of the Mississaugas. They moved south after 1649. By that time most of the Iroquois were living south of the St. Lawrence and Great Lakes.*
Right below: *Indian Rock Painting, Thousand Islands. Rock paintings can be found in many places in Ontario. This one was probably done by Iroquois artists before 1600. By that time most of the Iroquois were living south of the St. Lawrence and Great Lakes.*
Right below centre: *Distribution of Natives of the Algonkian Language Group c.1600 (after Leechman).*
Far right below: *Distribution of Natives of the Iroquoian Language Group c.1600 (after Leechman).*
Left below: *Queen Anne Silver Chalice. One of the most precious artifacts in Canada is the seven-piece (originally eight) silver communion set given to four Mohawk Kings after their visit with Queen Anne in 1710. Here, proudly stands one of the two silver chalices of this set, which has been in the possession of the Mohawks of Tyendinaga for 200 years.*

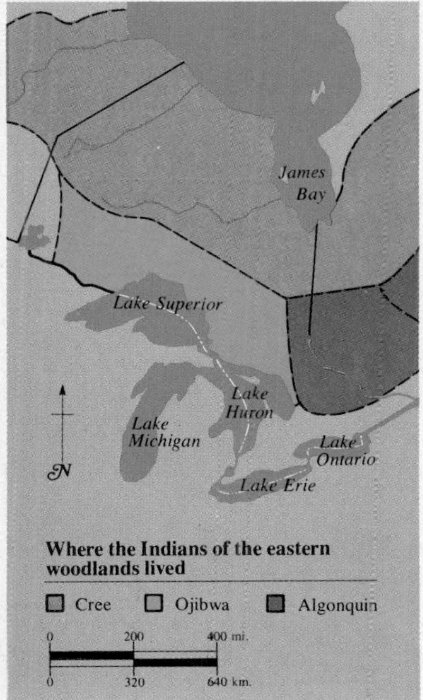
James Bay
Lake Superior
Lake Huron
Lake Michigan
Lake Ontario
Lake Erie
N
Where the Indians of the eastern woodlands lived
Cree
Ojibwa
Algonquin
0 200 400 mi.
0 320 640 km.

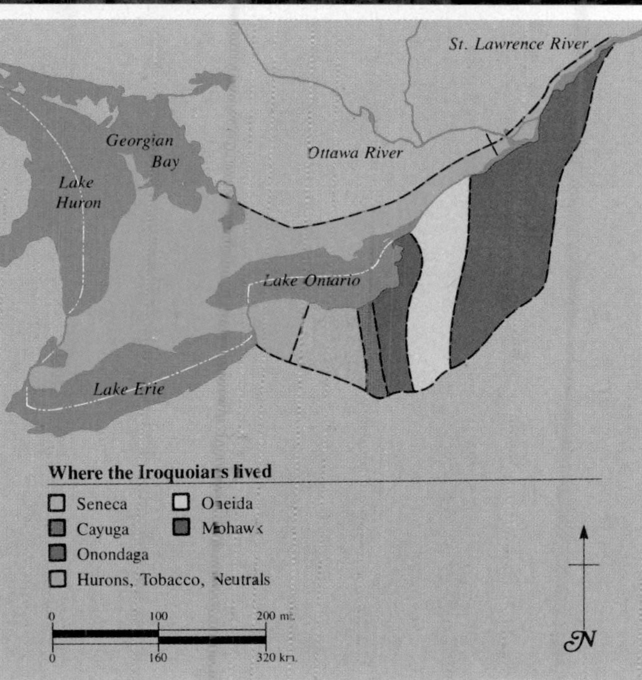
St. Lawrence River
Georgian Bay
Ottawa River
Lake Huron
Lake Ontario
Lake Erie
Where the Iroquoians lived
Seneca
Oneida
Cayuga
Mohawks
Onondaga
Hurons, Tobacco, Neutrals
0 100 200 mi.
0 160 320 km.
N

Ottawa River, and the Ojibwas, whose territory stretched north of Lakes Superior and Huron. The Ojibwas were subdivided into four distinct groups: the Ojibwas of the Lake Superior region, the Mississaugas of Manitoulin Island, the Ottawas around Georgian Bay, and the Potawatomis on the west side of Lake Huron (now the State of Michigan). All of them wandered over vast territories, aware of where the boundaries of their own lands were, occasionally having to defend them from neighbouring tribes. Exactly how many Algonkians were living in this large area is impossible to estimate accurately, but their numbers were not large. In Ontario there might have been 10,000 altogether.

To the south of the Algonkians lived people who spoke dialects of the Iroquoian language. Their territories corresponded roughly to the best agricultural land, from the south end of Georgian Bay across and eastwards along both sides of the St. Lawrence River, as well as south of Lake Ontario. They were an agricultural people, growing corn, beans, squash and pumpkins, all of which they dried as a source of winter food. Because they did not have to move as frequently in quest of food, the Iroquoians lived in stockaded villages of bark longhouses, each house shared by several families who were usually related to one another. Samuel de Champlain, the first governor of New France, described the longhouses as being "fifty to sixty yards long and twelve yards wide." A passageway extended the length of the house on which each pair of families shared a fire. In summer the Indians slept on raised benches which protected them from sand fleas. In winter they slept on mats below the benches where they were closer to the fires.

Like the Algonkians, the Iroquoians hunted for meat and used animal skins for clothing; they also fished and gathered fruits. Their religion was similar, but instead of the medicine men being the spiritual leaders they had "Keepers of the Faith" who supervised religious matters, and they called their Great Spirit "Orenda." In their countries, birch bark was not so plentiful, and they used elm bark for their longhouses and canoes.

The most powerful Iroquoian sub-groups were two confederacies — the Huron and the Iroquois. The Hurons founded a confederation of

Right top: *Rice Lake, South of Peterborough, c.1848. Caroline Hayward sketched Rice Lake, so named for its wild rice that grew in abundance along the shallow shoreline and which attracted the natives into the 20th century.*
Left below: *E. Pauline Johnson (1861-1913). No book of poetry by a Canadian has outsold* Flint and Feather, *the collected poetry of E. Pauline Johnson, a Mohawk from the Grand River Reserve near Brantford.*
Far right below: *Christ Church, Deseronto, 1843. The Mohawks have traditionally been Anglican. Led by Captain John Deseronto in 1784, one band of Mohawks settled in the Bay of Quinte area and built a chapel, called "Chapel Royal" because of the coat of arms presented to the church parish by George III. The present structure was built in 1843.*
Right below: *Original Mission House at Tuscarora. The Tuscarora village on the Grand River was established nineteen kilometres below Brantford in the 1780s. Anglican clergyman, Abraham Nelles (grandson of Hendrick Nelles who acquired 1,772 hectares of land on the Grand River from the Iroquois), was missionary to the Tuscaroras in 1831. The village then had a place of worship. The house shown here could also have been a Baptist mission, for one was started at Tuscarora in 1842.*

Left top: *Sha-Nah-Doht Neutral Indian Village. This typical Iroquoian longhouse village has been reconstructed at Delaware, Ontario. The Huron, Petun, Neutral and Iroquois nations built such villages, and grew crops outside the stockades.*
Far left below: *Ojibwa Indians on a Northern Lake. Here the natives celebrate their past with pageantry in Northern Ontario c.1900.*
Left below: *Indian Oval Storage Box. This small box is made entirely of wood, the sides of thick bark, the top and bottom of softwood, and the stitching from tough roots of a favourite tree. The artifact reflects Indian craftsmanship of the early 19th century.*
Right below: *Indian Family c.1900. These native parents and their children were photographed outside their log home on the Montreal River, 100 kilometres north of Sault Ste. Marie.*

four tribes — the Bear People, the Cord People, the Rock People, and the Deer People. They called their organization the Wendat Confederacy (from which some descendants are still known as Wyandots). The longhouse villages of the Hurons were located between Lake Simcoe and the southern end of Georgian Bay. The overall population at its peak has been estimated at 20,000.

To the south and west of the Hurons lived the Petuns — Iroquoians who, because they grew large quantities of tobacco which they traded to other tribes, were called the Tobacco Indians. South of the Petuns, along the north shore of Lake Erie, lived other Iroquoians known as the Neutrals, or Attiwandaraonk, meaning "stammerers," so called by the Hurons because of the way their dialect sounded. In turn, the Neutrals referred to the Hurons as stammerers for the same reason.

Last and most powerful, were the five nations of the Iroquois: Mohawk, Oneida, Onondaga, Cayuga and Seneca. They lived along the shores of Lake Ontario and the St. Lawrence in the late 16th century, but had moved south and built villages in the Mohawk Valley and around the Oneida and Finger Lakes by the 17th, except for one village somewhere in the Thousand Islands that was known as Toniata. In about 1570, the five nations formed their famous League of the Iroquois, mainly as a peace-keeping body which sought to negotiate from a position of strength.

The longhouse had, and still has, a special significance for the Iroquois people. Because their territory south of the St. Lawrence and Lake Ontario was rectangular, and wider from east to west than from north to south, the longhouse became the symbol of these lands. The Mohawks of the eastern portion were the Keepers of the East Door; the Senecas who lived at the far western end were the Keepers of the West Door. The Oneidas and Cayugas were the Keepers of the North and South Walls. The Onondagas, whose territory lay in the centre, were the Keepers of the Fire, which symbolized the fires that burned in all the longhouses. There the League members held their Council meetings. (Early in the 18th century the Tuscaroras, Iroquoians from farther south, joined, and the League became the Confederacy of the Six Na-

tions.) The population of the League was estimated at about 16,000 in the year 1685.

The League had the most sophisticated social and political organization of any of the northern natives. Each nation was divided into clans, each one headed by a senior woman who was the clan mother or matron. Each clan was entitled to a certain quota of chiefs, called sachems, and these were appointed, on an hereditary basis, by the clan matrons. The Council of the League consisted of sachems, but where these could not come to a decision, they referred the matter to the clan matrons. At the Council meetings, the League's sachems ruled on questions of concern to all the member nations; local matters were left to the rule of the individual nations. (When, in 1787, the new nation, the United States of America, wanted a constitution, the appointed committee drafting the legislation turned for a model to the system devised for the Iroquois Confederacy. The federal style of government had few precedents among European powers at that time.)

In addition to the sachems, each Iroquois nation had war chiefs chosen from among the most able warriors. These were not chiefs who sat at the council fires where the sachems made their decisions, but they led the men in battle. When the nations resolved on war, the women again had a unique role. While the men helped clear the fields and build the longhouses and stockades, the women were responsible for the planting, care, harvesting and storage of the crops. If the Council voted on war and the women disapproved, they could withhold the food the men needed to take with them, thus depriving the war parties of the supplies they required.

Despite their ties of language, the League of the Iroquois and the Wendat Confederation of the Hurons were enemies of long standing. The lands of the Petuns and Neutrals stood as a buffer zone between the two more powerful foes. Here was a rivalry which Europeans penetrating the interior of the continent would exploit to their advantage, with dire consequences for the Hurons. Involvement in white man's wars would, in less than 200 years, tear the League of the Iroquois asunder and divide it between the United States and Canada.

Left top: *St. Paul's Chapel of the Mohawks, Brantford, 1785. The first Protestant church in Ontario, it replaced the Queen Anne Chapel at Fort Hunter in New York State, following its plunder during the American Revolution. Named the Royal Chapel by Edward VII in 1904, it is one of the oldest wooden structures in Ontario today.*
Left Centre: *"Chiefswood," erected about 1853. Here was born the Mohawk poet E. Pauline Johnson. Built as a wedding gift for her English mother, a cousin of the American novelist William Dean Howells, it is now being restored.*
Left below: *Deseronto Council House, Built c.1840. Georgian in style, this council house for the Mohawks of the Bay of Quinte was demolished in the 1920s.*
Right below: *Oronhyatekha (1841-1907). This famous Mohawk was chosen to represent the Six Nations during the Prince of Wales' visit in 1860. Oronhyatekha studied medicine at Oxford University and this painting hangs in his* alma mater.

At the beginning of the 17th century, the native population of what became Ontario, including all the nations of the League of the Iroquois then living south of the St. Lawrence and Lake Ontario, might have numbered about 50,000. This indicates why the white man, with his firearms, more sophisticated knowledge of agriculture and animal husbandry, and ultimately overwhelming numbers, was able in a comparatively short time to destroy the native way of life. Even the agricultural Iroquoians required considerable space in comparison with their numbers. Their longhouse villages were not permanent.

After a few years the soil would begin to lose its fertility, and the wild fruit and animal population would be reduced. Then a village would be abandoned so that the area could regenerate naturally, and a new village would be built in an area which would be exploited, until the food supply was again used up. Thus, both the Algonkian and Iroquoian modes of living were extensive, rather than intensive, and could only prevail as long as plenty of land was available.

The first Europeans to enter what is now Ontario did so with the help of the natives. Much has been made of the heroism of white men who travelled great distances, laying the foundations of European knowledge of the vastness of the continent. In every case they were accompanied by native guides. Without them the explorers would not have found the way, nor would they have known how to survive on local food resources. European occupancy can be divided into two periods. The first was the era when the white men adapted to the native way of life. The second began when Europeans came in large numbers, as farmers, who brought their traditional methods, crops and livestock with them.

Right: *Field of Waving Corn. The climate and much of the soil of Southern Ontario is perfect for the ripening of high quality corn, or maize. The hybrid strains of today, that yield so many useful by-products, descend from the plant whose ears had kernels that were white, deep red and black, grown by the natives. The plant that was first cultivated by Indians has now become a valuable crop throughout the world.*

Left below: *The Indian Who Was Not an Indian. Grey Owl, lecturer and author of many books, did much to arouse sympathy for the native peoples and for conservation. After his death, the famous spokesman for the Indians was discovered to have been an Englishman named Archibald Belaney.*

1863

Far left top: *Six Nations Council House, Ohsweken. The Mohawks at Ohsweken on the Grand River, had their own council house, which was separate from the Mohawk council house at Deseronto.*

Far left below: *Old Moravian Church, Delaware. The mission church, and the reserve on which it was built, are reminders of the German-speaking Moravian missionaries who came into Upper Canada in the 1790s, accompanied by Delaware Indians who settled in the Thames Valley.*

Left top: *Moravian Village on the Thames River. This early painting by Philip John Bainbridge, shows the church and site of Fairfield, a settlement of Moravian missionaries and Delaware Indians, later called Moraviantown. Burnt by the Americans in 1813, it was rebuilt in 1815. Today it is a Delaware Indian Reserve.*

Left below: *Lacrosse at St. Regis Indian Reserve. The only place in the world where wooden lacrosse sticks are still made is here at St. Regis, just outside Cornwall. Iroquois still make the racquet-like implement for one of the oldest games played in North America.*

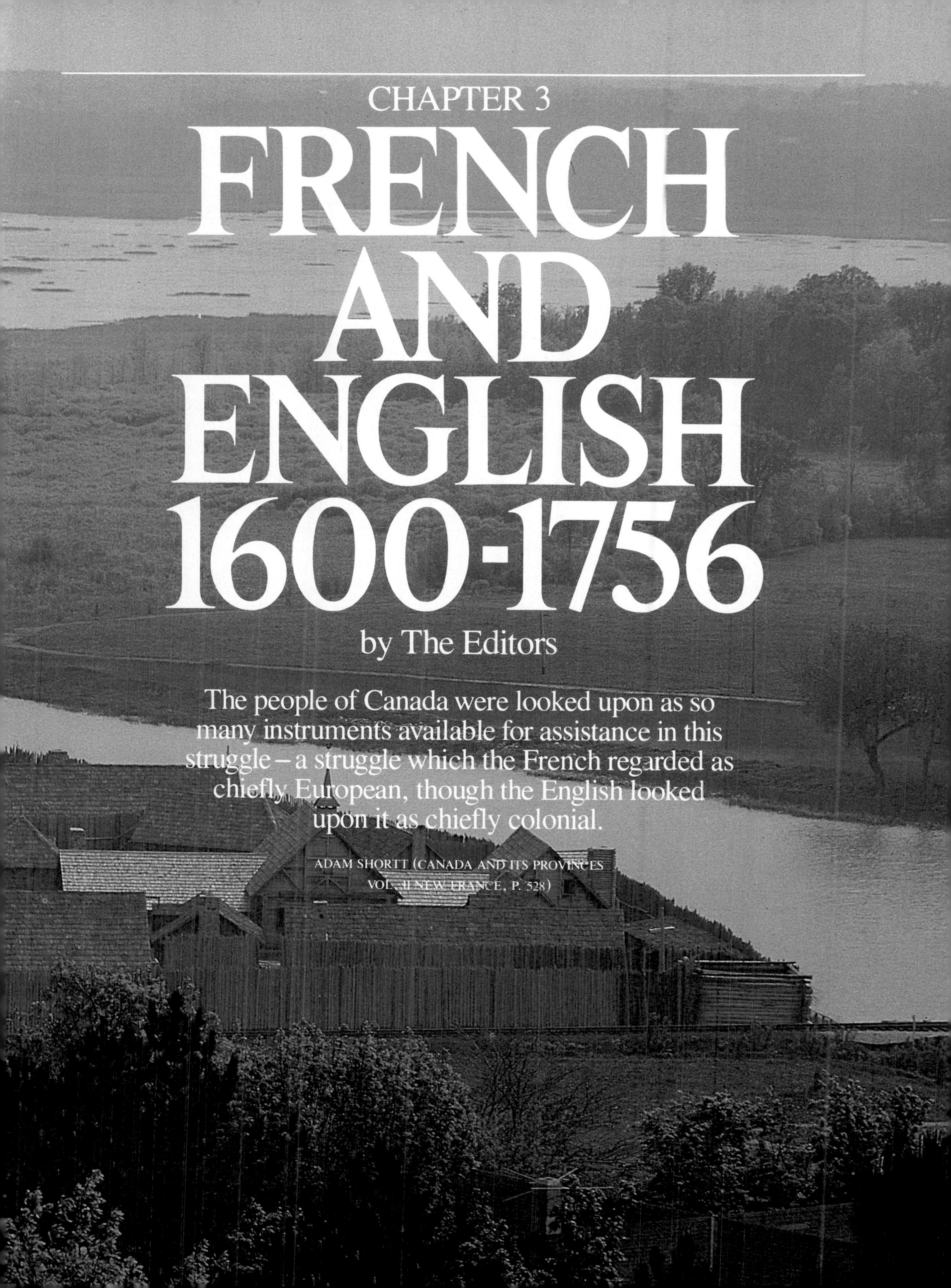

CHAPTER 3

FRENCH AND ENGLISH 1600-1756

by The Editors

The people of Canada were looked upon as so many instruments available for assistance in this struggle – a struggle which the French regarded as chiefly European, though the English looked upon it as chiefly colonial.

ADAM SHORTT (CANADA AND ITS PROVINCES VOL. II NEW FRANCE, P. 528)

The story of the French and English in Ontario is the story of the struggle to control the fur trade, the main reason why both France and England were interested in what Jacques Cartier once called "the land God gave to Cain." To any European the fur trade was a great bargain. Although some items exchanged for furs were useful, such as knives, axes, kettles, and cloth, many were cheap trinkets the traders got for a song, or liquor which did unpardonable harm to native people unaccustomed to "fire water." The European appetite for furs was insatiable, and the quest to find new areas where animals were plentiful, led to the exploration of more and more of the interior.

In the process the natives developed such an insatiable appetite for trade goods that competing European powers were able to form alliances with individual nations or tribes to keep the Indians divided. United, they might have been able to preserve their territories and way of life much longer. Ironically, the natives helped the newcomers by showing them how to live as they did; otherwise, the interlopers would not have taken control of the continent so easily. European penetration of the interior was done with native co-operation.

The French were Ontario's first permanent white settlers, but the first Frenchman and the first Englishman arrived in the province at about the same time. The Frenchman was Etienne Brûlé, a teen-aged servant of Samuel de Champlain, the first governor of New France. At Tadoussac, in 1609, the governor met Hurons who came to trade their furs and he decided to send young men to live among these natives to learn their language and customs. When more Hurons came with furs the following year, Champlain sent Brûlé home with them. He spent the winter of 1610-1611 in Huronia, but his exact whereabouts is unknown.

Henry Hudson, the English navigator who had explored the Hudson River for the Dutch in 1609, set out in 1610 on his voyage hoping to reach India by way of the northwest passage. That autumn he was at the southern tip of James Bay, his ship *Discovery* frozen in the ice. In June 1611, part of his crew mutinied and cast Hudson, his son and seven others adrift in a small boat, never to be seen again. Then in 1612-1613, another Englishman, Thomas Button, sailed into Hudson

Right top: *Henry Hudson Cast Adrift in Hudson Bay. The English mariner, Henry Hudson, first appeared in history in 1607 when he tried to find a northeast passage for the English Muscovy Company. In 1610 he set sail again from England in his new ship,* Discovery. *After a winter in Hudson Bay the crew mutinied in June 1611, and set Hudson, his son and seven others adrift. They were never seen again.*
Far right below: *Samuel de Champlain (1557?-1635). Known as the Father of New France, Champlain founded Quebec City and in 1610 he built a fur trading post at Montreal. In later years he explored Southern Ontario until 1616, after which he devoted his energies to Quebec.*
Right below: *Jean de Brébeuf, (1593-1649). Born in Normandy, Brébeuf was one of the first three Jesuits to be sent to Canada, where he arrived in 1625. He went among the Hurons, but Iroquois attacks intensified. Captured with his colleague Father Lalemant, they were taken to St. Ignace on the Sturgeon River and most cruelly put to death. Both were canonized in 1930.*
Left below: *French and English Forts Before 1756.*

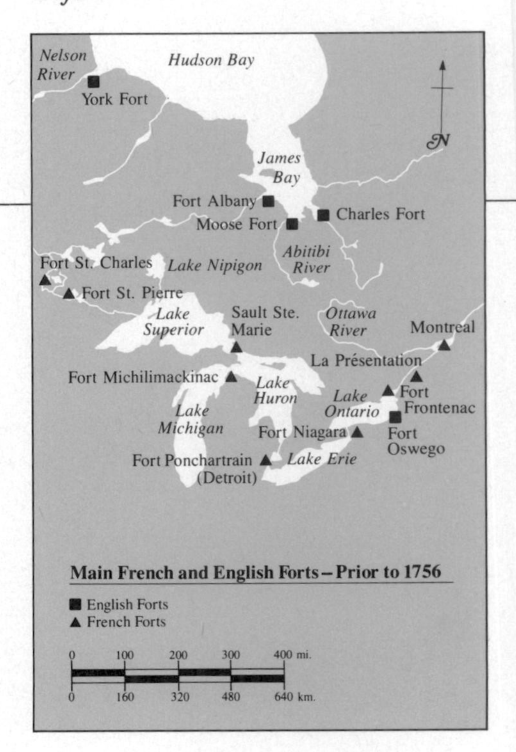

Left: ***The Martyrs' Shrine near Midland. On a hill overlooking the reconstructed Ste. Marie Among the Hurons, the Shrine was built to honour the eight Jesuit missionaries who were put to death over several years by the Iroquois. Work commenced on the Shrine in 1925, the year the eight Jesuits were beatified in Rome. In 1926 the church was opened, and 13,000 people attended the first Mass celebrated there. The eight Jesuit Martyrs became the first North American Saints in 1930. They were Fathers Jean de Brébeuf, Anthony Daniel, Noël Chabanel, Charles Garnier, Isaac Joques and Gabriel Lalemant, and two lay brothers, René Goupil and Jean de Lalande. At the time of publication, the Shrine was preparing for the 1984 visit of His Holiness, Pope John Paul II, the first pope to visit Canada.***

Right below: *Huronia in the 1640s.*

Bay and reached the Albany River.

In 1615 the first Catholic missionary to the Hurons, Father Joseph Le Caron, in the grey robes of the Récollet order, travelled with some guides up the Ottawa River, along Lake Nipissing and the French River to Lake Huron, thence to Huronia. Not many days later Champlain followed the same route accompanied by a party of Frenchmen and native guides. In Huronia he found that a large war party was assembling to attack the Iroquois in their own country. Impressed by the Frenchmen's "fire sticks," the warriors asked Champlain and his men to accompany them, and the governor agreed.

Huronia, the country of the four nations that made up the Huron, or Wendat Confederacy, lay between Lake Simcoe and the shores of Georgian Bay. South of Huronia was the country of the Petuns, and along Lake Erie that of the Neutrals. Like the Hurons, these people spoke an Iroquoian language, as did the Iroquois nations. The Petuns and as the name implies, the Neutrals, tried to avoid the rivalry that existed between the Wendat Confederacy and the Confederacy, or League of the Iroquois. The five nations that made up the League at that time lived in villages in northern New York State, some 300 miles (500 kilometres) distant from Huronia. The war party travelled by canoe through the Kawartha Lakes and the Trent River to Lake Ontario, and from there it ascended the Oswego River into the country of the Oneidas, one of the nations of the Iroquois Confederacy. Near Lake Oneida the Hurons clashed with the Iroquois. The Hurons were defeated and forced to withdraw. Champlain received an arrow in the leg and was taken all the way back to the Huron country to recuperate.

In 1616, the governor wanted to return to Quebec by way of the St. Lawrence River, but his Huron guides refused. Among the Thousand Islands was the Iroquois village of Toniata, and they were afraid to pass that way. Accompanied by Father Le Caron, Champlain returned along the Ottawa River instead.

Some years passed before other French explorers investigated the interior, for Champlain was worried about the safety of Quebec. In addition to the menacing Iroquois, the Dutch were approaching from the

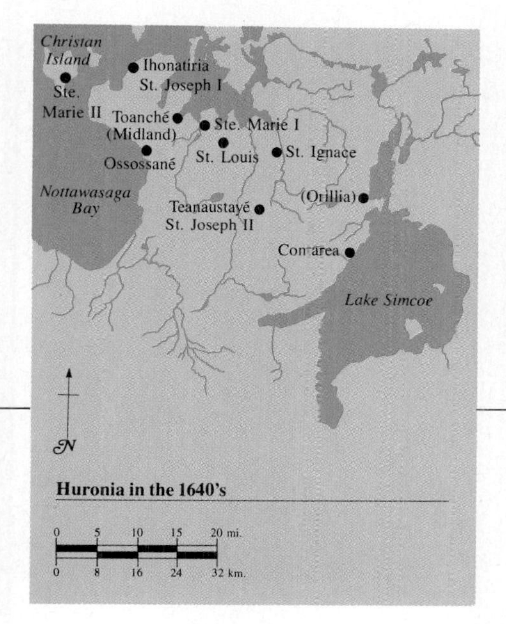

south, claiming the lands along the Hudson River. In 1615 they built a trading post called Beverwyck (now Albany, New York). The Iroquois, fearing the power of the French-Huron alliance, in 1617 made a treaty with the Dutch. Meanwhile, the French missionaries were active. They did not have much success in converting the tribes of the eastern woodland — nomadic hunters who were difficult to find. The missionaries hoped for better luck with the Hurons, whose agricultural villages were more sedentary. Several Récollets went to Huronia, and more of Champlain's young men — Nicolas Vignau, Nicolas Marsolet and Jean Nicolet — joined Etienne Brûlé. The freedom the youngsters enjoyed among the natives went to their heads, and the governor grew to mistrust them.

Champlain encouraged the Catholic missionaries who came to New France to go forth and save the souls of the "heathen" natives rather than remain at Quebec. The colony had been sponsored by wealthy Huguenots who founded the Company of St. Malo, and most of the colonists were Protestants. The Récollets were a very poor order, lacking the money for an effective mission, and they invited the wealthy Jesuit order to join them. The first black-robed Jesuits arrived in Quebec in 1625. At that time the Récollet, Nicolas Viel, living in a cabin at the Huron village of Toanché on the west shore of Penetanguishene Bay, was exhausted. He set out for Quebec to have a rest, but his canoe was swamped in the rapids near the Island of Montreal and he drowned.

In 1626 three priests went westwards — the Récollet La Roche de Daillon, and Jesuits Jean de Brébeuf and Anne de Rouë. They occupied Father Viel's cabin at Toanché, where Brébeuf remained three years; the other two left in 1628.

The Jesuits and the Récollets soon persuaded the French government to change its policy on Quebec. The charter of the Huguenots' company was revoked, and a new Company of New France sponsored by Catholics was set up to control the fur trade. In future, all settlers had to be Catholics. As this policy was being implemented, England decided to take over the French colony. In 1629 Captain David Kirke was sent with three ships to Quebec. Etienne Brûlé and Nicolas Marsolet, two of

Right: *Plan of Fort Frontenac, 1738. The original Fort Frontenac was built by LaSalle. Even after it was strengthened, with walls of masonry, it was vulnerable to attack. It stood on low ground and could be fired upon from heights to the west or from Point Henry (the site of Fort Henry) on the east. A British force under John Bradstreet captured the fort from the French in August 1758.*

Left below: *Tête du Pont Barracks, Kingston, 1789. By the terms of the treaty that ended the American Revolution, the forts that had been the British line of defence were on the United States side of the boundary. Kingston began as a new military base, and the Tête du Pont Barracks were constructed on the site of Fort Frontenac, started by the French the century before.*

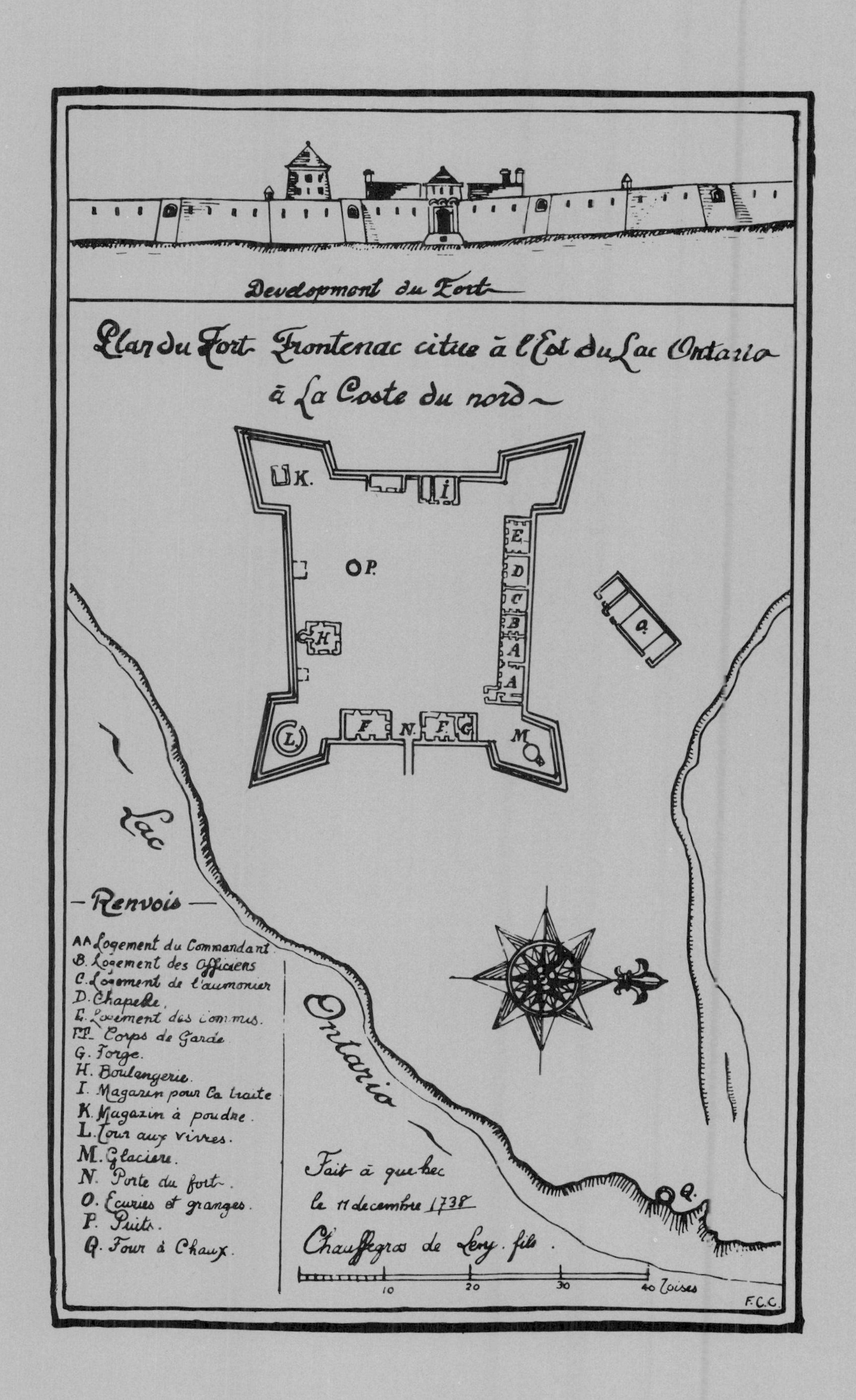
Developement du Fort
Plan du Fort Frontenac citue à l'Est du Lac Ontario à La Coste du nord
Lac
Ontario
Renvois
AA Logement du Commandant.
B. Logement des Officiers
C. Logement de l'aumonier
D. Chapelle.
E. Logement des commis.
FF. Corps de Garde
G. Forge.
H. Boulangerie.
I. Magazin pour la traite
K. Magazin à poudre.
L. Tour aux vivres.
M. Glacière.
N. Porte du fort.
O. Ecuries et granges.
P. Puits.
Q. Four à Chaux.
Fait à quebec
le 11 decembre 1738
Chaussegros de Lery. fils.
10
20
30
40 Toises
F.C.C.

MICHEL TSIOUI,
TEACHEANDALE.
CHIEF OF THE WARRIORS.
STANISLAS COSKA,
AHARATHAHA.
SECOND CHIEF OF THE COUNCIL.
ANDRE ROMAIN.
TSOUHAHISSEN,
CHIEF OF THE COUNCIL.
THREE CHIEFS OF THE HURON INDIANS RESIDING AT LA JEUNE LORETTE, NEAR QUEBEC,
IN THEIR NATIONAL COSTUME.

Left: Huron Chiefs at La Jeune Lorette. The Hurons who had escaped the Iroquois massacres of 1648-49, eventually settled close to Quebec City where their descendants intermarried with French Canadians. This picture by E. Chatfield was published in 1825. It shows Michel Tsioui, Teacheandale, Chief of Warriors (left), Stanislas Coska, Aharathaha, Second Chief of the Council (centre), and André Romain, Tsouhahissen, Chief of the Council (right).

***Right below:** Gabriel Lalemant (1610-1649). On becoming a Jesuit in 1630, at the age of twenty, Lalemant offered himself for foreign missions but due to poor health, he did not arrive in Canada until 1646. After a period in Quebec, he joined Brébeuf in Huronia only six months before their martyrdom at the hands of the Iroquois. After appalling torture he died on March 17, 1649, a few hours after Brébeuf. Sainthood was conferred upon both in 1930.*

Champlain's young men, went to pilot in a French fleet Champlain was expecting. Instead, they met Kirke's ships at Tadoussac and agreed to guide them into Quebec's harbour. Champlain surrendered, and Kirke sent the governor and all the missionaries back to France.

Two years later two other Englishmen visited Hudson Bay. Luke Foxe found the entrance to the Churchill and Nelson Rivers, and sailed north into the sea basin that bears his name. Less successful was Thomas James, who ran his ship on a shoal in James Bay. He survived to publish his memoirs, and the bay was named for him.

In 1632, by the Treaty of St. Germain en Laye, Canada was returned to France. Etienne Brûlé, living at Toanché, was murdered by the Hurons who feared Champlain's wrath if he caught them sheltering the turncoat. So ended the life of the first Frenchman to explore Ontario. Champlain returned from France, accompanied by black-robed Jesuits but no Récollets, for economy reasons. The wealthy Jesuits could pay their own way. In 1634 the Jesuit Fathers, Jean de Brébeuf, Antoine Daniel and Ambroise Davost, with some hired men, went to Huronia. At Ihonatiria, near the northern tip of the Penetanguishene peninsula, they started a mission named St. Joseph.

During the 1635 growing season, both drought and disease struck Ihonatiria, and the survivors left the village. When new Jesuits arrived, Brébeuf moved to the village of Ossossané on Nottawasaga Bay and opened a new mission, La Conception de Notre Dame. In 1637, Father Jérome Lalemant with two more priests came to be the Superior in Huronia. Lalemant opened another mission, Ste. Joseph II, at Teanaustayé on the upper reaches of the Sturgeon River.

Seeing the need for a well-fortified, centrally-located mission, Lalemant built Ste. Marie (now restored) on the shore of the Wye River. His workmen opened the first canal in central Canada, with three small locks to divert water within the stockade of Ste. Marie. The Hurons began to trust the missionaries but these were also years when new diseases swept the country. The well-meaning priests and their helpers, all unaware, were the cause of these misfortunes. Measles and smallpox introduced by Europeans, took a fearful toll despite the efforts of the missionaries to care for the sick.

In the 1640s when the Hurons had been weakened by disease, the Iroquois saw their opportunity to end the threat posed by the Wendat-French alliance. Both native confederacies wanted "fire sticks" but the French were reluctant to trade such weapons. The Dutch were not, and they supplied their Iroquois allies with muskets and ammunition. In 1642 the Iroquois attacked the Huron village of Contarea near the shore of Lake Simcoe (south of Orillia), killed everyone they found, and put the settlement to the torch. Next, the Iroquois isolated the Hurons by occupying lands along the Ottawa River that belonged to the Algonquin tribe, cutting off communication with Quebec for months.

In 1645, Father Jérome Lalemant left Huronia and the new superior became Father Paul Ragueneau, based at Ste. Marie. The Jesuits now had fifty-eight men in Huronia — twenty-two soldiers, eighteen priests, the rest "*engagés*" who were allowed to earn money trading, or "*donnés*" who were unpaid volunteers. The Jesuits had opened a dozen missions, nine to the Hurons, three among the Petuns and Algonquins. Land around Ste. Marie had been planted with crops so that the Black Robes could feed the hundreds who visited them.

In 1646, the Jesuits felt emboldened to attempt a mission to the Iroquois. They chose Father Isaac Joques, who had been in Huronia but was at the French village on the Island of Montreal, to go into the Mohawk Valley. In late August Father Joques set out with a lay brother named Lalande. The Mohawks killed them, placed their heads on a palisade, and threw their bodies into the Mohawk River.

At Teanaustayé, Father Antoine Daniel was in charge of St. Joseph II mission. On July 4, 1648, the Iroquois attacked and Father Daniel was among those killed. On March 14, 1649, they struck the mission of St. Ignace, on a tributary of the Coldwater River. Hurons fleeing to St. Louis mission to the west, warned Fathers Jean de Brébeuf and Gabriel Lalemant (a nephew of Father Jérome Lalemant), to escape. They refused to desert their flock and were subsequently tortured to death. Word reached Ste. Marie, where Father Ragueneau decided to evacuate the mission. A war party of Hurons headed for St. Louis to try and

***Right:** La Salle at Fort Frontenac 1675. In July 1673, Governor Frontenac visited Cataraqui (Kingston), and ordered the construction of a wooden fort. The following year, Sieur de La Salle was granted seigneury at Cataraqui. He returned in 1675 with a party of workmen and began work on a masonry stronghold, which he named Fort Frontenac in honour of the governor.*

turn back the Iroquois, and they fought furiously while Father Ragueneau and his followers burned Ste. Marie. They headed for Christian Island for safety, and there they started a second Ste. Marie.

While the destitute Hurons fled to this new Ste. Marie for succour, the Iroquois attacked the three missions to the Petun and Algonquin tribes and they killed Fathers Charles Garnier and Noël Chabanel. At Ste. Marie the winter was exceedingly cruel, for there was not enough food on the island for all the refugee Hurons. In the spring, Father Ragueneau evacuated the mission and with about sixty Frenchmen and 300 Hurons set off in canoes for Quebec. The Jesuits' plan for Huronia had ended in flames at the hands of the Iroquois.

Now the Iroquois turned upon the rest of the Petuns, and on the Neutrals, killing them and driving the survivors west and south; later they regrouped and called themselves Wyandots. When the warriors of the Iroquois Confederacy returned to their own country deep inside New York State, the lands of their fellow-Iroquoians lay desolate and deserted. Gradually the Mississaugas, who spoke an Algonkian language, drifted southwards and hunted through the once fertile fields.

With Huronia lost, the French became determined to wean the Iroquois away from the Dutch and form their own alliance. By 1654 Father Simon Le Moyne had ascended the St. Lawrence to establish a mission to the Onondagas, passing safely by the Iroquois village of Toniata because he was going to see people of their own confederacy. Father Le Moyne opened his mission on the site of Syracuse, New York.

In 1664 England wrested the New Netherlands from the Dutch, which only intensified the rivalry over the fur trade and convinced the French to move farther inland. In 1668 the Jesuit Father Jacques Marquette founded a mission on the site of Sault Ste. Marie for the Algonquins. Now members of the Order of St. Sulpice joined the Jesuits. Two Sulpicians, Dollier de Casson and René de Galineé, who combined exploration with religious zeal, charted Lake Erie and in 1669 visited Father Marquette's mission.

Meanwhile, there had been developments on Hudson Bay. Two French fur traders, wearied of the many regulations and heavy charges

Right top: *Champlain on the Shores of Georgian Bay, 1615. The original painting was done by Hummé.*

Right below: *Etienne Brûlé (1592-1633). one of Champlain's "young men," Brûlé wintered among the Hurons in 1610-1611, the first European to explore the interior. Here the artist, C.W. Jeffreys, shows Brûlé — the discoverer of Toronto — at the mouth of the Humber River with Huron guides.*

Far right below: *Robert Cavelier La Salle (1643-1687). La Salle was born in Rouen, France, and moved to Canada in 1666. He explored the lands south of Lakes Ontario and Erie in 1697-1680 and was later appointed commander of the new Fort Frontenac at Kingston, by Governor Frontenac. He subsequently explored extensively in the Mississippi valley and elsewhere. He was killed in 1682 when his party of explorers mutinied.*

Humme pinxt 1884.

imposed by the governor of New France, now Daniel de Rémy Sieur de Courcelle, went over to the English. While visiting London, Pierre Radisson and his brother-in-law Medard Chouart des Groseilliers, recommended bringing furs to Europe through Hudson Bay. As a result, under the patronage of King Charles II and his cousin Prince Rupert, the Hudson's Bay Company was formed. Groseilliers entered Hudson Bay aboard the ship *Nonsuch* and in 1669 he returned to England with a valuable cargo of furs. The following year the Company received a charter and started building fur forts, three on James Bay, and one north of the mouth of the Nelson River on Hudson Bay.

Far to the south the French continued reaching inland. In 1671 Governor Courcelle journeyed up the St. Lawrence and met the Iroquois at Cataraqui (Kingston) hoping to form an alliance. The Iroquois were hesitant. Then in 1672 Louis Jolliet, a Jesuit turned explorer, set out to look for the Mississippi River. At Sault Ste. Marie, Father Marquette joined him and they travelled down the Mississippi as far as the junction with the Arkansas River. That same year the new governor, Louis de Baude, Comte de Frontenac, sent Robert Cavelier Sieur de La Salle to the Council at Onondaga to invite the Iroquois to a meeting at Cataraqui. Frontenac arrived prepared to impress the natives with French power. He brought 400 men in 120 canoes and two flat-bottomed barges, each with a mounted gun.

The Iroquois, awed by the sight of so many Frenchmen in shiny breastplates and helmets, agreed to keep the peace and Frontenac returned to Quebec. La Salle stayed at Cataraqui to superintend the building of Fort Frontenac. It would serve to guard the entrance to the St. Lawrence and as a mission to the Indians. Some Senecas and Cayugas had now moved to the north shore of Lake Ontario and were growing more friendly towards the French, but the Mohawks who had had the longest contact with them, remained hostile.

La Salle soon returned to France where he was awarded a seigneury at Cataraqui. When he came back to Cataraqui in 1675, he was accompanied by Father Louis Hennepin, a Belgian Récollet. While Hennepin became the first white man to visit Niagara Falls, La Salle built the

Left: The Griffon. *To sail on the Great Lakes above Niagara Falls, La Salle built the "barque"* Griffon, *forty-five tons, five guns, in 1679, on Lake Erie. The artist, C.J.H. Snider, showed Father Louis Hennepin, who accompanied La Salle, standing on the quarter-deck.*
Right below: *The Christianity Group, Champlain Memorial, Orillia. This group of figures is at the base of Vernon March's statue in Couchiching Park. March also sculpted the Ottawa War Memorial and the United Empire Loyalist monument in Hamilton.*

Frontenac, a vessel of ten tons that carried two masts, each with a square sail — the first ship to sail the waters above the rapids of the St. Lawrence. By 1678 La Salle was planning to explore the Mississippi River. His chief assistant was Henri de Tonti, and the chaplain for the venture was Father Hennepin. To travel on the upper lakes, La Salle built on the Niagara River above the falls his ship *Griffon,* forty-five tons and five guns, the first sailing vessel above Lake Ontario. Father Hennepin explored the upper Mississippi for La Salle, but he was captured by Sioux Indians and did not escape from them until 1681. In 1682, having travelled through the upper lakes and down the Mississippi, La Salle reached the Gulf of Mexico.

The scene soon shifted to Hudson Bay because the French thought the English were taking away too many furs. In 1682, convinced that the Hudson's Bay Company was not paying them what they were worth, Radisson and Groseilliers went to France and helped form the Company of the North to trade on Hudson Bay. With Groseilliers' son, Jean Chouart, Radisson sailed into the bay and established a fur post up the Hayes River. They also captured the Hudson's Bay Company post north of the Nelson River, took the occupants prisoners, and with all the furs they could collect, Radisson sailed for Quebec leaving Chouart in charge of the French post. The governor at Quebec, then Lefebre de La Barre, demanded such a heavy tax that Radisson, in disgust, went to London and rejoined the Hudson's Bay Company.

In 1684 King Louis the Fourteenth, not wanting to risk an open war with England, ordered Chouart to abandon the post on the Hayes River and to return to the Hudson's Bay Company, the post he and Radisson had seized. The following year two French ships from Quebec attempted to trade, but were driven away by Hudson's Bay Company traders without obtaining any pelts. For the colonials, this was the last straw. Despite the French King's orders, a little army of thirty-three Frenchmen and sixty-six Indians, led by the Chevalier de Troyes and three Le Moyne brothers, Jacques, Paul and Pierre (the last, the legendary Iberville) marched 700 miles (nearly 1,200 km) overland from Montreal and attacked the English fur posts on James Bay from the

Right top: *Charter of the Hudson's Bay Company 1670.*
Right below: *Old Jesuit Mission, Sandwich. Father Armand de la Richardie landed at Sandwich (now Windsor) in 1728, and laboured among the Indians for many years. In 1746 he built this mission house overlooking the Detroit River. The house survived until it was destroyed by fire in 1912.*
Far right below: *Hennepin at the Falls of St. Anthony. In July 1680, Hennepin discovered and named the Falls of St. Anthony at the present site of Minneapolis. This indefatigable traveller was born in Ath (now in Belgium) about 1640. Believed to have been the first white man to see Niagara Falls, he mistakenly reckoned their height at 180 metres. He died in 1701.*
Left below: *Père Marquette Station in Leamington. Local residents, aware of the era of New France, commemorated one French missionary and explorer when the railway line reached their community.*

harles the Second By the

of God King of England Scotland France and Ireland defender of the faith &c To all to whome these present shall come greeting Whereas Our Deare and Entirely Beloved Cousin Prince Rupert Count Palatyne of the Rhyne Duke of Bavaria and Cumberland &c Christopher Duke of Albemarle William Earle of Craven Henry Lord Arlington Anthony Lord Ashley Sir John Robinson and Sir Robert Vyner Knights and Baronett Sir Peter Colleton Baronett Sir Edward Hungerford Knight of the Bath Sir Paul Neile Knight Sir John Griffith and Sir Phillipp Carterett Knight James Hayes John Kirke Francis Millington William Prettyman John Fenn Esquires and John Portman Cittizen and Goldsmith of London have at theire owne great cost and charges undertaken an Expedition for Hudsons Bay in the Northwest part of America for the discovery of a new Passage into the South Sea and for the finding some Trade for Furrs Mineralls and other considerable Comodityes and by such theire undertakeing have already made such discoveryes as doe encourage them to proceed further in pursuance of theire said designe by meanes whereof there may probably arise very great advantage to us and our Kingdome And Whereas the said Undertakers for theire further encouragement in the said designe have humbly besought us to Incorporate them and grant unto them and theire successors the sole Trade and Comerce of all those Seas Streight Bayes Rivers Lakes Creekes and Sound in whatsoever Latitude they shall bee that lye within the entrance of the Streight comonly called Hudsons Streight together with all the Land Countryes and Territoryes upon the Coast and Confynes of the Seas Streight Bayes Lakes Rivers Creekes and Sound aforesaid which are not now actually possessed by any of our Subiect or by the Subiect of any other Christian Prince or State Now Know Wee that wee being desirous to promote all Endeavours tending to the publique good of our people and to encourage the said Undertakeing Have of our especiall grace certaine knowledge and meere mocon Given granted ratifyed and confirmed And by these present for us our heires and Successors Doe give grant ratifie and confirme unto our said Cousin Prince Rupert Christopher Duke of Albemarle William Earle of Craven Henry Lord Arlington Anthony Lord Ashley Sir John Robinson Sir Robert Vyner Sir Peter Colleton Sir Edward Hungerford Sir Paul Neile Sir John Griffith and Sir Phillipp Carterett James Hayes John Kirke Francis Millington William Prettyman John Fenn and John Portman That they and such others as shall bee admitted into the said Society as is hereafter expressed shall bee one Body Corporate and Politique in deed and in name by the name of the Governor and Company of Adventurers of England tradeing into Hudsons Bay and them by the name of the Governor and Company of Adventurers of England tradeing into Hudsons Bay one Body Corporate and Politique in deede and in name really and fully for ever for us our heires and successors Wee Doe make ordeyne constitute establish confirme and declare by these present and that by the same name of Governor and Company of Adventurers of England tradeing into Hudsons Bay they shall have perpetuall succession And that they and theire successors by the name of the Governor and Company of Adventurers of England tradeing into Hudsons Bay bee and at all tymes hereafter shall bee personable and capable in Law to have purchase receive possesse enjoy and reteyne Land Rent priviledges liberties Jurisdiccons Franchises and hereditament of what kinde nature and quality soever they bee to them and theire Successors and alsoe to give grant demise alien assigne and dispose Land Tenement and hereditament and to doe and execute all and singuler other thing by the same name that to them shall or may apperteyne to doe And that they and theire Successors by the name of the Governor and Company of Adventurers of England tradeing into Hudsons Bay may pleade and bee impleaded answeare and bee answeared defend and bee defended in whatsoever Court and places before whatsoever Judges and Justices and other persons and Officers in all and singuler Accons Pleas Suites quarrells causes and demaund whatsoever of whatsoever kinde nature or sort in such manner and forme as any other our Liege people of this our Realme of England being persons able and capable in Lawe may or can have purchase receive possesse enjoy reteyne give grant demise alien assigne dispose pleade defend and bee defended doe permitt and execute And that the said Governor and Company of Adventurers of England tradeing into Hudsons Bay and theire successors may have a Comon Seale to serve for all the causes and businesses of them and theire successors and that it shall and may bee lawfull to the said Governor and Company and theire Successors the same Seale from tyme to tyme at theire will and pleasure to breake change and to make a new or alter as to them shall seeme expedient And further Wee Will And by these present for us our heires and successors Wee Doe ordeyne that there shall bee from henceforth one of the same Company to bee elected and appointed in such forme as hereafter in these present is expressed which shall bee called the Governor of the said Company And that the said Governor and Company shall or may elect seaven of theire number in such forme as hereafter in these present is expressed which shall bee called the Comittee of the said Company which Comittee of seaven or any three of them together with the Governor or Deputy Governor of the said Company for the tyme being shall have the direction of the

rear. The Hudson's Bay Company men were taken by surprise; they were prepared only for an attack from the water. The French and natives captured the three posts on James Bay, leaving that near the Nelson River in the Hudson's Bay Company's hands.

For the next ten years the French (led by Iberville) and the English swapped forts and stole each other's ships. The Hudson's Bay Company officers at the same time sought to extend the fur trade into the west. Young Henry Kelsey, stationed at the Nelson River post set out up the Hayes River in 1690. He followed the Saskatchewan River into the heart of the prairies, and returned to Hudson Bay in 1692.

In the south Governor La Barre had been recalled in 1685 and replaced by the Marquis de Denonville, who aggravated the Iroquois. After raiding some Seneca villages, he built Fort Niagara on their land without their permission. Then, acting on orders from King Louis that a more sensible governor would have ignored, in 1688 Denonville captured a large group of Iroquois men, women and children and imprisoned them in Fort Frontenac. Later, the men were sent to France to end their lives as galley slaves, a fate every bit as cruel as the torture deaths of Brébeuf and Lalemant. When they found out, the Iroquois went on the war path, isolated Fort Frontenac and forced the starving garrison to escape in boats to Montreal. Denonville was recalled and Frontenac returned to repair the damage. In 1692 the French attacked the Iroquois village of Toniata in the Thousand Islands. The survivors fled and the upper St. Lawrence became safer for French shipping.

In 1694 the French opened a fur post at Michilimackinac, and by 1697, the year before Frontenac died at Quebec, a garrison of soldiers had reoccupied Fort Frontenac. In 1701, Louis Hector de Callières, Frontenac's successor, ordered Antoine de La Mothe-Cadillac, the commander of the post at Michilimackinac, to build Fort Ponchartrain beside the Detroit River. France's position in southern Ontario was now much stronger, but she was soon to lose territory in the north.

In 1713, France and England signed the Treaty of Utrecht. Under its terms Ontario was partitioned. The French were confirmed in the south, but the English got the Hudson Bay lowlands. According to its

Left: *La Vérendrye at Lake of the Woods. Pierre Gaultier de Varennes, Sieur de la Vérendrye (1658-1749), was born in Trois Rivières, Quebec. He returned to Canada after military service in France and became a frontiersman. His explorations took him as far west as the Rocky Mountains. In 1732 he built Fort St. Charles on Lake of the Woods.*
Right below: *Ecole Secondaire Etienne Brûlé. The first French-language high school to be opened in Metropolitan Toronto was named after the first Frenchman to visit the area. In the 1920s the Ontario government passed Regulation 17, which adversely affected the right of Franco-Ontarians to be educated in their mother tongue. In 1968, the Robarts government, in which William Davis was Minister of Education, passed Bill 140 for elementary schools and Bill 141 for high schools, which restored that right. In 1969, the Ecole Secondaire Etienne Brûlé was begun in portable classrooms. The present building was ready for the school in 1973.*

Left: *Sainte Marie Among the Hurons. Father Jérome Lalemant (uncle of Father Gabriel Lalemant, the Jesuit Martyr) established his fortified mission in 1639 as the major one to the Indians of Huronia. Father Lalemant was succeeded, in 1645, by Father Paul Ragueneau. By 1649 the Iroquois attacks on the Hurons had grown in intensity. Soon after Fathers Jean de Brébeuf and Gabriel Lalemant were put to death by the Iroquois, Father Ragueneau and his staff burned Ste. Marie and withdrew to Christian Island for safety.*

Right below: *Champlain Monument, Nepean Point, Ottawa. Champlain is shown holding an astrolabe, an early navigation instrument. He lost his astrolabe on June 6th or 7th, 1613 near Cobden in Renfrew County. An ancient astrolabe, presumably Champlain's, was found in that area in 1867.*

charter the Hudson's Bay Company was granted all the land drained by rivers entering Hudson and James Bays. France refused to give up her claim to all of this territory, and the ownership of a wide belt of land was left unsettled. Now that England controlled all the fur trade through Hudson Bay, the rivalry shifted to the south.

In 1720, English and Dutch traders built a post at Oswego in order to be closer to the source of furs. French efforts to woo the Iroquois and their native allies were hampered because their trade goods were too expensive. In New France the administration was in the hands of appointed officials whose main reason for being in the colony was to become rich. They demanded a substantial share of each trader's furs, and the traders in turn had to raise the price of their goods. The natives were quick to notice that the goods they received at Oswego were cheaper and of better qualilty, and many avoided the French fur posts.

The French tried to catch up by going still farther inland, which involved more exploration. The white men who pushed farthest into the west were Pierre de La Vérendrye and his sons, Jean, Pierre and Louis-Joseph. In 1731 they opened a new post on the site of Fort William. The next year Jean reached Lake Winnipeg. These remarkable La Vérendryes explored as far south as the Black Hills of South Dakota and opened fur posts beyond the Red River.

More work was proceeding farther east. In 1749 the Sulpician Abbé François Picquet, opened La Présentation, a mission on the upper St. Lawrence (the site of Ogdensburg, New York) and encouraged Iroquois from the south to move there. Picquet's motives were to convert the natives and to have a strong fort. As much a soldier as a man of the cloth, Picquet opened shipyards at La Présentation and on the north shore of the St. Lawrence at Pointe au Baril. The same year the French began a substantial agricultural settlement on both sides of the Detroit River which already had a Jesuit mission. Farmers from the seigneuries along the lower St. Lawrence arrived to till the land. Before the resettlement of the American Loyalists in the 1780s, this was the first permanent white agricultural settlement in Ontario.

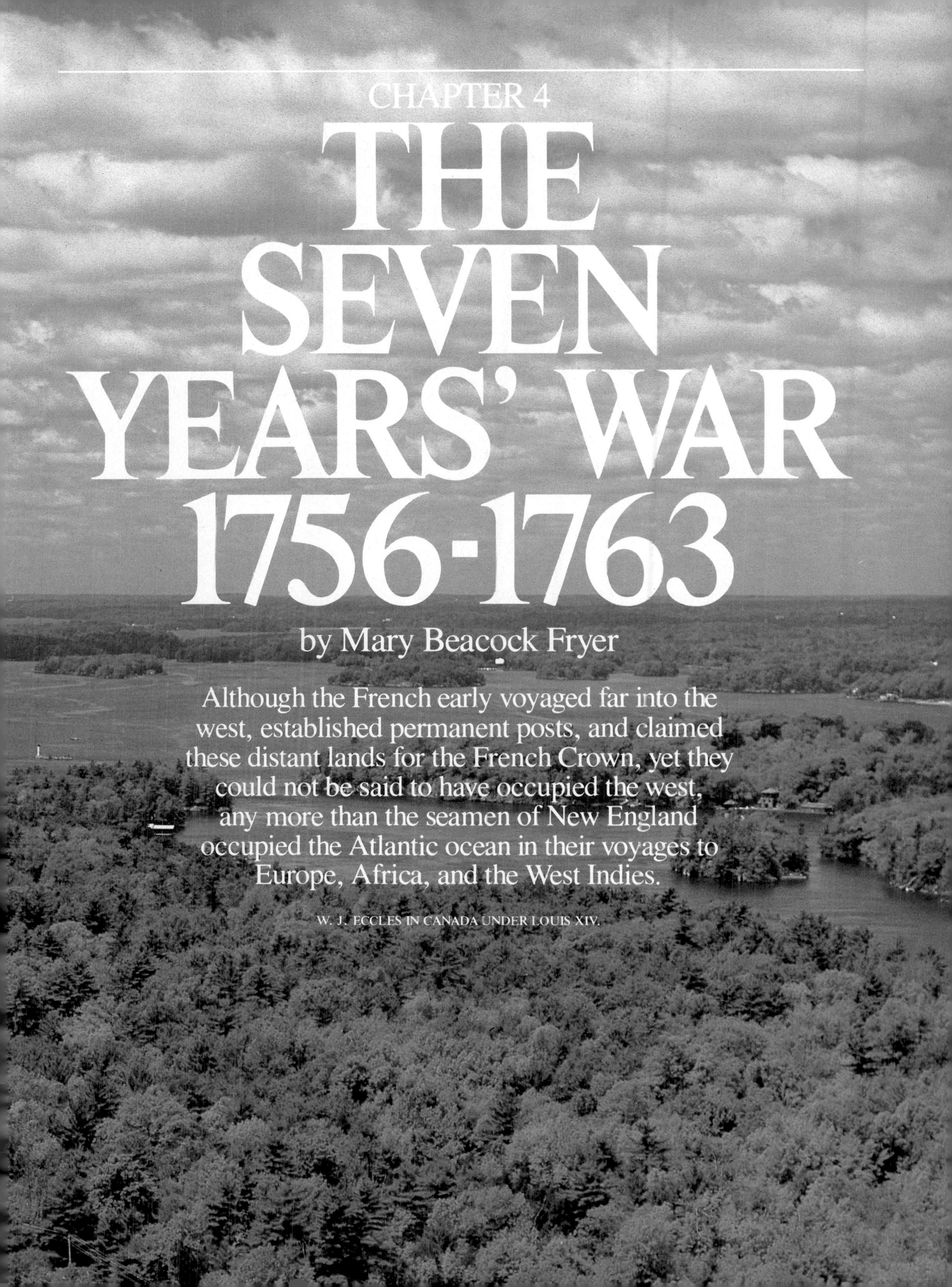

CHAPTER 4

THE SEVEN YEARS' WAR 1756-1763

by Mary Beacock Fryer

Although the French early voyaged far into the west, established permanent posts, and claimed these distant lands for the French Crown, yet they could not be said to have occupied the west, any more than the seamen of New England occupied the Atlantic ocean in their voyages to Europe, Africa, and the West Indies.

W. J. ECCLES IN CANADA UNDER LOUIS XIV.

By 1756 New France's days were numbered. The autumn before, General Edward Braddock led an expedition against France's Fort Duquesne (the site of Pittsburgh, Pennsylvania) to stop raids by the French and the Indians on the frontiers of Britain's colonies. Braddock was soundly defeated, and in May 1756, Britain declared war on France. At once Lake Ontario became a combat zone. Each side had a small navy. The British fleet operated from Oswego, the French fleet from Forts Niagara and Frontenac and Abbé Picquet's La Présentation. The French scored the first victory. In August, the commander-in-chief the Marquis de Montcalm, led an army of French soldiers, militia and Indian allies from the lower St. Lawrence against Oswego. Montcalm destroyed the fortress and incorporated the captured British vessels into the French fleet.

For two years the French were supreme on the Great Lakes, until in 1758 a force of British soldiers, colonials and Iroquois led by John Bradstreet captured Fort Frontenac and the entire French fleet. In need of a new navy the French built two corvettes, the *Iroquois* and the *Ottawa* in the shipyard at Pointe au Baril, opposite La Présentation. In 1759 the French evacuated tiny Fort Rouillé at the Toronto Carrying Place, and a British force under Sir William Johnson captured Fort Niagara. There the French had been building two "snows," a form of brigantine with three masts, which the British finished and launched as the *Mohawk* and the *Onondaga*. Shortly after Fort Niagara fell, Wolfe defeated Montcalm on the Plains of Abraham and took Quebec.

By 1760 only Montreal and the inland posts remained in French hands. In the summer General Jeffrey Amherst the commander-in-chief of British forces in America, assembled an expedition 10,000 strong at Oswego, preparing to descend the St. Lawrence. At the same time two other British armies were advancing on Montreal from Lake Champlain and Quebec. The Chevalier de Lévis, the French commander since the death of Montcalm at Quebec, ordered the French at La Présentation to delay Amherst as long as possible. They evacuated La Présentation and built a stronger post, Fort Lévis, on a small island close to the Galops Rapids (now Chimney Island, New York).

Overleaf: *The Thousand Islands. Here in 1760, General Jeffrey Amherst's only large sailing vessels got lost in the maze of channels, and did not find their way out for several days after the rest of the expedition had reached Pointe au Baril (between Brockville and Prescott). The plight of the vessels is remembered in the name "Lost Channel" that was given to some of the island passages.*

Right: *The Marquis de Montcalm. The French commander until his death in 1759, he led an army that captured Oswego from the British garrison in August 1756.*

Left below: *Plan of Fort de Lévis on Ile Royale (Chimney Island, New York). Chevalier de Lévis, the French commander after the death of Montcalm in 1759, planned to build this sturdy fort, but time ran out. When Amherst's whaleboats carrying 10,000 troops arrived off the island in 1760, the French garrison had erected a wooden stockade. The only large guns, five all told, had no carriages and were mounted on logs. Chimney Island, the scene of the last battle for New France, is a short distance downstream from Prescott, and can be seen from the International Bridge.*

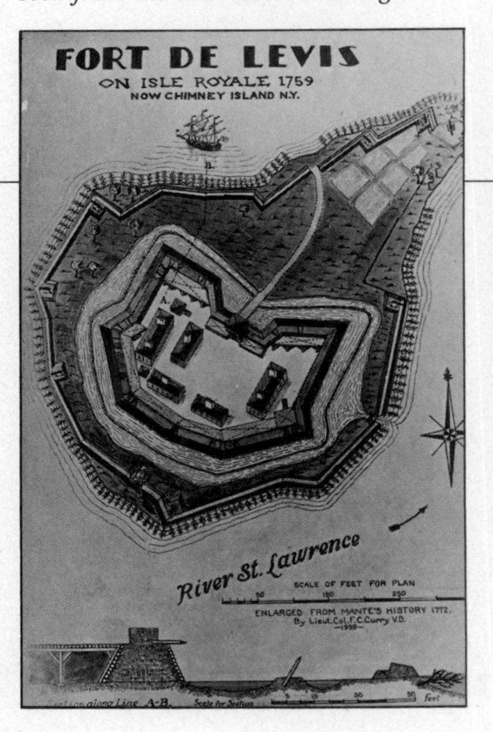

Three men stand out as heroes of the last battle fought for New France. They are Captain Pouchot, first name Pierre or François (depending on the source), Captain René La Force and Captain Pierre de Labroquerie. Pouchot was a French artillery officer; the other two were sailors born in Canada. La Force was the commodore on Lake Ontario and his flagship was the *Iroquois*. Labroquerie commanded the *Ottawa*.

On the small island Pouchot marshalled his resources. He had 200 soldiers — French and colonial — and the crews of the two corvettes, another 200 men. He put his soldiers and La Force and his crew at Fort Lévis. The *Iroquois*, leaking badly after hitting a shoal, had been beached below the five big guns of the fort. Meanwhile, Amherst was leaving Oswego, his 10,000-man army in whaleboats protected by the armed snows *Mohawk* and *Onondaga*. Amherst also had five small gunboats, each with a sail and several pairs of oars, commanded by Colonel George Williamson.

Among the Thousand Islands, the two snows got lost, an event commemorated in the name "Lost Channel." The rest of the expedition continued downstream. By August 16 the advance boats were near Pointe au Baril. There Captain Labroquerie patrolled in the *Ottawa*, and he was at a disadvantage. The corvette was unwieldy; the five oared gunboats could dart about avoiding Labroquerie's guns. Williamson's gunboats closed in on the *Ottawa*, firing a hail of shells on her deck. Wounded men fell, timbers splintered and crashed down. The *Ottawa* fought on for three hours, her deck slippery with blood and strewn with the dead and dying. At length Labroquerie surrendered.

The British repaired the *Ottawa*, renamed her the *Williamson* and sent her against Pouchot's soldiers and La Force's sailors on the island. Labroquerie, now a prisoner, watched as his former ship was hit forty-eight times by Pouchot's gunners at Fort Lévis. On the evening of August 19 the two snows *Mohawk* and *Onondaga* finally appeared, having found the way out of the maze of islands. On the 20th all three ships commenced firing upon Fort Lévis, joined by a gun battery the British erected on the north shore of the St. Lawrence. Amherst's ships boasted fifty guns to Pouchot's five, but the French artillerymen sank all three

Right: *The "French Castle" inside Fort Niagara, N.Y. The fort was begun as a trading post by Denonville, Governor of New France (1685-89) and completed later. The British flag was hoisted after its capture by Sir William Johnson in 1759.*

Left: *Blockhouse at French Fort Duquesne. The fort, on the site of Pittsburgh, Pennsylvania, was rebuilt by the British after they captured it in 1758 and renamed it Fort Pitt. The defeat of General Edward Braddock's expedition against Fort Duquesne, in 1755, led to Britain's declaration of war in May 1756.*

Left below: *Cairn at Pointe au Baril (Maitland, Ontario). In 1760 the French had a shipyard here, and in it two vessels, the* Iroquois *and the* Ottawa, *were built to replace the ships lost at Fort Frontenac in 1758. The* Iroquois *was badly damaged when she ran aground. The British captured the* Ottawa *and renamed her the* Williamson.

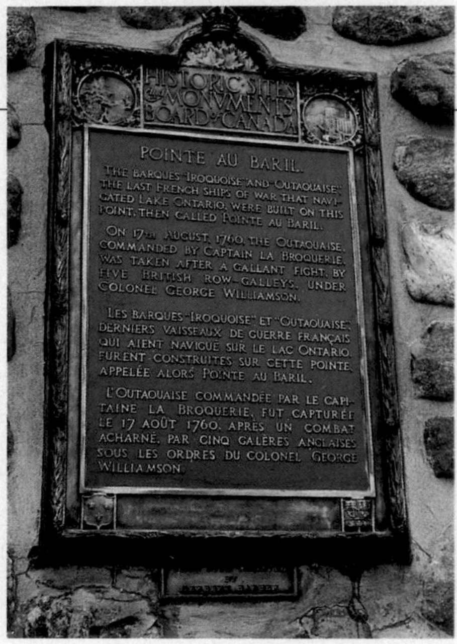

of them. Not until August 24, when he ran out of ammunition, did Pouchot surrender to Amherst. As he entered Fort Lévis, the British commander was confused.

"What have you done with your garrison?" he is said to have asked Pouchot.

"You have my garrison," Pouchot supposedly replied.

Of the 400 soldiers and sailors who fought on the French side in the Battle of the Thousand Islands, only twenty-five escaped death or injury. Pouchot himself had been wounded by flying timber. He could not have won, but he carried out the Chevalier de Lévis' orders to the utmost of his ability. Nor was his surrender the end of the delay. Amherst's men spent four days repairing the fort, renamed Fort William Augustus, in honour of the Duke of Cumberland. Leaving a small garrison the British expedition continued towards Montreal. All told, Pouchot's 400 men had delayed Amherst's 10,000 for twelve days.

On September 6, 1760, Montreal surrendered and Amherst dispatched Major Robert Rogers, the leader of the Queen's Rangers, to Detroit to arrange for the takeover of all the French inland posts. New France officially became a British colony in 1763, when the peace treaty was signed and the Seven Years' War ended in Europe. For some time the 90,000 people who remained in the former French colony were in a sort of limbo — a Catholic province ruled by a mother country in which Catholics had no civil rights. The Quebec Act of 1774 clarified the situation. French civil law remained in force, and Catholics were permitted to hold public office, while the seigneurial system of landholding was retained.

In North America the French were daring explorers, but France did not put enough colonists into the areas she claimed, to secure them. At the close of the French regime scarcely 120,000 colonists were living in New France and Acadia. By contrast, the population of Britain's colonies along the east coast approached 2,000,000. That the British captured Canada was hardly surprising. What was remarkable was that Britain had to fight four long years before she could defeat the French and their Indian allies.

Left: *General Jeffrey Amherst (later Lord Amherst). In 1760 Amherst was the commander of British forces in North America. He led the large expedition from Oswego down the St. Lawrence and captured Montreal. His last battle was fought in August, against a small force of French and Canadians who made a stand at Fort Lévis (on Chimney Island, New York).* ***Right below:*** *Major Robert Rogers (1731-1795). The hardy frontiersman commanded the first regiment known as the Queen's Rangers, more popularly Rogers' Rangers. Green-clad ranger companies operated in every theatre of the Seven Years' War. When the American Revolution began, Rogers raised a second regiment of Queen's Rangers, ultimately commanded by John Graves Simcoe.*

Left: *The British Fleet on Lake Ontario 1756. This painting by C.H.J. Snider, was incorrectly dated 1757, for the fleet was captured by Montcalm in August 1756. When captured, the British fleet consisted of eight vessels — the flagship* Halifax, *the* Oswego, Ontario, London, Mohawk, *and three small rowing schooners, the* George, Lively *and* Vigilant *that were used as tenders. Shown here are two small schooners and five vessels. The large "snow" in the centre is the* Halifax. *The others are difficult to identify. After the French captured the ships, they destroyed two schooners. The other vessels were incorporated into the French fleet and renamed. The* Halifax *became the* Montcalm, *the* London *the* George. *In 1758 all were sunk in Kingston harbour by the British.*

Left: *The French fleet on Lake Ontario in 1756. This painting, also by C.H.J. Snider, shows, from left to right, Commodore René La Force's flagship* La Marquise de Vaudreuil, *the schooners* La Hurault *and* La Louise, *and the sloop* Le Saint Victor. *Although the British had more ships, the French ships were larger and more heavily armed, and overwhelmed the British fleet in 1756. Two schooners were destroyed, and the other six ships (renamed) became part of the French fleet. All ten ships were sunk by the British at the capture of Fort Frontenac in 1758.*

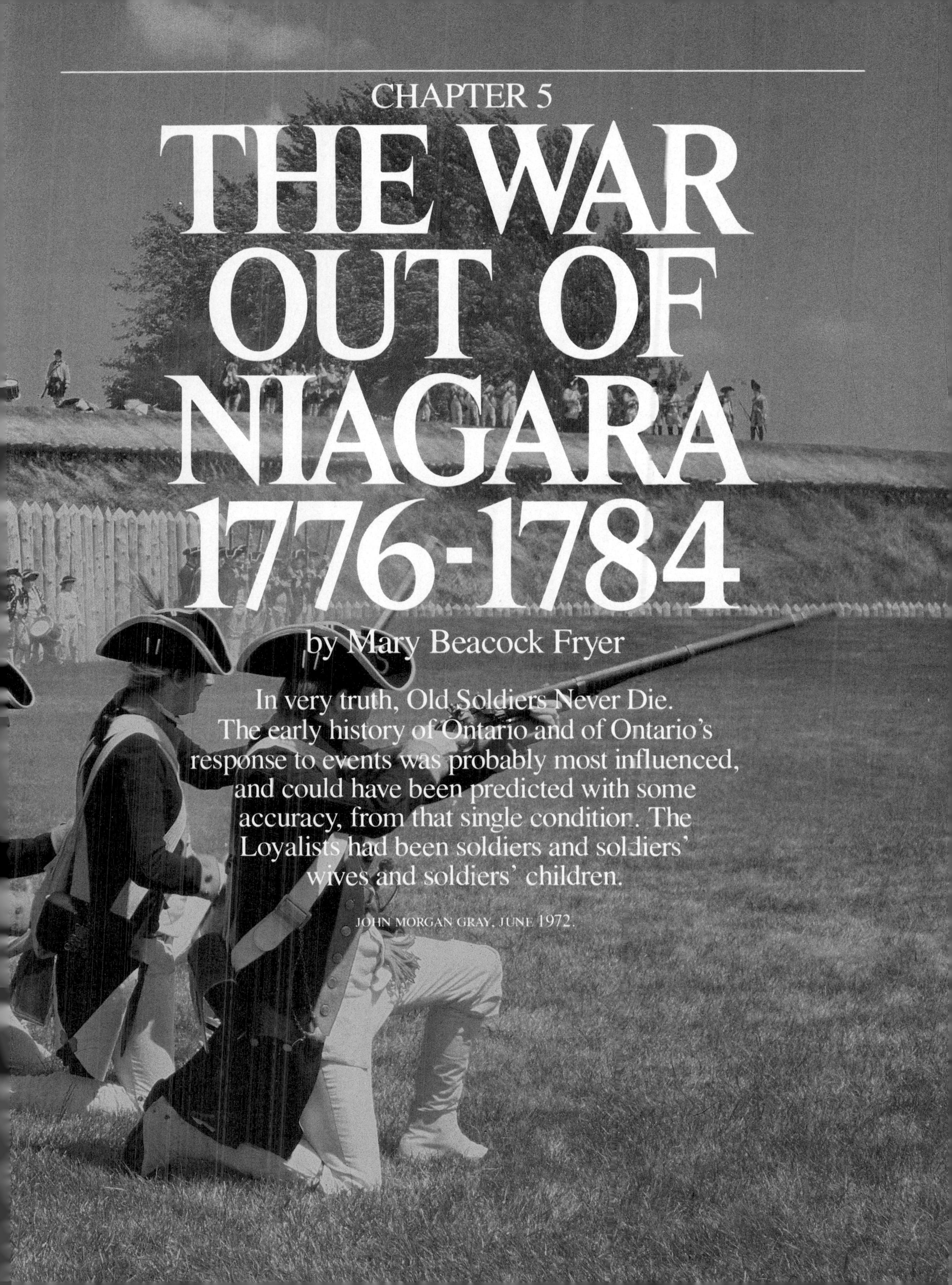

CHAPTER 5

THE WAR OUT OF NIAGARA 1776-1784

by Mary Beacock Fryer

In very truth, Old Soldiers Never Die. The early history of Ontario and of Ontario's response to events was probably most influenced, and could have been predicted with some accuracy, from that single condition. The Loyalists had been soldiers and soldiers' wives and soldiers' children.

JOHN MORGAN GRAY, JUNE 1972.

On the eve of the American Revolution the rebels in the Thirteen Colonies made overtures towards the province of Canada (now Ontario and Quebec) hoping to persuade the "Canadiens" to join their Continental Congress and fight for independence. They failed, and in the autumn of 1775 a rebel army began an attempt to annex Canada, which also failed. Afterwards, Canada became a base of operations against the rebels in the northern colonies.

During the war Canada had two governors. General Guy Carleton, knighted in 1776 after the rebel invasion was repelled, governed from the outset of the revolution until June 1778. His successor, General Frederick Haldimand, a Swiss professional soldier, governed until the autumn of 1784. He was knighted in 1785 for his services in Canada.

The security of Canada depended on Indian allies and on the garrisons of regular and provincial troops who were stationed at fortified posts — most of them inherited from the French régime — that extended from Gaspé Bay to Michilimackinac. Regulars were professional soldiers, usually recruited in Britain, who joined regiments that belonged to what was called the regular establishment. In addition to having names, these regular regiments were numbered. Provincial regiments were raised in the colonies. They had names but were not part of the regular establishment and were not numbered. Regular regiments tended to be permanent; provincial regiments were disbanded at the end of a war.

Important to the future province of Ontario were some of the forts from Oswegatchie (formerly La Présentation on the site of Ogdensburg, New York) to the westward, forts used for defence and from which offensive operations could be launched. The objective of these operations was the destruction of the rebels' food supplies to impede their war effort, especially the rich farmlands of New York's Mohawk Valley, called "the granary of the northern colonies." The provincial troops who fought in the campaigns staged from forts along the present southern boundary of Ontario were nearly all Loyalists from the northern parts of the rebelling colonies who had fled to Canada. They fought a cruel war, goaded by the memories of what they had suffered at the hands of

Far left top: *Guy Johnson (1740-1788). A nephew of Sir William Johnson, Guy became the Superintendent of Indian Affairs after his uncle's death in 1774. He was superseded in 1782 by his cousin, Sir John Johnson, Sir William's son.*
Left top: *Uniforms of the 84th Regiment Royal Highland Emigrants (1779-1784) and of the 8th (King's) Regiment, (1776-1784).*
Left below: *Re-enactment at Yorktown, Virginia, October 17, 1981. Men representing the Royal Artilllery took part in the march past during the American Bicentennial celebrations.*
Right below: *Joseph Brant (1742-1807). He was a subject for some of the best-known portrait painters of the 18th century. In addition to Charles Willson Peale's famous portrait shown here, others who painted Brant were George Romney, Gilbert Stuart, and William von Moll Berczy.*

their rebel neighbours, of public floggings, of women and children left destitute by parties of rebels who attacked their homes and stole everything they possessed. British regular officers were shocked at the cruelty of the colonials on both sides as they fought their bloody civil war. Governor Haldimand warned Loyalists in his provincial corps that he would not tolerate any atrocities against the rebels. Provincials had to abide by the rules of war.

The headquarters for the war in what the governors called the "upper country" was Fort Niagara, in the wilderness on Indian land. Other important posts above Fort Oswegatchie were Fort Pitt (formerly Fort Duquesne on the site of Pittsburgh, Pennsylvania) and Fort Detroit. Fort Pitt was seized early in the conflict and never retaken by the British. In 1778, Governor Haldimand added Carleton Island to his chain of posts, and in 1782 he ordered a garrison to occupy Oswego, empty since the Seven Years' War (1756-1763).

Carleton Island commanded the entrance to the St. Lawrence from Lake Ontario and had the finest harbour available. It was the main base of the Provincial Marine. Fort Niagara, a sturdy stone structure built by the French, was the headquarters of the Indian Department, and the British officer in command there was senior to those at the other inland forts. Fort Detroit (built by the French as Fort Ponchartrain) was a useful base for operating against the frontiersmen of the interior, and had the only agricultural settlement west of the seigneuries of the lower St. Lawrence, thus providing a local source of food.

Throughout the war, Carleton Island (where soldiers began building Fort Haldimand in 1778), Niagara, and to a lesser extent Detroit, provided safe havens for refugees, both Loyalist and Indian. At each place British regular troops, provincials and native warriors were stationed. Supplying these posts posed a problem in logistics. All goods had to be brought up the St. Lawrence from Montreal through rapids and over the lake. The farmlands of the lower St. Lawrence did not yield a substantial surplus, and most supplies for the inland posts were imported from Britain. Soon after he arrived, Haldimand resolved to have an agricultural settlement at Niagara, but he had to be diplomatic. The land

Right top: *Sphere of Operations Directed From Fort Niagara. Troops of the Northern Department (Canadian command), operating from Fort Niagara, campaigned south into the Kentucky Valley, west in Ohio country, and as far east as the border of New Jersey.*

Right below: *Council Chamber in Fort Niagara. The "French Castle," so called by the Indians, was the residence of the Superintendent of Indian Affairs when he was on duty. The military commanders of the fort used the chamber for meetings with their officers.*

Far right below: *Captain John Schanck (1740-1823). Born in Scotland, he joined the Royal Navy in 1758. He commanded the Provincial Marine on the upper lakes during the American Revolution.*

Left below: *Allan Maclean (1725-1798). A son of the Laird of Torloisk, Isle of Mull, Scotland, Allan Maclean came to North America during the Seven Years' War. He commanded an independent company under Sir William Johnson at the capture of Fort Niagara in 1759. During the American Revolution he raised the Royal Highland Emigrants (84th Regiment), and he commanded the inland forts from the spring of 1782 until the autumn of 1783.*

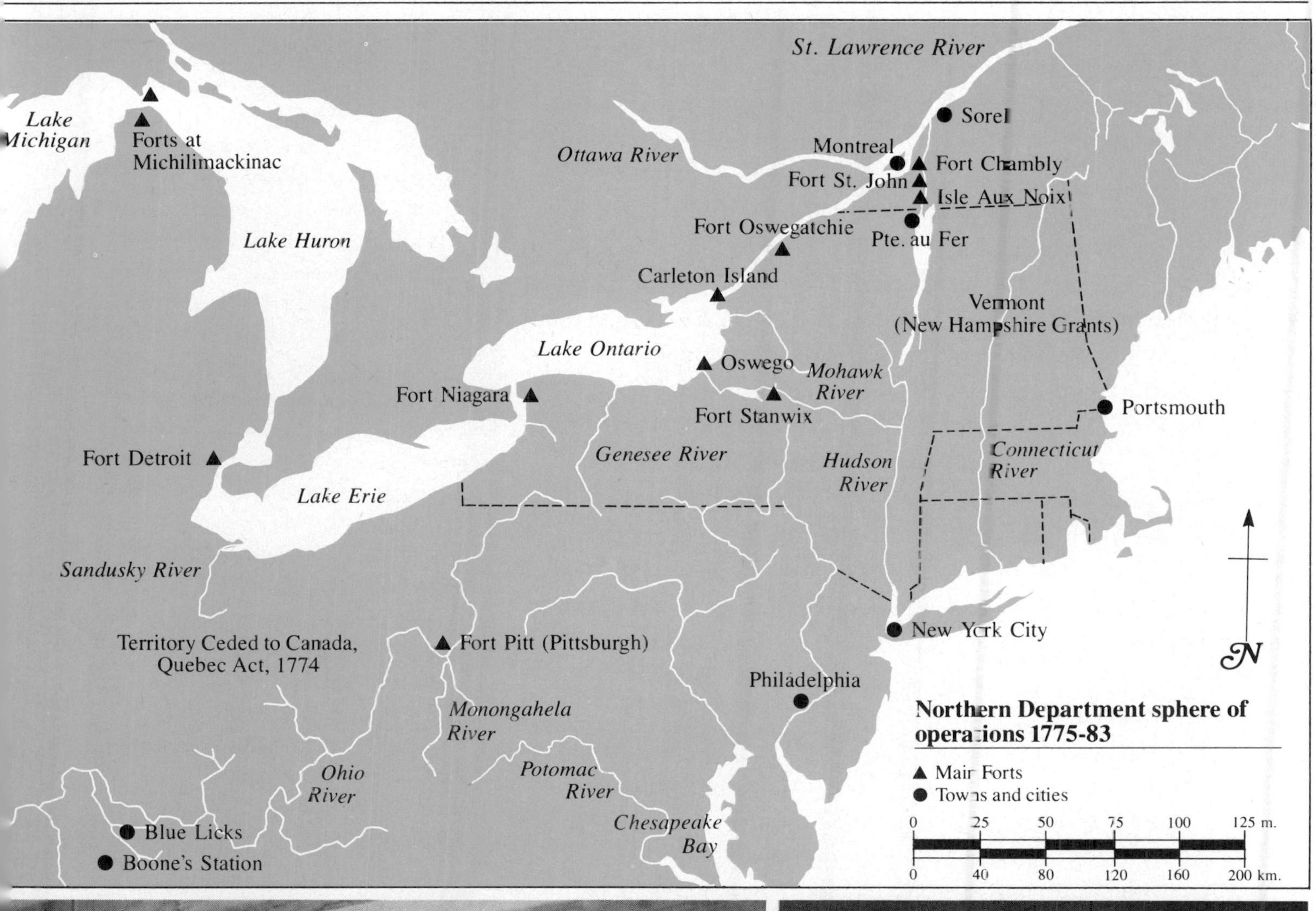
St. Lawrence River
Lake Michigan
Forts at Michilimackinac
Ottawa River
Sorel
Montreal
Fort Chambly
Fort St. John
Isle Aux Noix
Fort Oswegatchie
Pte. au Fer
Lake Huron
Carleton Island
Vermont (New Hampshire Grants)
Lake Ontario
Oswego
Mohawk River
Fort Niagara
Fort Stanwix
Portsmouth
Fort Detroit
Genesee River
Hudson River
Connecticut River
Lake Erie
Sandusky River
New York City
Territory Ceded to Canada, Quebec Act, 1774
Fort Pitt (Pittsburgh)
Philadelphia
Monongahela River
Ohio River
Potomac River
Chesapeake Bay
Blue Licks
Boone's Station
N
Northern Department sphere of operations 1775-83
Main Forts
Towns and cities
0 25 50 75 100 125 m.
0 40 80 120 160 200 km.

belonged to the Senecas, who knew that settlements started by Europeans tended to be permanent. In 1781, Haldimand purchased from the Mississauga Indians a strip of land on the west side of the Niagara River for food crops — and today Niagara-on-the-Lake occupies part of that land.

A series of British officers commanded each fort. At Niagara were Lieutenant-Colonel John Caldwell (1775-1776), Captain Richard Lernoult (1777), Lieutenant-Colonel Mason Bolton (1777-1780), Brigadier Allan Maclean (1782-1783), and Lieutenant-Colonel Arent DePeyster (1784). At Carleton Island were Captain William Ancrum (1778), Captain George MacDougall (1779), Major John Nairne (1780), Major John Ross (1781), Captain William Ancrum (1782) and Major John Adolphus Harris (1783-1784). At Detroit were Lieutenant-Colonel Henry Hamilton (1776-1778), Major Arent DePeyster (1778-1783), and Major Jehu Hay (1784). At Niagara the Superintendent of Indian Affairs had a suite of rooms, while a deputy, Alexander McKee, was on duty at Detroit, and Captain Alexander Fraser was the Indian agent at Carleton Island.

The Indian Department

Organized to control the fur trade, the Indian Department assumed a military role as unrest spread, and the officers received military ranks. Both sides wooed the native peoples, the British with more success than the rebels. Under the terms of the Quebec Act of 1774, Britain hoped to preserve the interior lands for the Indians. Land-hungry colonials, on the other hand, believed in their God-given right to encroach on the territory of the natives whenever they pleased. Initially Governor Carleton ordered Colonel Guy Johnson, the superintendent of Indian Affairs, Northern District, to keep the natives neutral, a policy that altered as events changed.

Guy Johnson, a nephew of Sir William Johnson, the superintendent until he died in 1774, lived at Guy Park, a manor in the Mohawk Valley. In May 1775, the rebel faction formed the Tryon County Committee of Safety, amidst rumours that plotters in Albany hoped to have

Right: *In 1710 four Mohawk leaders visited England and met with Queen Anne. They requested her to send Anglican missionaries among their people. The queen sent a seven-piece silver communion set for the Mohawks to use in their chapel at Fort Hunter. This is a portrait of one of the Indian leaders, Etow Oh Koam, who was given the name Nicholas when he became a Christian.*

Left below: *Early in the American Revolution, the Mohawk Indians buried the Queen Anne silver near Fort Hunter. It remained there until 1784 when a group of Mohawks paid a secret visit to New York and retrieved their treasure. They returned to Canada and divided the silver between the Grand River and the Deseronto bands. This is one of the pieces in the hands of the Mohawks from Deseronto.*

Guy Johnson kidnapped. Guy set out with his family and some 250 friends, among them officers in his department — John Butler and his son Walter, Gilbert Tice, Joseph Brant and John Deseronto — the latter two were Mohawk warriors. At Oswego, Guy's wife Mary, a daughter of Sir William Johnson, died. Her sorrowing husband continued down the St. Lawrence to Montreal, where he found Governor Carleton.

Guy wanted to unleash the fury of the natives against the rebels, but when Carleton refused permission he went on a leave of absence to England. Carleton consequently sent John Butler to Niagara to take over the Indian Department and carry out his orders to keep the natives neutral. Butler obeyed, until the autumn of 1775 when an army of rebels captured Montreal, and Carleton, who escaped to Quebec, changed his mind.

In the spring of 1776, Butler dispatched a detachment of the 8th (King's) Regiment and many native warriors to Oswegatchie to join Captain George Forster, the commandant. This force moved down the St. Lawrence and routed a rebel outpost at The Cedars, a short distance west of Montreal. That signalled the beginning of the rebel withdrawal from Canada. Afterwards, the Indian Department played a decisive role in the many excursions against the rebels in the northern colonies. Guy Johnson returned from England in 1776, and soon took up his duties. Haldimand was never impressed with Guy Johnson's performance, and in 1782 his cousin, Sir John Johnson, superseded him as Superintendent of Indian Affairs.

The Army in the Wilderness (The Professional Soldiers)

Detachments from two regular regiments served in what the governors called their "upper posts." These were the 8th and 34th Regiments. Two companies from the 47th Regiment helped build Fort Haldimand on Carleton Island in 1778. Also present at Niagara was a company of Hesse-Hanau Jaegers, riflemen from one of the regiments George III rented in his Hanover dependencies. One regiment, the Royal Highland Emigrants, began as a provincial corps. On December 24, 1778, it was

__Left top:__ Johnson Hall, Johnstown, New York. Built by Sir William Johnson in 1761, this mansion of square timbers flanked by stone blockhouses, passed to his son, Sir John, in 1774. Sir John escaped from the hall in May 1776, after Indians warned him that the rebels were coming to arrest him. He reached Montreal on June 18 with 200 followers — the first who enlisted in his regiment, the King's Royal Regiment of New York.

__Left below:__ "Royal Yorkers" at Yorktown, Virginia. Men uniformed as the first battalion, King's Royal Regiment of New York, paraded at Yorktown in October 1981, as a good will gesture. The original corps was not at the British surrender in Yorktown, in 1781. It operated in the northern colonies, was never defeated, and never surrendered.

__Right below:__ Plaque to Butler's Rangers. The plaque stands near Butler's burying ground, Niagara-on-the-Lake.

placed on the regular establishment as the 84th. Raised in the colonies, it consisted of two battalions. The first served in Canada, the second out of Nova Scotia. Detachments of the first battalion served from Oswegatchie to Michilimackinac. Most were residents of Canada, but about one quarter were Loyalists from the northern colonies.

The Provincials

To help subdue the rebellion, Britain raised many Provincial Corps of the British Army in her colonies. Popularly called Loyalist regiments, two operated from Canada's upper posts. Although these provincials thought of themselves as British Americans, in the ranks were men from every ethnic group living along the frontiers of the north. Amongst others whose origins did not lie in the British Isles were: Huguenot French, Germans, Swiss, Blacks, Alsatians and Dutch.

The King's Royal Regiment of New York

The commander of this corps was Sir John Johnson, the son of Sir William, the Superintendent of Indian Affairs who died in 1774, and his German wife Catherine Weisenberg. In June 1776, Sir John fled with 200 followers from his manor, Johnson Hall, at Johnstown in the Mohawk Valley. They crossed the Adirondack Mountains to elude their pursuers and arrived, half-starved, in Montreal on June 18. Governor Carleton gave Johnson permission to raise a provincial corps, which ultimately consisted of two battalions — the largest Loyalist regiment that served from Canada. The first battalion was based at Montreal, the second at Carleton Island. The regiment went on three major expeditions through the Mohawk Valley, two of which were staged from the upper posts.

Butler's Rangers

John Butler, whose home, Butlersbury, was at Fonda in the Mohawk Valley, was a major in the Indian Department, and later the lieutenant-colonel of a full-strength corps. He received permission to raise his regiment in September 1777. The first men who enlisted had seen action as

Right: *Tee Yee Neem Ho Ga Row (Hendrick). This John Verelst painting is one of the four Mohawk Kings who visited Queen Anne in 1810. Copies of the Verelst portraits of the Kings hang in the council chamber in the band council house on the Tyendinaga Reserve near Deseronto.*

Left below: *Fort Stanwix at Rome, New York. The fort was strategically placed at the portage between the Mohawk River and Lake Oneida, on the main route to Oswego. The reconstructed log fort is on the site of the original fort, in the centre of Rome.*

an unofficial unit at the Battle of Oriskany the month before. The regiment operated with native allies, and two companies were of men conversant in Indian languages. It was the most active against the rebels, and its base was Niagara. Companies of rangers were stationed at Detroit to assist the natives of the Ohio and Kentucky Valleys. Butler's Rangers usually operated in small detachments, accompanied by larger numbers of native warriors.

Scouts brought recruits, refugees and information to the upper posts, and a spy network existed between Fort Niagara and the southern colonies (word of the British defeat at Yorktown, Virginia, for instance, reached Niagara before the news was relayed to headquarters in Quebec). Rangers piloted escaped prisoners-of-war to Niagara. Some German regulars so rescued served in the rangers rather than return to their own Hanoverian regiments, a tribute to their hardiness. Haldimand wrote that a ranger must be able: "to shoot well, to march well, and to endure privation and fatigue." Records show that they made forced marches of better than twenty-five miles (forty kilometres), often dragging a three-pounder cannon nicknamed a "grasshopper." Unable to carry enough supplies, they often lived off the country and bivouacked without blankets. They returned to the forts mere wraiths, clothing tattered, shoes worn to ribbons. They did indeed range — from Niagara and Detroit to the boundaries of New Jersey and as far south as the Kentucky Valley (where they bested Daniel Boone).

Small Units

The Detroit Volunteers were French-speaking farmers whose homes were along the Detroit River. Like Butler's Rangers they went on raids along the frontier, penetrating deep into the Kentucky Valley, and terrifying settlers in the Daniel Boone country. The Loyal Foresters, recruited among frontiersmen in Pennsylvania, were formed into a provincial corps based at Fort Pitt. When that fort was taken by the rebels, some escaped to Niagara and joined the Indian Department. Joseph Brant's Volunteers formed a third small unit, of whites and natives, who also served with the Indian Department.

Right: *General John Sullivan (1740-1795). This officer in George Washington's Continental Army commanded, in 1779, the expedition that devastated the lands of the League of the Iroquois that lay south of the St. Lawrence and Great Lakes, to punish the natives for assisting the British against the revolutionaries. Sullivan's expedition failed. Native retaliation in 1780 and 1781, aided by provincial and regular soldiers, left many frontier settlements in flames.*

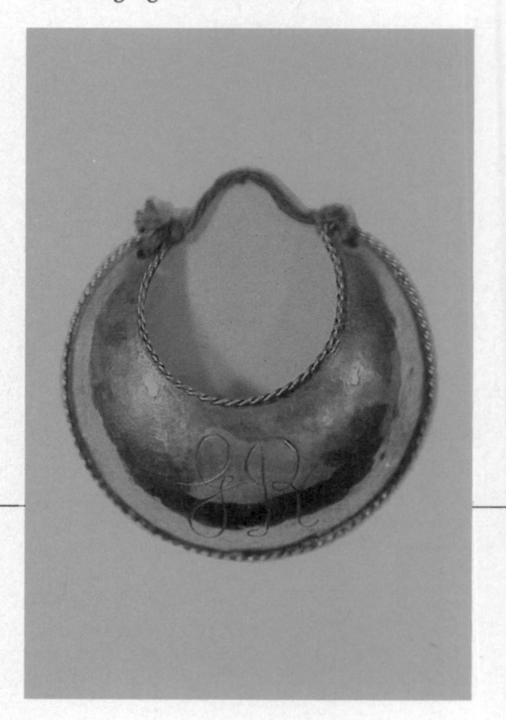

Left below: *Indian Department Gorget. All military officers wore half-moon-shaped gorgets suspended on their chests, usually of gold or silver and stamped with the Royal cypher. This Indian Department gorget is of copper, and smaller than most — about ten centimetres across. Officers in this department, both native and white, sometimes wore more than one gorget, one hanging below the other.*

Left: ***Sa Ga Yeath Qua Pieth Tow (Brant). Brant was one of the four Mohawk Kings who visited Queen Anne in 1710, and whose portrait was painted by John Verelst. Some sources claim that he was the father of the war chief, Joseph Brant, and his sister Molly, the second wife of Sir William Johnson. He may also have been their grandfather.***

Right below: *Peter Warren Johnson, Ensign in the 26th Regiment. Peter was the elder son of Sir William Johnson and his second wife, Molly Brant (she kept her maiden name because she would have been excluded from the society of Mohawk matrons if she took her husband's). Their son was named after Sir William's uncle, Admiral Sir Peter Warren. Young Ensign Johnson accepted Ethan Allen's sword when he surrendered outside Montreal in the autumn of 1775. In September 1776, Peter was killed in action at the Battle of Long Island, near New York City.*

The Native Allies

Tribes along the frontiers faced an insoluble dilemma during the quarrel between Britain and her colonies. Both sides have been condemned for their exploitation of the native peoples. Among those who suffered cruelly was the great Iroquois Confederacy of Six Nations — Mohawk, Oneida, Cayuga, Onondaga, Tuscarora and Seneca — whose lands lay to the south of the St. Lawrence and Lake Ontario. Unable to remain aloof, their confederacy was destroyed by the conflict. Many, notably the Oneidas, sided with the rebels, but the overwhelming majority favoured the British. Most active against the rebels were the Mohawks, whose long association with the Crown kept them on Britain's side.

Their friendship went back to the 1660s after the Dutch relinquished their colony of New Netherlands to Britain and it became New York. Having long opposed being converted to Catholicism by the Jesuits, in 1710 four Mohawk "Kings" went to England and met with Queen Anne. They asked the Queen to abolish the sale of liquor to the Indians, and to send Anglican missionaries among their people. The Queen did not have the power to grant the first request, but she supported the second. In 1712 she sent two sets of communion silver, engraved with the royal cypher, to their country. One set was for the Onondagas, who never used it, and today it is in a museum in Albany. The other set, given to the Mohawks, was placed in their chapel at Fort Hunter, and they brought it to Canada after the revolution.

In battle, the Mohawk warriors were led by the war chiefs Joseph Brant and John Deseronto, and they frequently joined forces with the more numerous Senecas and their war chief, Sayenqueraghta. Another native who was invaluable was Molly Brant, Joseph's elder sister, the widow of Sir William Johnson and Sir John's stepmother. She was known as Brown Lady Johnson to her neighbours around Johnstown, or Mistress Molly — the name she preferred. She kept her maiden name because she was a matron of the Wolf clan and would have had to give up her membership in the Society of Mohawk Matrons if she had taken her husband's surname. However, she departed from the Iroquois custom of matrilineal descent, for the six daughters and two sons she bore

Sir William were all called Johnson. Molly's status as a Mohawk matron placed her in a position of considerable influence over the warriors of the Six Nations. Whenever they wavered she persuaded them that supporting Britain was in their best interests.

In 1779, to punish the Iroquois for aiding the British, the rebels' commander-in-chief, General George Washington sent an expedition 5,000 strong to destroy the lands of the confederacy and end their participation in the war. Under General John Sullivan the expedition marched through the Iroquois lands, burning villages, chopping down orchards, burning crops and capturing livestock. Some of the rebel soldiers were astonished to find that these Indians had houses as fine as their white neighbours, with glass in the windows. Some Iroquois still lived in bark longhouses, but many had built more comfortable homes.

The warriors, aided by Butler's Rangers, tried to turn Sullivan's men back by hit and run raids since they were outnumbered. Afterwards, thousands of Iroquois women and children sought refuge at Fort Niagara, putting an impossible strain on the available supplies of food, clothing and blankets. Native retaliation almost emptied the rebel's settlements in the years that followed.

Farther west, the war between rebel and Loyalist, the latter assisting the natives, was a continuation of the struggle to keep settlers from moving west of the Allegheny Mountains. Among many bloody encounters, one stands out — the massacre of innocent Delaware Indians who had been Christianized by Moravian missionaries. In April 1782, a settler's family was murdered at Racoon Creek in the Ohio Valley, a few miles south of the Delaware village of Gnadenhutten. Looking for a scapegoat, a body of militiamen fell upon the Delaware people who had not taken part in the war. The frontiersmen beat and tomahawked to death ninety-six men, women and children, and burned their village. (In 1792, some Delawares and their missionaries started a settlement in Ontario which they named Moraviantown, now known as Thamesville.)

The Campaigns

The first action was the Battle of the Cedars in the spring of 1776 that

Right: *Lieutenant-Colonel John Butler (1725-1796). The commander of his own corps of rangers, Butler lived at Fort Niagara. His duties as Deputy Superintendent of Indian Affairs kept him occupied, and he was rarely able to lead his men on campaigns. This painting of the founder of Niagara-on-the-Lake belongs to his descendant.*

Far right top: *Women on Duty in Camp. Except when soldiers were in action, women formed an integral part of each regiment, attending to housekeeping chores, assisted by their children.*

Far right below: *General John Burgoyne's Surrender at Saratoga, October 19, 1777. Britain suffered two major defeats. Burgoyne's brought France into the war on the side of the rebels. Cornwallis' at Yorktown, two years later, brought down the war ministry of Lord North. His successor, Lord Rockingham, began peace negotiations in Paris.*

Right: *Fort Haldimand, on Carleton Island. The fort stood on a bluff, overlooking a low peninsula with a dockyard and good harbours on each side, where shelter could always be found.*

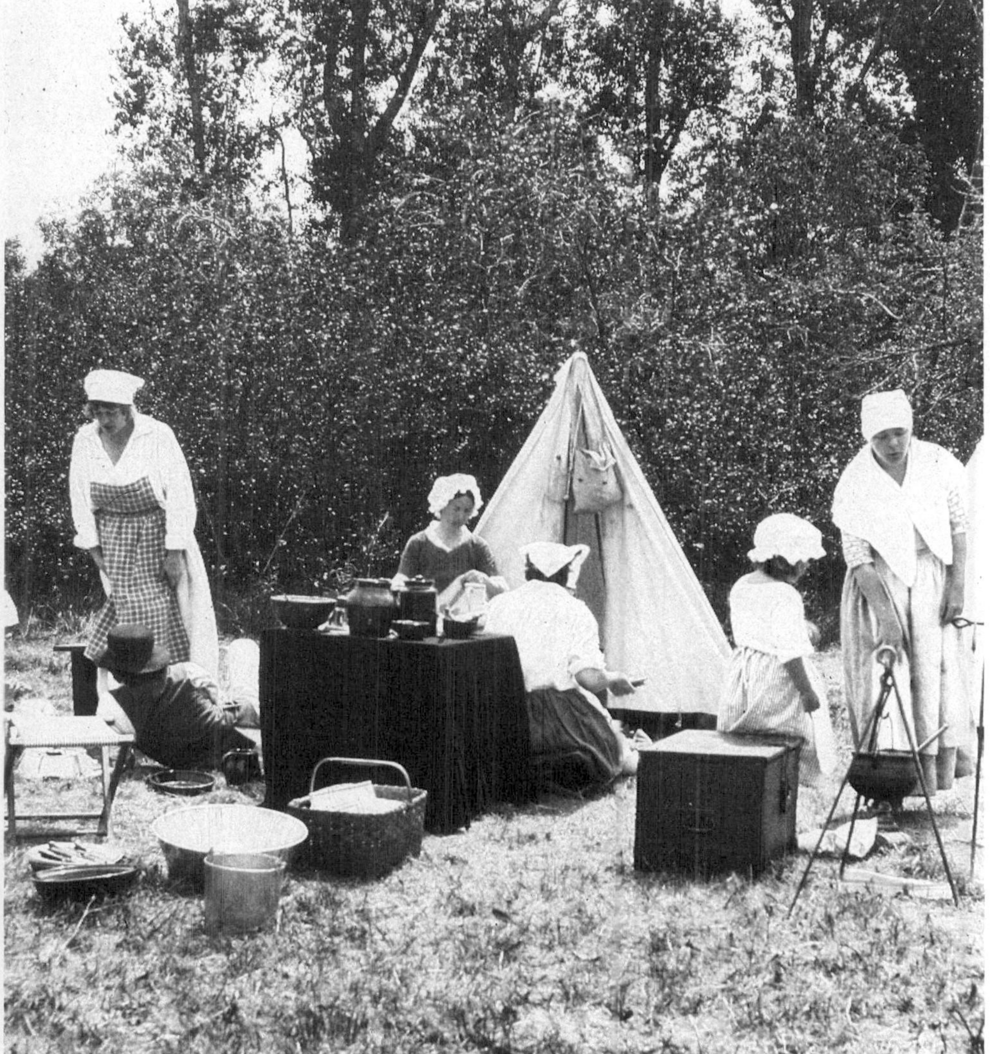

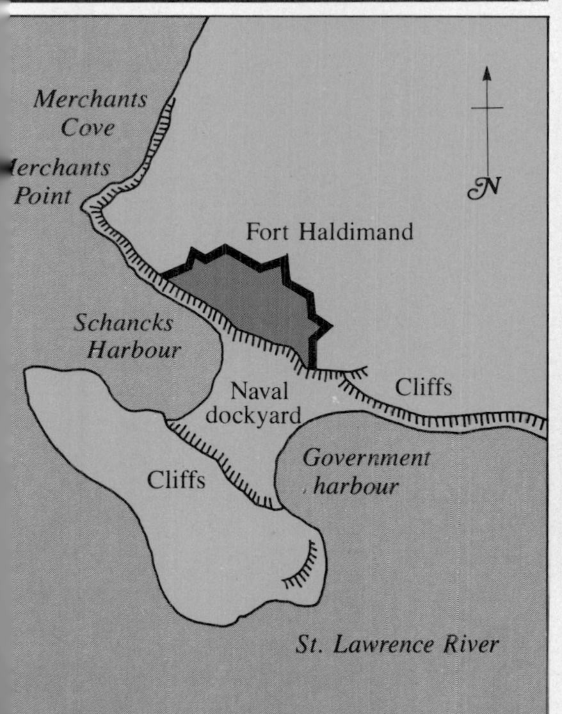
Merchants Cove
Merchants Point
Fort Haldimand
Schancks Harbour
Naval dockyard
Cliffs
Government harbour
Cliffs
St. Lawrence River
N
Southwest Portion of Carleton Island
0
500
1000 ft.
0
157.5
315 met.

drove the rebels from their outpost near Montreal. Next came the Battle of Oriskany in August 1777.

While planning his invasion of New York by way of Lake Champlain, General John Burgoyne decided to send a small expedition from Oswego through the Mohawk Valley to meet his main force at Albany. Commanded by Colonel Barry St. Leger, the expedition from Oswego consisted of: 133 King's Royal Regiment of New York with Sir John Johnson, 67 rangers under John Butler, 50 Canadians led by René de Rouville, 200 regulars from the 8th and 34th Regiments, 50 German riflemen, and 800 Iroquois with Daniel Claus, a deputy in the Indian Department as well as a son-in-law of Sir William Johnson. Assisting Claus were William Johnson, Sir William's half-Mohawk son, Sayenqueraghta of the Senecas, and Joseph Brant of the Mohawks.

St. Leger's expedition halted at rebel-held Fort Stanwix, between Oneida Lake and the headwaters of the Mohawk, because his guns were not heavy enough to reduce the fort. Molly Brant sent word that a supply train and reinforcements, under General Nicholas Herkimer, was approaching from the east. Sir John Johnson, John Butler, and Joseph Brant led a body of Loyalists and Indians to a gorge near Oriskany, and ambushed Herkimer's force. Loyalist and native losses were light, those of the rebels heavy — 500 killed and wounded — yet Oriskany was claimed as a victory by both sides. The reinforcements were turned back, but because St. Leger withdrew to Oswego until heavier guns could be brought from Niagara, Americans still claim Herkimer won. When St. Leger reached Oswego, Burgoyne sent word to abandon the attempt on Fort Stanwix and bring his men down the St. Lawrence to join him on the Hudson River. Before St. Leger could reach him, Burgoyne had surrendered at Saratoga that October of 1777.

In 1778 Butler's Rangers and the Indian warriors staged many raids. Best known were those on Wyoming and Cherry Valley, but other settlements in New York and Pennsylvania were also burnt. Even while the rangers and natives were trying to check General Sullivan's army in 1779, small parties were attacking rebel settlements.

The bloodiest time along the frontiers was from 1780 to 1781. The

Left: *No Nee Yeath Taw No Row (John). Artist John Verelst painted the portraits of the four Mohawk Kings who visited Queen Anne in 1710. After their visit, the Queen sent the communion silver that is now shared by the Mohawks of the Grand River and Tyendinaga Reserves.*
Right below: *Private in Butler's Rangers. The rangers were uniformed in green coats faced red, which were shorter than those worn in regiments of the line. The felt hats were made by cutting down standard issue bicornes, and trimmed with a belt or cartridge-case plate. While in action, some wore green-fringed hunting shirts and linen trousers.*

supply situation had improved, and Haldimand was able to equip larger expeditions. In the autumn of 1780, at Oswego, Sir John Johnson assembled a force 800 strong of regulars, provincials from his own regiment and Butler's Rangers, and natives under Joseph Brant. They marched through the Mohawk Valley destroying grain stored for Washington's army; they burned mills and barns, captured prisoners, and took all the livestock. Other companies of Butler's Rangers and natives continued their smaller scale raids on the rebels' food stocks.

In October 1781, Major John Ross of the second battalion King's Royal Regiment of New York led another expedition from Oswego through the Mohawk Valley. Ross' force, 740 strong, consisted of four companies of his own battalion, detachments of the 8th, 34th and 84th Regiments, three companies of Butler's Rangers under Captain Walter Butler, and 200 warriors under Captain Gilbert Tice of the Indian Department. Ross found the rebels better prepared than Sir John Johnson had the year before, and he fought a running battle near Johnstown. Ross withdrew directly towards Carleton Island, abandoning a cache of supplies he had left at Oswego. In the rearguard action at West Canada Creek, Walter Butler was killed.

Ross' men made such a fast withdrawal that even the pursuing rebel commander, Colonel Marinius Willett, could not help but admire them:

> Although they had been four days in the wilderness with only half a pound of horseflesh per man, yet they ran thirty miles in their famished condition.

Ross reported that his men did not leave a single prisoner behind. Men of his force who were missing when he reached Carleton Island turned up later there or at Niagara.

As 1781 drew to a close, the troops who had served from Canada's most strategic forts — those in the upper country and along Lake Champlain — had won a military victory. The rebels in the north were on the run. In Albany, New York, leaders were proposing a separate peace, and Vermont was neutral. The Loyalists and Indians serving from Canadian bases felt optimistic when, almost four years

Left below: *Winter Dress. In winter, the King's Royal Regiment of New York and other provincial corps used coats made from blankets that were called capotes.*

to the day after Burgoyne surrendered at Saratoga, the British suffered a major defeat at Yorktown, Virginia, in October 1781. In London, the war ministry of Lord North fell, and his successor, Lord Rockingham, opened peace talks in Paris. For many provincial troops the war was over, but not for Butler's Rangers.

Rangers based at Detroit continued to check the frontiersmen. In August 1782, Captain William Caldwell, with his company and 200 Shawnee warriors, was in Kentucky burning settlements. They were pursued to the Licking River by Daniel Boone and 200 mounted riflemen. At Blue Licks, Caldwell set up an ambush in which 150 of the frontiersmen were killed. Boone escaped, but his son Israel died. The last action took place in September when Captain Andrew Bradt, Colonel Butler's nephew, raided Wheeling (then part of Virginia colony, now in West Virginia).

At the peace table in Paris, eager to make concessions, Britain gave away the gains of the soldiers in the Canadian command, and the lands of her native allies. When the news of the formal cessation of hostilities reached Brigadier Allan Maclean at Fort Niagara, he warned Haldimand that the terms must be kept secret as long as possible. Haldimand himself was disturbed, and hoped he could make better arrangements for the native allies. When word did reach the Indian leaders, Maclean was worried they would turn on his small garrison, and he felt they would have been justified.

With the signing of the final peace treaty that September of 1783, the provincials at the upper posts, joined by provincials who had served along Lake Champlain, and certain of the natives, became the founders of Ontario. The Mohawks and some of the other Iroquois decided to accept a new homeland north of the Great Lakes. The Senecas, more remote from the white settlements, resolved to return and rebuild their shattered villages. The tribes farther west, the Shawnees and Wyandots, most of the Delawares and others, continued their war against the American frontiersmen.

Right below: *Butler's Rangers Belt Buckle. This artifact of brass was found at Fort Niagara, where the corps was stationed during the revolution.*

INDEFE
AN
EXPEN

This First Edition

of

LOYAL SHE REMAINS

is

presented to:

compliments of:

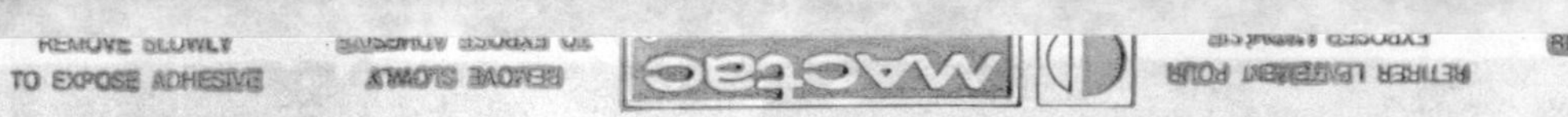

NSIBLE
ND
DABLE

CHAPTER 6

FIRST LARGE-SCALE IMMIGRATION 1784-1800

by Mary Beacock Fryer

Because they were Loyalists, we are Canadians...

W. S. MACNUTT.

People Awaiting Resettlement 1783

When the peace treaty was signed in September 1783, some 8,000 Loyalists were in what is now Ontario and Quebec, and most required government help to re-establish themselves. In addition, 2,000 displaced native allies needed assistance.

Most of the Loyalist men were still serving in the Provincial Corps of the British Army, the correct name for the regiments that Britain had raised in her colonies that are more commonly called Loyalist regiments. Their families were subsisting in refugee camps. Three battalions of provincial troops were on duty west of the rapids in the St. Lawrence. These were Butler's Rangers, the second battalion King's Royal Regiment of New York, and the first battalion Royal Highland Emigrants. Butler's Rangers were at Niagara; the second battalion King's Royal Regiment of New York was with Major John Ross at Cataraqui (Kingston), building a new military base because the boundary between Canada and the United States placed Carleton Island, Oswego and other British forts inside the new republic. The Royal Highland Emigrants were scattered from Oswegatchie to Michilimackinac. Most of the displaced Indians were near the inland forts, generally Niagara. There were about 500 Loyalist refugees, families of the provincials, at Niagara and Carleton Island, while a few were at Detroit.

In the lower part of the province were many more Loyalists, both civilians and provincial troops. The first battalion King's Royal Regiment of New York was near Montreal. Three companies of King's Rangers were at St. Jean. The Loyal Rangers were at the Lake Champlain outposts and at two blockhouses on the Yamaska River.

The Loyal Rangers were the youngest regiment, formed in 1781, but most were veterans of Burgoyne's campaign of 1777. Before Burgoyne surrendered, many of his provincials escaped from Saratoga to Canada. Others were freed later through prisoner exchanges. Governor Carleton, and later Governor Haldimand, regarded Burgoyne's provincials as refugees. When Burgoyne crossed into New York, his army became subordinate to the commander-in-chief at New York City, Sir William Howe. When they returned to Canada the corps leaders asked to have

Right top: *First St. Lawrence Canal. By order of Governor Haldimand, a canal forty-five centimetres deep was dug to by-pass the Cedars Rapids above Montreal. The work was carried out by British troops, provincials, and Loyalists in the* bateau *service. Loyalists who had gathered around Montreal travelled in flat-bottomed* bateaux *to reach the new settlements, and all passed through this canal at Côteau du Lac.*

Right below: *The Butler House, Niagara-on-the-Lake. The original owner is thought to have been William Johnson Butler, a son of Colonel John Butler. The main floor has four rooms, drawing room on the left, dining room on the right and two bedrooms at the back. The cooking hearth and bake oven were in the basement. The house first stood on the Butler land grant on the south side of town, and was later moved to Simcoe Street.*

Left below: *Loyalist Monument in Hamilton. Unveiled on May 23, 1929, it stood in front of the old City Hall in Hamilton. The hall has since been replaced by a new building, and the monument now stands in Prince's Square.*

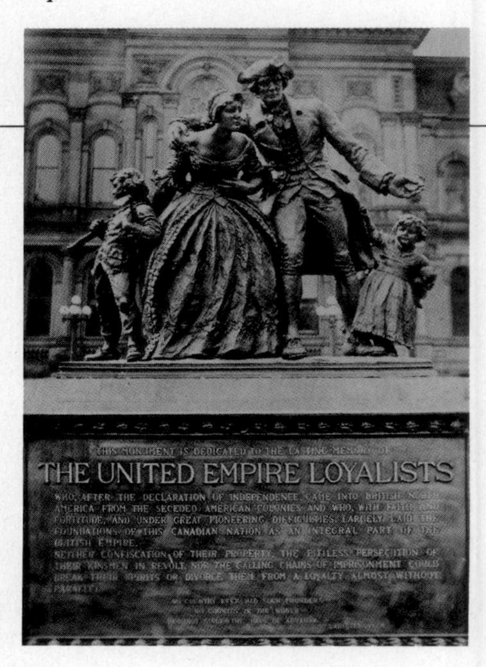

— CRAWFORD PURCHASE
CARLETON ISLAND
9th October – 1783
CRAWFORD
PURCHASE

Left top: *Loyalists at Cataraqui (Kingston) c. 1783. In the early 1780s James Peachy (or Peachey) was a surveyor-painter in the British army in Canada, executing water colours of historical and contemporary events. Here, one of his paintings captures Cataraqui (Kingston) shortly after the Loyalist landing there in 1783.*
Left below: *The Crawford Purchase, October 1783. The purchase of land along the St. Lawrence and Bay of Quinte was negotiated by Captain William Redford Crawford, of the second battalion King's Royal Regiment of New York, at the request of Sir John Johnson, Crawford's commanding officer as well as Superintendent of Indian Affairs. On October 9, Crawford reported to Johnson that the Mississauga Indians had agreed to sell the government a strip extending "from the lake back as far as a man can travel in a day."*
Right below: *Plaque on Site of Justus Sherwood's Loyal Blockhouse. The wording shows a Vermont bias, for the "British" refugees were American Loyalists. Sherwood was the head of the British Secret Service, and his Loyal Blockhouse stood on a secluded point on North Hero Island, Lake Champlain.*

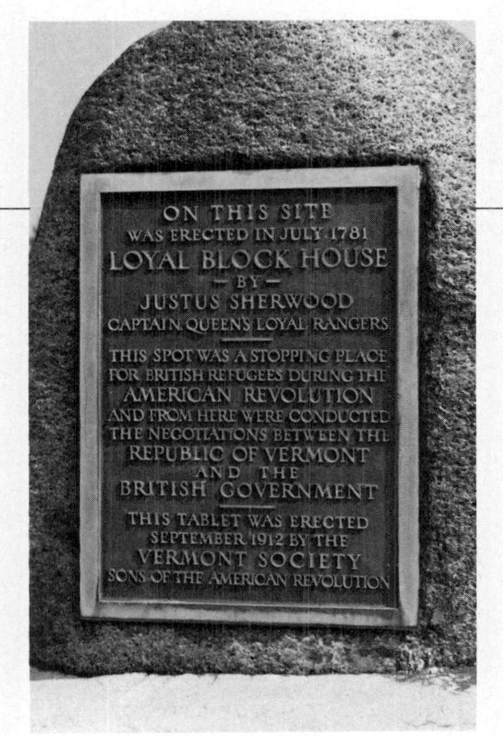
ON THIS SITE
WAS ERECTED IN JULY 1781
LOYAL BLOCK HOUSE
— BY —
JUSTUS SHERWOOD
CAPTAIN QUEENS LOYAL RANGERS
THIS SPOT WAS A STOPPING PLACE
FOR BRITISH REFUGEES DURING THE
AMERICAN REVOLUTION
AND FROM HERE WERE CONDUCTED
THE NEGOTIATIONS BETWEEN THE
REPUBLIC OF VERMONT
AND THE
BRITISH GOVERNMENT
THIS TABLET WAS ERECTED
SEPTEMBER 1912 BY THE
VERMONT SOCIETY
SONS OF THE AMERICAN REVOLUTION

their units brought to strength, but neither governor would permit recruits which they needed for their own regiments to be placed in corps that might be ordered to New York City.

By 1781, Haldimand had received assurances that he could keep these men, and he established the Loyal Rangers with Major Edward Jessup as the commandant. Amalgamated were the King's Loyal Americans led by Edward Jessup's brother, Ebenezer, and the Queen's Loyal Rangers led by John Peters. Other small units were commanded by Samuel McKay and Daniel McAlpin, both of whom had died by 1783, Samuel Adams who had retired, and Robert Leake who was still active. Most of the survivors of these units were placed in the second battalion King's Royal Regiment of New York under Major John Ross.

The main refugee encampments were around Sorel, where the government purchased the seigneury in 1780. Most were wives and children of the provincials, but some were elderly and included men who had retired from provincial corps. Two exiled groups came by sea from New York City when it was evacuated because they preferred Canada to Nova Scotia. Their leaders were Captain Michael Grass and Major Peter van Alstyne. As most were civilians, they did not enjoy the same status as the men who had served in provincial corps. Sir Guy Carleton, the former governor of Canada, who was in command at New York City in 1783, organized his refugees into militia companies and their dependants, and gave the leaders officers' ranks. As such they were not entitled to the half-pay which officers in provincial corps received when their regiments were disbanded.

Haldimand's Plans

In deciding where to put the Loyalists, Haldimand was guided by British policy, his Swiss background, and economy. Under the terms of the Quebec Act of 1774, the interior of the continent was to be preserved for the native peoples. Therefore, Haldimand was willing to allow the displaced Indian allies to settle inland, but the whites must be moved to the east coast. In the spring of 1783, Haldimand sent his Surveyor-General, Major Samuel Holland, to Cataraqui to select land for the displaced natives, and Captain Justus Sherwood, Loyal Rangers, to explore from Gaspé Bay eastwards.

Sherwood was one of the most interesting Loyalists to settle in Ontario. Although only a captain, he was Haldimand's Commissioner of Prisoners and Refugees, responsible for the safe conduct of hundreds of destitute Loyalists, and for exchanges through which prisoners were brought safely to Canada. In 1781 Haldimand appointed him head of his secret service. Sherwood's headquarters was the Loyal Blockhouse, on an island in Lake Champlain. His agents, all Loyalists who knew the country, carried messages that kept Haldimand in touch with New York City by land. Sherwood negotiated the truce that kept Vermont neutral for the last three years of the war.

On his return from exploring along the east coast, Sherwood reported that with the exception of Chaleur Bay, most of the good land was held by absentee owners, and Haldimand shied away from the legal complexities of dispossessing them. Therefore, the elderly could settle at Sorel, and a few could go to Chaleur Bay, but another plan was necessary for thousands of others.

Haldimand had the choice of settling Loyalists in the seigneuries or encroaching on Indian territory. The first solution repelled him. Although Loyalists spoke with many mother tongues, their common bond was English. Even the Catholic minority among the Loyalists was culturally different from the French-speaking Canadians. As in Switzerland "cantons" should be established on ethnic and religious lines. The governor consulted the natives, both Mississaugas, whose territory extended south to the shore of Lake Ontario and the St. Lawrence, and refugees, mostly Iroquois. The Mississaugas were willing to sell some land; the Iroquois felt that having Loyalists living near them would be a safeguard against depredations by the Americans. In September, Deputy-Surveyor John Collins and Justus Sherwood took a party of men to explore the upper St. Lawrence and the Bay of Quinte. While at Cataraqui, Sherwood laid out the boundaries of three American townships, each six miles square, for Haldimand considered these "the best to be followed as the people to be Settled there, are most used to it."

Right top: *Tapping Sugar Maples. Pioneers learned from the Indians how to make maple sugar, a substitute for cane sugar from the West Indies, which was very expensive.*
Far right top: *The Royal Townships. Because Lord Dorchester named many of the first townships after the children of George III, they were known as the Royal Townships. The New Johnstown settlement became, No. 1 Charlottenburgh, No. 2 Cornwall, No. 3 Osnabruck, No. 4 Williamsburgh, No. 5 Matilda. At New Oswegatchie were No. 6 Edwardsburgh, No. 7 Augusta, No. 8 Elizabethtown. At Cataraqui were No. 1 Kingston, No. 2 Ernestown, No. 3 Fredericksburgh, No. 4 Adolphustown, No. 5 Marysburgh. Surveyed later were Sophiasburgh and Ameliasburgh. Also shown are the first four town plots, from east to west: Williamstown in No. 1, New Johnstown (Cornwall) in No. 2, Johnstown in No. 6, and Kingston in No. 1 Cataraqui.*
Right below: *Servos Family Roots Can be Traced to Hungary. In the 17th Century the Servos family fled Hungary to the Rhine Valley and from there to the new world, settling at Schoharie in the Mohawk Valley. Following the American Revolution, this Loyalist family sought refuge in the Niagara Peninsula. Buried there on the farm, is Captain Daniel Servos of Butler's Rangers.*

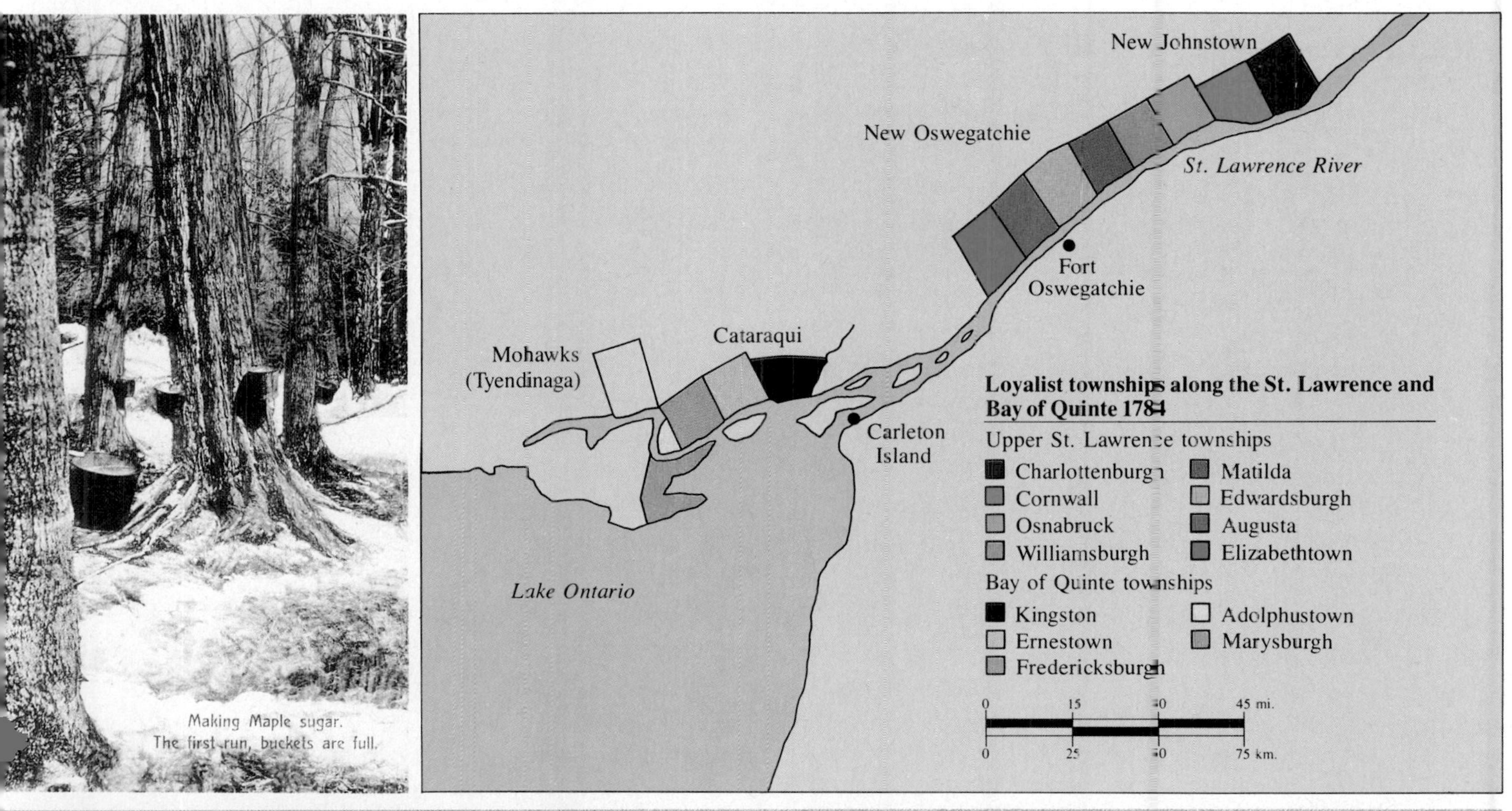

Making Maple sugar.
The first run, buckets are full.

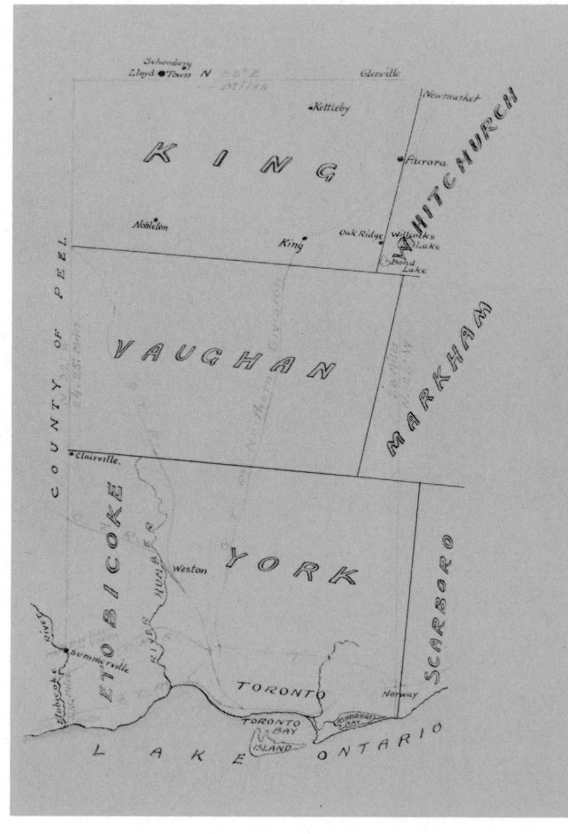
Schomberg
Lloyd Town
N
Glenville
Newmarket
Kettleby
KING
Aurora
WHITCHURCH
Nobleton
King
Oak Ridge
Willcocks Lake
Bond Lake
COUNTY OF PEEL
VAUGHAN
MARKHAM
Clairville.
ETOBICOKE
RIVER HUMBER
Weston
YORK
SCARBORO
River
Summerville
TORONTO
Norway
TORONTO BAY
ISLAND
LAKE ONTARIO

Left top: ***Historic Building at Kingston,*** *c.1890. This log-framed structure had for decades been locally known by several names associated with the 1792 Kingston visit of Governor Simcoe. Sold to the St. Lawrence Parks Commission as "the Simcoe House," it now stands at Upper Canada Village and was recently converted into a lockmaster's quarters.*

Left below: *John Graves Simcoe's Final Resting Place. A bit of Ontario was created in Devon, England, when Premier John Robarts accepted title to Wolford Chapel on September 27, 1966. Here, near Honiton, lie buried Simcoe, his wife Elizabeth and several of their children.*

Far left below: *The Toronto Purchase 1788. This tract was part of a land purchase from the Mississauga Indians. Tradition maintains that Lord Dorchester signed the purchase on a ship in Toronto harbour. More likely, Sir John Johnson, as Superintendent of Indian Affairs, negotiated the land purchase.*

Right below: *William von Moll Berczy Portrait of Peter Russell c.1803. Peter Russell became the Chief Administrator of Upper Canada, governing from 1796 to 1799.*

In November, the governor's plans were disrupted by the arrival of orders from the King, and the townships had to be enlarged. Land for Loyalists was to be divided into

> distinct seigneuries or Fiefs, to extend two to four leagues in front. If situated upon a Navigable River, otherwise to run square or in such shape and such quantities as shall be convenient . . . the propriety of which Seigneuries or Fiefs shall be and remain invested in Us, our Heirs and Successors.

Ten years after a tenant took up his land, an annual rent, called a "quit rent" of one halfpenny per acre was required of him. Loyalists were to exist under a modified form of the French system of land holding.

Although these exiles could not own their lands, the King's terms were generous. Each civilian head of a family was entitled to 100 acres (40 hectares). A non-commissioned officer would receive 200 acres, a private 100 acres. A field officer was entitled to 1,000 acres (400 hectares), a captain to 700 acres, a subaltern, staff or warrant officer to 500 acres. Each family member, whether of a private, non-commissioned or commissioned officer or civilian, was entitled to 50 acres.

Haldimand planned to have thirteen townships surveyed at first. Eight were along the upper St. Lawrence, five along the Bay of Quinte. He assigned them only numbers. In 1786, after Haldimand had left Canada, they were given names associated with George III and his children, and together with some townships surveyed later, became known as the Royal Townships.

Loyalists were to receive two thirds of the usual rations to May 1, 1785, and for the following year, one third. Each man and boy over ten years was entitled to a coat, waistcoat, breeches, hat, shirt, blanket, shoe soles, leggings and stockings. Each woman and girl over ten was allowed two yards of woollen cloth, four yards of linen, stockings, a blanket and shoe soles. Each child under ten was to receive one yard of woollen cloth, two yards of linen, stockings and shoe soles. Two children were to share a blanket, and for the journey every five persons were provided with a tent and a cooking kettle. Once cabins had been erected, all tents were to be returned to the quartermaster's department.

Haldimand received orders to disband his provincial corps by December 24, 1783, and he obeyed for those in the lower part of the province. However, because winter was close at hand, those in the upper country were not disbanded until June, 1784, by which time the migration in *bateaux* up the St. Lawrence from Lachine was under way. Sir John Johnson was the Superintendent of Loyalists, but he was busy with the affairs of the Indians. Thus, the work of organizing the *bateaux* at Lachine fell to Major Edward Jessup, Captain Justus Sherwood, and Major James Rogers, the commander of the King's Rangers.

To save transport costs, provincials near the inland forts settled close to the bases where they had served. Butler's Rangers remained at Niagara, the second battalion King's Royal Regiment of New York at Cataraqui. As a buffer zone between the last French seigneury and the first Loyalist township, Haldimand left a nine-mile-wide area vacant that was later surveyed as the Township of Lancaster. Above the vacant spot, the first battalion King's Royal Regiment of New York was moved to five townships (later Charlottenburgh, Cornwall, Osnabruck, Williamsburgh and Matilda). Most of the Loyal Rangers were sent to three townships farther west (Edwardsburgh, Augusta and Elizabethtown).

Towards the Bay of Quinte the first township (Kingston) was for Michael Grass' party, the second (Ernestown) for the Loyal Rangers, the third (Fredericksburgh) for the second battalion King's Royal Regiment of New York and the King's Rangers, the fourth (Adolphustown), a peninsula hardly a quarter the size of the other townships, was for Peter van Alstyne's group, and the fifth (Marysburgh) was for German regulars who wanted to stay in Canada and some Royal Highland Emigrants. Haldimand did not assign a township to the Royal Highland Emigrants because the majority of them had been recruited in Canada and had not lost their homes.

Two townships (Niagara and Stamford) were surveyed later for Butler's Rangers, although farm lots had been laid out in 1781. No townships were laid out at Detroit, for the numbers wanting to settle there were small. Those who did were men of the Indian Department, some

Right top: *British Naval Force on Lake Ontario, 1792. These vessels, drawn by C.H.J. Snider, are, from left to right, the schooners* Mississauga *and* Bear, *the sloop* Caldwell, *and the schooners* Onondaga *and* Buffalo.

Far right below: *Brant Monument. Attending the dedication service when the monument to Joseph Brant was unveiled in 1886, in Brantford, was ninety-four-year-old Chief John Smoke Johnson. As a boy, Johnson knew the famous Mohawk who had fought for the British Crown.*

Far right bottom: *Lord Dorchester's 1788 Toronto Purchase. Although no evidence exists that Lord Dorchester was ever at Toronto Harbour, the myth persists that he signed the agreement there.*

Right below: *Aeneas Shaw. A captain in the Queen's Rangers, Shaw left New Brunswick on snowshoes, met Simcoe at Quebec in the winter of 1791-92, and came with the governor to Upper Canada.*

Left below: *Queen's Ranger. Governor Simcoe commanded two regiments of rangers, one during the American Revolution, and a later one in Upper Canada. Both corps were uniformed in green jackets faced purple.*

Canada
Brant's Monument, Brantford, Canada.

THE HILL,
GLENO

Left top: *The Hill, Glenora, Ontario. Surveying new townships and assigning lots for settlement was a major job. Building the roads, mostly using labour provided by the settlers themselves, was another heavy burden. This photo illustrates the added problems found in hilly country.*
Left below: *Meyers' Mills. This stone building, part of Captain John W. Meyers' mills on the Moira River, Belleville, is still standing – one of the oldest industrial buildings in Ontario.*
Far left below: *The Meyers House, Belleville. Built by Captain John W. Meyers in 1796, and now demolished, it was one of the first brick houses in the province.*
Right below: *Loyalist From North Carolina, Reverend John Bethune. The chaplain of the 84th Regiment Royal Highland Emigrants during the American Revolution, Loyalist John Bethune (1750-1815), forefather of Dr. Norman Bethune, became the first Presbyterian minister in Upper Canada, settling in Glengarry County.*

Royal Highland Emigrants, and Captain William Caldwell's company from Butler's Rangers.

The first scuffle over whites purchasing land directly from the natives occurred at Detroit. By order of the King, no land was to be granted to whites until it had been ceded to the Crown, in order to prevent exploitation of the natives. Despite this, officers of the Indian Department purchased a tract from some Hurons in the vicinity, which was later confirmed. Because of this purchase near Detroit (later the Townships of Sandwich and Malden), Captain Caldwell's men were placed on the north shore of Lake Erie (the Township of Colchester).

Haldimand gave the natives a grant six miles wide on either side of the Grand River. Led by Joseph Brant, some were moving there, but dissent arose over that location. The Mohawks in particular were divided. One faction, led by John Deseronto, preferred the Bay of Quinte, where they could be on the shore. Inland along the Grand River they would be vulnerable to sneak attacks by the Americans. The Mohawks shared the communion silver Queen Anne had given them; four pieces went to the Grand River settlement, the other three to Tyendinaga, part of a township Haldimand assigned to them on the Bay of Quinte.

Resettlement proceeded despite shortages. Township surveys lagged behind the arriving settlers. As well, provisions and tools were slow to arrive. Settlers energetically cut down trees, but for many, seed did not come in time to be planted among the stumps. At Cataraqui, Major John Ross complained that refugees coming through Carleton Island had not received the clothing being given out at Lachine before Loyalists departed from there. As late as 1787, John Butler noted that Loyalists who had fled directly to Niagara never did receive this bounty.

A widely held opinion is that Loyalists were treated generously. This view is valid if only the half-pay officers are considered. The rank and file received barely enough to survive those first years, and the only thing they got in abundance was free land because it could be obtained cheaply from the natives. Most Loyalists had spent years in the various provincial corps, and they were treated no more generously than other disbanded soldiers. Land grants in America were awarded to soldiers after the Seven Years' War, and again after the War of 1812.

How many people today would feel abused if they were expected to winter in Ontario with the bedding and shelter the Loyalists had? Their survival was a tribute to their abililty to supplement from the wilderness the meagre provisions and clothing the government gave them.

The Dorchester Era

During the 1785 season, more Loyalists around Montreal who had not been able to get organized the year before made the journey by *bateau* up the rapids of the St. Lawrence to join the others. As well, the exodus from the northern states continued. Ultimately, some 10,000 genuine Loyalists had settled in the upper country by 1800. Once the earlier arrivals had time to produce enough food, they became concerned over the seigneurial restrictions and the continuance of French civil law. They petitioned for more congenial arrangements, and their spokesman was Sir John Johnson. Although he lived in Montreal, he had a manor at Williamstown in Charlottenburgh Township.

In 1786 Sir Guy Carleton returned to Canada as governor-in-chief, with a new title, 1st Baron Dorchester, a reward for his services at New York City in 1783. When Lord Dorchester arrived, Canada consisted of two administrative districts — Quebec and Montreal, and the Loyalists' settlements belonged to the latter. Local government was in the hands of a few appointed magistrates, and three men — Sir John Johnson, Justus Sherwood of Augusta Township, and James Baby of Detroit — were members of the legislative council.

Dorchester divided the upper country into four new districts, each one centred on a settlement. Luneburg was the upper St. Lawrence, Mecklenburg the Bay of Quinte, Nassau the Niagara area, and Hesse the settlement along the Detroit River. He chose German names to please the Hanoverian King, and from the same motives named the first townships after his children. Dorchester did not make local government democratic, but he brought the administration of justice closer to the people. Hitherto, the nearest court was in Montreal, but now courts would be held in the new districts. In addition, each district had a land

Right top: *Upper Canada's First Parliament Opens September 17, 1792. In a rendition of the opening of Canada's First Parliament, J.D. Kelly portrays Simcoe on a horse with his wife Elizabeth next to the flagpole, his secretary, William Jarvis, between him and the tree, and Chief Justice William Osgoode on the right holding a cane.*
Far right below: *Upper Canada's First House of Parliament, c.1900. Navy Hall, Upper Canada's first Parliament building, was in such a state of disgraceful ruination by 1895, Janet Carnochan undertook the formation of the Niagara Historical Society. Thanks to a generous donation from Toronto philanthropist, John Ross Robertson, the society restored the building.*
Right below: *William Jarvis, Mr. Secretary (1756-1817). Born in Stamford, Connecticut, Jarvis fought in the Queen's Rangers under John Graves Simcoe. In 1791, he was appointed provincial secretary, a post he held until his death. Jarvis Street, Toronto is named after his son Samuel Peters Jarvis.*

Negro burial ground 1830

Here stood a Baptist church erected in 1830 through the exertions of a former British soldier, John Oakley, who although white, became pastor of a predominantly negro congregation. In 1793 Upper Canada had passed an act forbidding further introduction of slaves and freeing the children of those in the colony at twenty-five. This was the first legislation of its kind in the British Empire. A long tradition of tolerance attracted refugee slaves to Niagara, many of whom lie buried here.

MISSISSAUGA ROAD,
NIAGARA-ON-THE-LAKE

board to award grants, the board members chosen from among half-pay officers. To supply the new settlements and protect the garrisons at the forts, the governor saw that the ships of the Provincial Marine were well maintained and manned.

He organized the first militia, thereby providing a direct link between the provincial corps and certain of today's militia regiments. The settlers may have felt burdened by militia duty, but other provisions Dorchester made were to their liking. The 84th Regiment Royal Highland Emigrants were permitted larger land grants, a source of envy for former provincials who had seen more active service. Dorchester solved this problem by raising all grants to match those of the 84th. Now a field officer was entitled to 5,000 acres (2,000 hectares), a captain to 3,000 acres, a subaltern to 2,000 acres, the rank and file to an extra 200 acres. All Loyalists' sons and daughters were entitled to 200 acres at age twenty-one, or for a daughter, earlier if she married.

The famous "Hungry Year" occurred between 1787 and 1789, depending on the settlement. Severe drought caused crop failures at a time when people had enough land cleared if the harvest was normal. The drought was worst along the upper St. Lawrence in 1787, and people suffered until the harvest of 1788. Dorchester visited these settlements and reported them flourishing. The drought struck Niagara in 1788, and conditions were grim until the harvest of 1789. Once these years passed, the settlers produced enough grain to supply the garrisons of regulars at the upper posts, which had not been withdrawn despite the boundary arrangements of the treaty of 1783. The settlers made potash, and some with river lots built timber rafts and sold logs at Montreal and Quebec. Both enterprises provided cash to an area where business was conducted through barter and promissory notes.

As the 1790s began, the British government passed the Constitutional Act to supersede the Quebec Act. The province was to be divided, to accommodate the aspirations of the Loyalists without interfering with the traditions of the French-speaking Canadians. The upper province would have freehold land tenure and English civil law, but the division could not satisfy everyone. Francophones in Upper Canada lost the rights

Left top: *Home of Matthew Elliott, Amherstburg. A captain in the Indian Department during the Revolution, Elliott settled at Amherstburg, developed a 1,200-hectare estate, and served as a Deputy Superintendent of Indian Affairs. Although in his seventies when the War of 1812 broke out, he went on active service and helped Brock capture Detroit.*
Left below: *An Early 19th Century Vehicle. In the early 1800s Waterloo County attracted more Pennsylvania Germans than did either the Niagara Peninsula or York County. Those trekking north would have used what has become known today as the Conestoga wagon. This one was used by the Weber family over 150 years ago.*
Right below: *Plaque at Niagara-on-the-Lake.*

guaranteed them by the Quebec Act, while anglophones in Lower Canada continued under the provisions inherited from the French régime.

Before the division of the province was made in 1791, Lord Dorchester had recommended that Sir John Johnson be made the first lieutenant-governor of Upper Canada, but the home government chose John Graves Simcoe. When Dorchester was informed, he again requested Johnson, suggesting that Simcoe take command of the Indian Department. This, too, was rejected by the home government. When Simcoe arrived, he had control over civil matters, but Dorchester, as commander-in-chief, was responsible for the defence of both provinces. Dorchester, peeved because Johnson had not been appointed to govern Upper Canada, seemed to delight in overruling Simcoe, perhaps in part because his subordinate was young enough to be his son.

The Simcoe Administration

John Graves Simcoe was energetic, enthusiastic, with a vision of what Upper Canada would become before he left England. He was well acquainted with Loyalists; he had commanded the Queen's Rangers, a provincial corps, during the revolution. He was invalided home after the defeat at Yorktown in 1781, and his rangers were disbanded in what became New Brunswick in 1784. His officers loved him and several left their clearings to join him in Upper Canada. One especially eager man was half-pay Captain Aeneas Shaw, who in the winter of 1791-1792, led twelve men on snowshoes overland and met Simcoe at Quebec.

Simcoe asked that a new Queen's Rangers of ten companies, each of 100 men, be raised in England for service in Upper Canada. He received permission, for reasons of economy, for only two companies. Records indicate 400 Queen's Rangers, suggesting that he raised two more companies in the Canadas. This item of budget-trimming was only one of many. If Simcoe regarded Upper Canada as something approaching the centre of the universe, the home government did not.

In June 1792, the Simcoes and their entourage began their royal progress up the St. Lawrence, welcomed warmly along the way by the Loyalists. Many half-pay officers donned shabby uniforms and shouted,

Left top: *Sketch of Log Huts or Barracks at Queenston, 1793 by Mrs. Simcoe. Elizabeth Simcoe says in her diary on Sunday, February 17, 1793: "I went to dine with some ladies of the Queen's Rangers at the Landing where the Rangers are quartered in huts."*
Left below: *Elizabeth Simcoe's Sketch of the Mill at Gananoque. One of Elizabeth Simcoe's many 18th century sketches of Upper Canada, a mill at Gananoque, is typical of the visual documentation she left for posterity.*

to His Excellency's delight, the old military slogans. At Kingston in July, Simcoe took his oath of office, and issued two proclamations. One divided the province into nineteen counties and allocated sixteen seats in the populated ones for the legislative assembly. The other proclamation called for elections. The Simcoes sailed to Niagara, sometimes called Butlersbury after John Butler's home in the Mohawk Valley, which the governor officially called Newark. The viceregal family took up residence in decrepit Navy Hall, used by the Provincial Marine during the revolution.

The elections were held, and the first session of the assembly began at Newark on September 17, 1792. The members alarmed Simcoe somewhat by proposing New England town meetings, which smacked of the "Elective principle" and he managed to postpone the bill.

Often overlooked is the fact that Loyalists brought with them two political traditions. Most were from New York and accustomed to appointed officials. But a minority were New Englanders, and those from Connecticut had known responsible government. Under Connecticut's charter, the enfranchised men elected all officers, including the governor. Connecticut families tended to congregate in Leeds and Grenville Counties, where the democratic-minded rallied around William Buell. By the 1830s the *Brockville Recorder,* owned by William Buell Jr., was the voice of reform in the eastern part of the province. Brockville also had a Yankee symbol, a New England square, as its focal point, the only one built in Ontario according to the original plan.

At the 1793 sitting of the Assembly, the members and Simcoe compromised. Simcoe wanted to abolish slavery, but the members objected. Some were slave owners, and with nearly every settler eligible for free land it was impossible to hire labour. Simcoe agreed to let the owners keep their slaves, but no more could be brought into Upper Canada. Children of slaves were to be free at the age of twenty-five, their children free from birth. In exchange, Simcoe agreed to a limited form of town meeting. Magistrates could issue warrants for meetings at which township officers such as tax collectors, pathmasters, fence viewers, assessors and clerks could be elected.

Right top: *Amherstburg, 1824. Settled after the revolution by Captain Matthew Elliott and other men of the Indian Department, strategically placed at the outlet of the Detroit River, Amherstburg was founded as a defensive site. When the fort at Detroit was amongst those handed over to the United States by Jay's Treaty in 1796, Amherstburg became even more strategic. Fort Malden, built there, was one of a new chain of forts, and was the headquarters of British operations on Lake Erie and in Southwestern Upper Canada during the War of 1812.*
Right below: *The Simcoes Lived in a Tent in Upper Canada. Before the Simcoes left England in 1791, they purchased Captain James Cook's tent and took it with them to Upper Canada, using it frequently as their abode, both at Newark (Niagara-on-the-Lake) and York (Toronto).*

York Pioneer's House, Exhibition Grounds at Sunset, Toronto, Canada

Left top: *The Scadding Cabin 1794. Built by John Scadding, who came to York from Devon in 1793 to manage Governor Simcoe's business interests, this log building stands today on the grounds of the Canadian National Exhibition, where it was moved in 1879 by the York Pioneer and Historical Society (founded in 1869).*
Left below: *Loyalist Box Stretcher Table. Few Loyalist pieces of furniture are extant today. This late 18th century box stretcher table, found on the First Concession of Adolphustown Township, has a provenance linking it with William Ruttan, of Huguenot descent, who came to the Bay of Quinte as a U.E. Loyalist in the spring of 1784.*
Right below: *Yonge Street and Sir George Yonge. Completed as a road of communication from York to Lake Simcoe on February 4, 1796, Yonge Street was named after Sir George Yonge, Britain's Secretary at War, 1782-1794.*

Simcoe continued his policy of having English names. The four districts became the Eastern (Luneburg), Midland (Mecklenburg), Home (Nassau), and Western (Hesse). As new townships were surveyed they were named after Simcoe's friends. Unfortunate was his fondness for John P. Bastard, a member of the British House of Commons, whose name still graces a township in Leeds County.

More important was the security of the province and, therefore, the need to increase the population and to develop a land policy. Since appeals to London and Quebec for more regular troops did not bear fruit, the governor reorganized his militia, appointing county lieutenants in the English manner to raise the battalions. The main source of settlers was the United States. Simcoe believed that the American Revolution had been the work of a minority and many Loyalists still in the republic would welcome the opportunity to reject congressionalism and live again under a British constitution. He advertised for settlers, stressing that Quakers would not be required to bear arms, a right not respected during the revolution. Quakers did respond. Many were of German origin and were considered the best farmers in the new world. Since many of the other Loyalists were also German, Upper Canadian agriculture tended to be superior to that of other provinces and many states.

As a further inducement to settlers, Simcoe enlarged all grants to 200 acres (80 hectares), and changed the method of applying for land. He abolished the district land boards and vested their responsibilities in himself, assisted by his executive council. His "open door" immigration policy was a mixed blessing. Many who came were more interested in cheap land than ideology; others were speculators. In some cases the governor granted whole townships to men who promised to bring in settlers. Many could not live up to their bargains and lost their titles.

Inconsistent with Simcoe's hope to expedite settlement was the way he handled reserves for a Protestant clergy and the Crown. Under the Constitutional Act, one seventh of the land was to support the clergy, and another seventh was to be sold to provide revenue for the Crown. Simcoe decided that reserved lots would be dispersed throughout the townships in a "checkerboard" pattern, rather than be set aside in blocks. Loyalists were entitled to free grants, while others were allowed 200 acres after paying a patent fee to have the lot registered. Strangely enough, for a man who understood the importance of roads, Simcoe did not foresee that the reserved lots would lie unsold and would be an impediment to the construction of roads. A settler did not mind cutting his share of a road past his farm, but he felt imposed upon when required to extend a road past vacant land.

Simcoe's relationship with Joseph Brant was marred by land issues. Brant allowed whites to buy substantial tracts of the natives' land on the Grand River. Simcoe disapproved, and Brant insisted that the "Haldimand Grant" had been an outright gift that his people could sell if they saw fit. Brant felt that the Grand River land, originally 570,000 acres (228,000 hectares), was not sufficient for the natives to continue their hunting and corn-beans-squash agriculture. He hoped that white farmers who settled among his people would teach them animal husbandry and build mills. (Parts of the Haldimand Grant continued to be sold until 1841, when the Iroquois ceded what remained to the Crown and the land became a reserve.)

Before Simcoe arrived, he had decided that the province's capital would be at the headwaters of the Thames River (the site of London), inland and difficult to attack. Neither Kingston, favoured by Dorchester, nor Newark was suitable. If the forts on the American side of the boundary were surrendered, Kingston would be too close to Oswego and Newark easily reduced to splinters by the guns of Fort Niagara. Thus, Simcoe decided that the Toronto Carrying Place, with a good harbour, was the logical spot for a naval base and for his temporary capital. In the summer of 1793 he moved there and named the new settlement York. Meanwhile, the Queen's Rangers started building a road from Burlington Bay to the Thames, which Simcoe named Dundas Street after the Honourable Henry Dundas, then a Secretary of State.

At York, the surveyor Alexander Aitkin, laid out a town plot and in sticky clay, sheltered behind a swamp that was to immobilize the populace periodically with "fever and ague," the future metropolitan city took root. The Simcoes wintered in 1793-1794 in their "canvas house"

Right: *The Roots of Toronto Planted in 1793. C.W. Jeffreys' early sketch shows Governor Simcoe inspecting the building of the fort at Toronto by the Queen's Rangers. The armed schooner* Mississauga, *which had brought Simcoe and his Rangers from Niagara, lies in Toronto harbour. Captain Cook's famous tent is in the background.*

Left below: *Colours of the Queen's Rangers, Revolutionary War Era. These regimental banners — the union flag prior to the addition of the cross of St. Patrick in 1802 and the blue ensign — were carried by the Queen's Rangers from 1777 to 1781, when the regiment surrendered at Yorktown, Virgina. The commander, John Graves Simcoe, saved the colours from the Americans. Because he was wounded, he was allowed to go to New York City, and the flags went with him, secreted in his baggage.*

that had once belonged to Captain James Cook, which the governor had purchased in London. The Queen's Rangers began opening a road from York to Lake aux Claies, which the governor renamed Lake Simcoe in honour of his father. The road became Yonge Street, after his friend Sir George Yonge, the Secretary at War.

The year 1794 was a tense one in Upper Canada. Britain and France were at war. In 1778, France had formed a military alliance with the rebels — an alliance the United States might renew. Also, an American army under General "Mad" Anthony Wayne was in the field against the western tribes and might menace Detroit. Lord Dorchester inflamed the situation by ordering Simcoe to build a fort on the Maumee River, as an outpost for Detroit. Simcoe obeyed with reservations. Like Detroit, the new Fort Miami was on land officially belonging to the United States. Building the fort was an act of hostility which Simcoe feared might lead to a declaration of war by the Americans.

Simcoe mobilized the Upper Canadian Militia, and his returns showed some 5,000 officers and men between the ages of sixteen and fifty. In addition, the governor planned a new Canadian Regiment, a provincial corps, and chose half-pay officers to raise recruits. His faith that many Loyalists were still in the former colonies was unshaken, for he suggested that Justus Sherwood and Hazelton Spencer (a member of the assembly) raise companies "from the States."

In order to concentrate on the war with France, Britain offered to negotiate evacuating the upper posts. President Washington sent his chief justice, John Jay to the Court of St. James in 1794. By 1796, Simcoe's last year in Upper Canada, Jay's Treaty had been ratified. Among others, Michilimackinac, Detroit, Niagara, Oswego and Oswegatchie were handed over to the Americans, although Carleton Island retained a caretaker garrison of British regulars. Both before and after Jay's Treaty, an alternative chain of forts took root on the Canadian side of the border — Fort Wellington for Oswegatchie, the base at Kingston for Oswego, Fort George for Niagara, Fort Malden for Detroit, and St. Joseph's Island for Michilimackinac. Carleton Island remained in British hands until 1812 when the Americans occupied it.

Left: Bateau *at Upper Canada Village. The* bateau *was the working boat between Montreal and Galops Rapids near Prescott, a stretch of the St. Lawrence where vessels of deep draft could not sail. The flat-bottomed* bateau, *about eight metres in length, oared and sometimes rigged for a lateen sail, stands as the symbol of the Loyalist migration into Ontario. The soldiers' uniforms shown here are from the 1816 era, possibly in keeping with the St. Lawrence Parks Commission's policy of having the village represent only the early 19th century.*

Right below: *Sir John Johnson's Manor House. Although Sir John made his home in Montreal, he had a manor and mills at Williamstown, Charlottenburgh Township. Few traces of the mills remain, but the manor house has been preserved.*

John Graves Simcoe was the most colourful lieutenant governor to rule Upper Canada between 1792 and 1841. He had come with ambitious plans which were only partially realized. The home government felt that many of Simcoe's ideas were too expensive. For example, he was unable to establish a system of grammar schools, as well as a university for the education of an upper class. Nevertheless, his impact on the province was profound. He remains the founder of Toronto, the man whose rangers built two famous roads—Dundas and Yonge Streets. He also left a part of himself in perpetuity. When John and Elizabeth and their two children sailed for home, they left at York the tiny grave of their Canadian-born daughter, Catherine Simcoe.

After the governor departed, the Receiver-General, Peter Russell, became the administrator. Elderly and timid, fearful of offending his superiors, Russell's was a caretaker government. Fortunately, Upper Canada was not threatened during his term, for Jay's Treaty had eased tensions with the United States. The clearings of the earliest settlers began to resemble farms, as the stumps gradually rotted and were removed from the fenced fields. The cabins of the first Loyalists were replaced by square-timbered homes, often symmetrical, with clean lines. One enterprising half-pay officer, John Walden Meyers (the founder of Belleville) had discovered the right kind of clay, and his Georgian-style home overlooking his mills was of brick. The framework of an urban pattern was emerging in the district seats and the many mill villages.

Upper Canada was still a frontier province where the easiest transport was by water, but life was more than mere survival for many inhabitants. More settlers flocked in and most were from the United States. From Pennsylvania came the Mennonites in their Conestoga wagons, following the trail of the black walnut, knowing that where walnut trees grew, they would find the best land. Some stopped near Niagara; others found what they wanted in Markham and Vaughan Townships; but in Waterloo County they formed their most distinctive settlements. By the turn of the century, other settlers of American origin outnumbered the original Loyalist stock, and on the eve of the War of 1812, the population had risen to 77,000 men, women and children.

Right: *Panoramic View of Upper Canada Village. Many water-side towns founded by Loyalist pioneers would have looked like this from a distance by about 1800, with a church or two silhouetted against the sky. Governor Haldimand wanted town plots to be centrally placed in each township, or on the centre of the waterfront, if it had one. The governor's instructions were not always feasible. The central place for the plot of Dundas, for example, was on the face of the Niagara escarpment and nearly perpendicular. A plot on level ground was selected.*

Left below: *Log Barn and Rail Fence. The timbers of this barn were squared by hand, a practice common to early structures before there were many sawmills in the new settlements.*

***Left:** Burgoyne's Provincials. In 1777, at the start of General John Burgoyne's expedition into New York from Canada, his provincial troops wore red coats faced green. Many Loyalists joined him as he marched south and never received full uniforms. War Office records show that nearly 800 of his provincials were alive after Burgoyne surrendered at Saratoga.*

Right top: *The Bethune House, Williamstown. Still standing, this house was built in the 1790s by Reverend John Bethune, chaplain to the Royal Highland Emigrants and the first Presbyterian minister in the province.*

Far right top: *Plaque in Augusta Township to Justus Sherwood. Some information on this plaque is not accurate. Sherwood was a captain in the Loyal Rangers, and in 1781 head of Haldimand's secret service. Captured at Saratoga, he was not exchanged, but returned to Canada as a paroled prisoner-of-war, a parole that was revoked in 1778. He did not die in 1798, for his will is dated August 1799, and was probated that November. The plaque stands at the foot of Merwin Lane, west of Prescott, named for Elnathan Merwin, an informer in Arlington, Vermont, who signed his messages to Sherwood, "Plain Truth."*

Right below: *Memorial to Governor Simcoe in Exeter Cathedral. John Graves Simcoe is buried in Wolford Chapel, Devon, in the southwest of England. This memorial in the cathedral, in the county town of Exeter, was erected by Simcoe's friends in 1812.*

Far right below: *Commemorative Stamp 1934. The Canadian Post Office issued this stamp, showing the Loyalist memorial in Hamilton, in the year of Ontario's Sesquicentennial, to honour the Loyalist resettlement of 1784.*

MAJOR-GENERAL FREDERICK HALDIMAND 1
ER) 1724-1808 SIR JOHN JOHNSON 1742-1830 HIS EX
OR-GENERAL ISAAC BROCK 1769-1812 MAJOR-G
GUY CARLETON (LORD DORCHESTER) 1724-180
JOHN GRAVES SIMCOE 1752-1806 MAJOR-GENE
EDERICK HALDIMAND 1718-1791 SIR GUY CAR
JOHNSON 1742-1830 HIS EXCELLENCY JOHN GR
BROCK 1769-1812 MAJOR-GENERAL FREDERICK
DORCHESTER) 1724-1808 SIR JOHN JOHNSON 174
1752-1806 MAJOR-GENERAL ISAAC BROCK 1769-
1718-1791 SIR GUY CARLETON (LORD DORCHEST
CELLENCY JOHN GRAVES SIMCOE 1752-1806 M
GENERAL FREDERICK HALDIMAND 1718-1791 SI
SIR JOHN JOHNSON 1742-1830 HIS EXCELLENCY
AL ISAAC BROCK 1769-1812 MAJOR-GENERAL F
TON (LORD DORCHESTER) 1724-1808 SIR JOHN JO
S SIMCOE 1752-1806 MAJOR-GENERAL ISAAC BR
DIMAND 1718-1791 SIR GUY CARLETON (LORD D
30 HIS EXCELLENCY JOHN GRAVES SIMCOE 1
MAJOR-GENERAL FREDERICK HALDIMAND 17
1724-1808 SIR JOHN JOHNSON 1742-1830 HIS EXCE
GENERAL ISAAC BROCK 1769-1812 MAJOR-GENE
CARLETON (LORD DORCHESTER) 1724-1808 SIR
GRAVES SIMCOE 1752-1806 MAJOR-GENERAL IS

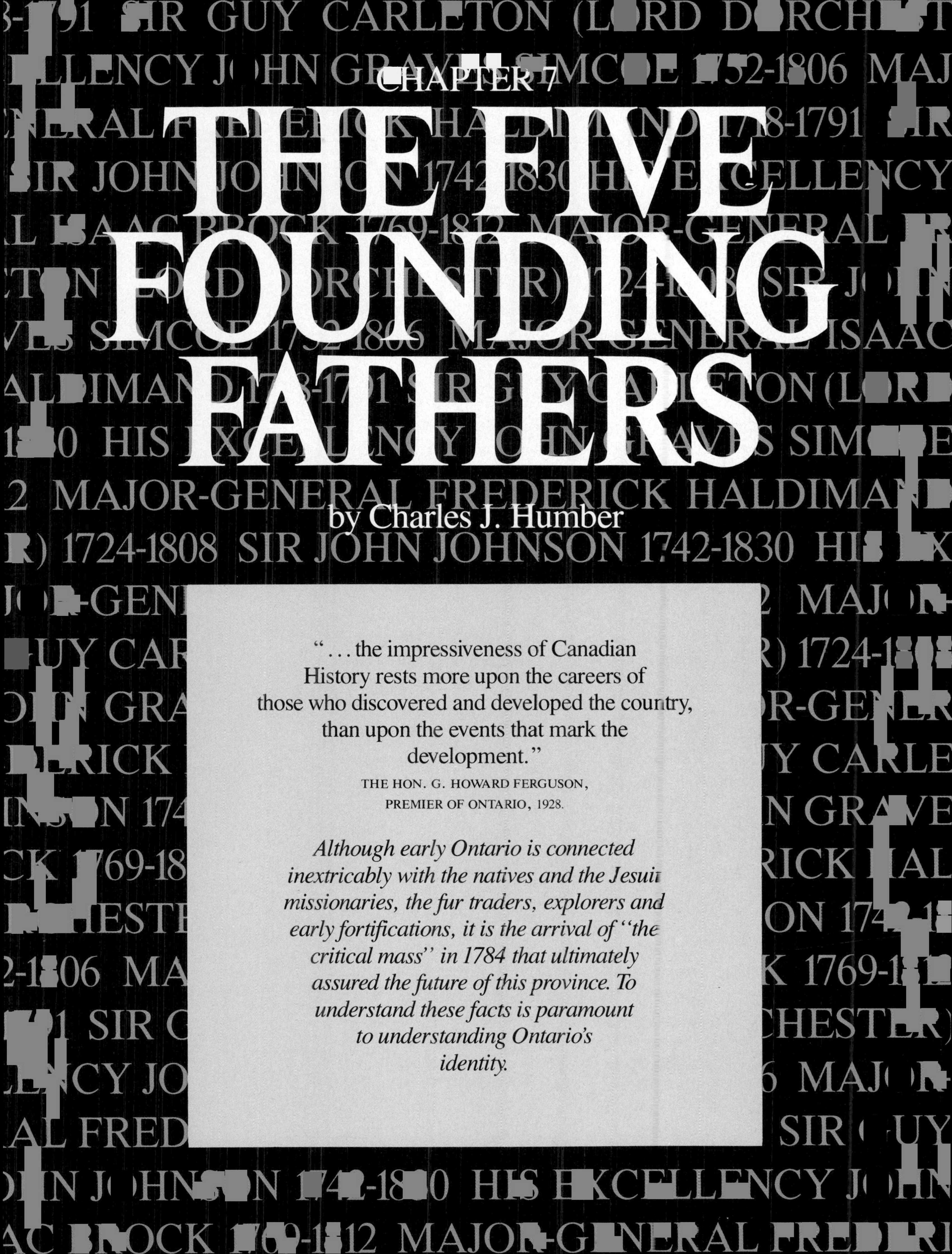

CHAPTER 7

THE FIVE FOUNDING FATHERS

by Charles J. Humber

"... the impressiveness of Canadian History rests more upon the careers of those who discovered and developed the country, than upon the events that mark the development."

THE HON. G. HOWARD FERGUSON, PREMIER OF ONTARIO, 1928.

Although early Ontario is connected inextricably with the natives and the Jesuit missionaries, the fur traders, explorers and early fortifications, it is the arrival of "the critical mass" in 1784 that ultimately assured the future of this province. To understand these facts is paramount to understanding Ontario's identity.

Major-General Frederick Haldimand 1718-1791

The painting of Major-General Frederick Haldimand, by Lemuel F. Abbott, is in the Canadiana Gallery, Royal Ontario Museum.

Frederick Haldimand, baptized Francois-Louis-Frédéric, was born August 11, 1718, at Yverdon, Switzerland. Although his military career prior to and including the American Revolution is noteworthy, his chief legacy is his role as a colonial administrator, particularly his resettlement of the disbanded Loyalist troops and the relocation of exiled Loyalist families during and immediately following the American Revolution and the 1783 Treaty of Separation.

A professional soldier, his career included service with the Prussian armed forces in the 1740s, the Swiss Guards in Dutch service in the 1750s, and the British army by 1755 at which time his career took him to America. There he served in the Seven Years' War, including service at Ticonderoga in 1758, the successful command and defence of Oswego in 1759 against 4,000 French and Indians, and the 1760 capitulation of Montreal, where he was General Amherst's emissary to the French.

From 1760 until the outbreak of the American Revolution, Haldimand served in various military and civil capacities, acting as governor of Trois Rivières (1762), and serving as the commandant of Florida (1767-1773), at which time he was commissioned major-general, and took command of New York from 1773-1775, following the absence of General Gage. By 1778, Haldimand was Governor-in-Chief of Canada (Quebec), an appointment important to the future of Ontario.

The resettlement of thousands of war and political refugees had to be handled by a man who understood the anxiety, anger, and frustration of these uprooted American Loyalists who had lost everything. They were significantly multicultural: Mohawk Indians, Gaelic speaking Highlanders, both Catholic and Presbyterian, German Lutherans, Dutch, "plain folk" such as Quakers, Blacks, as well as English, Welsh and Irish. The monumental task of resettling this "critical mass" along the upper St. Lawrence River, the Bay of Quinte region and the Niagara peninsula was accomplished by a leader whose difficulty with English fluency did not interfere with his expertise as a colonial administrator. At his insistence, Britain instituted two years (1784-1786) of food and seed supplied to all those who had lost their property because of loyalty and had fled to Canada, exiled, to begin anew in a new land.

With this massive task accomplished in 1784, Haldimand returned to England where in 1785 he was knighted. His papers, some of the most important in Canada, remain unpublished. To this date in Ontario, his legacy is neither honoured by historical plaques nor monuments, although a Regional Municipality as well as a township bears his name. He died in his beloved Switzerland in 1791, the year Quebec was divided into Upper and Lower Canada.

Sir John Johnson

Sir John Johnson's portrait, artist unknown, hangs in Johnson Hall, Johnstown, the house that was confiscated during the American Revolution. It is now maintained by the New York State Parks Commission, Peebles Island, New York.

Most of the important figures associated with early Upper Canada are identified with the colonies before or during the American Revolution as military officers or influential colonials. Sir John Johnson, born in New York in 1742, is no exception.

The son of Sir William Johnson, Superintendent of Indian Affairs until his death in 1774, Sir John fled the Mohawk Valley to Montreal in 1776 with a large number of tenant followers.

The same year he was granted permission to raise a Loyalist battalion. Called the King's Royal Regiment of New York or more frequently the Royal Yorkers, this corps was comprised of men with roots sunk deep in the Mohawk Valley. These Loyalists, mainly Scots Highlanders and German Palatines, were destined to settle as disbanded troops some eight years later in what is now Ontario.

With his battalion, his Iroquois allies and Butler's Rangers, Johnson moved through his homeland valley, confronting rebels with gunfire, protecting sympathizers, ravaging provisions meant for Washington's rebel army, and creating havoc for the revolutionaries. So effective were his efforts that he was granted permission to raise a second battalion in 1780. However "the world turned upside down" on October 17, 1781, when Lord Cornwallis surrendered all at Yorktown, Virginia. At the time, Johnson's struggle for control of northern New York was a toss-up.

The resettlement of the Loyalists took top priority after the 1783 Peace Treaty. Absolutely reduced to government dependence, the refugee Loyalists were placed in camps at such places as Machiche, Lachine, Sorel and Chambly. Land was hastily surveyed along the upper St. Lawrence and the Bay of Quinte regions. Plans were made for the anticipated *bateau* journey up the river the following spring. Initially, Johnson was placed in charge of the final disposition of the Loyalist regiments, including his own first battalion which took the most easterly five townships west of the Ottawa River, and his second battalion which took two townships west of Cataraqui (Kingston).

Because Johnson was Superintendent of Indian Affairs, he was also given the responsibility of resettling and reconciling his native allies.

Soon, centres such as Cornwall, Prescott, Brockville, Gananoque, Kingston, and Napanee among others, emerged as thriving Upper Canadian communities. This epic story, moreover, could never have happened without Sir John Johnson. This extraordinary Loyalist oversaw much of the 1784 resettlement of some 6,000 refugees, and his Royal Yorkers and their families comprised almost one half of the "critical mass" of 200 years ago.

Sir John Johnson died at Montreal in 1830.

His Excellency John Graves Simcoe 1752-1806

The portrait of John Graves Simcoe, c.1798, by Jean Laurent Mosnier, is in the John Ross Robertson Collection, Metropolitan Toronto Library.

John Graves Simcoe lived only fifty-four years (1752-1806) but accomplished more in his short lifespan than most great men achieve with longevity. Son of a naval captain who died off Anticosti Island in 1759 prior to the siege of Quebec, educated at Eton and Oxford, Simcoe was active throughout the American Revolution, arriving in Boston on June 17, 1775, the day the guns roared at Bunker Hill, and was with Cornwallis at Yorktown, October 17, 1781. Shortly after being wounded at Brandywine (1777), he was made commander of the Queen's Rangers, an elite corps given the status of First American Regiment by George III in 1779. Throughout the entire duration of the war, Simcoe's Queen's Rangers never lost a major battle. Military historians are unanimous in conceding his brilliance as a military strategist.

Returning to England in 1781 at the age of twenty-nine, he married Elizabeth Gwillim whose own legacy is a gallery of sketches unmatched in the visual documentation of Upper Canada.

When Britain divided Quebec on August 24, 1791, it appointed Simcoe as Upper Canada's first governor. Leaving his seat vacant in the House of Commons, Simcoe sailed for Canada, taking with him his future "home," a canvas tent formerly owned by Captain James Cook.

His mission was to implant a civilization. By strict definition not a "Loyalist," he came to govern a Loyalist province, to get things going, and to provide leadership for the struggling Loyalists.

Anticipating the War of 1812-15, Simcoe fortified Upper Canada and maintained friendly relations with the Indians. He also moved the capital from Newark to York to avoid close proximity to the robust republic below the border and built roads of communication — Yonge Street leading to future northern development and Dundas Street offering an east/west connection. With the re-activated Queen's Rangers, he effectively established the future city of Toronto and prepared for a naval establishment on the Upper Great Lakes.

Simcoe further realized the need for more people. Thus, he became the father of open door immigration, strongly believing that Americans from the south choosing Upper Canada as homeland were rejecting republicanism and embracing parliamentary government. This progressiveness annoyed the 1784 "critical mass" who vowed never to forgive the Americans for what had happened a decade earlier.

Although he divided the province into nineteen counties and provided representative government, liberalized land policies and encouraged educational opportunities, his most progressive act was prohibiting future slave importation, legislation that preceded the total abolition of slavery throughout the Empire in 1833.

Major-General Isaac Brock 1769-1812

This photograph of Major-General Isaac Brock's uniform shows the hole where the fatal bullet pierced his chest. The uniform belongs to the National Museums of Canada. Although artists have painted conceptions of Brock, none are authentic. Apparently he never sat for his portrait, and no true likeness of the general has been preserved.

The odds against the survival of Canada were high before the outbreak of the War of 1812. Thomas Jefferson exclaimed "the acquisition of Canada . . . will be a mere matter of marching." He was not whistling in the wind either, as there was considerable acrimony and division in Canada at the time. Brock even bitterly reflected about the worthwhileness of defending so many malcontents whose recent steady influx, mainly from the republic below the border, had created a different society from the one created by the "critical mass" that had come as Loyalist refugees some twenty-five years earlier. In the end, Canada did survive but suffered the great loss of a patriotic General frequently identified as the "Hero of Upper Canada."

The man after whom Brockville is named as well as Brock University, was born the same year, 1769, as both Napoleon and Wellington. By the age of fifteen he had joined the army. His love for the military led him to the West Indies, Holland and Denmark, the latter destination engaging him in the same conflict as Horatio Nelson.

On the eve of the impending war, Brock, commander of the troops as well as president and chief administrator of Upper Canada, knew that most second-generation Loyalists were eager to redeem their fathers' losses as a result of the American Revolution. His main worry was the disgruntlement, apathy and disloyalty in the more recently settled communities. He chafed about it continuously. Nevertheless, he forged ahead anticipating, as did Simcoe some twenty years earlier, an eventual American invasion.

A quick decision maker, he strengthened both Indian alliances and military fortifications, ordered the building of vessels, trained volunteers, created specially trained flank companies — all this despite the home government's refusal to send either men or money and the hostile attitude in the Upper Canadian Assembly.

On June 26, 1812, the inevitable war was declared by President Madison. Brock immediately and dramatically wrestled control of the vital northwest (Michilimackinac) out of American hands by mid-July. In August, with only 1,300 soldiers and Indians, he was able to force General William Hull to surrender his 2,500 men at Detroit. Although the brutal war was not to end for two years following the battle at Queenston Heights, Brock's untimely death there on October 13, aroused Upper Canadians and injected such a sense of fervour that they ultimately carried forward Brock's patriotic torch and vigorously fought for their country, ultimately assuring Canada's survival.

A great Indian ally and friend, Tecumseh, who died in the same war, said of Brock upon meeting him — "This is a man."

CHAPTER 8

THE WAR OF 1812: a "Mere Matter of Marching"

by Patrick C. T. White

At Queenston Heights and Lundy's Lane
Our brave fathers, side by side
For freedom, homes and loved ones dear
Firmly stood and nobly died;
And those dear rights which they maintained
We swear to yield them never!
Our watchword ever more shall be
The Maple Leaf forever!

ALEXANDER MUIR

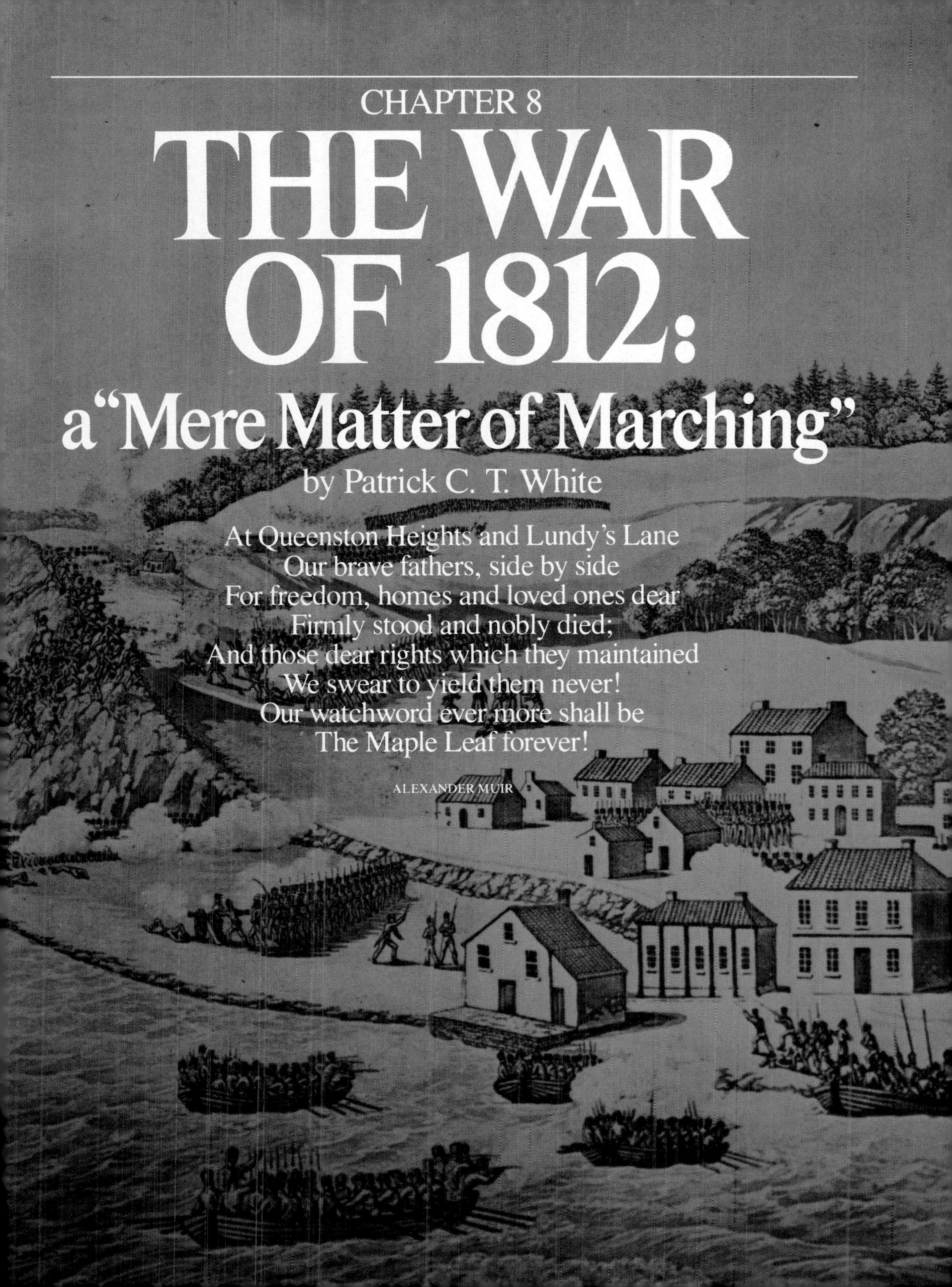

The War of 1812 was an extraordinary event both in the history of British North America and of the United States, for it was the first occasion in which the newly formed colony of Upper Canada suffered from an armed invasion, and it was the first foreign war into which the United States entered. The war and its invasion of Upper Canada did not spring from disputes between the United States and British North America, for the issues involving differences between the two had been substantially resolved by Jay's Treaty in 1794. Rather, the war arose from conflicts over maritime rights between Great Britain and the United States. These came from the terrible war between Britain and France which broke out in 1793 and lasted for over twenty years.

European wars in the past had been fought by relatively small armies and most frequently for political or imperial reasons. But the revolutionary and Napoleonic wars were fought by huge armies for ideological purposes. The introduction by the French of the *leveé en masse* — conscription — changed the nature of warfare, Lord Granville observed, and justified, therefore, the introduction of radical means to combat it. These included a fundamental change on the part of Great Britain in the usual rules of international law. It is true, of course, that this law was not statutory but rather customary. Nevertheless, it had been carefully documented in the writings of Vattel and it was generally followed by all nations. Under it, neutrals could trade with belligerents in goods other than contraband, which itself was restricted to arms and accoutrements of war. Naval blockades could be instituted but only against particular ports with an ever-present fleet to prevent the entrance and exit of ships from them. Trade by neutrals with belligerents' colonies was permitted, and coastal trade with warring parties was allowed.

But all this changed when Britain was driven to use her naval superiority to combat the military strength of France. For the first time in modern European history Britain extended contraband to include foodstuffs: she introduced the present conception of blockades by applying them to whole coastlines and countries: and she prohibited trade between neutral countries and a belligerent's colonies by enforcing the arbitrary but effective Rule of 1756. Damaging as these practices were to

Overleaf: *The Battle of Queenston Heights, October 13, 1812. General Brock, knighted for the capture of Detroit, was killed in one of the early assaults on the Heights. General Roger Sheaffe was awarded a baronetcy for completing the victory. When the battle was over, Sheaffe's 958 American prisoners out-numbered his own troops.*

Right top: *Ensign Archibald McLean's Commission. Brock signed this paper commissioning McLean an ensign in the Third Regiment of York Militia. It is counter-signed by James Brock, who was the general's cousin and secretary.*

Right below: *Captain John Brant (1794-1832). When Joseph Brant died in 1807, his youngest son, John, was chosen by his mother to succeed him. John Brant participated in all the major battles of the War of 1812, remaining true to the Mohawk tradition of throwing support to the King's forces. He was elected to the Provincial Parliament, but was unseated on a technicality.*

Far right below: *Baby House, Windsor. During the American invasion of July 1812, General William Hull established his headquarters in this house. Later, Hull withdrew and guns were mounted here to cover General Brock's crossing of the Detroit River to capture Detroit itself on August 16, 1812. The house was owned by François Baby (1763-1856), a member of the Upper Canada Assembly.*

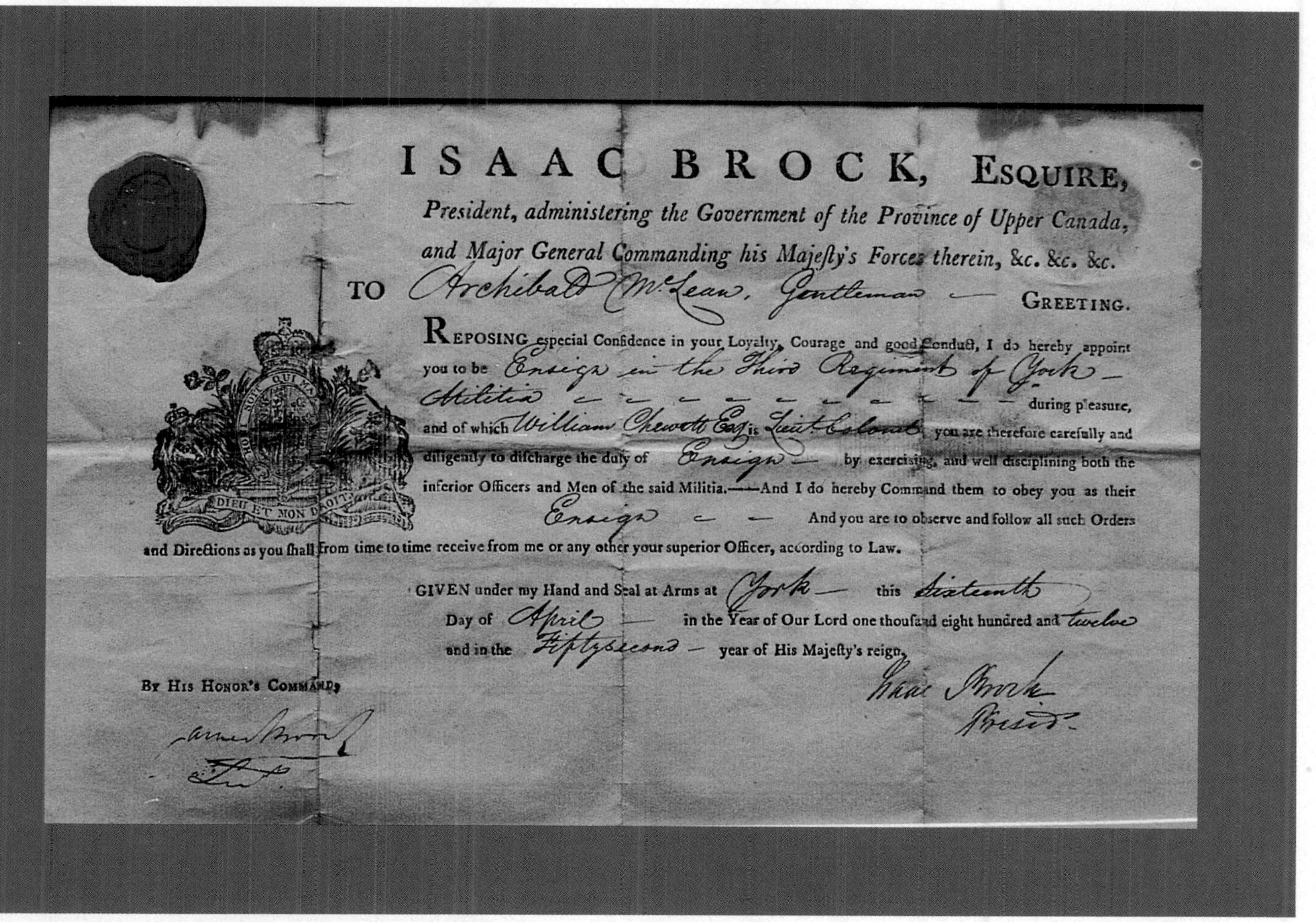

ISAAC BROCK, ESQUIRE,

President, administering the Government of the Province of Upper Canada, and Major General Commanding his Majesty's Forces therein, &c. &c. &c.

TO Archibald McLean, Gentleman — GREETING.

REPOSING especial Confidence in your Loyalty, Courage and good Conduct, I do hereby appoint you to be Ensign in the Third Regiment of York — Militia — — — — — — — — during pleasure, and of which William Chewett Esq. is Lieut Colonel you are therefore carefully and diligently to discharge the duty of Ensign — by exercising, and well disciplining both the inferior Officers and Men of the said Militia.——And I do hereby Command them to obey you as their Ensign — — And you are to observe and follow all such Orders and Directions as you shall from time to time receive from me or any other your superior Officer, according to Law.

GIVEN under my Hand and Seal at Arms at York — this Sixteenth Day of April — in the Year of Our Lord one thousand eight hundred and twelve and in the Fiftysecond — year of His Majesty's reign.

BY HIS HONOR'S COMMAND,

[illegible]

Isaac Brock
Presid.

AHYOUWAIGHS
CHIEF OF THE SIX NATIONS.

__Left:__ Tecumseh (1768?-1813). This artist's perception of the great Shawnee warrior is by F.H. Brigden. Tecumseh sought to unite the natives of the interior to check the advance of white settlement, and to preserve the integrity of the Indians' lands. With his native followers, Tecumseh was at least as responsible for the capture of Detroit in August 1812, as Brock's troops. Tecumseh was killed at the Battle of Moraviantown on October 6, 1813, a disillusioned man at the way the British had been routed by the Americans.
__Right below:__ Brock Leaving Fort George, October 13, 1812. There is no known portrait of Brock. In this representation the general is seen riding from his headquarters at Fort George, upon hearing guns from the direction of Queenston. He took command, exposing himself fearlessly. Although he fell, mortally wounded, the momentum he had set aflame sustained his men until they won the battle.

the United States, however, they could not be compared to the British practice of impressment, for this struck a blow at the very heart of American sovereignty. Impressment was the conscription of British seamen by force, either in ports and cities in the British Isles, or from vessels on the high seas. Its necessity was agreed upon by all sides in the British House of Commons, and its practice was pursued vigorously by all governments which held office in Westminster. But its consequences were profoundly felt by every segment of American society and deeply angered both the government and citizenry of the new republic.

There were two particularly contentious issues in impressment. In the first instance, Britain stopped American vessels on the high seas in order to recapture alleged deserters from the Royal Navy. As the United States took the view that her ships were sovereign portions of the nation, this practice was bound to cause serious friction. Far worse than this, however, was the British practice of stopping American ships on the high seas in order to remove British subjects from them for service in the fleet. It was the definition of a British subject which lay at the heart of the dispute. Britain, like all other nations, save the United States, believed in the doctrine of indefeasible nationality — that is, that an individual born in the country carried its citizenship to his death. Nothing, including the "novel doctrine of naturalization," as the law officers of the Admiralty wrote, could alter this fact. And as the Crown could call upon the services of all British subjects in wartime, it naturally followed that British ships could stop American ships on the high seas and remove from them naturalized Americans of British birth. To a nation built upon immigration this was intolerable.

Other issues between the United States and Great Britain, including British support for Indians, and western expansionism, paled into insignificance compared to disputes over maritime rights. No compromise could be reached by either nation on the central issues under consideration. Britain would not give up impressment, for victory over Napoleon depended upon the power of the Royal Navy. The United States would not surrender on the issue of naturalization, for that would mean that the American flag did not protect all the citizens of the republic. The question only remained as to when the United States would take the fatal step leading to war, and once having taken that step where would she fight it. The answer to the first question came on June 12, 1812, when President Madison sent his war message to Congress. The formal declaration of hostilities came on June 18. The answer to the second came when the United States invaded British North America.

That Upper Canada was the first and, indeed, most prolonged scene of battle has led some to believe that the United States was more interested in the acquisition of land than the defence of her sovereignty. But Upper Canada was selected as a target for purely tactical and strategic reasons. Because of Jefferson's policy of cutting back on the construction of frigates and the building instead of small coastal vessels, the United States could not challenge Britain on the high seas. But she could, as Henry Clay pointed out, strike Britain at her most vulnerable point — Canada. And the taking of that jewel in the imperial Crown, he continued, would compel Britain to address American grievances sympathetically. There was a further reason for the United States concentrating its attention upon Upper Canada. Its geographical proximity and the presence in it of a very large number of recent American immigrants made it seem to military planners and politicians alike an easy and certain target. The taking of Canada, Jefferson remarked, would be a "mere matter of marching." Clay himself insisted that he could take Canada with a file of Kentucky militia. To Americans, then, Canada would be theirs by merely strolling across the border.

What the Americans had failed to take into account in their calculations was the discipline and character of the forces facing them, and the skill and daring of the officers who led them. Nor had they judged correctly the surprisingly stable and resilient nature of the society they were attacking, or assessed properly the capacity of the United States to pursue a long and difficult war without creating a vocal and powerful opposition to its continuance. They made other mistakes, too. Their own forces proved to be too often undisciplined and too frequently led by incompetent commanders. And their failure to grasp at once the necessity of controlling the Great Lakes was almost criminal in its ignorance. A

Right top: *The Schooner* Simcoe, *November 10, 1812. The* Simcoe *was following the* Royal George *when the American fleet attacked her. Once that ship had eluded them, the American ships approached the* Simcoe. *Her captain, James Richardson Sr., ran her aground, confident the Americans would not risk going close to the shoal. Boats from Kingston rescued Richardson and his crew.*
Far right top: *Naval Engagement off Kingston, November 9-10, 1812. H.M.S.* Royal George, *flagship of the Provincial Marine, encountered the American Commodore, Isaac Chauncey's flagship* Oneida *and several smaller ships. The* Royal George's *sails were full of holes as she reached safety close to the guns of Kingston's shore batteries, and Chauncey withdrew.*
Right below: *Fort York in 1812. The fort was destroyed during the American attack on York on April 27, 1813. It was rebuilt on a larger scale in 1816. The restored fort of today and an historic site, is based on the 1816 plan, which does not resemble closely the fort of the 1812 era.*

Left top: *The* General Brock *at York, 1813. The hull of a new ship, named in honour of the slain hero of Queenston Heights, was burnt on the stocks by British and Canadian troops before the Americans captured York in April 27, 1813, to prevent it from falling into enemy hands.*
Left below: *The Battle of Fort George, May 27, 1818. On May 25, the American fleet arrived at the mouth of the Niagara River and began bombarding Fort George. On the 27th, American troops under Colonel Winfield Scott landed, and overwhelmed the now burning fort. The British commander, Brigadier John Vincent, tried to counter-attack, and after heavy losses withdrew his garrison to Burlington Bay.*
Right below: *Isaac Chauncey. On September 3, 1812, Chauncey was appointed Commodore of the American fleets on Lakes Ontario and Erie. He was based at Sackets Harbor, on Lake Ontario, and his flagship was the brigantine* Oneida.

war that began with a fair prospect of success and a high confidence in a happy outcome, proved to be difficult, costly, and in the final analysis, beyond the ability of the United States to win.

At the outbreak of the war Congress had provided for the raising of an army of some 35,000 soldiers, but by the end of June 1812, there were only 7,000 men in service. Madison was further authorized by Congress to enlist a force of 50,000 volunteers and 50,000 militia. This was an army, on paper at least, that was far larger than the one Wellington commanded in the peninsular war or even at Waterloo. Opposed to this potentially huge force was an army of 6,000 British regulars scattered across all of British North America. Only 1,600 of these men were stationed in Upper Canada. They were to be assisted, of course, by a local militia and a force of Indians led by Tecumseh. But the fact that the militia was drawn not only from Loyalists but also from recent American settlers created doubt in the minds of some as to its trustworthiness and reliability. These doubts proved without real foundation. It is true that some recent settlers joined the American forces and that some militiamen deserted, but the great majority of the population remained loyal to the Crown and the rate of desertion from the militia proved to be far lower in Canada than it was in the United States.

The British forces in Canada were led by the Governor-in-Chief of British North America, Sir George Prevost, a regular soldier who served in the British army and also had administrative experience in the West Indies. He was a cautious, prudent, even perhaps, a pedestrian figure; but when one's resources are meagre it is better to husband them carefully than squander them recklessly The commander in Upper Canada was an entirely different character. Major-General Isaac Brock was imaginative and bold in action, with a daring ability to calculate the enemy's plans and counteract them at a moment's notice. Opposing these two men were the Americans. At the head of the nation was James Madison, the president, who was one of the most original political philosophers of his age and the chief architect of the constitution of 1787. While he was a man of enormous intellectual gifts, he was a weak administrator; a man incapable of arousing his countrymen to meet the danger and challenges of war. The Secretary of War was William Eustis, who had been a surgeon during the Revolution, but had grown complacent with the passage of time. The commander of Detroit was General William Hull, the governor of the Michigan territory who had served as a lieutenant-colonel in the Revolution and who had only reluctantly accepted a command he knew he was not suited for. He had a force of some 2,000 soldiers including the United States Fourth Regiment — a formidable army compared to Brock's thin ranks.

Brock was not intimidated by the opposition. Rather, he swiftly acted to protect Upper Canada and attack the enemy. First, he secured the safety of his flank by ordering the seizure of Fort Michilimackinac. That brought not only security, but a flood of Indians to his side whom he could use in the south. Next, he turned his attention to Detroit. Hull had set out from Ohio with a force of 2,000 men for that fort, but disaster dogged his steps. The weather was abominable and when he finally reached the Maumee River he decided to send a vessel with his papers and dispatches, as well as sick troops, across Lake Erie to Detroit. That ship was captured by the British. Brock was now apprised of both Hull's strength and his intentions. Good soldiers do not ignore gifts from the gods and Brock did not intend to miss this opportunity. Meantime, Hull, innocent of impending disaster struggled on to Detroit. He reached his objective on July 12, crossed over the river and took Sandwich, thus forcing the British back to Fort Malden. A vigorous officer would have pressed on with his attack and tried to lay waste to the Niagara area, but Hull waited for more artillery to arrive before he began action. This reticence — indeed sloth — reaped a dreadful harvest. His troops' morale declined, and some began to desert; on the other side, British morale soared as they feared attack less and less. Worse, Indian attacks on Hull's line of communication persuaded him to withdraw all his troops into Fort Detroit. Brock's moment had come. He moved across the river with 300 regulars, 400 militia and 600 Indians, and laid siege to the fort, calling for Hull's immediate surrender. When his demand was rejected, Brock ordered a frontal attack upon the fort. Faced with this onslaught and terrified that the Indians might

Right top: *Stoney Creek Battlefield. Here, on June 5 and 6, 1813, British and Canadian forces, won a decisive victory over the Americans.*
Far right top: *The Secord House, Queenston. On the night of June 21, 1813, Laura Secord left this house for her walk to Beaver Dams.*
Right centre: *Inscription on the Monument to Laura Secord.*
Far right centre: *James Fitzgibbon. Shown in Later Life.*
Right below: *The DeCew House, Thorold. The house has since been demolished.*
Far right below: *Beaver Dams Battlefield. As a result of Laura Secord's information and other intelligence reports he received, Lieutenant James Fitzgibbon defeated a numerically superior American force under Lieutenant-Colonel Charles Boerstler.*
Left below: *Laura Ingersoll Secord (1775-1868). Wife of James Secord, Laura was the heroine of the Battle of Beaver Dams.*

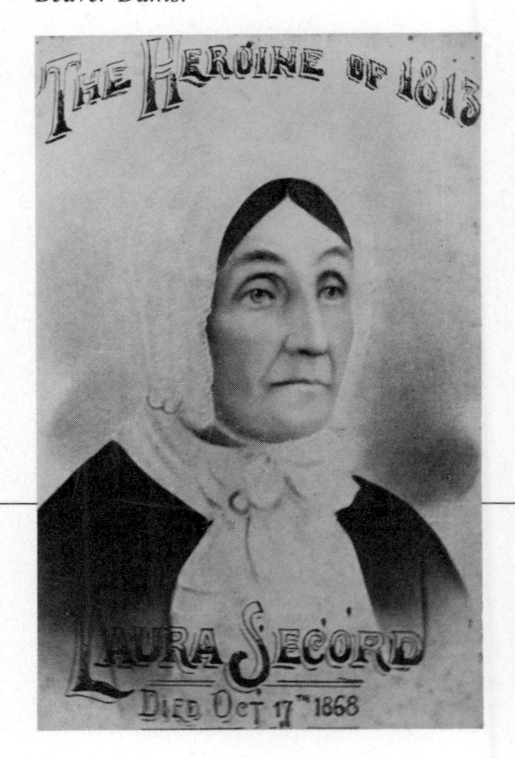

Laura Secord 1775-1868

To perpetuate the name and fame of Laura Secord who walked alone nearly 20 miles by a circuitous, difficult and perilous route through woods and swamps and over miry roads to warn a British outpost at De Cew's Falls of an intended attack and thereby enabled Lieut. Fitzgibbon on the 24th June 1813, with less than 50 men of H.M. 49th Regt., about 15 militiamen and small force of Six Nations and other Indians under Captains William Johnson Kerr and Dominique Ducharme to surprise and attack the enemy at Beechwoods (or Beaverdams), and after a short engagement, to capture Col. Boerstler of the U.S. Army and his entire force of 542 men with two field pieces.

The above is the text of the Laura Secord monument at Lundy's Lane, Niagara Falls, Ontario.

A. Buck. pinx.t
H.R. Cook. sculp.
ESTO PERPETUA
CONFIANCE
CAPT.N SIR JAMES LUCAS YEO, KN.T

Left: *Sir James Lucas Yeo (1782-1818). In this portrait, by A. Buck, Yeo is shown with his coat-of-arms. He joined the Royal Navy as a boy and saw much action as a young man. At age thirty-one he was placed in command of the British naval force on the Great Lakes.*

Right below: *The* Confiance *and the* Surprise. *On September 3, 1814, some seventy British soldiers and sailors, led by Lieutenant Miller Worsley, R.N., in four* bateaux, *captured the American schooner* Tigress *near Michilimackinac. She was renamed the* Confiance, *which was taken from Sir James Yeo's coat-of-arms. Two days later, deliberately flying the American pennant, Worsley's men in the* Confiance *captured the American schooner* Scorpion, *renamed the* Surprise. *Men from these vessels had, on August 14, participated in the destruction of the British schooner* Nancy *in the Nottawasaga River. Afterwards, they were the only sailing vessels above Lake Erie. Following their capture, Britain controlled the supply route to Michilimackinac.*

lose all control Hull succumbed; and on August 12, 1812, the first invasion of Upper Canada was broken. The ease with which this was done humiliated the government in Washington and lifted the spirits of Canadians.

Detroit was the point of only one projected American attack; two others were proposed. The first was aimed directly at Niagara, while the second was to follow the Lake Champlain route to Montreal. Washington would have been wise to concentrate upon the latter, for if the United States could have seized Montreal she might have starved Upper Canada into submission. To do this the Americans needed to gain control of Lake Champlain and this they could not do. So it was to Niagara, and for this General Henry Dearborn prepared himself. Brock, hearing of this gathering of forces, moved rapidly back to block it. On September 13, 1812, an American army of some 6,000 men under the command of Major-General Stephen Van Renssalaer launched an invasion across the Niagara River. Twin columns of 300 men each moved up the slopes of Queenston, and although they were fired upon more men were able to join them from the American side.

Brock, hearing the firing from Fort George rode over to take command of the British forces. When he arrived he found the Americans occupying the height of land at Queenston; he immediately counter-attacked to drive the invaders from their position. As he charged up the slope he was mortally wounded, as was his successor Lieutenant-Colonel John MacDonell. The British position seemed precarious, but the New York militia refused to join their comrades across the river, arguing that the militia was required by law only to serve in the state in which it was recruited. This passion for legal rectitude cost them the victory for now Major-General Roger Sheaffe hurried from Fort George with reinforcements, joined with the Indians, and launched a fierce attack upon the American position. The 1,000 men under his command broke the Americans, who fled back to the river, where they discovered that the boats which had brought them had retreated to the American side. The victory was complete; the Americans lost 30 killed in action and 900 regular soldiers as prisoners. Upper Canada had been saved in the first year of the war; and, as time was to show, this signal victory would preserve it throughout the conflict; for the United States was to find that if it could not conquer Upper Canada in the first year of fighting it would not be able to do it at all.

Nevertheless, America would try again and again and put to the test the quality of that colony's will and the determination of its soldiers. In December 1812, an army of some 5,000 soldiers attempted another crossing of the Niagara River but its efforts ended in utter confusion, despair and defeat. The onset of winter now made operations difficult, if not impossible. Further, the Americans were belatedly turning their attention to Montreal, but they only had an army of some 2,400 men on Lake Champlain — a force far too modest in numbers to undertake such an operation. Control of Lake Erie and Lake Ontario was recognized as holding the key to victory so that both sides began building ships in order to achieve this goal. But creating a navy was a slow and cumbersome business and by 1813 neither side was in a position to dominate the other.

The spring of 1813 arrived and once more the United States travelled a well-worn path. General Dearborn envisaged a series of attacks upon Upper Canada directed at York, Kingston, and the forts along the Niagara. On April 20, a force of 1,300 Americans sailed towards York, arriving on the 26th. They lay offshore overnight and on the 27th began landing west of the capital of Upper Canada. They were met with fire from Indians but a naval bombardment put a stop to it. Throughout the morning brisk fighting ensued with the British being slowly driven back to the town. Realizing they were outnumbered and losing the battle, orders were given to blow up the main magazine at York. In the explosion which followed, the American commander, General Zebulon Pike, and a number of his men were killed, but this did not prevent the invaders from pressing the attack and occupying the town.

General Sheaffe, commanding the British forces, retreated along the lake shore leaving a militia officer to arrange the terms of surrender. This involved turning over public but not private property to the Americans who then burned the parliament buildings and the barracks. There

Right top: *Captain Robert Barclay's Flagship, the Brig* Detroit. *The* Detroit *surrendered to the Americans during the Battle of Lake Erie, September 10, 1813.*

Right top centre: *Commodore Oliver Hazard Perry's Brig* Niagara. *At the start of the Battle of Lake Erie, Perry's flagship was the* Lawrence. *After that ship was badly damaged, Perry transferred to the* Niagara.

Far right top: *Death of Tecumseh. This stone tablet marks the spot where the great Shawnee leader was killed in action on October 6, 1813.*

Right below: *In this peaceful setting beside the Thames River, the American General and future President, William Henry Harrison, routed the army of General Henry Proctor, in the Battle of Moraviantown.*

Left below: *Fort Malden, Amherstburg. Built in the 1790s, Malden was needed after the British forts on United States territory were evacuated in 1796.*

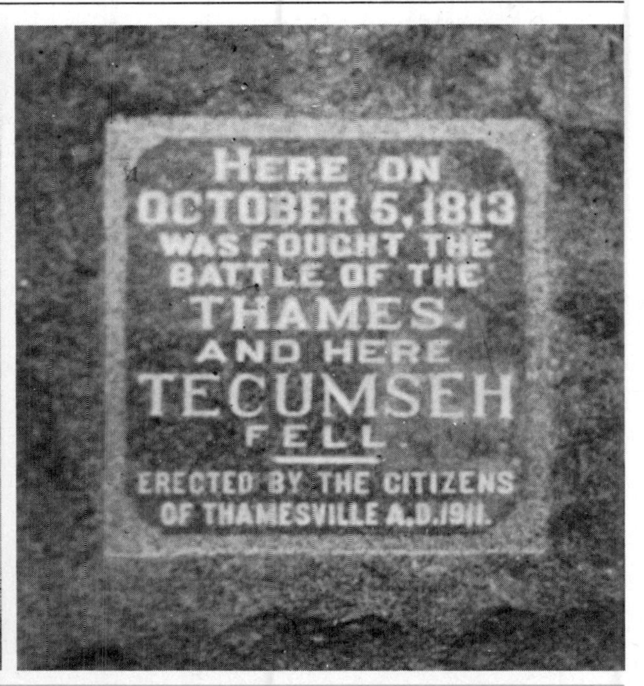
HERE ON
OCTOBER 5, 1813
WAS FOUGHT THE
BATTLE OF THE
THAMES.
AND HERE
TECUMSEH
FELL
ERECTED BY THE CITIZENS
OF THAMESVILLE A.D. 1911.

Lundy's Lane Battle Ground (July 25th 1814)
Soldiers' Monument at left. Niagara Falls, Canada.

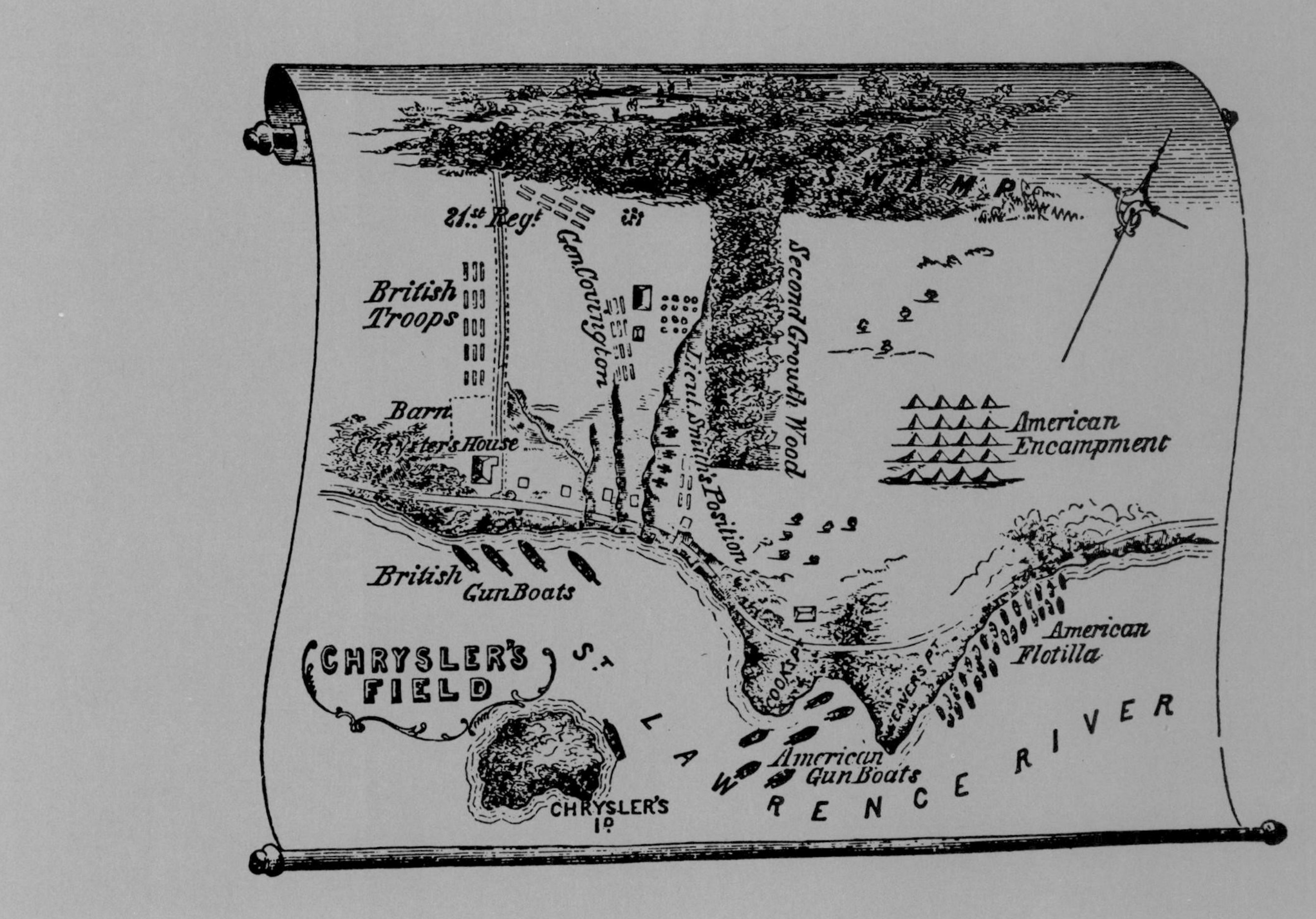
21st Regt
Gen Covington
British Troops
Second Growth Wood
Lieut. Smith's Position
American Encampment
Barn
Chrysler's House
British Gun Boats
CHRYSLER'S FIELD
ST LAWRENCE RIVER
American Flotilla
American Gun Boats
CHRYSLER'S Id

Left top: ***Lundy's Lane Battlefield, July 25, 1814.*** *The scene of one of the bloodiest battles fought on Canadian soil, all told, some 6,000 men were engaged. Each side lost about 800 soldiers in the six-hour struggle, and each claimed a victory. The British side had the edge — reserves to call upon; the Americans had none, and they withdrew to Fort Erie. The once-gory field is now a quiet cemetery.*

Left below: *"Chrysler's Field." This map from B.J. Lossing's* The Pictorial Field Book of the War of 1812 *(1869), illustrates the nature of the battleground, contained between the river and thick woods. Lossing misspelled the land owner's name, which was Crysler.*

Right below: *Crysler's Farm Old Monument. The field where the Battle of Crysler's Farm was fought was flooded during the construction of the St. Lawrence Seaway in the 1950s. A new monument in a memorial park was established nearby.*

was some looting and destruction of homes, although it was on a limited scale. Having completed their task the Americans moved off to attack the forts along the Niagara River. But they left behind a residue of distrust and anger. The destruction of towns, once begun, tends to escalate with calls for retaliation. Britain was determined to punish the United States for the attack upon York and did so in 1814, when an army of Wellington's veterans attacked and took Washington, dined at the White House, and then burned it and the naval yards.

By the end of May 1813, the Americans were ready to launch a major offensive in the Niagara area. A force of 2,000 men under General Winfield Scott attacked Fort George where Major-General John Vincent, realizing that his position was indefensible, spiked the guns and retreated in good order towards the head of the lake. He took with him the garrisons of Fort Erie and Fort Chippawa for they were equally exposed and vulnerable, and established himself at Burlington where he planned to take his stand. And a difficult one it seemed to be for the American forces had now risen to over 5,000 men. But numbers do not always count as Vincent was to prove. In the dead of night on June 6, he fell with his army upon the Americans at Stoney Creek; the battle was short, sharp and decisive. When it was over the Americans were in disarray, having lost two Brigadiers-General as well as a large number of troops. Once more calculated daring had been richly rewarded, and once again the American invasion had been blunted.

Equally successful although of less importance, was the defeat on June 24, of a superior force under Lieutenant-Colonel Charles Boerstler. The Americans attempted to capture a supply depot at Beaver Dams, near the DeCew house, south of St. Catharines. Of the action at Beaver Dams, an officer of the Indian Department remarked that the Indians fought the battle, while Lieutenant James Fitzgibbon, in command of the depot got the credit. As time passed credit for the victory went to a Queenston housewife named Laura Secord. Exactly how she learned of the impending attack has been clouded by time, but she did walk through the forest to the DeCew house to warn Fitzgibbon and she became the heroine of the War of 1812.

THE WAR OF 1812

***Left top:** British Assault on Oswego, May 6, 1814. Naval commander Sir James Yeo and land commander General Gordon Drummond struck Oswego and captured supplies of pork, flour, salt, and guns, but nineteen* bateaux *of vital naval stores eluded the British and reached Sackets Harbor.*
***Left below:** Survivors of the War of 1812. Ten veterans posed for this photograph on October 23, 1861, on the lawn of Sheriff Jarvis' home in Rosedale, Toronto.*
***Right below:** James Richardson Jr. James Richardson Sr. and Jr. were officers in the Provincial Marine. On May 6, 1814, James Jr. was aboard the sloop* Wolfe *at the attack on Oswego. During the engagement the ship was set on fire three times, and Richardson lost his left arm. Later, he was a Bishop of the Methodist Episcopal Church.*

led up a further 13,000 militia.

This was not a force which could be lightly broken. If Wilkinson had known what had happened to Hampton's forces on Lake Champlain his enthusiasm for this venture would have turned to utter despair. For the latter, with an insufficient army of only 4,000 had met with disaster. He had moved his army up the Chateauguay River and thence down to the St. Lawrence. There he had engaged Lieutenant-Colonel Charles de Salaberry who had entrenched himself with his soldiers in a near impregnable position. Some 400 of them were placed behind wooden barricades on one side of the river, while 160 of the others were concealed in woods on the other side of the stream; some 1,000 troops were held in reserve. Hampton's plan was simple: 1,500 men would swing behind de Salaberry's force and attack from the rear, while the main force would charge the wooden barricades in a frontal attack. So much for good intentions. The first part of the army got lost in the woods; the frontal attack collapsed in ignominy and his army fled the field in disorder. Hampton was so disheartened by these events that he withdrew his army up the Chateauguay River.

One calamity was now to follow another for Wilkinson decided to press his own attack forward without the support he needed from Hampton. On November 6, he sailed and marched his army down the St. Lawrence River passing Prescott and heading for Cornwall. He was hotly pursued by boats carrying 800 soldiers from Kingston, and subjected to increasingly ferocious fire from militia men along the way. It was below the Long Sault rapids that the issue was settled. The British, under Colonel Joseph Morrison, had chosen the ground of Crysler's farm as the place to take their stand. It was well suited for battle because open fields lay in front of the troops while their flanks were protected by the St. Lawrence River on the right and dense woods upon the left. It was into this position that the American General John Boyd, who was in charge of the battle, launched his soldiers. Superior in numbers, artillery and cavalry, the Americans might have expected to carry the day. But instead, the withering fire they met broke their spirits. They halted in their tracks; the British counter-attacked and drove them from the field.

Wilkinson was now desperate. His army had been badly mauled. Hampton could not and would not give him support and so he withdrew his army to the American side of the St. Lawrence River. It had been a disastrous campaign and he was consoled only by the thought that if he had reached Montreal, he could not have held it. And so 1813 drew to a close with victory no nearer than it had been a year and a half before. Upper Canada was still free of American troops; her people still stood fast; her government was still intact. Worse, reinforcements were on the way, for the war in Europe was winding down. Wellington was triumphant in the peninsular campaign and Paris would fall in 1814. What a prospect for Canada and what a nightmare for America!

The change of circumstances was soon seen in the plans which the British envisaged for Canada. There were to be three major offensives: the first was to be an attack upon Washington, the second a strike down Lake Champlain into New York, and the third a blow at New Orleans. The campaign against Washington was brilliantly executed and culminated in the burning of the White House and the naval yards, but the operation down Lake Champlain was a disaster. To succeed here, the British needed control of the lake, but this was lost after the British fleet was defeated in battle by the American forces skilfully and indeed brilliantly led by Captain Thomas Macdonough. There was nothing left for the British army but to retreat in humiliation back to Canada. The attack on New Orleans came three weeks after the Treaty of Ghent, and though a triumph for General Andrew Jackson, it had no effect upon the outcome of the war.

What had become clear by 1814, however, was the fact that neither side could win the war except at a terrible cost and each saw this as unbearable. The cost was clearly demonstrated by the casualties at the Battle of Lundy's Lane, north of Chippawa on the Niagara Peninsula. On May 25, some 2,650 Americans engaged a British force that ultimately numbered about 3,500. American casualties amounted to 853. British and Canadians, who won a tactical victory because the Americans withdrew, lost 878 killed, wounded, captured or missing.

Right: *H.M.S.* St. Lawrence. *Artist and author C.H.J. Snider called this first-rate ship-of-the-line "the silent* St. Lawrence" *because she never fired a shot in battle. She never needed to, for after she was launched on September 10, 1814, she was the largest wooden warship ever to sail on the Great Lakes. Over sixty metres long, manned by a crew of 1,000 and ultimately sporting 112 guns, she carried a heavier armament than Nelson's* Victory *at the Battle of Trafalgar. When rumours of the* St. Lawrence's *size reached Sackets Harbor, the Americans started building an even bigger vessel, but work ceased on it after the peace treaty was signed. Thus ended the naval arms race at the foot of Lake Ontario. The St. Lawrence became a floating barracks, and eventually the hull was sunk in Kingston harbour.*

Left below: *Anchor at Holland Landing Park. Planned for a future man-of-war on the Upper Great Lakes, this anchor, weighing nearly 2,000 kilograms, was abandoned at Holland Landing when peace was declared, and has been there ever since.*

Lord Liverpool, the British prime minister, did not feel that he could ask for further sacrifices from a nation which had been at war for over twenty years, and particularly so in the light of Wellington's advice to negotiate a peace because the object of the military — the preservation of British North America — had been achieved. President Madison was of a like mind, for a bitter opposition to the war had arisen in New England and the causes for which the war had been entered — maritime rights — had disappeared with the ending of the war in Europe. Now impressment, blockades, the seizure of American goods had all gone. And so on Christmas Eve 1814, the Treaty of Ghent, which called only for the restoration of the *status quo ante-bellum,* was signed.

What had this war done for America? Albert Gallatin, the great Secretary of the Treasury, said that it had renewed the spirit of the revolution and rekindled feelings of American nationalism. It had a similar effect upon Upper Canada, but the nationalism it fostered was imbued with a sense of anti-Americanism. The Loyalists had fled the Thirteen colonies in order to remain under British institutions, as well as to escape from American persecution. Further, it is clear that the institutions of Canada — representative government under the Crown — had proven to be remarkably resilient and strong. Had loyalty to the Crown been ephemeral, loyalty in its service would have been ephemeral, too, and the colony might have fallen to the American army. The opposite occurred. The deepest division in society appeared in the United States where opposition to the war hastened the negotiations for peace.

The Treaty of Ghent was agreed to by Britain because Canada was secure, not because she had lost the will to fight. It is perfectly true that desertions from both the British army and Canadian militia took place, but at no time did it match in numbers or degree the desertion rate from the American forces. It is true, too, that the heart of the army in Upper Canada was to be found in its core of British regular soldiers, but without the militia the outcome of many battles would have been in doubt and the prospects of final victory uncertain. Loyalty to constitutional monarchy marked the Loyalists in war and was to characterize their conduct in peace.

Right below: *Memorial Stone Where Brock Fell. Edward VII, when Prince of Wales, visited Ontario in 1860. On September 15, he dedicated this marker. The Brock monument column at Queenston Heights appears in the background.*

Main events of the war of 1812

1812	
June 19	United States declares war
July 17	British capture Michilimackinac
July 19	Americans defend Sackets Harbor, N.Y.
August 16	British capture Detroit
September 29	Americans raid Gananoque, U.C.
October 13	British win Battle of Queenston Heights, U.C.
November 9-10	Indecisive naval engagement off Kingston, U.C.
1813	
January 22	British win Battle of Frenchtown, Mi.
February 7	Americans raid Brockville, U.C.
February 22	British attack Ogdensburg, N.Y.
April 27	Americans capture York, U.C.
May 15	Yeo takes command of Provincial Marine
May 27	Americans capture Fort George, U.C.
May 29	British attack Sackets Harbor, withdraw
June 1	H.M.S. *Shannon* captures U.S.S. *Chesapeake*
1June 5-6	British win Battle of Stoney Creek, U.C.
June 24	British win Battle of Beaver Dams, U.C.
July 5	British raid Fort Schlosser, N.Y.
July 11	British raid Black Rock village, N.Y.
July 30	British raid Plattsburgh, N.Y.
September 10	Americans win Battle of Lake Erie
September 27	Americans capture Amherstburg, U.C.
October 6	Americans win Battle of Moraviantown, U.C.
October 26	British win Battle of Chateauguay, L.C.
November 11	British win Battle of Crysler's Farm, U.C.
December 10	Americans burn Newark and Queenston, U.C.
December 19	British capture Fort Niagara, N.Y.
1814	
February 6	British raid Madrid, N.Y.
February 19-24	British raids on Salmon River, Malone, Four Corners, N.Y.
March 30	Americans occupy Odelltown, L.C.
May 6	British capture supplies at Oswego, N.Y.
May 15	Americans raid Long Point, U.C.
May 20-June 6	British blockade Sackets Harbor, N.Y.
May 30	British ambushed at Sandy Creek, N.Y.
July 5	Americans win Battle of Chippawa, U.C.
July 25	Battle of Lundy's Lane, U.C., Americans withdraw
August 14	American capture British schooner *Nancy*
August 15	British begin siege of American-held Fort Erie
August 24-25	British burn Washington, D.C.
September 3	British capture American schooner *Tigress*
September 5	British capture American schooner *Scorpion*
September 10	H.M.S. *St. Lawrence* launched at Kingston, U.C.
September 11	British defeated on Lake Champlain
September 12-15	British attack Baltimore, Md.
October 1	Americans lift blockade of Kingston, U.C.
October 20	H.M.S. *St. Lawrence* lies off Niagara
November 5	Americans blow up Fort Erie, retire
December 24	Treaty of Ghent ends the war
1815	
January 8	Battle of New Orleans, La.

BRI
TAKES M
IN H

TAIN
IATTERS
AND

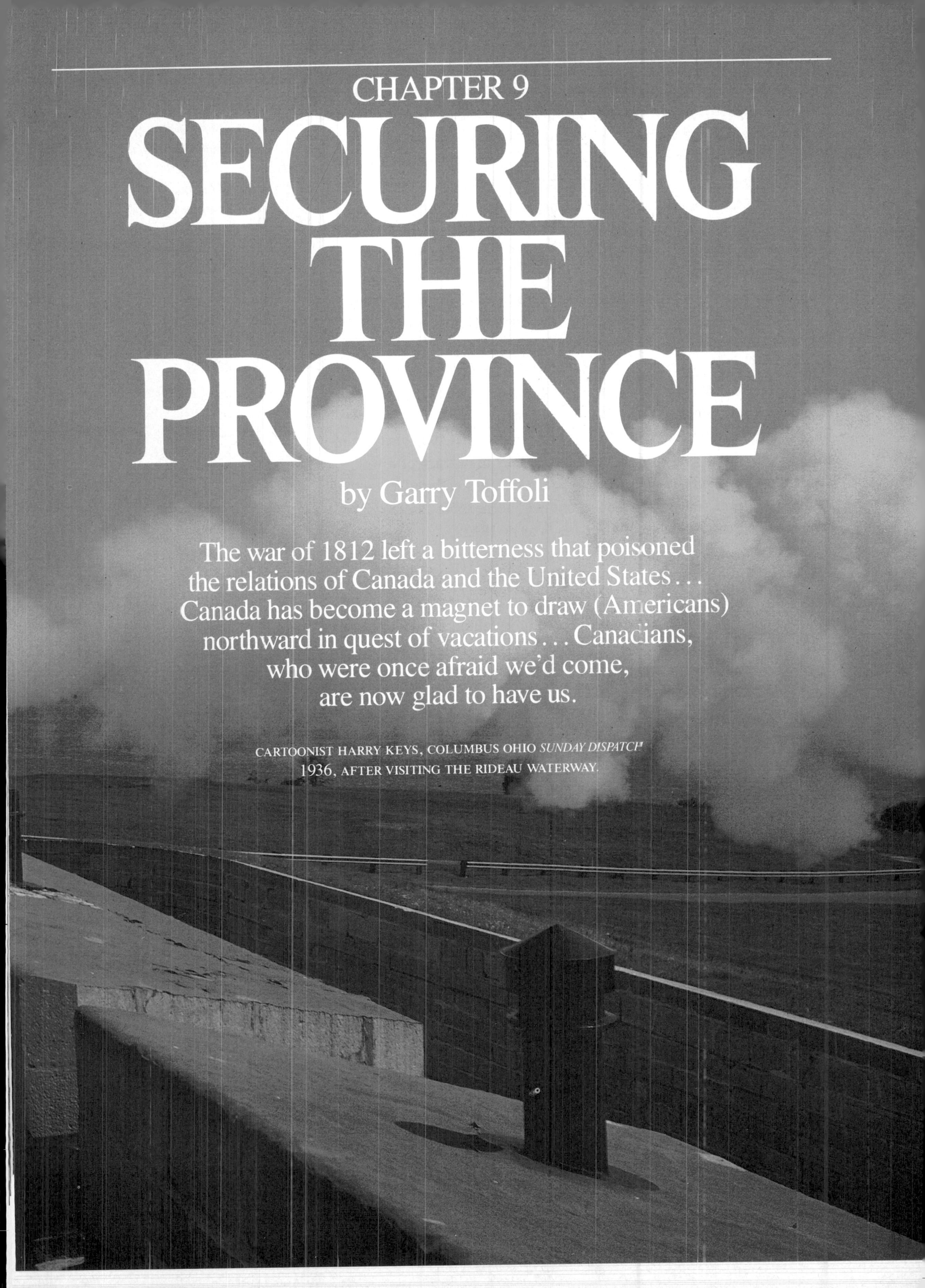

CHAPTER 9

SECURING THE PROVINCE

by Garry Toffoli

The war of 1812 left a bitterness that poisoned the relations of Canada and the United States... Canada has become a magnet to draw (Americans) northward in quest of vacations... Canadians, who were once afraid we'd come, are now glad to have us.

CARTOONIST HARRY KEYS, COLUMBUS OHIO *SUNDAY DISPATCH*
1936, AFTER VISITING THE RIDEAU WATERWAY.

CHAPTER 10

EARLY LAND DEVELOPERS

by Charles J. Humber

"The prosperity of the twentieth century is largely due to the foundation laid by the pioneers of the close of the eighteenth and the opening of the nineteenth century."

A. C. CASSELMAN, 1914

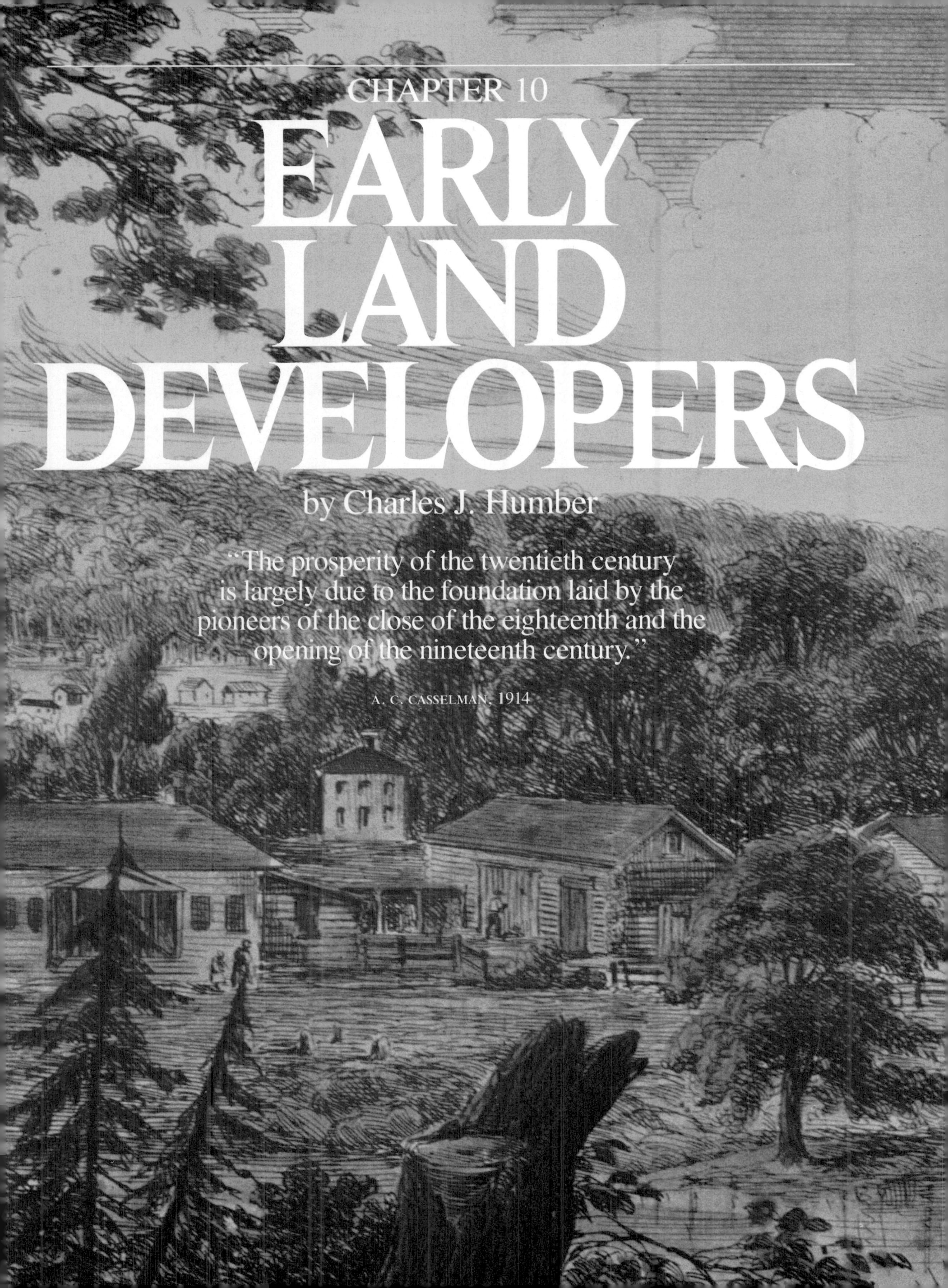

Crown land! Even today the very phrase evokes romantic aspirations for many and inevitably stirs the imagination for all. Crown land still exists, particularly in Ontario. Literally, there remains hundreds of thousands of lake lots, islands, river lots and countless woodland, brush and forest property as Crown land throughout this province.

Crown land was first distributed to settlers two centuries ago to accommodate the thousands of Loyalists who relocated along the water highways of future Ontario. At that time, the governor of Canada, General Frederick Haldimand, had no choice but to purchase tracts of land from the native peoples in the name of the Crown. Haldimand acted in accordance with British policy laid down under the Royal Proclamation of 1763, which specified that the natives were the legal owners of their tribal lands. Private individuals were not allowed to buy land directly from the natives; only the government could arrange for land purchases.

After this historic settlement occurred, only a sparse influx of settlers moved north, until 1792 when John Graves Simcoe came as the first governor to Upper Canada. Almost immediately Simcoe wanted to get the province on the move. He knew this was only possible by enticing massive settlement.

Perhaps the most famous group he attracted to Upper Canada was a party of settlers led by William von Moll Berczy, a portrait painter whose legacy in Ontario today hangs in many art galleries.

At the time he induced these people — who had come from Eastern Germany to the Genesee Valley in New York State — to move to Upper Canada, Simcoe envisioned connecting the fledgling capital, York, to Lake Simcoe. The Queen's Rangers had started building a road, and Simcoe offered substantial acreages of Crown land to Berczy to complete it. Berczy agreed to engineer the building of Yonge Street, and in so doing relocated his group in what is now the Town of Markham, northeast of Toronto. The Berczy settlers not only laid the foundations for the future and rapid growth of the Markham area but also began the immense task of pushing a road north through dense bush from York, the capital, to the lake named after Simcoe's father.

Although the original agreement between the two got caught up in a

Overleaf: *Engraving of Guelph. The roots of Guelph began on April 23, 1827, when Canada Company officials had a huge tree chopped down, signalling the beginning of land development.*
Right top: *William von Moll Berczy (1744-1813). He led a group of settlers from Germany to New York State in 1790, and Simcoe persuaded him to settle them in the Markham area, north of York. Gifted in many ways, Berczy painted this self-portrait c.1790.*
Far right top: *Site of German Mills. Built by the Berczy settlers in 1794-1795, this 1950 photograph shows what little remains of the mills, south of John Street in Thornhill on the east bank of the Don River.*
Right middle: *Yonge Street at Holland Landing, 1910. Started by the Queen's Rangers in 1793, continued by the Berczy settlers, and completed by Deputy Surveyor Augustus Jones to Holland Landing by 1795, Yonge Street linked York to the upper lakes.*
Far right middle: *Parade on Talbot Street, St. Thomas. The main street of many a town in the huge Talbot settlement that encompassed Elgin, Kent and Essex Counties, was often named after the colourful Irish land developer, Colonel Thomas Talbot.*
Right below: *Morpeth, Kent County. Like St. Thomas, Morpeth has its Talbot Street.*
Far right below: *Elgin County. Leamington, too, has a Talbot Street in memory of the early entrepreneur.*

HOLLAND LANDING.
ONT.

ERIE HOUSE

granted Crown land directly above these earlier settled townships. Here at St. Raphael, the first Roman Catholic parish in Upper Canada was established.

Like bees to honey, Scots attracted Scots and further emigration from Scotland to Glengarry continued in both 1792 and 1796. But it was the 1803 emigration that was the first really large-scale resettlement of Scots Highlanders in Upper Canada, following 1784.

Taking place under the auspices of another priest named Alexander Macdonell, chaplain of the Glengarry Light Infantry Fencibles raised in Scotland, this totally Roman Catholic regiment was untimely disbanded in 1802, following the Treaty of Amiens. Macdonell, destined to become in 1826 the first Roman Catholic Bishop in Upper Canada, recognizing that disbandment had placed extreme hardship on these men, persisted in relocating this regiment in Upper Canada. The Secretary of State for the Colonies, Lord Hobart, aware of the plight of the Fencibles, lent a sympathetic ear to the future Bishop, allotting him 1,200 acres (486 hectares) of Crown land in Upper Canada, and two hundred acres (80 hectares) for each of the men who went with him.

Shortly afterwards a shipload of disbanded Glengarry Fencibles, 1,100 souls, sailed for eventual resettlement in Glengarry County.

All were extremely loyal to the Crown. One of this later group, "Red George" Macdonell, became a hero at both Ogdensburg and Chateauguay, famous battle scenes of the War of 1812. Colonel John Macdonell, aide-de-camp to General Isaac Brock and Member of Parliament for Glengarry in 1812, was killed at the battle of Queenston Heights. Today, his body reposes with that of Brock at Queenston under the famous monument which honours "the Hero of Canada."

Although the moving spirit behind Scottish emigration to Upper Canada in 1803 was Bishop Alexander Macdonell, essentially he is not remembered as a land developer as much as he is a patriot, a military chaplain, an educator and a legislator. His leadership, nevertheless, in resettling on Crown land hundreds of Scottish refugees, should go down as one of the fortuitous events in the annals of Upper Canadian history. An 1852 census indicated that there were 3,228 Macdonell families liv-

Right top: *Guelph in 1908. The town where the Huron Tract Road was begun in 1827 celebrates Old Home Week nearly eighty years later.*
Far right top: *Goderich in 1907. The Lake Huron terminus of the Huron Tract Road welcomes passengers arriving on the CPR.*
Right middle: *Home of Comte de Puisaye, Niagara-on-the-Lake c.1900. This royalist in the French Revolution came to Upper Canada. After he failed to develop a settlement north of York, he moved to Niagara-on-the-Lake. In 1802 he went to England.*
Far right middle: *Home of Laurent Quetton de St. George, Toronto. This home since demolished, was built in 1809. St. George, for whom St. George Street, Toronto, is named, was one of the few* émigrés *who remained in Canada to seek his fortune.*
Right below: *Absalom Shade (1793-1862). Born in Pennsylvania, Shade became an agent for William Dickson. Shade established a community known as Shade's Mills in 1816, which was later named Galt, after Dickson's novelist friend.*
Far right below: *William Dickson (1769-1846). A prosperous Niagara merchant, Dickson puchased 36,500 hectares of land in South and North Dumfries Townships. Galt was the centre of his development.*

A ROYAL WELCOME
ROYAL CITY

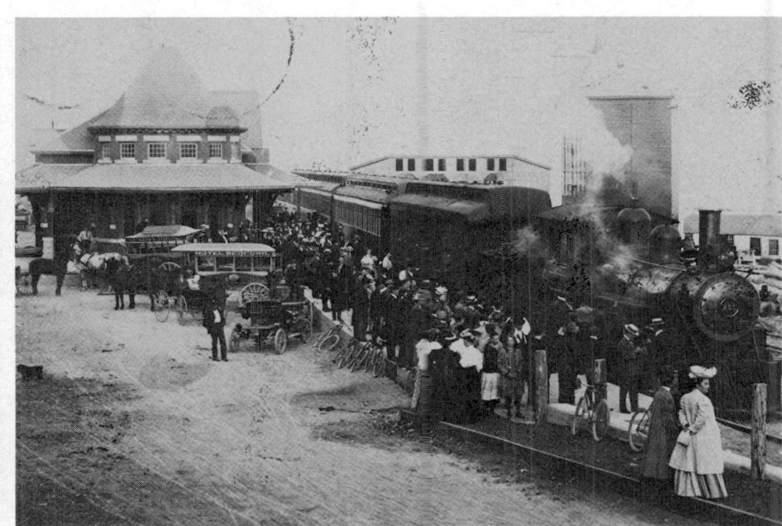

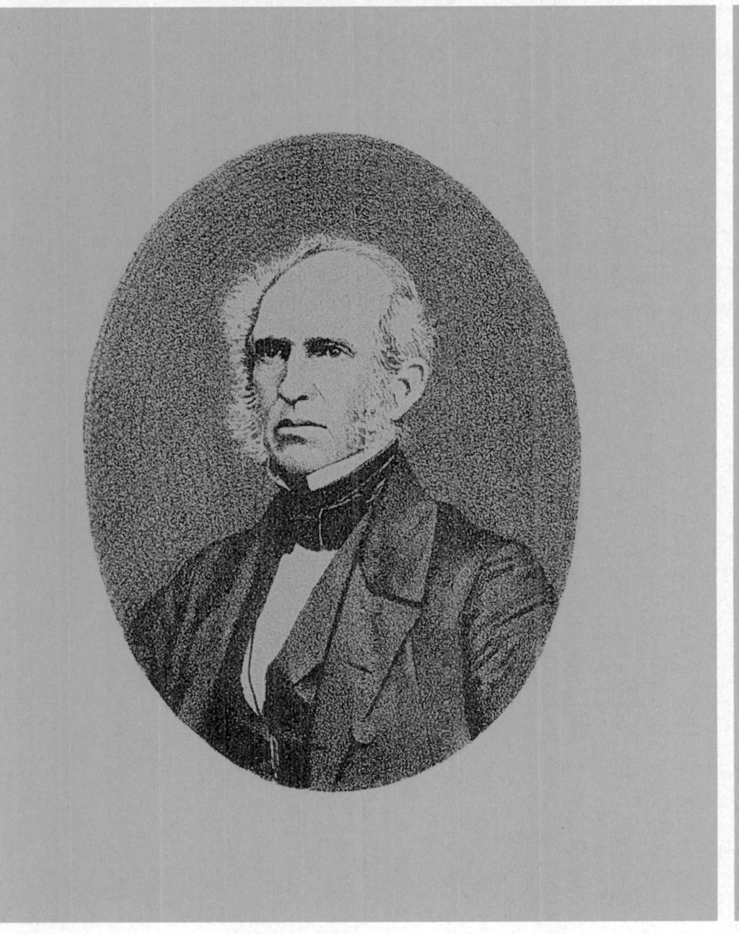

ing in Glengarry County.

Still another Scot, by the name of John Galt, became involved in one of the great land developing schemes undertaken in the upper province. A philanthropist and writer of renown in the early 1820s, a plan of his was to purchase a large tract of Crown land in Upper Canada and place upon it hundreds of people who had no particular occupation and who desired an opportunity to raise their families in some colony where they would not be a burden on the community.

Ironically, at first he did not wish to take any direct or active part in the formation of such a company, especially one that would develop land. He wished instead to devote his days to literature and the general education of his three sons, and offer only his influence from abroad in any relocation of settlers.

By 1824, however, and only after consulting with the Chancellor of the Exchequer, Frederick John Robinson (later, Viscount Goderich, for whom the city on Lake Huron would later be called), and such prominent Upper Canadians as Bishop Alexander Macdonell of Glengarry, Galt modified his original stance and became directly active in the formation and chartering of the Canada Company which immediately made him its first superintendent.

Shortly afterwards a government-appointed Commission sailed for Canada and visited Crown land in Upper Canada to determine the value of a particular tract. The final result was the purchase of the Huron Tract by the Canada Company in 1826, a huge triangle of Crown land nearly one million acres in size. The cost was approximately 1,000,000 pounds!

By April 1827, Galt set out to choose a suitable site to launch the operations of the Canada Company. With him went some Company officials, among them Dr. William Dunlop, affectionately known as "Tiger," who was "The Warden of the Canada Company's Woods." On April 23, late in the evening, the company's business was dramatically and romantically begun when a huge tree was chopped down. This signalled the beginning of a massive road-clearing operation which would soon attract thousands of settlers to the famous Huron Tract settlement

***Left below:** Susanna Moodie. One of the three famous Stricklands (Colonel Samuel Strickland was her brother), with her husband, Mrs. Moodie moved to Upper Canada from England in 1832. Her writings of her experiences in the bush, in which she usually stressed the harsh life of the hardy pioneer, served to prepare people wishing to emigrate for the life that lay ahead of them.*

for more than one hundred years. The site where the tree was felled became known as Guelph in honour of the Royal family.

Pushing northwest from this site through the Huron Tract would be the Huron Tract Road aimed at the deepest harbour on the Canadian side of Lake Huron. Now called Highway 8, its building was supervised by "Tiger" Dunlop and built by Anthony VanEgmond and his son Constant. It was to become one of the most important lines of communication in the province, passing through black walnut country from Guelph, through Waterloo County, Stratford, Sebringville and Mitchell, with its terminus at Goderich. The latter was to become a focal point of activity for the Canada Company.

In 1827, some 135 destitute Scots settlers arrived on the doorstep of the Canada Company in the newly created centre called Guelph. They had formed part of a group originally sent by still another land developing company to La Guaryra, Venezuela. Because the land there was so poor and the climate unsuitable they abandoned their settlement and hopes, and appealed for government assistance. Directed to New York, they were encouraged to try for the Huron Tract. Upon their arrival, John Galt, taking note of their destitute condition advanced them needed money to get them restarted. For this generosity he barely escaped censure by the company's directors in England who frowned on such acts. This alleged impropriety was enough for Galt. He consequently returned home. His good judgement of these impoverished souls, nevertheless, was totally correct. In a very short time they fulfilled all their obligations to the Canada Company, becoming as well, stalwart settlers and no government burden.

Many famous people became associated with this land developing leviathan, but none as famous as John Galt, friend of Lord Byron, father of Alexander Tilloch Galt and later one of Canada's Fathers of Confederation and still later the founder of Lethbridge, Alberta.

The last entry made on the books of the Canada Company was December 24, 1951 — for a desk, typewriter and chair . . . .

Large-scale emigration to large tracts of land are interesting, generally because of the abundant genealogical information associated with

***Right below:** Catherine Parr Traill, the sister of Susanna Moodie and Colonel Samuel Strickland. Mrs. Traill was not as critical of Upper Canadian life as was her sister. She accepted, in her book* Backwoods of Canada, *the new reality she faced after leaving the comforts of England. With her half-pay military husband, she arrived in Upper Canda in 1832, the same year as Susanna Moodie.*

ERBOROUGH WELCOMES HER VISITORS

POST OFFICE
CEYLON

Left top: ***Peterborough, Named for the Honourable Peter Robinson (1785-1838). The city shown c.1907, and the county surrounding it, commemorate the man who fostered migration of needy Irish to Upper Canada.***
Far left top: *Three Drawer Blanket Box c.1810. Skilled cabinet makers, Abraham and John Grobb, trekked north from Pennsylvania in 1800. John Grobb made this beautifully crafted 18th-century-style Chippendale blanket box.*
Left middle: *Ceylon, A "Sepoy" Town. Typical of communities in the region north of the Huron Tract known as Queen's Bush, Ceylon must have been named by half-pay officers who had served in India before settling in Upper Canada.*
Far left middle: *The Joseph Schneider House, Kitchener. One of the best preserved homes in Kitchener, it is a reminder of the German settlers who trekked north from Pennsylvania c.1800, planted roots and established businesses.*
Left below: *Auction Sale at Black Creek Pioneer Village. Each September blankets made in the traditional German way are auctioned. The village honours early settlers who came to Ontario at the invitation of land developers.*
Far left below: *Horning's Mills. Here is another tiny hamlet, dependent on an agricultural economy, that was established in Queen's Bush in the last half of the 19th century.*

such enterprises. However, sometimes the more modest attempts at land development reflect more accurately the human habitude in resettlement. The good luck or ill fortune comes into better focus.

One of the fortunate was William Dickson. When Joseph Brant, Chief of the Six Nations at Brantford, sold Block I on the Grand River, the purchaser, Philip Stedman, died shortly afterwards. After a series of transactions, the tract was eventually bought for 15,000 pounds by a veteran of the War of 1812, Upper Canadian William Dickson.

His purchase was pure speculation. Soon after, he met a young Pennsylvania German called Absalom Shade whose skills were quickly noted by Dickson. Hiring him as his agent the two set out to discover what future there was for this newly acquired 95,000 acres (38,460 hectares).

At the future site of Galt they noted there was sufficient water power for milling. Recognizing the future of their enterprise was here, Shade was left in charge to develop a town. He immediately set out and cleared land, built homes, and located settlers. By the end of the year a community named after John Galt, Dickson's favourite writer, was thriving with forty families.

William Dickson was fortunate in more than one way. He was not only able to spot talent when he saw it, namely, Absalom Shade, but he was also a good shot. The story goes that in 1806 he was challenged to a duel by William Weekes who had slandered the late Governor of Upper Canada, John Graves Simcoe. Each having offended the other, the two men came face to face with pistols behind the American Fort Niagara. One was killed — the other survived and became rich!

Bringing settlers a long way to replant their roots is often spotlighted by unfortunate circumstances. Two such examples are the ill-fated attempts to settle French *émigrés* north of the provincial capital late in 1798, and Lord Selkirk's failure to relocate in 1804 some Highland Scots on a tract of land in the extreme southwestern portion of Ontario on the shores of Lake St. Clair.

During the French Revolution (1789-1799), thousands of Bourbon supporters left France and relocated as *émigrés* in England, where they became a charge upon public and private charity. Governor Simcoe

EARLY LAND DEVELOPERS

Many others acquired Crown land in the early 19th century. They developed it, settled on it, and prospered from it. The total result has been the growth of the province over the years.

It is unfair not to mention every single group as they all form important links to Ontario's future identity and are the foundations upon which many Ontarians today proudly stand. Certainly the MacLeod and MacMillan emigrations to the eastern part of the province are as important as the other mentioned groups. So, too, are the Haliburton settlers north of Peterborough, the Lanark and Renfrew settlers to the east, and the pioneers who headed for the "Queen's Bush" north of the Huron Tract. The contributions to settlement made by railway, mining and lumbering magnates, the road and canal builders, and the religious leaders, such as David Willson in Sharon, are just as significant, but not as directly involved in land development as these others. There is, however, still one other important group in this epic story of Upper Canada settlement — the Germans.

A large number of German-speaking settlers had come with the Loyalists in the 1780s. Some, called Palatines, were part of Sir John Johnson's King's Royal Regiment of New York; some were German professional soldiers who went to Prince Edward County; still others were a cross-section of Germans with Butler's Rangers, original settlers on the Niagara frontier. These were quickly assimilated, their cultural identity disappearing as fast as the Crown land. But this was not the case with the Germans who began trickling in from Pennsylvania around 1800 and who collectively came in huge numbers throughout the first half of the 19th century, particularly to Waterloo County, the Twenty (Jordan), and the Vaughan/Markham township region.

Waterloo County is the largest centre in Ontario where German culture is most visible. Oktoberfest, Mennonite markets and buggies, and decorated barns exemplify this.

Settlers began arriving in the Waterloo region in 1799 from Franklin County in Pennsylvania. After several years a joint stock company called the German Company was formed to develop 60,000 acres (24,292 hectares) of land. Its directors were made up exclusively of Mennonites,

Right top: *Preston. Founded by John Erb, another Pennsylvania German, Preston lost its identity when it was amalgamated with Hespeler and Galt to form the City of Cambridge.*
Far right top: *Berlin, Founded in 1806. Settled by Germans from Pennsylvania, Berlin was incorporated in 1871, and became a city in 1912. Because of public pressure, during World War I the name was changed to Kitchener. Oktoberfest is the largest annual German festival in North America.*
Right middle: *Laskey Emporium c.1905. Moved from Laskey to Black Creek Pioneer Village, the building represents a Post Office and general store from the early days of settlement.*
Far right: *The Stallion Perfection. Good coach horses were in demand among the German settlers around Markham. They favoured a strain swifter than a plough horse and sturdier than a saddle mount. Such a horse was Perfection, advertised as a stud.*
Right below: *Lork Selkirk's Baldoon Settlement, 1804. Doomed because of low-lying land and poor drainage, the settlement failed. This lithograph c.1900, of the St. Clair Flats, suggests that it is a forlorn, haunted area. Today, after being drained it is a thriving agricultural region.*

THE CELEBRATED COACH HORSE

PERFECTION

Will Stand for Mares this Season as follows;

Monday, May 5, He will leave his own Stable, Lot 18, in the 5th Con., of Vaughan, and proceed to Samuel Stong's, and stop from 11 to 1; from thence to Mr. Cherry's Inn and stay from 2 till 3; thence down the Plank Road to Watson's Corners, thence to Sheppard's Inn, Yonge St for the night.

Tuesday, He will proceed to Mrs. Sullivan's Inn and stop from 10 to 11, thence down the Town Line to Mr. Sylvester's Inn and stop from 12 to 2, thence across to the Canada Road, to Mr. Glendenning's and stop from 3 to 4, thence to Mr. [illegible]' Inn, 6th Con. Markham, and stop the night.

Wednesday, He will proceed to Mr. Size's Inn, Unionville, and stop from 12 to 2, thence to Mr. Summerfelt's Inn, Cashel, and remain the night.

Thursday, He will proceed to the Town Line, to Mr. Lewis' from 10 to 11, thence to Gormley's Corners, 4th Con., Whitchurch, to Mr. Henry Hooper's from 3 to 4, thence to Bogertown, to Mr. Brows' Inn, and stop the night.

Friday, He will proceed to Newmarket to Mr. Belford's Inn, and stop from 10 to 11, thence to Mr. McLoud's Inn and stop noon, thence to Mitchel's Corners, and stop from 2 to 3, thence to Mr. Shuttle's Inn, and stop the night.

Saturday, He will proceed to Garret Haugh's Inn, King Horn, at noon, thence calling at different places to his own stable, where he will remain till the following Monday.

He will continue the above route during the Season, Health and Weather permitting.

PEDIGREE.

PERFECTION is a beautiful dark Bay, with black legs, mane, and tail. Stands fully sixteen and a half hands high. He is 7 years old this spring. He possesses great bone, muscle, and action, and has proved himself a sure foal-getter. He was got by *Old Perfection*, his dam by *Magerline*, grand-dam by *Messenger*. It is useless tracing Old Perfection any further, for it is well known that he was one of the best horses in Canada, and left the best stock of any other horse that travelled.

TERMS:—To insure a foal, $7; for the season, $5; Single leap, $3, cash down. Groom's fee, 25cts., to be paid at the time of service. Insured mares must be paid for on the 1st of January, 1863; season mares the two last rounds. Mares that are insured, must be returned regularly to the horse, or they will be charged as season mares. Persons disposing of their mares before foaling time, must pay the insurance, whether in foal or not. All accidents at the risk of the owners. No business done on Sundays.

John Snider Proprietor

April 24 [illegible] 1862 *Blackburn's City Steam Press, 90 Yonge Street, Toronto.*

principally from Lancaster County, Pennsylvania. Three prominent shareholders were Benjamin Eby, later co-founder with Joseph Schneider of Kitchener (Berlin), and the first Mennonite Bishop in Upper Canada, John Erb, the founder of Preston (part of Cambridge today) and Abraham Erb, the founder of the City of Waterloo.

Immigration to this county in the 1820s was very significant. Up to this time, the Germans coming to Upper Canada were from Pennsylvania. In 1824, this trend was reversed with the first of a series of settlers from Germany. When Christian Naf[f]ziger of Bavaria, an Amish Mennonite, led a group from Alsace Lorraine to Wilmot Township, he became the first individual within the German *milieu* to develop land. The 60,000 acres (24,292 hectares) in and around New Hamburg became the nucleus for these Germans and was the beginning of large-scale German emigration to Upper Canada, establishing such communities in the region as Heidelberg, Breslau, Mannheim, Baden, Wallenstein and Berlin, place names reflecting their roots on the Continent.

Close on the heels of the Loyalists who settled the Niagara frontier came the Plain Folk, most of whom were German Mennonites. A small group (eight families) had come in 1786 and purchased land from disbanded soldiers in Butler's Rangers. These were from Montgomery County, Pennsylvania, four hundred miles distant from the "Twenty," the community they founded in Lincoln County. In a short time still others came from Pennsylvania, and by the turn of the century the Mennonite Germans of the area were becoming a thriving agricultural community, anticipating by one hundred years or so the fruit- and grape-growing industries which so dominate the region today. In 1801 the first Mennonite Church in Canada had been established in this area and some very prominent surnames began to emerge, such as: Rittenhouse, Hunsberger, Housser, Fretz, Moyer, Hahn, Grobb and Albright, all identified today with science, law, education, craftsmanship and industry — the grist of Ontario social history.

Before Simcoe left Upper Canada in 1796, he assured the future growth of the north of York along both sides of Yonge Street. Encouraged to relocate as settlers, the Pennsylvania Germans began to migrate

Left below: *Surveyors in the Woods. This drawing by D.F. Thomson shows an early 19th century survey party, which usually consisted of fifteen members in order to handle all tasks. Equipment included a sextant shown here, a compass, a special surveyor's chain of one hundred 8-inch links that measured 66 feet (20 metres) — and rum. Data was recorded on the spot in field notebooks, and was incorporated into maps that were drawn afterwards in the surveyor's offices.*

north before 1800 and by 1804 Markham Township became dominated by one family, the Reesors, who had come in Conestoga wagons from Lancaster County. Other families associated with this area where Crown land was at a premium, are Stauffer, Barkey, Hoover, Burkholder, Wismer, Wideman, Raymer and Donner. A branch of this last family went west in a party that in 1846-1847 met a tragic death in the Rockies, in what was later named the Donner Pass. The area around Markham today is slowly giving way to urbanization, but still it clings to an agricultural landscape with prominent markets and fall fairs. The Markham fair continues to be a highlight of the year, while Stouffville has its market, and incidentally is named after the Stauffer family.

Vaughan was the sister to Markham Township, but now both are part of the Regional Municipality of York (formerly York County) and are officially called towns, no longer townships. Settled at the same time as Markham by Pennsylvania Germans, its early history is best exemplified by Jacob Baker who came in 1800 from Somerset County in Conestoga wagons with his wife, eight children and sixteen grandchildren. Other prominent German names in this region are: Cober, Keefer, Miller, Smith, Troyer, and Reaman. A prominent descendent of this last family was G. Elmore Reaman whose book, *The Trail of the Black Walnut* pioneered an interest in the German tradition in Ontario.

Black Creek Pioneer Village in Metropolitan Toronto, on land pioneered by the Stong family, commemorates these German-speaking people and each year the Black Creek Fall Festival is one of the most charming family outings anywhere in the province.

The story of the early settlement of this province frequently suggests romance and sentiment. Rarely does it examine the blood, sweat and tears that went into the building of roads and log homes and the clearing of Crown land. Perhaps it is best that today's generation does not have to duplicate these epic feats. Perhaps it is better that these pioneer forefathers never have to drive in traffic, endure line-ups at fast food outlets and television commercials . . . .

Right below: *Dominion Day Poster, Goderich. The town was named after the Right Honourable Frederick John Robinson, Viscount Goderich (1782-1859). As a member of the House of Lords and of young Queen Victoria's government, Goderich was involved in Canadian affairs during the rebellions of 1837 in Upper and Lower Canada. The poster shows the kind of events that were popular ways of celebrating in the late 19th century.*

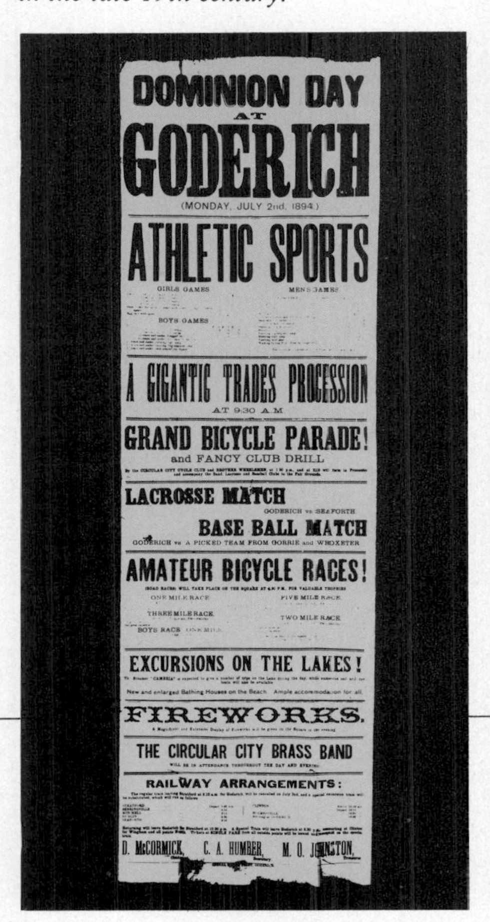

CAPREOL'S
COMMERCIAL SALE
20 ROOMS
PATERSON
JAMES CONNELL
E STEWARD
THOMPSON
WALKER

CHAPTER 11

"STEADFAST IN THEIR ALLEGIANCE"

by Colin Read

He (Mackenzie) as the oracle of discontent and no selfish personal motives blunted the edge of his tirades against monopoly and privilege.

DUNCAN MCARTHUR
THE REFORM MOVEMENT IN UPPER CANADA (1914)

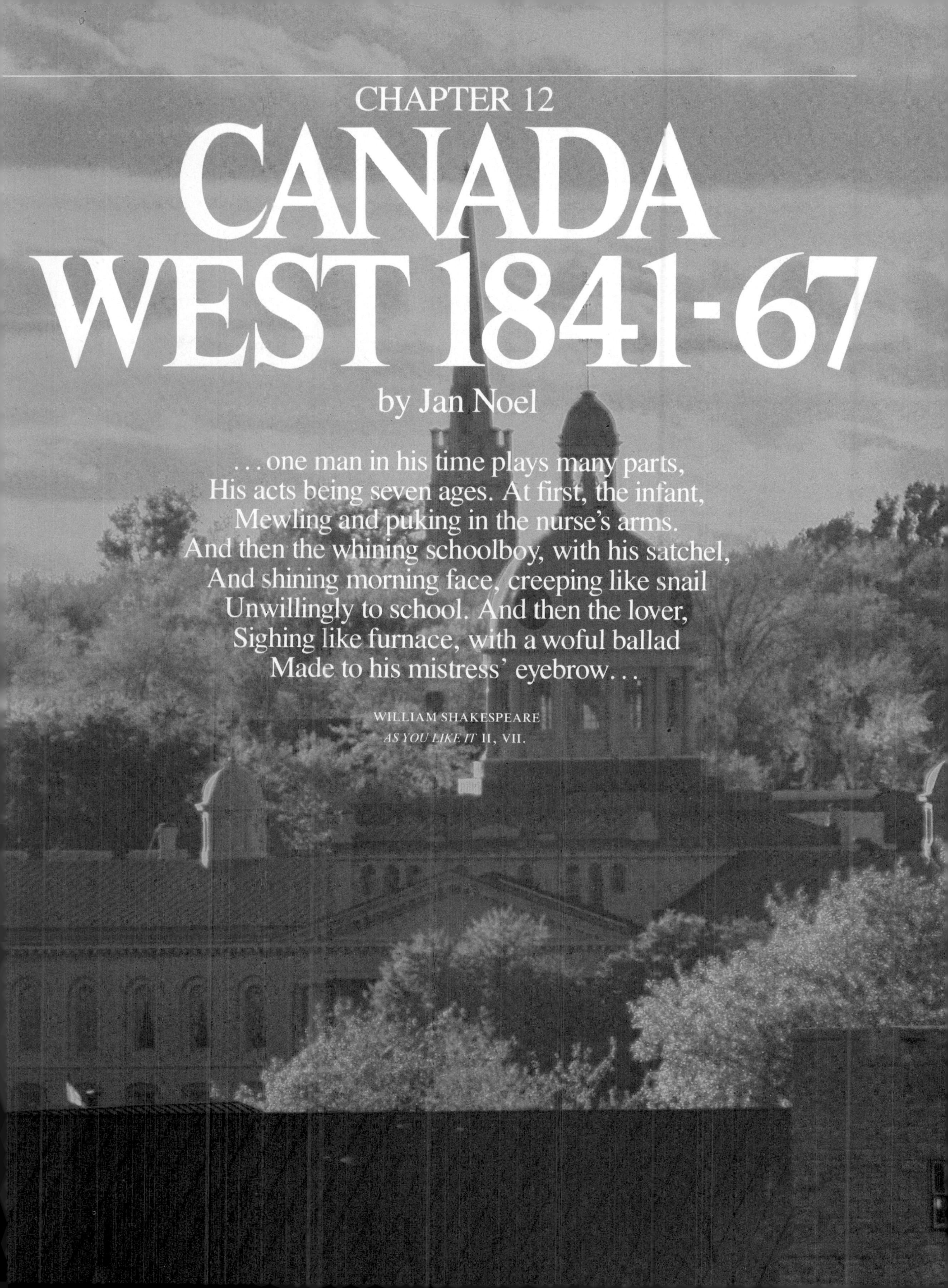

CHAPTER 12

CANADA WEST 1841-67

by Jan Noel

. . . one man in his time plays many parts,
His acts being seven ages. At first, the infant,
Mewling and puking in the nurse's arms.
And then the whining schoolboy, with his satchel,
And shining morning face, creeping like snail
Unwillingly to school. And then the lover,
Sighing like furnace, with a woful ballad
Made to his mistress' eyebrow. . .

WILLIAM SHAKESPEARE
AS YOU LIKE IT II, VII.

Ontario, then known as Upper Canada or Canada West, passed through three of the seven ages of man during the Union period, 1841-1867. In those brief twenty-six years she grew from infancy to young adulthood. Born in the 18th century, Upper Canada was still a brawling frontier baby when she was united with predominantly French Lower Canada to form the Union of the two colonies in 1841. Both colonies had recently misbehaved, rebelling in 1837. Now they were being closely controlled by their nursemaids — the governor and his councils. When the novelist Charles Dickens visited Toronto at the beginning of the Union, he was appalled by its "wild and rabid Toryism."

Despite this inauspicious opening of the Union period, Upper Canada was entering a time of growth that was truly remarkable. In the 1840s she learned to stand, politically, on her own two feet. The 1850s might be described as a period of troubled adolescence; in the 1860s the province emerged as a mature adult. There was rapid physical growth, with Upper Canada's population tripling between 1841 and 1867. While never severing the ties with Montreal, Ontario developed her own business enterprises. The energetic young province proved a driving force for economic expansion through railways, and later, through Confederation. Then too, in this Union period the basic lines of Ontario's character arose. The province's urban structure, basic transportation lines, the roles the major religious denominations were to play, the educational system, the social welfare institutions, the distinctive values, the systems of local and provincial government — all were inchoate or unclear at the beginning of the period, but by the time Ontario entered Confederation all these things were firmly established.

The child was brought forth, fine and fair in 1784 when the first Loyalists arrived. Of good family, she gave her first lusty cry from a bower deep in the woods of a fine estate. The lands stretched for hundreds of miles, rich arable lands, with magnificent stands of pine, oak and maple, and streams winding their way down into lakes of countless number. In her early years she was guided by the Family Compact. Some claim this high-born nanny was tyrannical, while others believe she merely supplied a needed discipline.

Overleaf: *Kingston, Capital of the United Province of Canada. The domed building to the right is Kingston City Hall, designed by George Browne, and built to house the Assembly of United Canada in 1843-1844. The large and small domes on the left belong to St. George's Anglican Cathedral.*

Left below: *Glenora, Near Picton. The old limestone mill buildings exemplify early industry in this Loyalist region, settled in the 1780s. The mill was started by Peter van Alstyne, and operated in the 1820s and 1830s by J. Hugh Macdonald, Sir John A. Macdonald's father. The buildings grace the Prince Edward County end of the Glenora Ferry, which crosses the Adolphus Reach of the Bay of Quinte. The view towards Adolphustown is one of the loveliest in Southern Ontario.*

The infant fussed and squalled but quickly grew out of this colicky stage and was ready for weaning. Mother England began the withdrawal of special trade privileges in 1846, the year she repealed the Corn Laws; by 1849 with the repeal of the Navigation Acts, the time of tender suckling was over. This experience was so traumatic for the Province of Canada (Upper and Lower) that the merchants of Montreal, feeling hungry and orphaned, sought adoption by the United States. Canada West showed little interest in the proposal. She looked across her lake and saw another source of nurture. Her bustling little towns along the lake sent their grain and potash down to the States by the Erie Canal, receiving in return the needed groceries and wares. Canada West's loyalty, stiffened by the alternate source of supply, enabled her to turn her back on the Annexation Manifesto.

Successfully weaned, infant Ontario grew rapidly. Population doubled in the single decade of the 1840s, from 480,000 to 952,000. This was the decade of the pathetic Irish Famine migration. Of the 90,000 who arrived at the port of Quebec, many found their way to the upper half of the Province; the dreaded cholera came along with them and took its toll of the frightened populace. Little Canada West tottered and reeled as she tried to keep her balance.

The province was, in the 1840s, brawling and noisy. Some of her primitive behaviour could be attributed to frontier conditions. Lumbering, which rivalled farming as the Province's major industry, was a boisterous and drunken business. It employed large numbers of men, away from their womenfolk, under dangerous conditions at the shanties and on the rushing waters. In the early 1840s the Irish Shiners battled with French Canadian lumberjacks for jobs in the Ottawa valley, carousing in the taverns and sending gangs of bullies to terrorize Bytown. A cruel climate, and unfeeling views of how much hardship the labouring classes could stand, saw canal workers digging from dawn until dusk, half-submerged in icy waters, with guards patrolling overhead to keep them quiet — small wonder that they drank, rioted and conducted some of Canada's earliest strikes. In the back townships, farm families still relied on their neighbours to help out with logging bees and barn

Right below: *Vankleek Hill, Eastern Ontario. Near Hawkesbury, Vankleek Hill was settled mainly by people of Dutch and German descent. The town derived its name from Simon Vankleek, a Loyalist from Dutchess County, New York. In the early days of Canada West, it had six stores, two taverns, a steam grist mill, a foundry, and assorted small factories.*

raisings. These too were often drunken affairs that ended in fighting.

Much of the rough-housing, however, sprang not from the North American frontier but from ancient customs and rivalries the immigrants had brought from Europe. Baby Ontario re-enacted many of them. The ghosts of Henry VIII and John Knox, Wycliffe and Wesley walked abroad as religious sects clamoured and clashed. The Methodist alliance of British Wesleyans and Canadians broke apart, and Free Kirk Presbyterians splintered off from the Church of Scotland. A cry of condemnation greeted Bishop Strachan's attempt to establish the provincial university at Toronto as a Church of England school. In town, and especially in Toronto, "The Belfast of Canada." Orangemen re-enacted the Battle of the Boyne, parading with King Billy astride his white horse, marching with fife and drum through the Green districts and banging the heads of any who objected. Hired bullies, many of whom had learned their arts of intimidation in oppressed Ireland, showed up at the open polling stations and tried to win the election by physically capturing the place and frightening all the opponent's supporters away. Electoral battles, metaphor now, were reality then.

Fortunately, this urchin could not move quickly enough to do any real harm to herself or the property. In the 1840s Canada West was only crawling along. She lumbered over dusty roads in ox-carts, laboriously hauling everything to and from water's edge. She got bogged down in mud on the Weller stagecoach that might take five days to reach Montreal from Toronto, at a speed anywhere from three to nine miles an hour. She steamboated along the lake at about the same pace it took to walk along the shore. Around the beginning of the Union period, Canada West still belonged to that ancient creeping world that would disappear later in the century. There was as yet no great difference between the quiet towns and the countryside. The sun and not the clock regulated the day and the year. Those were the days when, after the harvest was in, neighbours would "stop of a morning" and stay till dusk; a man would spend a whole day walking to the nearest post office to mail a letter, or to fetch a water witch with his hazel twig to discover where to dig the new well. Winter marched on and on, to the monoto-

Right top: *Log Cutting Near Westport. In Ontario, winter is a time when farm tasks are at their minimum, and other work can be done without the nuisance of insects and undergrowth. Log cutting in the woods has been a feature of pioneer life from the days of the earliest settlers, as a supplement to farm income.*

Right below: *Log Run at Yarker Falls. Originally known as Simcoe Falls, after John Graves Simcoe, this scene at Yarker Falls was typical of the era of Canada West and until after the turn of the century. Logs were floated down most streams in Southern Ontario, some to local sawmills; other logs were made into rafts for transportation down the St. Lawrence, or across the Great Lakes.*

Left below: *Orangemen Celebrate the 12th of July at Alliston c.1906. Protestant King William III's victory over the deposed Catholic King James II on the banks of the Boyne River in Ireland in 1690, is commemorated here beside Ontario's Boyne River.*

Far left top: Charles Poulett Thomson, Baron Sydenham (1799-1841). Poulett Thomson was appointed Governor-in-Chief of Canada in 1839, to carry out Lord Durham's recommendations to unite Upper and Lower Canada. He was created Baron Sydenham of Sydenham and Toronto in 1840.
Left top: James Bruce, 8th Earl of Elgin (1811-1863). Lord Elgin was Governor General from 1847 until 1854. During his term of office, Canada achieved responsible government.
Left below: Normal and Model Schools, Toronto. This combination of a teacher training college and a boys' private school, was founded by Egerton Ryerson, and built in 1851 to a design by F.W. Cumberland and T. Ridout.
Right below: Sir Francis Hincks (1807-1885). Elected to the legislature in 1841, Hincks worked for responsible government. He was Premier of Canada West from 1851 until 1854, and was knighted in 1869.

nous thump, thump of the flails on the barn floor or the trampling out of the grain by the horses' feet. Women in the remote districts might year after year retrace the same path from home, to church, to general store, to neighbour's house; some gave their first cries, bore their children and breathed their last, all within the same four walls. Sitting around the open kitchen fireplace at night, these farm folk still shivered when a wolf howled, a signal that one of the children would be snatched away. To learn when to wean the baby or sow the peas, they still turned to the almanac to see what counsel the ancient stars would give.

In one aspect Canada West was quite forward looking; she learned the basics of self-government. Prior to 1841, the centre of power in Upper Canada was the governor, advised by a council of appointed officials. In 1841 it was decided by the new governor of the Union, Lord Sydenham, that members of this council should be based on elected members of the Assembly. The passage of the "Resolutions of 1841" declared that these officials must maintain the confidence of a majority in the Assembly. The key question of the decade became whether the members of the council could be overruled on domestic questions by the governor. By the end of the decade, Reformers in the province were delighted with the British government's recognition that the governor would accept the advice of his local ministers on local questions, while they held a parliamentary majority for their policies. This was the essence of responsible government. It fell to Lord Elgin to recognize this new status in 1849 by allowing passage of the unpopular Rebellion Losses Bill when it was introduced by the majority Reform Party.

The leader of Ontario's crusade for local self-government was Robert Baldwin, head of the Reform Party of Upper Canada. Baldwin differed from most politicians of earlier years in his eminent respectability and unimpeachable integrity. He shaped anew the Reform support that had been shattered in the aftermath of the Rebellion of 1837. Fighting the perception that opposition and party were illegitimate, he established party government as the alternative to rule by officials of the Empire. As he and his chief lieutenant, Francis Hincks, argued through the 1840s, party government was the essence of responsible government.

They worked to build up a disciplined body of supporters in the Assembly and to secure the necessary control over positions and patronage. As pioneers in a period of constitutional change, Baldwin and Hincks pushed the party in a direction that anticipated the methods of John A. Macdonald. Under Baldwin's guiding hand Ontario also developed her local municipal institutions.

Another development of the 1840s was a burgeoning relationship with Canada East. Part of this was making a virtue of necessity since Britain had bedded the two Canadas down together in the Union of 1841. Since it was hoped that French Canada would be assimilated through this Union, she was rather upset about the new arrangement. Canada West reassured her friend that she did not intend to be an aggressive bedfellow. Francis Hincks, the Toronto reformer, wrote a series of letters to Louis Lafontaine, a leading French Canadian liberal in 1839-40 proposing that reform-minded Upper and Lower Canadians band together in the new Union Assembly. When Lafontaine did not secure a Lower Canadian seat in 1841, Baldwin found one for him in Fourth (later North) York, successfully persuading the farmers of Sharon and Stouffville to vote for the candidate from Terrebonne. Later, when Baldwin lost an election in Hastings, Lafontaine reciprocated by arranging a safe seat in Rimouski for his Upper Canadian colleague. More importantly, the two got their respective followers to synchronize their efforts during the seven-year struggle for responsible government. In the 1850s, politicians such as Hincks and Macdonald would continue this attitude of co-operation with the French, not least because it was so important for economic development that the two halves of the province work together. The relationship between Ontario and Quebec has been a long one and not without its tensions. In the 1840s, however, we see it at its best — a happy blend of idealism and enlightened self-interest for both sides, whereby the French warded off assimilation and the English warded off oligarchy.

It was in the 1840s, too, that the young colony first started attending school on a regular basis. Property tax meant that the fees dropped considerably. The tone of education grew more British as the frontier days

Right top: *Cobourg in 1841, After Bartlett. Victoria College (founded as Upper Canada Academy with Ryerson as the first principal) stands in the centre of this picture, which is virtually identical to W.H. Bartlett's work, dated 1841.*
Right below: *Perth in 1853. The county town of Lanark was laid out in 1816, in the Perth military settlement. Perth was connected to the Rideau Canal through the Tay River soon after the waterway was completed in 1832.*
Left below: *Sir Louis Hippolyte LaFontaine (1807-1864). He lost his seat in Terrebonne, and Robert Baldwin offered him York riding. Baldwin and LaFontaine were joint premiers in all but name in 1841-42. From 1848 to 1851, as premiers in reality, they formed "The Great Ministry" that brought about responsible government.*

THE TOWN OF PERTH, CO. LANARK, U.C. 1853.
from an oil painting by Field.

rtion of the John A. McLaren distillery
re and residence combined, erected by late
ex McLaren founder of McLaren distillery
nnas barber shop, a noted place in early days
hn Doran block, now stores and apartments.
meron Bros. store, afterwards a hotel, now a store.
mpbells hotel, remodelled and used as tenements.
yle's hotel, now a private residence.

8 *Residence of Wm Lock; owned & occupied by Mrs A.F. Goodman*
9 *Lock's brewery at present distillery of Spalding & Stewart*
10 *Steeple St. John's R.C. church, burned; residence on site.*
11 *Roof of post office; building used as store and dwelling*
12 *St. James church tower, replaced by steeple with belfry.*
13 *Cupola on roof of residence, late Danl McMartin.*
14 *A chimney on County Buildings.*
15 *Dr Thom's ice house.*

Left top: *The Main Street in Casselman c.1905. Founded by second generation U.E. Loyalists, Casselman, in Cambridge Township, County of Prescott and Russell, is now a French-speaking community. The Casselman family name is well known in Eastern Ontario. Author A.G. Casselman revised James Richardson's classic history of the War of 1812.*

Left below: *Main Street West, Hawkesbury. Situated on the Ottawa River, close to the Quebec border, Hawkesbury is another town that was founded by English-speaking settlers that is now a French-speaking community. In 1846, the village had only 250 people, and the biggest employer, Hawkesbury Mills, owned by the Hamilton family, was the largest lumber mill in Canada West.*

Right below: *Canada's First Electric Telegraph. A giant leap forward in communications is commemorated by this plaque on Toronto's 1844 City Hall (now part of the St. Lawrence Market). Only two years before, Samuel Morse transmitted his first message successfully.*

passed. American school readers of yesteryear were packed away in trunks and replaced by the Irish National Reader adapted for use here; and, while many of the earliest teachers had been American, after 1845 "Aliens" were no longer licensed to teach.

By the 1850s many Catholic pupils were going off to separate schools, which became well established in that decade. Universities, too, were opening their doors. In Toronto, in 1843, a Medical College and King's College (re-established as the non-sectarian University of Toronto in 1849) appeared. Queen's at Kingston and Victoria College at Cobourg (formerly Upper Canada Academy) opened in 1842. This important effort to "bend the twig" through schooling was largely due to the remarkable energies of Egerton Ryerson — one-time Methodist circuit rider, sometime opponent of Family Compact leader John Strachan, longtime editor of the widely circulated *Christian Guardian,* Superintendent of Education from 1844 until 1876 — and United Empire Loyalist.

The mid-century decades are notable for the 'taming' of Upper Canada. Besides being bundled off to school, she had many of her bad habits broken. The province was told to stop fighting and carousing. Drunkenness was common in those days when liquor sold for twenty-five cents a bottle and people drank it as a stimulant at work the way they drink coffee today. So many accidents, fights and family tragedies resulted that liquor became a monstrous social evil; thousands of Upper Canadians took the teetotal pledge. The tactful Lord Elgin, in response to public sentiment, curtailed the use of liquor at government banquets. In the 1840s, most of the emphasis was on voluntary abstinence to create a sober world; but by the 1850s, temperance people grew discouraged and asked for laws, hoping they would be harder to break than pledges. Eighty thousand people petitioned for Prohibition in 1852. The government responded with more restrictive laws but not Prohibition. The Sabbatarian Movement, which decreed all praying and no playing, loomed so large that children were occasionally arrested for swimming or for playing in the street on Sundays. Sabbatarians also objected to *working* on Sundays, which meant that some labourers got a badly needed holiday; and on many a farm, Sunday's potatoes were peeled and Sunday's water drawn on Saturday night so no finger would be lifted on the Sabbath. The Non-Conformist Protestant churches to which a majority of Upper Canadians belonged, especially Methodists, Baptists and Presbyterians, played a large role in creating this more sober climate.

There were other reforms as well. Institutions were created for the insane and the orphaned, instead of jamming them into the local jail. Or in the towns, the middle classes played an active part in promoting social welfare institutions, just as they had endorsed schools and sobriety. They were moved by some difficult-to-determine mixture of self-righteousness, fear of growing crime, and genuine concern. The reforming activity was probably, on balance, positive. Little Ontario found her surroundings safer as drunken accidents and brawling declined and the ill and the abandoned were sent to various institutions. The extremes of hilarity — but also those of misery — were disappearing.

Ontario was a bright, well-combed, well-scrubbed child by the end of the 1840s; in the 1850s she moved into her adolescent years. Mid-century found her troubled and temperamental, demanding her rights and quarrelling with the other members of her family at one moment, full of high dreamy, generous ideals the next. The province borrowed a lot of money and spent it wildly, building canals along the St. Lawrence and buying herself into the railway age. The 1850s also found her casting amorous eyes at her American cousin as railways and the Reciprocity Treaty greatly increased her coming-and-going across the border.

Adolescence is the season of idealism, and Ontario glowed with it around mid-century. She sided with the oppressed slave, and wept her way through *Uncle Tom's Cabin.* After the States passed the Fugitive Slave Law, Southwestern Ontario became a terminus for the Underground Railway. It has been conservatively estimated that forty thousand Blacks had arrived in Canada West by 1861.

Canada West was inspired, too, by her membership in the British Empire. Its remarkable factories produced cheap fabrics and iron tools for use around the world, as well as the engines to propel many a sleepy

Right top: *School for the Deaf in Belleville. Now known as the Sir James Whitney School in honour of a former Premier of Ontario, this school was opened as the Ontario Institute for the Education of the Deaf and Dumb on October 20, 1870.*

Right below: *Emancipation Day in Amherstburg. Ontario set her face against slavery almost from the beginning, with Governor Simcoe's ruling in 1793 that no more slaves could be brought into Upper Canada. This photograph was taken on August 1, 1894, the 60th anniversary of the abolition of slavery in the British Empire.*

Left below: *The Don Jail, Toronto. Built in 1858, the jail was designed by William Thomas, an English immigrant who also designed St. Lawrence Hall, St. Michael's Cathedral, and the last Brock Monument at Queenston.*

valid if one considered her alone, but not if one took responsibility for the whole family — i.e., the English and French halves of the Union. Voluntarism and Canada West preponderance in the Assembly were unacceptable to French Canada. She, too, took her religion quite seriously, and the ultramontane Catholicism of the day advocated very close connections between church and state — precisely the opposite of voluntarism. Moreover, Lower Canada had not, at the outset of the Union, been granted representation by population, when she had more people than the English half did; why should Upper Canada get it now that she had grown to be the bigger one? And yet . . . Quebec deserved not to be pushed around by Ontario when her ideas — and ideals — were so different.

Though he perhaps goaded Ontario a little too far on the French questions, George Brown was a fine fellow. He taught the young province to think of her future. Her quarters were growing cramped; her last wild acres on the Bruce peninsula being settled in the 1850s. George whispered sweet things into Ontario's ear (and broadcast them through the *Globe*) about fertile lands in the Northwest which could one day be hers. George also convinced her that she should reject the alternative of moving right out, that breaking up the Union might mean severing the British connection. He won the Clear Grits over to this point at the famous Reform convention held in Toronto in 1859.

As for all the family feuding, it never really did get settled in the 1850s. Representation by population was not granted, though in Canada West support for it grew every year. "Mother" proved rather more yielding — she finally did allow the Clergy Reserves to be sold off, though the proceeds didn't yield a great deal for Canada West, since many of them went to compensate contemporary and future parsons. Still it was a moral victory since the 1854 Act clearly stated that all "semblance of connexion between" Church and State should be removed. In the Assembly the two sisters still quarrelled and it was only with great difficulty — and frequent changes of ministry — that the family stayed together at all. It seemed that the old homestead was getting too small for someone of Canada West's size and spirit.

Right top: *Port Hope. One of the most attractive main streets in Ontario is in Port Hope, shown in this 1968 photograph. As one of the many busy ports of Canada West, the town's exports in 1844 included 58,000 bushels of wheat, 8,454 barrels of flour, 429 casks of whiskey, 78,000 shingles, 28,000 metres of sawn lumber, and 22 firkins of butter. The population in 1844 was 1,200.*

Right below: *Oakville Harbour. Oakville was founded by William Chisholm (1788-1842), born in Shelburne, Nova Scotia, of Loyalist parents who moved to the Niagara area in 1791. Chisholm participated in the cutting of a canal to Burlington Bay in 1824, and operated his own schooner,* General Brock, *which ran aground during opening ceremonies when the lieutenant governor, Sir Peregrine Maitland, was aboard as Chisholm's guest.*

Left below: *Edward Ermatinger (1797-1876). Born on the Island of Elba, Ermatinger settled in St. Thomas in 1830. In 1854 he pioneered banking in that part of the province and founded the Bank of Elgin.*

RANDALL'S
EXPORT
EXPORT
GIFTS RANDALL'S WALLPAPER
HOLMES SHOES
Coleman & Philp

LATEST ROLLER PROCESS
NIAGARA
Meadowvale Milling Co.
MEADOWVALE, ONT.
HIGH PATENT

Left top: Meadowvale Mill (Originally a Gooderham Mill). In the early days, mills were small, and scattered over the province at innumerable waterfalls that made good power sites. The Credit was one such river where this mill stood. Gradually, milling became centralized in large operations not dependent on waterfalls, and the old mills became derelict. The Meadowvale Mill was demolished in the 1950s by the local conservation authority, when it was regarded as a fire hazard.
***Left below:** "Niagara", Meadowvale Milling Company. This label was glued on each barrel of flour produced by the Meadowvale Milling Company. "Niagara" denoted the trade name of a special grade of flour.*
***Right below:** Grist Mill at Lyn, Near Brockville. This 1957 photograph is of the Cumming Mill, then falling into ruin. It has since been demolished.*

It was about the same time that Ontario began to display some outstanding talents. Once her broad acres were all cleared and settled, it became evident that they were able to produce great quantities of the grain the world wanted most. In the 1840s she had, as Stephen Leacock once said, watched American growth "from across a river, as people watch a fair and trudge home supperless." In the 1850s, she went to the fair beaming with pride, her wagon groaning with fat bags of golden wheat. The Crimean War cut off British supplies in eastern Europe and greatly increased the demand for Ontario's supply. Millions of bushels of wheat and flour poured out from the lake towns of Belleville, Port Hope, Whitby, Toronto, Port Credit, and Oakville. The wealth spurred the growth of small centres — the wheat boom largely accounted for the fact that Ontario had eighty-one towns in 1870 compared to thirty-eight in 1850. In these places businessmen produced field and household implements, woollens and specialty items for the newly prosperous farm families. The families, likewise, began to diversify in order to sell their raw wool, meat, and dairy products to the towns. As early as 1851 the upper half of the Province had a greater farm income and was clearly surpassing the lower half in processing the products of farm and forest. Canada West had 612 grist mills, of which 37 were steam driven; Canada East only 541, eight of which were steam driven. Canada West had 1,567 saw mills, 154 steam driven; Canada East 1,065, only four of which were steam driven. She had 925 foundries, 147 carding and fulling mills and 75 woollen mills. Canada East had more carding and fulling mills (193), but only 197 foundries and 18 woollen mills.

Ontario's earnings piled up. They financed the big town markets and town halls that appeared in the 1850s. Rumours of railways drifted through lace curtains. Suddenly, back streets turned into busy streets as town lots doubled and even quadrupled in price. Ontario turned up a trump; oil was discovered in the southwestern counties in the late 1850s and derricks began pumping up the black gold. Besides earning a lot of money, during the 1850s Ontario also borrowed a lot from England. Her capital imports tripled over those of the previous decade.

There was no doubt that Canada West was exchanging a portion of her brown homespun for imported finery, and was no longer content with a familiar fellow from the old country like George Brown (though the friendship continued). She was head over heels in love with the United States of America — and she was seeing a great deal of this suspect suitor.

The affair began one night in June 1854, when her governor, the suave Lord Elgin, took her down to Washington for a party. The champagne flowed 'til long past midnight, and Ontario was at her alluring best. When she woke up in the morning, she and America were going to exchange all sorts of things — farm and forest products, minerals, and fish. Moreover, they were both going to sail whenever they liked on Lake Michigan and the St. Lawrence, and no watchful coast guard or customs officer was going to collect a penny or say a word about it. Uncle Elgin, asked to explain, stammered that you couldn't lock up a spirited filly like that, that it was a choice between letting her have Reciprocity or calling out the British army to keep her quiet. Besides that, he and his home government believed in Free Trade, which many then saw as the vital step towards universal peace and brotherhood.

It soon became clear that Ontario had cast her lot with a very fast crowd. In the 1850s the steamboats on Lake Ontario got larger and faster. Smooth macadamized highways replaced the old bumpy roads that had mired in mud, spring, and fall. Along them rode Methodist preachers in comfortable steel-springed buggies, their lean days of riding the circuit on horseback a fading memory. The buggies sped past sawmills with boards spewing out of the new steam cutters. They sped on past wagons abandoned by farm boys who'd been struck with a vision, dumbfounded by the "great pillar of cloud and fire" as the first train they had ever seen shrieked by. Anxious parents received terse messages over newly-laid telegraph lines, "Don't wait up to me Ma, gone to Sarnia to help build the Grand Trunk."

There were plenty of jobs for Ontario lads and immigrant cousins in those days. Lady Elgin turned the first sod for the Northern Railway in 1851. By the summer of 1854 there were some 20,000 men a-building. At the height of the railway boom, between 1854 and 1856, 1,000 miles

Right top: *Oil Springs, Lambton County. This painting by Edwin Johnson shows the early type of oil drilling rig, the jerker lines that lead to the power house, and the gumbo clay fields. Here, in 1855, James Miller Williams, who came from New Jersey in 1840, opened the first commercial oil well in North America. By 1857, Williams was operating his own refinery. A museum now stands on the site of his early well.*
Right below: *Petrolia, Site of Oil Wells. Many of the men in this photograph could be oil pioneers at Petrolia, which took its name from the "black gold" found in the vicinity.*
Left below: *A Gusher at the Imperial Oil Works, Sarnia. In Sarnia's "Chemical Valley" modern oil refineries now process mainly imported oil from outside Ontario, but all this started with exploitation of local oil.*

JOHNSON
1965
J.C. HUCHSON & CO.
LUMBER & COAL DEALERS

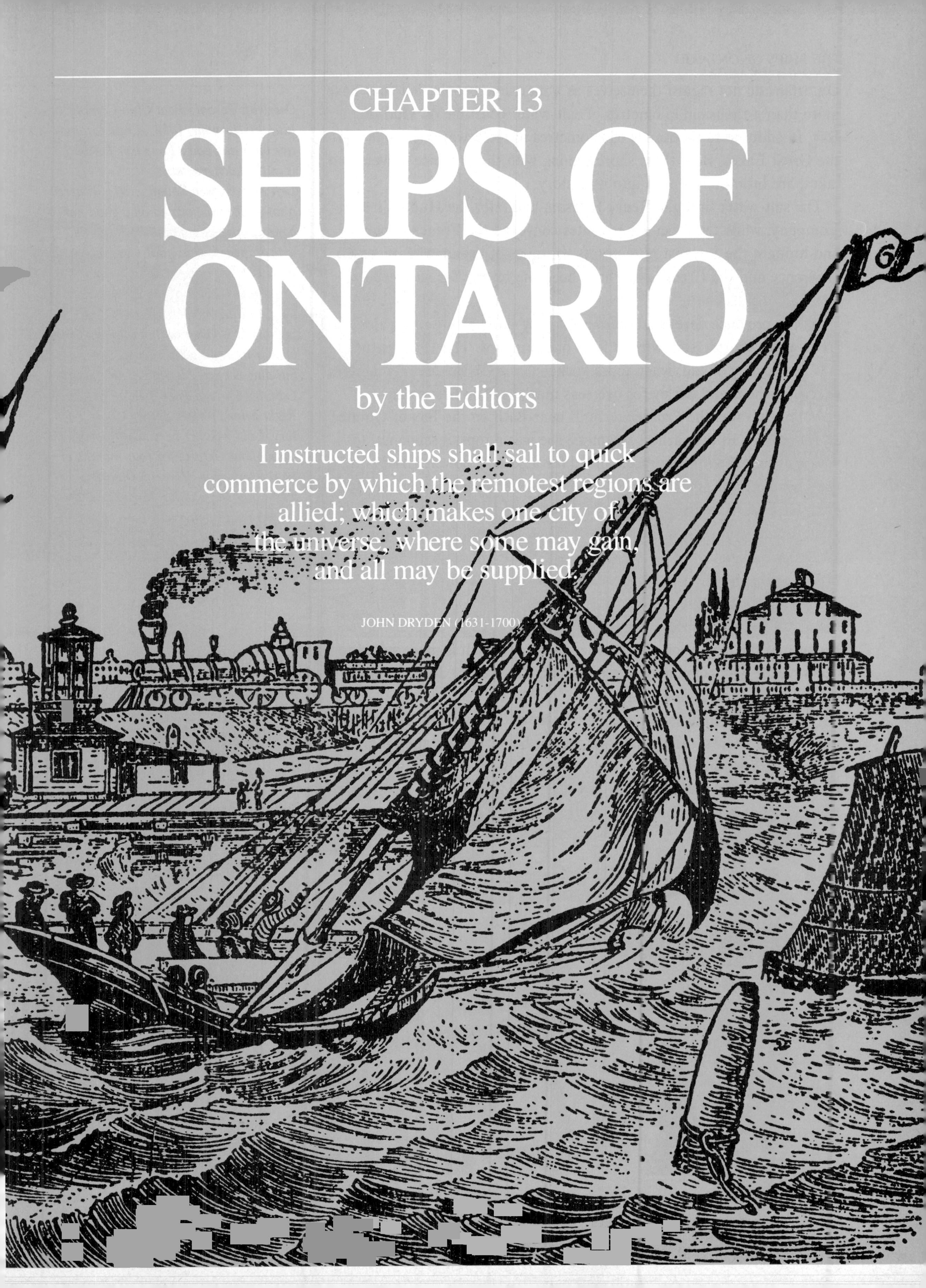

CHAPTER 13

SHIPS OF ONTARIO

by the Editors

I instructed ships shall sail to quick commerce by which the remotest regions are allied; which makes one city of the universe, where some may gain, and all may be supplied.

JOHN DRYDEN (1631-1700)

Lake Superior
Falls of St. Mary
L. George
Thessalon
R. Thessalon
Le Serpent
Minesou Bay
Lake Nipissing
French River
Lake Michagan
Old Michilimakinac
Abercroche Village
Middle I.
Thunder Bay I.
Thunder Bay
Lake Huron
White Rock
R. au Sable
County of Kent
only Sketch'd
River la Tranche or Thames
Lake St. Clair
County of Kent
County of Suffolk
R. Tonty
County of Essex
Detroit
Grand Marsh
Lake Erie
Endorsed. Canada
Upper
Case 37. No. 53.
(1793)
CANADA No. 59 (DUP.)

CHAPTER 14

DISTRICTS, COUNTIES, & TOWNSHIPS

by the Editors

> The climate here is very mild & good, and I think that Loyalists may be the happiest people in America by settling this Country from Long Sou (sic) to Bay Quinty (sic).
>
> JUSTUS SHERWOOD, SURVEYOR, TO GOVERNOR HALDIMAND'S SECRETARY, 14 NOVEMBER 1783

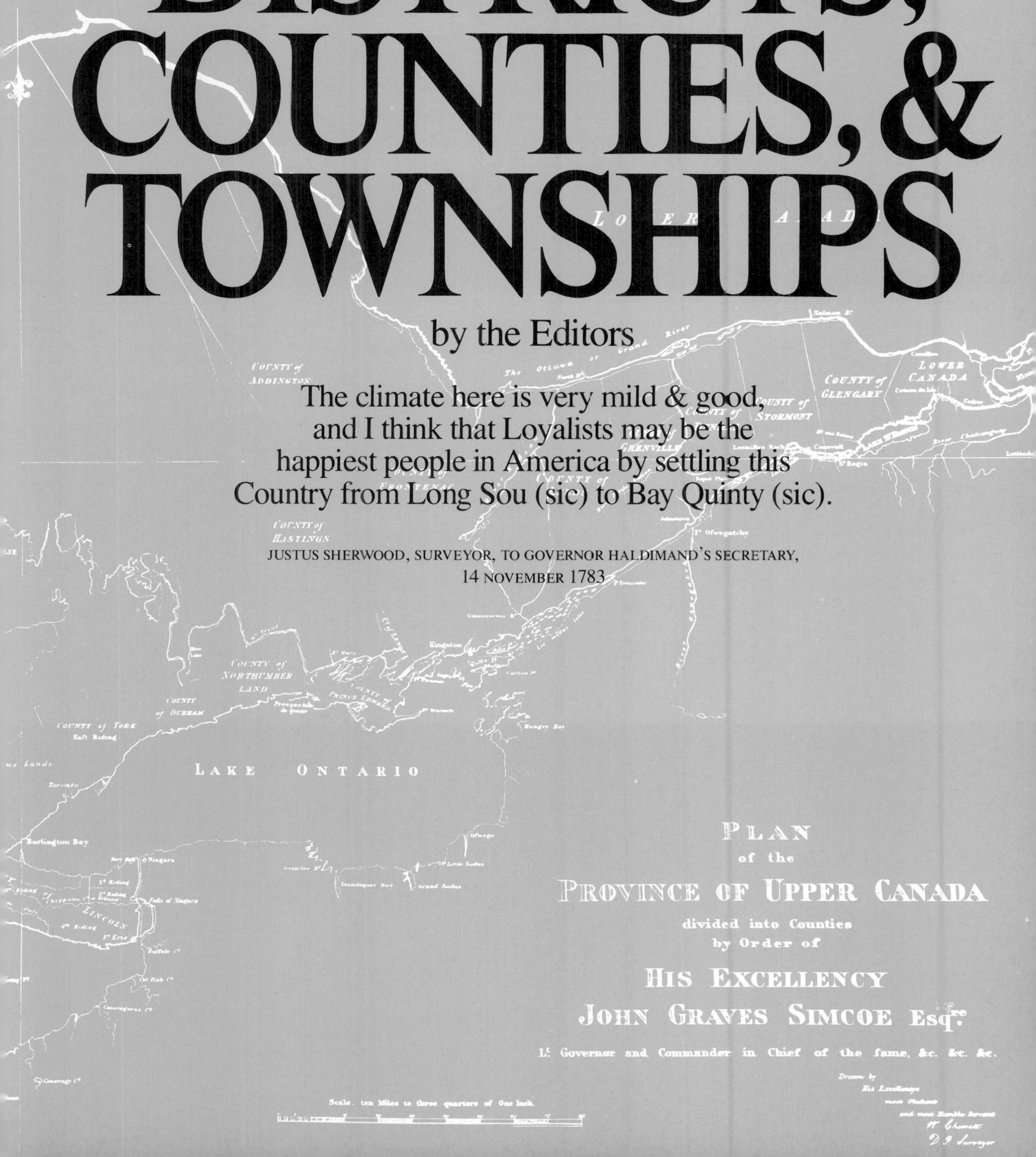

Land was first organized into townships, but these were not units of local government. They were officially seigneuries, with the government in Quebec City acting as the landlord for the King. By 1787, when Lord Dorchester named them, the townships were no longer considered as seigneuries, but they still had no role. The first local government was by districts, set up in 1788, and initially there were four. Each district had a court, the only form of local government for many years.

The main function of a district was law enforcement by appointed magistrates. In 1792, Governor Simcoe set up nineteen counties, but these were only electoral ridings. The first hint of democracy came in 1793, when Simcoe authorized a limited form of town meeting. Magistrates could call meetings at which minor township officers were elected by the property holders. Next, in 1832, urban centres were permitted boards of police which were appointed. The first place to incorporate was Brockville in 1832, followed by Prescott and Toronto in 1834.

The change from local government by appointees to that by elected officers began with the District Councils Act of 1841. Townships could elect representatives to a district council, but the warden (chairman) was appointed. Then, through the Municipal Corporations Act of 1849, passed by Robert Baldwin's ministry, all officials were elected. Districts were abolished except in thinly populated areas, and replaced by counties. Townships became rural municipalities, and in each county the townships sent elected representatives to the county councils. Separated towns which were independent of the counties, had mayors, while townships had reeves.

This system remained, with few changes for a century. Then the Ontario government decided to form regional municipalities, in which small municipalities would be grouped under a regional government. The first to be incorporated into this two-tiered system was the Regional Municipality of Metropolitan Toronto, formed in 1953 to cope with the problems of rapid urbanization.

Overleaf: *Simcoe's Nineteen Original Counties of 1792. Suffolk is now part of Elgin and Middlesex. Ontario was the large islands off Kingston, not the former Ontario County that is part of the Regional Municipality of Durham.*
Left below: *Belleville Town Plot, 1819. Belleville, originally Meyers Creek, began as a squatter settlement on land reserved for the natives. The survey was an afterthought.*
Right top: *Family of George III by Zoffany. Many early townships were named after the Royal family.*
Right middle: *The Districts in 1788.*
Far right middle: *The Districts in 1802. As the population increased, the districts were subdivided.*
Right below: *Cornwall, Seat of the United Counties of Stormont, Dundas and Glengarry. This photograph c.1913 shows Second Street and the main post office.*
Far right below: *The Districts in 1849.*

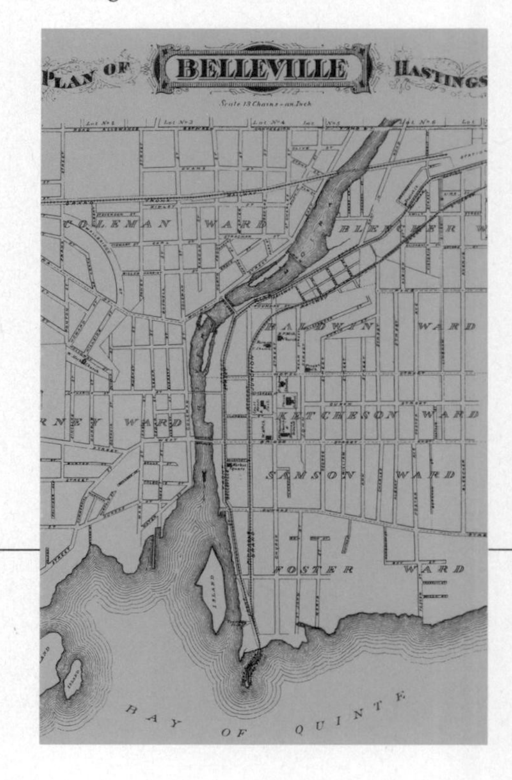

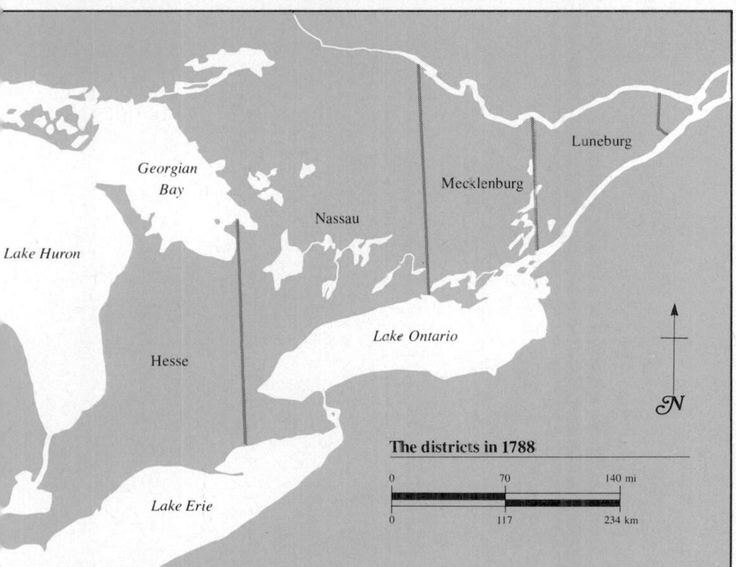
Georgian Bay
Lake Huron
Nassau
Mecklenburg
Luneburg
Hesse
Lake Ontario
Lake Erie
N
The districts in 1788
0 70 140 mi
0 117 234 km

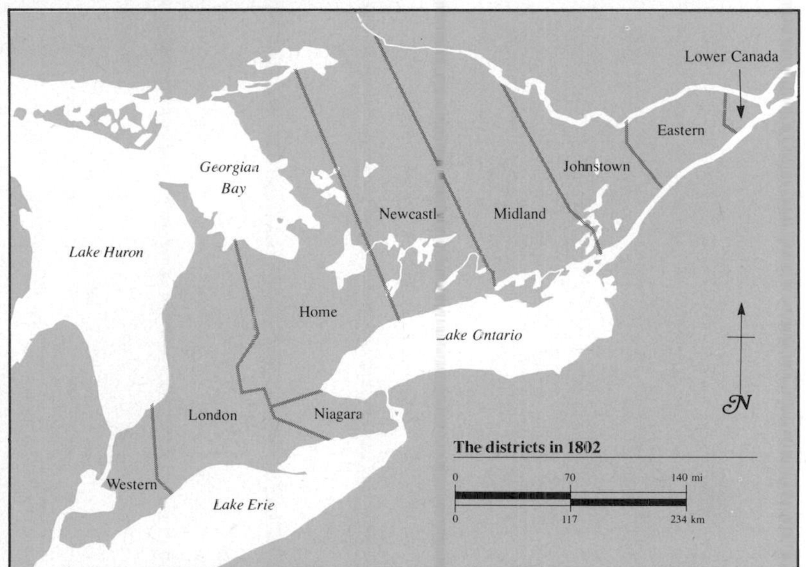
Lower Canada
Eastern
Johnstown
Midland
Newcastl
Georgiaa Bay
Lake Huron
Home
ake Ontario
London
Niagara
Western
Lake Erie
N
The districts in 1802
0 70 140 mi
0 117 234 km

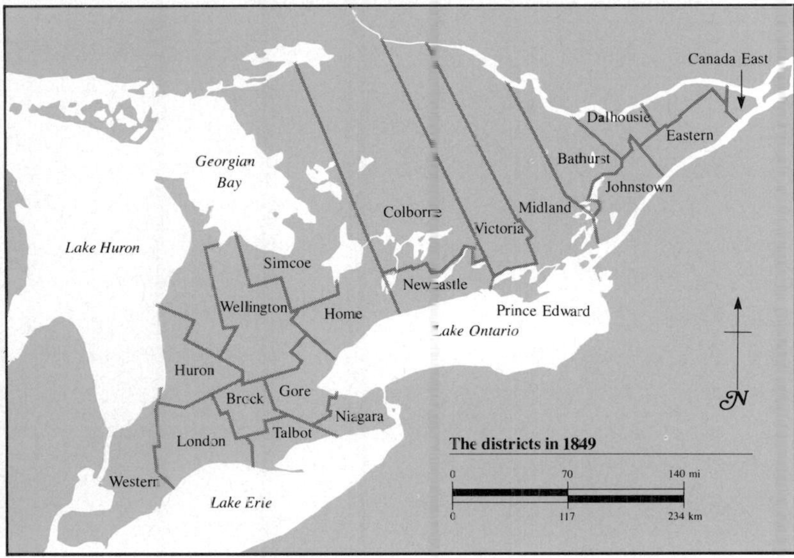
Canada East
Dalhousie
Eastern
Bathurst
Johnstown
Midland
Georgian Bay
Colborne
Victoria
Lake Huron
Simcoe
Newcastle
Wellington
Home
Prince Edward
Lake Ontario
Huron
Gore
Brock
Niagara
London
Talbot
Western
Lake Erie
N
The districts in 1849
0 70 140 mi
0 117 234 km

Far left top: *The Wharf, Lindsay, Scugog River c.1910. The seat of Victoria County, Lindsay was the home of Sir Sam Hughes (1852-1921), Minister of Militia and Defence during World War I.*

Left top: *Picton Welcomes Prince Edward's Premier Son. Rodmond Palen Roblin (1853-1937), Premier of Manitoba from 1900 to 1915, was born in Sophiasburgh and was given a royal welcome in Picton. Knighted in 1912, Sir Rodmond was the grandfather of Dufferin "Duff" Roblin, who became Premier of Manitoba in 1958.*

Far left below: *Cayuga, Bird's-Eye View. Cayuga, on the Grand River, is the administrative centre of Haldimand-Norfolk Region.*

Left and right below: *L'Original. Seat of the United Counties of Prescott and Russell, L'Original (which means "moose"), is on the Ottawa River where moose were wont to cross.*

Right top: *Air View of Parry Sound. This is the judicial seat of the District of Parry Sound.*
Far right top: *Ontario Street, Stratford c.1907. This seat of Perth County is a manufacturing town, and best known for the annual Shakespeare Festival.*
Far right below: *Cumberland Street, Port Arthur. The twin lakehead cities of Port Arthur and Fort William were combined, in 1970, to form the city of Thunder Bay.*

Far left top: *Parade on Dundas Street, Woodstock, Seat of Oxford County. This picture was taken looking west from East Market Street.*
Left top: *Picton, Seat of Prince Edward County c.1880. The town retains all the charm displayed in the painting of Lucius Richard O'Brien, first President of the Royal Canadian Academy.*
Far left below: *Newmarket, Former Seat of York County. Since 1971, Newmarket has been the headquarters of the Regional Municipality of York. The picture shows Main Street early in this century.*
Left and right below: *Court House, Brockville, Designed by John G. Howard (1803-1890). Brockville is the seat of the United Counties of Leeds and Grenville. The Court House faces the only New England style square in Ontario. One traveller called Brockville "the prettiest town I saw in Upper Canada."*

Right top: *Norfolk Street, Simcoe, Former Seat of Norfolk County. When the Regional Municipality of Haldimand-Norfolk was established in 1975, Cayuga became the administrative centre.*

Far right top: *Main Street, Belleville, Seat of Hastings County. Named after Sir Francis Gore's wife, Lady Bella Gore, this scene shows a pre-World War I parade.*

Far right below: *Barrie, Seat of Simcoe County. This parade featured a monster bottle of spirits.*

Far left top: *The seat of Lambton County. The town was named Port Sarnia (since shortened) by Sir John Colborne, in 1836, to settle an argument. Some residents favoured Buenos Aires; other were adamant for New Glasgow.*
Left and right top: *King Street, Chatham c.1906. Named Chatham by John Graves Simcoe, many fugitive slaves who reached Upper Canada by the Underground Railroad settled in the area.*
Far left below: *Dominion Day, St. Paul's Square, St. Catharines c.1908. Lincoln and and Welland Counties were combined in 1970 to form the Regional Municipality of Niagara, with administrative offices in St. Catharines.*

***Left and right below:** Orangeville, Seat of Dufferin County. Named after founder Orange Lawrence, the town staged a parade on West Broadway in 1900 to celebrate the relief of Ladysmith during the Boer War.*
***Right top:** Owen Sound, Seat of Grey County. This Grocers' Picnic Parade took place before World War I.*
***Right below:** Air View of Goderich, Seat of Huron County. Goderich was laid out in a radial pattern by John Galt in 1827. Many communities were photographed soon after World War I by the Owen Sound air ace "Billy" Bishop.*

MATU

RING

CHAPTER 15

WESTMINSTER IN THE WILDERNESS

by Arthur Bousfield

…and his dominion shall be from sea even to sea…

ZACHARIAH 9:10

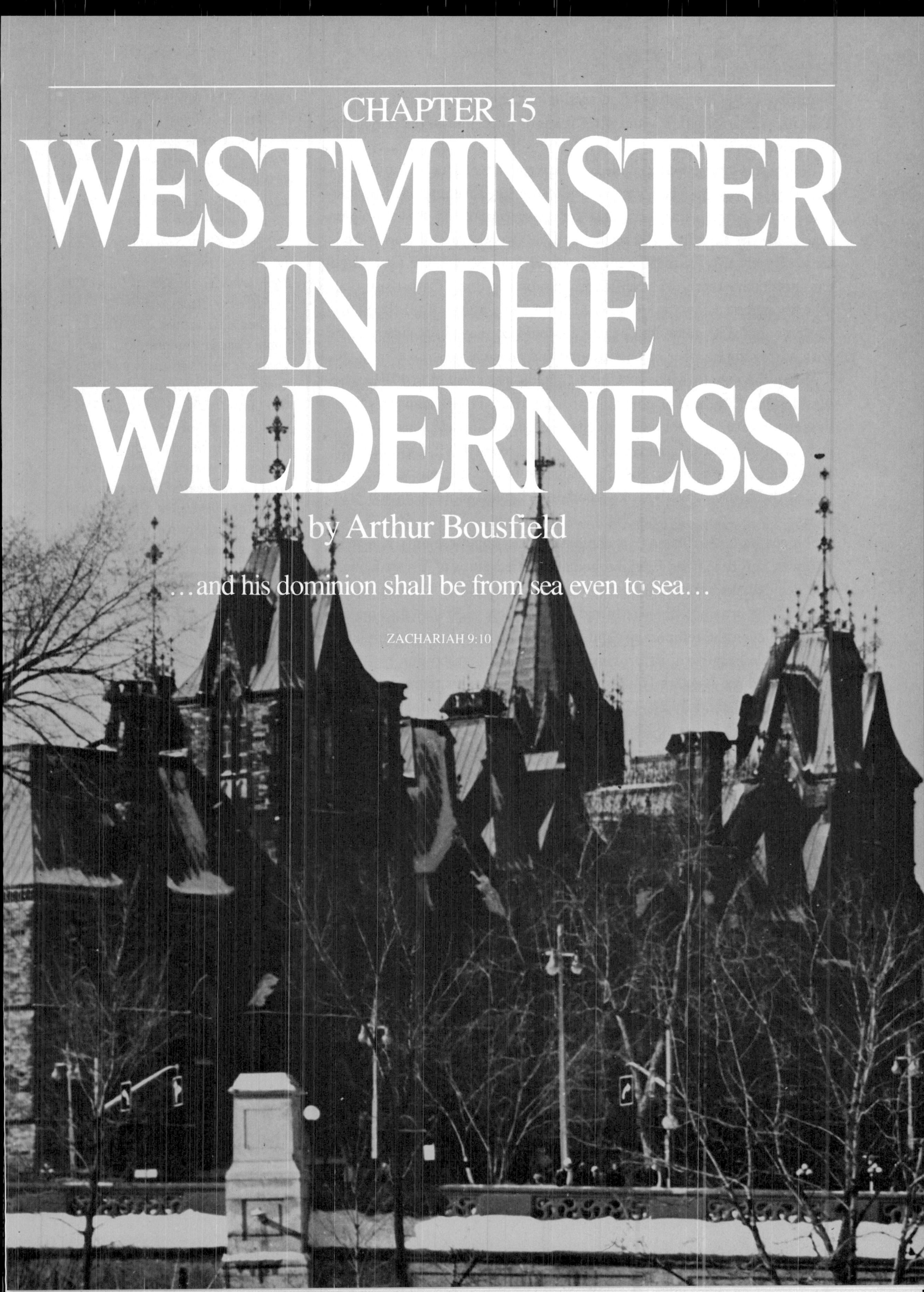

FIVE ROSES
F L O U R
HARVEST QUEEN

CHAPTER 16

NEW ONTARIO: The North Before and After 1884

by Laurel Sefton MacDowell

...the north opened a whole new vista before the industry and finance of the south.

G. P. de T. GLAZEBROOK
LIFE IN ONTARIO: A SOCIAL HISTORY

to separate the nickel from its ore so that it could be refined, and markets had to be found for this, as yet, little known metal. Both problems were resolved by the turn of the century. Production rose consistently, and the company eventually participated in the creation of the International Nickel Company (INCO) which went on to establish a virtual monopoly in the North American market and became an active competitor in Britain and Europe. Sudbury became the world's largest nickel producing centre and Canada's greatest mining area. Its success stimulated the development of the entire region of Northern Ontario.

For a northern population living in wooden buildings near dense forests, fires were a constant threat. As the population increased, so too, did the frequency of fires. Between 1910 and 1916 there were numerous bush fires, and in 1911 there was a major conflagration in Porcupine itself. At that time it was still no more than an isolated settlement on the edge of the lake, without any sophisticated equipment to prevent the fire from spreading. Flames quickly engulfed the town, destroyed the pit-heads of the mine, and burnt the railway cars, one of which contained 350 cases of dynamite. The resulting explosion created a hole six metres deep. More than seventy people were killed by burning or drowning when they rushed to the lake seeking relief. One hardy woman gave birth in the lake and both mother and child survived.

Ironically, the town of Cochrane experienced a massive fire on the same day. More than seventy people were killed and fifty stores, fifteen hotels, four churches, and two schools were destroyed. In both communities relief committees were formed to evacuate people, organize tents and cooking facilities for those who remained. Many relief supplies were generously donated by people in the south, and were carried to the devastated communities on the T & NO railway.

The same pattern was repeated in other northern communities. In 1912 and 1914, the towns of Timmins and Haileybury were burned. In 1916, a fire destroyed the settlements of New Liskeard and Cochrane (again), and the villages of Matheson, Nushka, Kelso, and Porquis Junction, killing between 300 and 450 people. In response, the government established a Northern Ontario Fire Relief Committee which

Left below: *Big Nickel, Canadian Centennial Numismatic Park, Sudbury. The only mining community that became a full-fledged city was Sudbury. S.J. Richie's Canadian Copper Company began mining nickel in the Sudbury Basin in 1886. The Big Nickel was a symbol of the world's largest nickel-producing region.*
Right top: *Teck Hughes Gold Mine, Kirkland Lake. Teck Hughes was next to Sir Harry Oakes' Lakeshore Mine. Now most of the buildings are gone.*
Right middle: *International Nickel Smelter, Copper Cliff. The smelter belched out smoke that destroyed nearby vegetation, but to the residents the smoke spelled prosperity.*
Right below: *Elk Lake. On the Montreal River west of New Liskeard, and not far from Gowganda, Elk Lake was one of many mining camps.*

CHAPTER 16

NEW ONTARIO: The North Before and After 1884

by Laurel Sefton MacDowell

. . . the north opened a whole new vista
before the industry and finance of the south.

G. P. deT. GLAZEBROOK
LIFE IN ONTARIO: A SOCIAL HISTORY

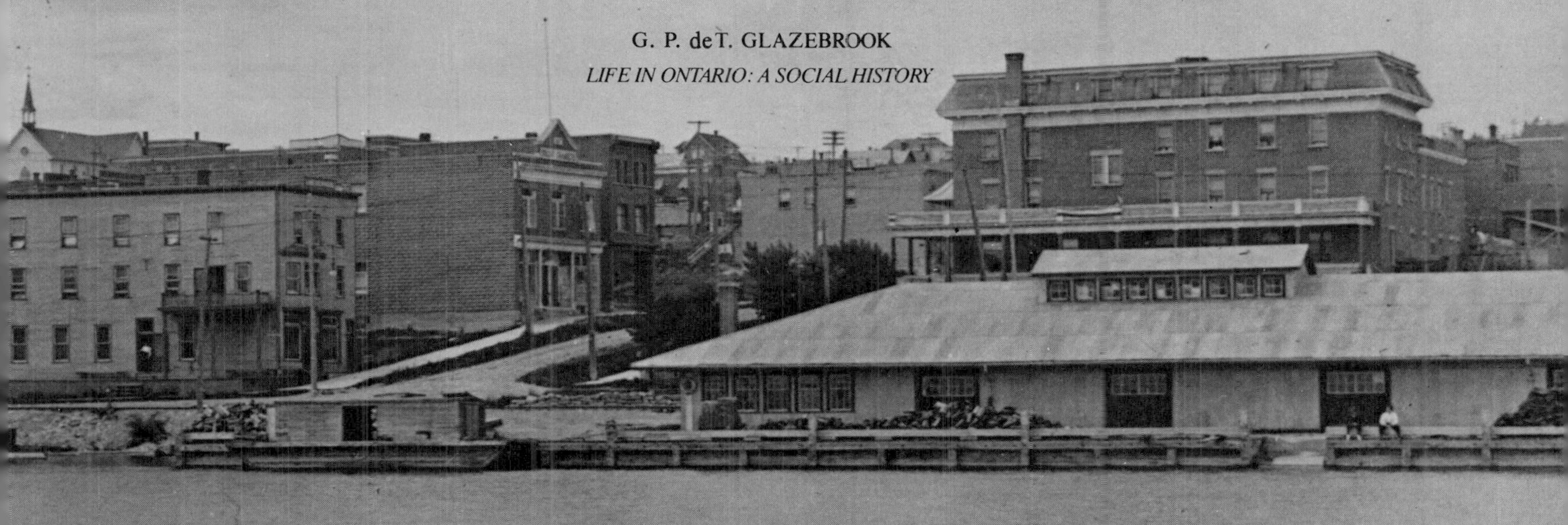

At the time of Confederation in 1867, Ontario with a population of about 1,500,000, generated over one third of Canada's total economic activity. But the northern portion — "New Ontario" — was still unknown and unexplored. By 1901, largely as a result of railway construction, the north had acquired a population of 100,401 and with the successful development of minerals and forest products it grew to 218,777 in 1911, and 267,388 in 1921. Ontario's six northern districts had almost ten percent of the province's total population. Economic growth had transformed the north, and contributed to the prosperity of the entire province. At the same time the northern climate shaped the region's distinctive cultural flavour with its emphasis on endurance, enterprise, independence, self-reliance, and an abiding love of liberty.

Overleaf: Haileybury. The founder, Charles C. Farr, named the town after Haileybury, his English public school. Farr emigrated in 1873 to work for the Hudson's Bay Company. In 1889 he moved to the site of Haileybury.
Left below: Map Showing Territory Claimed by Ontario and the Federal Governments, 1878.
Left bottom: Map Showing Area Given to Ontario Under the Canada Act of 1889. The present boundary between

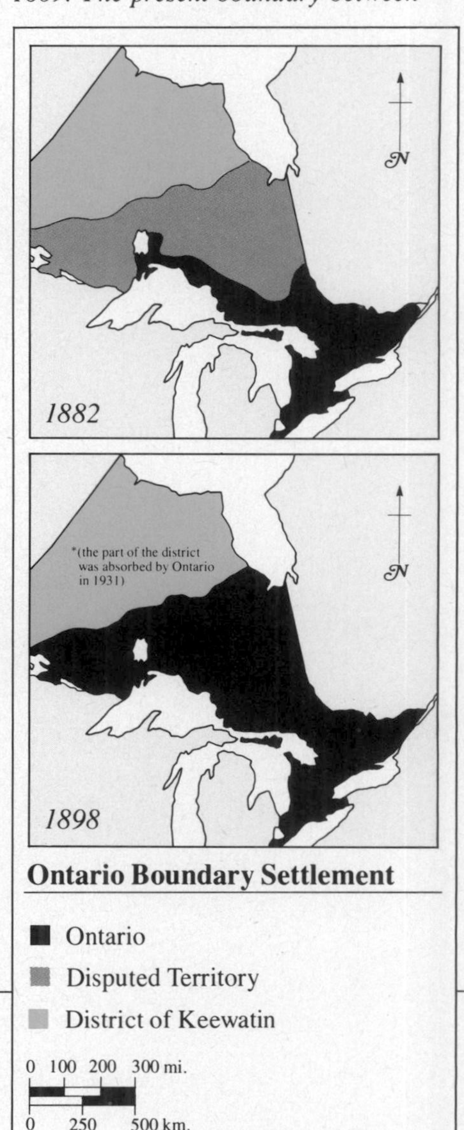

The Early Boundary Dispute

What is now Northern Ontario — or "New Ontario" as it was called in the 19th century — originally belonged to the Hudson's Bay Company, and was sold to Canada in 1870. However, the new territory quickly became a focus of dispute between federal and provincial governments, its northern and western boundaries remained unresolved for almost twenty years. But there was never any doubt that the sentiment of Canada West (as Ontario was called during the Union period) was decidedly "expansionist." Successive Ontario governments shared the view that Ontario's wealth should enure to the benefit of its inhabitants and should be controlled by their elected *provincial* representatives.

By 1871, John Sandfield Macdonald, Ontario's first premier, urged his legislature to facilitate the definition of Ontario's northern boundaries and assert provincial jurisdiction — not least because the federal government also claimed jurisdiction over the same territory. Oliver Mowat's government took a similar view, and actively encouraged both a "provincial rights" movement and the expansion of Ontario's boundaries north and west. In 1874, a three-man commission was established to adjudicate the boundary dispute between the two governments. It established an interim provisional boundary, agreed upon by both governments, pending a final resolutuion of the jurisdictional dispute.

Ontario and Manitoba was established in 1912.
Right below: *Engineers' construction camp. Tented camps sprang up wherever new projects started and were used for road construction as the work moved forward.*
Right bottom: *Old Stage Road (Highway 69) over Moon River, Muskoka. To encourage settlement, the provincial government built colonization roads to the north.*

In 1878 the Commission decided the boundary question in Ontario's favour; however, because the federal government refused to accept this decision, the matter proceeded to the courts. It was not resolved until 1884, when the Judicial Committee of the Privy Council in Britain (at that time Canada's final court of appeal) sustained Ontario's position that its northern boundary extended to James Bay and its western boundary extended to the Lake of the Woods area. But the federal government still laid claim to the natural resources of the disputed territory by virtue of its treaties with the region's Indians. In a further decision in 1888, the Privy Council held that title to the soil had rested with the Crown even before these treaties, and that Ontario, as the lawful agent of the Crown, owned and could control these resources. This decision was confirmed in 1889 by an Act of the Imperial Parliament (the Canada [Ontario Boundary] Act). This 19th century dispute between the federal and provincial governments over control of resource development, was but an early example of the kind of problem which has plagued federal-provincial relations well into the 20th century.

How was this victory accomplished, and with what local political posturing? In the decade following 1878, Premier Oliver Mowat continually urged the public to support the provincial position and demand the right to settle and develop New Ontario. The province decided to appoint two local territorial magistrates: E.B. Borron, who was to preside in the District of Nipissing (the northern section), and W.D. Lyon, who was to preside in the District of Thunder Bay (the western section).

Borron's territory consisted mostly of Indians, Hudson's Bay Company traders, and a few missionaries. His strategy was not to assert his authority overtly, but to co-operate with the local inhabitants. As a representative of Ontario, he put pressure on the federal government to fulfill its commitments to the Indians. He encouraged a more active provincial role, which included the construction of a school, a hospital, and a jail in the area's "capital" of Moose Factory. He also developed an administrative framework for law and order, claiming the right to appoint a constable, enforce the prohibition of liquor, and grant licenses to traders in order to protect native hunting and fishing rights.

The western region was much more heavily populated because it had attracted people to work in rail construction, lumbering, or gold prospecting. In that region, the two levels of government were in direct confrontation with each other, and there were disputes over the right to grant timber berths, mineral claims, and control the local liquor laws. In this situation of confused or conflicting authority, it was the local populace which suffered. Vast quantities of timber were removed, settlement was hindered, and lawlessness prevailed. In Rat Portage (now Kenora) outlaws were said to walk about "with knives and revolvers exposed in their belts" and challenged law officers "in true wild west fashion."

In 1883, both Manitoba and Ontario held provincial elections and while there remained some confusion as to the jurisdictions of the provincial authorities, both elections passed without violence and the provincial differences were resolved. As a result of the later *Imperial Boundary Act* of 1889, Ontario would encompass the entire Great Lakes system, and acquired what would prove to be immense wealth in pulpwood, minerals, and water-power. Its modern boundaries were established in 1912, with the acquisition of some portions of the Northwest Territories south of the sixtieth parallel, making modern Ontario three times larger than the old province had been.

Railways

With the resolution of the Ontario boundary dispute, the way was clear for the development of the new northern territories. The building of railways — beginning with the Canadian Pacific Railway (CPR) in the early 1880s — was a necessary preparatory step. The Transcontinental Railway would bind the west into Confederation, open new land for settlement, expose new mineral resources, and transport timber.

The construction of these railway lines was no mean feat, because much of Northern Ontario was still uncharted. In order to build the railway, engineers had to cut through the rock on the shore of Lake Superior, pour heavy fill in areas of muskeg, and construct a number of bridges. But the completed CPR provided access through the north

Right top: *Taking a Boiler to Porcupine, Cochrane District. This early photograph demonstrates vividly the difficulties settlers faced on primitive roads through wooded country — the roughness of the track, the muddy pools that formed on freshly cleared land. The same conditions applied during the pioneering phase in Southern Ontario.*

Right below: *The Polar Bear Express at Cochrane. Completed in 1932, the railway line follows the route of the Abitibi and Moose Rivers, the same path taken by Chevalier de Troyes and the legendary Iberville in 1686, from Montreal, to capture the Hudson's Bay Company fur posts.*

Left below: *Main Street, Cobalt, 1907. Rich veins of silver discovered at Cobalt in 1903 earned the town the nickname "the richest silver camp in the world."*

POLAR BEAR EXPRESS
1909

from Quebec to the Manitoba border and west of Cochrane. The upper reaches of navigable rivers running to James Bay became accessible for the first time. The new lines would link the South to its hinterland, provide markets for manufactured goods, and facilitate resource development.

The land north of the CPR line remained largely unknown until about 1900, when the Ontario government authorized a comprehensive plan of exploration across the northern part of the province to assess mineral, agricultural, forestry, and energy potential. The resulting positive reports and the need of the growing colony of Haileybury both contributed to the demand for better transportation.

Haileybury was the brainchild of Charles C. Farr who thought a small clearing on the west shore of Lake Temiskaming would be a perfect site for a model community, a "little England." He was a British Imperialist who had joined the Hudson's Bay Company at Fort Temiskaming in 1873, when he was only twenty-two. He bought land, moved to the future townsite in 1889, named the community Haileybury (after his English public school), and convinced A.S. Hardy, the Commissioner of Crown lands, to produce a pamphlet to attract settlers. But despite this aggressive promotion, relatively few people settled there, because the town was largely inaccessible. The trip from Mattawa took two days. By 1901, only three hundred people lived in Haileybury.

In 1884, to serve Haileybury's needs, the government built a road along Lake Temiskaming to North Bay. In 1902, construction was begun on the government-owned and -operated Temiskaming and Northern Ontario Railway (T & NO). It was completed in 1904 and over a period of twenty years would be extended from North Bay all the way to James Bay. Moreover, railway construction attracted immigrant workers to the North, which contributed to the local building boom and to the multicultural aspects of the northern population. Sault Ste. Marie became another rail centre with the construction of F.H. Clergue's Algoma Central and Hudson Bay Railway. A second railway, the Manitoulin and North Shore (renamed the Algoma Eastern in 1911) completed a line from Little Current to Sudbury in 1912.

Left and right below: *Fur Trading Post, Fort Albany. One of the earliest Hudson's Bay Company posts, Fort Albany was captured by the French in 1686. With their Indian allies they marched some 1,200 kilometres from Montreal and attacked the fort from the rear. The defenders were prepared only for an attack from the sea and were quickly overwhelmed.*

Right top: *Blacksmith's Shop, Moose Factory, c. 1849. Explored by Henry Hudson in 1611 and fortified by the Hudson's Bay Company in 1673, this English post pre-dates the 1749 French settlement in the Windsor area. The Blacksmith's Shop is the third on this site, the first having been destroyed by fire in 1735.*

Clergue was an American entrepreneur whose career was based upon a confidence in the north's potential. Following the success of his railway, he created the Consolidated Lake Superior Company, and is credited in this period with organizing "possibly the broadest group of integrated companies under a single man's control in Canadian history" (Morris Zaslow in *The Opening of the Canadian North).* Clergue's holdings were the industrial base for Sault Ste. Marie, which would become one of the major cities in the north, with a much more diversified industrial base than many of the smaller one-industry towns. But railway development was the common key to success.

Agriculture

The effort to develop a viable agricultural industry in the north was a mistake; yet, in its eagerness to encourage immigration and settlement, the government consistently extolled the potential of land which was unsuitable for agriculture. Indiscriminate agricultural settlement created hardship for many families who were convinced to settle there.

With the passage of the *Free Grants Act* of 1869, the government adopted a more active policy to promote the north as a farming frontier. The government built colonization roads, such as Bell's Line, and the Petersen, Hastings, and Bobcaygeon Roads; however, with stumps, rocks, and swamps to contend with, primitive building techniques, and only limited government financing, the solution was often the "corduroy road." One traveller described these roads as follows, and quoted by Nila Reynolds in *In Quest of Yesterday:*

> Holes masked by mud were of constant occurrence. Into these our vehicle plunged with a crash, threatening to reduce it to atoms but . . . it was dragged out by willing horses, apparently uninjured. Worse than the holes was the dreadful corduroy composed of large logs over which we bumped . . . So bad was the road that a dozen miles drive kept us five hours on the way.

Still, the government subsidized railways, established immigration bureaus in Great Britain, and sponsored experimental farms in remote regions to demonstrate the feasibility of modern agriculture. In 1900 there were ambitious surveys of northern agricultural potential which reported the presence of a vast, fertile, and a loudly touted "great clay belt" of some 16,000,000 acres (6,500,000 hectares).

These grand government settlement schemes were unsound and unsuccessful because much of the land was totally unsuitable for farming. The soil was thin and quickly eroded when the timber was removed by lumbermen or farmers. There were only a few fertile patches. Once Muskoka, Parry Sound, Haliburton, Nipissing, and Renfrew had been stripped of their pine cover or burned in one of the many forest fires, the land was found to be barren and simply abandoned.

The first settlers were often children or grandchildren of the first pioneers in the counties around the Great Lakes. Many were native Ontarians or of British origin, but the north also attracted Americans, North Europeans, and French Canadians. South and Central Europeans came north to work in the resource industries but they were less actively involved in agricultural settlement.

The problems of the northern settler were particularly acute. They were almost always poor for they literally had to cut their farm out of the bush. To subsist they often worked in the logging industry part-time. Their homes were isolated from each other in small clearings surrounded by dense forest. During the winter when the men were away working in the logging camps, the women had to make out as best they could.

The settler's lot was aggravated by rough terrain and extremes of climate. Early frosts restricted the variety of crops. Unexpected rain could be a disaster at harvest time. As settlers cleared land, they had to cope with hoards of insects and the constant problem of the thin shield soil heavily interspersed with rocks. Despite these difficulties, agriculture on the Canadian Shield enjoyed small temporary successes. There was an active social life organized around the raising of cabins, logging bees, church socials, dances, and regattas. Small villages grew up with schools, churches, libraries, and even local newspapers.

The settlers had always welcomed railway development but ironically, when the railways did come, they contributed to the decline of

Right top: *Barn Raising at Emo. This turn-of-the-century photograph shows a long-standing method of setting a barn frame in place — by the use of many hands.*
Right middle: *Katrine. On Highway 11, a continuation of Simcoe's Yonge Street, Katrine is a hamlet south of Burk's Falls, District of Parry Sound.*
Right below: *CNR Elevator, Port Arthur. The largest elevator in the world when it was built, it was used to store western grain.*
Left below: *Francis Hector Clergue. In the early 1900s, Clergue, an American, built his industrial empire at Sault Ste. Marie. He erected a power plant, paper mill and steel mill. His enterprises flourished during the building of transcontinental rail lines, but ran into difficulties when World War I began. In 1935, Sir James Dunn took over the steel works and began updating them.*

northern agriculture. As the railways opened more fertile land to the west, the northern farms were abandoned and population declined. Between 1901 and 1941, the population of Ontario increased seventy-two percent, but there was negligible increase in the northern counties of Haliburton, Muskoka, Parry Sound, and Renfrew. Since the Second World War, the population has remained almost static.

Indiscriminate agricultural settlement wasted the resources of the Canadian Shield. There was no place for the self-sufficient, subsistent farm. Some farmers continued on scattered fertile plots on a specialized basis, raising livestock and a few field crops. But agriculture could never provide an economic basis for the region.

Mining

The early history of the mining industry was a story of frustration, fate, and fortune, and when valuable discoveries were made it was often more a matter of good luck than good management. Yet, once gold and silver were found, those involved tended to forget the difficulties of the past, and the amount of indirect government assistance which was a prerequisite for their success. Instead, they revelled in optimism about the promise of "New Ontario" and clung to the myth that it was all the result of individualism, self-sufficiency, and hard work.

The construction of the railways set the stage for this drama of discovery. The T & NO railway was not originally conceived as an adjunct to mining development. It was built because of the clamour of settlers who still lived precariously in an isolated country "where canoes and flat boats, horses and oxen, snow shoes and cutters were the only modes of transportation" (Albert Tucker in *Steam into Wilderness*). Initially, there was little expectation that the construction of the T & NO would generate sufficient rail traffic to make it profitable. As each advance of steel disclosed new wealth, the mining industry became an ever more important aspect of the railway's business. In less than ten years, the Cobalt region — justly claimed to be "the richest silver camp in the world" — produced ore worth five times the cost of constructing the railway line from North Bay to Cochrane.

Left and right below: *"His First Discovery" at Gowganda 1909. Somewhat off the beaten track, Gowganda is southwest of the main Kirkland Lake gold fields. Here, K. Farah, a Syrian nicknamed "Big Pete," built and ran the Canada Hotel. Later, he developed the Big Pete silver mine at Cobalt.* ***Right top:*** *"Four Foot Wide" Vein of Gold, Dome Mines Near Timmins. Dome Mining Company took its name from the gold-rich quartz dome. Timmins was named for Noah and Henry Timmins, storekeepers in Mattawa before they joined the Cobalt silver rush and made huge personal fortunes.*

Prior to the discovery of silver in Cobalt, a group of New Liskeard businessmen and farmers formed the Temiskaming and Hudson Bay Company to promote mining exploration in the Cobalt area. Prospectors staked a number of claims, which proved to be "rich." The "lucky Hudson" as it was called, made its original investors millionaires.

The folklore of the 1903 Cobalt silver rush attributes the first discovery to a local blacksmith named Fred Larose. The story goes that he threw his hammer at a passing fox, missed, and struck a huge nugget of silver. In fact, the first claim was filed by J.H. McKinley and E. Darragh, who were contractors supplying wooden ties to the railway. They became the founders of the successful McKinley-Darragh mine.

By 1904, the initial scepticism of the public and the T & NO Rail Commission was replaced by a mood of excitement. The Cobalt silver rush was on, as discoveries continued to be very rich. William Tretheway developed a mine where, it was said, one load of ore consisted of "slabs of native metal stripped off the walls of the vein, like boards from a barn." The silver produced increased until 1911, and became the basis for huge personal fortunes — like those of Noah and Henry Timmins, who were originally storekeepers in Mattawa and John and Duncan McMartin, who were tie contractors for the railway.

The T & NO Railway responded to this burgeoning mining industry in several ways. In addition to the freight cars filled with ore, timber and pulpwood, and the cheap coaches for the miners and their families, from March 1907, the railway provided a service for wealthy businessmen, brokers, engineers and entrepreneurs, known as "the Cobalt special." This elegant train left Toronto every evening at 9:00 p.m. and arrived in Cobalt at 8:45 the next morning. It included Pullman sleeping cars, a library car, and luxurious dining facilities.

While some businessmen whose fortunes depended upon local silver mining took up residence in new spacious homes along "millionaires' row," in Haileybury or in New Liskeard, most did not. They were non-residents who periodically visited the source of their wealth, arriving on the Cobalt special, and returning by the same means. They stayed at the elegant Matabanick Hotel in Haileybury.

The discovery of gold came somewhat later, although, after uncertain beginnings progress was as sensational as it had been in Cobalt. In 1907, several claims were staked in Whitney and Tisdale townships, but they were subsequently abandoned. Later, Alex Gillies discovered the ore body which was to become the basis for the Hollinger mine. He and young Benny Hollinger, then aged nineteen, worked for two "grubstakers," and routinely tossed a coin to resolve claims for payment of their expenses. In this way Hollinger came to own six claims which became the mine bearing his name. It was developed by the Timmins-McMartin-Dunlop syndicate.

Other gold finds led to the development of Porcupine. Exploration revealed a dome of quartz plastered with gold. This mineral dome became the basis for the Dome Mining Company.

Sandy McIntyre gave his name to the second largest gold producer in the Porcupine area. As a henpecked husband, he had escaped domesticity by fleeing to Canada where he worked for a while for the T & NO Railway. He joined the prospectors going to Porcupine and eventually staked four claims north of those earlier discovered by Hollinger. His name remains in the corporate name of McIntyre-Porcupine Mines Limited, which, like Dome, continues to be active in the mining industry.

Although there were some who struck it rich, the lucky ones were few. In general, most early prospectors did not become rich from their claims. In 1910 for example, Sandy McIntyre received no more than $8,000 for his original half interest in the McIntyre mine. He died a penniless pauper at the age of seventy.

Harry Oakes was the exception. In Kirkland Lake he was "the only prospector on record to have staked claims, financed them, and brought them into production" (O.T.G. Williamson in *The Northland Ontario).* Oakes had some fifteen years of mining experience and had learned that some promising claims originally staked by the Burrows brothers were due to expire. Oakes was on hand to restake them, and with the Tough brothers he developed the largely successful Tough-Oakes mine. There were other amalgamations and business ventures but Oakes never

Left below: *Bird's-Eye View of McIntyre-Hollinger Mine Near Schumacher. The McIntyre Mine was named for Sandy McIntyre, who sold his interest in 1910 and died penniless. The ore body for the Hollinger Mine was discovered by Alex Gillies, on claims that belonged to Ben Hollinger.*
Right top: *King Cobalt Silver Mine. Residents of Cobalt called it "the best little town on earth."*
Right middle: *Dome Gold Mine, South Porcupine. This Dome mine is situated on land that is now part of Timmins. Today, Dome is a vast conglomerate known as Dome Petroleum.*
Right below: *Silver Street, Cobalt. By 1915, sixteen silver mines were in operation in and around Cobalt, their shafts sunk below the town's streets, their towers dominating the landscape.*

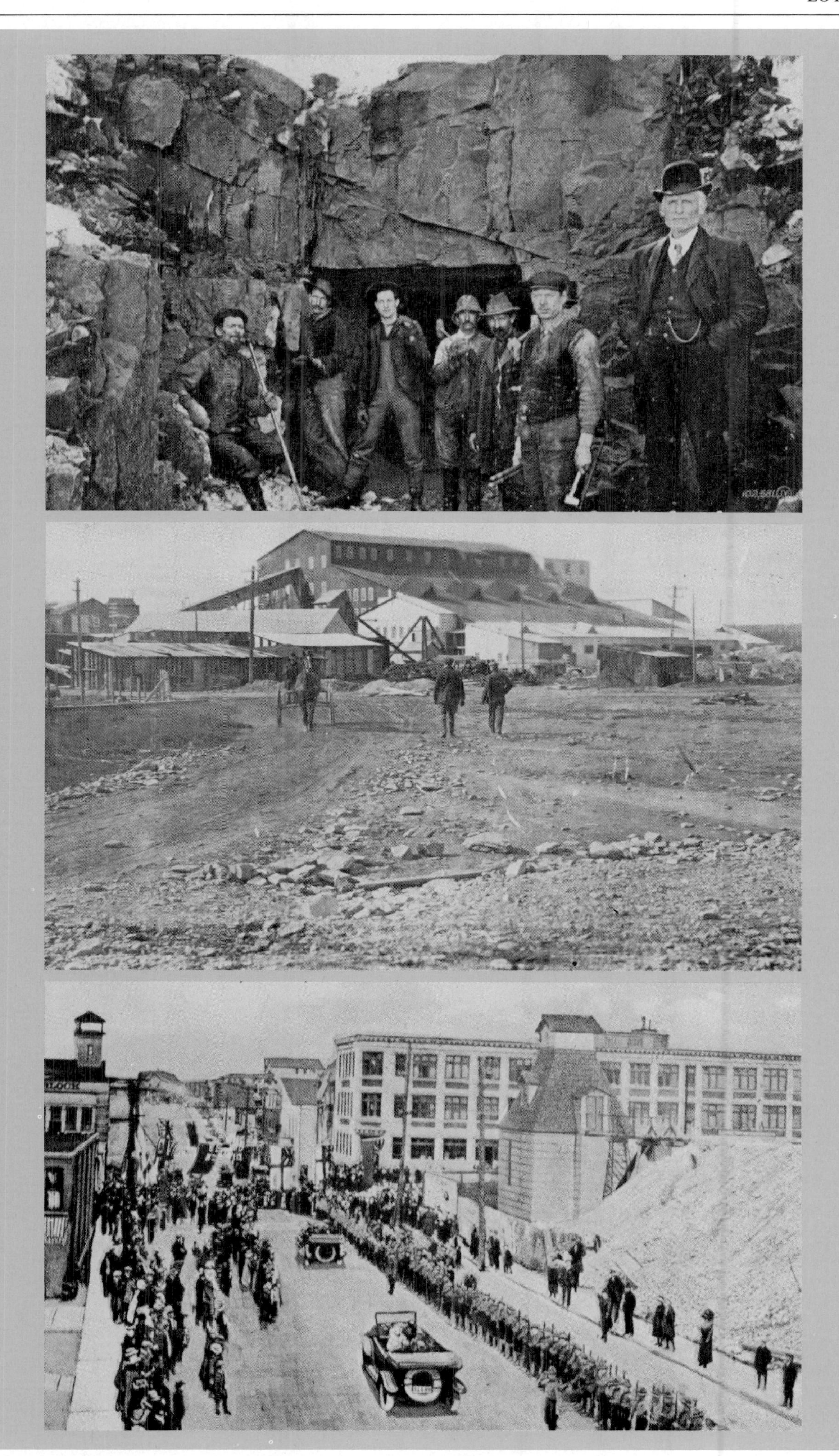

gave up his lucrative financial interest in this one.

William H. Wright was the other person to profit from his claims on what became known in this gold camp as "the main break." When he came to Canada in 1907, he had no mining experience at all, but went to Cobalt where he secured a job painting mining buildings. With his brother-in-law, Ed Hargreaves, he staked what became the Wright-Hargreaves mine. Hargreaves sold his half interest for $6,000. Wright retained a quarter share and became a millionaire.

"Characters" are always present in mining camps and Northern Ontario had its fair share of them. Gowganda was the home of K. Farah, better known as "Big Pete," one of the most successful businessmen in all of New Ontario. He was reputed to be the "man with the gold touch" — a Syrian from Mount Lebanon who arrived in New Liskeard in 1899. He recognized that the town needed a hotel and built "The Canada." When silver was discovered in Cobalt he joined the rush, filed some successful claims, and developed the "Big Pete" mine.

The gold mining town of Kirkland Lake also had certain citizens of some local notoriety. There was Charlie Chow — a hotel dealer who allowed itinerant prospectors to pay for their meals with mining shares. He died a millionaire. Another folk heroine was Roza Brown, an old woman (also reputed to be rich) who built a shack on Government Road and tried to avoid taxes by presenting her abode to the British Crown.

These stories invariably stress a rags to riches theme and reflect the Northerner's admiration for ingenuity and endurance. Hardy individualists are part of the real or imagined past. The reality was somewhat more prosaic and depended more upon government encouragement and assistance than is usually acknowledged.

After the discovery of silver and gold, the local towns grew rapidly. When silver was discovered in Cobalt in 1903, Haileybury and New Liskeard were transformed from agricultural villages into bustling towns. Haileybury's population increased dramatically as engineers, speculators, businessmen, and some miners took up residence. A railway line from North Bay to New Liskeard was opened in 1904, and a street

Left and right below: *Ferguson Avenue, Haileybury. This quiet agricultural village boomed with the discovery of silver at Cobalt. Since Cobalt was "dry," Haileybury was the local liquor outlet and did a thriving hotel business. A railway line reached nearby New Liskeard in 1905, and a street railway nine kilometres long linked Haileybury with Cobalt. Some businessmen built homes along "millionaires' row" in Haileybury. Others were non-residents who stayed at the elegant Matabanick Hotel. The Temiskaming and Northern Ontario Railway provided a service for businessmen, brokers and engineers — a train called the "Cobalt special," with Pullman cars — that left Toronto in the evening and reached Cobalt the next morning. Those who stayed over chose hotels in Haileybury.*

railway system was built linking Haileybury to Cobalt. Haileybury also became a local liquor outlet (Cobalt was dry), and did a thriving hotel business. It was here that "in busy barrooms of the hotels, spectacular mining deals were settled and fortunes won and lost" (T. Tait in "Haileybury: The Early Years," *Ontario History,* 1963).

Cobalt was described by its citizens as "the best little town on earth." It grew quickly and eventually acquired curved streets and a variety of buildings of haphazard construction. Cobalt drew prospectors and miners, drifters and dreamers, from all parts of the world. It was a typical mining camp with a spirit of recklessness, and in the bunkhouses at night miners exchanged tales based on their experience in similar camps in Scotland, Nova Scotia, and Butte, Montana. Cobalt was perhaps unique among mining camps of the world because, by law, no intoxicants were allowed. But, of course, bootleggers plied a profitable trade.

Cobalt was a reflection of the mining industry in economic, social, and even physical terms. Two blocks from the railway station there was a steep hill on which many of the great mines, such as the Silver Queen, the City of Cobalt, and the Nancy-Helen were located. Their shafts were sunk beneath the town's streets, and their towers dominated the landscape. By 1915 there were sixteen mines operating in and around Cobalt. The town became a training ground for many of those who later worked in the mining industry.

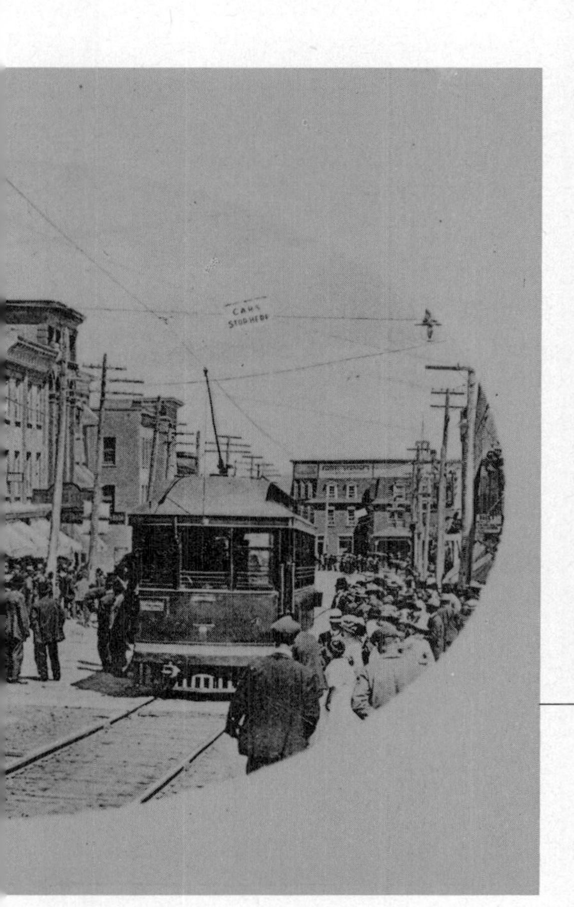

After the initial successes in Cobalt there were further mineral discoveries in Porcupine Lake, Swastika, Larder Lake and Kirkland Lake. Mines and servicing towns sprang up at Elk Lake, Gowganda, and in the Larder Lake district, so that by 1908, the town of Larder Lake was a bustling place. By 1914 Kirkland Lake had only one mine site in production (the Tough-Oakes), and other future mines were, as yet, still "holes in the bush" (S.A. Pain, *Three Miles of Gold).*

The only mining community which developed into a city was Sudbury, which was also an "east-west rail junction," and the centre of a prosperous lumbering area. In the 1880s, S.J. Ritchie created the Canadian Copper Company which purchased land in the Sudbury basin and began mining nickel in 1886. However, there had to be a cheap process to separate the nickel from its ore so that it could be refined, and markets had to be found for this, as yet, little known metal. Both problems were resolved by the turn of the century. Production rose consistently, and the company eventually participated in the creation of the International Nickel Company (INCO) which went on to establish a virtual monopoly in the North American market and became an active competitor in Britain and Europe. Sudbury became the world's largest nickel producing centre and Canada's greatest mining area. Its success stimulated the development of the entire region of Northern Ontario.

For a northern population living in wooden buildings near dense forests, fires were a constant threat. As the population increased, so too, did the frequency of fires. Between 1910 and 1916 there were numerous bush fires, and in 1911 there was a major conflagration in Porcupine itself. At that time it was still no more than an isolated settlement on the edge of the lake, without any sophisticated equipment to prevent the fire from spreading. Flames quickly engulfed the town, destroyed the pit-heads of the mine, and burnt the railway cars, one of which contained 350 cases of dynamite. The resulting explosion created a hole six metres deep. More than seventy people were killed by burning or drowning when they rushed to the lake seeking relief. One hardy woman gave birth in the lake and both mother and child survived.

Ironically, the town of Cochrane experienced a massive fire on the same day. More than seventy people were killed and fifty stores, fifteen hotels, four churches, and two schools were destroyed. In both communities relief committees were formed to evacuate people, organize tents and cooking facilities for those who remained. Many relief supplies were generously donated by people in the south, and were carried to the devastated communities on the T & NO railway.

The same pattern was repeated in other northern communities. In 1912 and 1914, the towns of Timmins and Haileybury were burned. In 1916, a fire destroyed the settlements of New Liskeard and Cochrane (again), and the villages of Matheson, Nushka, Kelso, and Porquis Junction, killing between 300 and 450 people. In response, the government established a Northern Ontario Fire Relief Committee which

Left below: *Big Nickel, Canadian Centennial Numismatic Park, Sudbury. The only mining community that became a full-fledged city was Sudbury. S.J. Richie's Canadian Copper Company began mining nickel in the Sudbury Basin in 1886. The Big Nickel was a symbol of the world's largest nickel-producing region.*
Right top: *Teck Hughes Gold Mine, Kirkland Lake. Teck Hughes was next to Sir Harry Oakes' Lakeshore Mine. Now most of the buildings are gone.*
Right middle: *International Nickel Smelter, Copper Cliff. The smelter belched out smoke that destroyed nearby vegetation, but to the residents the smoke spelled prosperity.*
Right below: *Elk Lake. On the Montreal River west of New Liskeard, and not far from Gowganda, Elk Lake was one of many mining camps.*

DRUG STORE
GRAND VIEW

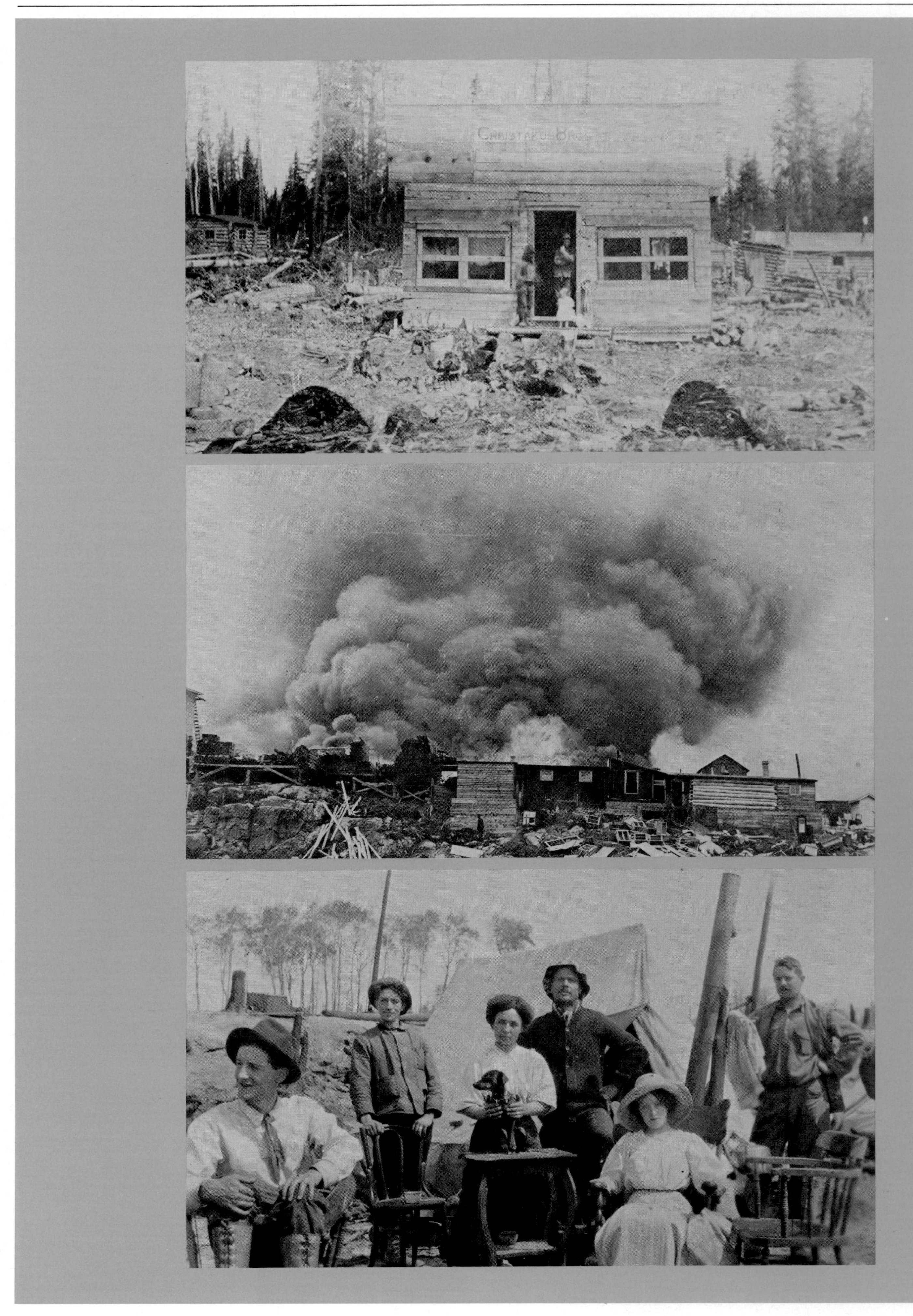
CHRISTAKUS BROS

Left top: *Golden Avenue, South Porcupine, Before the Fire. In heavily forested country, where nearly all buildings were of wood, fires took a heavy toll. South Porcupine was burnt soon after this photograph was taken.*
Left middle: *The Cobalt Fire. Cobalt was swept by a disastrous conflagration in June 1912.*
Left below: *After the Porcupine Fire. In 1911, a major fire swept Porcupine, an isolated settlement on the shore of the lake. More than seventy people died, some in the fire, while others drowned after escaping into the lake.*
Right below: *Traders' Bank of Canada, Porcupine. Bank architecture in mining towns was functional. Perhaps large buildings were not needed. Too many spendthrift miners saw their earnings vanish before they could get near a bank.*

raised over $200,000 and provided quantities of food, clothing, and medical supplies. In 1922 another fire burned Haileybury and the surrounding areas. This time, forty-three people were killed, and 6,000 left homeless, so that after the fire, eighty-five discarded Toronto streetcars had to be transported north to serve as temporary shelters.

These repeated disasters sparked widespread concern and during World War I, the Ontario government introduced more stringent fire protection measures, including the appointment of fire rangers and stricter controls on the burning of brush. In the 1920s — partly as a result of Premier Howard Ferguson's interest in renewed northern development — bush pilots, many of them war veterans, began a regular patrol of Ontario's northern mining and lumber camps.

More difficult to control, but in some respects just as devastating, were the vagaries of the marketplace. By the 20th century Ontario had established itself as a leading supplier of minerals to the world market, but that market proved to be inherently unstable and precarious. Thus, periods of prosperity and growth were frequently followed, often unexpectedly, by periods of recession, unemployment and hardship — posing social and economic problems which have yet to be resolved.

The lumber, pulp and paper industries

Provincial plans for the development of "New Ontario" also depended upon the successful exploitation of the forest reserves. The growth of the lumber industry was an integral part of the government's overall development strategy, because its requirements were expected to stimulate the construction of waterways, roads, and railways which would be economically advantageous to the entire region. Between the 1830s and World War I, for example, locks were built to create the Trent Canal system, and the various slides and dams were constructed of sufficient dimension to ensure the ready passage of timber. Steamers along the Trent Canal system carried to market, farmers' grain, and lumbermen's sawlogs, just as the railways would do in a later period.

The early lumber industry influenced the settlers' lives in many ways, not all of which were amicable. The local population supplied the companies with a much needed source of labour, and the lumber companies furnished farmers with part-time employment and an additional source of income when they would otherwise be idle, as Nila Reynolds observed:

> In the old days, logging gangs entered the bush as early as the first of September for cutting and skidding, road making and camp building and all stream improvements such as dam building and clearing of debris could be more economically accomplished before the snow fell.

The lumber camps provided markets for the produce of local farmers and the nearby towns benefited from the business of woodsmen who frequently squandered their wages on liquor. Concerns about law and order, however, were tempered by a realization that the return of the loggers meant an infusion of ready cash into the local economy.

There were also periodic conflicts between the interests of the settlers and the lumber companies. Farmers had to clear their land, and in so doing, destroyed the native forests; moreover, when the agricultural frontier was pushed beyond its natural limits there was a waste of forest resources. When commercially valuable white and red pine, spruce and balsam were removed, they did not grow back but were replaced by less valuable species like poplar and birch. For a long time this uneconomic waste of forest resources was condoned by the Ontario Crown Lands Department, which considered the lumber industry to be only a transitory stage preceding agricultural settlement.

Lumbering, land clearance, and fires all took their toll of the northern forests; yet, despite much careless treatment in the early years, Northern Ontario remained a treasure house of forest wealth. Gradually, this was recognized as a distinct asset and the government began to segregate lands for agricultural and lumbering purposes so that the two industries would not impede each other's development. Encouragement of the lumber industry became part of the government's development strategy. Revenue in the form of bonuses, Crown timber dues and license fees was a major source of government income until the 1920s.

The lumber industry prospered in the early period for there was a

Left and right below: *Log Jam, Mississauga River, Near Blind River. Logging was regarded as a prelude to agriculture, until the forests were seen as a valuable resource in themselves. Log jams formed easily; and lumbermen developed great skill in breaking them and keeping the logs moving.*
Right top: *Logging Near Port Arthur. The lumber industry began with the square timber trade, based on tall white pines. When these had been removed, smaller trees became the basis for the pulp and paper industry. Hydro-electric plants were built, for the large pulp and paper mills required a source of energy. The pulp and paper industry was more regulated from the start than the square timber trade had been, but it generated pollution. Wood scraps and chemicals were dumped into streams.*

ready market for sawlogs and squared timber in Quebec, the United States, and in Britain. However, this early success was achieved at considerable long-run cost. The timber forests were treated as an inexhaustible resource. There was no interest in forest renewal. Historian Arthur Lower's classic, *The North American Assault on the Canadian Forest*, describes this wasteful exploitation, praises the early efforts at conservation, and portrays the lumbermen as buccaneers.

By the 1880s the industry began to suffer from inefficient overproduction, American competition, and depressed prices. By the turn of the century the great pine forests in Northern Ontario were substantially depleted, and in this period government and industry representatives became increasingly oriented towards conservation. The lumbermen sought greater predictability and stability in the industry, which they hoped would lead to its orderly expansion. From 1900 there was a much more sophisticated approach to the use of timber resources with controls on cutting and more effective land classification.

Gradually (and particularly between 1909 and 1921), there emerged a national conservation movement to which the industry gave its support. Trees were not in unlimited supply and came to be regarded, as they are today, as a "renewable resource." Still, it took a sequence of forest fires between 1910 and 1916 to create a public fire protection system. With the conservationist movement came the concept of the "scientific management" of forests, and the Conservative Whitney government even established a forestry school at the University of Toronto.

In co-operation with the local lumbermen (particularly those in the northwest), the province also sought to promote industrial development by encouraging the local processing of timber. In 1897 new Crown Timber regulations included a "manufacturing clause" on all sawlogs cut in Ontario, to promote the pulp and paper industry, then still in its infancy. It was hoped that restrictions on the export of unprocessed raw materials would attract capital (particularly from the United States), into sawmill and factory development.

By the early 20th century the square timber trade had given way to sawlog and pulpwood industries. The rise of the pulp and paper industry was a direct response to an insatiable appetite for paper in American cities, and resulted in the building of enormous mills and hydro-electric power projects to supply them with energy. And, as expected, new roads, railways and local service centres accompanied the industrial development. As early as 1901 so many new pulp and paper mills had been built that there was a local shortage of labour. In 1911 alone, eighty-one new companies were formed to exploit Canadian pulpwood resources. In 1913 a rail line was built from Porquis to Iroquois Falls to serve the mill of the Abitibi Power and Paper Company. Efficient rail transportation continued to be a prerequisite for economic success.

From the very beginning the pulp and paper industry was more regulated than the early timber trade had been, with the result that there was less friction with local agricultural settlements. More difficult to resolve, however, were the marketing problems raised by protectionist American tariff policies which restricted entry of Canadian products into the American market. Finally, with the 1912 Underwood tariff, rates levied on Canadian newsprint were reduced, establishing virtually free trade in mechanical pulp and newsprint. The market for Ontario products was expanded, and American capital attracted to the North to finance the construction of new paper mills.

The pulp and paper industry boomed during World War I, overproduced in the 1920s, and foundered during the Depression. On one occasion, to stabilize the industry, the provincial authorities intervened to impose a government-regulated cartel. At other times, particularly during Howard Ferguson's tenure as Minister of the Department of Lands, Forests, and Mines, government regulation was relaxed. The primary concern was to keep the industry prosperous and Ontarians at work. Conservation was a decidedly secondary goal.

As in the mining industry, the pulp and paper industry spawned a series of "company towns" like Espanola, Sturgeon Falls, Spruce Falls, Iroquois Falls, and Fort William, which prospered or failed, depending upon the commercial success of the local (and usually only) employer. However, unlike the mining towns, the new pulp and paper towns were often established as attractive and well-maintained company communi-

Left below: *Spanish Mills, Spanish River Near Espanola. Unlike the mining towns, the pulp and paper towns tended to be attractive, well-maintained, company communities.*
Right top: *Latchford Saw Mill, Latchford, Near Cobalt. "Had a $10,000 fire today which totally destroyed our planing mill. Our saw mill as shown on the other side is safe so is the stock of lumber." This excerpt is dated September 28, 1908.*
Right middle: *An Early Log House at Dryden. At first called Lake Wabigoon, Dryden began as an experimental dairy farm. Now it is better known as a town in the pulp and paper region of Northwestern Ontario.*
Right below: *Scott Street, Fort Frances. This town is the administrative centre for the District of Rainy River. The only other town is Rainy River itself.*

THE DOMINION BANK
RECORDS
GRADE CHINA
JEWELER
Scott Street. Fort Frances, Canada.

ties. Espanola, for example, illustrates the vulnerability of a community dependent upon one main industry.

Between 1903 and 1929, Espanola was not incorporated, nor did it have a municipal council. It was run jointly by the Spanish River Pulp and Paper Company, and the Abitibi Power and Paper Company. In 1911, the erection of a paper mill had coincided with the construction of the Manitoulin and North Shore Railway, and an upswing in the economy following World War I resulted in an expansion of the mill and an influx of new citizens. But by 1921, the economy was in a recession, the pulp and paper industry was overextended, and the companies were engaging in intense competition to maintain their share of the shrinking market.

In 1928 the Abitibi company negotiated a merger with the Spanish River Company, and acquired control of five Canadian newsprint firms and their subsidiaries. This consolidation was initially grounds for considerable optimism, although the company had, in fact, overextended itself financially and there were soon more layoffs. In 1929, the mill was closed permanently, and in 1932 it went into receivership. "Any hope among the town's people regarding re-opening of the mill was abandoned. Espanola had lost its reason for existence" (Eileen Gotz in "Espanola," *Laurentian Review*).

Espanola experienced a severe depression until the Second World War and was, for a time, considered an appropriate isolated location for a prisoner-of-war camp. In 1943 a new American company (the Kalamazoo Vegetable Parchment Company) bought the Abitibi timber concessions with a view to supplying high-grade pulp to its parent firm in Michigan. KVP entered into agreements with the Ontario government for larger timber limits, remodelled the old Abitibi mill, and opened for business in 1946. KVP in turn was later to be purchased by the E.B. Eddy Forest Products Company which runs it today. The experience of Espanola is characteristic of that of other one-industry towns, whose continued existence still depends upon the success of that single industry or firm.

Left below: *Sturgeon Caught in Georgian Bay. Many early tourists came for the fishing and hunting. Sturgeon was a popular game fish, but other species were also favourites — northern pike, bass, pickerel. The first tourist accommodation was in boarding houses or primitive camps. These were followed by resorts, large summer hotels often with cottages to rent.*

In contrast to agriculture, which was never very successful in the North, tourism became an important part of the northern economy. Tourism united the South and the North and exposed many urban Ontarians to the beauty of their own wilderness.

The tourist trade developed on a sporadic basis, beginning with the occasional vacationer in the 1860s. In these early days, vacationers travelled by stagecoach — which could be dangerous. Accidents were frequent, as wheels sometimes came off. Visitors also travelled by steamboat over canals and waterways originally built to facilitate commercial traffic and industrial development. However, increasingly, waterways like the Trent-Severn system were used to promote the tourist industry, and steamers came to be used more for pleasure cruises than the transportation of goods. When the last lock on the Trent system was completed in July 1920, the first vessel to pass through the entire system was not a commercial steamer but a private motor launch named the *Irene.* Early guidebooks describing these routes and the historic sites of what was known as "the Northern tour" all included such places as Fort Erie, Niagara Falls, Queenston, Kingston, and Toronto.

As early as the 1830s, there were reports of good fishing in the North, and throughout the 19th century fishing came to be regarded as an increasingly important recreational asset. In the 1850s, retired British officers travelled north to hunt and fish on Rice Lake. There were early cottagers on Lake Erie — including educator Egerton Ryerson — and residents of Toronto became regular summer visitors to the North. In the 1870s resort lands were developed on Lake Erie, Georgian Bay, Lakes Simcoe and Scugog, and in the Kawartha area. In 1870 the first resort hotel was built in Muskoka at the north end of Lake Rosseau. Muskoka became a popular destination, since it was only a few hours from Toronto and could easily be reached by railway, steamship, and later by automobile.

By the 1880s Muskoka had lost much of its wildlife and timber, and had proved to be a poor area for farming. Tourism emerged as an industry with potential. That industry grew quickly, and Gravenhurst,

Right below: *French River, District of Nipissing, Path of Voyageurs. The link from Montreal to Georgian Bay and the upper lakes was by way of the Ottawa and Mattawa Rivers, Lake Nipissing and the French River. Along this waterway paddled explorers, fur traders and government officials, who portaged around many sets of rapids. North Bay, "gateway to the north," is the seat of the District of Nipissing.*

Bracebridge, and Huntsville all became flourishing resort towns.

As a result of the prolonged economic boom between 1896 and 1914, the 1890s saw the development of elegant resorts catering to wealthy patrons with the time and means to holiday in the North. Fashionable cottage areas emerged on Lake Simcoe and there were grand sailing regattas on Stoney Lake. Such developments were available only to a limited class in society. Tourist development required an appeal to a broader base, and conscious of the growing economic potential of the industry, the Ontario government created Algonquin Park in 1893. As early as 1907, the Kawartha area was advertised as "the bright waters and happy lands, where nature lies in sweet abandonment and laughing waters kiss a hundred shades" (John Marsh, in *Kawartha Heritage).* These assets, together with deep winter snows suitable for skiing, and proximity to the thickly populated south, gave the northern tourist industry a secure base.

With the advent of the automobile in the 1920s, the tourist industry experienced a boom. Ontario became the destination for two out of every three American visitors. The recreational lands were all served by roads, of a sort. Established tourist areas like Lakes Simcoe and Couchiching already had good provincial roads, and the road system was being continually improved. Mass tourism became a viable possibility — especially as the workers began to take holidays too. There was an increase in both the number of campers and provincial parks to accommodate them. Resort hotels gave way to cheaper food and accommodation, so that roadside cabins (which later evolved into motels) became much more common.

The Depression brought an end to this recreational boom and during the Second World War, restrictions on gasoline and building materials inhibited the growth of tourism. At the end of the war, however, the tourist industry rebounded with renewed vigour as the country experienced its greatest period of economic expansion, and in *Profiles of a Province,* R.I. Wolfe wrote:

> The summer cottage remains as it has been almost since the time of confederation, the single most important character-

Left below: *Largest Speckled Trout on Record. This specimen, weighing fourteen and one half pounds (about seven kg), was caught in the Nipigon River in 1916 by Dr. W.J. Cook.*
Right top: *Preparing a Shore Dinner, Temagami. The area around Lake Temagami is still relatively unspoiled, better known to residents of Northern Ontario than to those in the South because of its remoteness.*
Right below: *Main Street, Kenora. The seat of the District of Kenora, the town is in the Lake-of-the-Woods region, one of the routes used by voyageurs, now an area greatly favoured by tourists, particularly Americans and residents of Southern Manitoba.*

PORT ARTHUR 315 M.
FORT WILLIAM 315 M.
SIOUX LOOKOUT 151 M.
FORT FRANCES 140 M.
DRYDEN 89 M.
TOPPER RETURNS' PALACE
JACKSON
HERE'S TO YOUR GOOD
SAFEWAY

> istic and desired place of recreation for the people of Ontario, and for the vacationing visitors from beyond its borders.

Although Northern Ontario failed to develop a viable agricultural industry, it found in the tourist trade a more successful alternative.

To sum up, through successive periods of rapid development, recession and recovery, Northern Ontario has become a defined region with distinctive economic and social characteristics. With economic successes came established communities — scattered and isolated at first — but all sharing the same hopes for their future. As these communities became more settled and secure, they lost their frontier quality, and their very isolation contributed to the development of a lively local community life. There were numerous fraternal orders (Masons, Elks, Lions, Kinsmen), sports clubs, and hockey teams which became the pride of the local population and the origin of generations of hockey heroes.

Yet despite the natural beauty and natural resources which provided the basis for the region's economic development, its real wealth has been in its people. Harry Oakes, industrialist Sir James Dunn, and media magnate Roy Thompson, all started on the road to riches in Northern Ontario and went on to pursue careers on a larger stage. Finns, Swedes and Italians were attracted to the North, along with retailers and professionals drawn from old Ontario. Together with the Franco-Ontarians, who still make up a significant portion of the population, these many people have contributed to a multicultural mosaic, infused with a spirit of individualism which is uniquely northern. In *The Northland Ontario,* O.T.G. Williamson has concluded:

> The Northland is a country with a personality. It is compounded of optimism, fortitude and a gay willingness to take a chance . . . Northern Ontario is perhaps more typically Canadian than any other comparable area in Canada . . . but its true grandeur rests firmly on its people's character . . . Its spirit is still that of the pioneer and warrior, the two elements in Canadian life that have led to nationhood.

Most Ontarians would agree.

Right top: *Mount McKay Near Fort William. Mount McKay is part of the Nor'Westers, of the barrier wall of plateau along the north shore of Lake Superior. The name Nor'Westers commemorates the men of the North West Company who established a headquarters at Fort William in 1804.*

Right below: *Temagami Summer Resort. Tourism added a vital dimension to the economy of the North. In the late 19th century, Southern Ontarians discovered the beauties of the North, and they required places to stay. Huntsville, Gravenhurst and Bracebridge all became flourishing resort towns for people from Toronto, while northern residents often favoured such places as Temagami.*

Left below: *"Good Finish" at Byng Inlet, Magnetawan River. In the District of Parry Sound and west of Algonquin Park, Magnetawan lies in the heart of good hunting and fishing territory.*

Mt. McKay Fort William.

SHELL
GRILL
TEA ROOMS
GENERAL STORE
CANOES
ETC:
KODAK
FILMS
FISHING
TACKLE
GENERAL
STORE

CHAPTER 17

THE RISE OF KING STREET

by Michael Bliss

I look for companies that will not only grow with the country, but faster than the country

E. P. TAYLOR

The Loyalists began turning the wild forest into a bounteous garden. The work was long and hard. Several generations had to pass before all the stumps and stones were gone; the wells and root cellars dug; the drainage ditches and concession roads built; and the big barns and the "red-brick-with-gingerbread-trim" houses dotted the Ontario countryside. By the 1890s the job was largely done. The foundations of Ontario's wealth had been laid well and truly in its fields and farms, in what everyone recognized as its greatest industry, agriculture.

Make no mistake about this. Ontario's prosperity originated in the land and the sweat of the men and women who cleared and worked it. Canadians were starting to talk about the great wheatfields of Manitoba and the Northwest Territories, but in 1891 it was Ontario that produced three fifths of Canada's grain, half the country's hay, half the sheep and cattle, and more than two thirds of all the fruit, swine, and dairy products of the Dominion. In 1900, Canada's greatest exports to the Mother Country were agricultural products from Ontario: cheese, butter, and bacon for the British breakfast table. It was not until 1906 that Manitoba, Alberta, and Saskatchewan combined, grew enough wheat to edge that product ahead of central Canada's cheese as the nation's number one export. A lot of good things grew in Ontario.

The big city of Toronto got its nickname, of course, from its role as an exporter of farm products. In the 1850s, the farmers in the townships around the city raised good pigs, hogs with flesh made lean and firm by eating pea-meal mash. In 1860 a young British immigrant, William Davies, shipped a case of this Canadian back bacon back home for his brother to sell. Fifteen years later, William Davies was slaughtering and curing 30,000 hogs a year in his packing house on Toronto's Front Street. A quarter-century later his business was being run by Joseph Wesley Flavelle, the son of Irish-Protestants from the Peterborough region, who had learned his trade as a provision merchant before coming to Toronto. In 1900, Flavelle's William Davies Company, Ltd., shipped over 400,000 hog carcasses to Britain. It was the largest pork-packing company under the Union Jack, making Toronto the hog butcher to the Empire. That is why the city began to be called "Hogtown."

Overleaf: *Toronto c.1891. Ontario then produced three fifths of Canada's grain, half the hay, sheep and cattle, and more than two thirds of all the fruit, swine and dairy products. The financial district was spreading along Toronto's King Street.*
Left below: *William McMaster (1811-1887). Arriving in Canada from Ireland in 1833, McMaster started a wholesale dry-goods business, founded the Bank of Commerce in 1867, and was appointed to the Senate that year. He provided McMaster University, named in his honour, with a large endowment.*
Right top: *World's Largest Cheese. Weighing ten tonnes, this cheese, made at Perth in 1892, was sent to the Chicago World's Fair.*
Right middle: *Lean pigs made the best quality bacon, and were the basis for Toronto's meat-packing industry.*
Right below: *Tomatoes for the Heinz Factory, Leamington.*

CITIZENS BAND
PERTH

***Left top:** Niagara Peaches Ready for Shipment. The "tender fruit soil" and the protection against severe frosts afforded by the Niagara Escarpment, combine to make one of the best areas for peach growing on the continent.*
***Left middle:** Tobacco Field Near Leamington.*
***Far left middle:** Harris Open-End Binder, Brantford 1890.*
***Left below:** Steam Threshing Machine. A great advance in technology; these machines toured neighbourhoods at harvest time to thresh grain. Farmers shared the labour, and the day was a busy one for the women. Huge roasts and vast amounts of potatoes, pickles and pies were a "must" for men doing heavy work.*
***Right below:** Senator E.D. Smith of Winona. The founder of the jam-making firm, Smith's factory was in the heart of the Niagara Fruit Belt, close to the source of supply.*

(One of the little-noticed reasons for the pork packers' success was that Ontario farmers had been persuaded to switch from raising American breeds of round, fat hogs to the lighter, leaner British strains. Even the hogs in Ontario were Loyalists.)

William Davies and Joseph Flavelle made substantial fortunes exporting the bacon (proving, in a way, that you really could make a silk purse out of a sow's ear). Many other businessmen did well as importers and distributors of products that Ontario's farm families needed. The first great "merchant princes" of Toronto, men like (Senator) John Macdonald and (Senator) William McMaster, imported the dry goods and hardware and jewellery that the prospering Ontarians wanted. The wholesalers sent their merchandise on to the country general storekeepers and the small town retailers.

By the mid-1880s, rural Ontarians were ordering their goods by mail from the "World's Greatest Store," Timothy Eaton's giant department store in Toronto. When Eaton, an Ulsterman, moved into Toronto from St. Mary's, Ontario, in 1868, he was backed by his fellow Methodist, John Macdonald. His dry goods store grew into a department store, at first on the basis of his Toronto trade: Eaton had a good location, he sold everything at fixed prices (instead of forcing buyers to haggle), and he kept his customers happy. Business boomed when he discovered that thanks to his catalogues, the province's fine railway network, and a good postal service, he could sell to everyone in Ontario — and then, of course, all across Canada. If you didn't like Timothy Eaton's merchandise, you could always see what his canny competitor and imitator, Robert Simpson, had to offer. By 1900, Eaton's and Simpson's were the greatest retailers in Canada; their catalogues would have been the nation's bestsellers, except that they were given away free.

Of course, if you ran a farm you would buy that gold watch for your son or the English china for your wife only *after* the farmyard was properly equipped with mowers, binders, rakes, and other implements necessary to keep on top of the business of farming. The demand for farm implements created Ontario's most flourishing manufacturing industry. These agricultural implement factories, started by tinkers and craftsmen like Daniel Massey and Alanson Harris, turned into great businesses by their sons and grandsons. By the 1880s, the Masseys of Toronto and the Harrises of Brantford were shipping their products all over the world, and when they joined forces in 1891 to create the Massey-Harris Company, Limited, capitalized at the astonishing sum of $5,000,000.—that was Canada's first truly big manufacturing business.

Manufacturing — making things in factories — seemed to be the wave of Ontario's future in the 1880s. The prosperous countryside needed everything from pots and pans to pumps and pianos, and there seemed to be no good reason why they should not be made at home in Canada. The infant Ontario Manufacturers' Association stood four-square behind John A. Macdonald's "National Policy" of high tariffs against most imported products. Implemented in 1879, it gave a tremendous boost to domestic manufacturing (some said it was too much of a boost, for the farmers had to pay higher prices for goods "Made in Canada," and many of them did not like it). The "tall chimneys" of new factories sprouted like weeds across the province in the eighties — textile mills in Cornwall and Belleville; carriage works in Oshawa; the foundries and machine shops of Galt and Guelph; leather shops and furniture factories in Berlin; Labatt's and Carling's breweries in London (not factories, exactly, but the workingman needed his refreshment). In Windsor, Welland, St. Catharines, and other cities, the Canadian branch plants of big American firms were being forced to manufacture in Canada.

American enterprises were welcome to come to Ontario, just as the Loyalists had been, and if they brought their money and jobs with them, so much the better. American enterprise and capital were critical to founding the great blast furnaces in Hamilton in the 1890s, and there was that fantastic industrial wizard from Maine, Francis Hector Clergue, who used American investors' money to turn Sault Ste. Marie into the show-case city of "New Ontario" at the turn of the century.

Wait a minute. The wealth is supposed to be in agriculture. What are we doing in Sault Ste. Marie, among the rocks and trees and rapids of that unpopulated Northern Ontario wilderness?

It was turning out that modern Ontario was much more than a gar-

Right top: *St. Lawrence Paper Mill, Mille Roches.*
Far right top: *Chair Factory, Wingham. Craftsmen made the first chairs in small shops. Gradually, factories began to mass-produce furniture.*
Right middle: *Quaker Oats Mills, Peterborough.*
Far right middle: *View of Blind River. On the north shore of Lake Huron, Blind River is a centre for the pulp and paper industry.*
Right below: *Two Manufacturing Plants at Welland. The upper picture shows the Plymouth Cordage Company, maker of rope and string. The lower is Canada Steel Foundries, at a location convenient for the assembly of iron ore and coal.*
Left below: *Trenton Cooperage Mills. Barrels were needed for storing many items — flour, apples, nails.*

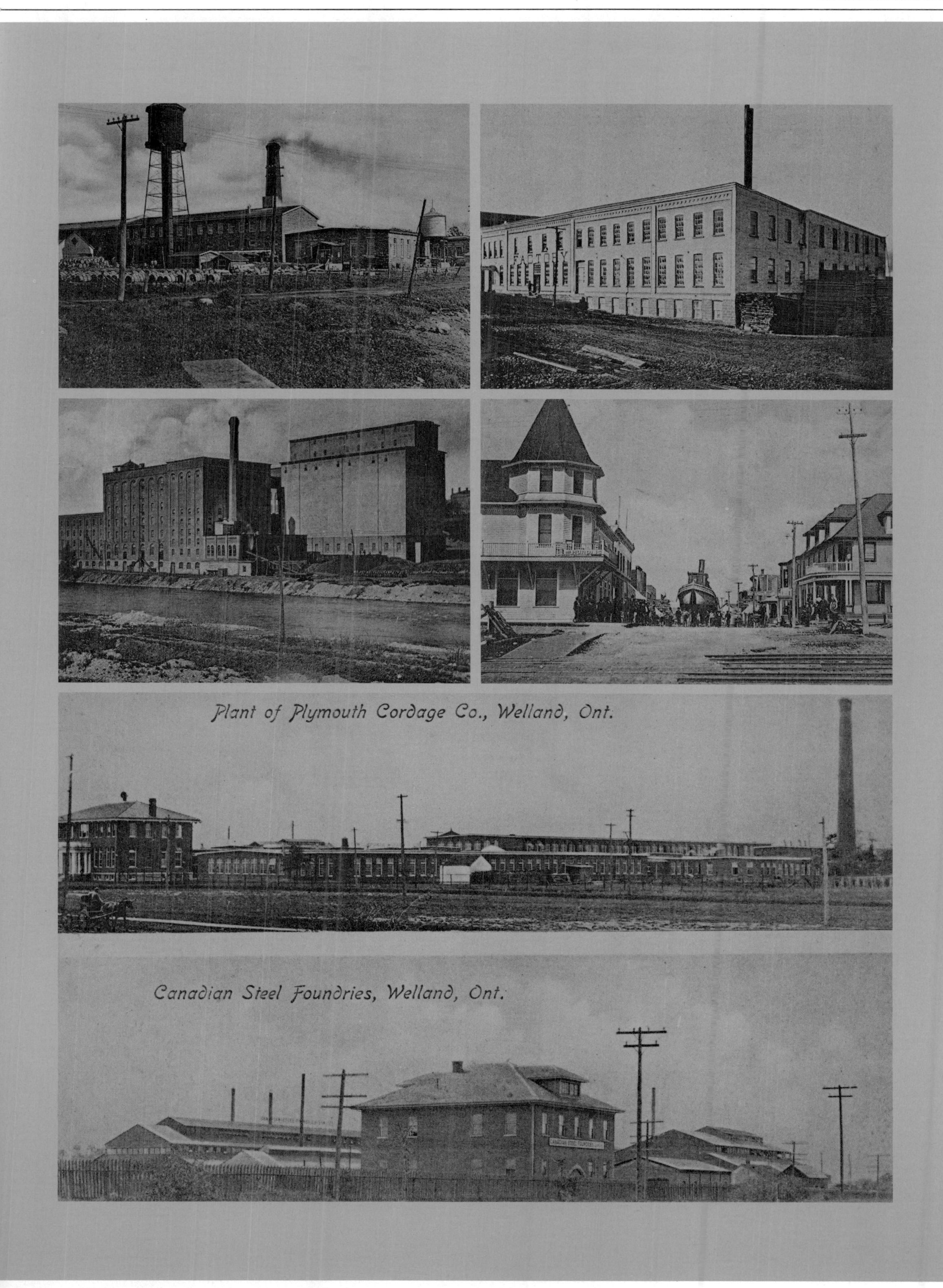
Plant of Plymouth Cordage Co., Welland, Ont.
Canadian Steel Foundries, Welland, Ont.

CANADIAN GENERAL ELECTRIC COMPANY

Left top: ***Electrical Development Company Power House, Niagara. The power house utilizes the drop of the great waterfall.***
Left middle: *Big Chute Power House, Severn River. Many power houses, large and small, were built on waterfalls to supply electricity to nearby towns, villages and farms.*
Left below: *Canadian General Electric Plant, Peterborough. With the development of hydro-electricity came improvements in small electrical appliances. In 1910, the Toronto Electric Light Company began a campaign to market 2,000 irons. Each weighed six pounds (more than two kg), and sold for $60.*
Right below: *Electric Car. The first streetcar is shown entering Port Stanley on Lake Erie on October 29, 1907.*

den carved out of a wilderness. It was not only the soil that was fertile in Ontario, but the trees, the rocks, even the waterfalls were becoming sources of great wealth. Don't think of Ontario as just that strip of farm country along the shores of Lakes Ontario and Erie. Think of the North, the vast territory around the shores of Huron and Superior, the Canadian Shield all the way up to Hudson Bay. Think of Ontario as Canada's agricultural heartland, yes, but also its timber capital and mineral treasure-house and hydro-electric powerhouse, too. Think of Empire Ontario.

The earliest settlers made a little money from potash as they cleared their land. Then the loggers moved north to hurl down the pine; hew it into great square timbers for the British market, and then into deals to go to the States. Wrights, Bronsons, Rathbuns, and Boyds made their good livings in the hard business of lumbering, and there was a real basis to Bytown/Ottawa's wealth before it started to flourish on tax money. The big stands of pine were becoming fewer and farther between by the end of the 19th century, but a whole new industry was developing to take those puny little spruce trees of the Shield; mash them into pulp and then roll them into paper. F.H. Clergue's first great factory at the Sault was a pulp and paper mill. The townsfolk literally danced around the machinery at its opening in 1896 because of the prosperity the enterprise would bring to the region.

The Sault had to keep pace with Sudbury, which was becoming the mining capital of Canada ever since they found all that copper and nickel ore along the main line of the CPR in the mid-eighties. No sooner said than done, it seemed, for F.H. Clergue's prospectors found major iron ore deposits in Algoma. They provided the raw material for his great steel mill in the wilderness. *Wilderness!* How can you call a country with so much wealth a wilderness? A few years later, over in Northeastern Ontario, the rocks of Cobalt turn out to be laced with silver. Then there seems to be gold everywhere — at Porcupine, Larder Lake, Kirkland Lake. You can have real mining booms, real gold rushes, just like they'd had in far-off California and the romantic Klondike, right here in Ontario, just an overnight train ride up from Toronto. It seemed that just about everywhere in Northern Ontario when a prospector threw his hammer it would strike something silver or yellow.

Then there was the "white gold" or the "white coal" to get Ontarians even more excited. This was power . . . energy . . . the new 20th century fuel . . . the hydro-electricity created when falling water turned turbines. Ontario had to import all its coal. But it had falling water all over the province, in the great rivers of the North, along the Ottawa and St. Lawrence, in the rapids at Sault Ste. Marie (which F.H. Clergue harnessed to drive all his other industries), and in stupendous quantities at Niagara. Niagara Falls had been awesome to look at, but had also been the worst darned obstacle to trade and commerce and the prosperity of the province. Now Niagara would drive the machinery in Ontario's factories, light the province's offices and parlours, and replace horse-power to drive the cars along the street railways of every city and town within 150 miles of the Falls. Is it any wonder that the dawn of the 20th century in Ontario glowed with currents of excitement?

Ontarians still relied on money from abroad — the province was a good place to invest in — to finance most of these new industries. But fascinating things were starting to happen with the handling of money. As the farm communities prospered, the merchants who served them also flourished and little pools of domestic savings were created. So was a demand for financial agents, people who could buy and sell mortgages, provide insurance, offer banking and trust services, sell stocks and bonds. At first it was outsiders, like U.S.-based insurance companies, or Quebec's Bank of Montreal, that provided most of Ontario's financial services. But gradually local people began to create their own institutions. The decrepit Family-Compact-founded Bank of Upper Canada collapsed in 1866, but within a year Senator McMaster and other Toronto merchants had founded the Bank of Commerce to take its place. Hamilton's Canada Life Assurance Company had been writing policies for almost twenty years before Confederation, and flourished in the decades afterwards as the farmers who had paid for their land began to think about their families. Banks, insurance firms, mortgage companies, real estate brokers, and financial agents sprang up like

Right top: *Imperial Oil Company, Sarnia. Sarnia is still the centre for a petrochemical industry.*
Far right top: *Talc Mine, Madoc. Talc is an ingredient of soaps, lubricants, pigments and talcum powder.*
Right middle: *Marmoraton Iron Mine, Marmora, 1972. The mine has closed since this photograph was taken.*
Right below: *Miners' Houses at Atikokan, 1968.*
Far right below: *Steel Plant, Sault Ste. Marie.*
Left below: *Sir Adam Beck (1857-1925). Born at Baden, of German descent, he was the son of Jacob Beck and Charlotte Hespeler. Elected to the Legislature in 1902, Beck introduced the bill that set up the Ontario Hydro-Electric Power Commission in 1906, and was its first chairman. He was knighted in 1914.*

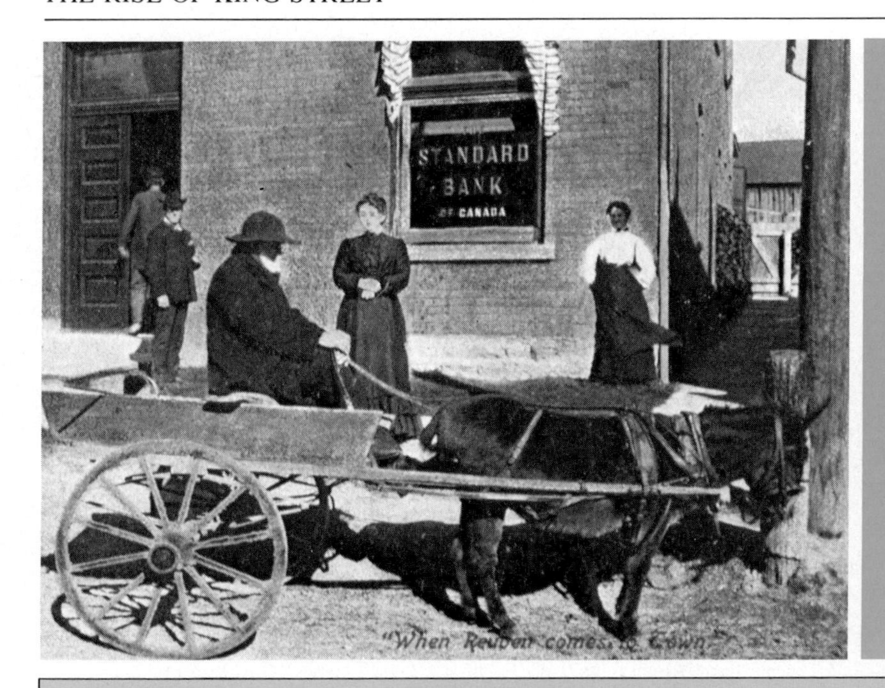

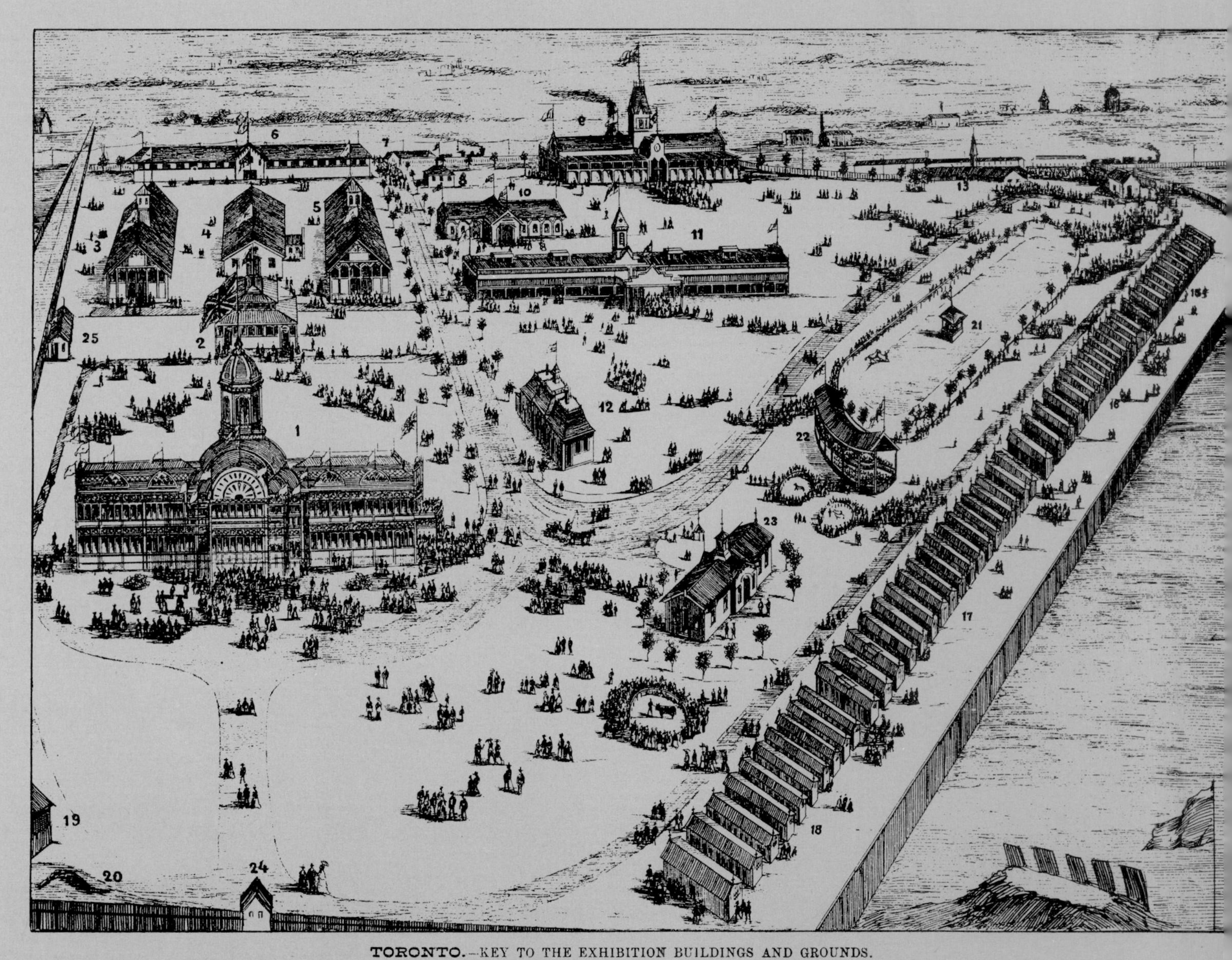

TORONTO.—KEY TO THE EXHIBITION BUILDINGS AND GROUNDS.

1. Main Building.
2. Dairy.
3. Agricultural Hall.
4. Restaurant with Kitchen.
5. Horticultural Hall.
6. Carriages.
7. Great Western Railway Ticket Office.
8. Hatching House (Chickens).
9. Machinery Hall.
10. Stoves.
11. Agricultural Implements.
12. Association Offices.
13. Poultry.
14. Strachan Avenue Lodge.
15. Pigs.
16. Horses.
17. Cattle.
18. Sheep.
19. Pioneers' Log Huts.
20. Cairn.
21. Judges' Stand (Horse Ring).
22. Grand Stand.
23. Police and Department of Public Comfort.
24. Wharf Station and Office (Comfort).
25. Dufferin Avenue Lodge.

Left top: **Molson's Bank, Morrisburg.** *Finance in Eastern Ontario tended to be tied to banking firms in Montreal, which was closer than the financial district on King Street.*
Far left top: *"When Reuben Comes to Town." The donkey and cart interested the photographer, but of more significance is the Standard Bank, Markham village, in the background.*
Left below: *Canadian National Exhibition. This annual fair is descended from the Crystal Palace Great Exhibition of 1851, of which Prince Albert was the chairman.*
Right below: *Toronto Board of Trade Building, 1900. The Board of Trade was a symbol of the city's role as a financial centre that began towards the end of the 19th century.*

mushrooms in the seventies and eighties. Even the fledgling Toronto Stock Exchange, founded in 1852, but moribund as often as not through the sixties and seventies, finally began to show some life (though even in a good year in the eighties the *total* volume of shares traded was less than 200,000!)

The liveliest single financier in all of Ontario, perhaps all of Canada, got his start in life insurance, real estate and mortgages in Peterborough, in the 1870s. George Albertus Cox came from a family of British immigrants who tried the United States in 1810 and then crossed the border in 1818, settling in Northumberland County. Born in 1840, George Cox began his Peterborough career in 1858 as a telegraph operator. Thirty years, six terms as mayor, innumerable real estate deals, life insurance policies, and railway promotions later, Cox and his family moved to Toronto to centralize their business interests. In 1900, Senator George A. Cox was president of the Canada Life, president of the Bank of Commerce, president of the Central Canada Savings and Loan Company, and president of half a dozen assorted lesser firms. His son-in-law, A.E. Ames, headed one of the most prominent stock-broking firms in the province, largely because so much of his father-in-law's business came his way. To handle bonds and debentures, George Cox set up Dominion Securities in 1901, which soon became the largest bond trading house in Canada — even after two of its employees broke away to form Wood Gundy and Company in 1905. In 1898, Cox also created the National Trust Company to do that kind of business. All the Cox companies' head offices were on King Street, the financial heart of Toronto. The Toronto Stock Exchange, located on King Street, rented its quarters from George Cox. He was the godfather of Toronto finance, his "family" of companies dealing in all kinds of transactions, controlling well over $50,000,000 in investment funds, a huge sum for the time.

All across the province prosperity led to the creation of a comfortable middle class and scatterings of a rich upper class — not to mention the considerable number of fairly well-off farm families who were beginning to send sons and daughters to university and take once-in-a-lifetime trips back to the Old Country. But it was Hogtown, more royally known as the Queen City, that stood at the centre of so much of the growth, and itself grew with dazzling speed. Toronto developed around a beautiful harbour, right in the centre of the province, a port for goods moving to and from Montreal, the Canadian terminus for produce being shipped down from the North and across Lake Ontario to New York and other American destinations. Then it became the railway hub of the province. All tracks seemed to lead through Toronto: the city had a hinterland to its east, a hinterland to the southwest, and two or three layers of hinterland to its north. Its population soared — from 86,000 in 1881 to 206,000 in 1901 and 375,000 in 1911, far outpacing disappointed rival centres like Hamilton. Toronto became the commercial, financial, even the manufacturing capital of the province, as well as its seat of government. The city was cleanly, godly, and very, very prosperous. Toronto the Good was Ontario's imperial capital.

Toronto's big businessmen had their sights set on new fields to conquer. If the Bank of Commerce could prosper in Ontario, surely it could compete with the Bank of Montreal right across the Dominion. There was a growing demand for life insurance around the world, and the Canada Life (which George Cox had imperiously moved from Hamilton to Toronto in 1899), had agents eager to sell their product anywhere. Many investors, foreign as well as Canadian, seemed to be fascinated with the coming new industries of the 20th century, and why shouldn't Toronto's financiers be the organizers of this great boom?

The Toronto financiers and industrialists seemed to be everywhere in Canada in the prosperous first decade of the new century. They were promoting bicycle and automobile companies (Canada Cycle & Motor — CCM — was launched in 1899 to do both), making strange new business forms for typewriters and duplicating machines (eventually that printer who had come out from England, S.J. Moore, would head the world's largest business form company), and founding streetcar and electrical companies everywhere — not just in Toronto, but in far-off Brazil, where the enterprises that became Brazilian Traction and finally Brascan were begun with Toronto financing, in the early 1900s.

The fine hand and cool smile of Senator Cox was everywhere in these

Right top: *Bank of Hamilton. Businessmen in towns and cities started local banks, but generally they were short-lived as independent operations. Many were bought out by larger banks as branches.*

Far right top: *Confederation Life Building c.1900. Still standing at Richmond and Yonge Streets, Toronto, the building was a symbol of the growth of the money economy.*

Right below: *Mutual Life Insurance Building. Not all head offices were near King Street. The Mutual Life head office is in Waterloo.*

Left below: *The Mail Building, King and Bay Streets, Toronto. Founded in 1872, in opposition to George Brown's Liberal* Globe, *the* Mail *was a Tory paper. The editor and manager, Thomas Patterson, was a friend and supporter of Sir John A. Macdonald.*

14

Left top: ***Sir Henry Pellatt (1859-1939). Commander of the Queen's Own Rifles from 1901 to 1921, Pellatt was knighted in 1905 for his service to the militia. He was a founder of the Toronto Electric Light Company, which brought the first hydro-electricity from the power plant at Niagara to Toronto.***

Far left top: *Casa Loma. This familiar landmark in Toronto was built by Sir Henry Pellatt. His first wife, Mary Dodgson Lady Pellatt, helped start the Girl Guide movement in Canada.*

Left below: *The Gzowski Family, 1855. Sir Casimir Gzowski (1813-1898), son of a Polish nobleman, came to Canada in 1842, worked as a government engineer, and formed his own company in 1853. He was the first chairman of the Niagara Parks Commission, and after serving as Queen Victoria's aide-de-camp in Canada, he was knighted at Windsor Castle in 1890.*

Right below: *Advertisement for Photography Firm, Richmond Hill, 1887.*

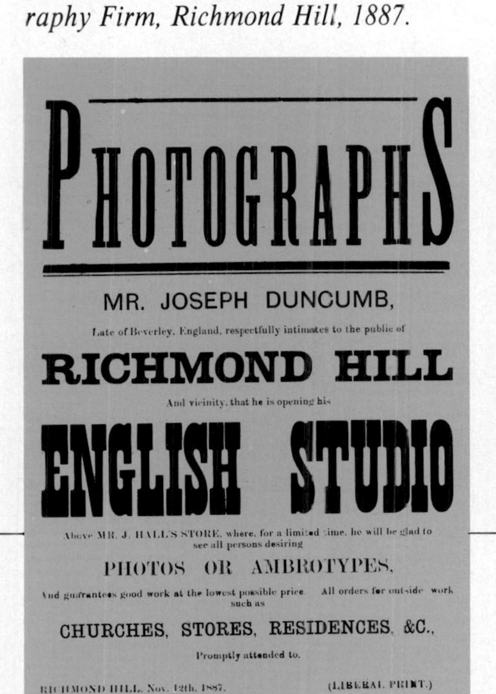

enterprises, but there were other "household" names on King Street: Ames, Massey, Flavelle, Frederick Nicholls, E R. Wood, E.B. Osler, the Pellatts — not the Eatons, who tended to mind their store — and the dynamic duo of railway contractors, William Mackenzie and Donald Mann. Like almost everyone else in the Toronto group, Mackenzie and Mann came out of small-town Ontario (was Toronto really such a great city, or was it just lucky to be surrounded by so many really productive communities?), made their first fortunes near home, and then decided there was no limit. Mackenzie and Mann were railroaders first and foremost: They saw no reason why two Ontario boys shouldn't build and own a transcontinental railway system to compete with the mighty Canadian Pacific. Backed by the Bank of Commerce, Mackenzie and Mann turned 125 miles of bankrupt Manitoba railway track into almost 10,000 miles of transcontinental railway (the Canadian Northern) by 1910. Most of the new track was west of the Great Lakes — in Manitoba, Saskatchewan, and Alberta. But wasn't that appropriate? Call it Hogtown or something even less flattering. You had to admit that it was Toronto's destiny to be the commercial, financial, and railway metropolis of Canada. Let the old money and cautious companies of Montreal slumber on in Quebec. Upper Canada's Loyalists had settled on the western frontier of British North America. Now their descendants lived in the vital centre of the great Dominion.

The great visions did not always work out exactly as the dreamers intended. The incredible American promoter, Clergue, tried to do far too much too soon at the Sault; he overexpanded, ran out of money, and watched his northern industrial empire collapse in bankruptcies and worker riots in 1903. Fortunately, little Canadian money was lost in the debacle, for the Toronto financiers had always suspected that Clergue was unsound. In turn, though, there were a lot of Ontario manufacturers who suspected that the private, Toronto-based companies, trying to develop Niagara's hydro-electric power, were bound to put their own profits and dividends before low rates and prompt service. Led by a cigar-box manufacturer from London, Adam Beck, the advocates of "public power" got the provincial government on their side, beat the

Nicholls-Pellatt-Mackenzie companies in the court of public opinion (the hustings rang with attacks on the "electrical ring" and counter charges of "socialism" and "confiscation"), and by 1910 had succeeded in creating Ontario Hydro, the world's first publicly-owned electricity distribution system. About that time, too, the handwriting was just starting to appear on the railway station wall, hinting that Canada had too much track, that the bottom line for the Canadian Northern might someday be bankruptcy (as it was in 1919, followed by reincarnation a few years later, under the same initials, as part of the CNR).

For the most part it was onward and upward in these heady Edwardian years of economic growth and social and political stability. There were no income or corporate taxes and while native-born Canadians were too proud and demanding to make good servants, the Motherland sent out a steady stream of maids, valets and chauffeurs. Most of the well-to-do were devout churchgoers, imbued with a sense of stewardship, who generously gave time and money to build the hospitals and universities and cultural institutions befitting a civilized Christian province. There was usually enough money left over to live very comfortably in mansions and country homes with good British names—"Oaklands," "Glendon Hall," "Holwood," "Oak Wold," and "Glen Stewart."

At the extreme, the Loyalist province had created so much wealth that one of her more eccentric sons, Colonel Sir Henry Mill Pellatt, a stock-broker and promoter who liked to demonstrate his loyalty by taking his regiment to England for a coronation and army manoeuvres, saw no reason why he should not live in his own "Old World" castle. He built it overlooking Toronto with towers, turrets, secret passages, oak and armour — part fairy-tale castle, part architectural monstrosity.

Sir Henry and Lady Pellatt moved into their "Casa Loma" in 1914. It was the same year that Senator George Cox died; the same year the Toronto Stock Exchange left King Street for new quarters on Bay Street. It was the same year the guns began to go off in Europe. Henry Pellatt's simple world of hard-working farmers and millionaire financiers started to collapse. Loyalty came to mean much more than spending your profits play-soldiering and building castles.

Right: *Bay Street Looking North Towards Old City Hall. Today, the name "Bay Street" is synonymous with high finance. To turn-of-the-century Ontarians, and to many others in Canada, that symbol was King Street.*
Left below: *King Street Looking From Yonge Street c.1914. Here lay the heart of the Ontario business community in the late 19th century, before the financial district spread up Bay Street.*
On pages 354-355:
Map of Ontario's Railway Network in 1899. Railways may have been instrumental in transporting passengers — but they were crucial in developing a thriving industrial economy throughout Ontario.

TRUSTS
GUARANTEE

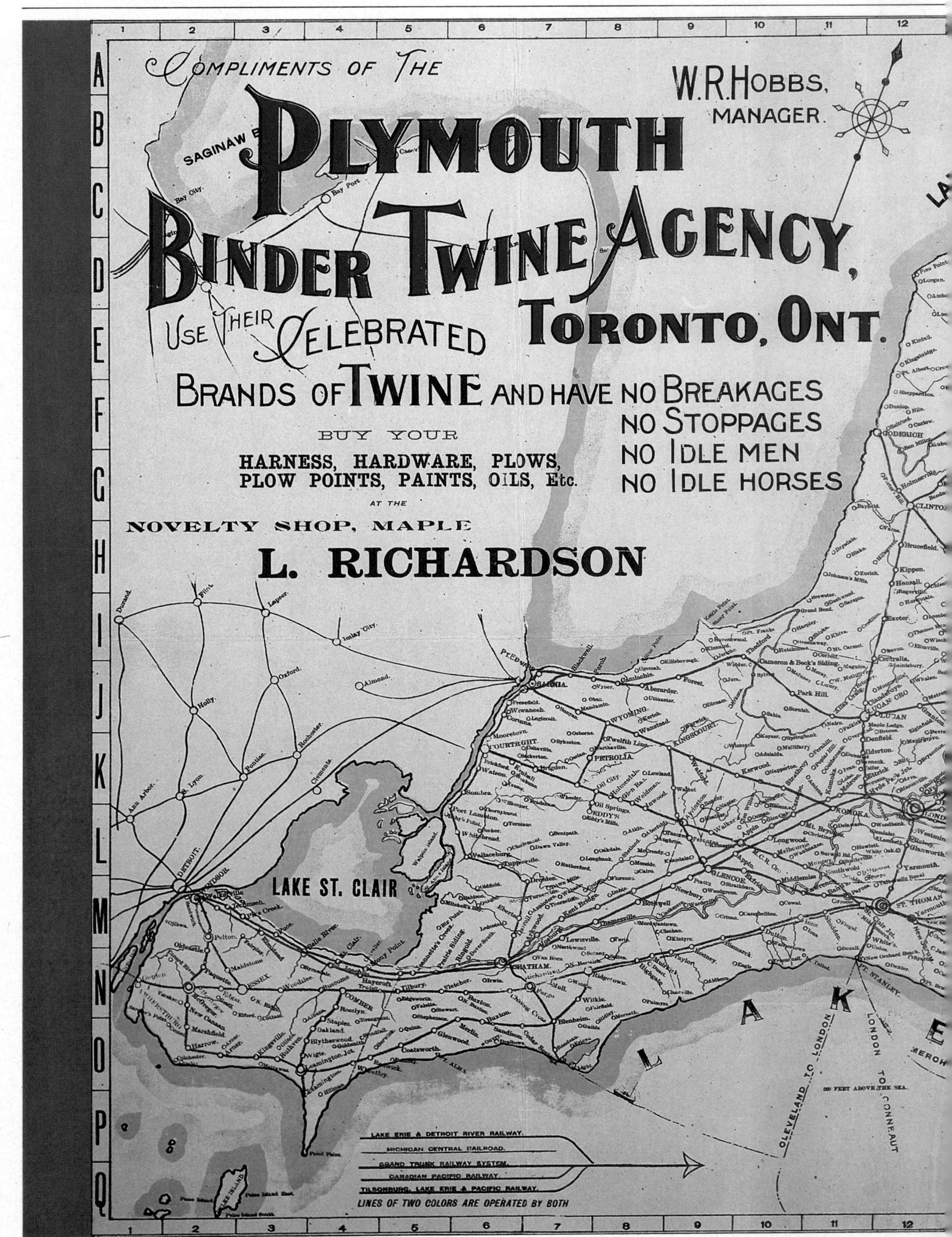

COMPLIMENTS OF THE
PLYMOUTH
BINDER TWINE AGENCY,
TORONTO, ONT.
W.R.HOBBS,
MANAGER.
USE THEIR CELEBRATED
BRANDS OF TWINE AND HAVE NO BREAKAGES
NO STOPPAGES
NO IDLE MEN
NO IDLE HORSES
BUY YOUR
HARNESS, HARDWARE, PLOWS,
PLOW POINTS, PAINTS, OILS, Etc.
AT THE
NOVELTY SHOP, MAPLE
L. RICHARDSON
LAKE ST. CLAIR
LAKE
SARNIA
CHATHAM
DETROIT
LAKE ERIE & DETROIT RIVER RAILWAY.
MICHIGAN CENTRAL RAILROAD.
GRAND TRUNK RAILWAY SYSTEM.
CANADIAN PACIFIC RAILWAY.
TILSONBURG, LAKE ERIE & PACIFIC RAILWAY.
LINES OF TWO COLORS ARE OPERATED BY BOTH
CLEVELAND TO LONDON
LONDON TO CONNEAUT

14 15 16 17 18 19 20 21 22 23 24 25
A B C D E F G H I J K L M N O P Q
RON
NOTTAWASAGA BAY
LAKE SIMCOE
OWEN SOUND
SOUTHAMPTON.
MEAFORD.
COLLINGWOOD.
ORILLIA
BARRIE
ORANGEVILLE
GUELPH
GALT
BERLIN
STRATFORD
WOODSTOCK.
BRANTFORD
MILTON
TORONTO
LAKE ONTARIO
NEW YORK
E R I E
LONDON TO MONTREAL
TERED ACCORDING TO ACT OF PARLIAMENT OF CANADA IN THE YEAR ONE THOUSAND EIGHT HUNDRED AND NINETY-NINE, BY THOS. A. BROWNE, LONDON, ONTARIO, IN THE OFFICE OF THE MINISTER OF AGRICULTURE.
London Printing and Lithographing Co., LIMITED, PUBLISHERS.

Left top: *Gray's Carriage Works, Chatham. Factories like Gray's built magnificent vehicles with leather hoods.*
Left below: *McLaughlin Carriage Company, Oshawa. Founded by Robert McLaughlin, his son R.S. (Colonel Sam) McLaughlin, soon got interested in automobiles. In 1908, he built 154 F cars. These caught the eye of three Brockville brothers, Bill, Charlie and Fred Beacock, who had been selling Fords since 1903. Beacock and Company became McLaughlin's first dealership outside Oshawa. The Beacocks had been "selling cars when McLaughlin was still making buggies."*
Right top: *Tudhope Car Factory, Orillia. Henry Ford produced his first experimental car in 1896, and Ontarians were not far behind. Long-forgotten makes were made in small factories such as Tudhope's.*

Far right: *Traders Bank, Toronto — A Comparison. The Traders Bank is compared to a New York building and the new steamer* Cayuga.
Right middle: *Talbot Street East, Leamington, When Automobiles Were a Novelty.*
Right below: *Goodyear Rubber Works, Bowmanville. The rubber industry grew with the expansion of the automobile industry. Bowmanville, close to Oshawa, was a good location for tire production.*

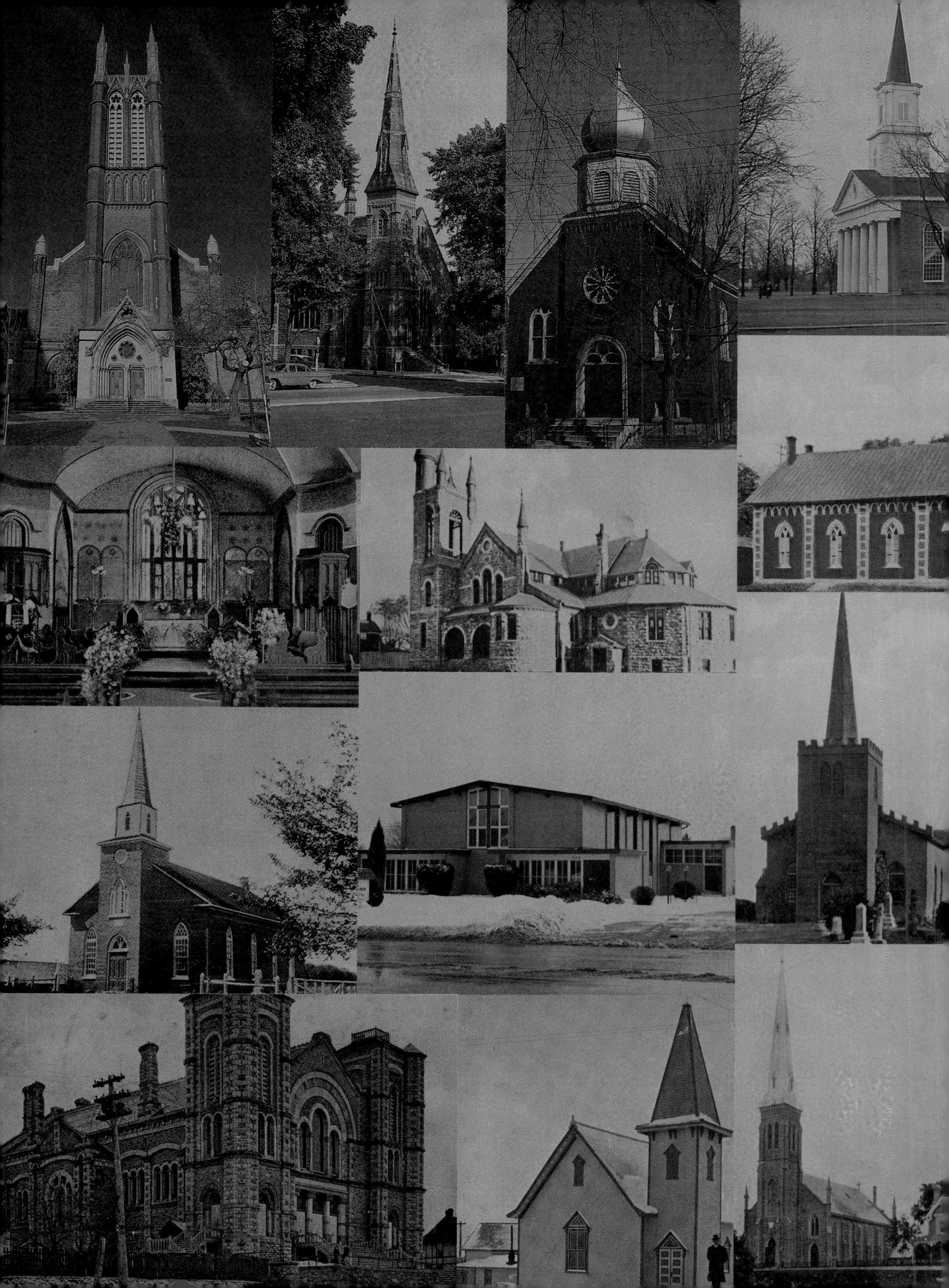

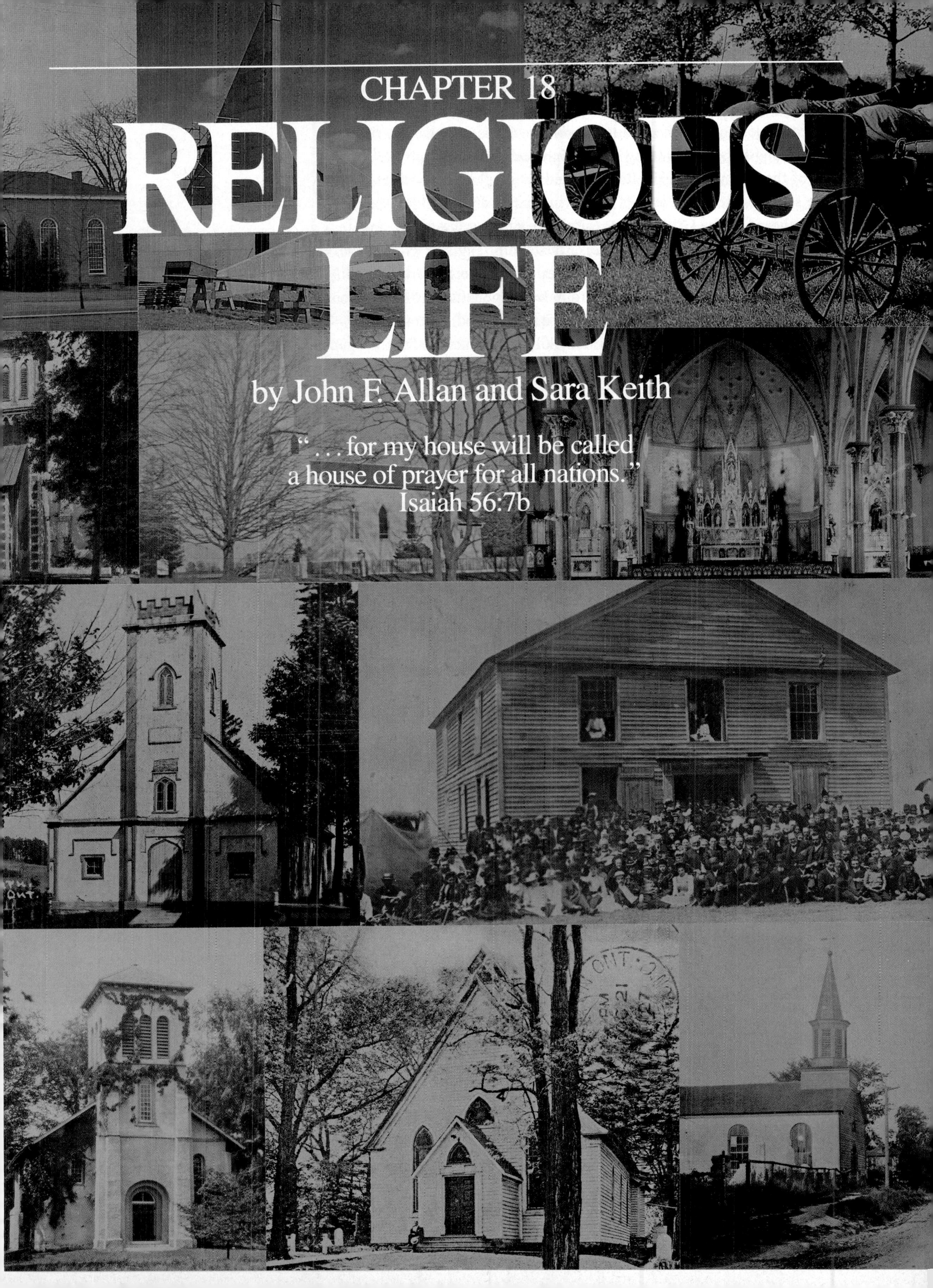

CHAPTER 18

RELIGIOUS LIFE

by John F. Allan and Sara Keith

"...for my house will be called
a house of prayer for all nations."
Isaiah 56:7b

there she was sent on with other refugees to Montreal. Paul retired from the army in 1779, and worked as a carpenter until they decided to take up land in Augusta.

At first, the Methodists were served by lay preachers, as were the Mennonites who came north soon after the Loyalist migration, and the earliest Baptists. Among the first Methodist preachers was William Losee, from New York State, who toured the St. Lawrence settlements in 1790 while on his way to the Bay of Quinte. The following year, by popular request, he was appointed missionary to the latter settlement by the New York Conference of the Methodist Episcopal Church.

The Church of England soon sent a missionary to assist Reverend John Stuart. He was Reverend John Langhorn, who arrived in Kingston in 1786. He travelled throughout the Bay of Quinte settlements, and in 1791 his parishioners opened St. Paul's Church in Fredericksburgh. By 1793 he had a two-point charge when St. John's Church in Bath was completed.

In 1784 there were two Roman Catholic priests in the western wilderness. One was Father John St. Hubert, at Detroit, who cared for his French-speaking flock in the Parish of Assumption, across the Detroit River. The other was Father Roderick Macdonell, missionary to the Indians of St. Regis, who visited the settlers in Charlottenburgh Township in 1785. The following year Father Alexander Macdonell of Scotus led a group of Highlanders from Scotland to what became Glengarry County. They settled among their fellow Highlanders who had served in Loyalist regiments. The priest soon founded the Parish of St. Raphael, in Charlottenburgh. In the churchyard lie Simon Fraser, the explorer, and John Sandfield MacDonald, Ontario's first premier.

The next priest was Father Edmund Burke, from Ireland, who toured the settlements from 1794 until 1801. Then he left for Nova Scotia, where he became Bishop of Halifax, and he encouraged a lad named Michael Power to enter the priesthood.

In 1789, the German-speaking Lutheran settlers of Williamsburgh Township, Dundas County, invited Reverend Samuel Swerdfeger, a Loyalist still in Albany, to come as their minister. He arrived in 1790

__Left top:__ Barbara Heck (1734-1804). The grave of the "Mother of Methodism in North America" is in the Blue Church cemetery, west of Prescott.
__Left below:__ The Blue Church. In 1809 residents of Augusta and Elizabethtown Townships built a chapel on the New Oswegatchie town plot, which caught fire in 1840. The present church was built in 1845.

***Right:** U.E.L. Memorial Window, Grace United Church, Napanee. Donated and unveiled on October 16, 1983, by George L. van Koughnett, the window was designed by Theo Lubbers of Montreal. It commemorates the Loyalists, especially the men of the King's Regiment of New York and their families, who settled around Napanee in 1784.*

and dedicated Zion Church. The Dutch Reformed Presbyterians, too, received ministers quite early. The Reverend John Ludwig Broeffle served in Williamsburgh for thirty years, while Reverend Robert McDowell was sent by the Albany Synod to the Bay of Quinte, where three congregations were organized — in Adolphustown, Ernestown and Fredericksburgh.

The Mohawks and other members of the League of the Iroquois had resettled in Ontario because they had been military allies of the Crown. A different group of natives arrived by way of Detroit in 1791, as much refugees as the others. They were Delawares, led by their missionary, David Zeisberger, of the Moravian Church. They settled on the Thames River, where they proceeded to clear land and cultivate it — a mixed community of Old World and New World Christians. They called their settlement Fairfield, but today it is known as Moraviantown, on the Indian Reserve above Thamesville. Fairfield was on the path of east-west travel to and from Detroit, and during the War of 1812 the settlement of the Moravians, who were pacifists and exempt from military service, was sacked and burned by the Americans. Led by the missionary of the Chippawa Indians, Christian Frederick Denke, the surviving Moravians took refuge in Burlington for the duration of the war. In 1815 they returned to rebuild New Fairfield on the south bank of the Thames opposite the old site.

After 1791, the year Vermont joined the American Congress as a state, many Loyalists who had hoped that Vermont might become a British province left for Canada. Among them came a party of Baptists, led by their elder, Abel Stevens. They settled in Bastard Township, Leeds County, and the congregation they organized in 1803 still exists as the Philipsville Baptist Church. Another Baptist congregation was organized near West Lake, Prince Edward County, where the missionary was Reuben Crandel and he began his work in 1799.

Upper Canada became a separate province in 1791, and the following year Lieutenant Governor John Graves Simcoe arrived, expecting that the Church of England would be the established one. One seventh of the land was to be reserved for the support of a Protestant clergy under the terms of the Constitutional Act that set up the new province. Simcoe interpreted this as meaning the Church of England, and to encourage allegiance to that church, in 1793 he had an act passed by the Legislature stipulating that only Anglican clergymen could perform marriages. Where no clergyman resided within eighteen miles, marriages could be conducted by the magistrates. Roman Catholic priests were exempt, but ministers of other denominations were not, especially lay preachers such as Methodists and Baptists, who were not required to study theology. (In 1798 ministers of the Church of Scotland were allowed to perform marriages, but the others were not so empowered until 1831.)

Simcoe also advertised that Quakers in the United States would be welcome in Upper Canada, and exempt from bearing arms. Although Simcoe needed settlers to serve in the militia, his plan was not without logic. He needed a "land army" of farmers to stay home and produce food. Some Quakers went to Prince Edward County, others to the Niagara Peninsula or north of York on Yonge Street. Among the Quakers was David Willson, a resident of Newmarket, who regretted that music was not part of the Friends' meetings. In 1812 he founded his own sect, the "Children of Peace," in order to have instrumental and vocal music in his services. In 1825 he built the now-restored temple in the village of Sharon.

Even before Simcoe encouraged pacifist sects, which included Mennonites as well as Quakers, to come to Upper Canada, Anglicans were numerically a minority. Reverend John Stuart, reporting to the Society for the Propagation of the Gospel in 1787, noted with disapproval that most Upper Canadians were Presbyterians, Anabaptists, Dutch Calvinists or New England "Sectaries," and that such had been encouraged when the government allowed John Bethune, the Presbyterian minister at Williamstown, a stipend of fifty pounds. Not long before Simcoe left Upper Canada, Thomas Raddish, an Anglican clergyman, arrived to be the missionary in York, the capital. Raddish stayed only six months, long enough to obtain grants of land, before he returned to the comforts of England in 1797.

Left below: *Reverend Samuel Swerdfeger. By 1789 the Lutherans in Williamsburg, Dundas County, had built a small frame church. They invited him to be their pastor. He arrived in 1790 and dedicated their building Zion Church.*

Left and right bottom: *Synagogue at 25 Richmond Street East, Toronto. The first Jewish congregation in Canada West was formed in 1856. In 1876 the*

first Holy Blossom Temple, shown here, was built. The congregation moved to the present building on Bathurst Street in 1937.
Right below: *Lewis Samuel (d.1888). Born in England, Samuel came to Toronto in 1856. With his wife Kate (d.1904), Joseph Lyons and others, Samuel helped found the first Jewish congregation in the province.*

The Simcoe family's interest in Upper Canada did not end with its departure in 1796. At Sibbald Point, on Lake Simcoe, is St. George's Anglican Church. A member of the founding family, Mrs. Susan Sibbald, was a friend of the Simcoes. The governor's daughters painted a stained glass window that was installed in St. George's in 1845.

Qualified religious leaders were thinly spread for the first few decades, but churches were even slower to materialize. Barbara and Paul Heck were quick to hold Methodist classes in their cabin, and other denominations also held services in their homes. The first church actually built was the Anglican St. Paul's Chapel of the Mohawks at Grand River. In it were placed four pieces of the communion silver that had been sent by Queen Anne in 1712. The other three pieces went to Tyendinaga and were later kept in Christ Church, Deseronto.

The second church was built by Roman Catholics in the Parish of Assumption (Windsor) in 1787, although the congregation was much older. In 1789 the Lutherans built a chapel on Bowerman's Hill, Marysburgh Township, Prince Edward County. Two Methodist churches were erected in 1792, one at Hay Bay, Adolphustown, generally considered the older, and the other not far away in Ernestown Township. Quakers who settled in Prince Edward County formed a congregation in the 1790s, but they did not build a meeting house until 1803.

On the Niagara Peninsula, a Presbyterian congregation was formed in Stamford Township in 1785, but the first church, St. Andrew's, was built at Niagara-on-the-Lake about 1794. During the War of 1812 it was destroyed by the Americans because its steeple gave the British a clear view of the fortifications on the New York side of the Niagara River. An Anglican clergyman, Reverend Robert Addison, started a congregation at Niagara-on-the-Lake in 1792, but the first church, St. Mark's, was not built until 1807. Like St. Andrew's, St. Mark's was destroyed by the Americans and later rebuilt. In 1786 George Neal, a Methodist, began preaching at the home of Christian Warner near Queenston. The first Baptist congregation on the peninsula was organized at Beamsville by Jacob Beam in 1788.

Of interest is the Blue Church, built on the town plot in Augusta

Township, Grenville County, for its founders were ecumenical. Known for its colour through three successive buildings, the first dated from 1809, the third from 1845. Officially it was a Church of England, but of the twelve original subscribers, nine may have been Anglicans. James Breakenridge was a Presbyterian, Paul Heck a Methodist, and Elijah Bottum a Baptist. The final church, still standing, is very small, for by 1845 it was obvious that no village was ever going to grow on the town plot. Now services are held there only occasionally, but the burying ground is large. In it lie members of many pioneer families, and the Methodists of North America have erected a monument to Barbara Heck, in memory of her contribution to the founding of the church in the new land.

Until the middle of the 19th century, by which time parts of Ontario were acquiring an aura of civilization, church architecture was not imposing. For instance, the first building used as a church in Carleton County, of logs, was in March Township and was originally a home. Many of the large churches near the cores of Ontario's cities, and the smaller but often fine ones dotted about in rural hamlets, date from the second half of the last century.

A feature in the lives of all who preached the gospel was travel — journeying over long distances to visit members of denominations in their settlements. Reverend John Stuart, based in Kingston, could reach his Mohawk flock at Tyendinaga easily, but he went occasionally to minister to the Iroquois at Grand River. Father Alexander Macdonell wrote a description of his work in 1826, the year he became Bishop of Kingston:

> For several years we had to travel of the whole Province from Lake Superior to the Province line of Lower Canada in the discharge of our pastoral duties, carrying the Sacred Vestments, sometimes on horseback and sometimes in small Indian birch canoes, crossing the great lakes and descending the rapids of the Ottawa and St. Lawrence in those miserable crafts, living with the Indians and sleeping in the woods.

Best known for their itinerant habits were the Methodist saddlebag

Right top: *St. Edward's Catholic Church, Westport. Built in 1859, the church stands close to Upper Rideau Lake.*
Far right top: *Quaker Meeting House, Newmarket. Like the dress of the "Plain Folk," the Quakers' meeting houses were plain.*
Right middle: *Sharon Temple, North of Toronto. The temple was built by the followers of David Willson (1778-1866), who formed a sect that broke away from the Quakers.*
Right middle centre: *Holy Trinity Church, Chippawa. Among those who worshipped here were: the singer Jenny Lind in 1851; Edward Prince of Wales in 1860; and parishioner Laura Secord.*
Far right middle: *Church of Our Lady Immaculate, Guelph. This Gothic church, on its hilltop, is one of the most attractively sited churches in Ontario.*
Right below: *Altar, Christ Church (Anglican), Deseronto. The tablets, in Mohawk, are copies of tablets in the Mohawk chapel at Fort Hunter, New York, that were destroyed during the American Revolution.*
Far right below: *A Polish Church in Wilno, Renfrew County. Wilno, east of Barry's Bay, was settled in the 1860's by immigrants from Poland.*

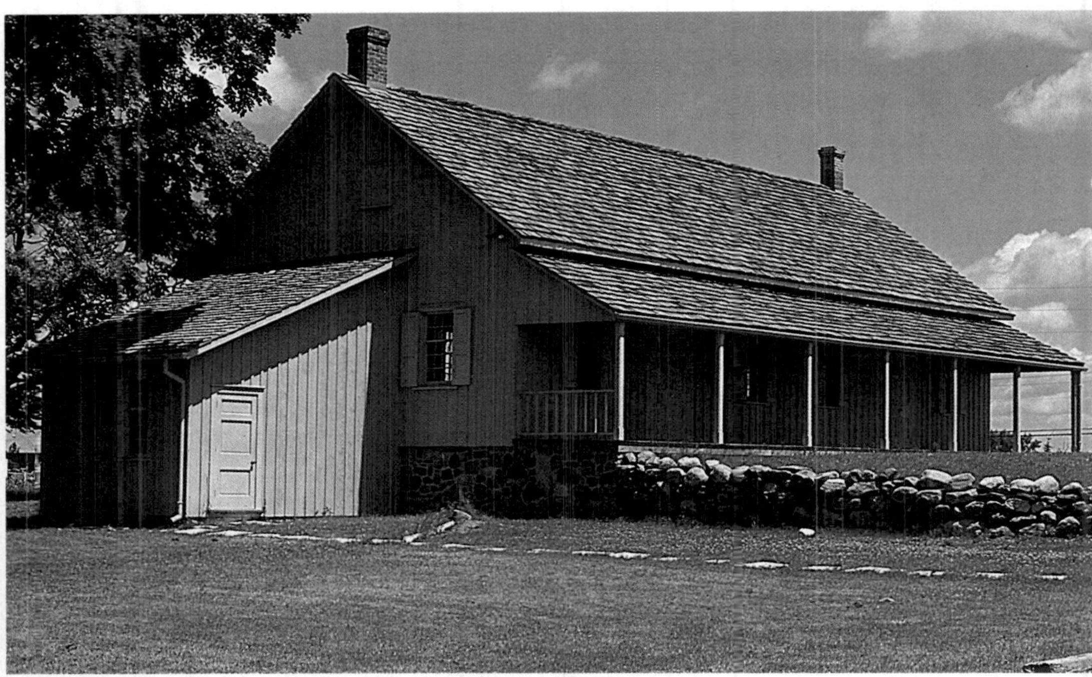

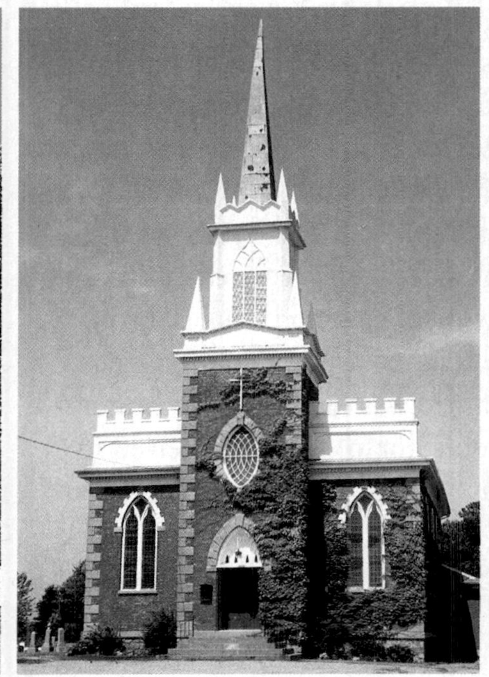

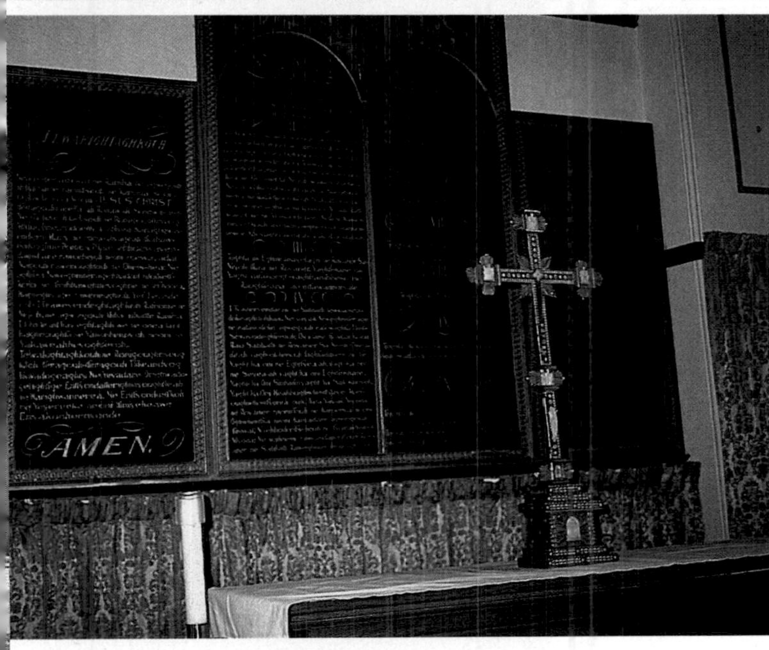
AMEN

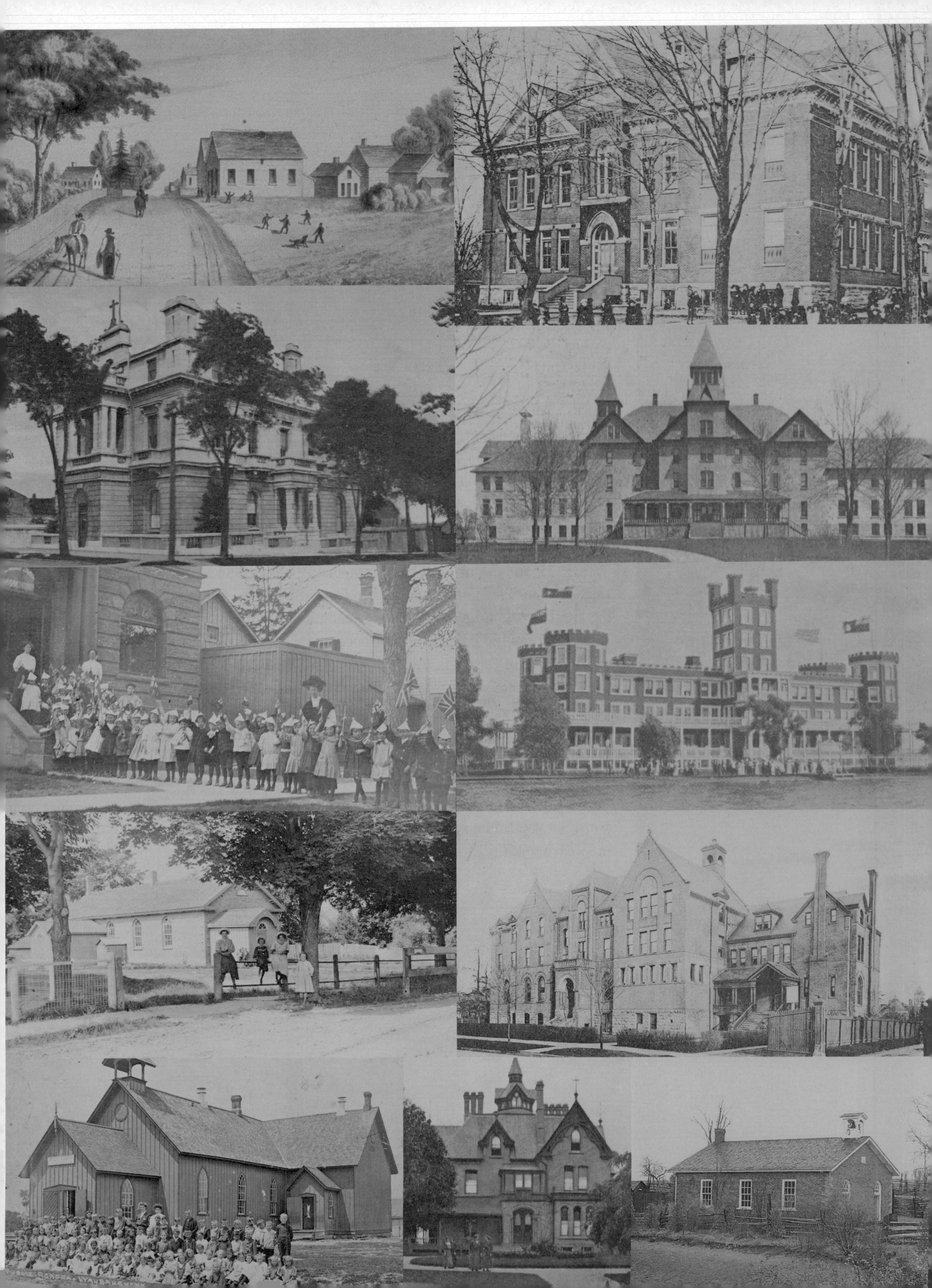

CHAPTER 19

EDUCATION & SOCIETY IN THE 19th CENTURY

by Paul Axelrod

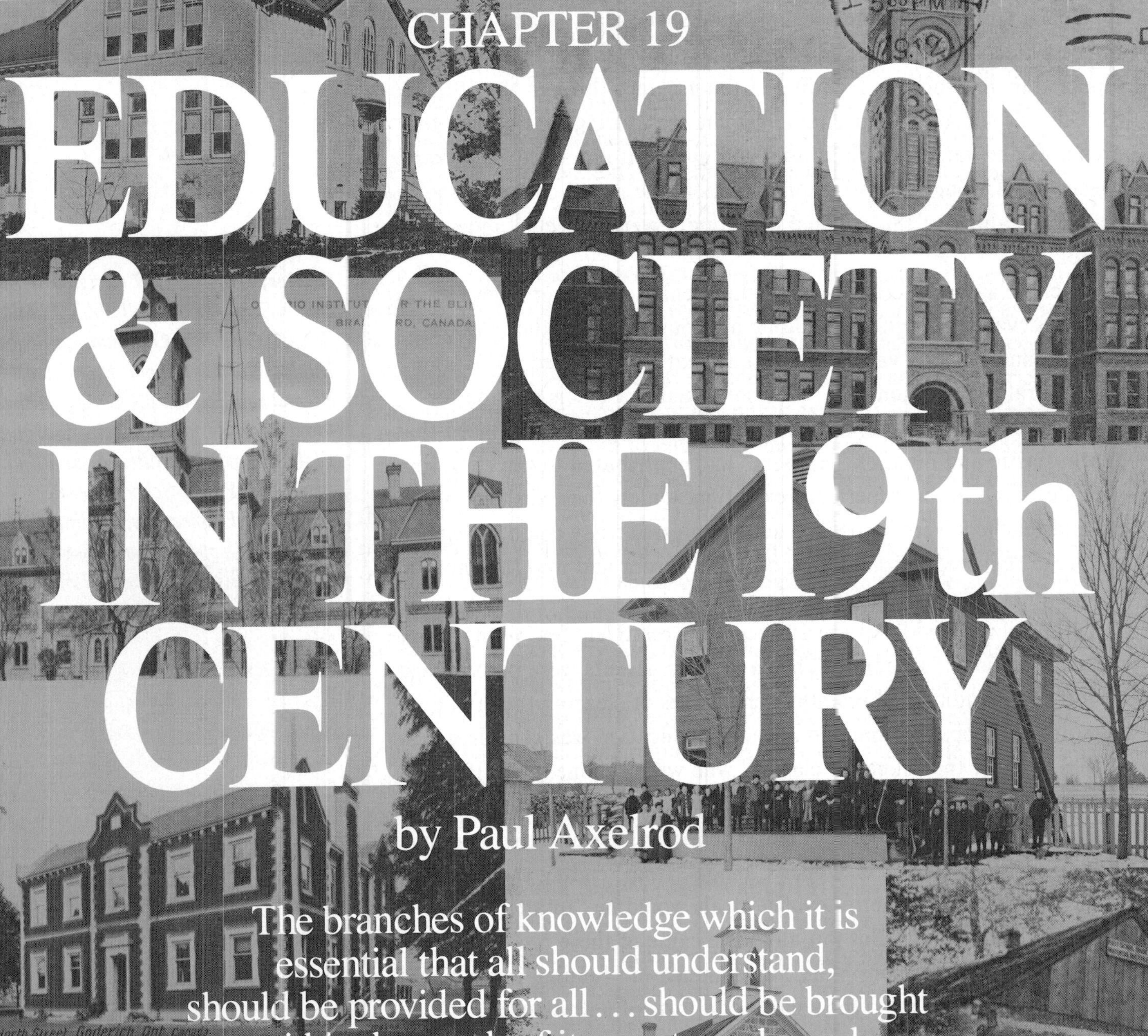

The branches of knowledge which it is essential that all should understand, should be provided for all . . . should be brought within the reach of its most needy, and forced upon its most careless.

EGERTON RYERSON, 1846

utilitarian, educational system.

Universities, too, felt the impact of the industrial revolution. While retaining their highly elitist character, developments in their own professional programs reflected the growth of the major resource sectors of the economy. Queen's opened a school of mining in 1893 and an engineering faculty in 1905. The University of Toronto established a school of forestry in 1907.

New pressure, however, did not displace old and cherished values. The resurgence of British imperialism towards the end of the 19th century tapped the deeply rooted Loyalist heritage of the province. The glories of the British Empire were already celebrated in school textbooks. The Diamond Jubilee of 1897 inspired an enthusiastic reassertion of that faith. Empire Day in the schools of Ontario honoured the past and hailed the future with a massive display of speeches, sporting events, and military rituals that became an annual event on Queen Victoria's birthday. For George Ross, the Minister of Education, the commitment to imperialism sustained and fired a passionate devotion to Canadian nationalism. He was proud of having helped "instill into the half million school children of the Province a greater love of Ontario, for Canada, and for the Empire than was previously entertained."

The principles of imperialism, capitalism and Christianity formed the core of school programs designed to "Canadianize" the legions of foreign students whose families settled in Ontario after the beginning of the great immigration wave of 1896. Quickly, they were "singing God Save the King, saluting the flag, reciting the Lord's Prayer and a short Bible reading." Like their Canadian classmates, they were taught to be punctual, obedient, and respectful of the law.

The world had changed since the Loyalists first entered the province, but education inherited and upheld the ideals they treasured. While the 20th century might diminish, it would never eliminate their influence on the cultural and political life of Ontario.

Right top: *Lutheran Seminary, Waterloo. The seminary became Waterloo Lutheran University, renamed Wilfred Laurier when it became secularized.*
Far right top: *Summerhill, Queen's University, Kingston. The building became part of Queen's after 1842.*
Right middle: *McMaster University, Toronto. Founded as the Toronto Baptist College, it moved to Hamilton in 1930. The Royal Conservatory of Music now occupies the building.*
Far right middle: *Royal Military College, Kingston. The college was founded in 1876 to train officers for the newly formed Canadian army.*
Right below: *Laurentian University, Sudbury, in 1968. Laurentian was established in 1960.*
Far right below: *Trent University, Peterborough. The buildings were designed by two firms — Ron Thom, and Thompson, Berwick and Pratt.*
Left below: *Brock University Poster.*

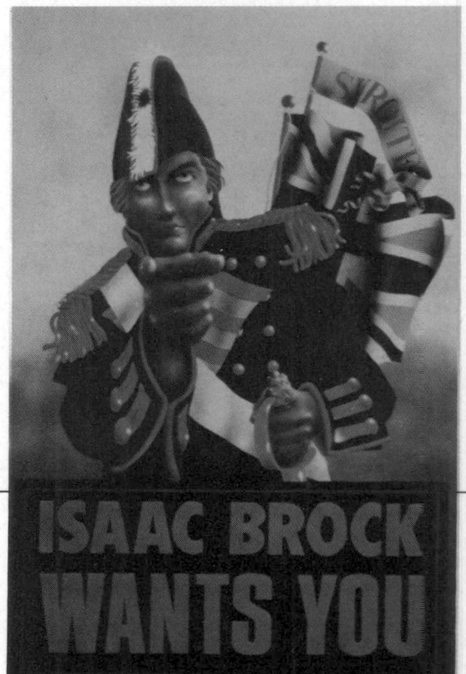

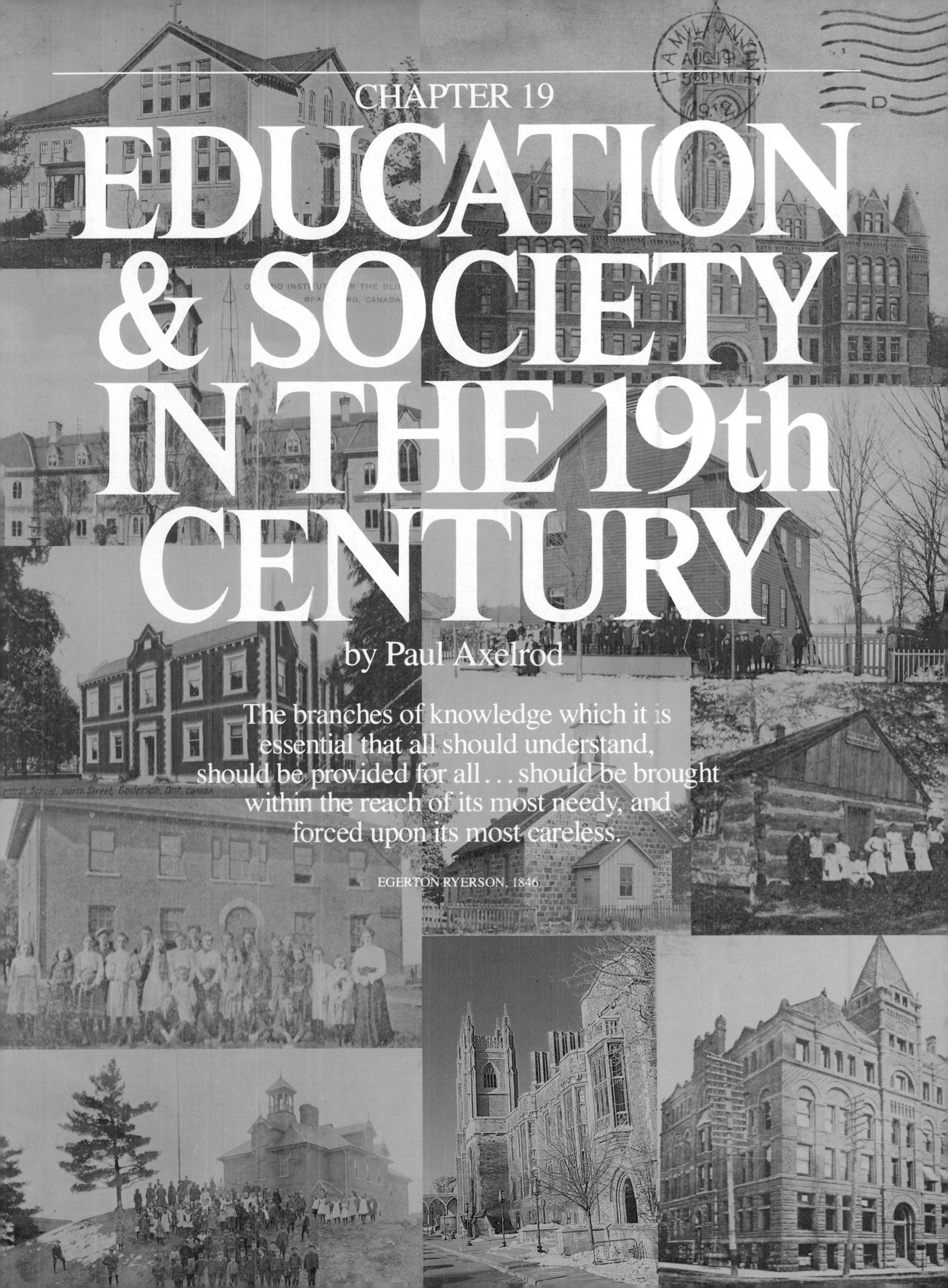

CHAPTER 19

EDUCATION & SOCIETY IN THE 19th CENTURY

by Paul Axelrod

The branches of knowledge which it is essential that all should understand, should be provided for all . . . should be brought within the reach of its most needy, and forced upon its most careless.

EGERTON RYERSON, 1846

Loyalism, Christianity, the economy, and social class — these were the forces which shaped the development and orientation of education in Upper Canada from the founding of the province through the 19th century. While schooling underwent vast changes during that period, the pressures and values which infused and guided it remained remarkably consistent. Through the prism of education, the moral concerns and the material realities of this colonial community were reflected and exposed.

When he assumed office in 1791, Lieutenant Governor John Graves Simcoe devoted himself to moulding a colony which fit the religious, political and military values of the time that he cherished. Education was central to his vision. His successors would carry his mission forward. With other like-minded compatriots, Simcoe was convinced that "enthusiastic and fanatick Teachers" had contributed to the conspiracy which erupted in the American revolution. Unless these disloyal preachers and teachers were unmasked and suppressed, they could be expected to spread their republican heresy over the border and into the churches, homes and classrooms of Upper Canada.

Yet, until the middle of the 19th century relatively few young people received "official" schooling. They and their parents were preoccupied with the demanding and relentless challenges of clearing the land and planting the crops. Formal and advanced education was considered essential only for the "superior classes" who were destined to guide and govern society. In this spirit Simcoe had sought direct support from the British government for both grammar schools and a university designed to keep the "Gentlemen of Upper Canada" from sending their children to the United States where Loyalist ideals would be "totally undermined and subverted." But initially little came of these projects, with the result that the responsibility for founding and funding institutional education depended upon the voluntary efforts of ambitious educators and committed parents. By 1800 about twenty privately run schools had been started by Loyalists throughout Upper Canada.

The most influential of the province's early teachers was John Strachan. A Scottish immigrant who converted from the Presbyterian to the

Overleaf: *Top row (left to right): Strachan's School, Cornwall 1803; Public School, Cornwall; Continuation School, Dublin; Normal School, Hamilton.*
Second row: *Regiopolis College, Kingston; Indian Residential School, Mount Elgin; Ontario Institute for the Blind, Brantford; Public School, Keene.*
Third row: *Empire Day, Collingwood; Foresters' Orphans' Home, Deseronto; Central School, Goderich; Wyndham's Centre School; Old School House, Waterloo.*
Fourth row: *Public School, Cedar Dale; Wycliffe College, Toronto; Public School, Bath; Hart House, University of Toronto; College of Physicians and Surgeons, Toronto 1891.*
Fifth row: *Public School, Waubaushene; Bishop Bethune Anglican College, Oshawa; Black Creek Village School, Toronto; Public School, Tweed.*
Right below: *Statue of Robert Raikes (1735-1811), Queen's Park, Toronto. Raikes, of Gloucester, England, founded the Sunday School movement, originally intended to provide some education to children for whom schools were not available.*

Anglican faith, he opened a grammar school in Cornwall in 1803. There the traditional offering of classical education was supplemented by more practical training suitable for the business and political careers its students were destined to occupy. Its graduates included an impressive list of individuals — many, incidentally, did not come from Loyalist families — who later joined the ranks of the Family Compact.

In 1807 the province's first important school legislation was passed. The District Public School Act called for the creation of a grammar (or secondary) school in each of the province's eight districts. These schools would continue to charge tuition fees, rendering them still inaccessible to those of humble means, but for the first time teachers' salaries were to be partially subsidized from the public treasury. Through this Act the principle of state aid to education had come to Upper Canada.

But education for all was far from reality. While there is considerable evidence that voluntary efforts and informal training in private homes, Sunday schools, and church-run settings provided many Upper Canadian children with some basic experience in reading and writing, pressures began to build for more systematic changes. Anglicans had never been numerically superior in the province, and communities of Methodists, Presbyterians, Baptists and Roman Catholics grew to resent being excluded from clergy reserve entitlements. Elementary or common school facilities remained expensive, inaccessible, or entirely unavailable. From the Anglican — and Loyalist — perspective, John Strachan, like Simcoe before him, feared the continuing influence of "Yankee adventurers" among the ranks of itinerant teachers. His concerns deepened as a result of the War of 1812.

The Common School Act of 1816, sponsored by Strachan, extended state aid to those communities which hired teachers and resolved to provide regular instruction to the young. The Act required instructors either to be natural-born subjects of Great Britain or to have taken the oath of allegiance to the Crown. There were severe limitations in the scope of the legislation. No grants were provided for building or maintaining schools, and most communities continued to charge tuition fees. Teachers' salaries remained low; teachers themselves had little prestige;

and common school facilities were unevenly distributed throughout the province. Furthermore, the legislation banning American teachers was ineffectively enforced. By the mid-1820s, universal education for the youth of Upper Canada seemed a distant prospect. Financial crises rendered government aid unreliable. According to Strachan, the common schools served a total of only 7,000 pupils and grammar school training was available to just 300 boys. University education, first proposed by Simcoe, and long sought by Strachan, had yet to arrive on the scene. While Strachan succeeded, in 1827, in obtaining a charter from the British government for the creation of the University of King's College, an institution intended mainly to train Anglican clergymen, non-Anglicans within the province fought the project, and sixteen years would pass before King's would open its doors.

Fierce debates about the development and funding of education gripped the province during the 1830s. While a loose consensus was evolving about the need for improvements in the quality and extent of public schooling, the protagonists found no agreement on the form and content of those changes. Reformers demanded that education (and other public works) be funded from the entitlement of the Clergy Reserves, while Tories insisted that the people tax themselves. The former sought more direct control over public education through the Assembly, while the latter favoured maintaining authority through the non-elected Councils. When Lieutenant Governor John Colborne established Upper Canada College in 1829, he was attacked by his opposition for extending higher educational privileges to the children of the aristocracy. On the eve of the 1837 rebellion, the controversies had been aired but the problems had not been resolved.

The defeat of the rebellion introduced an air of sobriety into the politics of the province, weakening the influence of the radical reformers and strengthening the hands of the moderates and conservatives. American ideology, once again, was considered by many to have been the cause of Upper Canada's recent political woes. Lieutenant Governor Arthur denounced the "madness allowing Americans [still] to be the instructors of the Youth of the Country." The persistence of these con-

Left below: *Doorway, University College, Toronto. Designed by F.W. Cumberland and W.G. Storm, the college building was opened in 1856. Standing in the doorway is James Loudon, professor of physics.*
Right top: *Enoch Turner School House 1848, Toronto. Turner donated funds for this school after the Toronto council refused to open free common schools. In 1851, the Toronto Board of Education agreed to turn it into a free school. Today it is an historic site.*
Right below: *Upper Canada College, Toronto, Founded 1829. In 1891 the college moved from its original site on King Street to a site north of St. Clair Avenue. The 1891 building shown here was demolished and replaced by the present one in 1958.*

cerns accounted, in part, for both the development of a more centralized school system, and the attempt in the late 1840s to eliminate all American textbooks from the classrooms of Canada West, in favour of the pro-British, Irish National Readers.

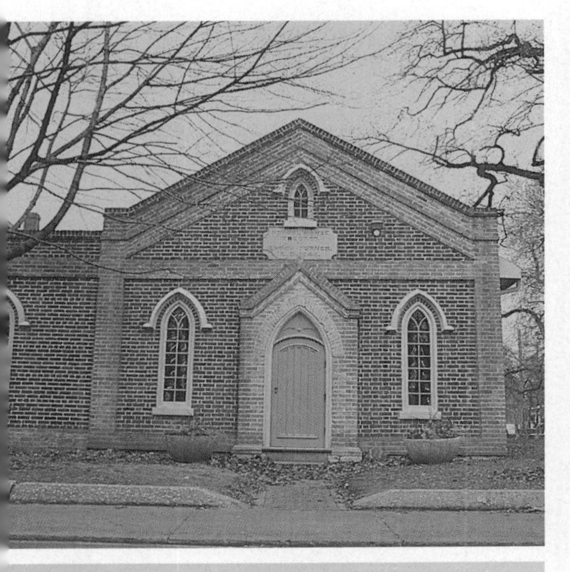

If Loyalism remained a powerful force in the shaping of educational policy, so too, did Christianity. The growing diversity of the population no longer allowed Anglicans a certain monopoly over the religious, cultural, and political life of the province. For one thing, the terms of the Act of Union of 1841 forced the leaders of Canada West to recognize the religious and educational rights of the minority of Catholics in exchange for the similar protection of Protestant rights in Canada East. Thus the School Act of 1841 effectively guaranteed the survival of "separate schools" on the grounds that "any number of inhabitants of a different faith from the majority in (either) township or parish might choose their own trustees . . . and might establish and maintain one or more schools" under the same terms as other common schools.

Other religious groups were equally determined to ensure that God watched over the classrooms of the public school system. Competing Christian denominations might disagree on matters of doctrine, but all accepted the responsibility of the public schools to provide students with a sound moral training, based in Egerton Ryerson's words, on "the general system of truth and morals as taught in the holy scriptures."

The development of colleges and universities was a further indication of the continuing relationship between education and religion in the province. Methodists, Presbyterians, Baptists and Roman Catholics all established colleges in the 1840s and 50s in which clergymen from these denominations could be trained. The creation of the non-denominational University of Toronto in 1849, and the dispersal of the Clergy Reserves in 1854, symbolized not the victory of secularization, but instead the achievement of religious pluralism within a distinctly Christian framework.

When Egerton Ryerson became Superintendent of Education in Canada West in 1844, he inherited the cultural and social traditions and faced the educational challenges of his predecessors. He was by no means out of place. The son of a Loyalist who had fought in the American Revolution and had emigrated from the Maritimes to Upper Canada in the 1790s, Ryerson had already made his mark on religious and political affairs in the province. As a widely known Methodist minister and the first editor of the Methodist newspaper, the *Christian Guardian,* he became an eloquent spokesman for Upper Canadians seeking educational reform, religious equality and the preservation of cultural identity. Though fostering an English school system, he felt that French-speaking children should be educated in their mother tongue, a right that was curtailed after his time. Though dismissed by some as a disruptive radical, in truth he was a social conservative who had firmly dissociated himself from the militants involved in the 1837 rebellion. Though he favoured more self-government for the colony, he was devoted to the Crown. Though he challenged religious exclusivism, he was as righteous a Christian as John Strachan. As the dominant figure in education for three decades, he sought (in his own words) to "lay the basis of an Educational structure . . . as broad as the population in the country . . . the whole based upon the principles of Christianity and uniting the influence and support of the Government and the people."

Ryerson did not singlehandedly mould the educational system. Instead, he guided his charges through the social currents that swept through the province (and the continent) at mid-century. While he encouraged change, he responded to and sometimes resisted demands for it as well. As much as he influenced the direction of education, he was shaped philosophically by the environment in which he lived and worked.

Mid-19th century Canada was a society in flux. Most Upper Canadians, of course, still worked on farms, but agriculture was augmented by the growth of urban centres where the patterns of community living were very different. Roads and railways increased the mobility of people seeking new occupational outlets, the use of steam power introduced new forms of industrial labour, and the influx of hungry immigrants from the British Isles deepened the society's class divisions.

Those who governed Upper Canada, somewhat paradoxically, both

Left and right below: *Village School at Scotland, Near Brantford. Today this attractive wooden frame building would be considered a fire trap.*
Right top: *Statue of Egerton Ryerson, First Superintendent of Education. The statue stands in the grounds of Ryerson Polytechnical Institute, founded in 1948 as Ontario's first post-secondary technical college. The Institute was named in honour of Dr. Egerton Ryerson (1803-1883), widely recognized as the founder of the educational system in Ontario.*

favoured and feared the social and economic changes through which society was moving. While the comfortable and prosperous welcomed new opportunities for earning money, frequently they could be found lecturing others on the spiritually corrosive and corrupting influence of obsessive materialism. They employed immigrants and the poor as transportation and factory workers (at low wages), but at the same time they expressed concern about the alien habits, the rugged lifestyles, the crowded living conditions, and the class conflict generated by the presence of the working poor. While encouraging economic growth, society's leaders sought ways of protecting themselves and the community from what were seen as its most unpalatable consequences.

Egerton Ryerson was a typical and influential exponent of this point of view. He believed that the solution to society's problems could be found in the promotion and achievement of a broad system of public schooling. Schools were the instruments through which the traditional values associated with God, Queen and country could be passed on and perpetuated. Delinquent children could be controlled, "saved," and retrained, and ideally, subject to the positive influence of their classmates from "respectable" families. According to Ryerson, it was the duty of education to develop "all the intellectual powers of man, teach him self-reliance as well as dependence on God, excite him in industry and enterprise, and instruct him in the rights as well as the duties of man." Where parents proved unwilling or incapable of providing such training, it was the duty of the state, through its schools, to carry out the task.

These were ambitious, sweeping goals, and for the school promoters, attainable only through an educational system requiring both compulsory attendance and public funding at the elementary level. The struggle to achieve these measures carried on for over two decades as many property holders fought to keep the state out of the classrooms and beyond the reach of the people's pocketbooks. To opponents of compulsory taxation who accused Ryerson of pandering to the "brats" of the community, the Chief Superintendent responded: "to educate all the brats in every neighborhood is the very object of [the] . . . bill; and in order to do so, it is proposed to compel selfish rich men to do what they ought to do, but what they will not do voluntarily." The authority of the province was emboldened by the Common School Act of 1846, empowering the government to plan the curriculum, inspect the schools, and certify the teachers. In 1847, Ontario established a "normal" school for the training of teachers, one of the first in North America, and a step forward in the professionalization of teaching.

Still, the long tradition of local autonomy and volunteerism in educational affairs could not be easily displaced by provincial administrators. Thus, the 1846 Act created a Board of School Trustees (whose members were elected from each school district) which had the power to hire and fire teachers, maintain school buildings, and implement the school laws of the province. These activities were to be overseen by the Superintendent of Education and a General Board of Education whose members were provincial appointees.

With respect to funding, the Common School Act of 1850 preserved the local option by allowing, without requiring the constituents of each school board to impose a property tax upon themselves for the purpose of financing the schools in their district. The growing acceptance of this approach was obvious; by 1870, 4,244 of 4,400 school sections in Ontario had adopted the local assessment procedure voluntarily. One year later the Common School Act made the practice compulsory, thereby guaranteeing that throughout the province elementary education would be tuition-free. In addition, the law stipulated that children between the ages of seven and twelve must attend school for at least four months per year.

The accomplishments of Ryerson and the school promoters should not be understated, but neither should the continuing deficiencies of the educational system be overlooked. Perhaps the gravest problem was the failure of compulsory attendance legislation to ensure equality of educational opportunity. Despite the steady growth of industrialization and urbanization, the rewards of economic progress were by no means shared equally by the citizens of the province. While factory owners, affluent farmers, and professionals lived relatively prosperous lives, the unskilled, the seasonally-employed, the poor and the dispossessed (in

Left and right below: *Mrs. Forster's School (Pinehurst) Toronto, 1864. This private school for young ladies was on McCaul Street, near the Grange (now part of the Art Gallery of Ontario). Before the advent of common (now public) schools, individuals started small private schools, sometimes in their own homes. Many such schools were short-lived.*

Right top: *School in Port Ryerse. This is the quintessential "Little Red School House" which is part of Ontario folklore. Port Ryerse, on Lake Erie, was founded by Samuel Ryerse, a Loyalist who came to Upper Canada in the 1790s.*

country and city) struggled simply to survive. The schools captured and in some ways perpetuated these class disparities.

The official statistics showed that by 1887, over 400,000 students were enrolled in the province's elementary schools. However, between 1872 and 1887 the attendance percentage of school-aged children had risen from forty-two percent to slightly less than fifty percent. With half of the province's children attending school irregularly or not at all, the cynic might have concluded that the legislation of 1871 was simply ineffective. The elimination of tuition fees removed from elementary schools direct financial barriers, but the children of the poor could not always pay for incidentals such as books and supplies. Many farmers kept their children at home during the planting and harvesting seasons, and even during the winter, poor weather hindered access to schools in remote areas. The high degree of transience among job-seeking parents interrupted the schooling of their children as well. In cities, working-class children, instead of going to school, frequently performed unskilled labour in factories under cruel conditions at exploitative wages in order to supplement family incomes. It was estimated that in the 1880s, children constituted eleven percent of Toronto's labour force.

Furthermore, educational facilities were strained to the limit. In 1877 the pupil-teacher ratio in elementary schools stood at 72:1 (though it improved to 49:1 by 1902), with conditions especially inadequate in the crowded cores of urban centres. In a beginners' class at Borden Street School in Toronto "the little things are packed so closely upon the benches that they often have to sit with their shoulders fitting in towards the back of the seat sideways." In more affluent areas, however, better equipped schools were more common.

The training of teachers, too, left considerable room for improvement. Since the demand for teachers outstripped the supply, thousands were hired with minimal qualifications. In the late 1870s, only one quarter of the elementary teachers had received advanced training in the Normal Schools at Toronto and Ottawa (the latter opened in 1875). The remainder usually proceeded through a fourteen-week course in one of fifty-two county "model" schools, where entrance requirements were low, and opportunities for practice teaching were severely limited.

The salaries of school teachers did little to raise the standards of the profession. County male teachers saw their average incomes decline from $404 per year in 1884 to $344 in 1899. For female teachers, average salaries dropped from $270 to $250 over the same period. An exasperated inspector grumbled: "Labourers and domestic servants are paid higher wages than many of our teachers."

The disparity in male-female wage rates, combined with the rapid growth of the student population, accounted in large measure for the "feminization" of the teaching profession in the last quarter of the century. To cope with higher enrollments, and to preserve the status of male teachers, men were commonly promoted to the higher grades or to administrative positions (at higher salaries), and women were hired to teach in the lower grades. At a time when other occupational avenues opened to women were restricted mainly to domestic or factory work, thousands streamed into teaching despite the appalling and discriminatory wage rates. By the mid-1870s there were more female than male teachers in the elementary schools of Ontario.

The progress of secondary education was especially uneven in Ontario in the latter half of the 19th century. Legislation in 1853 had brought the grammar schools under public authority with respect to the regulation of courses and the appointment of teachers. But the quality of education continued to concern provincial officials. The number of grammar schools had grown to about 100 by the 1860s, but many were inadequately staffed and served a bewildering variety of functions. Frequently, classical education, the *raison d'être* of these schools in Ryerson's mind, was taught poorly or not at all. Attempts by Ryerson to tighten regulations provoked a storm of protest in the late 1860s from local groups stubbornly protecting their community schools and the eclectic form of secondary education they offered.

Forced to respond to social realities, Ryerson, and the province's grammar school inspector, George Paxton Young, adopted a new policy which became law in 1871. The grammar schools were replaced by two streams of secondary education: high schools (for boys and girls) which

Left below: *Public Library and Bell Tower, Uxbridge. Public libraries were established under the Ontario Free Libraries Act of 1882. Earlier, libraries were provided within mechanics institutes.*

Right top: *George Paxton Young, Inspector of Provincial Grammar Schools, 1870s. During Young's tenure, in 1871, grammar schools were replaced by two streams — high schools for girls and boys, and elite collegiate institutes that prepared boys to enter university.*

Right below: *Jarvis Collegiate Institute, Toronto. The roots of this school go back to the Home District Grammar School, that started in 1807. John Strachan was headmaster in 1812. The building shown here was replaced by the present one in 1924.*

stressed the teaching of English, commercial subjects and natural science; and the more elite collegiate institutes, designed to teach Latin and Greek to boys intending to enter university. Public education at advanced levels for women remained limited. In addition, fees were not abolished, and as late as 1905, sixty percent of Ontario high schools were still charging private tuition.

Apart from the University of Toronto which opened on a non-denominational basis in 1850, higher education remained under the private control of a variety of religious groups. By 1881, twelve such colleges were scattered throughout Ontario in Windsor, London, Berlin, Toronto, Kingston, Cobourg and Ottawa. (Also, the Royal Military College was opened under federal auspices in Kingston in 1876.) Strongly committed to their particular modes of Christian teaching, these institutions began and survived in the face of formidable financial obstacles. The pressures increased after 1868 when the Ontario government settled a long-standing political dispute by withdrawing financial support to church-run universities, leaving the University of Toronto as the exclusive recipient of public grants. By the late 1880s the economic plight of several colleges was desperate. As a result, an arrangement was struck with the University of Toronto. In exchange for financial support and the right to continue offering theological degrees and some instruction in the humanities, the "federated" colleges would agree to surrender to the University the authority to teach and provide degrees in virtually all other academic fields. Victoria College (Methodist) was the first to federate with Toronto (1890), followed soon after the turn of the century by Trinity (Anglican) and St. Michael's (Roman Catholic). Queen's (Presbyterian) and Western (Anglican) yielded in their own ways to the pressures of economic exigency. In 1908 and 1912 respectively, they divested themselves of religious control and were entitled to public funding.

Whether denominational or not, the universities approached the knowledge explosion of the Victorian era in a cautious, often sceptical manner. New discoveries in physical and natural science, particularly the stunning, controversial claims of Charles Darwin, tested the spirit and parameters of critical inquiry in the lecture halls of the nation. Could materialistic interpretations of man's evolution be reconciled with the traditionally idealistic views about the immanence of the Christian God in the affairs of the world, past and present? Respected professors like William Lyall, James George, and John William Dawson by no means denied the need to study and address these intellectual challenges. Instead, they sought to contain examination of them within highly disciplined and moralistic boundaries. Students were encouraged to help push back the frontiers of knowledge so long as they retained their ethical sensibilities. But the pursuit of knowledge for its own sake was unacceptable and dangerous, the precursor to intellectual anarchy and social disorder.

Canadian universities also had a strong reluctance to enrol female students. Mount Allison University in Halifax broke tradition by admitting its first woman in 1862 (though its first female graduate did not appear until 1875). Queen's University allowed women to enrol in 1878 as did the University of Toronto in 1884.

While traditionalists had accepted the value of educating girls at the elementary levels, they could see no good reason for more advanced training. Women, after all, were destined to continue in their roles as housewives and mothers. Higher education was, therefore, perceived as a frivolous, expensive, or unnecessary venture. What was the point, they argued, of training women for professions and careers for which they were mentally ill-equipped, and which were rightly occupied exclusively by males? Advocates of university training for women did not entirely escape these dominant cultural prejudices. Few argued that men and women should have equal educational and career opportunities. But society, they contended, could only benefit from the extension of culture, refinement, and propriety to intelligent women.

Even after the doors had opened, university women faced considerable discrimination. Entry to many professions remained closed to them until the turn of the century, and many departments even refused to allow men and women to be taught in the same classrooms. Significantly, co-education in Canadian universities took root only when financial

Left below: *Port Arthur Collegiate Institute. Collegiates taught classics. High schools taught English, commercial subjects and natural science. Education provided by collegiates was not considered necessary for girls until towards the end of the century.*
Right top: *Technical School, College Street, Toronto. Designed by E.J. Lennox and erected in 1892 for the short-lived Toronto Athletic Club, the building was subsequently used by the Technical School. Later it housed various government activities and a police headquarters. Now it is part of the Ontario College of Art.*
Right below: *Alma College, St. Thomas. Founded in the 1870s by the Methodists, Alma College is a private school for girls, now operated by the United Church of Canada.*

pressures made segregated classes impractical. By 1900, ten percent of Canadian university students were female, compared to over thirty percent in the United States.

In the absence of other alternatives for advanced education, numerous ladies colleges and academies, run privately by religious denominations, were created in Ontario in the last half of the 19th century. These included the Loretto Academies in Toronto, Hamilton, Niagara Falls, Guelph, Stratford and Belleville (Catholic); Alma College in St. Thomas (Methodist); and the Ottawa Ladies' College (Presbyterian). They offered a wide variety of courses, not all of which would be considered advanced, and depended for their survival on a combination of church support and private tuition fees. Moral, religious, and mental training as opposed to career preparation (with the possible exception of teaching), constituted the main function of these institutions. Those that survived into the 20th century became convents or private girls' schools.

The turn of the century imposed new demands on the schools and universities. By 1900, over forty percent of Ontarians lived in urban centres. The rise of the mechanized factory system displaced craftsmen and tradesmen as major producers of finished goods, and diminished as well, their roles as instructors of apprentices. Increasingly, schools were called upon both to teach young people the skills of specific vocations. In 1891, the Toronto Technical School opened for the purpose of offering theoretical and laboratory instruction in such subjects as physical science, mechanical instruction, architecture and building. In 1899, manual training for boys was introduced into the elementary schools, and by 1900, subjects such as chemistry, physics, botany and zoology had all gained an entrenched place in most Ontario high schools.

Still, employers complained about the inadequate preparation of students destined to work in industry. Manufacturers in Toronto and Ottawa initiated a campaign for technical and industrial education which culminated in the Industrial Education Act of 1911. Industrial schools, trade schools, and technical education departments within high schools quickly emerged throughout the province. The public had become convinced that a prosperous economic future depended upon an adaptable, utilitarian, educational system.

Universities, too, felt the impact of the industrial revolution. While retaining their highly elitist character, developments in their own professional programs reflected the growth of the major resource sectors of the economy. Queen's opened a school of mining in 1893 and an engineering faculty in 1905. The University of Toronto established a school of forestry in 1907.

New pressure, however, did not displace old and cherished values. The resurgence of British imperialism towards the end of the 19th century tapped the deeply rooted Loyalist heritage of the province. The glories of the British Empire were already celebrated in school textbooks. The Diamond Jubilee of 1897 inspired an enthusiastic reassertion of that faith. Empire Day in the schools of Ontario honoured the past and hailed the future with a massive display of speeches, sporting events, and military rituals that became an annual event on Queen Victoria's birthday. For George Ross, the Minister of Education, the commitment to imperialism sustained and fired a passionate devotion to Canadian nationalism. He was proud of having helped "instill into the half million school children of the Province a greater love of Ontario, for Canada, and for the Empire than was previously entertained."

The principles of imperialism, capitalism and Christianity formed the core of school programs designed to "Canadianize" the legions of foreign students whose families settled in Ontario after the beginning of the great immigration wave of 1896. Quickly, they were "singing God Save the King, saluting the flag, reciting the Lord's Prayer and a short Bible reading." Like their Canadian classmates, they were taught to be punctual, obedient, and respectful of the law.

The world had changed since the Loyalists first entered the province, but education inherited and upheld the ideals they treasured. While the 20th century might diminish, it would never eliminate their influence on the cultural and political life of Ontario.

Right top: *Lutheran Seminary, Waterloo. The seminary became Waterloo Lutheran University, renamed Wilfred Laurier when it became secularized.*
Far right top: *Summerhill, Queen's University, Kingston. The building became part of Queen's after 1842.*
Right middle: *McMaster University, Toronto. Founded as the Toronto Baptist College, it moved to Hamilton in 1930. The Royal Conservatory of Music now occupies the building.*
Far right middle: *Royal Military College, Kingston. The college was founded in 1876 to train officers for the newly formed Canadian army.*
Right below: *Laurentian University, Sudbury, in 1968. Laurentian was established in 1960.*
Far right below: *Trent University, Peterborough. The buildings were designed by two firms – Ron Thom, and Thompson, Berwick and Pratt.*
Left below: *Brock University Poster.*

ENLIST NOW
COULTHARD'S
MACS CLOTHING PARLOR

CHAPTER 20

THE FIRST WAR TO END ALL WARS

by Strome Galloway

The British citizen army. . .was dogged and resolute, but not very dashing. Dash was the specialty of the Canadians and Australians.

CORELLI BARNETT ON WORLD WAR I
BRITAIN AND HER ARMY 1509-1970

bayonets — came from Ontario.

When victory was finally achieved, the entire Canadian Expeditionary Force in France and Flanders, numbering well over one hundred thousand front line troops, was commanded by Ontario-born Lieutenant-General Sir Arthur Currie. Except for around 10,000 men in the Royal Canadian Navy, all Canada's service men were in the army, there being no air force the flyers belonging either to the army or the navy. The outstanding Canadian air ace, and possibly the Allies' top scorer, with seventy-two *confirmed* enemy aircraft shot down, was Lieutenant-Colonel William A. "Billy" Bishop, V.C., an Owen Sound boy of United Empire Loyalist descent. What probably became the most famous war poem of all times, *"In Flanders' Fields"*, was written in the heat of battle by Lieutenant-Colonel John McCrae, a military doctor whose birthplace was Guelph. In addition to Bishop, of the sixty-nine other Canadian Victoria Cross winners, fifteen were officers or men serving in Ontario-raised Battalions.

Such were the exciting results of the early patriotic response to the romantic call, "Your King and Country Need You."

There was a grim side too. For, with all its glamour and patriotic fervour and the glory that some gain, war also brings forth agony and heartbreak and the shedding of much young blood. Of this great host of Ontario's heroes, 68,000 were killed, wounded or listed as missing. The "missing" were those whose bodies could not be found, thus there was no proof that they were dead. (The bodies of unknown soldiers, the "missing" of 1914-1918, were still being dug up in the old battlefields sixty-five years after the war ended.)

Thousands of Ontario homes were saddened, knowing that they would never see their loved ones again. But the stout-hearted among the bereaved took pride in these deaths, believing that those who had lost their lives had done so in a noble cause. They had fought for the honour of their King and Country, and in perhaps so terrible a war that it would put an end to all wars. And so they consoled themselves that the thousands of lost lives and the many aching hearts left behind had not been in vain.

Left and right below: *2nd Battalion, Queen's Own Rifles. This Toronto regiment, dating from 1860, was with the Canadian Expeditionary Force in France and Flanders, World War I, and in the D Day landings, World War II.*

Among the First to Fight

Ontario units were among the first Canadians to fight, going into action near Ypres, Belgium, in April 1915. Of the twelve Canadian infantry battalions which withstood the first gas attack in the history of warfare, five were from Ontario. The conduct of one of them, the 2nd Battalion, which had been recruited in Ottawa and Peterborough, earned it the title the "Iron Second." Of the four Victoria Crosses awarded to Canadians for valour during the first three months of battle, one went to Lieutenant F. W. Campbell, of the 1st Battalion, recruited in London and other Western Ontario centres. Equal gallantry was displayed by Toronto's 3rd Battalion, the "Mad Fourth" Battalion from Hamilton and Brantford, and the 15th Battalion, also from Toronto.

Although the Canadian infantry battalions were designated by numbers, they were, in fact, built around the old historic militia regiments of the Dominion. The 1st (Western Ontario) Battalion was formed around the 7th Canadian Fusiliers of London; the 2nd (Eastern Ontario) Battalion around the Governor General's Foot Guards of Ottawa and the Peterborough Rangers. The 3rd (Toronto Regiment) was a combination of the Queen's Own Rifles and the Royal Grenadiers, whereas the 4th (Central Ontario) Battalion was the disguise given to the Royal Hamilton Light Infantry and the Dufferin Rifles of Brantford, of which units it was composed. The 15th Battalion managed to retain its old name in brackets, being known as the 15th (48th Highlanders of Canada) Battalion.

Ontario's artillery batteries came from such centres as Toronto, London ánd Guelph, whereas numerous Ontario men found their way into all manner of supporting units. But the bulk of Ontario manpower was found in the numbered infantry battalions based on the old familiar militia units which in the past had countered the Fenians at Ridgeway, or fought Poundmaker and his braves in Saskatchewan, or supplied drafts for the Canadian contingents which fought the Boers in South Africa only a dozen years before. As in all previous wars, the foot soldier was the backbone of the army.

Left and right bottom: *Camp Borden. This postcard was sent to May Cockburn of Toronto on August 14, 1916, by her father. The photographer superimposed the plane, which explains the soldiers' lack of interest in it.*

War on the Home Front

Wars are not won only by soldiers on the battlefield, sailors at sea, or aviators in the skies above. There is a home front, too. On the home front patriotism and a will-to-win must be the driving force behind the men and women in the factories, on the land, and in the supportive roles needed to keep the nation going under the stress and strain of war. Much of this work is brought to nothing by enemy action. Munitions, war supplies, and tons of foodstuffs were lost on the way to Great Britain and Europe when the merchant ships were sunk by German submarines, or U-boats as they were called. Indeed, Germany almost won the war by starving the people of Great Britain and France, in cutting off their needed food importations from across the Atlantic. This meant increased food production by Canada's farmers, increased work in the food processing industries, as well as increased work in factories which turned out war materials for the battlefield.

Conditions such as these make new and almost unbelievable demands on the time and energy of a nation's workers. They call for new workers from all levels of society. It can be recalled with pride that the people of Ontario responded to these demands in splendid style. But all these things soon change the face of a nation, and between 1914 and 1918 the face of Canada, and perhaps most of all Ontario, the industrial heartland of the Dominion was greatly changed.

Canada's economy was depressed in 1914 and there was much unemployment. But soon enlistments in the army, new jobs in munition plants and other war-oriented industries, and demands for more and more farm workers took up the slack. This recovery was gradual. Ontario industry had to tool up to get into war production and this lasted during most of 1915. However, things were in full swing by 1916, and in that year there was no unemployment worth noting. By 1917 there was such a shortage of labour that women were entering the labour market in thousands, and young people were taking part-time employment during school holidays, not primarily to earn pocket money or help out at home, but because the country needed every additional pair of hands to keep from "losing the battle of the home front."

__Left below:__ Victory Bonds Poster. Submarines were first used in World War I. As illustrated, their sinkings provoked outrage.
__Right top:__ Sir Samuel Hughes (1853-1921). Born in Darlington, Hughes joined the militia at age thirteen. He commanded the 45th Regiment in 1897. He was Minister of Militia and Defence in the Borden government (1911-1916). Always controversial, he was forced to resign, but was knighted in 1915 for his services.
__Right below:__ Sir Arthur Currie (1875-1953). Born in Napperton, Middlesex County, he commanded the First Cana-

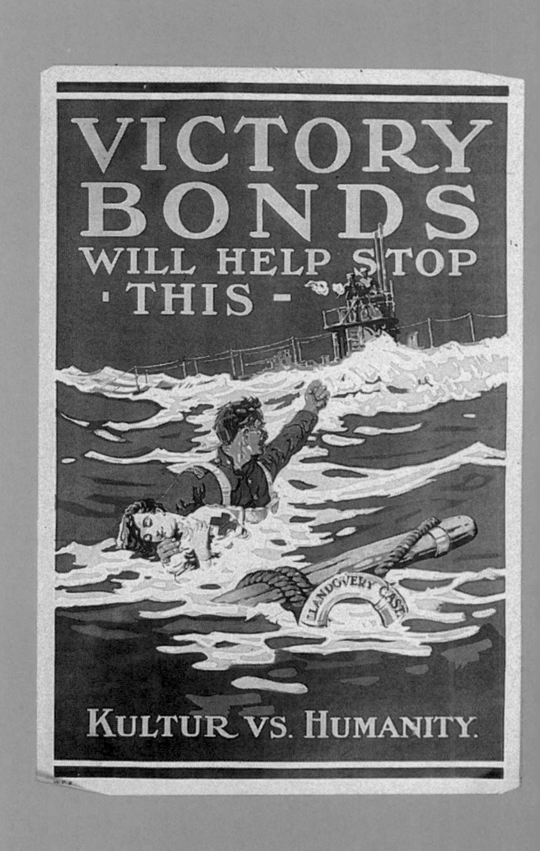

dian Army overseas in 1915. After the victory at Vimy Ridge in 1917, he was made lieutenant-general and placed in command of the Canadian Corps. In 1919 he became the first full general in the Canadian army.

The industrial structure of the province was much altered by the final years of the war. Fortunes had been made in many areas which had been far from prosperous before the war. The woollen and textile industries boomed. Thousands of blankets were needed for the army both at home and overseas. Thousands of uniforms and other items of clothing had to be manufactured. Much of these items were quickly used up and had to be replaced over and over again. In the world of leather, not only millions of pairs of boots had to be issued and stocked, but leather equipment such as belts, bandoleers and pouches were needed. Additionally, since it was largely a horse-drawn war, and with many cavalry and particularly horsed artillery regiments, the manufacturers of saddlery, harness and leather accoutrements prospered greatly. Again, much of this equipment was constantly destroyed in battle and had to be replaced. The manufacturers of tentage and canvas items created riches for some. Ontario flax growers found that their crops had to be increased to produce the drying oil from which was made the 'dope' used to preserve the wings and fuselages of the aircraft of the day.

The manufacturing economy expanded unbelievably. New skills were developed when motor vehicles and aircraft began to go into large-scale production as war-winning items. The manufacturers, like many food producers, became war 'profiteers' and were criticized for money they made. Factory workers got high wages and were scorned by those whose menfolk were fighting in the trenches for a dollar or two a day. Yet, without these industrialists and their workers on the home front, the war could not have been won.

By 1917 Ontario had become a veritable arsenal and one of the prime sources of supply for many of the war materials needed by the Empire and its allies. Nickel was vital for the manufacture of ammunition and Ontario's nickel mines produced most of this metallic element used in the Allied war effort. Ontario's timber industry was revitalized, since lumber was needed in vast quantities for the construction encampments and military housing. Between the outbreak and the end of the war, in Ontario the number and capacity of Ontario manufacturing establishments more than doubled.

Great Social Changes

By the middle years of the war it became apparent that great social changes were taking place. Fortunes were made, wages were high, so inevitably prices rose. Special war-inspired taxes were levied, particularly on amusements, which raised millions of extra dollars for the war effort. With so much ready money young workers married in increasing numbers. In Toronto there were ten times more marriages than in similar periods before the war. The demand for housing was great, but because of all the marriages and because men could not be spared from war work to do civilian construction, the housing shortage was acute. Domestic upsets resulted. Farmers were pressed to produce more and more farm products. Yet, they were constantly deprived of farm workers because of enlistments in the army, or moves by young farm hands into the better paying war factories.

Trade unionism grew and some strikes took place, but in the main, the wave of patriotism which characterized 1914 did not ebb. The population was overwhelmingly behind the war effort and only a very few people questioned the need for hard work and long hours as being necessary to achieve victory.

One big change that took place was the introduction of prohibition. The Ontario Temperance Act was the manifestation of a strong belief that alcohol hampered industrial efficiency and put undesirable temptation in the way of young soldiers and war workers, separated from the restraints of family life. By September 1916, liquor could be obtained in Ontario only by a doctor's prescription, and consumed only in the private home. All bars, liquor stores and drinking clubs were closed. Boarding houses and hotels were prohibited from selling alcoholic beverages. Only native wine could be consumed in public. The cry was that the $30 million spent annually on 'booze' in Ontario might better be spent to help win the war. Amazingly enough, there was little opposition to the ban. In fact, 825,000 Ontarians put their signatures to a petition for a dry Ontario. One tiny bit of humour came out of the temperance drive. When Toronto's 201st Battalion tried to recruit 'temperance men' only, it was singularly unsuccessful and had to be disbanded

Left below: *164th Battalion Parades Through Milton.*
Right top: *Parliament Building Fire, February 3, 1916. The Centre Block, except for the library, was destroyed, with some loss of life. Parliament sat in the National Museum, as told in an amusing article in the* Toronto Star *the following day.*
Right below: *Poster Promoting Sale of Victory Bonds. People made great sacrifices both in time and money in the cause of winning the war.*

only a few months after being organized.

Life on the home front had its difficulties. There were hydro shortages, which in 1917 led to lights being turned off in manufacturing plants for three days at a time — though not of course in war plants. Street lighting was prohibited between certain hours. Places of amusement had to be closed because no heat was available, and many offices, shops and warehouses were denied heat and workers shivered through the winter months at desk, and counter, and work bench, in overcoats and mufflers.

Wars cannot be won without the spending of huge sums of money. That money has to come from the people, either by taxation or donation. Early in the war a Canadian Patriotic Fund was established. With less than one third of the entire population of Canada, Ontario subscribed more than one half of the total amount of the Fund. By the sale of Victory Bonds, the Dominion Government raised one billion, seven hundred and ten million dollars. Ontario people purchased eight hundred million of that amount.

Part of the province's war effort was also found in the many outright gifts which were made. Within sixteen days of the outbreak of the war, the Ontario Government had granted half a million dollars to the Imperial War Fund and shortly afterwards sent 250,000 bags of flour overseas to feed beleaguered Britain and her army in the field. Ontario also contributed immense amounts of money through donations from Women's Institutes, the Imperial Order Daughters of the Empire (I.O.D.E.) and other organizations. Endless hours were spent by many women's organizations in knitting socks and sweaters, in making bandages and wrapping parcels of comforts for the men in camps or overseas. These activities became the social events of the times, and frivolous, non-productive social gatherings were frowned upon. But Ontario's women, or the younger ones at least, soon found they were needed in more strenuous tasks than these. The increased demands for 'manpower' called them to take their place in the foremost ranks on the Home Front, in industry and in agriculture, filling jobs normally held by men.

OTHER FOSSILS MAKE WAY FOR SENATE AT THE MUSEUM

Description of the Building in Which the Commons Meet This Afternoon.

COME ON!
Let's finish the Job
BUY VICTORY BONDS

Ontario's Women Join In

Ontario's men enlisted in large numbers. But it was often difficult for a man to decide where his duty lay. The demands for men for war industry and food production vied with the military for the available manpower. The heavy casualties on the Western Front meant more and more men must enlist to keep Canada's fighting forces up to strength. The government urged the farmers to greater levels of production, yet many farmers' sons were eager to join the army.

Conscription was introduced in August 1917, and this caused further shortages in the labour force. Already many women were at work in war plants and on the land. Now more and more of them quit their traditional roles and undertook to do "a man's work." Many of the conscripts were given harvest leave in season, but this disrupted their training, and either kept them from going overseas when required, or saw them dispatched to the trenches without enough training. So women war workers were vital to the pursuit of victory.

Women were especially successful in munitions factories and as full-time farmerettes. There was still a place for part-time volunteers, and countless committees prepared supplies for hospitals, collected comfort for the troops, raised money by various means, looked after the wounded in hospital and convalescent homes, which helped in the prosecution of the war, or in relieving the suffering of the fighting men.

Many Ontario women served overseas, not only as nurses in the Medical Corps, but in such organizations as the St. John Ambulance and the Red Cross. School children also joined in, and in 1917 alone, more than 8,000 girls and boys from Ontario's high schools gave up their summer vacation to help provincial farmers produce more food.

In the early days of the war some women, more military-minded than most, attempted in both Toronto and Hamilton to form a Women's Home Guard, teaching rifle shooting and other defensive skills. These groups were unofficial and were raised in the fear that raids might be made on Canada by Germans or Austrians from across the American border. When these raids did not materialize, the Women's Home Guard idea soon died. Similar organizations cropped up all over Ontar-

Right top: *William Avery Bishop V.C., D.S.O. and Bar, D.F.C. (1894-1956). Born in Owen Sound, Bishop joined the Royal Flying Corps in 1915, and was credited with downing 72 enemy aircraft.*

Far right top: *"Billy" Bishop and his Nieuport. Bishop joined 60 Squadron in March 1917, and flew this French-designed fighter until August, when he switched to a British S.E.5.*

Right middle: *Overseas Contingent on Parade — The Largest Ever Staged in Toronto.*

Right below: *Conscription Poster Showed That Canada Was Involved in a Major War.*

Far right below: *The Dumbells. This Ontario group was formed by Captain Merton Plunkett to entertain Canadian troops overseas. After the war they toured many Canadian and American centres before disbanding in 1929.*

MILITARY SERVICE ACT, 1917.

IMPORTANT NOTICE.

Every male British subject resident in Canada who was born on or since the 13th day of October, 1897, and who was unmarried or a widower without a child on the 20th day of April, 1918, must report to the Registrar or Deputy Registrar under the Military Service Act, 1917, of the district in which he resides, on or before the 1st day of June, 1918, or within ten days after the man reporting shall have attained his nineteenth birthday, whichever date shall be the later. The report must be in writing, and it must state the name in full, the date of birth, place of residence and usual post office address of the person reporting. It may be sent to the Registrar or Deputy Registrar by registered post, free of postage. The address of the Registrar or Deputy Registrar to whom the report should be sent may be obtained from any postmaster. Failure to comply with these requirements will be visited by severe penalties.

ISSUED BY THE DEPARTMENT OF JUSTICE, MILITARY SERVICE BRANCH.

OTTAWA, 17th MAY, 1918.

io in the first year or so of the war. There was a Women's Recruiting and Patriotic League, a Suffragists' War Auxiliary, and a Women's Emergency Corps, all with rather ill-defined war aims, but helpful in many ways.

Because of their energetic entry into war services of various kinds, Ontario women were given the right to vote in 1918. The year before, those women who had a husband, brother or son overseas were given the franchise. But Ontario was a bit behind in this area. Women of the four Western provinces had been casting their ballots at the polls.

Ontario takes to the Air

By 1917 aerial warfare had become an important part of the battle scene. Aircraft were little more than a military novelty in 1914, when first used as flying observation posts. But the succeeding three years saw the development of photographic reconnaissance machines, heavy bombing planes and swift fighters. Men had to be trained for this new dimension in warfare.

Many young Canadians were joining the British Royal Flying Corps or the Royal Naval Air Service, as Canada had no military air service. An Ontario flyer, Bishop, became an outstanding aerial fighter during the first few months of 1917. Another Ontarian, Major Andrew McKeever, born in Listowel, held the Allied record as the top-scorer pilot of a two-seater. Piloting this much more cumbersome type of aircraft, carrying a passenger for observation and photography, limited the pilot's ability to engage an enemy plane successfully. Despite this, the Listowel boy managed to shoot down thirty German machines.

In December 1916, the British War Office authorized the establishment of the Royal Flying Corps Canada. In January 1917, the construction of fifteen flying sheds was begun at Camp Borden, some fifty miles north of Toronto. By June 1918, according to the *Canadian Magazine*, Camp Borden had become "the largest aerodrome in the world."

Early in 1917 an aerodrome was begun at Long Branch, a suburb of Toronto, and in May of that year work began on flying camps at Leaside and Armour Heights, also close to Toronto. As time went on,

Left below: *Canadian Infantry World War I. Artist Harry Payne recorded many features of a soldier's equipment – standard British Empire uniform, steel helmet introduced late in the war to reduce head wounds, and Lee Enfield rifle (not the Canadian Ross rifle that jammed when it grew hot from repeated firing).*
Right top: *Decorated in the Field. A lance-corporal receives the Distinguished Conduct Medal.*
Right below: *George V Reviews Canadians at the Front. Deeply sympathetic*

to his servicemen, the King paid many visits to them. On one occasion he was injured when his horse fell and rolled on top of him.

camps to train airmen were established on two other Ontario sites, one near Deseronto, the other at Beamsville. Ontario was rapidly becoming the air training centre for the Empire. Instruction in airplane engines was given at Leaside, whereas aerial gunnery was taught at Beamsville, and aerial bombing practice took place in Lake Ontario against towed targets. One of the first Ontario-trained pilots was Donald MacLaren, a Westerner. He "received his wings" at Toronto and although he arrived at the Front only in time to have his first aerial combat in February 1918, by the Armistice in November his Ontario training had paid off by his having shot down forty-eight enemy planes!

Ontario Indians Also Served

Ontario's Indian population joined in the war in a most patriotic manner. Ojibwas and Chippewas sent extremely high proportions of their men into the army. Many served with the 52nd (New Ontario) Battalion, the "Bull Moose Battalion" and the names of every Indian in the battalion appeared on its casualty list. The Six Nations, or Iroquois, were mostly found in the 114th Battalion, "Brock's Rangers," so named because many of the Indians in its ranks were descended from warriors who had fought under Major-General Isaac Brock at Queenston Heights in the War of 1812.

In the early days of the war, individual Indians enlisted in the various units raised near their homes. One of the most notable, Corporal Francis Pegahmagabow, was awarded the Military Medal for Bravery in the Field, three times over. He enlisted in the 1st (Western Ontario) Battalion in 1914, became a sniper and is reported to have killed 378 Germans. On one occasion he is credited with capturing 300 of the enemy by clever stalking tactics. While these figures may be somewhat wild exaggerations, it is apparent that Pegahmagabow's personal contribution towards the destruction of the Kaiser's army was well above that of the average soldier.

Many Indian bands sent as high as sixty to seventy percent of their able-bodied males into the army. The enlistment record was probably achieved by the Scugog Mississaugas which had a total population of thirty, of which only eight were adult males. All eight enlisted. The Golden Lake Algonquins made another record, sending twenty-nine soldiers to the Front which left only three men on the reservation.

Ontario's Indian women responded as did their white sisters, by providing for the needs of their men at the Front or in camp. One group of Oneida women sent twenty-five boxes of comforts overseas in 1916, increased their total to 104 boxes in 1917, and during the first ten months of 1918 before the Christmas period, sent seventy-four boxes to their men across the Atlantic. Money was also raised by the women of various bands through the sale of baskets and beadwork.

Still in at the End

From the beginning to the end, Ontario's soldiers were where they were needed. Ontario Front Line infantry battalions, other than those already mentioned were: 18th (Western Ontario), 19th and 20th (both designated Central Ontario), 21st (Eastern Ontario), 38th (Ottawa), 52nd (New Ontario), 58th (Central Ontario), 75th (Mississauga) and 4th Canadian Mounted Rifles, half of which came from Toronto as the result of an amalgamation. In addition, Princess Patricia's Canadian Light Infantry, although originally recruited from British Army reservists and Boer War veterans living in all parts of Canada, and later McGill University students, latterly became classed as an Ottawa unit and was reinforced from that city and area. Canada's only professional infantry, The Royal Canadian Regiment, went overseas with companies from Toronto and London. Of the 260 infantry battalions organized across Canada, 95 were Ontario-raised. Four fifths of these battalions were used as draft-finding units for the fifty "fighting battalions" in France and Flanders. Few of them reached more than half strength.

On November 11, 1918, when the bugles sounded the "Cease Fire" on the Western Front, the troops who had driven deepest into the enemy's territory were those of the 116th (Ontario County) Battalion. The 116th halted on a line north of Mons on the main Mons-Brussels road at the hamlet of Casteau, the exact spot where, by historical coincidence, the first rifle shot of the British Empire was fired by a trooper

Left below: *An Afternoon at Home c.1915.*
Right top: *Bust of Kaiser William II, Berlin (Kitchener). Before the war, the Kaiser (George V's first cousin) was revered in this community with German roots. Early in the war, local men dumped this bronze bust into the nearby lake. It was reclaimed and used to make shoulder flashes for Canadian soldiers. In 1916, Berlin was renamed to honour Lord Kitchener, drowned that year when the cruiser* H.M.S. Hampshire *was sunk.*
Right below: *Prisoner-of-War Camp, Kapuskasing, 1916. Captured German soldiers put a strain on Britain's food supply, already curtailed by enemy submarines. Many prisoners-of-war were sent to Canda and were sometimes kept in former lumber camps in remote areas, making escape difficult.*

of the 4th Royal Irish Dragoon Guards on August 23, 1914. Since that day, more than 750,000 British Empire warriors had been killed and about one million five hundred thousand wounded.

In Ontario, news of the armistice brought people out into the streets cheering, beating tin pans, blowing whistles and waving flags. In Windsor it was reported that 10,000 citizens jammed Ouellette Square and joined in a spontaneous outburst of thanksgiving to Almighty God because of the termination of hostilities. In Kingston, the whole city was on the streets from early morning. At night a huge bonfire burned on the Market Square and 25,000 people cheered themselves hoarse. In newly-named Kitchener, an alderman with a German name, whose loyalty had been suspected by some, was taken from his office in the City Hall and compelled to kiss the Union Jack amid the tremendous cheers of the crowd. Churches of every denomination held services of thanksgiving, and the jubilant crowds burned effigies of the Kaiser and sang the same songs they had sung on August 4, 1914.

Shortly after the Armistice the victorious allies followed up the retreating German Army. The first Canadian infantry unit to cross the German frontier was the 2nd (Eastern Ontario) Battalion on December 4. The first Canadian infantry unit to reach the Rhine was the 3rd (Toronto Regiment) Battalion, which arrived at the river line at Wesseling, five miles south of Cologne, on December 9.

And so ended the war which cost the civilized world more than ten million dead and double that number wounded — a war so terrible that men did not believe it could ever happen again. So they called it "the war to end all wars."

Yet, as Ontario's sons turned their backs on Europe and embarked on the ships that would take them back to their mothers, wives and sweethearts, and back to the shop, the office and the plough, there lay on a hospital bed in Germany, a young enemy corporal. In less than twenty years, he would rise from obscurity to such great political power that he would be capable of seeking his defeated nation's revenge, and plunging the whole world into war again.

BUCKINGHAM PALACE.

1918.

The Queen & I wish you God-speed, a safe return to the happiness & joy of home life with an early restoration to health.

A grateful Mother Country thanks you for faithful services.

George R.I.

In Flanders Fields

In Flanders fields the poppies blow
Between the crosses, row on row,
That mark our place; and in the sky
The larks, still bravely singing, fly
Scarce heard amid the guns below.

We are the Dead. Short days ago
We lived, felt dawn, saw sunset glow,
Loved and were loved, and now we lie,
In Flanders fields.

Take up our quarrel with the foe:
To you from failing hands we throw
The torch; be yours to hold it high.
If ye break faith with us who die
We shall not sleep, though poppies grow
In Flanders fields.

JOHN McCRAE 1872-1918

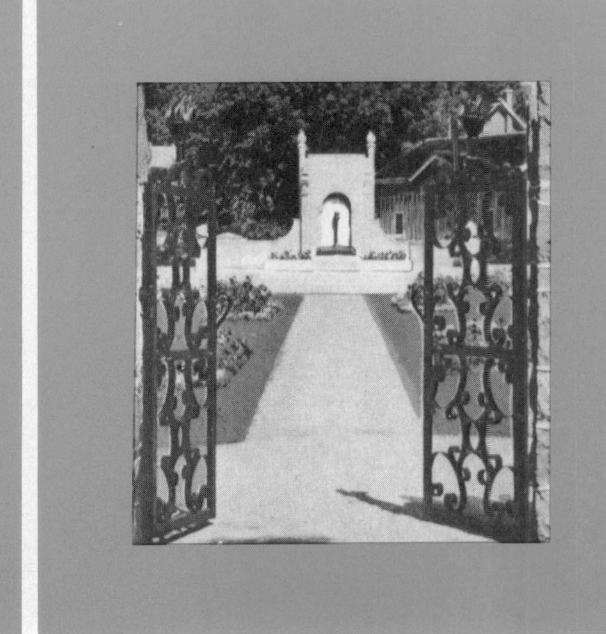

Far left top: *George V's Letter to Edward William Low of Port Perry, 1918. The King spent many hours writing personal letters to families of the dead, and to soldiers severely wounded. He wrote to Mr. Low, who recovered. His daughter donated the King's letter to the Monarchist League.*
Left top: *Colonel John McCrae's Poem.*

Left below: *Memorial to John McCrae, Guelph. McCrae (1872-1918), born in Guelph, was a medical officer, who composed his poem in a dugout near Ypres, 1915. He died of pneumonia in 1918.*

THE TORONTO DAILY STAR

TWENTY PAGES. TORONTO, MONDAY, NOVEMBER 11, 1918. 5 O'CLOCK EDITION TWO CENTS.

THE ARMISTICE IS SIGNED

Canadian Troops Capture Mons as the Last Act of the Great World War

Right top: *Headline From* Toronto Star.

Right middle: *"Halifax Welcomes Her Fighting Sons," May 16, 1919. A year-round port, Halifax was the main point of departure and return for Ontario's soldiers, sailors, airmen and nurses.*

Far right: *Unveiling of Canadian War Memorial, Vimy Ridge, July 26, 1936. Thousands watched as King Edward VIII unveiled the monument and Royal Air Force planes flew past in tribute to Canada's war dead.*

Right below: *Galt Peace Day Parade, July 19, 1919. Every Ontario municipality celebrated the end of the war. Many, like Galt, took time to make lavish preparations.*

WORKERS OF THE WORL
UNITE
FOR

CHAPTER 21

VOICE OF LABOUR

by Laurel Sefton MacDowell

The last century made the world a neighbourhood; this century must make it a brotherhood.

J.S. WOODSWORTH, FEBRUARY 17, 1917

The working class in Ontario evolved as the province changed from an essentially agrarian society to an urban industrial one with a growing manufacturing sector. For workers, this process of change was traumatic. Ontarians were accustomed to job security and paternal relationships with a familiar employer. In industrialized society, however, workers became dependent on wages in an impersonal labour market where labour surpluses resulted in frequent periods of unemployment. And to those accustomed to the pre-industrial rhythms of life on the farms of Ontario or Europe, factory discipline proved almost intolerable. The result was an increasingly dependent and impoverished sector of society, where the exploitation of women and children, long workdays, harsh working conditions and low wages were prevalent.

There were several effects. The crowding of workers in dirty, disease-ridden slums became a catalyst for change. Labour reformers were opposed to the values and inequities of the new industrial system and middle-class social reformers were motivated by humanitarian concern for the plight of the workers and by their fear that the industrial working class would revolt. Both became vocal in their criticisms.

By the 1880s, governments felt impelled to study industrial conditions and the reasons for increasing industrial conflict, and provincial legislatures enacted the first standards legislation, called Factory Acts. In 1886, Oliver Mowat's government prohibited the employment of boys under twelve and girls under fourteen years of age. This legislation was inadequately enforced, but it was an important precedent.

In 1889, the federal government's Royal Commission on the Relations of Labour and Capital published its report. Terrible abuses were revealed in the evidence of a woodworker from London, Ontario:

> Q. Are there any boys running machinery in your shop?
> A. Yes.
> Q. What kind of machinery do they run?
> A. They work on the planer, the rip-saw, the cross-cut saw, sand papering machines and jointers; in fact there are boys who can run almost any machine. Every week or two an accident happens.
> Q. The boys get hurt?
> A. Yes, their fingers are cut off.

Overleaf: *Cobalt Miners' Strike Parade, Timmins, January 14, 1913. The Cobalt union, which belonged to the World Federation of Miners, included the Timmins area.*

Left and right below: *Poling a Raft c.1900. The last raft of squared logs went down the Ottawa River in 1901.*
Left and right bottom: *Bunkhouse Men. This crowded bunkhouse was better than many, an attempt to allay criticisms of bad living conditions. In isolated locations, where men did not stay long, forest workers were difficult to unionize.*

Q. What becomes of the boys when they get their fingers cut off?

A. I saw a case of an apprentice to the woodworking business. After he had been working four weeks he had been put to running a machine: probably he had never seen a machine before, and four of his fingers were cut off. The boys in this town and the firm kept him about a month and then discharged him, and this boy is now working at painting.

Working women in Ontario were particularly disadvantaged members of the labour force. Often the Factory Acts were either unenforced or they covered companies larger than the sweatshops in which many women worked. Thus, despite some legislative improvements, most working women in Ontario remained largely unprotected. They were regarded by employers as a form of cheap labour, and in all types of employment where both men and women participated they were paid less than men for the same work.

There was little inclination to improve their lot. Female employment was regarded as marginal and temporary. In the prevailing view of middle-class society, the workplace was 'not a proper sphere' for women whose primary role was in the home as wife and mother. Royal commissioners, factory inspectors and middle-class reformers concentrated on such relatively unimportant matters as the lack of lunchrooms, seats for shop girls and clean washrooms. Women continued to work in poorly ventilated and badly lit factories for long hours and little pay.

With the exception of the Knights of Labor, few efforts were made to unionize women. Male trade unionists (like the rest of society) thought that it was undesirable for women to work in factories although they believed that women who were forced to do so should be better paid. Craft unionists in particular, regarded female labour — which was usually unskilled — as unfair competition. Women remained largely unorganized, and dependent on labour standards legislation.

This early legislation and the work of government inspectors had even less impact on the conditions of labourers in the hinterland of Ontario. These were the men who built the roads and rail lines (the CPR and the Transcontinental, for example), worked in the mines, and cleared the forests for the lumber trade and hydro developments. The employers relied upon private agents who did a lucrative business recruiting workers. There were always written agreements which the workers were required to sign, but such gave little protection and were often quite misleading. In *The Bunkhouse Man* Edmund Bradwin wrote:

> Many such agreements used by private employment agencies . . . were emphatically one-sided. The rate of pay and the charges for board were alone expressly stated, but the dozen and one discrepancies and minor losses usually incurred in camps were not fully anticipated by newcomers to forms of frontier work. Too commonly things were skillfully misrepresented . . . and men engaging thus were hastily bundled off to find out for themselves the conditions of work and pay at isolated camps . . . . The contract is vague enough except that it articles a man for work at a set wage per day to some employers, and states clearly the advances so far made. Such a form, however, has little to indicate what will be the real wages when actual conditions are later encountered at camp.

Edmund Bradwin worked in the camps as an instructor for Frontier College, an organization dedicated to raising educational levels of the workers. When he published his exposé of the evils of the camp system in 1928, it created a furor and resulted in some much-needed reform. Nevertheless, these unskilled, transient, largely immigrant workers, remained well behind their urban counterparts.

The workers' most effective response to their inferior position in industrial society was the organization of trade unions. Having lost their agrarian and small town communities, workers began to construct new social organizations based on their mutual interests in the work place. Trade unions were defensive organizations which resisted the pressures of exploitative employers, competition in the labour market and the ravages of technological change.

The first unions were formed as early as the 1830s. The York Typographical Society (YTS), for example, was started in 1832 when York was little more than a frontier village. The reason for forming the society was clearly set out in the preamble of its constitution:

> Owing to the many innovations which have been made upon

__Left top:__ Phillips Thompson. A qualified lawyer, Thompson became an outspoken labour journalist.
__Left below:__ Daniel O'Donoghue (1844-1907). O'Donoghue was the first labour representative in the Ontario legislature, 1873.

Right top: *James Simpson, Toronto Labour Leader. He was mayor in 1935.*
Right below: *Mr. Justice C.P. McTague. Chairman of the National War Labour Board during World War II, he was the architect of Canada's modern industrial relations system.*

> the long-established usages of the professors of the art of printing, and those of a kind highly detrimental to their interests, it is deemed expedient by the journeymen printers of York that they should form themselves into a body similar to societies in other parts of the world in order to obtain that honourable station and respectability that belongs to the profession.

The YTS temporarily lapsed in 1837 after a disastrous strike against the master printers in which the union had sought a ten-hour day, eight dollars a week, and limitations on the use of apprentices. Ironically that strike was defeated, in part, because of the efforts of William Lyon Mackenzie. One of the leading political reformers of the day and publisher of the *Colonial Advocate,* he was, nevertheless, adamantly opposed to the union's demands. The union reorganized in 1844, and for the next thirty years there were periodic confrontations with George Brown, who was publisher of the Toronto *Globe,* leader of the Liberal Party, and another leading opponent of the union's claim for higher wages. The local union, affiliated with the International Typographical Union (ITU) in 1866, played a leading role in the Nine Hour Movement. In 1872 it struck successfully for the nine-hour day. This victory put the ITU in the forefront of the international movement for shorter hours, and had an impact on other Toronto workmen, who had just joined together in a new city-wide trade union organization.

Most unions were organized later in the 1860s, among skilled workmen such as shoemakers, iron moulders, tailors, who had bargaining power because they could not be easily replaced. The goal of these craft unions was to organize all workers in a trade, to establish a price for labour, and to control the supply of labour. This objective was hindered by the efforts of employers, who wanted to introduce labour-saving machinery, and hire cheap, unskilled labour to run it.

Technological change was a persistent feature of 19th century industrial society. Skills were being swept away as innovating employers introduced mechanization. Some trades — like tailors, shoemakers and coopers — were particularly hard hit and suffered considerable unemployment. In 1852, the Toronto Journeymen Tailors' Operative Society persuaded a local firm to get rid of its new sewing machine, however, this success was temporary. Two years later the employees struck over the same issue and were replaced by women. When the union members drove a wagon through the streets proclaiming that their employer was unfair, he took legal action. The tailors were found guilty of conspiracy and their society was dissolved.

In the shoemaking industry, the introduction of sewing machines had similar effects. It was more efficient for manufacturers to establish factories and replace skilled craftsmen with women. In 1867, the Knights of St. Crispin was formed to try to preserve what in retrospect was acknowledged to be "a proud but obsolete craft." Other crafts, less vulnerable to rapid mechanization, fared somewhat better.

The development of the labour movement followed a definite pattern. Unions initially organized as small, independent locals located in different communities. By the 1890s as locals within a trade began to exchange information, links developed on a national or even an international basis. Common union affiliation and a union travel card could facilitate the search for work on both sides of the border and help meet the challenge of larger, more sophisticated employers.

Larger unions also became necessary as employers went further afield to hire their work force or employ strikebreakers. Communication between locals kept members informed of strike situations so that they could not be readily recruited by employers. The impulse towards national or international unions was a necessary response to the expansion of the labour market.

Despite fierce employer opposition, these craft unions did not embrace a socialist philosophy or espouse a connection with any specific political party. They have sometimes been termed "business unions" because, in keeping with the philosophy of Samuel Gompers, then president of the American Federation of Labor, they concentrated upon organizing along craft lines, and a limited number of "bread and butter" issues. It was a matter of "reward your friends and punish your enemies." In Canada, unions have been influenced by the British experience and are more inclined to support a social democratic party.

Left and right below: *Strike of Chesterfield Furniture Workers, Stratford 1934. One issue was the lower wages paid to women.*

Left and right bottom: *Workers' Parade, Nipigon, May 1, 1926. May Day remains a traditional time for such parades.*

In the 1880s a new kind of union burst upon the scene. It was known as the Holy and Noble Order of the Knights of Labor and differed from the existing craft unions in a number of important respects. It was committed to changing society. The Knights of Labor believed in organizing all workers, including women, into a single union.

The Knights began as a secret society in Philadelphia, and to counteract employer opposition, they employed a ritual involving passwords, oaths and special handshakes combined with the phrase "I am a worker." The ritual reiterated the beliefs of the order — and the appeal to pride of the Order's membership undoubtedly contributed to its allure. However, despite its dynamism and idealism, the Knights of Labor had internal contradictions which undermined its effectiveness as a trade union movement. When it did conduct strikes (for example, the 1883 telegraphers' strike and the 1886 strike of Toronto street railwaymen), they often failed.

Within the labour movement itself, the Knights were a divisive force, challenging the craft unions which considered the organization of unskilled workers (their competition) to be a threat to the job security of their members. Thus, when the craft unions gained a majority of delegates at the 1902 Trades and Labour Congress (TLC) convention in Berlin (now Kitchener), the Knights were expelled. Though the union was already in decline by that time, it left a positive legacy. It developed an articulate critique of industrial society and a vision that all workers should be organized into industrial unions. This latter idea was far ahead of its time and would not be achieved in Canada until World War II.

With the broadening of the franchise and the introduction of the secret ballot, industrial workers also came to play a larger role in politics. Job consciousness had created union organization amongst skilled tradesmen but their common problems prompted the emergence of a broad perspective (which some historians regard as "class consciousness") and overt political activity.

Skilled workers — part of the "labour aristocracy" — provided leadership for the entire movement, and they were sufficiently effective that politicians of the day began to respond to "labour" as a political interest group. In 1872, Sir John A. Macdonald, calling himself "the workingman's friend," introduced the Trade Unions Act which freed unions from criminal sanctions for conspiracy in restraint of trade. At the provincial level, Oliver Mowat passed the Ontario Factory Act to demonstrate his sensitivity to workers' needs and interest. In *Dreaming of What Might Be,* G. Kealey and B. Palmer quoted from Phillips Thompson, an outspoken labour journalist. In 1885 Thompson claimed that "a determined effort is now being made by the Grit party to capture the labour vote."

Increasingly, workers began to speak with one voice. They organized labour councils in urban centres, so that representatives of all unions in an area could meet regularly to discuss issues of mutual concern. In 1871, the first such council, the Toronto Trades Assembly, was founded by five locals from different craft unions. In 1873, the recently formed Ottawa Trades Council succeeded in getting its president Daniel O'Donoghue elected as the first labour representative to the Ontario Legislature. O'Donoghue was an Irish-born printer who is sometimes called "the father of Canadian labour."

Canadian workers initially practised what was then called "partyism," which Martin Robin, author of *Radical Politics and Canadian Labour,* defined as supporting old-line parties if they proved to be sympathetic to labour. However, when a labour representative was elected, he was invariably absorbed into the existing party system. O'Donoghue, for example, was an ally of Mowat's Liberal government, and was rewarded after his defeat in 1879 with a succession of government jobs. In 1873 The Canadian Labour Union (CLU) was founded by thirty-one Ontario locals at a convention called by the Toronto Trades Assembly. It was really more of a regional than a national body and it did not last long, but it was an important precedent. The CLU would be succeeded by other national labour congresses. The most enduring one was the Trades and Labour Congress (TLC) which was founded in 1883, and lasted until 1956, when it merged with the Canadian Congress of Labour (CCL) to form the modern Canadian Labour Congress (CLC).

Left and right below: *Weekly Meeting, Windsor, 1947. The management of the Ford Motor Company met with the negotiating committee of Local 200, United Auto Workers (UAW-CIO).* ***Left and right bottom:*** *Ford Strike,*

These central labour bodies made submissions to federal and provincial governments on such issues as: improved labour standards legislation, the abolition of immigration, female suffrage, equal access to education and opposition to business monopolies.

Windsor, 1947. Striking workers jammed the approaches with their cars to prevent access to the Ford plant.

Labours' political role extended beyond simply lobbying governments. In the 1870s, both organized and unorganized workers participated in the Nine Hours movement and organized parades, meetings and support for the Toronto printers' strike. In this same period a new labour newspaper, the *Ontario Workman* was established, and later such newspapers grew in number partly as a result of the intellectual ferment stimulated by the Knights of Labor. These small papers (like the *Palladium of Labor* and the *Labor Advocate*) often propounded minority views on such topics as the "National Policy" of Macdonald's Conservatives. The labour press was critical of the co-option of labour's political representatives and the pace of reform. Phillips Thompson, writing as "Enjolras" in the *Palladium of Labor* exclaimed:

> Just let us think for a while what the effect upon government and society would be supposing the great majority of working men everywhere were thoroughly educated in the principles of Labour Reform, and determined at any sacrifice to carry them into effect. Let us picture to ourselves the social condition that would result were our ideals realized by the resolute determination of the masses in all civilized lands to use their power for the good of the whole people, instead of letting the selfish few play upon their prejudices and passions, and rule them for the benefit of the upper class.

By the 1880s, the political climate was changing dramatically. It had become increasingly apparent that the interests of labour and capital were not the same, and labour reformers began to advocate an independent political platform for Canadian labour. These ideas were eclectic in the late 19th century, but they were all sharply critical of the *status quo.* By the turn of the century these ideas had evolved into a socialist critique of capitalist society.

In 1906, delegates to the TLC convention voted to launch their own political party. This experiment was short-lived, but in Ontario it did result in the formation of the Independent Labour Party (ILP). However, the ILP had little initial success.

The ferment surrounding World War I and labour's opposition to conscription launched the TLC once again into independent politics. The result was that the Canadian Labour Party (CLP) contested the 1917 federal election. Though none of the labour candidates was elected, there were strong showings in Hamilton and Temiskaming. However, many workers had voted for the government or for the opposition Liberals. In the 1919 Ontario election, members were elected and formed a coalition with the farmers in E.C. Drury's farmer-labour government. There were two Labour members in the cabinet, including Walter Rollo as the Minister of Labour. It was an important achievement for the fledgling party but it could not last.

The decade of the 1920s was characterized by consolidation, growth and mergers in the business community, greater American investment in the economy and rapid technological change. It was a period of boom and the beginning of the modern consumer society. But for all this expansion, the prosperity would prove precarious and unstable. There were serious imbalances which would later become evident.

It was a decade of contrasts. There was prosperity but also high unemployment. While everyone aspired to own a car (and by 1930 one in seven adult Canadians did), "consumerism" made workers more conservative, and the number of trade union members in Ontario declined substantially. Workers also responded positively to an aggressive employer campaign to avoid the formation of independent unions by establishing "employees' committees." The "industrial council" movement was commonly associated with subsidiaries of large American corporations but it also included some Canadian firms like Massey-Harris.

Despite the decline in union membership, there were improvements. The eight-hour workday became the norm in some sectors of the economy. By the end of the 1920s it was possible for the average male manufacturing worker to raise a family solely on his own wages. The average female worker's wages also rose but only slightly. On the political scene, post war cynicism, and disagreements between the farmer and

Right top: *Strike at Stelco Plant, Hamilton, 1945.*
Right bottom: *Demonstration by East York Teachers, Queen's Park, December 1973. Bills 274 and 275, affecting teacher-trustee negotiations, were withdrawn after first readings.*
Left below: *James Shaver Woodsworth (1874-1942). Born on a farm in Etobicoke (now in Metropolitan Toronto), of Dutch and Mennonite Loyalist origin on his mother's side, Woodsworth's family moved to Manitoba. In 1921, he became a Labour M.P. for Winnipeg North Centre, a seat he held until his death. He was a founder of the CCF Party (now the NDP).*

labour representatives in Drury's government accompanied waning support for independent labour politics within the TLC.

In the depression of the 1930s, the labour movement was further devastated. Neither traditional organization models nor more radical Communist alternatives seemed to provide an answer. This situation changed as a result of the 1937 strike of Oshawa autoworkers. The Congress of Industrial Organizations (CIO) — an aggressive, democratic, industrial union movement — had come to Ontario.

Despite the active opposition of businessmen and the hostility of Premier Mitchell Hepburn (who ran his 1937 election campaign more against the CIO than Earl Rowe's Conservatives), the CIO grew. Later, when the war brought full employment, the CIO successfully organized the workers of Ontario's manufacturing sector into strong permanent unions. Organizations like the United Auto Workers (UAW), the United Steelworkers of America (USWA) and the United Electrical Workers (UEW) are still prominent in the private sector today.

The Co-operative Commonwealth Federation (CCF), a new national party, was founded in Regina in 1933. Under the leadership of Manitoba Labour M.P. James Shaver Woodsworth, a section of organized labour, the farmer's movement, intellectuals and middle-class progressives all came together. In Ontario, despite early internal divisions between farmers, labour and some Communist interlopers (who were ejected), the CCF gained support dramatically during the Second World War.

Following the example of the British unions' relationship with the British Labour Party, the new industrial unions increasingly supported the CCF. In 1943 they formally endorsed that party as the "political arm of labour," as they would later endorse the New Democratic Party (NDP), the CCF's successsor. In the 1943 Ontario election, the CCF, with labour support, became the Official Opposition. This election was significant in that it began a unique feature — the three-party system. By 1980, more than a million Ontario citizens were members of trade unions. The "voice of labour" could claim the right to be heeded on matters affecting the welfare of Ontario workers.

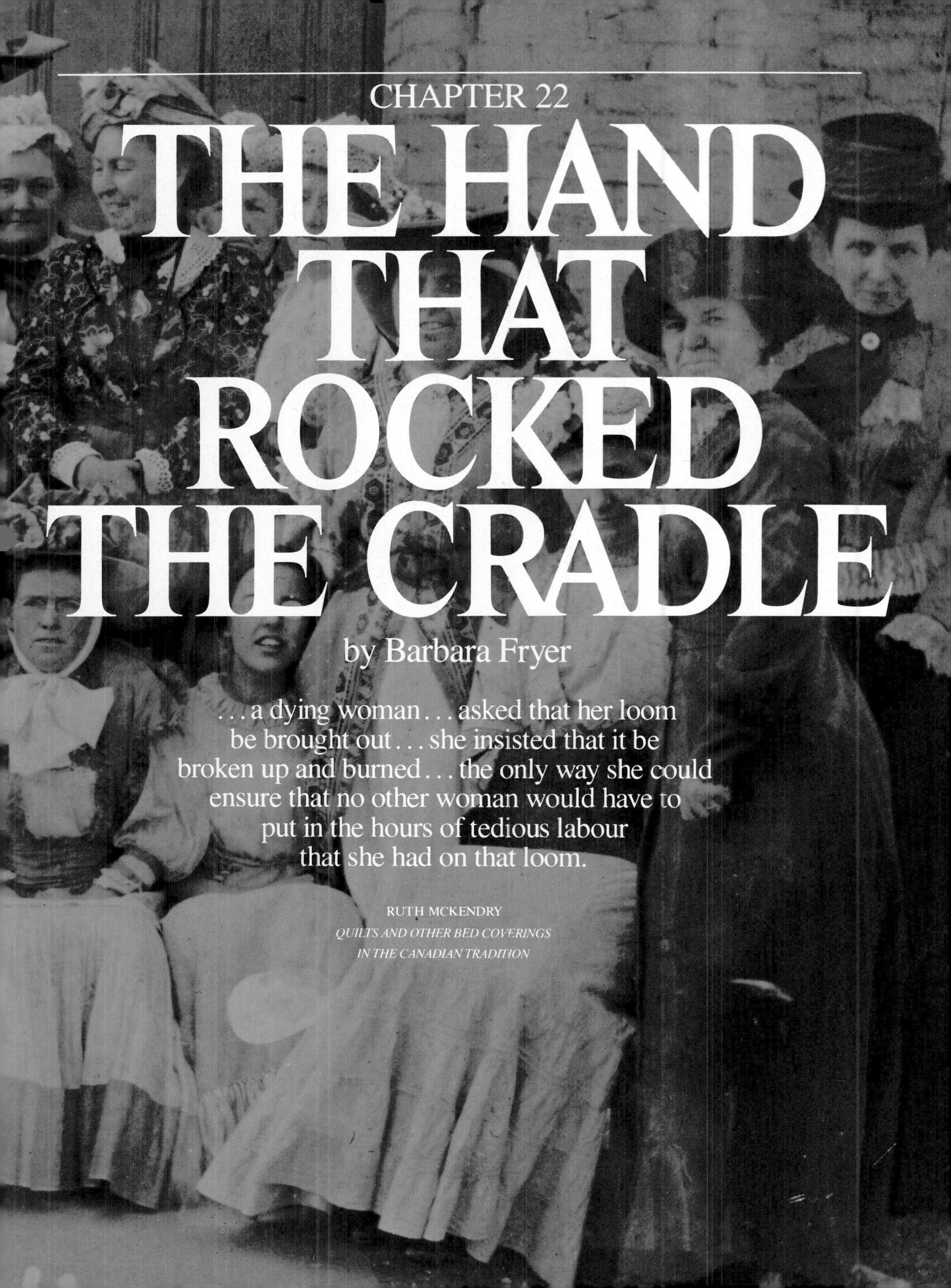

CHAPTER 22

THE HAND THAT ROCKED THE CRADLE

by Barbara Fryer

. . . a dying woman . . . asked that her loom be brought out . . . she insisted that it be broken up and burned . . . the only way she could ensure that no other woman would have to put in the hours of tedious labour that she had on that loom.

RUTH MCKENDRY
QUILTS AND OTHER BED COVERINGS IN THE CANADIAN TRADITION

In the introduction to *The Proper Sphere,* Editors Ramsay Cook and Wendy Mitchenson point out that many people who write about women feel that the subject really belongs in accounts dealing with the development of the whole human race. But because females have been ignored in many history books, such writers feel that there is a need to catch up. Since women appear in other parts of this work, the following chapter is not an attempt to explore the entire history of women in Ontario. Rather it is an effort to trace the movement of women from their traditional role, tending to children and domestic duties to their ever increasing participation in the outside domains of politics and paid work.

In 1856, Reverend Robert Sedgewick told a Young Men's Christian Association audience in Halifax that women and men should operate in separate spheres. Government, he said, "is naturally divided between the two sexes, the noble government of children belonging to women, the less noble government of adults to man."

While Sedgewick's beliefs were shared by many Ontarians in the 19th and 20th centuries, they were roundly criticized by a growing number of women who were agitating for the vote. Some feminists even went so far as to suggest homemaking was not the ideal occupation for women. In *A Not Unreasonable Claim: Women and Reform in Canada, 1880s-1920s,* is a piece by Deborah Gorham on Flora MacDonald Denison. A prominent Toronto feminist, Denison wrote:

> Now we all know there is a great deal of maudlin sentiment written about the home, for we see on all sides, women whose lives are dull and monotonous if not tragic, just on account of this wonderful talk of the sacredness of the home. The only sacred spot is the place where human beings are so circumstanced that they can live up to their own ideals to the end of attaining happiness . . .

It is no secret that women have normally been thought well-suited to home-related activities. It has been that way since the days when Woodland Cree occupied a vast stretch of what is now Northern Ontario. These native people survived on deer, caribou, moose and small game. Women cared for the home, cooking, sewing and watching over young children. Farther south, the Ojibwa and Algonquin Indians also

__Overleaf:__ Ladies' Aid, Wardsville, February 11, 1914. Ladies' Aid volunteers formed an integral part of many church congregations. Wardsville is on Highway 2 west of London.
__Left below:__ Elizabeth Posthuma Gwillim Simcoe (1766-1850) in Welsh Dress. Wife of the first lieutenant governor, she was an accomplished artist, diarist and spoke both French and Welsh.
__Right below:__ Jane Okill Stuart. The wife of Reverend John Stuart, first Anglican clergyman in Upper Canada, Jane journeyed with her husband and children from Schenectady, New York, to Montreal in 1781. In 1785 they settled in Kingston. George Okill Stuart, later Archdeacon of Upper Canada was their son.

hunted, bolstering their food supply with fish, berries and wild rice. The division of labour was much the same as with the Woodland Cree. The political structure was one of male dominance.

The Neutral, Tobacco and Huron Indians along the Great Lakes practiced agriculture, growing corn, squash, beans and tobacco. Their way of life was similar to that of the League of the Iroquois which consisted of five, and later six nations and had a representative council which determined external policies, such as whether to go to war.

Within the clans, the families were matrilineal — a child belonged to his or her mother's clan and inherited its customs and name. Each bark longhouse accommodated up to twenty families, and was run by an older woman or two. Most of the food was acquired as a result of female labour, as women were responsible for agricultural activities. Men occupied themselves with war, trading, hunting and fishing. In his writings about the Hurons, Samuel de Champlain praised the women of Huronia, who bore the brunt of the work.

The matrilineal family structure and the power wielded by women at lower levels of authority did not stop females from being considered inferior to men, nor did the vital agricultural work performed by women. Though they possessed a good deal of say in how their societies were run, a separation was still drawn between the woman's concern for the home and the outer masculine realms of hunting and external politics.

Generally speaking, among the native people living in what was to become Ontario, marriages could be informal if the couple desired, and dissolved at the wish of either partner. The native concept of marriage was significant to the French fur trade, which began in the 17th century. Many French traders married native women "*à la façon du pays.*"

As well as being a loving partner to the fur trader, the native woman had the appropriate skills to help him survive the natural elements, and she facilitated his communication with his Indian trading partners. With the woman tending to domestic work and helping her husband with his job, one can see that when the two cultures mixed the conventional division of labour between the sexes was retained.

According to Gaetan Vallières, in *L'Ontario français par les docu-*

ments, there had been some French women in a small number of colonies in present-day Ontario. The arrival of the Loyalists in the late 18th century was followed by the coming of immigrants, mostly of British, European or African origin and many from the United States, bringing Ontario's population to more than 1,500,000 by 1871.

Up to the middle of the 19th century the predominance of rural life made it fairly easy for all to see that a woman played a valid economic role in a family's struggle to make a living. In the wilderness or on a farm, wife and husband could observe one another at work and understand how major the achievements of the other were. The joint effort between men and women to stay alive in the natural elements was chronicled by many a female writer, including Mary O'Brien and the sisters Susanna Moodie and Catharine Parr Traill.

Though being a homemaker and raising children was the conventional goal for females, there were women who worked for money. They were mostly single and had to support themselves, or mothers whose economic circumstances made participation in the labour force a necessity. After 1830 it became increasingly difficult for a man to acquire land, and hence fewer women had the chance to become farm wives. Many men went west in search of new opportunities. As a result, more and more women had to work for wages either to tide themselves over a long engagement or because they would never marry.

The Proper Sphere included an article by M. Phelps, originally published in 1890, which cited a visitor to America who found that in the America of 1840 seven paid occupations were available to women, including domestic service, factory jobs, teaching, sewing, book-binding, being a compositor and keeping a boarding house. The Canadian census indicated that, by 1881, women were active in 227 different occupations.

As the 19th century wore on the concentration of women in teaching grew rapidly. Concerning the feminization of teaching in *The Neglected Majority,* Alison Prentice noted that in the Upper Canada of 1851, women made up 22.2 percent of the teachers in public or common schools. By 1871, 50.2 percent of the teachers in the same network of

Right top: *Municipal Elections Goderich, 1894. Candidate C.A. Humber solicited votes from both ladies and gentlemen. Women owning property had voting privileges in municipal elections.*
Right below: *Model School, Parry Sound, 1906. Model schools were attached to provincial teacher training institutions, first called Normal Schools.*
Left below: *Silhouette, Canadian National Exhibition, 1909. This pretty silhouette was on a card advertising an antique gallery.*

schools were female. A big factor in the switch was that women were paid less than men and were often in higher demand. Some people tried to rationalize the discrepancy in pay by saying women were best suited to teach very young children, while men were better at the more demanding job of instructing more advanced students.

The invention and proliferation of new machinery made way for new forms of women's employment in the latter part of 19th century Ontario. Sewing machine sales rocketed in the 1870s, leading to the ready-made clothes industry. The garment industry which followed, was one of many with a bad reputation for dehumanizing women, children, and men. Sixty-hour weeks and unhealthy working conditions were not unusual and the pay was low.

Nursing was expanding around the time Canada's first school for nurses was established in 1874 in St. Catharines, Ontario. Office work was quickly becoming a woman's field. In the Canada of 1881 there were 1,573 employees — mostly men — taking care of such office duties as handwriting letters and bookkeeping. Some women saw that office work could open into a domain for females, and soon, the Young Women's Christian Association started classes in business English, bookkeeping and shorthand.

The first typewriters hit the Canadian market in 1879, and as business after business acquired the new machines, there grew a demand for people who could touch-type. Women taught themselves to type in order to get jobs, and the Y.W.C.A. introduced typing courses. When women entered a labour field the increase in manpower supply made it possible for an employer to find people willing to work for less.

The growth of urban areas and wage work contributed to the lowering of the status of women. Those who cared for home and children while their husbands earned wages did not appear equal to their partners — they were not making any money. Women in paying jobs earned less on average than men. Some people succumbed to the temptation to translate the pay gap into a difference in capacity and worth.

While many women had jobs and were removed from the traditional full-time role as housewife, earning wages in the outside world was still

Municipal Elections 1894.

Ladies and Gentlemen:

At the request of several prominent ratepayers of our town to allow my name being brought before you as Mayor for the ensuing year, have given my consent and will, if elected, devote, to the best of my ability and judgment, the necessary time and attention pertaining to that office and would therefore respectfully solicit your vote and influence for me as Mayor for 1894.

Respectfully yours,

Goderich, December, 1893. C. A. HUMBER.

not an ideal after which most strove. Being married and a full-time housewife appealed to the majority. Meanwhile, labour-saving devices and technology that removed some work from the home and into the factory gave some women spare time. This meant many could join organizations, and a multitude of women's groups sprang up. They included the Woman's Christian Temperance Union, established in 1883; the National Council of Women of Canada, 1893; the National Council of Jewish Women, 1894 and the Y.W.C.A.

By getting together with other women and pooling their "feminine" capacities for tenderness and clean living, they could put their talents to good use. These women felt the home was their domain, and now that they were stepping out, they were protecting homes in general.

Of course, the aim of many organizations was reform by advocating help for the poor, promoting laws for clean water, temperance, and so on. In *A Not Unreasonable Claim: Women and Reform in Canada, 1880s-1920s,* one writer commented on a common characteristic of the reform groups: "Each organization was originally formed to right a specific wrong, but once formed, each tended to involve itself in a number of reform enterprises." For example, the W.C.T.U. was started in 1883 to agitate against the consumption of alcohol, and three decades later it was involved in more than twenty-five causes.

Though the accomplishments of some of these groups were impressive — relief for the poor, helping immigrants — the predominantly middle-class members have been criticized in some circles for imposing their moral values on others, and they have been accused of addressing some societal ills in a superficial manner.

The very successful Women's Institutes differed from many of the reform groups in their objectives and approach. The first of the Women's Institutes — now a world-wide movement — was founded in 1897 at Stoney Creek, Ontario, by Adelaide Hunter Hoodless, and it was her hope that the organization would improve the living standards in rural areas by teaching women better homemaking techniques. According to the constitution presented at the first meeting:

***Left below:** First Harem Skirt in Canada, 1911.*
***Right top:** Card of Admission to Teachers' Course in Elementary Household Science, 1912.*
***Right below:** Adelaide Hunter Hoodless (1857-1910). Born on a farm near St. George, Brant County, Adelaide and her husband, John Hoodless, farmed near Stoney Creek, where she founded the first Women's Institute in 1897, now a world wide movement. She introduced home economics into Ontario's schools, and helped obtain funds for the Macdonald Institute, Guelph.*

> the object of this Institute shall be to promote that knowledge of household science which shall lead to improvement in household architecture with special attention to home sanitation, to a better understanding of economics and hygenic value of foods and fuels, and to a more scientific care of children with a view to raising the general standard of health of our people.

The death of a young son from impure milk spurred Hoodless on to founding an organization that now has branches across Canada and around the world.

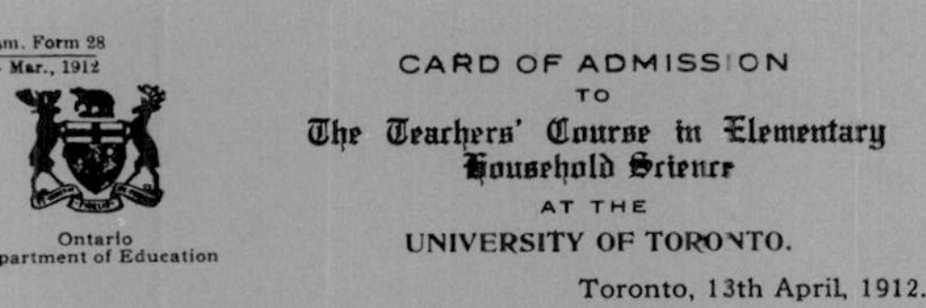

xam. Form 28
o. Mar., 1912

Ontario
epartment of Education

CARD OF ADMISSION
TO
The Teachers' Course in Elementary
Household Science
AT THE
UNIVERSITY OF TORONTO.

Toronto, 13th April, 1912.

The Minister desires me to inform you that, on presenting his card to Miss A. L. Laird, Associate Professor, at the Faculty of Household Science, University of Toronto, you will be admitted to the Short Course for Teachers in Elementary Household Science, commencing on April 20th.

iss Hazel K. Seaman.

A. H. U. COLQUHOUN,
Deputy Minister of Education.

Although a lot of women's groups had no interest in female suffrage when they started, some eventually incorporated it into their demands. The Woman's Christian Temperance Union was among them. A provincial plebiscite on prohibition in 1894 and a federal plebiscite in 1898 resulted in victories for the temperance movement. But a lack of government action followed, prompting the president of the W.C.T.U. to say in 1904: "If we dropped every other Department in our organization, and worked for woman's enfranchisement, we should be farther ahead in ten years than we will be in fifty years without it."

Other organizations had suffrage in their platforms right from the start. One of the most important was founded in 1876 by Dr. Emily Howard Stowe in Toronto. She had graduated from the Women's New York Medical School in 1868 (Canadian medical schools would not accept her), and came to Toronto as Canada's first female doctor, supporting her invalid husband and three children. Stowe was disturbed that Canadian women were not showing much interest in women's rights.

This inspired her to found the Women's Literary Movement in 1876. The name of this female rights group was meant to head off shock waves that a more radical-sounding name might cause. Public education was a major club activity. In 1881, a Toronto weekly newspaper, *Canada Citizen,* gave the group its own column.

Stowe's organization was the first to go to the Ontario legislature to ask for votes for women (provinces were then in charge of federal and provincial voting eligibility). This helped pave the way, in 1882, for the

MOD
ONT

> the object of this Institute shall be to promote that knowledge of household science which shall lead to improvement in household architecture with special attention to home sanitation, to a better understanding of economics and hygenic value of foods and fuels, and to a more scientific care of children with a view to raising the general standard of health of our people.

The death of a young son from impure milk spurred Hoodless on to founding an organization that now has branches across Canada and around the world.

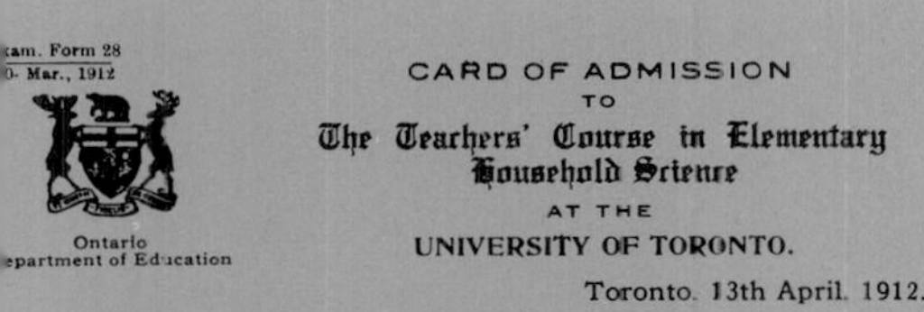

Exam. Form 28
6 Mar., 1912

CARD OF ADMISSION
TO
The Teachers' Course in Elementary Household Science
AT THE
UNIVERSITY OF TORONTO.

Ontario
Department of Education

Toronto, 13th April, 1912.

The Minister desires me to inform you that, on presenting this card to Miss A. L. Laird, Associate Professor, at the Faculty of Household Science, University of Toronto, you will be admitted to the Short Course for Teachers in Elementary Household Science, commencing on April 20th.

Miss Hazel K. Seaman.

A. H. U. COLQUHOUN,
Deputy Minister of Education.

Although a lot of women's groups had no interest in female suffrage when they started, some eventually incorporated it into their demands. The Woman's Christian Temperance Union was among them. A provincial plebiscite on prohibition in 1894 and a federal plebiscite in 1898 resulted in victories for the temperance movement. But a lack of government action followed, prompting the president of the W.C.T.U. to say in 1904: "If we dropped every other Department in our organization, and worked for woman's enfranchisement, we should be farther ahead in ten years than we will be in fifty years without it."

Other organizations had suffrage in their platforms right from the start. One of the most important was founded in 1876 by Dr. Emily Howard Stowe in Toronto. She had graduated from the Women's New York Medical School in 1868 (Canadian medical schools would not accept her), and came to Toronto as Canada's first female doctor, supporting her invalid husband and three children. Stowe was disturbed that Canadian women were not showing much interest in women's rights.

This inspired her to found the Women's Literary Movement in 1876. The name of this female rights group was meant to head off shock waves that a more radical-sounding name might cause. Public education was a major club activity. In 1881, a Toronto weekly newspaper, *Canada Citizen,* gave the group its own column.

Stowe's organization was the first to go to the Ontario legislature to ask for votes for women (provinces were then in charge of federal and provincial voting eligibility). This helped pave the way, in 1882, for the passage of a law allowing single women with property to vote on municipal by-laws, a drop in the bucket in what was to be a long struggle.

A year later the Women's Literary Club disbanded and formed the Toronto Women's Suffrage Association, which, of course, embraced the goals of its predecessor. A slight gain was made in 1884 when unmarried, propertied women were given the right to vote in municipal elections. The Toronto group evolved into the Dominion Women's Enfranchisement Association in 1889.

Over the next quarter-century several members of the Ontario legislature introduced bills that would enfranchise women. But these got little support. The helpful members included Liberals John Waters and John Smith, and Labour member Allan Studholme. The successive Conservative premiers, Sir Oliver Mowat and J.P. Whitney (who came to power in 1905), did not support votes for women.

In 1907 the Dominion Women's Enfranchisement Association became the Canadian Suffrage Association. One of its eminent members was Flora MacDonald Denison, a dressmaker and journalist who grew up in Belleville and Picton. Denison, who became president of the new association in 1911, was more radical than the mainstream of women pushing for the vote. She did not support some of the moral goals of many suffragists, such as temperance, and she was critical of the church, which to her unfairly down-played the women's political position.

Denison attacked the traditional division of labour in families, telling women not to be afraid to relinquish household work. She believed meal-getting and child care could eventually be taken over by trained specialists. She could have had something along the lines of today's day-care centres in mind.

Among many other important characters in the suffrage movement were Dr. Augusta Stowe Gullen, following in her mother's footsteps, and from 1893 to 1898 Lady Aberdeen, the wife of the Governor General of Canada. She founded the National Council of Women of Canada in 1893. The council supported giving women the vote.

Arguments against enfranchising females were abundant: it was not

Left below: *Dr. Emily Jennings Stowe (1831-1903). She was trained at the New York Medical School, was the first woman to practice medicine in Canada, and a leader in the women's suffrage movement.*
Right below: *Dr. Augusta Stowe Gullen (1857-1943). Daughter of Emily Stowe, Augusta was the first woman doctor trained in Canada. She, too, favoured*

women's suffrage, and helped found the Women's College Hospital, Toronto.

Left and right bottom: *Norwich, Where Emily and Augusta Stowe were born. Both were descended from the Quaker founders of Norwich, who believed that men and women were equal, a tradition that may have propelled the Stowes to seek votes for women.*

lady-like; women were physically weaker; they had smaller brains than men. Sometimes the same notion was twisted to support both sides of the struggle: some claimed women would clean up politics with their gentle qualities; others countered that politics would rob women of their so-called feminine characteristics.

In 1915, the Conservative party in Ontario was led by Sir William Hearst, who let on he was not convinced women wanted the vote. Ontario's suffrage movement was lagging behind the west, where Manitoba, Alberta and Saskatchewan women were enfranchised in 1916. The rural life of many prairie province residents helped bring this about; men could see that their wives made a crucial economic contribution to farm living. In the more urban Ontario, females were not taken as seriously.

The victories in the prairie provinces did nothing to sway the Ontario government. Premier Hearst said that as Liberal and Conservative women were peacefully performing war work side by side, it would be foolish to risk giving them something that might cause them to squabble. Soon, however, Hearst did an about-face. On February 27, 1917, bills for provincial enfranchisement that had earlier been introduced by Liberal William McDonald, and private Conservative J.W. Johnson were scheduled for second reading. Hearst got up, praised the contribution females were making to the war effort and endorsed giving women the vote. Ontario women had the provincial franchise as of April 12, 1917, and they could sit in the legislature beginning April 24, 1919.

Hearst's abrupt change has been attributed to what was happening on the federal scene. Robert Borden's Union government, a coalition of the Conservatives and Liberals, was about to grant some women the federal franchise, and Hearst risked alienating women from the federal Conservative party in the upcoming national election if the provincial Conservatives were to withhold suffrage.

While Ontario's politicians grappled with the female suffrage issue, Members of Parliament had their hands full with it also. When women in the prairie provinces were enfranchised by their provincial governments, there was some argument as to whether this meant they should also be able to vote in dominion elections. In 1917, war-related issues arose that would ease some women into voting in the next federal election. Borden was in favour of conscription and with an election on the horizon, he had to find a strategy to deal with the issue. He negotiated with [some] pro-conscription Liberals to form a coalition. In addition, he devised the Wartime Elections Act which removed the vote from conscientious objectors (including Mennonites and Doukhobors), as well as Canadian citizens born in enemy countries who had been naturalized since 1902. The Act also gave the vote to women who were British subjects, twenty-one years and older, and were closely related to someone in the armed forces of Great Britain or Canada.

This Act, which was only to last until demobilization after the war, was criticized by opponents as a ploy to ensure Borden's re-election. It would disenfranchise many people in the west opposed to conscription who might vote against him, while bestowing the vote upon women likely to be in favour of conscription, as they would want troops to support their loved ones overseas.

Other women were able to vote in the 1917 election because the Military Voters Act enfranchised any British subjects who had taken active part in military service. This Act gave the vote to some people under twenty-one years of age, and to a number of women, notably army nurses.

Borden promised that if he were elected, women would soon have the federal franchise. He was returned to power and made good on his promise. Women got the dominion franchise on May 24, 1918, and by 1920, they had the permanent right to sit in the House of Commons. The first woman to win a seat was from Ontario — Agnes MacPhail. Elected in 1921 as an independent, her parliamentary career spanned nineteen years, after which she joined the Co-operative Commonwealth Federation and was elected to the Ontario legislature in 1943.

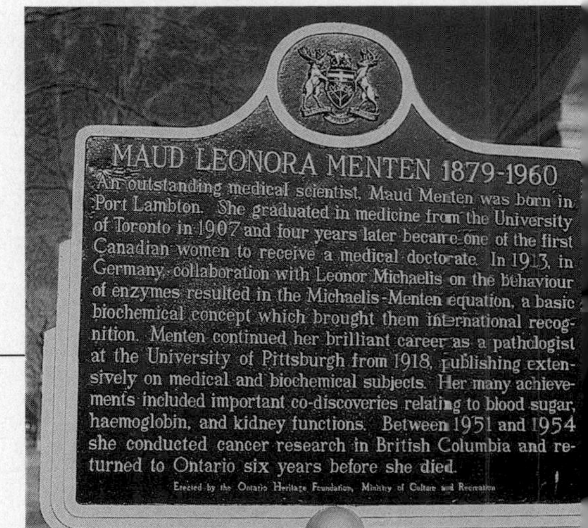

MAUD LEONORA MENTEN 1879-1960
An outstanding medical scientist, Maud Menten was born in Port Lambton. She graduated in medicine from the University of Toronto in 1907 and four years later became one of the first Canadian women to receive a medical doctorate. In 1913, in Germany, collaboration with Leonor Michaelis on the behaviour of enzymes resulted in the Michaelis-Menten equation, a basic biochemical concept which brought them international recognition. Menten continued her brilliant career as a pathologist at the University of Pittsburgh from 1918, publishing extensively on medical and biochemical subjects. Her many achievements included important co-discoveries relating to blood sugar, haemoglobin, and kidney functions. Between 1951 and 1954 she conducted cancer research in British Columbia and returned to Ontario six years before she died.
Erected by the Ontario Heritage Foundation, Ministry of Culture and Recreation

Women were allowed to be senators in 1929, after a struggle led by Alberta and Quebec women which centred on whether the word "person" in the British North America Act applied to female persons.

Over the years, the number of female politicians in Canada has been

Left below: *Postage Stamp Honouring Nellie Mooney McClung (1873-1951). Born in Chatsworth, her family moved to Manitoba in 1881. Author and fighter for women's rights. Nellie sat in the Alberta Legislature, 1921-1926, and helped get women appointed to the Senate of Canada.*
Left bottom: *Plaque to Maud Leonora Menten (1879-1960). Queen's Park, Toronto.She graduated in medicine in 1907, and in 1911 became the first Canadian woman to earn a medical doctorate.*
Right below: *Clara Brett Martin (1874-1923), First Woman Lawyer in Canada. The Mowat government had to pass legislation before the Upper Canada Law Society would accept her as a student.*

small. Charlotte Whitton, a former mayor of Ottawa, lamented in a 1946 article in *Saturday Night,* that not a single woman was sitting in a provincial legislature or the House of Commons. The situation has improved only slightly; about a dozen out of 282 federal constituencies sent women to the House of Commons in the 1980 national election and subsequent by-elections.

If Reverend Sedgewick's idea that only men should take part in organized politics seems to be dying an excruciatingly slow death, perhaps the other side of his belief, that women should stay home and care for children, is losing ground more rapidly. On December 11, 1981, the *Toronto Star* reported that for the first time in Ontario more than half (58.2 percent) of the mothers of children aged sixteen and under were working outside the home. The article also showed that in 1951, in Ontario, fifteen percent of married women were in the labour force and that by 1980, 58.5 percent of wives were employed.

Adjustments still need to be made to accommodate women who want to have jobs, so that women, children, and men alike, will be content with this trend. The 1981 census indicated that at the beginning of the decade, on average, women in Canada earned less than half (49.7 percent) of what men were paid. Women are still struggling to land jobs that have traditionally been done by men.

The women's movement in Canada is going strong and nowadays it is starting to embrace the broad spectrum of Canadian society. It started out as a predominantly middle-class, white organization in which the involvement of many women — native, immigrant, and Franco-Ontarian, for example — was lacking. Feminists would like to see all women in Ontario reach out and get involved in the movement.

Women have moved a substantial distance from their homes into the spheres of politics and the labour force. A passage written by Flora MacDonald Denison in the early 20th century seems to apply to today:

> Women are at last in the commercial arena and each day becoming more independent. Their final salvation will be achieved when they become the financial equals of men.

MOD
ONT

ERN
ARIO

CHAPTER 23

THE 1920s

by the Editors

I refuse to dance – Blues.
Black Bottoms, Charlestons, what wind blew
them in. Monkeys do them in zoos.

NOEL COWARD, *THIS YEAR OF GRACE!* 1928

WE WANT TO BE
CITIZENS
not
TRANSIENTS

CHAPTER 24

THE GREAT DEPRESSION

by Michiel Horn

Our world stopped and we got off.

JAMES GRAY
THE WINTER YEARS

have. Whether further studies would lead to a job was questionable, but studying seemed better than sitting around doing nothing.

People learned to make do with little. Churches were important social centres as well as places of worship and agencies of charity. Sports and games were important, though professional spectator sports had a tough time surviving the early 1930s. Among the National Hockey League franchises to fold was one in Ottawa. Radio was a means of familiarizing many with the NHL, however, as hundreds of thousands of Canadians learned to watch through the eyes of Foster Hewitt, reporting from the new Maple Leaf Gardens in Toronto.

The movies were popular, though the quarter or fifty cents admission was too expensive for those on relief. Like the films, the stars were mostly American, though Canadians like Raymond Massey and Walter Pidgeon were also on the screen. After May of 1934 Ontarians, like people the world over, watched with fascination the newsreels that preceded the featured films as the story of the Dionne quintuplets unfolded. Born to a French Canadian couple near Callander in Northern Ontario, the quints were brought into the world by a country doctor, A.R. Dafoe. The chances against identical quintuplets being born, let alone surviving, were astronomically high, but survive they did. Raised apart from their parents, Annette, Cécile, Emilie, Marie and Yvonne were for years a major tourist attraction. To many they were a symbol of hope in a world that otherwise seemed to offer little.

The Depression did not end immediately at the outbreak of war in Europe and Canada's entry in it in September 1939. Some of the young men who lined up to enlist were motivated less by patriotism than steady work and wages. Within two years unemployment ceased to be a problem and a labour shortage had taken its place. Moreover, deflation had given way to inflation as an economic plague.

Neither the war's prosperity nor its sadness could dim the memory of the "dirty Thirties." An entire generation of Canadians remembered the Depression as an economic disaster whose return should be avoided at almost any cost. The memory persisted and influenced government policies into the 1970s. It has not disappeared even today.

Right top: *Opening North End Gates, Welland Canal, Humberstone Township, 1932. On January 1, 1970, the township ceased to be a municipality. Under regional government it was divided between the Cities of Niagara Falls, Port Colborne and Welland. The present Welland Canal was completed in 1932, except for the Welland bypass, added by 1973.*

Right middle: *Elevator No. 7, Port Arthur, 1930s. At Port Arthur western grain is still loaded into "lakers" for transport down the St. Lawrence Seaway. On January 1, 1970, Port Arthur and Fort William, jointly called the Lakehead, amalgamated to form the City of Thunder Bay.*

Right below: *Queen Elizabeth Way, Port Credit, 1940. In 1931, work began on this limited access highway, which was eventually completed from Toronto to Fort Erie. On June 7, 1939, it was opened by King George VI and Queen Elizabeth (now the Queen Mother) and named in her honour.*

Far right below: *Canadian Bank of Commerce Head Office, Toronto. Planned during the good times of the 1920s, the building was finished in November 1930, just as the serious recession set in following the stock market crash of 1929. Until the 1960s it was the tallest building in the Commonwealth.*

POOL TERMINAL
7

units in action against the enemy. Of these, twenty-six, or forty-five percent of Canada's front line fighting units came from Ontario.

Naturally, Ontario men were also fully represented in the multitude of support and administrative units needed when an army takes the field. Dozens of engineer, signal, artillery and medical units are required in the combat zone. Thousands of supply, services, and auxiliary personnel were needed on European battlefields or close behind, and a comparable percentage of these troops also came from Ontario. The Royal Canadian Navy, the Royal Canadian Air Force, volunteer home defence units of the reconstituted unmobilized part of the Militia, renamed the Reserve Army, the Veterans' Guard and the three women's services, the Canadian Women's Army Corps, the Women's Royal Canadian Naval Service (the 'Wrens') and the Women's Division of the R.C.A.F. contained thousands of the province's fair sex.

Ontario on Hostile Shores

Ontario's fighting men were in the thick of it from the very beginning. Three Ontario infantry battalions, The Royal Canadian Regiment (mostly from Toronto and London), the Hastings and Prince Edward Regiment (from the Belleville-Trenton-Bancroft area), and the 48th Highlanders (from Toronto), were all in France before that country fell in June 1940.

On August 19, 1942, the ill-fated Dieppe Raid saw three other Ontario infantry battalions wiped out on the shores of France. These were Toronto's Royal Regiment of Canada, the Royal Hamilton Light Infantry and the Essex Scottish Regiment, of Windsor. Embarking with a total combined strength of 1,326 officers and men, these three units returned after nine hours of war with only 323, some of them wounded.

When Sicily was invaded on July 10, 1943, more than one third of the Canadian assault force was composed of Ontario units, three of which were those who had been in France in 1940. Now, they were in the forefront of General Eisenhower's armies which had begun the liberation of Europe. Two months later, having been victorious in Sicily, they landed on the Italian mainland. There they fought for the next eighteen months; were then moved to Holland, where they took part in the final defeat of the German Army in May 1945.

On D-Day, June 6, 1944, when the Normandy landings took place, the Queen's Own Rifles, a Toronto unit; the Highland Light Infantry from Galt and Kitchener; the Stormont, Dundas and Glengarry Highlanders from Eastern Ontario; all splashed ashore in the very forefront of the attack on Hitler's vaunted Westwall, piercing it the first day of their battle.

Later, in both the Mediterranean and Northwest European campaigns other Ontario regiments distinguished themselves, several of which bore unmistakably provincial names, such as the Ontario Regiment, whose home town was Oshawa, and the Lake Superior Regiment from Northern Ontario.

Wartime Industry and Finance

Wars are not won only on hostile shores and angry seas, or in flaming skies. They are won by resolute populations, by industrial production, and by the pouring out of money, as well as of blood.

The urgent demands of the war industry quickly cleared unemployed men off the streets. War plants needed men as much as the armed forces did. Women too, as in the first war, moved out of their homes into the labour force — this time in even greater numbers. Ontario's industry, suffering from ten years of economic depression, quickly revived. Machinery and patriotic student labour aided the normal rural work force to reach new peaks of production on the province's farms, to help feed beleaguered Britain. There was far better planning than there had been in 1914-18. After all, the experience of the earlier war was to be found in government and industrial filing cabinets.

Two examples of Ontario's wartime industrial expansion are — Victory Aircraft and John Inglis Company. The former, a Crown company with factories at Malton, near Toronto, reached a total of 9,500 employees who eventually turned out Lancaster bombers at a rate of one a day. The latter, at Long Branch a Toronto suburb, had 17,000 workers. They produced more machine guns during the war than any other indi-

Left and right below: H.M.C.S. Wallaceburg ***J336****. Built at Port Arthur and commissioned August 11, 1943, the* Wallaceburg *escorted convoys from Halifax and New York halfway across the Atlantic, and sank one, possibly two, German submarines. In the crew was a descendant of Joseph Brant.*
Left and right bottom: H.M.C.S. M C ***110****. Launched at Honey Harbour, July 1943, this submarine detector patrolled from Labrador to the West Indies.*

vidual firm in the Empire. Some 500,000 weapons, Bren guns, Browning aircraft machine guns, the .55 calibre Boys' anti-tank rifle and the 9 mm pistol became the tools of victory in Canadian and Allied hands. Other plants turned out many varieties of warlike items, both weaponry, miscellaneous items of equipment and wheeled and tracked vehicles. The labour force was almost totally employed. Only the unemployable were without jobs.

In less than three years Ontario, as did its sister provinces, ceded provincial rights and tax fields to Ottawa. Personal income and corporation taxes were collected by the Dominion Government, with a portion of each returned yearly under a system of fixed grants. The war had to be financed, and it could be done effectively and reasonably economically only by centralized methods. The needs of 1939-45 were essentially the needs of 1914-18, as have been already described in an earlier chapter, and the temporary social and industrial re-adjustments of the two periods were almost the same. However, the magnitude of the second struggle, the immense strides in science and technology since the Armistice of 1918, and the vastly increased geographic areas of the war itself meant that, in many respects, the war efforts of the first conflict although similar, were dwarfed by those of the second. Indeed, Canada's dollar expenditure in the Second War was ten times that of the First.

Since most of the province's work force was engaged in producing military items, there were no new cars, no new home appliances such as refrigerators, electrical gadgets, stoves and the like. The building of private homes was at a halt, for construction for wartime needs took not only the labour but the materials as well. Consequently, the population became cramped in inadequate housing as it flocked in its thousands to factory sites, or wartime administrative centres from the smaller places of the province. This had a disquieting effect on the normal tenor of family life, added to which there was the problem of domestic separations caused by almost a million men in uniform, hardly any of them stationed anywhere near their homes.

When Premier George Drew came to power in succession to Premier Hepburn, Ontario waged war on the home front with renewed vigour.

Drew was intensely loyal to the Crown, firm in his belief in the Empire and in Canada's and Ontario's role in it. His patriotic and dynamic leadership, a bit too much for the average Canadian to digest in peacetime, increased the confidence in final victory. Under Drew's guidance an Ontario Service's Club was set up in London, England, for Ontario's fighting sons and a War Bride's Bureau was opened to counsel British wives of Ontario servicemen.

When the war began, Ontario's manufacturing complex was just beginning to emerge from the Great Depression. By the war's end, immense enlargement had taken place — chemicals, synthetic rubber, steel and textiles required by the armed forces gave manufacturing a tremendous fillip. Munition plants as in the first war, only greater in size and more efficient in operation, were established everywhere. They were just as upsetting to the social and economic life of the province as they had been a score or more years before, but men and women who served in them were as necessary to the winning of the war as the marching battalions on the field of battle. In the forests of Ontario more men revived the pulp, paper, and lumber industries from the slump of the 1930s, for war devours all manner of things, animal, mineral and vegetable.

The N.R.M.A.

In June 1940, because of the serious situation in Europe, the National Resources Mobilization Act came into force. This brought thousands of young males into the army for home service, first on a part-time training basis, then as full-time soldiers. These men were called "zombies," but in the end 16,000 of them were found to be sufficiently alive that they were sent to the front, where some made the supreme sacrifice in the last days of the war. In August 1943, one Ontario-raised battalion of these N.R.M.A. conscripts commanded by active force officers, took part in the unopposed invasion of the Aleutian Island of Kiska. An active force officer with service in Britain and northwest Europe, has since said that this was the "toughest, best trained unit" he had encountered during the war.

Women Help as Before

Repeating their Great War performance, Ontario women from all social levels responded quickly to the demands of war. They devoted their spare time to a multiplicity of voluntary tasks; knitting socks, mufflers, sea stockings for the navy, and gloves; rolling bandages and assisting the war effort in countless ways.

Many teen-age girls, for instance, joined the Ontario Farm Service Force to help harvest the crops. Serving in servicemen's canteens and entertaining the troops, especially Commonwealth and foreign servicemen training in Canada was another place where Ontario's women shone. Ontario was sprinkled with air training centres full of lonely lads from Britain, Australia, New Zealand and other Commonwealth countries or Empire possessions. In Toronto, members of a Royal Norwegian Air Force establishment known as "Little Norway" found life in a strange land pleasant indeed, because both matron and maid remembered that they had these strangers within their gates, and considered it a duty to be hospitable.

Thousands of Ontario women, of course, donned the King's uniform, or the uniforms of the Red Cross, St. John Ambulance or other auxiliary or government organizations, such as the Wartime Prices and Trade Board and served their country both at home and abroad. Their entry into war production has already been mentioned. Probably seventy-five percent of munition workers in Ontario's plants were women.

Left top: *Canadian Nursing Auxiliary. As in World War I, nurses were vital to the care of the troops.*
Left below: *Canadian Women's Army Corps. In World War II, women became an integral part of the army for the first time.*
Right below: *Major-General Guy Simonds Wading Ashore on Sicily From a Landing Craft. When the allies landed in Sicily, July 10, 1943, Simonds, educated in Ontario, commanded the Canadian First Division, which later took part in some of the toughest fighting of the Italian campaign.*

Two Days to Remember

Finally, after almost six years of war, victory in Europe came with Germany's unconditional surrender on May 7, 1945. The next day was celebrated as the official VE-Day. In the Empire's capital hundreds of thousands of the King's subjects came out into the streets, filling Trafalgar Square and Piccadilly Circus and surging down The Mall, where they called for the King and cheered him for hours as he appeared again and again on the balcony of Buckingham Palace. In the May 7 edition of the *Toronto Daily Star* the headlines read: "Toronto Goes Wild with Joy, German Surrender Brings Mass Celebrations" — "Canadians wept, sang, prayed at peace news." At Toronto's city hall on May 8, some 20,000 people joined in a mighty chorus of "Praise God from Whom all Blessings Flow," and the previous night 250,000 people thronged the city's parks to witness fireworks displays, or to cram the churches, where many "givers of thanks" found that the pews were packed and they had to stand outside. Throughout the province local papers reported the same things going on.

Three months later, in early August, the United States Air Force dropped atomic bombs on Germany's oriental ally, demolishing the cities of Hiroshima and Nagasaki and killing thousands. The Japanese sued for peace. VJ-Day was proclaimed on August 14, 1945. The second war to end all wars had come to its end. The outbursts of public joy and thanksgiving which had characterized VE-Day were repeated throughout the Allied nations.

During the next six months Canada's overseas units, the men packed like sardines in every available ocean liner, returned home. Among them was General H.D.G. Crerar, the Ontario-born commander of the victorious First Canadian Army.

On January 26, 1946, *The St. Thomas Times-Journal* published a special edition welcoming the local unit, the Elgin Regiment, back from the war. On its front page the paper saluted the city's returning heroes, using the words, "They did their bit, and gallantly, to keep the Old Flag Flying." A picture of the flag, almost filling the page, as though billowing in the breeze, depicted the proper patriotic symbol as Ontario saw it then. The flag was the Union Jack.

Another era in the long history of the province of Ontario had come to its end.

Right top: *The Beach, Dieppe, August 19, 1942. In the aftermath of the disastrous raid on the French coastal town, tanks and landing craft burn. The 1,326 men of Toronto's Royal Regiment of Canada, the Royal Hamilton Light Infantry, and the Essex Scottish Regiment of Windsor, who took part, suffered seventy-five percent casualties.*
Right middle: *Canadians on Normandy Beaches Following D-Day Landings of June 6, 1944. Going ashore at Bernières, the Queen's Own Rifles encountered withering fire. They moved so rapidly against the Germans that the Régiment de Chaudière, landing fifteen minutes later, met only sniper fire.*
Right below: *War Cemetery, Bergen-op-Zoom. Among the Canadians buried here are men of the Algonquin Regiment of North Bay and the Lake Superior Regiment of Port Arthur, who were killed in November 1944, in the Netherlands.*
Far right below: *Canadian Troops Marching Through Dieppe. On September 1, 1944, Canadian forces captured Dieppe, scene of the unsuccessful raid of August 1942.*

SERGEANT
C.C. IRWIN
THE ALGONQUIN REGIMENT
3RD NOVEMBER 1944 AGE 24
"YEA, THOUGH I WALK
THROUGH THE VALLEY

CHAPTER 26

NEW FACES

by Margaret Penman

We are all immigrants to this place.

MARGARET ATWOOD
FROM *"THE AFTERWORD," JOURNALS OF SUSANNA MOODIE*

"Chinese Smörgasbörd" reads the billboard outside Wingham. The visitor may well wonder whether he or she is getting a crazy salad of chow mein, Swedish meatballs, and dim sum washed down by aquavit. This kind of sign is not unusual in places like Wingham, nor in the "sepoy" towns close to Lake Huron, such as nearby Lucknow. The sign's seeming schizophrenia reflects Ontario's rich cultural mix.

Two hundred years ago Loyalist refugees from the United States included Huguenot French, Germans, Swedes, Blacks, Alsatians, Dutch and other ethnic groups. They spoke, like today's newcomers, many mother tongues, but their common bond and their language of communication was English. While the majority were Protestants, the exodus included some Roman Catholics and a few Jews. The migration into what is now Ontario consisted of members of Christian denominations. Nearly all were frontier farmers whose main need for survival was a good piece of land. The Jews were urban merchants, and they tended to remain in Montreal. They had the contacts and expertise to establish new enterprises, and had little need for a free grant of land.

Loyalists may well have been the first political refugees from a republican form of government. And while some people of today may joke that because of the American Revolution the rich Loyalists went to England, the smart to the Caribbean, and the rest to Canada, our most recent newcomers, many of them political refugees as well, clearly demonstrate that Canada, especially Ontario, is their first choice.

Ontario has experienced two multicultural migrations — that of the Loyalists, which was on a small scale but had considerable impact, and the migration that began after World War II. The latter was on a much greater scale but not necessarily of more profound impact, since the migration of 200 years ago created the need for a separate province. At the time when the post-World War II influx began, Ontario was a province whose people were almost solidly of British stock. This came about because of the origin of most immigrants between 1816 and 1930.

Following the Napoleonic Wars, Britain was struck by a depression at a time when thousands of men had been discharged from the army. Unemployment was very high, and a solution to the distress was migra-

Overleaf: *Chinese Men Entering Canada, 1900. This group of immigrants went to Sarnia from Port Huron, Michigan, after travelling through the United States.*
Right top: *Anderson Ruffin Abbott in United States Civil War Uniform. Abbott, who was born in Toronto in 1837, graduated from the University of Toronto in 1861 — the first Canadian Black to become a doctor. One of eight Black surgeons in the Union Army, he later practised medicine in Ontario.*
Left and right below: *Jewish and Chinese Restaurants on Toronto's Spadina Avenue. Successive waves of immigrants have opened restaurants to serve their own ethnic foods — menus that often appeal to a wider public.*

tion to Upper Canada. Commencing in 1816, people from the British Isles arrived in ever greater numbers, while the potato famines of the 1840s, that affected Scotland as well as Ireland, brought many thousands of newcomers in search of a better way of life. By 1884, when the time came to celebrate the centennial of the Loyalists, Ontario had become a province wherein the majority of the population could trace its roots to the mother country.

There were some notable exceptions, although the overall numbers were not large. Because of Governor Simcoe's legislation to phase out slavery after 1793, Upper Canada soon became a haven for Blacks from the United States. After slavery was abolished in the British Empire in 1834, Blacks formed their Underground Railroad to assist escaping slaves to reach freedom on British soil. Many Blacks assumed roles of leadership for their expanding communities.

Mary Ann Shadd, who helped found the abolitionist *Provincial Freeman* in Chatham in 1853 (which was moved to Toronto in 1854), was the first Black newspaperwoman in North America. Anderson Ruffin Abbott, born in Toronto in 1837, graduated in Medicine from the University of Toronto in 1861, the first Canadian-born Black to become a doctor. Abbott, one of eight Black surgeons who served in the Union Army during the American Civil War, later practised in Chatham, Dundas, Oakville and Chicago, before retiring to Toronto. Delos Rogest Davis, born in Colchester Township in 1846, was admitted to the Law Society of Upper Canada in 1885. He practised in Amherstburg, the first Black lawyer in Canada. In 1910 he was made a King's Counsel.

Other exceptions were a trickle of immigrants from several European countries, and a few of Chinese origin. One migration, although of Britons, deserves special mention. From 1869 until stopped because of high unemployment during the 1930s, some 80,000 children were brought by a variety of sponsors — the best known was Dr.Thomas Barnardo — and placed on Canadian farms as a form of cheap labour. More than half of these children, orphans or from impoverished families, were sent to Ontario. They were called "home children" because they were gathered into special houses before emigration, and received in similar "homes" in Canada before they were placed. Some were accepted as part of the families to which they were sent, but too often the memories of their early years in Ontario were filled with sadness.

Since the Second World War, thousands of West Indian, Chinese, Portuguese, and Indo-Pakistani immigrants have joined the earlier waves of English, Irish, Jewish and Italian immigrants to give the province an even wider ethnic mix. Ontario traditionally takes in about fifty percent of all immigration to Canada and at least half of these settle eventually in Metropolitan Toronto. The complexion of the city and of the province has changed; Ontario may be said to have come full-circle. Multicultural she began, multicultural she is again.

Metropolitan Toronto, popularly known as "Metro," has become one of the most racially diverse cities in the world. It is not just in the rural areas that you can eat "Chinese Smörgasbörd." In Metro there are about fifty different nationalities represented in the restaurant scene, from Armenian or Yugoslavian to Thai. Some thirty languages are taught to 8,500 children through the Toronto Board of Education's Heritage Language Programme, which was introduced in 1977. The programme, set up across the province, allows for instruction in a heritage language where there is a minimum of twenty-five students. Major languages taught in Toronto schools are Chinese, Greek, Portuguese and Italian. As well, throughout Ontario, French programmes have expanded, to allow francophone children to be taught in their mother tongue and anglophone children to become bilingual.

Statistics compiled for the Ontario Ministry of Citizenship and Culture indicate that the largest ethnic group in the Toronto area remains people from the British Isles. The 1981 Census showed about 913,000 people of English, Scottish, Welsh and Northern Irish origin, or a combination, which accounts for forty-three percent of Metro's population. But the introduction in 1967 of the immigration point system, which made Canada more accessible to non-Commonwealth immigrants has changed Ontario, especially Toronto. The point system rewards people for speaking English and for having skills that are needed.

In the last ten years, the number of Portuguese has almost doubled

Right top: *Bilingual Brochure on Exchange Programme Between the University of Sudbury (now Laurentian) and the Catholic University of Lublin, Poland. Many Polish people settled in the Sudbury area to work in the mines. This programme, arranged by the two universities, was developed to maintain cultural links between the Polish community and the ancestral land.*

Left and right below: *Hungarian Refugees, Toronto, 1957. The demonstrations in Hungary for a democratic government were put down by Russian tanks. Many Hungarians fled the country, and large numbers came to Canada. The former residence of Ontario's lieutenant governors, Chorley Park, was used as a reception centre for these refugees.*

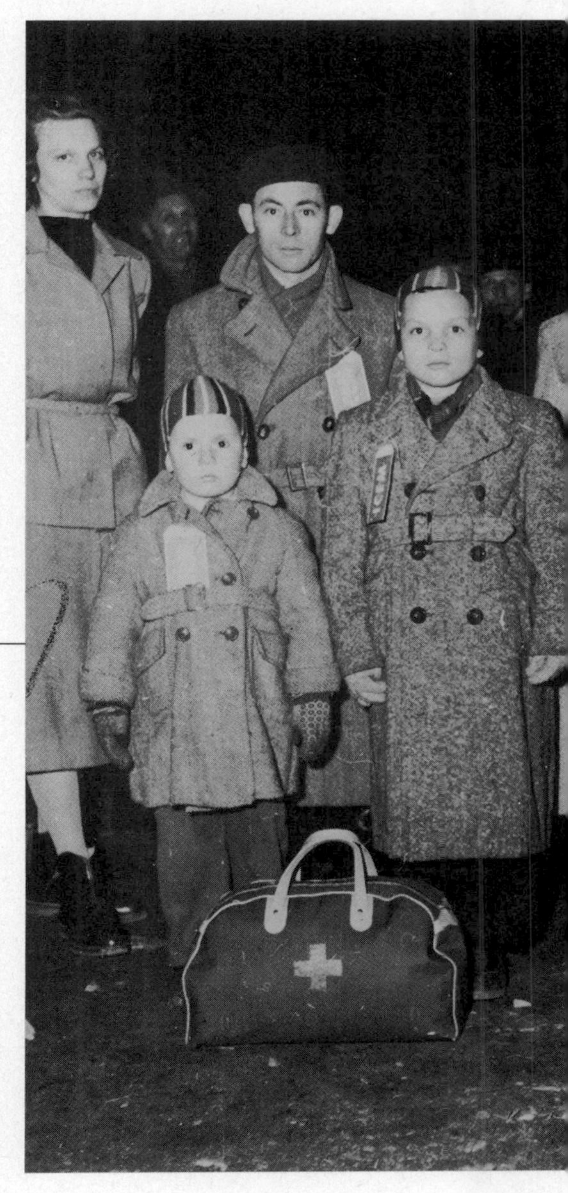

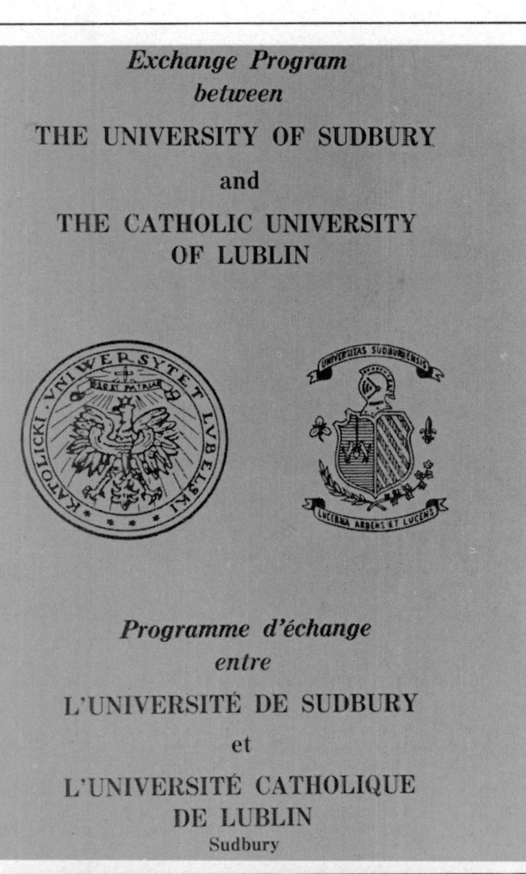

and the Indo-Pakistani population has more than tripled. There has been a big increase in the numbers of West Indians, Chinese and other Asiatic groups. The Filipino group has also increased significantly.

Of the fifty-seven percent of Metro's people who do not trace their families to the British Isles, Italians are the largest group, numbering 232,000 in 1981. They are followed by the Jews (98,000); Chinese (78,000); Portuguese (70,000); Greeks (59,000); and Germans (53,000). Metro's French-speaking population numbers 51,000. Small pockets of Eastern Europeans include 39,000 Ukrainians and 37,000 Poles.

In 1981 a change in the collection of census data made the West Indian population, which potentially outnumbers the Jewish and Chinese communities, one of the most poorly documented groups in Metro. That census allowed for the identification of immigrants from the Caribbean and Guyana only as "Black Caribbean," rather than by country of origin. The resulting figure of 43,710 people excludes the large number of West Indian immigrants to Metro who are ethnically East Indian, Chinese, or white. It is generally thought that in 1981 there were about 120,000 West Indians of all ethnic backgrounds in Metro and that about eighty percent of Metro's Black population was West Indian.

This cultural change in the city and the province is the result of Canadian immigration policy since World War II. Canada has admitted 4,500,000 immigrants and refugees since the end of the war. This compares with 3,500,000 for Australia and approaching 11,000,000 for the United States, the other two major immigrant receiving countries in recent times. Table 1 shows Canada's annual intake of immigrants and refugees between 1946 and 1980.

The critical dates in Canadian post-war immigration policy are 1947, 1962, 1966-67, and 1977-78. Each marks the beginning of a significant new stage in policy development and/or management. In 1947, Prime Minister Mackenzie King made a statement outlining the major features of the Liberal Government's post-war immigration policy — essentially a continuation of the inter-war "White Canada" policy. This was followed by the creation of a new Department of Citizenship and Immigration in 1950 and a new Immigration Act in 1952.

Table 1 — Canada: Immigration 1946-80

Year	Immigrants	Year	Immigrants
1946	71,719	1964	112,606
1947	64,127	1965	146,758
1948	125,414	1966	194,743
1949	95,217	1967	222,876
1950	73,912	1968	183,974
1951	194,391	1969	161,531
1952	164,498	1970	147,713
1953	168,868	1971	121,900
1954	154,227	1972	122,006
1955	109,946	1973	184,200
1956	164,857	1974	218,465
1957	282,164	1975	187,881
1958	124,851	1976	149,429
1959	106,928	1977	114,914
1960	104,111	1978	86,313
1961	71,689	1979	112,196
1962	74,568	1980	143,117
1963	93,151		

Source: Canada Employment and Immigration Commission

In the new Immigration Regulations of 1962, the Diefenbaker Government abandoned an immigration policy based on racial discrimination in favour of a universal policy based on skills and talents, family reunification and compassionate considerations mainly relating to refugees. Immigration became part of a new, high-priority Department of Manpower and Immigration in 1966-67, with a mandate to upgrade and develop the skills and mobility of the Canadian labour force. Special Immigration Regulations issued in 1967 contained an entirely new "Canadian point system" which had been worked out by Canadian immigration officials for the selection and admission of immigrants.

In the years 1976-77, a new Immigration Act was passed by Parliament introducing significant changes in immigration and refugee policy and management. It had been preceded by a major review of Canada's immigration and population policies, which began in the fall of 1972, followed by a Green Paper on Immigration Policy tabled in the House of Commons in February 1975. This led to the appointment in March of a Special Joint Committee of the Senate and the House of Commons

***Left below:** Lebanese Family Portrait, London, c.1921. Coming to Canada in the 1920s was a lonely experience for Lebanese people, for their numbers were small in those years. Although wearing national dress would have caused stares at the time, the post World War II immigration has changed this considerably, as Ontarians become more accustomed to seeing immigrants from a great variety of countries.*

***Right below:** The St. George's Greek Orthodox Ladies' Auxiliary. Here the ceremony of cutting the* Vassilopita *— New Year's Bread — is about to be performed in the presence of Father Stavrou.*

to examine the Green Paper and to hold public hearings across Canada on the fundamental questions it raised of immigration policy and population growth and distribution. The Committee presented its Report to Parliament eight months later. Sixty out of sixty-five of the Committee's recommendations were accepted by the Liberal Government and formed the major elements in the new Immigration Act passed in the following year. It provided for the amalgamation of the Department of Manpower and Immigration and the Unemployment Insurance Commission to form a new and very large quasi-independent agency, the Canada Employment and Immigration Commission, with a small supporting Department of Employment and Immigration.

The Commission consisted initially of ten regions, organized mainly on provincial lines, and an eleventh region formed by Manpower and Immigration's Foreign Service. In April 1981, however, as part of the accelerated process of consolidation of Canada's overseas operations, made known by the Prime Minister on March 21, 1980, it was announced that the Foreign Service, consisting of some 350 immigration officers, would be transferred to the Department of External Affairs.

Although, under the British North America Act, Canada's basic constitutional instrument, immigration is a concurrent responsibility of the federal government and the provinces, it is the federal government which has controlled and managed immigration until the passage of the new Immigration Act. This has been due, in large part, not to any intransigence on the part of the federal government, but to a general unwillingness on the part of the Canadian provinces, until recently, to become involved or to spend any money in this area of public policy.

There are two exceptions to this — the Provinces of Ontario and Quebec. Throughout the post-war period, beginning in 1946, Ontario, which had immigration agents in Britain and Europe for a very long time, developed its own immigration programme in collaboration with the federal government, organizing a very valuable flow of professional and skilled immigrants to the province. This programme became less important in the early 70s, by which time Ontario had developed a highly skilled labour force. In the late 50s, however, Ontario created her own Citizenship Branch and her own language training programme intended to supplement the existing federal-provincial programmes.

In addition to language training, Ontario has set up a variety of programmes to support ethnic groups, ethnic cultural activity, and intergroup relations. The province has provided translation and interpreter services for immigrants and now has very active Citizenship and Multicultural Branches within its Ministry of Citizenship and Culture.

As part of the extensive review, the development of progressive immigration policies and programmes in Canada, which began in the fall of 1972, improvements have also occurred in the refugee policies and programmes. Since that date Canada has admitted significant numbers of political and war refugees, including some 8,000 Ugandan Asians, 7,000 Chileans, 15,000 Haitians, 9,000 Lebanese and substantial numbers from Cyprus, Portuguese Angola and other areas. Although not directly involved with the war in Vietnam, Canada admitted 13,500 Indo-Chinese refugees by 1980. As a member of the Executive Committee of the Office of the United Nations High Commissioner for Refugees, Canada recently doubled its contribution to the UNHCR budget. Refugees are well accepted in Canada and the concept of an active and continuing role for Canada in the permanent settlement of refugees receives very definite public approval.

Dr. Freda Hawkins of the University of Toronto, a recognized expert on immigration, has concluded that in general, immigrants have been absorbed into the overall community with comparatively little friction. However, the liberal atmosphere on which Canadian cities pride themselves has been somewhat tarnished of late. In Toronto, forms of racism, albeit on a small scale, have surfaced. Instances of racist sentiment and a few racist incidents have occurred in some Toronto schools. In smaller cities and towns, too, reflecting a small "c" conservatism, people have been prone to show resentment of the newcomers.

These have been worrying developments, and although not widespread, a number of ameliorative measures have been taken by municipal authorities, especially in the Toronto area where most of the immigrants have settled. A special study on this subject, entitled *Now is Not*

Right top: *Italians in Fort William (now Thunder Bay) in 1924. Peter Trevisano and Saturno Marchiori are engaged in a game of bocce, a game much like bowling.*
Left and right below: *Lithuanian Language School, 1962. One of the small Baltic countries, Lithuania has a long, proud history. In the 20th century it was independent from 1918 to 1940, and is now part of the Soviet Union. Lithuanian Canadians strive to maintain their homeland cultural traditions.*

Too Late was carried out recently on behalf of the Metropolitan Toronto Council. One of the recommendations of this study was for a major across-the-board increase in services for immigrants in this city.

Whipple Steinkrauss, Director of the Citizenship Development Branch, Ontario Ministry of Citizenship and Culture, describes the province's growth as:

> A steady progression. You came from a culture but you got rid of it very quickly. That has provided the framework or mind-set that is most receptive to newcomers. The framework reflects different kinds of influences. Institutional framework adapts, too. It is not *rational,* not tidy, not consistent. But it is part of the history of compromise.

To ease immigrants into a bewildering new world, the Ontario government has established Welcome House at Dundas Street and University Avenue in downtown Toronto, the heart of the area where many immigrants first settle. There, at any given moment on any given day you will find counsellors who speak some nineteen languages and dialects. Refugees themselves, the counsellors (now Canadians) are there to interpret Canadian ways to newcomers, and to help them register for services such as family allowances and OHIP.

"Our business is to help people to help themselves as fast as possible," said Peggy Mackenzie, Director of Welcome House.

Here language classes are conducted for landed immigrants who have been in Canada less than three years and are not eligible for Employment Canada's vocational classes. Welcome House handles an average of 1,000 new Ontarians a month. There are similar centres in Ottawa, Hamilton, Windsor, Sudbury and Thunder Bay. Peggy Mackenzie speaks with special feelings of the refugees:

> The Salvadoreans are very poor because they have been brought in by the churches. The Southeast Asians are being bounced out of dishwashing jobs because of the economy. The message is always there: last in, first out. But they have tremendous motivation. Refugees are survivors after all. They would not be here otherwise.

Of course there are problems. If that were not the case there would be no need for the kind of help Welcome House offers. Rosanna Scotti, Co-ordinator of Multicultural Relations for Metropolitan Toronto, said:

> You can take the girl out of the country, but not the country out of the girl. With all groups of immigrants and refugees, whoever is here longest and first is king of the castle. Group displacing group is the history of the province. It's a constantly evolving process. Now there are so many newcomers of so many different kinds.

While some might argue that there is integration, for example, intermarriage, Scotti's opinions reflect the Ontarian self-image of a mosaic rather than a melting pot. The Canadian mosaic implies cultural survival, the opposite of the American approach that favours newcomers becoming Americanized as quickly as possible.

The largest groups now entering Ontario are West Indians, Vietnamese, and Hispanics from Central and Latin America. Ontario is also getting special refugees such as Poles, Russian Jews, and Chileans. The Vietnamese need a variety of services. For them there has been both an immigration trauma and "the Boat People" trauma. Women immigrants have more problems, too. Women are the most exploited in the labour market. They are often the most oppressed at home, do not speak the language and have no knowledge of their rights as citizens.

A series of reports by sociologists at the Centre for Urban and Community Studies at the University of Toronto, completed in 1979 and published in 1981, showed that there is inequality and segregation in jobs according to ethnic groups.

Since 1979, Metro's Chinese community has absorbed 20,000 refugees from Southeast Asia, eighty percent of whom were ethnic Chinese. The next big impact on the community could well come from a wave of migration from Hong Kong. Immigration lawyers in Metro are already processing a string of inquiries from Hong Kong entrepreneurs who are nervous about China repossessing the colony when the ninety-nine year British lease expires in 1997. Canadian immigration policies allow prospective immigrants to apply for admission as entrepreneurs if they can establish a business that would employ at least five Canadians.

Left below: Programme Cover on Malta. Consisting of three tiny islands between Sicily and the North African coast, Malta was for a long time a British naval base in the Mediterranean. This sunny, small country has contributed its share to Ontario's rich cultural heritage. Severely bombed during World War II, the country is also a place of very early civilization. The Maltese trace their beginnings back to the days of the Phoenicians, who established a colony on their islands in 1,000 B.C. Malta became a Crown colony in 1814, and became independent in 1964, within the commonwealth.

Although unemployment and under-employment remain problems in difficult economic times, there are many success stories, too. Celebrations in 1984 include not only popular perennial festivals such as Caribana and Caravan and Scottish Tattoos, but also the triumphs of individual immigrants and their children who have reached pre-eminence.

Here are just a few examples: Federal Cabinet Minister Charles Caccia; Members of Parliament Nick Leluk and Jesse Flis; Member of the Ontario Legislature Yuri Shymko; Dean of the University of Toronto Law School Frank Iacobucci; Judge Stanley Frizell and Queen's Counsel Stanley Frolik; architects Ray Moriyama, Eberhard Zeidler and Uno Prii; literary figures Peter Newman, Joy Kogawa and Ken Adachi; mining engineer Steve Roman; opera director Lofti Mansouri; Catholic Bishop the Most Reverend A.M. Ambrozic; Eddie Goodman, chairman of the Royal Ontario Museum; Dan Lanuzzi, whose television station, MTV, broadcasts in twenty-five languages; Steve Stavro of Knob Hill Farms and Ed Mirvish, the great shopkeeper and theatre owner; Toronto Alderman Ying Hope. The list could go on and on.

In May 1948, four months after the Communists seized control of Czechoslovakia, Henry and Jarmilla Jelinek and their five children escaped from Prague to Switzerland. The following year they settled in Oakville, Ontario. Two of the children, nine-year-old Otto and seven-year-old Maria, were already promising skaters. Thirteen years later Otto and Maria returned to Prague, after the Czech authorities promised that their Canadian citizenship would be respected, and became the World Figure Skating Pairs Champions of 1962.

A truly distinguished career is that of a son of Russian Jewish parents, Max Laskin and his wife, Bluma Singel, who came to Ontario in the early 1900s. The Right Honorable Bora Laskin, P.C., C.C., late Chief Justice of the Supreme Court of Canada, was born in Fort William in 1912. His most distinguished career began in 1937 when he was called to the bar. A leading authority on constitutional issues, he was the Chief Justice during the issue of "constitutional patriation."

__Right below:__ Krishna Indian Movie Theatre, Toronto. Since the 1960s, people from the Indian sub-continent have come to Ontario in increasing numbers. They include many well-educated people, usually with an excellent command of English. Nevertheless, they enjoy seeing movies in their mother tongue. The motion picture industry in India is one of the largest in the world.

Far left top: *Otto Jelinek, Conservative M.P. Otto and his sister Maria (World Figure Skating Pairs Champions in 1962) were born in Czechoslovakia and came to Canada in 1949. He has represented the Halton riding since 1972.*

Left top middle: *Yuri Shymko, Conservative M.P.P. Born in Poland, of Ukranian parents, Mr. Shymko came to Canada with his family in 1953.*

Left top: *David Lewis (1909-1981). A former federal leader of the New Democratic Party, Mr. Lewis was born in Imperial Russia of Polish Jewish parents. He came to Canada in 1921, and later won a Rhodes Scholarship to Oxford.*

Far left below: *Tony Lupusella, New Democratic Party M.P.P. Mr. Lupusella was born in Italy and came to Canada in 1969, at age twenty-five. His main interest is social progress.*

Left below middle: *Hon. Susan Fish, Minister of Citizenship and Culture, Ontario Government. Mrs. Fish was born in Rio de Janeiro, grew up in New York City, and came to Canada in 1968.*

Left below: *Michael A. Spensieri, Liberal M.P.P. Born in Italy in 1949, Mr. Spensieri came to Canada in 1962.*

Right top: *Ernest Annau, Award Winning Architect. Born in Hungary, Mr. Annau lived in several countries before coming to Canada in 1951. He studied architecture in Toronto, and in Munich, West Germany.*

Far right top: *Frank A. Bazos, Businessman. Born in Greece, Mr. Bazos is a founder and present Chairman of the Becker Milk Company, Scarborough, Ontario.*

Right below: *Carlos Ott, Architect. Mr. Ott, born in Uruguay, was the winner of the international competition for a new opera house in Paris, France.*

Far right below: *Cecil Smith, Executive Director of the Ontario Track and Field Association. A former resident of Wales, Mr. Smith came to Canada in the early 1970s.*

CHAPTER 27

THE LEADERS

by Brian Land and Deborah Forman

Ask most Canadian school boys who D'Arcy McGee was and they'll probably say he was a hockey player!

JOHN W. FISHER ("MR. CANADA")

THE LEADERS

Speakers of the Legislative Assembly of Ontario since 1867

Hon. John Stevenson 1867-1871
Hon. Richard William Scott 1871
Hon. James George Currie 1871-1873
Hon. Rupert Mearse Wells 1874-1879
Hon. Charles Clarke 1880-1886
Hon. Jacob Baxter 1887-1890
Hon. Thomas Ballantyne 1801-1894
Hon. William Douglas Balfour 1895-1896
Hon. Francis Eugene Alfred Evanturel 1897-1902
Hon. William Andrew Charlton 1903-1904
Hon. Joseph Wesley St. John 1905-1907
Hon. Thomas Crawford 1907-1911
Hon. William Henry Hoyle 1912-1914
Hon. David Jamieson 1915-1919
Hon. Nelson Parliament 1920-1923
Hon. Joseph Elijah Thompson 1924-1926
Hon. William David Black 1927-1929
Hon. Thomas Ashmore Kidd 1930-1933
Hon. Norman Otto Hipel 1935-1938
Hon. James Howard Clark 1939-1943
Hon. William James Stewart 1944-1947
Hon. James de Congalton Hepburn 1947-1948
Hon. Myron Cooke Davies 1949-1955
Hon. Alfred Wallace Downer 1955-1959
Hon. William Murdoch 1960-1963
Hon. Donald Hugo Morrow 1963-1967
Hon. Frederick McIntosh Cass 1968-1971
Hon. Allan Edward Reuter 1971-1974
Hon. Russell Daniel Rowe 1974-1977
Hon. John Edward Stokes 1977-1981
Hon. John Melville Turner 1981-

***Right top:** Hon. Louis Orville Breithaupt (1890-1960), Lieutenant Governor of Ontario, 1952-1957.*
***Far right top:** Hon. John Keiller MacKay (1888-1970), Lieutenant Governor of Ontario, 1957-1963.*
***Right below:** Sir George William Ross (1841-1914) and Cabinet 1903. Premier in 1899, Ross' defeat in 1905 ended thirty-four years of Liberal rule in Ontario.*
***Left below:** Hon. Thomas Ballantyne (1829-1908), Speaker of the Ontario Legislature 1891-1894.*

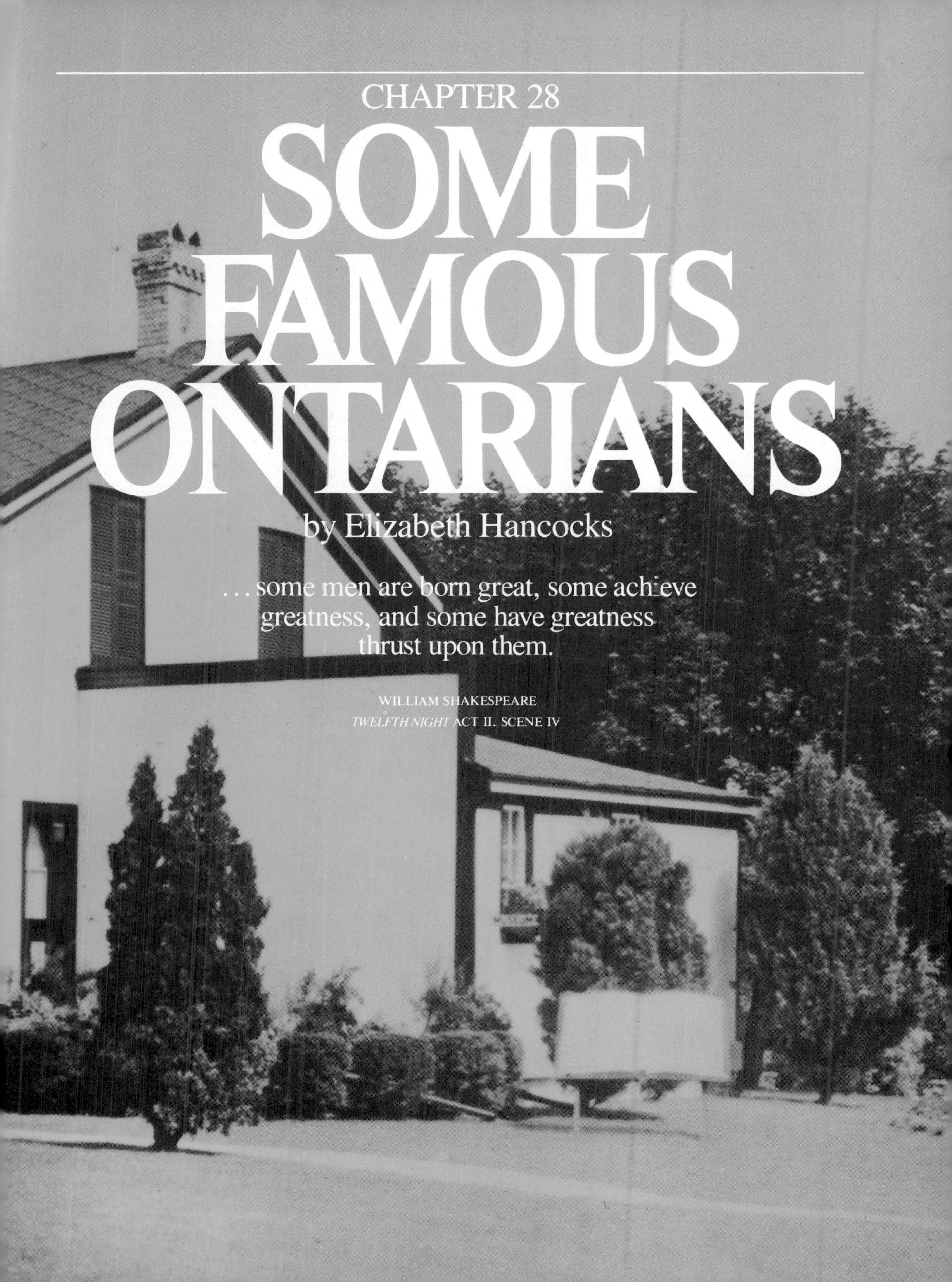

CHAPTER 28

SOME FAMOUS ONTARIANS

by Elizabeth Hancocks

. . . some men are born great, some achieve greatness, and some have greatness thrust upon them.

WILLIAM SHAKESPEARE
TWELFTH NIGHT ACT II. SCENE IV

Alexander Graham Bell (inventor of the telephone), Lucy Maud Montgomery (author of *Anne of Green Gables)*, and actress Marie Dressler (better known for her starring role in films such as "Tugboat Annie") shared something in common. They were all Ontarians.

Some Ontarians came here; some were born here; some stayed; and some went on to make their name in other lands — but all shared a common heritage with the province that is sometimes called the "Heartland of Canada." They were of every background imaginable, black and white, male and female, Loyalist and rebel, but they all tried to be the best, often were the best in their fields, and every one of them desired to make their province and their country, even the world, a better place in which to live.

They succeeded admirably, in fields as diverse as agriculture and poetry, transportation and business, communications and painting, sports and mining. Some of them (such as Bell and his telephone) have determined the entire structure of our world today. Others, important leaders in their time, are less well known. But the accomplishments of these remarkable individuals deserve to be graven on the pages of our heritage, and remembered whenever the words "excellence" and "achievement" are spoken.

A Scot, adventurer Captain Miles Macdonell (1769-1828), settled near Cornwall at St. Andrews West following the American revolution, and in 1811 became agent for Lord Selkirk's ill-fated Red River colony. He led the first band of settlers there, and was arrested when the North West Company tried to destroy the settlement. Released without trial and returned to his farm in Osnabruck Township, he later moved to his brother's farm in Point Fortune, where he died.

One of Canada's greatest explorers, David Thompson (1770-1857), fur-trader, geographer and adventurer, lived in Williamstown from 1815 to 1835. Thompson travelled more than 5,000 miles (3,000 km) in the service of the Hudson's Bay Company, exploring and mapping with remarkable accuracy much of the Canadian West. Born in England, apprenticed in 1784 to the Hudson's Bay Company, later (1797) transferring to the North West Company in which he became a partner,

Overleaf: *Alexander Graham Bell Homestead, Brantford (1847-1922).*
Right top: *Simon Fraser (1776-1862), Fur Trader and Explorer.*
Left and right below: *Weller Stage Coach. The stage is shown passing Little Trinity Church, King Street East, Toronto, on a winter journey to Kingston.*

Thompson was the first white man ever to descend the Columbia River from its source to its mouth. When he left his beloved west in 1812 he prepared a map, now on permanent display at the Public Archives of Ontario, which became the basis of all subsequent maps of the area. From 1816 to 1826, Thompson surveyed the boundary between Canada and the U.S., but never lived to profit from his work. He died in poverty at Longueuil, near Montreal.

Another name that rings clear through the "discovery" period is that of Simon Fraser (1776-1862), born in Vermont, the son of a Loyalist officer who came to Canada in 1784. Fraser entered the fur trade with the North West Company in 1792, and by 1805 was in charge of operations west of the Rocky Mountains. In 1808, while searching for a water route to the Pacific Ocean, he descended the thundering river which now bears his name. The skill and daring required to traverse the boiling Fraser make his feat one of the most outstanding in the exploration of Canada. Fraser retired in 1817, and settled on his property near St. Andrews West in Stormont County.

If you like apples, you'll know the name McIntosh — the sweet/tart fruit whose juicy taste is almost a hallmark of the bountiful Ontario autumn. What you may not know is that it's named for John McIntosh (1777-1846), whose parents emigrated from Inverness, Scotland, to the Mohawk Valley in New York. John came to Canada in 1796 and in 1811 obtained a farm lot near Dundela in Dundas County. While clearing the land he found several apple seedlings, and since orchards were a feature of every pioneer farm in those days, he saved and transplanted them. One bore superior fruit, which ultimately became the McIntosh Red apple. John's son Allan established a nursery, and promoted the new species extensively. Its popularity in North America has led to its propagation in many lands — a true testament to the sensitivity, initiative, and skill of Ontarian John McIntosh and his sons.

In the days before cars and trains, the fastest method of transportation was by stage coach. William Weller (1788-1863), thrice mayor of Cobourg, chairman of its Harbour Commission, president of the Cobourg-Rice Lake Plank Road Company, and organizer of the Inter-

national Telegraph Company, was also Ontario's leading stage-coach proprietor between 1830 and 1856. In February of 1840 he drove Governor General Charles Poulett Thomson from Toronto to Montreal in the record time of thirty-seven hours, forty minutes.

Josiah Henson (1789-1883), a black slave born in Maryland who escaped to Upper Canada in 1830 was a leading abolitionist of his day and in 1841, on 200 acres of land near Dresden, helped build the British-American Institute, a vocational school for escaped slaves. Henson's life in slavery provided much of the material for Harriet Beecher Stowe's politically powerful novel *Uncle Tom's Cabin.* Henson is buried in Dresden.

Ogle R. Gowan (1796-1876), born in Ireland, emigrated to Upper Canada in 1829, settling at Brockville. Here he established the Brockville *Statesman*, and was instrumental in the formation of the Orange Lodge in British America in 1830. This association played an active part in suppressing the Rebellion of 1837. Gowan served twenty-seven years as the Brockville area's parliamentary representative after being elected to the Legislative Assembly in 1836, and served at the Battle of the Windmill in 1838. He died in Toronto.

Allan Napier MacNab (1798-1862), born at Niagara, enlisted in the army at 18, and distinguished himself for bravery during the War of 1812. Called to the bar in 1826, he entered politics, was elected to the Legislative Assembly for Wentworth, and became a noted supporter of the Family Compact. During the Rebellion of 1837 he was one of the government's most active military supporters and was knighted for his services. MacNab was leader of the Tory-Conservatives, and Prime Minister of Canada (1854-1856). His most enduring legacy to the province, however, is his monumental home in Hamilton, Dundurn Castle, built in 1832. Today, it is restored as a museum. He resigned from the government in 1856, and was named baronet in 1858.

Sisters Susanna Moodie (1803-1885) and Catharine Parr Traill (1802-1899) can scarcely be mentioned separately, so intertwined were their lives. Members of the literary Strickland family, they both emigrated to Upper Canada in 1832. Efforts to develop a wilderness prop-

Left below: *Ogle R. Gowan (1796-1876).*
Left and right bottom: *Third Home of Samuel Strickland, Lakefield.*
Right top: *Rev. Josiah Henson (1789-1883).*
Right below: *Josiah Henson's Home Near Dresden, Now a Museum.*

erty resulted in Susanna's best-selling book *Roughing it in the Bush.* The story of Catharine's pioneer experiences appears in *The Backwoods of Canada.* Unable to make their farm property pay, the Moodies moved to Belleville in 1840 where they edited and wrote the short-lived *Victoria Magazine.* Susanna wrote many novels and poems, and her contributions were the mainstay of the Montreal publication *The Literary Garland.* Catharine remained in the Wakefield area, and in her *Studies of Plant Life in Canada,* and other works, proved herself a gifted botanist. The latter work was illustrated by her sister's daughter Agnes Moodie Fitzgibbon who herself published what has been called "Canada's First Coffee Table Book" – *Canadian Wild Flowers.* Today the original illustrations for this and many other works, are in the University of Toronto's Fisher Rare Book Library.

An often overlooked Ontarian is Bishop Joseph-Eugene Guigues (1805-1874), who in 1848 established the University of Ottawa, Ontario's first bilingual university. Guigues, born in France, entered the Oblate Order and was ordained in 1828. In 1844 he came to Canada as provincial in charge of missions, and in 1847 was appointed Bishop of Bytown, the first Roman Catholic bishop of Ottawa.

William Pope (1811-1902), born in Kent, England, settled permanently at Port Ryerse, on Lake Erie, in 1859. A talented artist who worked with pen and ink and watercolour, Pope was keenly interested in ornithology. He first visited Canada and the United States in 1834, when he began his many drawings of bird life, returning for many long visits before he decided to make his home in Ontario. Although he painted the occasional landscape, his special field was birds, and he has been called the "Audubon on Canada." The Metropolitan Toronto Library has a collection of Pope's watercolour sketches.

Ontario has a long history of helping abolitionist causes, but William King (1812-1895), did more than just offer moral support. King was born near Londonderry, Ireland, educated at Glasgow University, and emigrated to the United States. In 1846 he was sent as a Presbyterian missionary to Canada where, in 1849, he founded the Elgin Association. This group purchased 4,300 acres of land near Buxton, Kent County, on which were settled freed and fugitive slaves. Descendants of the original settlers still live in the area.

Sir Casimir Gzowski (1813-1898), born in Russia of Polish parents, distinguished himself as a pioneer engineer. Forced to emigrate following his participation in the Polish Rising of 1830, he came to Canada in 1841 and eventually organized the company which built the Grand Trunk Railway from Toronto to Sarnia (1853-1857), as well as the International Bridge across the Niagara River at Fort Erie in 1873. Gzowski founded the Canadian Society of Civil Engineers in 1887. He was first chairman of the Niagara Parks Commission (1885-1893), a colonel in the Canadian militia, appointed Honourary Aide-de-Camp to the Queen in 1879, knighted in 1890, and was Administrator of Ontario (1896-1897).

Another Ontarian of Polish descent who played an important role in Ontario's development was the Right Reverend Isaac Hellmuth (1817-1901), who emigrated to Canada in 1844. Hellmuth, educated at Breslau University, was ordained in the Church of England in 1846, and in 1861 appointed Archdeacon of Huron. He assisted Bishop Benjamin Cronyn in establishing Huron College, and served as its first principal (1863-1866). Hellmuth succeeded Cronyn as Bishop of Huron in 1871, and in 1877 the professors and alumni of Huron College, strongly supported by Hellmuth, proposed the establishment of the Western University of London, now the University of Western Ontario, founded in 1878, of which Hellmuth became the first chancellor (1878-1884).

Before Sir Sandford Fleming (1827-1915), came on the scene, the 24-hour day was unknown. Fleming, born in Kirkcaldy, Scotland, died in Halifax, Nova Scotia. He was the engineer in charge of surveys and construction for virtually every important railway built in Canada, as well as designer of the first Canadian postage stamp in 1851. His proposal for a worldwide, uniform system of reckoning time was first made before the Canadian Institute on February 8, 1879, in a building on the corner of Richmond Street in Toronto. His ideas eventually gave rise to the International Prime Meridian Conference in Washington in 1884, at which the basis of today's system of Standard Time was adopted.

Left below: *Niagara Memorial Hall, Niagara-on-the-Lake. First local museum built exclusively to house Ontario's artifacts.*
Left bottom: *Janet Carnochan (1839-1926).*
Right top: *Sir Sandford Fleming Commemorative Stamp.*
Right below: *"Pure Canadian Honey" Tin.*
Right bottom: *Title Page of William Canniff's* History of Upper Canada.

HISTORY

OF THE

Settlement of Upper Canada,

(ONTARIO,)

WITH SPECIAL REFERENCE TO

THE BAY QUINTE.

BY

WM. CANNIFF, M.D., M.R.C.S.E.,

PROFESSOR OF SURGERY UNIVERSITY VICTORIA COLLEGE, AUTHOR OF THE "PRINCIPLES OF SURGERY."

TORONTO:
DUDLEY & BURNS, PRINTERS, VICTORIA HALL.
1869.

The conference also endorsed Fleming's idea of a "Universal Day" or 24-hour clock. Fleming was a founder of the Royal Canadian Institute, a proponent of world cable communications systems, and chancellor of Queens University for thirty-five years.

Physician-turned-historian William Canniff (1830-1910), was born in Thurlow Township, Hastings County, a grandson of Loyalist James Canniff of Adolphustown. Educated at Victoria College in Cobourg, the Toronto School of Medicine, the University of New York and in 1855 admitted as a member of the Royal College of Surgeons in England, Canniff, after serving in a number of hospitals in England, Germany and France, returned to Canada and became a professor of surgery at Victoria College. He was Toronto's first Medical Officer of Health (1883-1891); wrote *A Manual of the Practice of Surgery,* the first text-book of its kind ever published in Canada, and was one of the founders of the Canadian Medical Association. Canniff is, however, best known for his historical works, and in 1869 published *A History of Settlement in Upper Canada,* the first major history of the province. In 1894, he published *The Medical Profession in Upper Canada,* recording the lives of medical men who might otherwise have been forgotten, reprinted as recently as 1981. He died in Belleville in 1910.

Bees were what made David Allanson Jones (1836-1910) world famous, and because of him there is even a town in Ontario named Beetown (formerly Clarksville, now Beeton). Jones, one of eleven children, was born in Whitchurch Township, and was Canada's first major commercial honey producer. As a breeder he scoured the Old World for species of bees, and brought queens for isolated breeding to an island in Georgian Bay. He was president, in 1881, of the Ontario Beekeeper's Association, and in 1885 founding editor of the *Canadian Bee Journal.* His birthplace, on a farm north of the town of Ringwood on Highway 48, to this day harbours masses of beehives which can be seen from the road.

Janet Carnochan (1839-1926) was founder and for 30 years curator of the Niagara Historical Society, and it was thanks largely to her efforts the society built the first building in Ontario to be used solely as an historical museum — the Niagara Memorial Hall, which opened in

1907. Born in Stamford Township, she taught school at Niagara-on-the-Lake, and on retiring devoted herself exclusively to historical work. She edited a wide range of publications for the Niagara Historical Society, and wrote the history of St. Mark's Church, St. Andrew's Church, and the history of Niagara.

Christened Peter Martin, a name he refused to accept, Dr. Oronhyatekha or Burning Cloud (1841-1907), was a Mohawk and a physician who became president of the Grand Council of Canadian Chiefs, and was largely responsible for the successful organization of the Independant Order of Foresters. Born on the Mohawk Grand River Reservation, he attended college in Ohio and Massachusetts, Oxford University, and the University of Toronto, the first member of his race to receive a Canadian university degree. He married a great-granddaughter of Joseph Brant, practiced medicine in Frankford, then in London, Ontario; was a devout Anglican, a Mason, and an Orangeman. In 1878 he was invited to become a member of the first Canadian lodge of the new Independent Order of Foresters, and his work for this remarkable organization filled the rest of his life. The order, which has its roots in the medieval England of Robin Hood, is designed to provide assistance for widows and orphans through a co-operative scheme for life insurance. Oronhyatekha became one of the most ardent proponents of the society, and in 1881 was appointed its Supreme Chief Ranger, a position he held until his death. When he began his work, the society had fewer than 400 members. He raised the membership to more than 250,000, and a fund of more than $11 million. Today, there are nearly 2 million members around the world, with headquarters in Toronto.

The name Alexander Graham Bell (1847-1922), needs no introduction to Canadians. The inventor of the telephone was born in Edinburgh, Scotland, and in 1870, came to Canada with his father and settled at Brantford. On July 26, 1874, he disclosed for the first time, his concept of the principle of the telephone, and his call to Paris, Ontario, from Brantford, on August 10, 1876, is now recognized as the world's first long distance call. Bell was founder of the Bell Telephone Company, and explored not only the world of sound but also the world of

Left and right below: *Funeral of Dr. Oronhyatekha in 1907. The funeral procession is shown passing the now-demolished Independent Order of Foresters' Temple Building on Toronto's Bay Street. The memory of Dr. Oronhyatekha is still treasured by his fellow-Mohawks on the Tyendinaga Reserve on the Bay of Quinte.*
Right top: *Stamp Commemorating the Famous Oarsman, Ned Hanlan.*

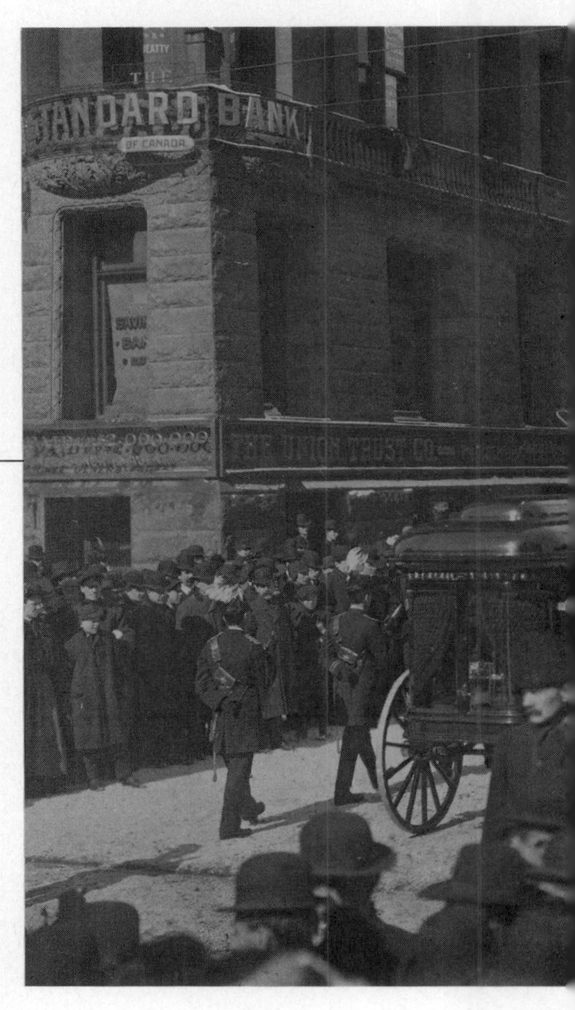

flight. The Silver Dart, an airplane of his design, built and flown at Baddeck, made Canada's first powered flight

Lucy Maud Montgomery (1847-1942), may not be well known herself, but her fictional counterpart, Anne of Green Gables, is probably more real to generations of Canadians than many people. Lucy was born in Prince Edward Island, educated at Charlottetown and Halifax, and lived at Cavendish, Prince Edward Island from 1898 to 1911, where her career as a novelist began. In 1911 she married Presbyterian minister Reverend Ewan Macdonald, and moved with him to Leaskdale, Ontario where, during her fifteen years of residency, she wrote eleven of her twenty-two novels. In 1926 they moved to Norval, a small town adjacent to Georgetown, Ontario, and in 1935 Lucy was awarded the Order of the British Empire by King George V.

At one time, the greatest oarsman in the world was an Ontarian, Ned Hanlan (1855-1908). Born in Toronto, he took up rowing as a child when his family settled on the Toronto Islands at a place now named Hanlan's Point. In 1875 he won the amateur rowing championship of Toronto Bay. In 1876 he defeated all opponents in the Philadelphia Races of that year. In 1880 he won the World Single Sculls Championship in England, retaining his title until 1884. He was an alderman in Toronto between 1883 and 1899.

Sir Adam Beck (1857-1925), made Ontario one of the first places in the world to benefit from inexpensive hydro-electric power. Born in Baden, Wilmot Township, Waterloo County, Beck was elected mayor of London in 1902, and the following year appointed to the provincial commission to investigate the development and distribution of power from Niagara Falls. He served as a member of the Ontario legislature where, in 1906, he introduced the bill that created the Hydro-Electric Power Commission of Ontario, a body of which he was chairman from 1906 to the year of his death. Under his guidance, Ontario Hydro grew to be one of the most respected public utilities in the world. Beck was knighted in 1914 in recognition for his services.

Thomas 'Carbide' Willson (1860-1915), was a homespun inventor of a different sort. Born at Princeton, Oxford County, and educated in

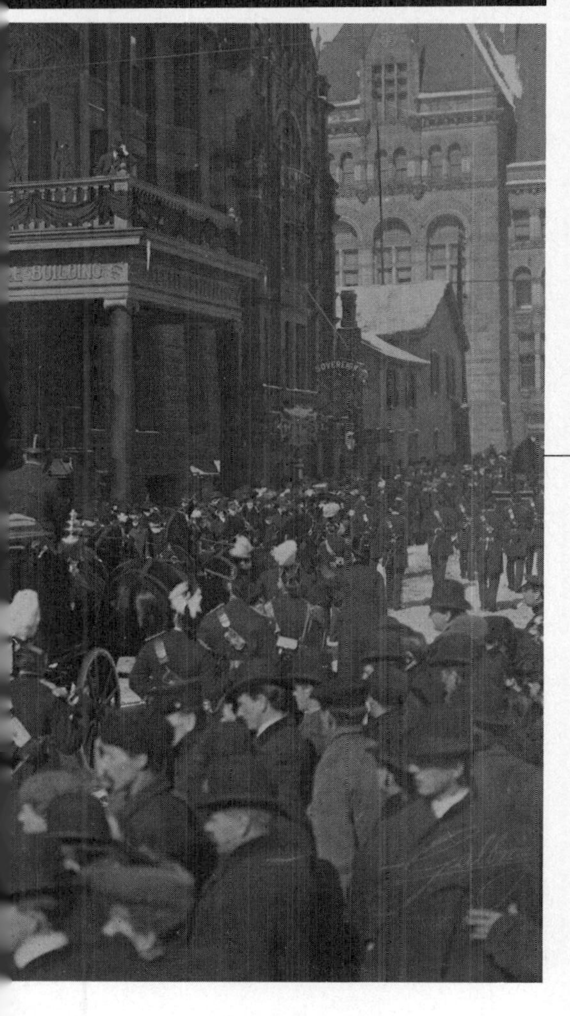

Hamilton, he became an electrical engineer and discovered the first commercial process for the production of calcium carbide, used in the manufacture of acetylene gas. By 1892 he had established a carbide works at Merriton, Ontario, and shortly thereafter a similar plant in Shawinigan, Quebec. He settled in Ottawa in 1901, and in 1909 the University of Toronto awarded him the first McCharles Prize.

Mention Reverend Charles W. Gordon (1860-1937) and most Canadians may be forgiven a blank look. Mention Ralph Connor and faces will light up. Ralph Connor, the pen name of Reverend Gordon, was the author of *The Man from Glengarry*, *The Sky Pilot*, and *Glengarry School Days.* Born at St. Elmo in Glengarry County, ordained a Presbyterian minister in 1890, Gordon served as a missionary in the Northwest Territories until 1893, was a chaplain during World War I, and Moderator of the Presbyterian Church in Canada (1921-1922). Son of Reverend Daniel Gordon, a famous minister himself, and Mary Robertson (whose sister Margaret Murray Robertson was a prolific novelist at a time when Canada was just struggling into existence), Gordon left Glengarry at the age of ten when his father moved to Western Ontario. One of Canada's most successful novelists, he relied on his own and family remembrances, although he considered himself a minister first, and used his writing to teach, rather than as an art form.

The inventor of basketball, one of North America's most popular sports, was an Ontarian. Dr. James Naismith (1861-1939), was born near Almonte and in 1883 entered McGill University. He graduated in theology from Presbyterian College in Montreal, and then enrolled at the International YMCA Training School, Springfield College, Massachussetts. In 1891 he devised the game of basketball in answer to the need for a team sport that could be played indoors during the winter. He was director of physical education at the University of Kansas for thirty-six years, and died at Lawrence, Kansas.

Poet Pauline Johnson (1861-1913), was another Mohawk who made an enormous contribution to Canadian life. She was born in Chiefswood, near Brantford, in a house built by her father, Chief G.H.M. Johnson, a greatly respected leader of the Six Nations, as a wedding

Left below: *Almonte, Birthplace of Dr. James Naismith. Originally called Waterford, the name had to be changed to avoid duplication. In 1855, the residents chose Almonte, in honour of Juan Napomucene Almonte, a Mexican general, Ambassador to Washington.*
Left and right bottom: *Princeton, near Woodstock, Birthplace of Thomas "Carbide" Willson.*
Right top: *Title Page of Margaret Marshall Saunders' Novel,* Beautiful Joe.

gift for his English wife — a cousin of the American novelist William Dean Howells. Pauline attended Brantford Model School, and from her youth contributed verses to periodicals. Her first volume of verse was *White Wampum,* followed by *Canadian Born* By her writing and the dramatic recitations of her own works in Great Britain and North America she made herself the voice of the Indian race in the English tongue. No book of poetry by a Canadian has ever outsold her collected verse, *Flint and Feather.*

Another writer, not as well known as her fictional creations is Margaret Marshall Saunders (1861-1947). Born in Milton, Nova Scotia, she taught school briefly before starting her career as a novelist. Her second book *Beautiful Joe* achieved international fame. Inspired by a visit to Meaford c.1892, the book is based on the story of a dog rescued from a brutal master by a local miller. First published in 1894, the novel appeared in several editions and by 1939 had been printed in at least ten languages. Miss Saunders settled in Toronto in 1914, and was awarded the C.B.E. in 1934 in recognition of her contribution toward securing humane treatment for animals.

Canadian Favourites

Beautiful Joe

Marshall Saunders

McClelland and Stewart Limited

Sir Gilbert Parker (1862-1932), was an Ontarian who largely made his mark outside his native province. Parker was born in Camden East, and educated at the University of Toronto. In 1885 he travelled to Australia as a journalist, then in 1889 to England where he wrote fiction and achieved great success as an historical novelist. He became a member of the British House of Commons in 1900 and in 1902 was knighted for his literary achievements. He was a leading figure in the British Unionist Party, created baronet in 1915, and privy councillor in 1916.

The name Jack Miner (1865-1944), is synonymous with wild geese. Miner, born in Dover Centre, Ohio, settled in 1878 on property near Kingsville, Ontario and in 1904 established the Jack Miner Bird Sanctuary to aid in conserving migrating Canada Geese and ducks. A few years later he began a program of bird banding to determine wildfowl movements, and during his life lectured extensively on wildlife conservation. The Jack Miner Migratory Foundation was incorporated in the U.S. in 1931, and in Canada in 1936. Miner was awarded the O.B.E. in

1943 for "the greatest achievement in conservation in the British Empire." The sanctuary today is a mecca for birdwatchers.

Marie Dressler (1868-1934), née Lalia Maria Koerber was born in Cobourg, educated in Toronto, and began her career as an actress on the local stage. About 1883 she joined a touring stock company and rapidly gained recognition on Broadway as a comedienne. She made her first film in 1914, although real film success eluded her until 1930. Among her best remembered character roles is "Tugboat Annie." She was named best actress of 1931 by the Motion Picture Academy of Arts and Sciences. Dressler followed two other Canadians as best actress — Toronto's own Mary Pickford (1929) and Montreal-born Norma Shearer (1930).

Stephen Leacock (1869-1944), Canada's most famous humourist, was born in England, but raised near Lake Simcoe, Ontario. He was educated at Upper Canada College, as well as the Universities of Toronto and Chicago. He taught first at Upper Canada College, then in the Department of Economics and Political Science at McGill (1901-1936). He wrote in his own field of economics, but is best known for his popular books. *Literary Lapses,* appeared in 1910. *Sunshine Sketches of a Little Town,* published in 1912, became a classic. His genius in applying "exaggeration and incongruous juxtaposition to ordinary people in every-day situations" gained him a world-wide reputation.

"In Flanders Fields the poppies blow, between the crosses, row and row, that mark our place . . ." Who can forget, having once heard them, the emotional lines penned by Canada's war poet Lieutenant-Colonel John McCrae (1872-1918), born in Guelph, Ontario. Physician and poet, graduate of the University of Toronto, McCrae penned his famous lines in a dugout near Ypres in 1915. He was medical officer in the First Canadian Contingent in World War I, and was posted to a hospital at Boulogne where he remained until his death from pneumonia. For many years before the war he had contributed occasional verses to the *University Magazine* and other periodicals. His famous "Flanders Fields" poem was first published anonymously in the English periodical *Punch,* on December 8, 1815, and is considered by many to be

Left below: *Jack Miner (1865-1944), Ontario's "Bird Man."*
Left and right bottom: *Birthplace of Marie Dressler, Cobourg.*
Right top: *Sir Gilbert Parker (1862-1932).*
Right below: *Marie Dressler (1868-1934).*

the finest verse written in English during the Great War.

Clara Brett Martin (1874-1923), born in Toronto of Irish and Hungarian ancestry, was a brilliant student. She became the first woman lawyer, not just in Canada but in the British Empire. Beforehand, she waged a fierce battle, backed by Premier Oliver Mowat, against the Upper Canada Law Society, whose leaders believed that a woman would never be a competent lawyer. Premier Mowat had an act passed by the legislature enabling women to be students-at-law. The Law Society decreed that women could only become solicitors, because a court of law was no place for a lady. Martin appealed again to Mowat, and the legislature passed an act permitting women to become barristers. On February 2, 1897, Miss Martin entered Osgoode Hall, and she joined the firm of Shelton and Wallbridge. She was so successful that the firm became Shelton, Wallbridge and Martin. She also served on the Toronto Board of Education, and was known for her progressive ideas.

Edmund John Zavitz (1875-1968), known as the father of reforestation in Ontario, graduated from McMaster University in Hamilton, Yale, the University of Michigan, and taught forestry at the Ontario Agricultural College. He entered the province's public services in 1905, became deputy minister of Lands and Forests (1925-1934), and was Chief Forester until 1953. He started the St. Williams' Forestry Station in Norfolk County, the first in Ontario, and through his leadership large areas of waste land have been restored to productivity.

Tom Thomson (1877-1917), probably Canada's most famous painter, was born at Claremont, Ontario, but lived in the village of Leith near Owen Sound. He taught himself painting, and worked in Toronto as a commercial artist until 1913. His distinctive style of landscape painting influenced the work of the Group of Seven. Among his better known works are *West Wind*, *Jack Pine*, *Spring Ice*, and *Northern River*. He drowned, tragically, in 1917 in Canoe Lake, Algonquin Provincial Park.

Dr. Mahlon Locke (1880-1942), was a pioneer in the treatment of arthritis. Locke was born in Matilda Township, Dundas County and studied medicine at Queen's University and in Scotland. In 1908 he opened a practice in his home in Williamsburg and became interested in arthritis, which he believed was caused principally by fallen arches, so he treated arthritics by manual manipulation of the feet. Many of his patients claimed to be cured or helped by this method of treatment and his fame spread throughout North America and overseas. From 1928 onwards, thousands of sufferers visited him at his Williamsburg clinic where he treated hundreds of patients daily.

Boxer Tommy Burns (1881-1955), born Noah Brusso near Hanover, Grey County, became Canada's leading heavyweight though only 5′7″ in height and weighing 170 pounds. In 1906 he defeated Marvin Hart and became the first Canadian to win the heavyweight championship of the world. Defeated in 1908 by the Black American Jack Johnson in Australia, he did not retire from boxing until 1920, when he entered the ministry. Brusso's training methods were widely admired and emulated, and he wrote a book on scientific boxing. He died in Vancouver.

Lawren Harris (1885-1970), became, along with Tom Thomson and others, one of Canada's best-known painters. Born in Brantford, he studied in Germany and began working in Toronto in 1910. He was a founding member of the Group of Seven, and is famous for his paintings of the Precambrian Shield and the Arctic. His best-known works include *Shacks*, *North Shore*, *Lake Superior*, and *Bylot Island.*

Athlete Tom Longboat (1886-1949), born at Ohsweken, became one of the greatest marathon runners of all time. From 1906 to 1912 he consistently defeated most of the leading amateurs and professionals at distances of 12 to 26 miles. He won the Boston Marathon, represented Canada in the 1908 Olympic Games, and served overseas with the Sportsmen's Battalion and the Canadian Engineers (1916-1919).

Dr. Henry Norman Bethune (1890-1939), was a descendant of Loyalist Reverend John Bethune (1751-1815). Bethune was born at Gravenhurst, Muskoka District, graduated from the University of Toronto, saw extensive service during World War I and later gained widespread recognition as a thoracic surgeon. His increasing concern with social and political issues took him to Spain in 1936 where he set up the world's first mobile blood transfusion unit. In 1938 he went to China where he worked with Mao Tse Tung's National Revolutionary Army as a sur-

Left top: Dr. Edmund J. Zavitz (1875-1968).
Left below: Dr. Mahlon Locke (1880-1942).
Right top: Tom Longboat (1886-1949) in Hamilton, Followed by Competitor March.
Right below: Tommy Burns (1881-1955), World Heavyweight Champion.

geon and medical adviser until his death from septicemia on the field of battle. Revered by the Chinese as a national hero, Bethune is buried in the Mausoleum of Martyrs, Shih Cha Chuang, China.

The first woman elected to the parliament of Canada and a redoubtable spokesman for women's rights was Agnes Campbell Macphail (1890-1954), born near Hopeville, Grey County. In 1919 she joined the United Farmers of Ontario, was elected as a Federal Progressive from Grey in 1921, and retained her seat until 1939. A strong speaker, she always maintained her independence of party politics, and was concerned mainly with agricultural affairs, prison reform, and welfare of the aged. Following her defeat in 1939, she joined the CCF party and represented East York in the Ontario legislature (1942-1951).

Dr. Sir Frederick Grant Banting (1891-1941), was born in Alliston, and educated at local schools and the University of Toronto. There, under the direction of Dr. J.R.R. Macleod, Banting began work in 1921 on diabetes, then incurable. His assistant was Charles Best, whose story follows. They succeeded in isolating insulin, one of the most important medical discoveries of the 20th century that would save the lives of thousands of diabetics throughout the world. In 1923, Banting and Macleod were awarded the Nobel Prize for Medicine, and in 1934, Banting was knighted by King George V. Banting had served overseas during the First World War, and he volunteered for the Canadian Medical Corps in the Second. He was killed in a plane crash in Newfoundland in 1941, while on his way to Britain.

One of Canada's outstanding economic historians, Harold Adams Innis (1894-1952), was born in Otterville, Oxford County, graduated from McMaster University in Hamilton, obtained his doctorate from the University of Chicago and in 1920 joined the Department of Political Economy at the University of Toronto. He ultimately became department chairman and Dean of Graduate Studies, profoundly influencing Canadian historical writing with the publication of his *Fur Trade in Canada*, 1930. His *Empire and Communications*, 1950, investigated the effects of communications technology on cultural values and social institutions, and helped establish international communications theory.

Innis College, University of Toronto, is named in his honour.

Tremendously important to Canada in the 20th century has been the development of aircraft. William Avery Bishop, V.C. (1894-1956), one of the country's greatest fighter pilots, was born in Owen Sound. "Billy" Bishop, was attending the Royal Military College when war was declared in 1914. He first joined a cavalry unit, but in 1915 transferred to the Royal Flying Corps. He was credited with the destruction of seventy-two enemy aircraft, and became the youngest lieutenant-colonel in the air force, and won the Victoria Cross, Distinguished Service Order, and the Military Cross. During World War II he became director of recruiting for the RCAF with the rank of Air Marshall.

Dr. Charles Herbert Best (1899-1978), was born in West Pembroke, Maine, the son of Nova Scotian parents. He attended Harbord Collegiate in Toronto, and graduated from the University of Toronto in medicine in 1925. While a graduate student, he assisted Dr. Frederick Banting in isolating insulin in 1922, a discovery that gave new hope to people afflicted with diabetes, but for Best, recognition came slowly. He was not knighted with Banting in 1934, but because he lived many years after the other's death in 1941, Best made other important discoveries. He developed a means of storing blood serum that was beneficial during World War II, for which he was made a C.B.E. in 1944. He helped develop a variety of drugs, and was awarded the C.C. in 1968.

This chronological roll call of Ontarians who made their mark on the province, the country, and the world represents barely a fraction of those who deserve to be mentioned, for example, Prime Ministers John Diefenbaker and Lester Pearson. These few, however, truly represent the genius that continues to stimulate Ontario, as well as the love and concern with which her able citizens regard her.

Canadians, never overly emotional about their "native land," nevertheless, feel a strong and deep attachment to their province and country, and when challenged, rise to heights as great as those of the citizens of any country in the world. Ontario is, indeed, "a place to stand, a place to grow" — but it was made so by her citizens, who have worked hard at it for more than two centuries.

Left below: *Harold Innis Cartoon from the Innis College* Herald.
Right: *The Great Canadian Flag Debate 1964 by* Toronto Star *Cartoonist Duncan Macpherson. Prime Minister Lester Pearson (born at Newtonbrook, now in Metro Toronto) argues with former Prime Minister John Diefenbaker (born in Neustadt). New Democratic leader, Tommy Douglas, is on the right.*

MAYALASIA
CONGO
CYPRUS
VIET NAM
CANADA
Macpherson TORONTO STAR

Far left top: *Mary Pickford (1894-1978). Born Gladys Marie Smith in Toronto, she was a child actress. In 1909, she appeared in the first of 194 movies. "American's Sweetheart" was also a shrewd businesswoman, who in 1919, joined her husband, Douglas Fairbanks Sr., D.W. Griffith and Charlie Chaplin, to form United Artists.*

Left top middle: *Raymond Massey (1896-1983). An internationally revered actor and movie star, Massey was born in Toronto and began his acting career at Hart House, Universtiy of Toronto. He served with the Canadian Army in both World Wars, and is best remembered for his movie portrayal of Abraham Lincoln. He was a brother of Vincent Massey, the first Canadian to be Governor General.*

Left top: *Robert Samuel McLaughlin (1871-1972). The first President of General Motors of Canada, Oshawa, Colonel Sam, or R. S., as he was known, was a well-known philanthropist and a benefactor of the United Empire Loyalists' Association of Canada.*

Far left below: *Neustadt, Grey County, Birthplace of Prime Minister John George Diefenbaker.*

Left below: *Two Ontario-Born British Press Lords. Left, Roy Thomson (1st Baron Thomson of Fleet, 1894-1976) was born in Toronto and built a newspaper chain before going to Scotland in 1953. There he began a business empire that eventually included the London* Times. *Right, W. Maxwell Aitken (1st*

Baron Beaverbrook, 1879-1964) was born in Maple, although he spent his early years in New Brunswick. He went to England in 1910 and founded newspapers. Lord Beaverbrook served in British cabinets in both World Wars, and was Churchill's Minister of Aircraft Production during the Battle of Britain.
Right top: *Dr. Charles H. Best, Co-Discoverer of Insulin.*
Far right top: *Dr. Sir Frederick Banting, Co-Discoverer of Insulin.*
Right below: *Joseph Burr Tyrrell (1858-1957), Explorer of the Barrens. Born in Weston (now in Metro Toronto), Tyrrell joined the Canadian Government Geological Survey. He discovered dinosaur bones in the Red Deer Valley and also the Drumheller coal seam. In 1893, and 1894, he led two expeditions which explored the Dubawnt and Kazan Rivers, to the west of Hudson Bay.*
Right below middle: *Dr. Abraham Groves (1849-1934). This Ontario medical doctor performed the first appendectomy operation in North America, a procedure that has saved many lives.*
Far right below: *Guy Lombardo (1902-1977). Born in London, Ontario, Guy Lombardo, with his popular band, the Royal Canadians, was remembered throughout North America for over fifty years, especially for New Year's Eve celebrations.*

CHAPTER 29

THE ARTS

by Donald Blake Webster

Art . . . begins with the world
we construct, not with the world we see.

NORTHROP FRYE
THE EDUCATED IMAGINATION

How long does it take for a new frontier territory, populated as abruptly as Upper Canada was by the Loyalist influx of 1784, to get beyond the level of bare subsistence, and to begin development as a full society? How long does it take to pass from the stage of isolated raw settlements to the beginnings of economic infrastructures, on which all arts and cultural activities depend? In the example of Upper Canada, we can pretty well conclude that the transition, from scratch and marginal existence to the development of a society, proceeded over approximately twenty to thirty years — the first generation.

Perhaps as much as by its natural blessings, and partition as a separate province in 1791, new Upper Canada was boosted economically by the Napoleonic Wars and the resulting huge British demand for North American commodities. Upper Canada passed the subsistence stage to become a timber and grain exporter before 1800. Great rafts of logs were floated down the St. Lawrence to Montreal, there to be loaded for British ports. In 1802 alone, English-bound exports of wheat and flour exceeded 8,000,000 bushels.

Travel to and from, and within Upper Canada, particularly for cargoes, was by water, by virtually every form of craft and raft that would float. It was the accessibility of water power and transportation, not roads, that in fact governed settlement patterns. In effect, transport isolation created a fortunate (through hindsight) condition. It necessitated the establishment of indigenous commercial crafts and manufacturing far sooner after the first settlement than was the case with the more eastern import-accessible provinces.

Since Upper Canada, in its isolation, was forced to go-it-alone to a large degree (even the canal systems did not come until the 1820s and 30s), the region also created a substantial market for its own products, providing a solid economic incentive for entrepreneurs, craftsmen, and small manufacturers of all descriptions. While settlement in Quebec and the Maritimes remained clustered on the coasts for many decades, the isolation of Upper Canada was also a boost to interior settlement, away from the lake shores. Following the Lake Ontario and Erie drainage rivers, all good water-power sources, and available agricultural

Overleaf: *Festival Theatre, Stratford. Ontario's first annual festival theatre was founded in 1953.*
Right top: *Passenger Pigeons, Old Fort Erie, 1804, Watercolour by Military Artist, Edward Walsh, Regimental Physician.*
Right below: *Windsor Chair, York, c.1800-10. Possibly by Daniel Tiers, this American-type chair belonged to the Jarvises.*
Far right below: *Low-Back Windsor Chair, Kingston. This chair was made and signed by Chester Hatch, c.1825.*
Left below: *Three-Legged Round Table, c.1795-1810, York Region, belonging to William Jarvis.*

few notices or records of independent specialist craftsmen before the 1810-1820 period. Virtually all artisans, whether land grantees or tenants, farmed at least to a self-sustaining level, and often practiced their crafts seasonally, primarily in winter. Word-of-mouth was sufficient notice for the small areas they served. Even when access to a newspaper existed, few craftsmen advertised at all, except when they were establishing a new business, or changing location. (Of more than 500 cabinetmakers working in York-Toronto before 1865, less than ten percent ever advertised in any form, and this pattern is probably applicable to other artisans.) Business directories were not to exist for several decades, and craftsmen were not required to list their occupations on tax rolls. Thus, unless they left journals, ledgers, or other documents which have survived, no written records of their occupations exist.

Certainly the largest output of artisans was furniture, an essential in every household. Most was home-made, crude, and discarded when loose or broken. This throw-away furniture was neither stylized nor sophisticated, and virtually all has long since disappeared. No surviving examples of indigenous Upper Canada furniture have yet appeared either documented or reliably datable as earlier than 1800, and pitifully few existing pieces are datable before 1812. What was not ultimately discarded seems to have disappeared in the house fires that occurred with great regularity.

Stylized or formal furniture, derived from design forms then current in Britain and the United States, appeared first only in the 1800 to 1810 period, but then increased in production very rapidly. It was this furniture, and not the rough self- or carpenter-made basics, that reflected a growing economy. This was the sort of furniture ordered, from skilled and at least semi-specialist cabinetmakers, by millers, merchants, shippers, or more prosperous farmers, people who for the first time since 1784 were generating discretionary income available for desires beyond just bare necessities. This also had, of course, the spin-off effect of attracting additional artisans and merchants to Upper Canada, not only cabinetmakers but all manner of other skills as well.

The better cabinetmakers utilized native hardwoods — they had no

Left below: *Silver Teaspoon, c.1790-95, and Silver Sugar Tongs, c.1790-1810. Maker unknown, the spoons were made for John Aikman, New Jersey Loyalist who settled in Upper Canada. The sugar tongs were made by Jordan Post, York's first silversmith.*
Right top: *Bow-Front Curly Maple Sideboard, Eastern Ontario, c.1800-20, Reflects the Earlier Hepplewhite Period.*
Right below: *Tall Chest of Drawers Inlaid, 1821, Niagara. Niagara area furniture, in the Germanic tradition, is finely crafted and highly collectable.*
Far right below: *Bureau Desk of Curly Maple, Niagara, Reflecting English Craftsmanship and Style of the 1820 Period.*

M · M 1821

choice — which they bought or took in trade from farmers clearing the old-growth forests. Fashionable mahogany, like other bulky imports, was available only in port-of-landing cities such as Halifax, Saint John, Quebec, and Montreal, but not in Upper Canada. Home or carpenter-made furniture was generally of pine, or pine mixed with a straight-grained hardwood such as maple or ash.

The cabinetmakers needed better wood, and thus wild black cherry became the poor man's mahogany (though it is a finer wood) of Upper Canada, and figured maple (curly or bird's-eye) its foil or contrast, the equivalent to the Ceylonese satinwood then so popular in Britain. Singly or in combination, cherry and figured maple became *the* primary woods of the best stylized Upper Canada furniture, as well as walnut, preferred by Upper Canada-Germanic makers.

The earliest *recorded* cabinetmaker in Upper Canada was Pennsylvania-born Daniel Tiers, who came to York with the Berczy settlers, and in 1798 established a chair-making business. He advertised just once, in the *Upper Canada Gazette* in 1802, noting "armed chairs, sittees [sic] and dining ditto, and fan-back and brace-back chairs," probably all Windsor types. Tiers gave up chair-making in 1808, to buy a tavern in Yorkville.

Largely because of its location at the head of the St. Lawrence, and its garrison and naval dockyard, Kingston remained the major town in Upper Canada through the 1820s. Unlike York, with a newspaper since 1793, Kingston had no newspaper or advertising medium until the Kingston *Gazette* was founded in 1810. Three cabinetmakers then advertised within two years. Loyalist Abia Sayre, who had opened shop about 1805, produced, or at least offered, an unusually wide range of furniture, from clock cases to bureaus to dining tables. Grenno & Sawyer began a chair-making shop in 1811, and Samuel Howe, the son of a Loyalist, opened a full-range furniture shop the same year.

As with all artisans, it is impossible to determine just what cabinetmakers actually produced themselves, and what simply passed through their shops. They all imported and sold furniture, particularly chairs, from both Montreal and New York State; increasingly they sub-

Left top: *The Poplars, Grafton, Built by Eliakim Barnum, 1817.*
Far left top: *Front Doorway, John Beverley Robinson House, Toronto, 1822. The Georgian doorway is on display at the Royal Ontario Museum, Canadiana Gallery.*
Left below: *Union Station, Toronto, Built Between 1915 and 1927.*
Left below middle: *Trinity College, University of Toronto. The college moved from Queen Street to the present Hoskin Avenue site in 1925.*
Far left below: *Sharon Temple, Built Between 1825 and 1831.*
Right below: *The Grange, Toronto, Built by D'Arcy Boulton, 1818.*

contracted furniture components from outside piece-workers, and also bought and sold "used" furniture after repair and refinishing. They typically, as well, had parallel businesses, as upholsterers, house joiners, or sign painters, and as dealers in paints and varnishes, hardware, and lumber. The single most constant and staple business was serving the continuous demand for coffins.

Since the makers rarely marked their products in any case, and discards and fires have taken such an extreme toll, few surviving pieces of Upper Canada furniture made before 1820 have been positively identified to a specific maker. Among the earliest, in fact, are a few chairs of Chester Hatch who, at the age of nineteen, went to Kingston and opened a chair-making shop in 1815, and imported as well. Hatch is known through marked chairs of the 1820s and 30s, and continued in business until 1857.

Lieutenant-Colonel William Armstrong, in 1814, advertised in the Kingston *Gazette* for a local contractor to make for the garrison 100 barracks tables, 100 officers tables, and 200 cane or rush-seated chairs. It would be interesting to discover if any of those still exist.

Other than furniture, another absolute essential in every household was utility pottery (now also heavily collected) for preparing and preserving foods. Few families could afford white English tableware, particularly given the hazards and cost of getting it to Kingston or York from Montreal. Wooden trenchers and bowls, and horn cups, often served instead. Food preparation, and salted or vinegar-pickled winter storage, however, required liquid-tight utility and container vessels. Earthen pottery was far simpler and cheaper than wooden cooperage, but unlike furniture, neither could be home-made. Both called for specialist craftsmen and equipment.

While multi-skilled men such as John Smith and others like him could produce cooperage, potters became essential. Unlike expensive tableware, heavy, cheap, and fragile pottery was not worth the breakage cost of shipping from Britain and transporting up the St. Lawrence to Lake Ontario. As with mahogany logs, the importing of English utility earthenware was just not economically feasible. Upper Canada in its

Left below: *Sugar Bowl and Cover, Mallorytown Glass Works, 1839-40. This footed free-blown aquamarine bowl represents the earliest glass produced in Ontario. For many years all glass used in Upper Canada was imported. The Mallorytown works lasted only one year, and the next known glass works was opened in Hamilton in 1865.*

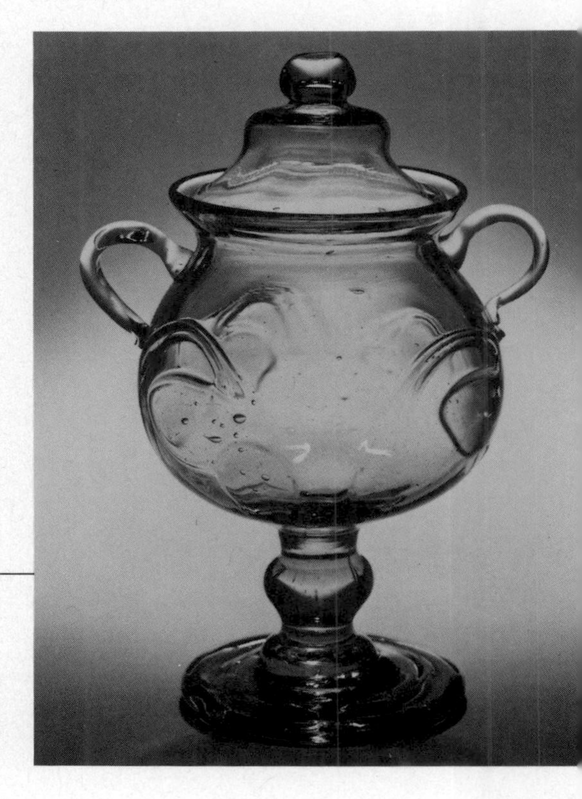

early years undoubtedly was at times in difficult straits for winter food-storage containers, and winter diets were extremely limited.

The first *known* potter to establish a commercial pottery was Samuel Humberstone, English-born, who came from Pennsylvania to Augusta Township, near Prescott. He established his pottery sometime before 1796, and produced utility wares of local red-firing clay until his death in 1823. His son Thomas moved to York in 1798, acquired a 200-acre farm, and established a family pottery that continued in operation, through four generations, until 1919, the longest-lived pottery business in Canada.

***Right below:** Decorated Pottery Jar, Waterloo County, 1825. The earliest dated examples of Ontario pottery are several pieces made by the Mennonite potter Jacob Bock (1798-1867). Pottery was made in Upper Canada earlier than glass, because it was both breakable and cheap to produce. Fragile pottery was difficult to transport, and many potters began making it locally, although the earliest pieces did not survive long. Much of a potter's work was replacement of breakages.*

Early potters, like cabinetmakers, only rarely marked their work, so it is often impossible to connect surviving pieces to their makers. In fact, virtually no Upper Canadian pottery survives intact from much earlier than about 1840. Utility earthenware was as fragile as it was inexpensive, and potters depended on loss and replacement for much of their business.

Glassmakers, or Glasshouses, as the factories were called, were even scarcer than potteries in Upper Canada. By 1839, Amasa W. Mallory was making free-blown bottles and tableware near Mallorytown, west of Brockville. Although this is the earliest known glass operation in Upper Canada, some evidence suggests that glassworks may have operated on the north shore of Rice Lake, and near DeCew's Falls in the Niagara region, some time before the Mallorytown operation. A few pieces, tinted aquamarine, from the Mallory works, are in the collection of the Royal Ontario Museum.

Beyond necessities, amenities and luxuries, mostly of English origin, were imported in great variety and sold by numerous merchants. Craftsmen soon followed, initiating local production. Even silver, particularly table flatware, was widely stocked by shopkeepers, and was probably in wider use than the limitations of a frontier society might suggest. Numbers of Loyalist silversmiths had come to Canada, though most went to the Maritimes.

Jordan Post, however, came to Upper Canada from Connecticut in 1787, eventually settling at York, and is the earliest *recorded* silversmith in the province (though he was probably not the first). In a period when silversmiths had migratory habits, Post remained in York, married Melinda Woodruff in 1807, and was still apparently in business at his death in 1853. Jordan and Melinda Streets in Toronto are named after Post and his wife.

Elisha Purdy opened a shop in Niagara in 1799, as a watchmaker and repairer, and also advertised as doing gold and silver work. By 1800 he was in York, advertising as a watchmaker and jewelery dealer. Purdy shortly gained a competitor in the silver and watchmaking business, John Alexander Mackenzie, who, in York in 1801, advertised that he had worked in Edinburgh and London.

There is no doubt that Upper Canada depended heavily on imported goods before local production gained headway. In the realm of heavy and/or inexpensive commodities, however, that were not feasible to import — furniture, pottery, metal work, and iron — native industry gained the balance of what we now call "market share," before 1820.

In all the various commercial crafts, only those makers are known who left records of themselves through advertising or other documents that have survived. Advertising is a primary source for artisans of the Loyalist period, but was possible only after the establishment of newspapers. No business directories were published until the 1840s.

The obvious need and market created by a very rapidly expanding population was certainly served by far more craftsmen than are in any way known today. The example of cabinetmakers, fewer than ten percent of whom ever advertised, is probably applicable to most other crafts — word-of-mouth was sufficient. There also exist numerous examples of good and stylized, signed and dated pieces of furniture, made before 1825, by otherwise unrecorded cabinetmakers, as well as a few pieces of silver by unknown makers. From this, and also considering the loss of many written records over the years, it is probably safe to assume that the number of artisans actually practicing, if only on a part-time basis, was probably at least double the number recorded, and in some crafts perhaps ten times as many.

On this basis, virtually every town or area attracted its essential sup-

Right top: The Mill Ford *(1898) by Homer Watson (1855-1936). The painting is in the Art Gallery of Hamilton.*

Right below: *The Artist Painting Queen Victoria, 1895. Frederick Bell-Smith. Director of Fine Arts, Alma College, St. Thomas, became the first Canadian artist to paint a reigning monarch at a live sitting.*

Left below: *Portrait of the Hon. Henry Ruttan (1792-1871) by Paul Kane, c.1850. Son of William Ruttan, a Loyalist who settled at Adolphustown in 1784, Henry was Speaker of the Legislature in 1837.*

port skills and facilities. Specialized artisans, by a combination of farming for basic subsistence, and spreading their crafts into parallel trades and businesses, survived and prospered. Though much of what they produced has disappeared over the years, that which remains is today treasured as part of the physical heritage of Ontario's origins.

While at first the craftsmen's efforts were functional, as the 19th century progressed, craftsmen embellished their work to make it more pleasing to the eye. Included as craftsmen were the many homemakers who wove and spun, and who, too, wanted their efforts to look attractive. Bed coverings were made from colourful fabrics and embroidered; pottery became ornaments to display; a cupboard was more interesting with architectural detail, or with inlays of contrasting woods.

One exceptional art form was found among German settlers. Known as *fraktur* because letters were broken for ornamentation, it was used to decorate handwritten or printed documents. Letters were embellished and watercolour pictures particularly of flowers and birds, were added. Some of this decoration was amateurish but some was done by itinerant professional artists who toured German-speaking communities.

Some religious sects disapproved of music, but many of the first settlers brought their musical heritage with them. Singing was popular, and a fiddler was a necessity at a country dance. The first instruments were imported and scarce, of course, but by the 1830s pianos were being made in Canada. By the 1850s, many small towns had opera houses. Some productions were locally cast, but most were provided by touring companies from the United States. Importing culture was a good deal cheaper than fostering indigenous talent, a situation not unknown in later times. Ontario was part of the regular circuit of Dockstader's Minstrels. In 1851, sponsored by P.T. Barnum, the "Swedish Nightingale" Jenny Lind sang in Toronto's St. Lawrence Hall (she later became a naturalized British subject).

Painters and architects could flourish at home but they followed current trends. For architects, the earliest styles were late Georgian, neoclassical designs such as St. Andrew's Church at Niagara-on-the-Lake or "The Grange" in Toronto, derived both from England and from the

Left & right below: *Markdale Citizens' Band, 1909. Every community struck up the band and blew their own horns as an expression of their love for music.*

colonies the Loyalists had left. By the time the first Parliament Buildings were erected in Ottawa, the Gothic Revival was in vogue.

Left and right bottom: *Pembroke Boys Brass Band c.1910.*

The first painting in Upper Canada was topographical. Mrs. Simcoe belonged to this school doing a blend of accurate drawing and watercolour. Military artists like James Peachey, Edward Walsh and Edward Henn, were required to make accurate drawings, but they also painted for pleasure. Niagara Falls was a favourite subject, as were various aspects of Upper Canadian life.

Portraiture here, as everywhere, was the artist's bread and butter, as William von Moll Berczy learned. Other portraitists were Georges Berthon, who arrived from France in 1844, and William Sawyer. Their contemporary, Paul Kane, sketched the natives of Ontario and the West and his finished oils were done in Toronto.

Egerton Ryerson, the educator, helped Upper Canadians appreciate art. In 1857 he opened at the Toronto Normal School, the Canadian Educational Museum, exhibiting oil copies and prints, and plaster casts of European masterpieces, the only public display of art in the province.

Painter John Fraser founded the Ontario Society of Artists in 1872. In 1876, the OSA, the Ontario School of Art (now the Ontario College of Art) was founded. The Royal Canadian Academy began in 1880, and Lucius R. O'Brien, born at Shanty Bay, was its first president. Fraser, O'Brien, and John Verner, the latter born in Sheridan, Ontario, made a concerted attempt to express the Canadian experience in the type of luminous landscapes that were popular in the United States in the 1870s and 1880s.

The next crop of painters felt that they had to find inspiration by going to Paris — a sentiment shared by writers such as Morley Callaghan. The first to go to France was William Brymer of Ottawa, who was followed by J.W.L. Forster of Norval. Others who went were Paul Peel of London and George Reid of Wingham. One who stayed behind was Homer Watson of Doone, whose unaffected landscapes prompted Oscar Wilde to call Watson the "Canadian Constable." In 1900, Sir Edmund Walker and George Reid, then the president of the OSA, founded the Toronto Museum of Art (now the Art Gallery of Ontario).

Far left top: *Dora Mavor Moore (1888-1979) as a Young Woman. A "First Lady" of Ontario theatre, Dora Mavor Moore was an actress in her own right, as well as a promoter of other Canadian talent and of the production of plays. She founded the New Play Society that staged many classical productions in the Toronto of the 1940s and 50s.*

Left top: *St. Lawrence Hall, Toronto. Completed in 1850, the hall was long the social and cultural centre of the city. It was designed by William Thomas, from Stroud, Gloucestershire, England. The hall was restored by the city in 1967 as a centennial project.*

Far left below: *Royal Alexandra Theatre, Toronto. One of Ontario's most famous theatres, many first-rate companies have played here. The tradition continues through the foresight of Ed Mirvish, who saved it from demolition and restored it to its former grandeur. Honest Ed Mirvish also restored London's Old Vic.*

Left below: *Victoria Opera House, Prescott. Actually Prescott Town Hall, which housed an auditorium, the building was erected in 1874. Many of Ontario's smaller towns and cities have similar impressive public buildings reflecting a neo-classical influence.*

Right top: *Roy Thomson Hall, Toronto. The home of the Toronto Symphony Orchestra, this concert hall opened in September 1982, and was named for the late Canadian newspaper magnate, Baron Thomson of Fleet.*
Right below: *Shaw Festival Theatre, Niagara-on-the-Lake. Ontario's second annual festival theatre began in 1962, nine years after the Stratford festival was launched. Stratford had its large theatre open by 1957; the main building for the Shaw Festival was opened in 1972. Both now present a mix of classical plays and some light, more contemporary works.*

Left: La Malbaie, *Quebec, By A.Y. Jackson, 1947. Alexander Young Jackson (1882-1974) was a member of the Group of Seven, joining in 1920, who painted the Ontario landscape as well as other parts of the country.*
Right: Flight Lieutenant Carl Schaefer, RCAF *1948, by Charles Comfort. Carl Schaefer was a fellow artist and friend of Charles Comfort. The latter was a war artist who painted overseas in the 1940s. In addition he was a powerful landscape painter. All told, Comfort did three portraits of Schaefer. Comfort was Director of the National Gallery, Ottawa, 1959-65.*

Right below: *Price List at 1934 Exhibition of Ontario Society of Artists in Toronto's Centennial Year. The exhibition at Eaton's College Street offered paintings for sale at prices such as these:*

A. J. Casson's "In Lloydtown" $35.00
A. Y. Jackson's "St. Urbain, Quebec" $35.00
Arthur Lismer's "Mountain Lake, Ontario" $70.00
Charles Comfort's "Debris" $40.00
Fred S. Haine's "Wet Day, Minden" $35.00
Tom Stone's "Evening Shadows" $35.00

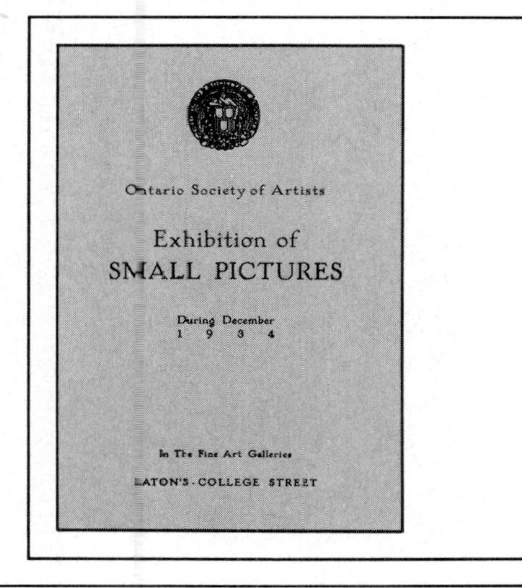
Ontario Society of Artists

Exhibition of
SMALL PICTURES

During December
1 9 3 4

In The Fine Art Galleries
EATON'S - COLLEGE STREET

The Passing of Spring

No longer in the meadow coigns shall blow
The creamy blood-root in her suit of gray,
But all the first strange flowers have passed away,
Gone with the childlike dreams that touched us so;
April is spent, and summer soon shall go,
Swift as a shadow o'er the heads of men,
And autumn with the painted leaves; and then,
When fires are set, and windows blind with snow,
We shall remember, with a yearning pang,
How in the poplars the first robins sang,
The wind-flowers risen from their leafy cots,
When life was gay and spring was at the helm,
The maple full of little crimson knots,
And all that delicate blossoming of the elm.

ARCHIBALD LAMPMAN

Far left top: *Stephen Leacock by William Notman and Son, Montreal. Stephen Leacock (1869-1944), though an economist and historian, is one of Canada's best-known men of letters and a widely loved humorist. Born in England, he grew up on a farm near Lake Simcoe. Orillia provided the model for his* Sunshine Sketches of a Little Town *(1912).*

Left below: *Stephen Leacock's Summer Home, Brewery Bay, Lake Couchiching. The kindly humorist, former teacher at Upper Canada College and McGill professor, spent many years in this house near his mythical Mariposa (Orillia). The house is now open to the public.*

Left top: *Archibald Lampman (1861-1899) and Poem. Born in Morpeth, of Loyalist Dutch and German descent, Lampman was a nature poet. His interest in the Canadian landscape is the common denominator linking many of Canada's 19th century poets.*

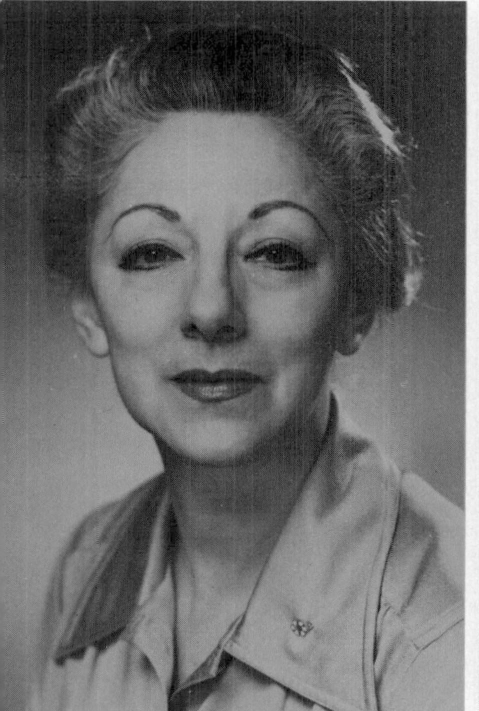

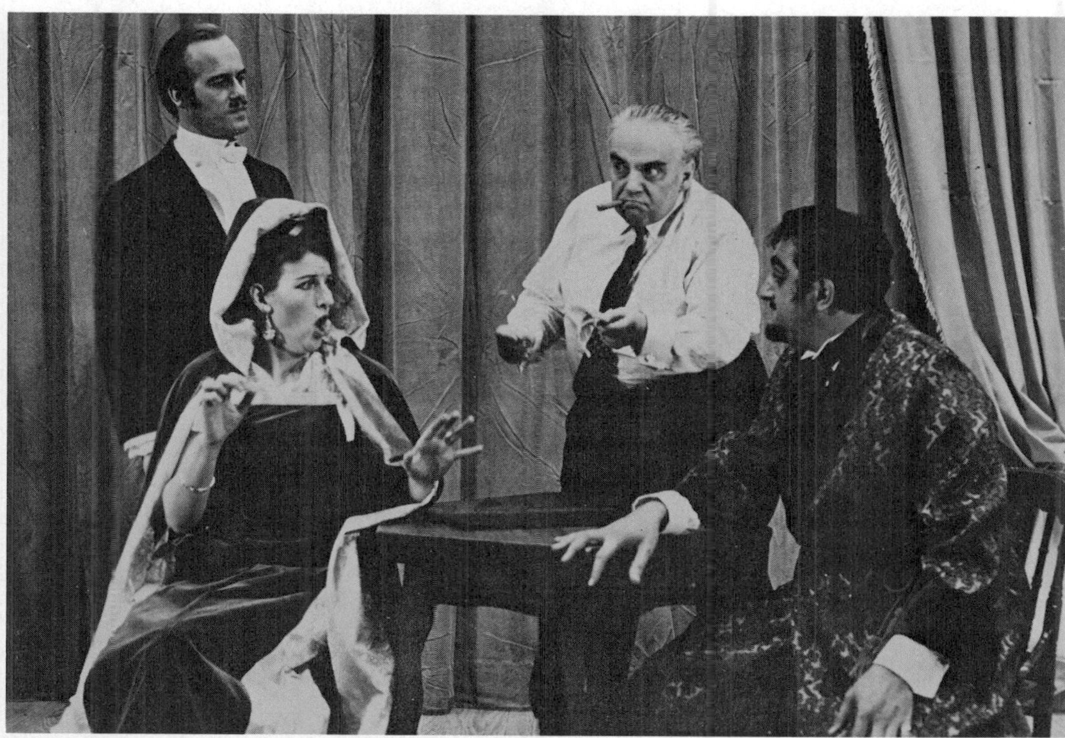

Right top: *Celia Franca, Founder of the National Ballet of Canada. As well as the founder, Miss Franca was Artistic Director of the Ballet from its beginnings in 1951 until 1974. An officer of the Order of Canada and recipient of many other honours, she is a member of the Board of Directors for the Theatre Ballet of Canada, with headquarters in Ottawa.*

Right below: *National Ballet Company of Canada in Performance. Here the now internationally renowned company dances "Napoli Pas de Six." Young dancers train at the National Ballet School, Toronto.*

Far right top: *Herman Geiger-Torel Directing a Rehearsal of* Die Fledermaus, *Canadian Opera Company. Herman Geiger-Torel (1907-1976) was born in Germany and fled Nazi persecution to South America. He settled in Toronto in 1948, and from 1950 until his death he was stage director and eventually general director of the Canadian Opera Company.*

NEW ERA
KINGSTON

CHAPTER 30

ROYAL VISITS

by Gary Toffoli and Arthur Bousfield

. . . when we speak of the Queen as the Queen of Canada it is no mere empty formality but a simple affirmation of the fact that we have a royal and not a republican form of democratic government.

JOHN FARTHING

FREEDOM WEARS A CROWN

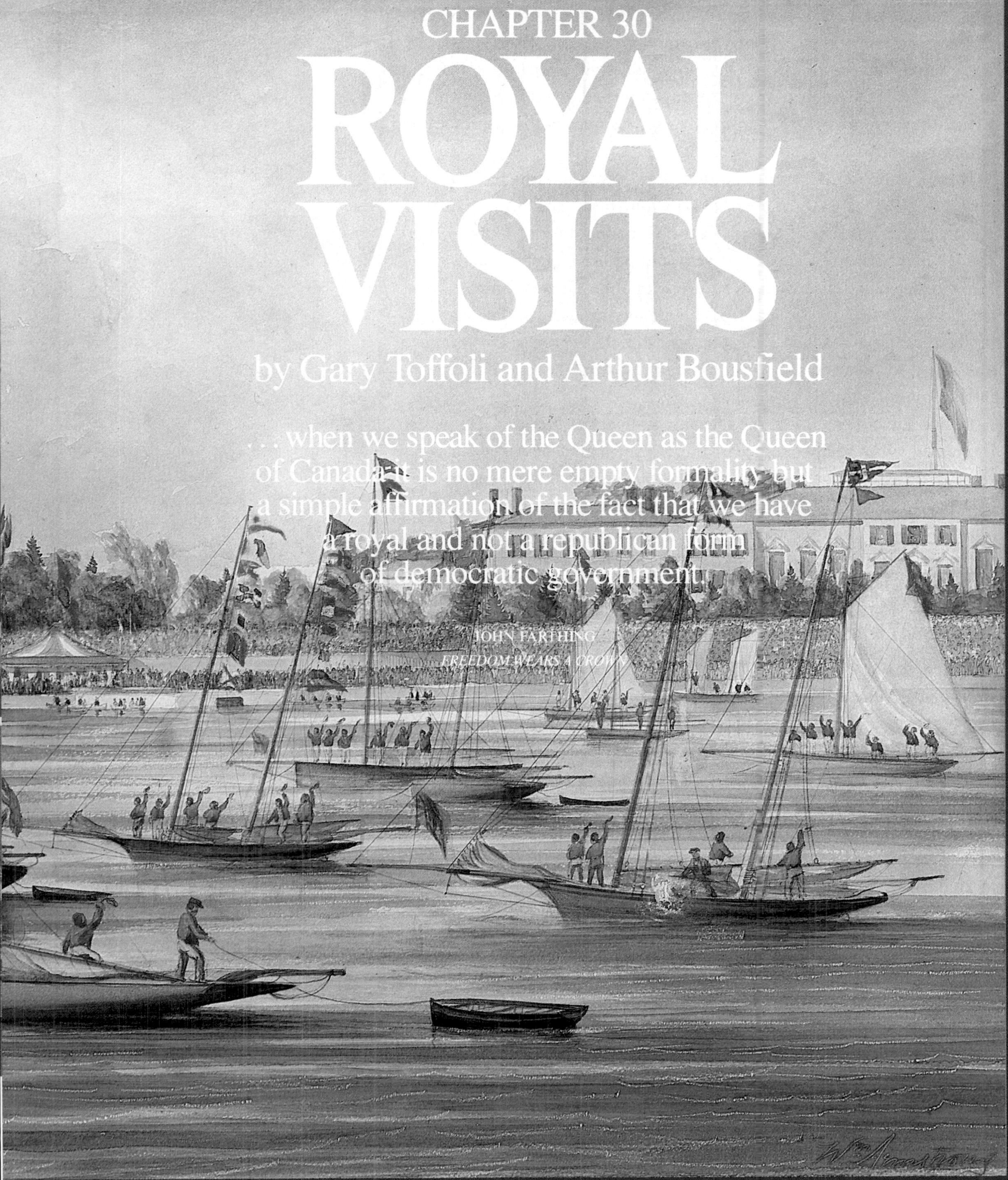

Family among them again yet, but that did not dampen their loyalty. Had not the new town founded by Galt in 1827 been named Guelph after the Royal House? As if to make amends, the new King, William IV, was the first Sovereign who had been in North America. As Prince William he was at Quebec before Upper Canada was created.

William IV's reign lasted seven years and ended the year the province exploded. Princess Victoria, who became Queen on June 20, 1837, had grown up knowing about British North America. Although not a year old when her father the Duke of Kent died in 1820, she had learned about his career in Canada. One day in 1832, her mother sent for Victoria (then fourteen) to present Joseph and Robert Bouchette to her. The Duke had assisted the topographer, Joseph Bouchette, in publishing his first work on Lower Canada in 1815. Father and son now returned to London for the publication of an expanded edition entitled, *The British Dominions in North America or a Topographical and Statistical Description of the Provinces of Lower and Upper Canada.* Dedicated to William IV, this book contained the first full-scale geographical account of Upper Canada together with accurate maps.

Queen Victoria's first diaries as Queen are full of the rebellion in Upper Canada. The Palace appreciated that the uprising was more against local powers than in opposition to the Queen's authority, and the Queen herself influenced events. She personally convinced a reluctant Lord Durham to accept the post of Governor in Chief. Durham returned the compliment by issuing his controversial amnesty to the rebels on Victoria's Coronation Day, June 28, 1838.

The Queen's marriage to her good-looking, intelligent German cousin, Prince Albert in February 1840, marked a new era. The second Royal Family was about to play its part on the Ontario scene. All told, the families of six different monarchs have known the people and places of the province firsthand. Upper Canada celebrated Victoria's wedding with great gusto when the news arrived.

The royal union was followed closely by the political marriage of Ontario and Quebec by which Upper Canada became Canada West. Prince Albert, meanwhile, helped the Queen recover her proper influ-

Left and right below: *Meeting of the Duke of Kent and Governor Simcoe at Newark (Niagara-on-the-Lake), 1792.*
Left and right bottom: *Painting by J.D. Kelly of the Proclamation of Queen Victoria's Coronation at Fort York, June 28, 1838.*

ence as constitutional sovereign. Late in 1841 she reprimanded Peel, the British Prime Minister, for offering the post of Governor General to Sir Charles Bagot, before consulting her. Victoria was a warm partisan of another governor, Lord Metcalfe, and in 1845 after his resignation because of ill health worried:

> that there will not be too great a delay in making the new appointment, as experience has shown that nothing was more detrimental to the good government of Canada than the last interregum after Sir Charles Bagot's death.

The year of the Montreal Annexation Manifesto, Toronto showed Ontario's fervent loyalty by holding the first major public celebrations on Victoria Day, May 24, which soon became *the* great Canadian holiday. Popular enthusiasm towards the Monarchy in the fifties is usually attributed to the jingoism of the Crimean War of 1854-1856 in which many Ontarians served, but, in fact, it was a personal project of Prince Albert's that brought Ontarians closer to the Royal Family three years before. All Prince Albert's love for science, capacity for detail and fertile imagination went into the Great Exhibition of 1851, the direct ancestor of the Canadian National Exhibition, Central Canada Exhibition, Western Fair and succeeding world expositions. Canada — that is Ontario and Quebec — sent 345 crates of goods to be exhibited in the Crystal Palace. She ranked second among the colonies and seventh of all contributing countries, surpassed only by France, Belgium, the United States, Austria and India. (One gold-medal winner from Ontario was Thomas MacKay, a builder of Rideau Hall.) Before long, crystal palaces were springing up in Toronto and Hamilton.

Renewed patriotism prompted new requests from Ontario for the Queen in person. In 1859 both houses of the provincial parliament passed an address asking the Queen to come and open the Victoria Bridge at Montreal. Five delegates took the address to the Queen. Leading them was Hon. (later Sir) Henry Smith of Kingston, the Speaker of the Assembly.

The Queen declined. Not the perils of the journey, but reluctance to leave London to the ever-suspect politicians for so long was her real reason. But next year the Prince of Wales would make a tour. In this way, after much importunity by the province, the 1860 tour, a landmark for Ontario and the Monarchy came about. After spending August in the Maritime colonies and Canada East, Albert Edward, Prince of Wales, arrived in Ottawa on September 1.

A colourful reception awaited him. Brashly self-confident in its new status as capital, Ottawa sent 1,200 brightly dressed lumbermen and Indians in canoes to escort his steamer. Next day, with great pomp the Prince laid the cornerstone of the new Parliament Buildings. From Ottawa he travelled to Brockville by the newly-built railway, which was proving such a benefit in linking the far-flung corners of the province, proceeding up the St. Lawrence into the heart of Ontario. Angered by the Prince's cordial association with the Roman Catholic Church in Quebec, Ontario Orangemen decided to turn his presence into a protest. This led the royal party to boycott Kingston and Belleville, when arches with anti-Catholic slogans were not removed. In Toronto, on September 10, a single offending arch was left up. The Prince cancelled the corporation's invitation to his levee, but apologies were tendered and he held a special reception for the city fathers later in the day. The incident showed the Crown's resolve to remain strictly neutral in the face of rabid provincial sectarianism.

From Toronto the Prince travelled north to Collingwood, stopping at small communities on the way. Newmarket, Aurora, Bradford and Barrie proudly received their first royal visitor. Returning to Toronto, the Prince agreed to become patron of the Royal Canadian Yacht Club, opened Queen's Park, reviewed the volunteer corps, visited the university (where he was admitted as a second-year man), and opened Allan Gardens. In the evening he attended a ball at Toronto's Crystal Palace.

In London, he danced with Miss Gzowski *twice* at the Tecumseh House ball. At Niagara, his horrified entourage stopped him from taking up aerialist Blondin's offer to wheel him in a barrow across the Falls on a wire. In more normal circumstances, he later laid the foundation stone for the new Brock monument, leaving participants with as civilized a statement of patriotism as they would ever hear:

Right top: *Bust of Albert Edward Prince of Wales, St. Lawrence Hall. This likeness by Norton Edwards was presented to the City of Toronto in 1866.*
Right bottom: *The Marquis and Marchioness of Lorne (Princess Louise) at Niagara Falls, Canada, February 15, 1879. Princess Louise was a daughter of Queen Victoria.*
Right below: *Funeral Service for Queen Victoria. The service in Toronto for the Queen, who died on January 22, 1901, was held at the same hour as the service in Britain.*

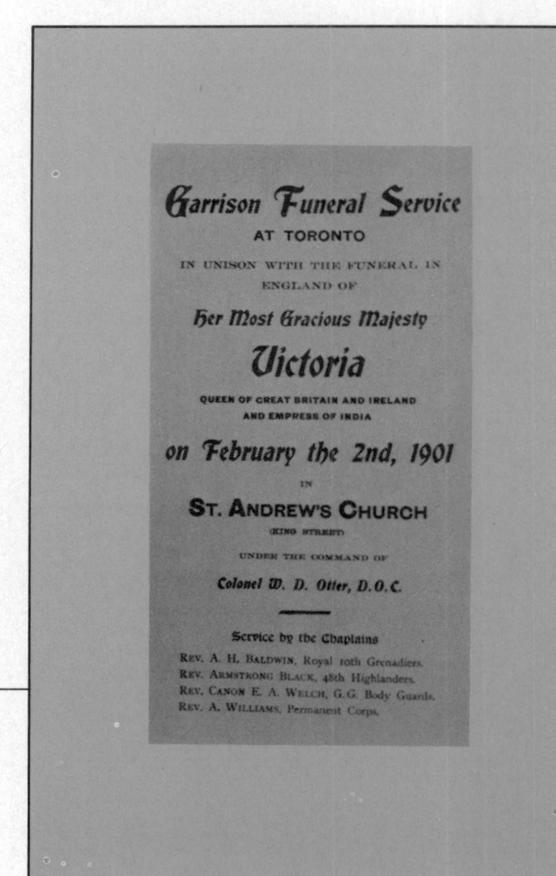

Garrison Funeral Service
AT TORONTO
IN UNISON WITH THE FUNERAL IN ENGLAND OF
Her Most Gracious Majesty
Victoria
QUEEN OF GREAT BRITAIN AND IRELAND AND EMPRESS OF INDIA
on February the 2nd, 1901
IN
ST. ANDREW'S CHURCH
(KING STREET)
UNDER THE COMMAND OF
Colonel W. D. Otter, D.O.C.

Service by the Chaplains
REV. A. H. BALDWIN, Royal 10th Grenadiers.
REV. ARMSTRONG BLACK, 48th Highlanders.
REV. CANON E. A. WELCH, G.G. Body Guards.
REV. A. WILLIAMS, Permanent Corps.

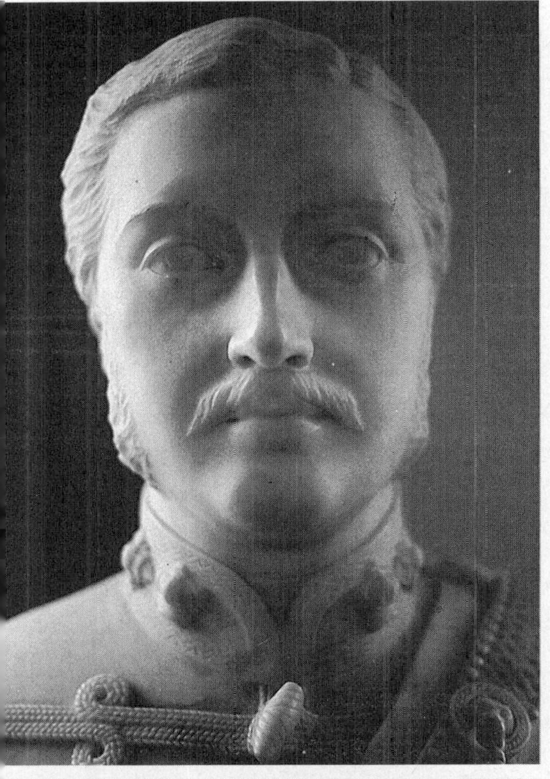

> Every nation may, without offence to its neighbours, commemorate its heroes, their deeds of arms and their noble deaths. This is no taunting boast of victory, no revival of long passed animosities, but a noble tribute to a soldier's fame; the more honourable, because we readily acknowledge the bravery and chivalry of that people by whose hands he fell.

Hamilton, where a crowd of 50,000 awaited him, was the last stop before the Prince crossed into the United States at Windsor.

Despite its troubled beginning, the tour was a tremendous success. It became one of Ontario's legends, gathering its store of colourful anecdotes, apocryphal or otherwise. One told how the Prince sampled a peach in a Niagara orchard. "How I wish my mother could taste such delicious peaches!" he exclaimed. The owner of the orchard, who was up in the tree from which the fruit had come, overheard the remark. He called down, "Why didn't you bring the old woman along with you?" (not knowing who the visitor was). In practical terms, the tour opened British North America to Queen Victoria's family, four more of whom shortly arrived.

In 1861 the second brother, Prince Alfred, later Duke of Edinburgh, a midshipman, toured Ontario in May with the Governor General, Sir Edmund Head. Prince Arthur, Victoria's third son, was in the province in 1869 when his regiment, the Rifle Brigade, was stationed at Montreal. That same year His Serene Highness Prince Louis of Battenberg, future husband of the Queen's granddaughter, Princess Victoria of Hesse, and father of Earl Mountbatten of Burma, visited Toronto in 1872. Never again would a decade pass without some member of the Royal Family being in Ontario.

At last, in 1878, came what many people really wanted — residence of a member of the Queen's family in the province. Princess Louise, fourth daughter of Victoria, settled into Rideau Hall, and Ontario communities got a generous share of her attention and that of her husband Lord Lorne, the Governor General. Clever and energetic, the Princess, as a talented sculptor and painter quickened the cultural life of the province. She also grasped what was most needed for the Monarchy.

Writing to her brother Prince Arthur, she told him:

> I think it possible you may come here one day. Canada is so loyal, so interesting, and with such a marvellous future that it really seems as if the Governor Generalship should always be filled by a member of our family.

Unfortunately, the Queen made this impossible. Her youngest son, Prince Leopold, visited Princess Louise in Ottawa in 1880. He returned to the United Kingdom set on being made Governor General, but Victoria found him too useful as her secretary and conspired with her British Prime Minister to frustrate his ambition to succeed Lorne.

During the 1860 tour, the Prince of Wales decided that his sons should grow up with a first-hand knowledge of the overseas possessions. Thus, Prince George, his second son, came to Ontario in 1883 when he stayed at Rideau Hall and visited Toronto and Niagara.

In 1890 the Prince of Wales's brother, Prince Arthur Duke of Connaught, toured Ontario, crossing the province by train as part of a trans-Canada railway journey. Queen Victoria found that her own life was interwoven with the lives of individual Ontarians. She acquired *Pioneer Mill* and *The Last of the Drought,* two paintings by Kitchener artist Homer Watson who, in 1887, went to Windsor Castle to revarnish them. She commissioned Lucius O'Brien, first President of the Royal Canadian Academy, to paint her two landscapes. Sir Casimir Gzowski, the Polish engineer who immigrated to Ontario, was appointed her personal aide-de-camp and did service at Windsor. After her son's 1860 tour, Queen Victoria sent Laura Secord a much needed gift of money, just as earlier she had sent a similar present to Abigail Becker, heroine of the Long Point Island disaster. Even the bizarre life of James Gay, the Guelph eccentric, touched the Queen's. This self-appointed Poet Laureate of Canada and by contemporary standards, writer of the worst doggerel in the province, not only wrote to his Queen, but received carefully preserved replies. In 1882 he got to London and called at the Palace, but the Queen was at Balmoral.

Frederic Martlett Bell-Smith, another artist who taught art in Hamilton, St. Thomas and Toronto, painted a famous picture of the Queen.

Right top: *Prince Arthur, Duke of Connaught. Queen Victoria's third son visited in 1869, and returned as Governor General, 1911-16, to represent his nephew, King George V.*
Right bottom: *The Prince of Wales (Edward VIII) at Kingston, 1919.*
Left below: *T. Eaton Store Decorations 1919, in Honour of the Prince of Wales. The big flag is 39 metres wide and 19.5 metres high.*

When the Prime Minister of Canada, Sir John Thompson, died suddenly at Windsor Castle in 1894, and the Queen personally laid a wreath on his coffin, it was suggested to Bell-Smith that he paint the historic scene. He travelled to London to seek a personal sitting from Her Majesty but was told it was impossible unless be bribed the Munshi, the Queen's Indian Secretary.

Bell-Smith decided on a bold stroke. He would write to Princess Louise through the Marquess of Lorne (whom he had met in Canada) and also ask Princess Beatrice, youngest daughter of the Queen, for a sitting. Princess Beatrice agreed, and Bell-Smith requested her help with the Queen. Through the two princesses, the astute Ontarian outmanoeuvred the Munshi and became the first Canadian artist and one of the few in the world to receive a sitting from Queen Victoria.

In 1901 the Prince of Wales at sixty became King Edward VII and the first great event of his reign for Ontario was a tour by the Heir to the Throne, Prince George, now Duke of Cornwall and York, and his wife Princess May. In Ottawa, the Duke unveiled Hébert's statue of Queen Victoria and was empowered by the King to hold an investiture of the Orders of the Bath and of St. Michael and St. George, the first time such a ceremony had taken place here.

When the Duke and Duchess arrived in Toronto, a quarter of a million people greeted them on their way to the City Hall despite heavy rain. Toronto was lavishly decorated with arches, including a magnificent one erected by the Independent Order of Foresters on Bay Street. Enthusiasm reached such a pitch that Oliver Howland, the Mayor, was drowned out by the choir of 1,000 which began to sing at the wrong moment. His Royal Highness noted that the first name of Toronto was "the first title conferred upon me by my dear grandmother." Despite confusion that left high officials, their wives and daughters struggling for admission with those of no rank, a reception for 2,000 in the Legislative Chamber was the greatest social event in the history of the city.

Leaving Toronto, the royal couple visited Brampton, Guelph, Berlin, Stratford, London, Ingersoll, Grimsby, Niagara-on-the-Lake, Niagara Falls, St. Catharines, Hamilton, Brantford (where they inspected the communion plate presented to the Mohawks by Queen Anne in 1712), Paris and Woodstock. Returning through eastern Ontario, they stopped at Belleville and were presented with an address in sign language from the children of the Ontario Institute for the Deaf and Dumb.

From Belleville, the party travelled to Kingston, then through the Thousand Islands to Brockville, Cardinal and Cornwall where the Duke received lacrosse sticks for the royal children and the Duchess a bouquet "with as much apparent interest as though it were the first one that had ever been offered to her." Thus ended the Ontario portion of the tour, a tour which became the pattern for all the cross country tours that were to follow in 1919, 1939, 1951 and 1959.

In August 1905, Prince Louis of Battenberg returned to Ontario accompanied by his nephew Prince Alexander of Battenberg, eldest son of Princess Beatrice. Prince Louis was now a rear-admiral, and would eventually be First Sea Lord. He travelled to Ottawa and Toronto and met fellow subjects of German descent at Berlin. In the spring of 1906, Prince Arthur of Connaught, only son of the Duke, obeying the King's wish, returned from a state visit to Japan through Canada.

In 1908, the Duke of York, now the Prince of Wales, returned to Canada for the Quebec Tercentenary. Although he did not come to Ontario, the Queen's Own Rifles of Toronto, headed by their Colonel Sir Henry Pellatt, led the military parade before him on the Plains of Abraham. Sir Henry, one of the keenest royalists of his day, was building his great Casa Loma as a place to entertain the Royal Family when they came to the provincial capital, a dream he only realized once when the next Prince of Wales (Edward VIII) stayed there.

It was indicative of Ontario's growing prosperity that the King received a delegation of the Canadian Manufacturers' Association at Windsor in 1905 headed by Kingstonian William Kerr, President of the C.N.E. Ontario-born artist John Colin Forbes followed in Bell-Smith's footsteps and received sittings at the Palace from the King and Queen when commissioned by the Canadian Government to paint their portraits. The Queen gave him extra sittings and the King sent cigars each day. Forbes also painted their daughter, Queen Maud of Norway.

***Left below:** King George VI and Queen Elizabeth Aboard the Royal Train at Brockville, 1939. This was the first visit of a reigning monarch to Canada. The violets, presented to the Queen by local Brownies, were from the garden of Mrs. Dwight Mallory.*
***Right below:** Governor General The Earl of Athlone and Princess Alice at the Opening of Parliament, September 6, 1945. Princess Alice was a daughter of Prince Leopold Duke of Albany, youngest son of Queen Victoria. The governor general was the former Prince Alexander of Teck, brother of Queen Mary, who took the title Earl of Athlone because of anti-German feeling during World War I.*

Ontario's next royal chapter opened in 1911, with the return of the Duke of Connaught who now, as uncle of the new King, George V, belonged to the older generation of the family. But at last a member of the Royal Family was Governor General. The Connaughts brought to Rideau Hall their beautiful, shy daughter Princess Patricia, whose impact was comparable to that of Lady Diana Spencer, the ninth Princess of Wales, more than half a century later.

The Duke remained from 1911 to 1916 and in 1913 introduced his young nephew Prince Albert, who was to become King George VI, to the ways of the province. That same year, the centenary of the War of 1812 was underway. Queen Mary unveiled the Stoney Creek memorial on June 6, the anniversary of the fateful battle, by pushing a button at Buckingham Palace.

Had not World War I broken out in 1914, this period of royal residence would have been the happiest so far recorded in Ontario. The war, however, was a personal tragedy for the Connaughts (as for many other members of the Royal Family) because the Duchess was the daughter of a German Prince. Connaught was to have been succeeded at Ottawa in the spring of 1914 by Queen Mary's youngest brother, Prince Alexander of Teck, who had been with her in Ontario in 1901. Anti-German bigotry in some quarters in Canada led the Canadian Government to change its mind. Prince Alexander, who was born at Kensington Palace, was to come as Governor General in 1940 under the less German title of Earl of Athlone.

Ontarians in the forces were inspected by the King in Britain, visited by him at the Front or consoled by him in places like the Ontario Military Hospital at Orpington. Many Ontario wounded received handwritten notes from George V, who spent hours at his desk paying this personal tribute to the troops who had served him. The post-war era was the era of the dashing Edward, Prince of Wales. He had served in the Canadian Corps during the war, and from 1919 to 1927 he spent six months of his life in Canada. Before becoming King he was four times in Ontario: the first occasion being his triumphant tour of 1919, the second in 1923, the third in 1924 and the fourth in 1927, for the sixtieth anniversary of Ontario's entry into Confederation, when he opened the Princes' Gates at the C.N.E. in Toronto.

In 1919, his natural manner took public affection by storm. He visited the mines at Cobalt and Timmins, chatted with disabled veterans in Toronto (even running after one crippled man's cap blown off by the wind), and took a leading part in the Labour Day parade in Ottawa only months after the Winnipeg General Strike. As his grandfather laid the cornerstone of the old Parliament Buidlings in 1860, the Prince of Wales did the same for the new structure on September 1, 1919.

Two other sons of King George V came to the province in the Twenties. Prince George, soon to be Duke of Kent, the most charming and brilliant of the four royal brothers, accompanied the Prince of Wales in 1927, while the more reserved Prince Henry, Duke of Gloucester, had a painful visit to Ottawa in the summer of 1929, having broken his collar bone in Vancouver which spoiled his hope of seeing much of Ontario. Prince Albert, the second brother, nearly became a resident of Ottawa in 1931, but his appointment as Governor General was thwarted by interference from the British Secretary of State for the Dominions.

Between world wars, two grandchildren of Queen Victoria visited the province. Queen Marie of Roumania, daughter of the Duke of Edinburgh and heroine of the war, made a tour in 1926, wishing to see the province where Joe Boyle, her country's knight errant, was born. And in 1934 Charles Edward, Duke of Saxe-Cobourg-Gotha, the only son of Prince Leopold, Duke of Albany, passed through en route to Japan to represent the German Red Cross.

Canadian public opinion, strongest in stolid, Loyalist Ontario, was a key factor in the abdication of King Edward VIII in 1936. For Ontarians, an American socialite as Queen was unthinkable. The popular Prince whom Canada regarded as "one of her own," had come to an unexpectedly tragic end, barely months after veterans from the province gathered at Buckingham Palace to exchange banter with their monarch. This had followed the King's unveiling in France of the grand Vimy Memorial designed by Toronto sculptor Walter Allward.

To whatever degree his abdication tarnished the Crown, its lustre was

Left and right below: *Some Canadian Stamps Commemorating Special Events in the History of the Canadian Monarchy.*

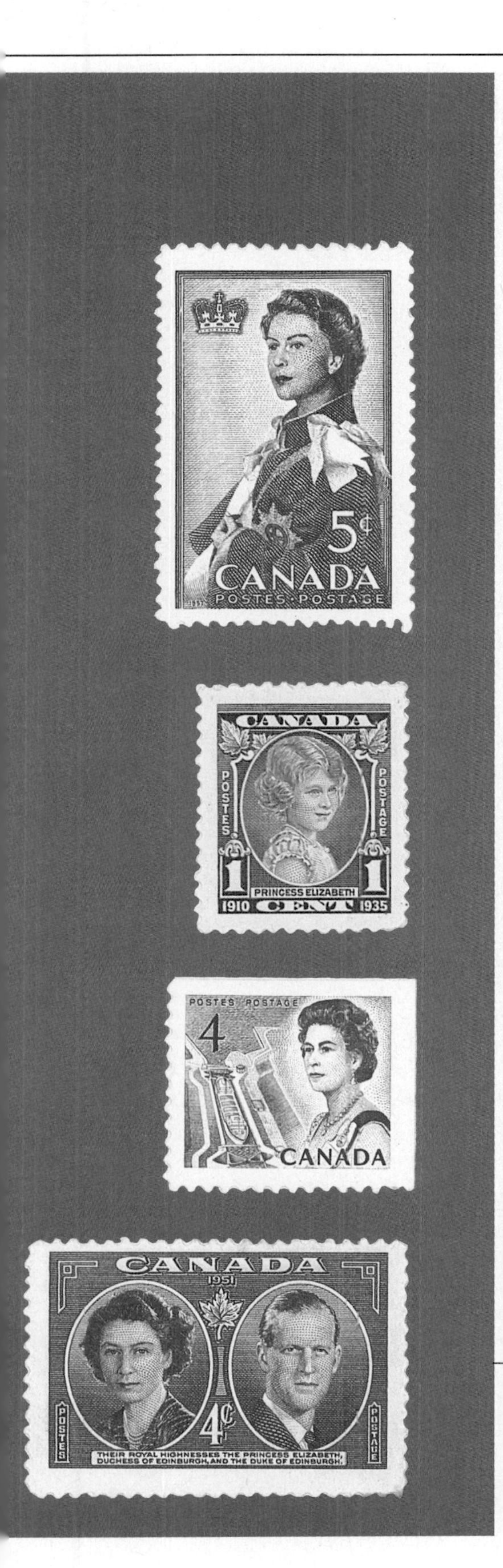

quickly restored by the great 1939 tour of King George VI and Queen Elizabeth which brought the reigning Sovereign, after nearly a century of waiting, to his province of Ontario for the first time. The King visited many Ontario centres, addressed the Legislature in Toronto and gave Royal Assent to bills in his Parliament in Ottawa. At the unveiling of the National War Memorial in Ottawa he told his sister, "One old fellow said to me, 'Ay, man, if Hitler could see this!' It was a wonderful proof of what a people's King means."

The Earl of Athlone, Governor General from 1940 to 1946 and his wife Princess Alice, daughter of Prince Leopold, presided over the war years in Ottawa. War brought several other members of the Royal Family to Ontario on active service. In August 1941 the Duke of Kent returned to Ottawa for liaison with the R.C.A.F. and was also in Toronto, a month before he was killed in an air crash in the United Kingdom. Two years later Alistair, the rather feckless second and last Duke of Connaught (son of Prince Arthur who predeceased the first Duke) arrived as A.D.C. to Athlone. After becoming ill from exposure, he died in Ottawa in April 1943. From 1945 to 1946 George, 7th Earl of Harewood, the eldest son of Princess Mary the Princess Royal, George V's daughter, served in the capital as A.D.C. to his great uncle.

The reign of King George VI, whose self-sacrificing wartime leadership had inspired Ontarians in the province as well as overseas, closed with the cross-country tour in 1951 of Princess Elizabeth and the Duke of Edinburgh. Her Royal Highness arrived with a draft accession declaration in her luggage in case the ailing King should die suddenly. This was the first of the Queen's many sojourns in Ontario, for the present reign has ended all disadvantages of a so-called absent monarchy.

Modern transportation has erased the ocean that once separated Upper Canada from George III's family. Since 1951 the Queen has been in Ontario in nine different years: 1957 (the first Sovereign to open Parliament), 1959, 1964, 1967, 1973 (twice), 1974 (a stopover), 1976, 1977 and 1982. Other years have taken her to other parts of the country. The Royal Family today is more numerous and younger than it has ever been and consequently more peripatetic. Snowdons, Gloucesters, Kents and Harewoods have all been in Ontario. Prince Philip has come to the province more often than any other member of the Royal Family in history.

The Queen has joined her Ontario subjects for the great events of their life as a community, such as the opening of the St. Lawrence Seaway in 1959, Centennial Year celebrations in 1967 and yachting events at Kingston in the Olympic Games in 1976. The Queen gave special permission in 1965 for the Royal Union badge to be included in the new Ontario flag, along with the provincial coat-of-arms whose Cross of St. George is an illusion to King George III. In 1977, Prince Andrew became the first royal Prince to attend school in Ontario.

For two hundred years the Royal Family has come to Ontario not just to see and be seen; they have come as participants in provincial life, for military, diplomatic or government service, to organize and preside at meetings such as the Duke of Edinburgh's Study Conference, to give their patronage or for private purposes. Ontario in its turn has influenced the Royal Family. Edward VII, George VI and Elizabeth II each gained much needed self-confidence on their first tours in Canada. Even royal tragedy has run its dark course on the Ontario stage. Princess Louise lost an ear in a sleighing accident in the streets of Ottawa which embittered her and destroyed her marriage. Victoria's granddaughter, Princess Marie Louise, saw her life's course altered one day in 1900 at Rideau Hall where she was staying, ready to begin a trip to the Rockies. She was suddenly summoned by rival telegrams to Germany by her father-in-law, the Prince of Anhalt, and to London by Queen Victoria. Returning to the Queen, she learned that the prince had annulled her marriage to his son.

The Monarchy is the key element in the Ontario identity. The Royal Family has always been intimately involved in their subjects' lives, but their frequent presence in the province has reinforced and enhanced that intimacy by allowing the great majority of their subjects to see them as they are. When the Queen returns in 1984 for the provincial bicentenary, she will be continuing Ontario's royal saga, begun in 1792.

Right top: *Canada's Birthday Cake. On July 1, 1967, Queen Elizabeth II cut the huge cake at a Centennial party on Ottawa's Parliament Hill.*
Far right top: *Prince Philip at Upper Canada College, 1979. The Prince, who holds the title "College Visitor," greeted the football team during the celebrations of the school's 150th anniversary jubilee.*
Right bottom: *The Queen and Her People, Upper Canada Village, July 21, 1976.*

Left top: *First Visit of Charles, Prince of Wales to Toronto, April 1979. At the Fort York Armouries, the Prince wore the uniform of Colonel-in-Chief of the Royal Regiment of Canada.*

Bottom left: *July 1, 1983, Edmonton, Alberta. At the World University Games, Diana, Princess of Wales on her birthday, greets a member of Canada's gymnastic team, Elfi Schlegel of Toronto.*

Right top: *Banner Embroidered by Queen Mary When She Was Princess of Wales. The motto "Ich Dien" (I serve) and the three feather emblem are thought to have originated when Edward III presented his son, Edward Prince of Wales (the Black Prince), with the banner of the defeated King of Bohemia after the Battle of Crecy in 1346. The embroidery work depicts this occasion, and also incorporates the arms of Ontario. The banner was presented to the University of Toronto in 1908, three years before the Princess of Wales became Queen Mary, consort of George V.*

Right bottom: *Royal Yacht* Britannia, *July 1967. The Queen and Prince Philip, with their guests, Prime Minister Lester Pearson and Mrs. Pearson, sailed up the St. Lawrence. This photograph of the yacht and her escort of small boats (many of them from the New York shore) was taken at Brockville.*

***Top:** Square Dance at Rideau Hall, October 11, 1951. This well-remembered view of the Queen and Prince Philip was photographed during their first visit to Canada when the Queen was still Princess Elizabeth. The above painting by Hilton Macdonald Hassell (1910-1980) was completed in 1958.*

***Left bottom:** The Queen Mother, 1981. The Queen Mother took part in Niagara-on-the-Lake's Bicentennial (1781-1981). Lieutenant Governor John Aird and Cabinet Minister Thomas Wells greeted her at the airport.*

***Right bottom:** Queen Elizabeth The Queen Mother, Toronto, 1979. The Queen Mother has made many visits to Ontario since she first came with King George VI in 1939. Here she is accepting flowers from young folk dancers while Lieutenant Governor Pauline McGibbon and Premier William Davis watch.*

NDREWS JEWELLER
SMITH JEWELLERS
Brockville DRUGS
HUB
STORE FOR MEN & BOYS

CHAPTER 31

HERITAGE AWARENESS

by the Editors

"A wise nation preserves its records, gathers up its muniments, decorates the tombs of the illustrious dead, repairs its great public structures, and fosters national pride and love of country by perpetual references to the sacrifices and glories of the past."

JOSEPH HOWE

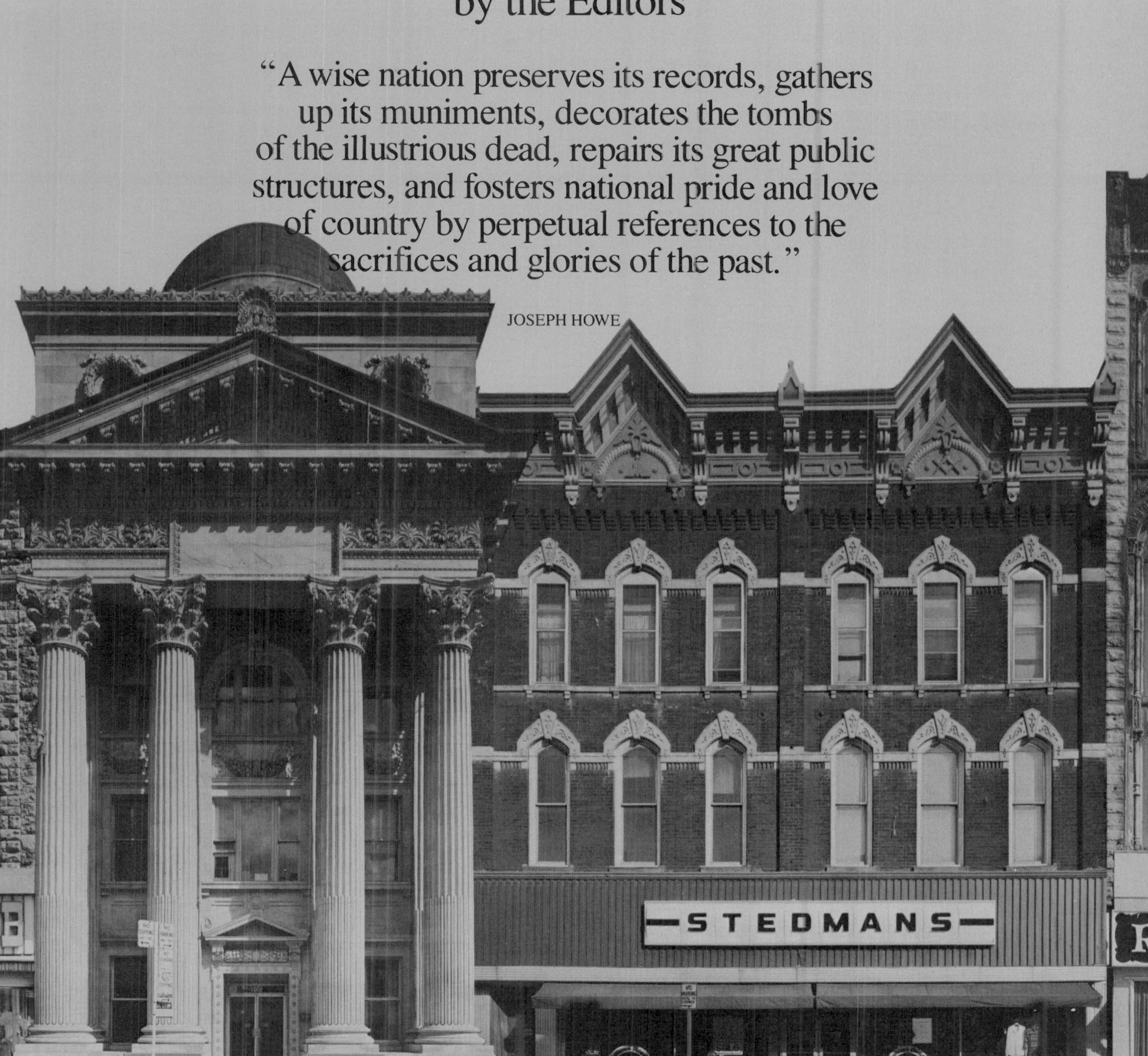

In 1967, Centennial Commissioner John Fisher, "Mr. Canada," scolded Canadians for not taking their history seriously. He said, "How can we be true or strong when we, through neglect, rob tomorrow's citizens of links with the past." Robertson Davies recently echoed these sentiments to an American audience: "The odd thing is that so many Canadians who are eager to bring forth a new spirit seem to think that we have no past or that it is unworthy of consideration."

In turn they were re-echoing Joseph Howe, the Maritimer and newspaper magnate, who exhorted Canadians early in the 19th century to preserve their material history. Since Canadians have been making these kinds of observations for generations, why are so many still nonchalant about their heritage? This remains so, despite the existence of the Heritage Canada Foundation and the Ontario Heritage Foundation that have been created to foster the same kind of heritage awareness that John Fisher advocated as a broadcaster for forty years.

One might argue that a solid base had been formed in the 19th century, and that the 20th century should have been a time when generations knew and treasured their history. Certainly there were enough historical societies to promote heritage awareness. The Historical Society of Upper Canada was established in 1861, the York Pioneer and Historical Society in 1869, the Ontario Historical Society in 1888, as well as eighty or more similar societies set up in the 1880's. Barely populated by 1900, Ontario faced two world wars, a serious depression, rapid expansion of both an industrial society and an educational system, and a rootless society moving from community to community because of greater job opportunities. These factors, and others, have encouraged a greater emphasis on "tomorrow," not a return to "yesterday."

Yet the future looks bright for Ontario's heritage. No one today would permit Thomas Edison's summer home in Vienna, Ontario, to be taken to Greenfield Village, near Detroit. The recent upsurge of interest in nostalgia, antiques, main street preservation, and historic sites in general, suggests that our heritage is secure. Schools are placing greater emphasis on Canadian history. A generation is emerging with an interest in heritage awareness, a "growth industry" of the 21st century.

Overleaf: *An Ontario Heritage Foundation poster advocating architectural preservation.*
Right top: *Applewood, Etobicoke, Metropolitan Toronto. Birthplace of James Shaver Woodsworth, a founder of the Socialist movement in Canada, this house was moved 200 metres to its present site on West Mall where it was restored.*
Right middle: *English Morris Dancing at London Folk Festival.*
Far right middle: *Oktoberfest, Concordia Club, Kitchener.*
Right below: *William Hamilton Merritt Commemorative Stamp, November 20, 1974.*
Far right below: *Yorktown, Virginia, October 17, 1981. Ontario Cabinet Minister Dennis Timbrell and Captain-Lieutenant Edward Anderson, King's Royal Regiment of New York, were present at the re-enactment of the October 17, 1781, surrender of the British army.*
Left below: *Stores at Pioneer Village, Fanshawe Dam, London.*

ROBIN

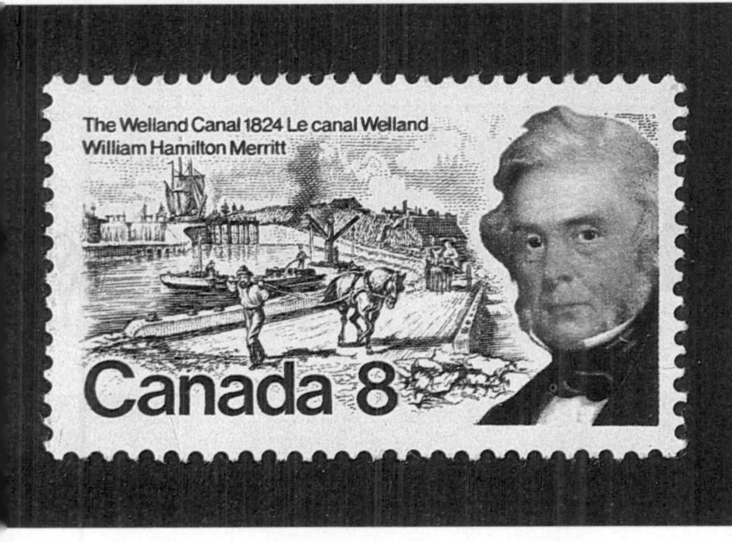

The Welland Canal 1824 Le canal Welland
William Hamilton Merritt
Canada 8

BLACK HISTORY IN EARLY ONTARIO

An exhibition sponsored by the Ontario Black History Society and the City of Toronto Archives celebrating Black History Month, February 1981.

THE MARKET GALLERY
of the City of Toronto Archives
South St. Lawrence Market
95 Front Street East
Toronto, Ontario M5E 1C2

February 7 — March 15, 1981

Far left top: *York Pioneers, 1879. The York Pioneer and Historical Society was founded in 1869. Ten years later they saved the historic Scadding cabin by having it moved to the grounds of the Canadian National Exhibition.*
Left top: *Black History. In 1978 the Ontario Black History Society was founded to preserve the Black legacy in the province that goes back to the Loyalist era.*

Far left below: *Unveiling of Plaque to John Brant, Ohsweken. Left to right are: Hon. Harry Nixon, M.P.P. (Brant); R.J. Smallwood, Six Nations Agent; Mrs. Howard Disher, Brant Historical Society; Prof. T.F. McIlwraith, Historic Sites Board; Mrs. Ethel Brant Monture, author: E.P. Garlow, Chief Councillor; Dr. John Charlton, M.P. (Brant-Haldimand).*

Left below: *Royal Ontario Museum, Toronto. The museum has a wealth of Ontario material and artifacts. Opened by the Duke of Connaught in 1914, the museum was expanded in 1936 and 1981. It is one of the world's largest general museums.*

Right top: *The Fight to Save Fort York, Toronto. In the 1950s, the fort was to be demolished to make way for an expressway. Members of the Women's Canadian Historical Society, and others, protested, and the route of the expressway was altered.*
Far right top: H.M.S. Nancy *(1789-1814). Sunk in 1814, the schooner was raised in 1927, and placed at the Marine Museum of the Upper Lakes, Nancy Island, Wasaga Beach.*

Right below: *Huron County Museum, Goderich. Many artifacts and local history documents are now preserved in former schools turned into museums sponsored by counties and municipalities and supported by public funds.*
Far right below: *City of Hamilton celebrated its centennial in 1913.*

PART
IN GR

NERS
OWTH

AIR ONTARIO

however, and it was soon in financial

service to Ottawa in 1976, with a man-

ANDEN HOLDINGS LIMITED

Anden Holdings Limited is a corporate partnership which has been growing for more than twenty-two years.

The name Anden was derived from the two owners, Andrew M. Spriet and Dennis F. Plowright, known better as Andy and Denny.

In 1962, Andy, a professional civil engineer operating his own consulting firm, started his first investment company called London Building Products.

The company's first general manager was Denny, who at the age of twenty-one took the newly-formed company into the home improvement business, a field he'd been in since sixteen.

London Building Products sales for the first year of operation were $90,000. The home improvement company grew and in 1967, just five years old, with sales of more than $1 million, the company introduced solid vinyl siding to the Canadian marketplace. Shortly thereafter, the company became the national distributor of Mastic vinyl siding in Canada.

The name was changed to Anden Vinyl Products Limited, with Denny becoming the president and general manager, and Andy taking the position of chairman of the board.

In 1970, with sales exceeding $3 million yearly, Anden purchased from the Case Tractor Company its 229 Adelaide Street location. It became, and remains, the corporate headquarters of Anden Holdings Limited.

In the following years, Anden's Vinyl Division opened offices in London, Sudbury, Windsor, St. Catharines, Oshawa, Kitchener and Belleville.

It added a finance company, Charleton Building Credits, to provide a financial package for home improvement loans to its customers.

The inception of The Common Market in 1971 filled a growing need in Southwestern Ontario for a fine furniture store and interior design service. In beautifully restored premises in one of London's oldest buildings, Helen and Joyce, wives of Andy and Denny, manage the retail outlet.

Denny's love of antique cars brought a new division into the group, a company called The Automotive Affair. from it evolved two new car dealerships, B.M.W. and Jaguar, now known as Grand Touring Cars.

Andy and Denny's interest in cars also led them into Classic Cars of London, manufacturing the 1935 Auburn Boat-tail Speedster replica. More than thirty cars were sold.

Other divisions of the company included The Printers Shoppe, Atlantic Door Company, Anden Wholesale, Custom Installations, Datsun on York and Marc Christopher Yachts.

In 1972, Anden approached its supplier, Mastic Corporation of South Bend, Indiana, to manufacture vinyl siding in Canada under a joint venture. An agreement resulted in the formation of Mastic Manufacturing Limited. A new 30,000-square-foot plant was built at 25 Midpark Crescent in London. The success of the Canadian firm (now known as Mastic Inc.) is a matter of record. Mastic became and remains one of the major manufacturers of vinyl siding in Canada. It is interesting to note that shortly after the joint venture agreement was signed, Mastic Corporation of South Bend was purchased by Bethlehem Steel, a multimillion dollar American corporation.

Mastic Inc. grew and prospered in Canada for more than ten years, but in 1982, Bethlehem Steel triggered a provision in the joint venture calling for the 'buy out' of Anden's shares. After great deliberation on Anden's future, one solution prevailed. In the fall of 1982, Anden Holdings Limited purchased the outstanding shares held by Bethlehem Steel. Mastic Inc. was now totally Canadian owned, a subsidiary of Anden Holdings Limited.

Mastic Inc. continued to manufacture solid vinyl siding in London, Ontario, with wholesale warehousing in Ontario, Quebec, Nova Scotia and Alberta, supplying distributors and dealers from coast to coast. Mastic Inc. exports to its own distribution company, Mastic PTY Limited in Australia, as well as exporting to Europe, the United Kingdom, and South America.

The Anden Group today employs some 400 people and has combined sales of $40 million annually. It is an example of free enterprise and the contribution of small business to the province's growth and financial well being. Andy M. Spriet and Denny F. Plowright are partners that have made it work. They are continuing to expand their companies.

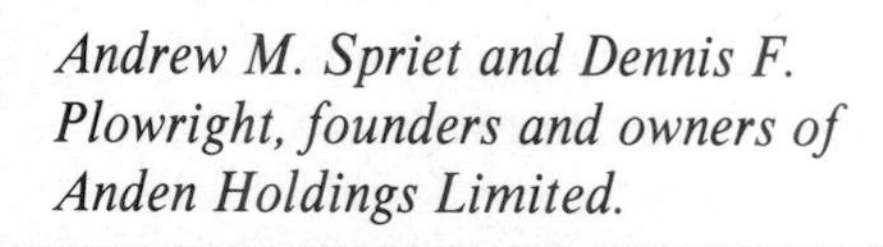

Andrew M. Spriet and Dennis F. Plowright, founders and owners of Anden Holdings Limited.

ANDREW ANTENNA COMPANY LIMITED

Andrew Antenna Company Limited, a wholly-owned subsidiary of Andrew Corporation, was incorporated in Canada in 1953. Two years later, it took possession of a new 4,200-square-foot building in Whitby. When it celebrated its 30th anniversary in 1983, it could boast more than 200 employees, and a modern plant in excess of 138,000 square feet, most of which is on the same site it had established three decades previously.

Andrew is primarily involved in the design and manufacturing of point-to-point microwave and satellite earth stations, as well as radar and navigational aid antenna systems used throughout the world. In addition, Andrew has a complete range of transmission lines available for use in microwave antenna systems, and its RADIAX slotted coaxial cable is designed to function as a continuous antenna, making it an ideal choice for use in mines, subways and tunnels.

Andrew is one of those companies whose history is short, but which, in its own field, is a pioneer. It established an engineering department in Whitby, in 1963, primarily to design and test VHF, UHF, and microwave antennas and systems, but it also led to many innovative communications developments. The high performance antenna concept used in frequency congested applications, and the novel 'wind-scoop' on shielded antennas which takes the wind load off radome membranes are two such examples.

One of AACL's manufacturing-engineering highlights was the development of the modern spinning machine, the success of which saw similar machines built for plants in Texas, Scotland and Australia.

The company's manufacturing facilities include an extensive machine shop, a welding shop with equipment for tungsten/inert gas and arc welding, silver bronzing and soldering departments, facilities for metal finishing and painting, assembly and fitting shops.

Earth station antennas by Andrew can be found in almost every country in the world. During the successful 1982 Canadian Mount Everest Expedition, for instance, it was Teleglobe Canada utilizing an Andrew earth station antenna located at the Sheraton Everest Hotel in Kathmandu, Nepal, that beamed television coverage of the event around the world via the INTELSAT satellite. In this remote country where there is no radio or television, and only one land line telephone and telex service to India, the broadcast was a major breakthrough in providing immediate, interference-free contact with the rest of the world.

Top: *Andrew's earth station antenna on location at Kathmandu, Nepal.*
Middle: *Hugh J. Swain, president and general manager.*
Bottom: *"Troposcatter" microwave antennas at Fort Smith and Pine Point, N.W.T., on the CNT network. These unique microwave antennas were installed to avoid building line-of-sight repeater stations through the nesting areas of the Whooping Crane in Wood Buffalo National Park.*

ASTRO DAIRY PRODUCTS

When George and Alex Karkic came to Canada twenty years ago, they brought with them the accumulated experience of seven generations of dairymen from their native Macedonia. But both decided they'd seen enough of dairies to last them a lifetime and at first opted for different ways to earn a living. George operated a supermarket, and Alex managed a chain store.

But they were always irked by the fact that the type of yogurt they were used to couldn't be bought anywhere in Canada — so they decided to put their knowledge to work making the kind of yogurt they really liked. They quit their jobs, and with their father Blagoya, in 1972, obtained a one-year lease (just in case things should go wrong . . .) on a small building in Scarborough, acquired the necessary equipment, and started to make yogurt.

They had one big advantage. There are more than half a million yogurt-loving Macedonians living in the Toronto area, all potential customers for the Balkan-style product.

They needn't have worried. Astro yogurt took off from the start, and sales mounted steadily.

Their first plain Balkan-style yogurt was made mainly for customers of European origin who were knowledgeable about yogurt and hungry to taste it again.

As demand grew, Astro introduced a flavoured yogurt to appeal to sweeter Canadian tastes, and by 1981, business had expanded to the point that Astro moved into a spanking new plant in Etobicoke. Its product line has also expanded to include sour cream, cottage cheese and juices.

The secret to their success, the family believes, is not merely the fact that there are a lot of yogurt-lovers in the area, but also the fact that the company uses only natural ingredients in its product.

To make the point, they cite the instance of a committee of parents monitoring their children's school lunches, which protested when the school served a yogurt filled with sugar and stabilizers. "We want Astro," they demanded, and kept at it until one parent tracked down the Karkics at their dairy, and ordered 200 yogurts twice a week for the remainder of the school year.

Members of the Karkic family enjoy a yogurt break. Left to right: brother George, Walter, father Blagoya and brother Alex. The company first started making Balkan-style yogurt in 1972.

The use of all natural ingredients has also had an influence on the total market for yogurt, and has proven such a success that the rest of the industry had to follow suit.

The family is quick to credit Agriculture Canada and its provincial counterpart with tremendous assistance in their first development phase. Courses provided by the provincial ministry, and field inspectors from the federal government, were a great source of information in helping them make a better product, they believe.

Major outlets for the firm's products now include privately-owned grocery stores, supermarkets, convenience stores, delicatessens, caterers, health food stores and a variety of ethnic stores and churches. They are distributed throughout Ontario and parts of Quebec, and Alex is proud of the fact that he has received phone calls from as far away as Vancouver, enquiring about the product.

The Karkic family has controlled the business since its inception, and a third generation is now being groomed to take over.

But the family has made other contributions to the community, as well. They sponsor the Astro West Mall Hockey Team, and St. Andrews' Soccer Team in Scarborough, and often provide gifts of food to the Scott Mission.

They are proudest of the fact that their yogurt helped a young Scarborough boy who was allergic to food to survive. So important was it considered by the hospital, that it was delivered by ambulance when a regular Astro driver was unavailable.

With the new plant successfully on stream, the Karkic family is looking forward to more growth through a variety of new products. But it also takes quiet satisfaction in the fact that its Balkan-style yogurt (a product with a 4,000-year history) has literally introduced Ontarians to a unique new taste — one that in a few short years has become part of our own culture.

BLAKE INDUSTRIES LTD.

Some of the country's most successful young businesses begin in basements, and because they're so new people tend to feel they "have no history." Nothing could be further from the truth.

The early days of a company's development are crucial for its future, and often set the pattern for later, sometimes explosive growth.

That's certainly the case with Blake Industries Ltd., and a basement is exactly where it started.

Specifically, Gordon Blake, a former Columbia Metal Rolling Mills supervisor, began Centrifugal Coaters in 1963 (now a division of Blake Industries), painting the heads of screws for decorative and architectural applications in the basement of his Oakville home.

It was only a few months, however, before he was forced to move into a 3,000-square-foot plant on Highway 122 near Ford's Oakville assembly line.

By 1968, his brother Robert joined the venture, and the company moved to Speers Road, more than tripling its floor space. In 1973 the company again expanded — again tripling in size.

Today, Centrifugal Coaters Division of Blake Industries employs 100 in a 50,000-square-foot plant with four production lines and some of the most modern robotic coating equipment in the world.

You'll see the company's primarily protective coatings on buildings and products everywhere: the orange bands on the CN Tower in Toronto, for instance; the big 'M' on the Bank of Montreal building; on IBM terminal housings, and on equipment from AES, Mitel and Xerox, as well as in dozens of architectural applications.

By itself, the story of Centrifugal Coatings is one of exciting development in a very short time, but the Blakes think big.

As a result of their interest in the outdoors and boating (Gordon was a director of the Canadian Wildlife Association for two years, and also president of the Anglers & Hunters of Ontario), in 1978 Robert, in his capacity as the financial officer in charge of development, led the company to purchase a small marina at the mouth of the Wye River. Using their knowledge of construction and development, the Blakes set out to turn the Wye Heritage Marina into one of the finest boating facilities on the Great Lakes.

In 1978, the marina had slips for 150 boats. By July of 1983 it had space for 780, with 300 more under construction.

With the aid of the Ontario Government's BILD program, Wye Heritage Marina is now a rendezvous of the Great Lakes Cruising Club. It's become the largest marina in the province, with repair and service facilities for vessels of up to 100 feet in length.

And the Blakes still aren't finished. There's a second generation on the way — Robert and Gordon each have four children — beginning to learn the ropes in sales, factory and office.

The company plans to expand into other related types of business — it would like to manufacture some of the products it's now only painting, for instance. It would like to make castings, and sell completely finished products. It also has a completely new painting facility on the boards.

Top: *Robert Blake, president of Blake Industries; Gordon Blake, president of Wye Heritage Marina.*
Bottom: *Wye Heritage Marina, the largest marina in Ontario — and still expanding.*

BLUE CROSS OF ONTARIO

When Ontarians count their historical blessings they often forget to include prepaid hospital and medical care among them. Such services are now so firmly established in this country citizens regard them as a right.

Today, health plans offered by provincial governments throughout Canada provide varying degrees of 'basic benefits' to every Canadian. By law, no insurance organization may sell what government plans provide. Blue Cross, therefore, concentrates on the provision of supplementary medical benefits, and has pioneered coverage for a wide range of drug, dental and major medical benefits plus coverage for visitors to Canada and for Canadians travelling abroad on business or vacation.

Yet, barely four decades ago this was not the case. Then, Ontarians could still be crushed under the debt load caused by hospital/medical care, or worse still, have to wait until hospitalization literally became a matter of life and death and successful treatment uncertain.

It was bad for hospitals, too. During the Great Depression of the 1930s, hospitals (then, as now, private institutions) were collecting less than fifty percent of the bills they were accumulating and struggling to avoid bankruptcy. Hospital rates were running anywhere from $4.50 to $5.00 a day for standard ward accommodation, and an additional $1.00 or $2.00 a day for semi-private care. Yet, most workers were lucky if they were earning twenty-five cents an hour.

In many instances, a patient would be admitted as a "public charge," and the hospital "wrote off" expenses incurred by his inability to pay. Yet, hospitals still required funds to operate, and those funds had to come from somewhere.

Whichever way you looked at it, the situation was bad and getting worse.

Today, things are vastly different, and it is clearly recognized that the inception of the Blue Cross Plan for Hospital Care (now simply Blue Cross of Ontario) was the major catalyst for as profound a social change as our province has seen in its 200-year history.

To understand the difference between the disastrous days of the 30s and the situation now, it's necessary to have an idea how Ontario's (and Canada's) prepaid medical care system evolved. Then, there was no such thing as government prepaid hospital care. In fact, there was no prepaid hospital care at all, public or private.

The concept was first proposed by a group of teachers at Baylor University in Dallas, Texas, in 1929. They agreed to pay a small fee each semester (fifty cents a month) in exchange for twenty-one days of care for any sick or injured teacher.

The first Blue Cross Plan in Canada began in Manitoba, in 1939. Then followed plans in Ontario (1941), Quebec (1942), Atlantic Canada (1943), and Alberta (1948). More recently, long-established health and dental underwriters in British Columbia (1980) and Saskatchewan (1980) have joined the Blue Cross organization.

In Ontario, the Ontario Hospital Association, the private, voluntary body representing Ontario's hospitals, recognized the need for a similar prepaid concept to make hospital/medical treatment affordable to the people of Ontario and, at the same time, guarantee payment to the providers of service, the hospitals and doctors. OHA launched a group hospitalization plan — Blue Cross — to provide prepaid insurance protection. Offices opened on April 1, 1941 in the Excelsior Life Company building at 36 Toronto Street; Blue Cross had come to Ontario.

The first group to enrol comprised twenty-two employees of the Cunard-Donaldson steamship line on March 17, 1941, and in April 1941, nine-year-old Sam Beattie, hospitalized at Toronto's Hospital for Sick Children, became the first patient to benefit, thanks to his family's premium of $1.00 a month.

Ontarians knew a good thing when they saw it. Enrolment in the early 1940s was so fast it was almost impossible to handle. By the end of 1942 there were 42,000 participants; by the end of 1943, 137,000. In 1944 enrolment passed the 500,000 mark. An employee of the era recalls: "Enrolment was so fast, group application

Left to right, the five founders of Blue Cross in Ontario: R. Fraser Armstrong; Arthur Beaton Whytock, M.D.; J. Clark Keith; G. Harvey Agnew, M.D.; John Wallace McCutcheon, M.D.

cards simply piled up in a corner of one of the offices for two or three months before we could get around to processing them. In the meantime, we paid the hospital's bill as long as the employer's name on the claim form was in fact enrolled in the group plan."

The postwar era was traumatic for Blue Cross — especially so when it discovered that the legislative authorities had postponed a decision on a critical rate increase to cover rising hospital costs. In desperation, Blue Cross moved unilaterally and increased rates. The government said nothing about the increase, but sent in auditors who, after examining the books, declared the increase insufficient to cover costs, and recommended a second.

In the early 1950s, the government, with the active assistance of Blue Cross, drafted and enacted legislation to govern prepaid hospitalization plans. Under the act, non-profit plans are operated as a service to the people of Ontario.

By the end of the decade it looked as if the end was in sight for Blue Cross. The provincial government was planning to take over the provision of basic health care for the people of Ontario. In fact, it had made the decision to do so in 1956, and asked for Blue Cross assistance in developing the public plan, and in training staff (since Blue Cross already covered nearly half the residents of the province). Thus, on December 31, 1958, the Blue Cross Plan for Hospital Care employed 703 people. One day later, Blue Cross had 93 employees — and the Government of Ontario had a universal hospital insurance plan (now called OHIP), with fully experienced former Blue Cross staff to operate it. To say that the changeover was again traumatic would be to understate the case. Yet Blue Cross still felt it had a role to play in medical care for Ontarians: the provision of health insurance benefits not included in the basic government plan.

The same year Blue Cross introduced its plan for semi-private accommodation in hospital. In 1960 it developed a major medical plan to cover private nursing, wheelchairs and special appliances, and a year later entered the prescription drug insurance field. In 1967 it pioneered the introduction of a dental plan in Canada, and in 1968 improved its major medical program, the 'Extended Health Care Plan,' to pay, in effect, 100 percent of all eligible claims made by subscribers.

From what had appeared to be the end of the road in 1959, Blue Cross of Ontario had emerged as a major, and still growing provider of supplementary health care benefits — with its original non-profit principles and expertise still intact.

Blue Cross Chief Operating Officer Brian Mead.

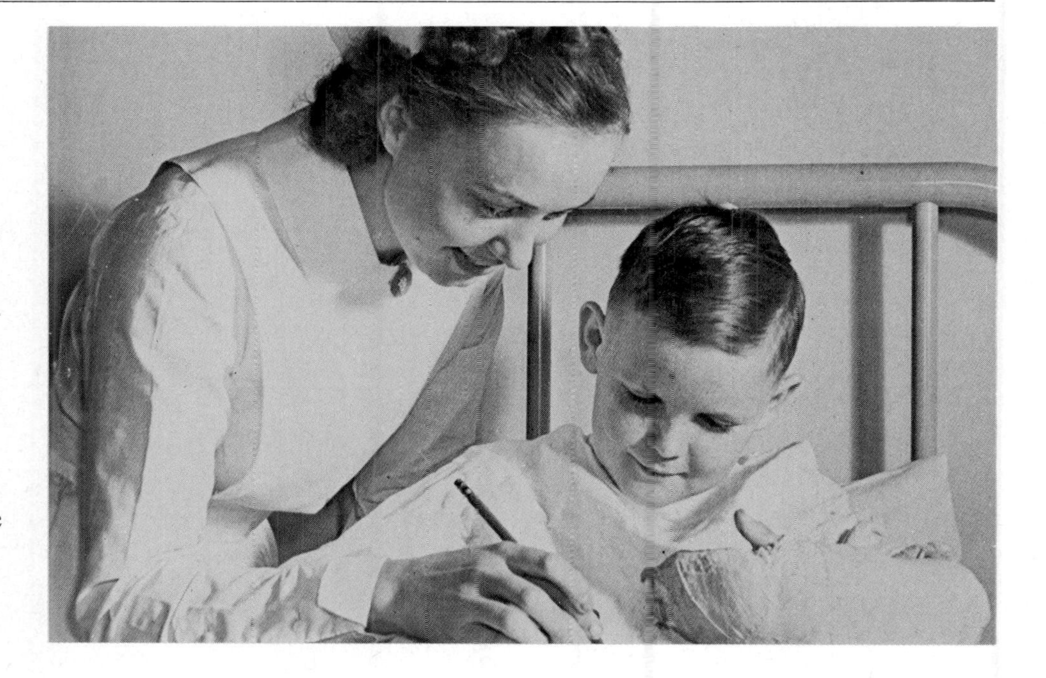

Sam Beattie, nine years old, the first patient ever helped by Blue Cross in Ontario back in 1941.

As if to demonstrate its new muscle, the 14-storey Ontario Hospital Association/Blue Cross Centre was officially opened in October 1972, at 150 Ferrand Drive in Don Mills, where it has become a familiar landmark to the millions of people who each year drive Toronto's Don Valley Parkway.

During the 70s, Blue Cross continued to develop new insurance programs, such as coverage for visitors to Canada, and coverage to protect Canadians touring abroad in cases of sudden illness and travel emergencies.

Under Chief Operating Officer Brian Mead, Blue Cross of Ontario is planning to expand again — this time into the life insurance field, in collaboration with Canada's other provincial Blue Cross operations.

Blue Cross remains Canada's largest non-government health benefits provider with executive offices in eight key Canadian cities, and branch locations in 25 more. Regionally administered, but nationally co-ordinated, Blue Cross is a private business which stands on its own.

When Ontarians count their historical blessings, among the foremost should be listed freedom from fear of overwhelming debt, by reason of illness. Blue Cross helped make it so.

BROWNLINE INC., A BOORUM & PEASE COMPANY

When Thomas Brown started his office supplies store in 1846, a full twenty-one years before Confederation, he had no way of knowing that his company would outstrip his most optimistic appraisal of the future.

Today, Brownline Inc., as the company is now known, manufactures and distributes some 8,000 products, has a head office and plant in Toronto, a warehouse in Vancouver, and employs 200 people.

At age twenty-two, Thomas Brown left his home in the north of England, and accompanied by his family, came to Toronto where he purchased a stationery store from a Mr. Payne. At this time, Toronto was a promising town of 20,000 people, and the stationery business was located on King Street on the site of the present King Edward Hotel. It was a line of business Brown knew well, because it was the business his father had been in.

Thomas Brown had three sons, Thomas, John, and Richard, and each of them succeeded him in the business. When Thomas Brown died in 1856, the business was directed by his son, Richard, who carried on and developed it for 63 years until his death in 1920 at age 86.

Richard Brown was a man of genial disposition and great integrity. Under his direction the company grew from a local firm to one that had business dealings from one end of Canada to the other.

As the business grew, it moved to the north side of King Street, and later, additional adjoining premises were acquired. Expansion took place so regularly that, by 1900, the company was obliged to build a five-storey warehouse and factory on Wellington Street East. This building, however, was completely destroyed in the 'Great Fire' which ravaged the business section of the city in 1904, but was soon rebuilt on the same site.

A second fire occurred the same year, completely destroying the temporary premises, the Queen City Curling Rink on Church Street. Undaunted by such disasters, Brown found other premises, and with comparatively little interruption, the operations of the firm continued until the new building was ready for occupancy. Meanwhile, since the business continued to grow, management found that by 1913, still larger premises were required, and the company relocated to 100 Simcoe Street, Toronto.

In the early years, bookbinding played an important part in operations, and Brown Brothers Limited had a high international reputation for this activity. Evidence of the company's skill and workmanship is provided by the number of diplomas, medals and other honours it won at many exhibitions.

It won the first prize for bookbinding at the first industrial exhibition held in Toronto in 1846, for instance. It won a medal at the exhibition held in Montreal in connection with the opening of the Victoria Bridge in 1860; and one at the Philadelphia Centennial. It won three diplomas at different exhibits in Paris, and a medal at the Indian and Colonial Exhibit held at London in 1886, as well as at the Chicago World's Fair of 1893.

Exhibit of Paris Exposition 1867.

When Richard Brown died on February 14, 1920, his elder son, T. Albert Brown, became president and thereby became the fourth generation in the business. On his death, September 9, 1930, his only brother, R. Norman Brown, assumed office as president. 'Mr. Norman,' as he was known to the staff, had been associated with the firm since 1895. The fifth generation, represented by J.L. Brown, son of T. Albert Brown, joined the firm in 1929. J.H. Chipman, son-in-law of T. Albert Brown, joined the company in 1932.

Some interesting historical notes are provided by the company's earliest accounting records. These records show that in March 1874, the payroll was divided into 'men' and 'girls,' each working six days a week, for at least nine hours a day. On average, the men earned $1.29 a day; the girls ninety-three cents. Total gross pay for the week amounted to $228.34; that was the full payroll for twenty-two men and twenty-one girls. Also noteworthy is the pay of the company's secretary-treasurer: $800 a year.

Divisional activity of the company today is similar to what it has been throughout its history. The company is divided into five departments.

The Account Book and Loose Leaf department offers a complete range of multi-columnar and account books and associated lines, as well as office forms, binders, and all modern loose-leaf items.

The Factory and Special Order department is responsible for the manufacture of account books, special forms, loose-leaf supplies and catalogue covers.

The Stationery department offers a varied selection of commercial stationery, office supplies and sundries. New items are constantly being added. The Seasonal Department offers the widest range of calendar pads, journals and diaries manufactured in Canada. This line has expanded to total needs of the office, products for home and personal use, plus the advertising promotional field.

The newest department is the manufacturing of storage and media housing for the high technology industry.

In addition, the company is the sole Canadian distributor for numerous American and British manufacturers of office supplies, paper and bookbinding materials.

Brownline Inc. has a policy of continuing to seek new methods, techniques and new materials, not only to keep abreast of progress in its industry, but also to keep ahead of its field. Over the years, Brownline Inc. has maintained a good reputation for enlightened management practices, and because of this, many employees have spent their entire working lives with the company.

In May 1972, after 125 years of private Canadian ownership, Brown Brothers Limited was sold. The new American owner was the Boorum Pease Company, another family firm that has been in the same business as Brown Brothers since 1842, and is recognized as the largest manufacturer of blank book products in the United States.

Boorum and Pease employs some 1,000 people in the U.S., and has its head office and manufacturing plant in Elizabeth, New Jersey. Two other plants are located in Syracuse and Brooklyn, New York. In addition, the company has warehouses in Los Angeles and in Atlanta, Georgia.

Brown Brothers changed its name to Brownline Inc. in 1980, when it came under the direction of a new president, Canadian Steve Smerek.

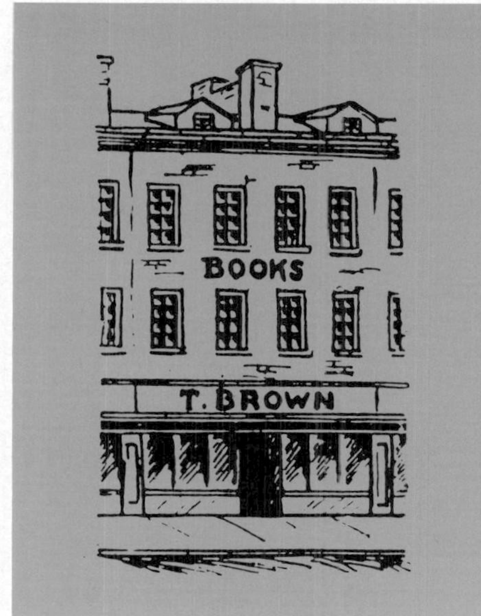

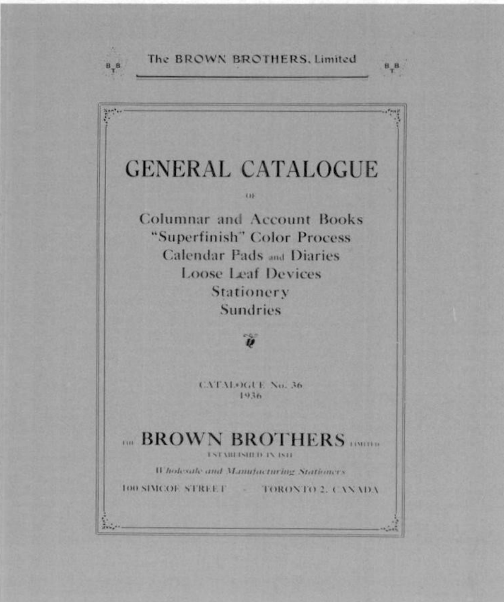
The BROWN BROTHERS, Limited

GENERAL CATALOGUE

OF

Columnar and Account Books
"Superfinish" Color Process
Calendar Pads and Diaries
Loose Leaf Devices
Stationery
Sundries

CATALOGUE No. 36
1936

THE BROWN BROTHERS LIMITED
ESTABLISHED IN [illegible]

Wholesale and Manufacturing Stationers

100 SIMCOE STREET - TORONTO 2, CANADA

The Simcoe Street location, occupied in 1913

Pages from the company's 1936 catalogue showing its original premises.

Waterman Avenue premises of Brownline Inc. today.

BOMAC BATTEN LIMITED

Bomac Batten is the direct descendant of five Canadian firms whose collective service to the Canadian newspaper and advertising business spans more than a century. That is remarkable enough in itself, but its immediate forbear, Grip Limited, also has the distinction of providing employment, at least for a time, to four of Canada's best known painters — J.E.H. MacDonald, Tom Thomson, Arthur Lismer, and Franklin Carmichael.

It was in 1841 that Charles Dickens wrote *Barnaby Rudge* and gave to the cynical little figure of a raven in that story the name 'Grip.' In 1873, John W. Bengough, a famous Canadian cartoonist of the day whose work had appeared in the Montreal *Star* and the Toronto *Globe* began a humorous Toronto political weekly whose masthead displayed the name 'Grip' and Grip Limited was born.

By 1894, *Grip Weekly* had discontinued publication, but by then a lively business had grown up around it. To facilitate making engravings for the paper, the company had originally established a small engraving department. It immediately stimulated the demand for illustrations from other newspapers and commercial houses, and from this little plant came the first printer's plates to be made on metal in Canada. By 1905 Grip had also produced its first set of quadricolour (four-colour) plates.

Two years later J.E.H. MacDonald joined the company, then Tom Thomson, and by 1911 Lismer and Carmichael were all employed. Thus, this small 'state-of-the-art' engraving plant can claim that the nucleus of the Group of Seven was all at work on its premises just at the time of some of the group's most important artistic development.

By 1909, in a parallel but unrelated development, two other platemaking firms, one in Toronto and one in Montreal, had merged. National Electrotype Company, and Canada Newspaper Syndicate Limited (which made stereotype plates) amalgamated under the name of Rapid Electrotype Company of Canada Limited.

But Rapid was prevented from offering full plate service by lack of an engraving plant, so it negotiated the purchase of Grip Limited in May 1926. The corporate name changed to Rapid Grip Limited.

On January 9, 1931, a third name — that of Batten — was added to the firm. In 1910, A.C. Batten had established a company to distribute Canadian and British world news to Canadian papers. Originally functioning as a wire service under the name Colonial Press, it also developed a ready set or 'boiler-plate' service and a news mat and stereo service specializing in British and Canadian features for distribution to daily and weekly newspapers.

With the establishment of the Canadian Press wire service, Batten discontinued this, instead concentrating on ready-set features. In 1913 he started an engraving and art department, and established a Montreal branch in 1917. Early in 1924 he changed the firm's name to Batten Limited.

Thus, it was a natural merger that took place between Batten and the owners of Rapid Grip Limited, and when the deal was completed, a new firm emerged with the name Rapid Grip and Batten, Limited. It was to last for forty-one years, until 1972, when the name Bomac came into the firm.

In 1931, the same year as the Batten merger, C.H. McNellen, an employee of Rapid Grip and Batten saw an opportunity to launch out on his own, so with three partners he began Bomac Electrotype Company. Again, to offer a complete service, the partners bought Service Engravers Limited in 1933, and changed its name to Bomac Engravers Limited. By 1937 McNellen was sole owner of Bomac Electrotype, and by 1956, sole owner of Bomac Engravers. In 1965, he changed the name of the two companies to Bomac Graphics Limited.

Mr. McNellen acquired control of Rapid Grip and Batten, Limited on January 7, 1971, and the name was changed to Bomac Batten Limited May 1, 1972. The company is a Canadian leader in the manufacture of quality offset separations, platemaking and engraving.

Tom Thomson (foreground) around 1910 at his drawing board.

Today's artist at his electronic palette which can transfer an image by laser beam to film.

BUTLER METAL PRODUCTS, DIVISION OF GCIL

In 1892, when William Butler Sr. opened his first machine shop on York Street in Hamilton, he purchased the entire operation for $6,000.

Although by the turn of the century the company still only employed between seven and ten people turning out small custom machine parts, it couldn't have started in business at a better time. The Automotive Age was about to begin, and it would see Butler grow from a single-shop company to a major manufacturer of automotive parts, both in the United States and Canada.

By 1929, the auto industry had grown to enormous proportions. William Butler Jr. had become a full partner in the business, and in 1932, sole owner of the company, following the death of his father.

Even though the Depression was making life tough for everyone, William Jr. began looking for a site on which to expand the business. He finally settled, in 1938, on the premises of a former hockey-stick company located on Guelph Street North in Preston, Ontario.

That same year, Butler purchased several screw machines, and changed its name to Butler Stampings and Machine Screws Limited.

The growing enterprise scarcely had time to get settled when the Second World War burst upon Europe in all its fury. With growing war orders from the Canadian government, Butler rented the premises of the Rock Spring Brewery until the end of the war, and there produced ammunition boxes.

Meanwhile, the main plant concentrated on war orders for General Motors, producing stamped metal parts for army trucks and other vehicles.

In 1949, the company was sold to the Mindustrial Corporation Limited, a Canadian holding company, and changed its name to Butler Metal Products, the name it bears today.

By 1957 it had built an additional 20,000-square-foot plant on a 29-acre site on Eagle Street (now Cambridge), and expanded dramatically by acquiring Advanced Steel Products of Chatham, combining the operations in the one Cambridge location.

It then began to pursue an aggressive research and development program, and in the early 1970s applied its stamping techniques to a process for stamping thermoplastic materials.

A second take-over occurred in 1972, when the Guthrie Corporation of London, England, acquired control of Mindustrial, and thus of Butler.

The take-over allowed Butler to expand again, this time with its thermoplastic stamping process. So successful was the development that a new division came into being in 1979, and is now a separate company within the Guthrie Group known as Butler Polymet. It operates out of the old Guelph Street plant, and a new facility in Lenior, North Carolina.

Today, Butler is a leader in the stamping industry in North America, and supplies other major industries with a huge range of stamped metal parts.

The automotive business is still a mainstay of the company, and some 40 percent of its products are exported to the United States.

Butler now employs 500 people in a 170,000-square-foot plant on Eagle Street in Cambridge. It continues to expand its facilities and upgrade its equipment, and utilizes transfer presses, CAD/CAM (computer-aided design/computer-aided manufacture) techniques, and robots in its modern manufacturing operations.

The latest in modern equipment: a 1000-ton six-stage transfer press producing deep-draw stampings.

William Butler's first machine shop on Mary Street in Hamilton, Ontario, c.1910. In the photo, left to right: Tom Arkwright, Harry Plasteau, William Butler (standing), William Butler Jr. (as a child, and sitting by his father), unknown machinist.

CANADIAN GENERAL ELECTRIC

In 1882, fifteen years after Confederation, the companies which were to become the roots of Canadian General Electric were federally incorporated.

They included the Edison Electric Light Company of Canada, established in Hamilton, Ontario (which listed Thomas Alva Edison as one of its shareholders) and the Thomson-Houston Electric Light Company of Canada, headquartered in Montreal.

A decade later these companies were welded together to become Canadian General Electric, when their parent companies in the United States were merged to form the General Electric Company. CGE had 500 employees, a small factory in Peterborough, and a Toronto head office.

Canada's population was about 5,000,000. Most of her citizens were farmers, labourers and lumbermen. Alberta and Saskatchewan did not exist as provinces. Newfoundland was a Crown colony that would not join Canada for another sixty-seven years.

For artificial light, heat, and power, Canadians depended on oil and gas lamps, the wood stove, the water wheel and steam engine.

Since then, Canada has become a modern industrialized nation, and CGE, with about 14,000 employees today, has helped make the country into a world technological leader in the fields of power generation, and the recovery and processing of resources.

Its first Canadian president, Ontarian W.R. Brock, shepherded the company through nearly two decades of major expansion in the foundry and heavy machinery engineering businesses, and saw CGE become an important supplier to the developing electrical energy sector.

By 1907 CGE was capable of making everything electrical from filaments for light bulbs to 20,000 horsepower electric generators. Its Canada Foundry Company (later to become the Canadian Allis-Chalmers group) churned out equipment for the building of a nation — generator frames, structural steel, railway bridges, steam shovels, cranes, streetcars, stonecrushers — and a host of other items from screws to locomotives.

In 1912, British-born Frederic Nicholls succeeded Brock and by the end of 1913 CGE was manufacturing all its electrical products in plants at Peterborough, Montreal and Toronto; its non-electrical products in Toronto, Stratford, and Bridgeburg, Ontario, and Montreal.

It plunged into World War I manufacturing munitions, like other companies drawn into the war effort, and by the end of the war emerged as an industrial giant in Canadian terms.

Under the presidency of A.E. Dyment, the company continued to grow — even during the recessionary years of 1922-24 — by acquiring the Canadian Edison Appliance Company which manufactured household appliances.

By 1925, D.C. Durland was appointed president and General Electric (U.S.) had acquired ninety percent of CGE's stock.

Durland served the company for two decades — until the end of World War II, in fact — and presided over growth his predecessors would have envied. In spite of the Depression, the company was successful as a supplier to Canada's industrial and resources sectors, and by the mid-1940s had achieved the highest volume of production in its history.

Its products continued to involve electrical apparatus and appliances, and during the war, munitions. It was

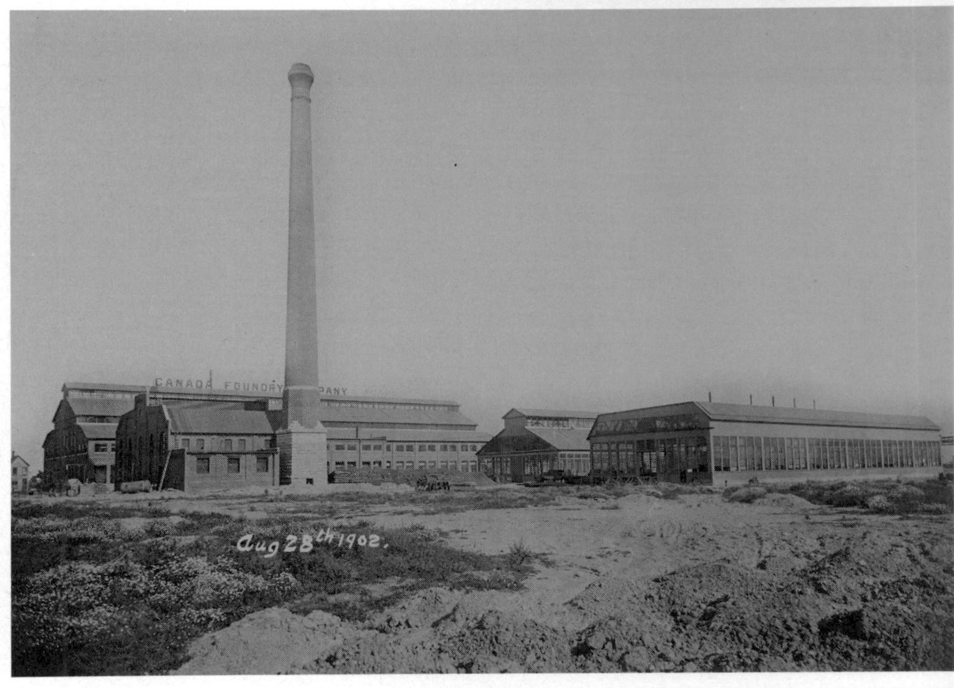

Top: Frederick Nicholls, President (1912-1921).
Bottom: The Canada Foundry Company, a CGE subsidiary, became the nucleus of the Davenport complex in Toronto. Photo c. 1902.

Interactive graphics play a key role in the design of higher tolerance, higher performance molded parts at the CGE CAD/CAM Moldmaking Centre. The Centre has the most sophisticated computerized system for mold design, analysis and manufacture in Canada, and is staffed by engineers and technicians with wide experience.

also noted for its architectural bronze casting, and one of its achievements included the bronze castings for the Sir Adam Beck memorial on University Avenue in Toronto.

In 1946, Harold M. Turner was appointed president, and the twelve years of his regime marked the company's transition to peacetime manufacturing. Expansion to service pent-up wartime demand saw the addition of manufacturing and distribution facilities throughout Canada.

CGE's product range expanded to include fluorescent lamps, watthour meters, and a host of new electrical appliances, as well as television tubes.

By 1955, when James. H. Goss succeeded Harold M. Turner as president, CGE had undergone a major reorganization and divisionalization, and under Goss this process continued. When J. Herbert Smith assumed the presidency in 1957, CGE was poised to enter the nuclear age, and became expert in technologies of special value to Canada and other developing countries, including long distance power transmission, mine hoist technology, hydro-electric and Candu nuclear power.

Under Smith CGE acquired Dominion Engineering Works, as well as a number of other companies in related electric and electronic fields.

It was turn-key contractor for the 20 MW Nuclear Power Demonstration station at Rolphton, as well as a 168 MW station in Karachi, Pakistan. It provided equipment for the St. Lawrence Seaway Power Project, constructed the first heavy-water plant in Canada, and designed and installed at Churchill Falls one of the most powerful hydro-electric generating units ever built in North America.

Walter G. Ward's appointment as president in 1972 began a period of consolidation. CGE was involved in the startup of Ontario Hydro's Pickering nuclear station in 1972, in the manufacture of hydro-electric equipment for export, and the sale of high-technology heavy equipment in foreign markets.

Today, under chairman Alton S. Cartwright, the company has streamlined itself to deal with the speed of technological change in the 80s. Since early in the decade it has focused on restructuring, developing new businesses, and repositioning or dropping weak product lines.

The resulting strategy saw it concentrate on developing what it calls "high technology, world class competitive products and service businesses."

Within a decade, it ceased making some forty-four products, but added or repositioned forty-one. The company withdrew from manufacturing and selling such products as television sets, building wire, power cable and television and radio broadcast equipment, for example. At the same time, it increased its investment in Canadian designed and developed world-class high technology products, high volume products, and technical service businesses, all targeted towards increased export opportunities.

In 1984, the CGE reputation for strength in technology is known around the world. As CGE heads into its second century, it would appear that the company's ability to change and grow remains as solid as its name.

CANADIAN NATIONAL

The coming of the railway to Ontario marked the province's transition from a colonial to a modern industrial society. In this process, CN has played a major role since 1853 – when the Ontario, Simcoe and Huron Railway (the ancestor of the CN System in Ontario) opened for business.

The year 1853 is one of the great watersheds in Ontario history, because in that year not only did the 'Oats, Straw and Hay,' as it was called, open to Allandale, but workers were preparing to build the Grand Trunk from Quebec and Montreal to Toronto and Sarnia; the Great Western was under construction from Suspension Bridge (Niagara Falls) to Windsor; and the first steam locomotive built in Canada – the *Toronto* – emerged from the works of James Good on what is now downtown Queen Street East in Toronto.

Formed in 1919 to consolidate a near bankrupt group of five major railroads and some 195 smaller ones, CN has worked steadily through the years pruning, rationalizing and systematizing the once-fragmented roads until it has become one of the world's great railways. But it is more than a railway. In order to compete effectively and efficiently in a competitive environment, CN has had to adapt and adopt. It has become a diversified transportation and communications enterprise with a number of complementary interests: telecommunications, trucking, shipping, resource development, real estate, hotels and international business consulting.

Few would have suspected the future, however, when Lady Elgin, amid the cheers of 2,000 Torontonians who turned out for the occasion, on October 15, 1851, turned the first sod for the OS&H, while her husband, the Earl of Elgin and Governor General of British North America, wheeled away the sod in a wooden wheelbarrow.

Today, in Ontario as in the rest of Canada, CN Rail is the largest of several CN divisions. CN Rail provides all the company's rail freight services. It also operates inter-city passenger trains under contract with VIA Rail Canada, and GO commuter train services in the Toronto area on behalf of Government of Ontario Transit. Toronto is the headquarters for CN Rail's Great Lakes Region, which generally encompasses the entire province. The Region has a work force of some 11,000 railroaders with a payroll well in excess of $300 million annually.

CNX/CN Trucking, CN Communications, CN Hotels and Tower, and CN Real Estate are other sectors of this profitable Crown Corporation that are critical to Ontario's continued development.

Right from its inception, CN was noted for its technical innovation and expertise.

In 1929, for instance, it gained the world speed record for a diesel-electric locomotive. Following World War II it was among the first railroads in the world to revitalize its war-worn plant: it experimented with, and then installed train radio; it installed automatic signalling systems; it phased out the steam locomotive in favour of cleaner, more powerful diesels; it began laying welded rail on mainlines; it invented, then put into service new types of roadbed maintenance equipment; and it either designed itself, or participated in designing a whole range of new freight equipment and systems.

Intermodality became CN's watchword. It looked at the transportation pattern of the country as a whole, and utilized those modes of transport that most efficiently and effectively got the job done. It used trucks where they were effective; interchanged them with rail at key points; and (in other parts of Canada) with CN Marine. It developed unit-train systems, piggyback operations (truck-on-rail), and experimented with new types of passenger equipment.

The entire history of the company has been one of innovation and diversification based on the natural interconnection between transportation and communication.

Since 1964, when the company opened its CN Rail Research Centre, it has been hard at work pursuing innovations that, when taken together, may well result in what its current president, J. Maurice LeClair, calls the 'Electronic Railroad of the future.'

This will be " . . . a railway operation in which the key operating personnel will be computer operators and

Toronto station in 1857 shortly after the railroad opened. The Grand Trunk became part of the CN system in the early 1900s.

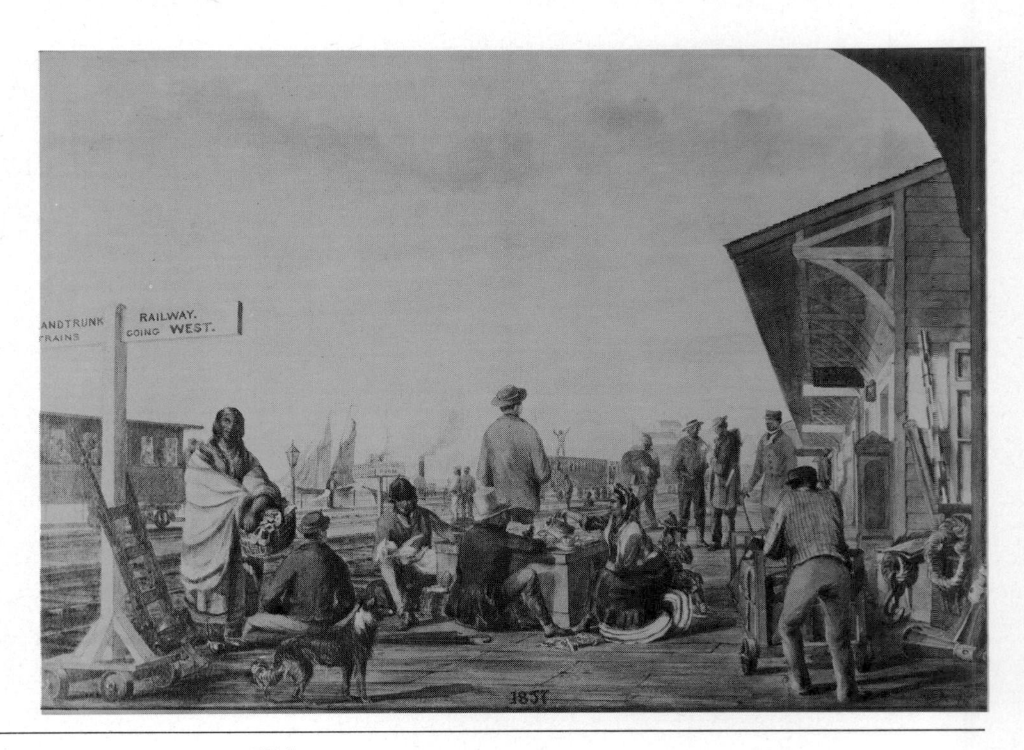

programmers communicating with each other via desktop terminals rather than by the present systems of signal lights, telephone or radio," says LeClair.

CN developed and implemented positive traction control for locomotives, a system which improves the control of wheel slippage on diesels pulling heavier train loads.

It introduced the first crew-crane transporters in North America, special tamping machines for railbeds, and other specialized road-maintenance and repair equipment that is recognized as the best in its field.

It extensively utilizes computer-assisted design models to enable it to simulate and plan its main-line expansion programs.

It designed, developed, and built a revolutionary new type of train dispatcher's rail traffic control system that may well become an industry standard.

It has developed and implemented new computerized systems for yard inventory, traffic reporting and control, and is now working on an even more sophisticated car identification and location system.

It has been 131 years since the OS&H first saw the light of day; then was reorganized into the Northern Railway of Canada; then amalgamated with the Hamilton and North Western Railway in 1872; which was swallowed, in turn, by the Grand Trunk Company; which in 1922, bankrupt, became part of the CN system.

Those first seventy years were ones of construction, development, and growth. The decades that followed saw more development, as well as rationalization of the entire system. The decades to come may well see a railroad run on what, only a few years ago, would have been described as 'science fiction' concepts.

As one of the oldest companies in Ontario, CN may also fairly be described as one of the newest. It is no exaggeration to say that if the railway was pivotal to the shift of the province from a colonial to an industrial society, it may well play a similar role in the transition of Ontario to an electronic society in the decades to come. CN's record of experimentation, innovation, and implementation stands the province in good stead.

Top left: *Increasing volumes of trucks are moving off the highway and onto CN Rail flat cars for the trip between Toronto and Montreal. Gantry crane lifts trailer for placement aboard 60-car Laser piggyback train which provides overnight service between the two cities. Use of piggyback reduces truckers' line-haul costs, as well as wear-and-tear on the highways.*

Top right: *This trainload of iron ore from Northern Ontario bound for the foundries at Hamilton passes over a trestle at South River — tough railroading country.*

Bottom: *The use of computers has resulted in greater productivity and hundreds of millions of dollars saved at CN Rail. The company uses them in almost every facet of its operations.*

THE BRYANT PRESS LIMITED

By the turn of the century, Toronto had become the graphic arts capital of Canada. Its first printers had established themselves in the 1830s, and by the 1890s several major printing companies were founded. One of these is The Bryant Press Limited.

Many Canadians who may never have heard of the company have, nevertheless, been closely associated with its products. Bryant is today, the largest printer/binder of hardcover books in Ontario, many of which are textbooks used by students in every province of the country.

The Bryant Press began in 1895, when the company occupied a building on the present site of Union Station in Toronto. Of J. E. Bryant, the man who gave the firm its name, little is known. Printing then was quite different from what it is now, machinery was just beginning to come into general use. As a rule, all type was set, and all books bound by hand.

The Bryant Press became The Bryant Press Limited in 1903 under the management of John Weld, President.

During its eighty-nine-year history the company has relocated several times, first in 1895 to Richmond Street, where the Robert Simpson Company now stands. Between 1913 and 1925 it made four moves, first to Spadina Avenue, then to George Street, next to Jarvis Street in 1915, and in 1925 to 360 Adelaide Street West, where it remained until 1970.

John Weld died in 1931 and his son, Douglas S. Weld, succeeded him as President. This family tradition was to continue: since the beginning there has been at least one member of the Weld family active at Bryant Press. In 1969 John D. Weld, Douglas's son, became President and is currently active in the company as Chairman of the Board and Chief Executive Officer. Ronald F. Port the current President was elected in 1977 (the only person outside the Weld family to hold this office). The fourth generation of Welds in the company is represented by Thomas J. Weld, a great-grandson of the firm's first President, and Wendy Lee Weld, a great-granddaughter.

By World War II the company did a brisk business producing high quality commercial printing by the letterpress process, as well as tickets for milk, bread and ice (all of which were home-delivered), tea bags, theatre and other amusement tickets; butter, sugar, tea and coffee ration coupons which were issued to Ontario residents during the Second World War.

A list of some of the more colourful items from Bryant's printing history includes racing programs for Ontario Jockey Club meets at Woodbine, Thorncliffe, Long Branch and Dufferin race tracks; *Esquire* Magazine which was printed by Bryant during a short period of industry unrest in the United States; Watsons Compound Interest and Annuity Tables; fibreboard, a material that was waxed after printing and used by the dairy industry for milk and cream cartons; Collins White Circle pocket novels (25,000 copies each of twelve titles a month) printed by sheet-fed letterpress.

Post-war automation revolutionized the printing industry, and by 1949, the firm's hardcover binding operations became fully machine controlled. Offset printing was a further advance that offered great savings in time and money. Bryant purchased its first sheet-fed offset press in 1953, and today runs a complete multicolour sheet-fed pressroom which includes presses capable of printing 4 colours at a time on sheets up to a maximum size of 55″ x 77″.

In 1971, the firm moved to its present location at 260 Bartley Drive, Toronto, following its purchase of the printing division of McCorquodale & Blades, Canada. This plant occupies more than 100,000 square feet on a single floor, and employs 175 people.

In 1983, Bryant purchased the binding equipment of The Hunter Rose Company of Toronto when that firm fell victim to Canada's toughest depression since the '30s.

The Company, over the years, has trained excellent tradesmen in the Graphic Arts Industry. Loyalty to the firm is high; 7 employees have served the company for more than 50 years.

The skills and traditions of binding craftsmanship that have served customers over the years are revealed by the book you have in front of you. It was bound by The Bryant Press Limited.

The Weld family with one of the company's large four-colour presses.
Left to right: Wendy Lee Weld
John D. Weld, Chairman and C.E.O.
Thomas J. Weld.

CERTIFIED BRAKES, A LEAR SIEGLER COMPANY

Certified Brakes is now the largest manufacturer of automotive brakes in Canada, and exports to sixty-five countries around the world. In the last fifteen years the company's gross revenue has risen to $50 million from $4 million — a far cry from the company's humble beginnings in 1948, says Canadian Albert McAra, Certified's current president.

Thirty-six years ago, Certified Automotive Replacements of Toronto, opened above a market on Toronto's Spadina Avenue. At that time, six employees struggled in a one-room workshop to produce ten reconditioned master brake cylinders a day. The company's co-partners were Jack Hernick, sales manager and founder; Sam Sperling, plant manager; and Bill Sokoloff, office manager.

The business was essentially founded on the solution to a simple but widespread problem. In those days — the late 40s — it was found that after one or two years, corrosion took place inside the brake cylinders of most automobiles.

Jack Hernick devised a way of putting a sleeve inside the cylinder, an innovation that was basically a rebuilding operation, since the non-corrosive alloy sleeve put into the rebuilt cylinders eliminated the corrosion problem.

In the early days, Hernick tried to interest several large manufacturers in handling the re-sleeving operation, but was told that it was impossible to rebuild brake cylinders by sleeving on a mass-production basis.

The three men, however, remained unconvinced, and by sheer persistence, a small company once again showed large manufacturers that, with a lot of faith, small miracles can be coaxed into existence.

Within ten years the company's red, white and blue label became a familiar sight on the shelves of automobile repair shops throughout the country.

Bill Sokoloff had previously owned a cable manufacturing plant, but disposed of it in 1951, when he joined Certified on a full-time basis. Sam Sperling came to the firm with considerable technical expertise. Hernick recalls how, years ago, Sperling went home tired after a day's work at his own business, and he (Hernick) would urge him to come down to Certified's Spadina Avenue plant where they would work until the early hours of the morning in an attempt to get cylinders ready for the day staff to complete.

The dedication was rewarded by a steady increase in the company's sales, which enabled it to move to larger premises on McCormack Street in Toronto. Today, the company occupies a 180,000-square-foot manufacturing plant on Kimbel Street in Mississauga, Ontario. This plant is considered to be the most modern disk-brake-pad manufacturing facility in the country.

The company has a second plant, located at 1000 Martin Grove Road, Etobicoke. This 100,000-square-foot facility has been in service for twenty years, manufacturing Certified's brake shoes, brake cables, strip and rolled lining.

In 1969, the original partners sold the company to Royal Industries, an American company. The previous year, Royal had also purchased Krasne Manufacturing Inc., a firm whose product range is similar to that of Certified. During this period of ownership, the Krasner company was known as Royal Brake Products, but has now been re-named Certified Brakes. It's located at Danville, Kentucky.

In 1977, Lear Siegler Inc. merged with Royal Industries, and assumed control of Certified Brakes. By then, both Hernick and Sperling had retired, but Sokoloff, one of the original partners, who had been president of the Certified Division of Royal Industries, remained president of the division under Lear Siegler from 1977 to 1982.

The current parent company was founded in 1954 and is headquartered in Santa Monica, California. Lear Siegler manufactures and markets a wide range of technical and automotive products including products for the aerospace industry. Present sales of the company are in excess of $1.5 billion.

Brake shoe manufacturing at the company's Martin Grove Road plant.

Canadian offices of Lear Siegler's Certified Brakes division.

CUDDY FARMS LIMITED

The 'open door' policies affected by corporate chief executive officers in media interviews often stretch belief. Yet an 'open-door' policy was the making of A.M. (Mac) Cuddy, who credits the success of Cuddy Farms to the unwavering commitment of his employees. His affectionate, back-slapping, elbow-squeezing style is genuine in its application, and his employees appreciate that fact.

Says Cuddy: "Had someone screened calls or refused to see me while I was on the road, I would never have made it this far. I'll be damned if I'll stop anyone from pulling himself up by his own bootstraps."

The same grass roots philosophy has been the trademark of Cuddy Farms' 35-year history. The road from obscurity to international prominence in the agribusiness has been a long and rough one for Mac Cuddy and his clan of six, but something he looks back on with satisfaction.

"We would rise at two a.m., load the truck with about 200 freshly dressed birds, and take Highways 2 and 5 to Toronto. The trip would take about five hours. We'd sell to Canada Packers and Burns, and be back home by three or four p.m. Then, of course, we had to kill and dress birds for the next day. Those were long, long days," says Cuddy with a grin.

"This was shortly after I had left my job as a Veteran's Land Act Settlement Officer, a posting I received after returning from the Second World War."

Cuddy smiles again as he remembers his days with the V.L.A. "I'm not sure what I hated most – working for someone else, or working for the government. It was probably the latter."

"When we began growing commercial turkeys for processing in the early 1950s, we used every available blade of grass. The work was never finished. That's why I'm in favor of large families. An instant labour force at your disposal."

Yet, as Cuddy surveys the acres of landscaped lawns and horse-dotted pastures that surround his Strathroy-based firm today, he says he believes his company survived where other independent producers didn't because it was able to adapt to a changing marketplace.

In 1952 he met George Nicholas, a California-based turkey-breeding pioneer. It marked a turning point in his business.

"That's when I decided to become a hatcheryman, to improve the breed, and not just remain a supplier," he says.

Today, the Cuddy-Nicholas relationship remains steadfast, and even though faces change, their commitment to the breeding industry remains the same. While both companies have flourished over the years, Cuddy has surged to the forefront – becoming the largest producer of turkey eggs and poults in the world. More recently, it has become a serious contender for the top spot as a processor in the United States.

"We've been referred to as the IBM of the turkey industry," quips Cuddy. "I like to think of ourselves as a sort of turkey Avis – we try harder."

Highway view of Cuddy Farms, 1951. Steel posts and runaway weeds have been replaced by landscaped grounds and rolling pastures.

But it hasn't all been unbroken success and growth. In the mid-60s, Cuddy was involved with a processing company in London, Ontario. It purchased a controlling interest in the firm, and opened a further processing line – a move that established Cuddy as an innovator. The plan failed, and the plant closed in 1971 – only to be reopened in 1976 as Cuddy Food Products Ltd., with a complete line of food service products.

Similar investments made throughout the 1960s, in an attempt to vertically integrate the company, proved only marginally successful, and were sold.

Yet Cuddy isn't sorry about the results. "The industry wasn't ready for our type of processing," he says.

"We tried to bite off more than we could chew. Selling the plants provided an impetus to expand into the U.S. and establish a foothold in the eastern and mid-western markets."

Always a burgeoning market for day-old turkey poults, North Carolina seemed an ideal location to establish an American base. Hatcheries and farms were purchased; customers established; and, as expected, a Cuddy sent to manage the operation.

In the fifteen years that have since passed, the U.S. subsidiary has maintained a friendly rivalry with its Canadian parent. It has also firmly established the Cuddy name in six states, with vans and refrigerated tractor-trailers criss-crossing another fifteen.

At one point, the company considered going public, but decided that family control was too important to sacrifice.

Strong Italian and German markets are the nucleus of Cuddy's international business, although inquiries from South America and Eastern Bloc countries are routine events. To supply both domestic and international customers, Cuddy massively expanded his facilities, and built a laboratory and research department that rivals any government-sponsored facility.

Cuddy Food Products of London, Ontario, reopened in 1976 as a further processor of deboned turkey meat. A reputation for quality that began in one industry quickly moved into another — an indication why the giant McDonald's Restaurant chain chose Cuddy Food Products to be the sole Canadian supplier of the restaurant's line of chicken products.

Originally an agricultural-based organization, Cuddy Farms has returned to its origins with the addition of a frozen food plant, scheduled to open in mid-1984. The plant will process a variety of vegetables for Canadian and overseas markets.

Mac Cuddy's real love is horses, however, and he can't remember a time he wasn't involved with them. As might be expected of a breeder, he doesn't take them lightly. Today, Cuddy is regarded as one of the standardbred industry's leading authorities — as a breeder, owner, and spokesman. He owns a blue-ribbon racing stable, and a small, but select nursery that includes three World Champions. His reputation is international, and he currently serves as a director on the Hall of Fame, Hambletonian Society, and the Ontario Jockey Club.

Yet Cuddy is modest, some would say to a fault. At a recent Ontario Chamber of Commerce Awards Dinner he was presented with the first Outstanding Business Achievement Award. He accepts the accolades given to him by his peers and profession, but prefers anonymity. "I put my pants on the same way everyone does," he quips. "One leg at a time."

A.M. (Mac) Cuddy surrounded by his five sons, key managers within the expanding organization.
An aerial view of Cuddy Farms today.
In the early days, the farm was a family affair. Barbara Cuddy with 'a friend,' Cuddy Farms, 1953.
Ranging bronze turkeys prior to construction of the Hatchery, Cuddy Farms, 1952.

CUTLER BRANDS AND DESIGNS INC.

DIVISION OF CANADIAN CORPORATE MANAGEMENT CO. LTD.

If you visit the souvenir section of virtually any store in Canada today, chances are that somewhere your eye will fall on an all Canadian-made product from Cutler Brands and Designs. Yet, a corporation that today supports more than 200 people originated because one man lost his job – victim of a recession

In 1934, at age fifty-four, Harry Cutler, father of ten children, abruptly found himself unemployed when the glass company he'd worked for since age eighteen fell victim to the Depression. Unemployment didn't cause him to despair, however – it spurred him on to found a company that today makes a wide array of glass and textile products and employs more than 200 people.

Harry Cutler had arrived in Toronto from England with his parents in 1883, at age four. By 1897 he was employed with a major Toronto glass company, but the move that was to dominate his life was the partnership he entered with his boyhood friend Eddie Memberey in the formation of Bent Glass Specialties Company.

The first thing the pair did was to build an 1,800-square-foot sheet metal building with a small coke-fired, glass-bending machine. Here, they were able to manufacture convex picture-frame glass, as well as curved glass for windows and greenhouses, by heating the glass to 600°C and sagging it into cast iron or boiler-plate molds. Total cost of the new building and oven was $1,100 but the move was successful and Bent Glass Specialties Company was later incorporated (1945) as Cutler Brands Limited.

In 1938, Cutler's two sons, Arthur and William, joined the firm to help with the expanding business on day-to-day transactions and product development. A year later the firm expanded, building a one-storey plant to house a kiln capable of bending large store-front plate glass.

A particularly significant expansion took place in 1944. That was the year the company acquired several properties on Geary Avenue, Toronto, to accommodate further expansion. However, in July of that same year, a plant fire caused building damage that ran to $7,684.

In 1944 Harry Cutler died at age sixty-four, and it was shortly after this that his sons Lloyd and Ned joined the business. In 1950, a second major building expansion took place – to accommodate the new textile division of the company. Cutler Designs Limited was incorporated in 1951 and headed by Arthur Cutler, who expanded the company into the silk screen printing of T-Shirts, blouses, towels and other items.

During the 1950s, other important developments occurred. The company installed a 95-foot electric lehr for glass bending, and Wesley Cutler, another son, joined the business.

In the 1960s the company installed a six-colour textile printing machine, and throughout the decade continued to add other equipment to help deal with the continued growth of Cutler's textile division. By 1972, Cutler Brands Limited and Cutler Designs Limited had both expanded to occupy a total of 85,000 square feet – an entire block of Geary Avenue, Toronto.

In 1975, Canadian Corporate Management Co. Ltd. acquired fifty percent of the two Cutler operations, and the remaining fifty percent on December 31, 1978. On March 9, 1979, the four Cutler brothers – Arthur, William, Lloyd and Ned – retired and pursued new interests.

The overall success of the company is generally credited to its founder, Harry Cutler. He was a man so well grounded in his business that he placed the company on a firm foundation right from the beginning. He was also a strong family man with family-oriented sons, who, in their turn, operated the company in such a way that all employees felt they were part of an extended family, and many remained

Harry Cutler, front row, centre, when he was employed by the Toronto Plate Glass Company, a firm that went under during the Depression.

loyal to the company their entire working lives. As a result of this easy and friendly interface between management and workers, the company has had virtually no labour difficulties throughout its entire history.

Cutler's sons, who ran the business after his death, are remarkable in themselves. Wesley, following university graduation, worked for a number of major Canadian companies, and was also an advisor to his father's firm. He was, moreover, one of Canada's all-time great football stars, and during the 1930s participated in three Grey Cup Games. He was later elected to the Canadian Football Hall of Fame.

Arthur and William worked in their father's company for 41 years and retired in 1979. Arthur specialized in hand-painted trays and screened textiles. William was chiefly involved with glass products and the development of a complete line of decorated tableware.

Twins Lloyd and Ned, who were with the company 34 years, also retired in 1979. Lloyd helped develop production techniques for decorated textile products. Ned, a commerce and finance graduate, was responsible for personnel, finance and systems, mainly in the glass field.

Although the company was well run, its success is equally attributable to its innovative initiatives. In the 1930s and 40s, for instance, it made bent-glass windows with the aid of three large coke-fired ovens, often to sizes as large as 120 by 144 inches.

It developed a line of beautiful hand-painted bent-glass serving trays — the first in Canada. Decorating was first in oil colours, but later made use of ceramic colours which fused into the glass during the bending operation, much like colour is fired into china under heat.

Later, it decorated lighting glassware using the silk-screen process, and in parallel with this creativity, the firm developed equally creative ideas in the textile division.

Over the years, Cutler Brands and Designs Inc. has served companies from one end of Canada to the other, and count among their customers such well-known companies as O'Keefe, Molsons, Caldwell, and Wabasso, as well as numerous advertising specialty companies.

The present direction of the company is the responsibility of Mr. A.R. Tressel, a colleague of the Cutlers since 1955, their personal choice for the position.

Mr. Tressel has a wide background in both sales and manufacture of glassware and from the time he took over as president and general manager in 1979, successfully adopted the Cutler family tradition of team spirit that worked so well in the past.

He succeeded in expanding the company's base by broadening its ceramic, plastic and textile lines, especially in patterns and products for the retail and advertising specialty trade.

Cutler Brands and Designs Inc. factory at 136 Geary Avenue, a far cry from the first 2,000-square-foot building.

The picture's battered, but the pride is evident. Left to right Bill Cutler, Al Lehane and Ernie Lamountain examine a set of newly-fired tankards in 1956 — the first year the company began decorating tableware.

The year 1984 marks a special anniversary for the company — its 50th. There seems little doubt that with long-term employees determined to make the company succeed 'for everyone's sake' Cutler will continue expanding in the decades to come.

L. DAVIS TEXTILE CO. LIMITED

Throughout the years, the L. Davis Textile Co. Limited has grown from a three-employee business located in a small 3,000-square-foot warehouse in Toronto, to a total of 134,000-square-foot manufacturing, distribution and sales facility employing 450.

Established by the late Louis Davis in 1942, the original company manufactured men's overalls and uniforms, but today has the reputation of being the largest manufacturer of children's sleepwear in Canada, exporting to countries such as Australia, New Zealand, England, Ireland, Holland, Belgium and France.

The company began its expansion in 1945, when it moved to Wellington Street, Toronto. Mr. Davis hired an additional employee and began selling jackets and shirts wholesale for men and boys, and in an indication of things to come, sewing flannelette diapers that were contracted out through a homemaker service.

During the years 1945 to 1947, the company was incorporated and another company founded under the name of Clover Linen, which manufactured Plymouth pillow cases, sheets, and also imported linen tablecloths.

By 1954, the company had settled into larger premises on Noble Street. It had fifteen employees, with Louis Davis working alongside them. As the manufacturer of children's sleepwear grew, Davis began producing private label brands for national retailers, as well as his own brands. He also began to market household kitchen items and toys under the name Giftex.

In 1957, he added an adult sleepwear division to his children's wear line when the company moved to new premises, with 8,000 square feet on Geary Avenue.

By 1965, however, the children's wear had become so successful that the Giftex operation was discontinued. With the company continuing to expand (it now occupied 77,000 square feet), its managers made a major decision to focus attention totally on infant and children's products.

In December 1970, Louis Davis sold the assets and complete control of the company to his sons, Michael and Kenneth. He died on June 14, 1971.

During the 70s, the company merchandised and marketed in six divisions: Sleepwear, Playwear, Underwear, Bedding, Diapers, and Infant Accessories. In 1975 it decided to become a national brand in Canada, and all its children's sleepwear products became known by the Snugabye label.

Realizing what requirements for future expansion this move could mean, the company bought a parcel of land adjacent to its Geary Avenue property. In 1976, as demand for its products continued to increase, it also leased 22,000 square feet of warehouse space on St. Clair Avenue.

By 1980, the company felt it had such a recognizable product that it was ready to introduce an additional size range (eight to fourteen) to its already booming children's sleepwear division. Thus, in the winter of 1983 L. Davis Textiles Co. Ltd. opened a new 54,000-square-foot plant in Toronto that included new showrooms and boardrooms.

Davis sees itself as a pioneer in the industry in the areas of machinery and computer use. In fact, the Davis factory has a world-wide reputation for productivity, and tour groups from as far away as Japan, Finland, and England have visited the facilities.

The L. Davis Company points to its fine employee relations as a major factor in its success. It proudly points out that many people in middle management have been with the company since its inception. The company means it when it says that its first commitment is to maintain its people in a safe and contented environment.

Louis Davis founder.
Michael Davis, President, and Kenneth Davis, Vice-President.

DEACON BROTHERS LIMITED

Since 1897 there has been a Deacon making fine clothing in Belleville, Ontario, but the family traces its Canadian roots to Thomas Deacon, an officer with Burgoyne's army at the time of the American Revolution, an early settler, around 1778, and first postmaster of Kingston.

The father of the Belleville Deacons – William B. – was a grandson of Thomas. He began as the proprietor of a men's wear store on Front Street in 1897.

William, grandfather of the present executive trio, was an enterprising merchant, and found a ready market for the custom-made dress shirts he made in the back room of his shop. So good were they, in fact, that demand soon exceeded his ability to supply. So William closed the store and became an industrialist.

The Deacon Shirt Company first opened for business from a plant on Coleman Street in 1903, and even though the building was destroyed by fire in 1910, it was rebuilt and operating again by 1911.

By 1914, Fred S. Deacon joined his brother William in the operation – just in time to help with a tremendous spurt in the company's business as a result of clothing orders for the Canadian armed forces.

The founder's son, Fred H., joined the firm during the 1920s – and realized the growth potential for the company in the demand for sportswear. Deacon's golf jacket, for instance, designed in this period, has literally become a Canadian classic – so crisp and neat in appearance, its style has changed very little over the years. Winter sportswear furthered the fame of the Deacon label.

During the 1930s, the plant moved to Front Street, and John Deacon, the founder's second son, returned to the firm. Again, he was just in time to help with a burst of war orders as Deacon's operation burgeoned to two shifts to make special clothing for the Armed Forces.

By 1941 the company had moved into a new and larger plant on Dundas Street, and the Deacons were deeply involved in the design and production of electrically heated flying suits for the allied air forces.

Deacon's designer, Reg Hinchey, and the Deacon flying suit designs were eventually loaned to American firms for production, and Mr. Hinchey and Mr. Fred H. Deacon both received citations from the American government for their work.

The firm's founder, William B., died in 1944, followed by Fred S. in 1946 – but they had seen their firm grow from a single store to one of Canada's most important clothing manufacturers.

Following the war it fell to Fred H. and John to reorient the company's activities. They put their wartime "warmth without weight" expertise into making protective outdoor apparel, and led the way in producing new types of outdoor sportswear.

Two British fabrics, Grenfell cloth from Burnley, England, and Viyella from Paisley, Scotland, were fashioned into a wide range of windbreakers, parkas and sportshirts. Natural fibers, wool, cotton and duck down were emphasized in styling, directed to a growing leisure market.

Today, the company is owned by the three sons of Fred H. Deacon: Fred, general manager; Donald, production manager; and Eric, in charge of design.

Since all three Deacon brothers have sons (named for their fathers in the traditional Deacon manner), it appears Deacon Brothers will remain a family firm whatever the future holds for this expanding Canadian enterprise.

Left: *Original plant of Deacon Shirt Company on Coleman Street.*

Right: *The Deacon brothers: left to right, Don, production manager, Eric, general manager, and Fred, in charge of design.*

DOULTON CANADA INC.

English ceramic tableware has been part of the Canadian scene for almost two centuries, and the Doulton Group of Companies has made a significant contribution to this heritage.
English tableware became part of the trading medium of the earliest merchants. Documents show that members of renowned English potting families made the hazardous sailing voyage to the 'new world' early in the 19th century to strengthen their hold on the market.

For the most part, trading was maintained by factory salesmen campaigning for orders. Eventually, however, agency houses were established in Canada, and from this bridgehead came the wholly-owned subsidiary companies of the great potting houses.

Doulton Canada Inc. takes its name from the Royal Doulton of international fame. Doulton, in fact, was founded in 1815 – on the eve of Waterloo – when Loyalist settlers had been in Canada barely three decades. The origins of some of the famous names sharing the Doulton umbrella began about the same time as the revolution that was to result in the settlement of Canada. Royal Crown Derby, then in London, started in 1750; Minton in 1793. The 19th century produced the Royal Albert, Paragon and Beswick potteries.

Today, the Royal Doulton Tableware Group not only represents a third of the manufacturing capacity of the British tableware industries, it is also a worldwide marketing organization. It, too, has carefully nurtured its traditions, yet, while revering its past, is forward looking in its thinking and planning.

The Royal Doulton Group has had a dedicated presence in Canada since the early 1930s. Then, the importing house of Parson-Steiner Limited served not only Ontario, but all of Canada until 1955. Other members of the present group were established in 1935, 1941, 1945, 1950, and later. Out of the beginnings of a few has grown the 200 or more people who today service the Canadian consumer through Doulton Canada's network of distributors, its 'Doulton Rooms' in stores, and its 'Lawleys of London' stores.

Doulton established its own presence in 1955, when it set up showrooms and offices on Wellington Street. By 1960, these were inadequate and new headquarters were built in Don Mills.

Mergers, acquisitions and a rapidly expanding market led, in 1979, to yet a larger facility at 850 Progress Avenue in Toronto's suburban Scarborough. Here, on an eight-acre lot is probably the most modern facility of its kind in the world. It was opened in 1981 by the Honourable John Black Aird, Lieutenant Governor of Ontario, in the presence of Sir Richard Bailey, C.B.E., Chairman of Royal Doulton Tableware Ltd., and G.W. Churton, President of Doulton Canada Inc., who came to Canada in 1955 to set up the original company.

Indian Brave, a ceramic sculpture to mark Canada's Centennial Year, is a magnificent equestrian model of a North American Indian. Designed by Mrs. Peggy Davies at Doulton's Burslem factory, the Sioux warrior required a special kiln and six firings to achieve the correct colouring and texture. It is totally hand painted.

DUNWOODY & COMPANY

It was in the buoyant business environment of 1921 that the late Col. James M. Dunwoody opened his firm's first office in Winnipeg, Manitoba. The next sixty years have seen the firm of Dunwoody & Company grow from this modest sole-practitioner beginning to its present status as one of Canada's most prominent chartered accounting firms, with twenty-nine offices across Canada, including the firm's largest, in Toronto.

Now located in the Royal Bank Plaza in the heart of Toronto's financial district, the Toronto office is the flagship of the firm. But it wasn't always so.

The Dunwoody firm really began in Western Canada, and expanded steadily from its founding. By 1938 it had offices in Kenora and Fort Frances, and its staff had grown from Col. Dunwoody, a clerk, a secretary and one client, to fourteen people — a significant growth during the depression years.

It was also attracting prestigious major clients, among them the Canadian Wheat Board administration, Canadian National Railways, and Claude Neon Ltd.

At the outbreak of World War II, James Dunwoody volunteered for service, and worked for more than two years setting up control systems for the military.

When he retired from the army in 1943, he decided to open an office in Eastern Canada. He chose Toronto, called the new firm James M. Dunwoody & Company, and set up shop at 330 Bay Street. Like its Winnipeg forerunner, it had modest beginnings, with himself, one staff member, an audit clerk and a stenographer as the entire staff.

With its personal and practical approach to dealing with client problems, the firm grew rapidly, establishing traditions along the way which were carried on by subsequent partners. By 1954 there were offices in Oakville and Welland, as well as the head office in Toronto, while the western region consisted of offices in Winnipeg, Kenora, Fort Frances, Fort William (now Thunder Bay), Atikokan, and Dryden.

In 1958, Dunwoody Limited was incorporated to carry on practice as a licensed trustee in bankruptcy.

The year 1959 saw the opening of an office in Vancouver. By 1965 Dunwoody & Company consisted of twenty-three partners and 163 employees in eleven offices throughout Canada.

Yet even as a new national partnership was being formed, the firm realized that it was embarked on a major growth pattern and it had to expand outside the country by acquiring multinational connections. Consequently, on March 31, 1964, the firm was party to the creation of the international association, which is now Dunwoody Robson McGladrey & Pullen. Dunwoody & Company was and is the leader and moving force of an association which now extends into sixty countries around the world.

Since that time, Dunwoody & Company in Canada has grown by mergers, as well as by internal growth. Today, the firm also has offices in Ontario at Sault Ste. Marie, Kitchener/Waterloo, Hamilton, Markham, Oshawa, Cornwall and Ottawa.

In the years ahead, the company intends to continue to offer the same personalized approach to services which have marked its last sixty years. These include auditing, accounting, tax consulting, insolvency, financial advisory, and other services to the business and financial community.

The firm's growth in Ontario from the first small practice in Fort Frances to the thirteen busy offices of today, is a proud and integral part of its history.

Colonel James Dunwoody, D.S.O., D.C.M., E.D., C.A., founder of Dunwoody & Company. The painting, which was commissioned to mark Col. Dunwoody's 50th year in public practice, hangs in the boardroom of the Toronto office. The work of artist Erik Dzenis, it depicts him wearing the regimental tie of the Fort Garry Horse, the regiment of which he was Colonel.

Scott Street, Fort Frances, around 1927 when Dunwoody & Company opened its first Ontario office.

ELGIN HANDLES LIMITED

Elgin Handles is the oldest woodworking industry in St. Thomas, and still operates from the site on which it began in 1887.

It began as John Heard and Company, which started at Lambeth in 1866, moved to Amherstburg in 1878, then on November 26, 1886 signed an agreement with the City of St. Thomas in which it promised to erect a two-storey brick building, 40 by 100 feet, for "manufacturing wheels and other wooden work for carriages," and to employ an average of forty men daily.

The company purchased property adjacent to the London & Port Stanley Railway on January 14, 1877, and erected a factory in December that same year.

The deaths of John Heard Jr. in 1896, Heard Sr. in 1897, and the early withdrawal of the two sons-in-law finally left William the only member of the original partnership.

He was soon joined by his younger brothers Richard and Robert, additional property purchased, new sheds erected, and by 1906 the firm was employing an average of fifty men.

But it fell on difficult times, and by 1912 had only twelve employees. The advent of the motor car, and failure to develop new product lines may have caused the decline.

Meanwhile, in 1915, George P. Smith, Joseph Lewis and his son Charles had formed "The Elgin Handle Company, business to be carried on in the premises of Heard and Company or some other premises." Smith was the business manager. The Lewises, who had worked for the J.H. Still Handle Company, were the operators. At first, the new company operated in premises rented from Heard, but on December 2, 1918 Elgin Handles purchased the Heard property from Molson's Bank.

The new firm erected a warehouse which was burned in 1933 and rebuilt immediately. After the Second World War it carried out extensive renovations on the old Heard building.

Like its predecessor, Elgin Handles purchased most of its material locally, but a bird and a pest changed all that.

In the early 1930s a pest killed the chestnut trees which had been a favourite of the sapsuckers. These birds then turned their attention to the local hickory trees, eventually making them unsuitable for handles, and the firm had to purchase hickory from Tennessee.

In 1957, after a long and successful career under the ownership of George Smith and Harvey Jay, the firm was sold to businessman Hap Day, who had operated a sand and gravel business, but was better known for his career as an outstanding player and coach of the Toronto Maple Leafs. He and his son Kerry expanded Elgin Handles into the largest handle factory in Canada, and one of the largest in North America.

In 1974, the firm made a breakthrough crucial to its success. Instead of providing handles to other manufacturers, the firm imported sledges, heavy hammers and small hand tools from Japan. Handles are now installed in the plant, and the finished product distributed to the retail trade.

In 1977, Hap Day retired, and was succeeded by his son Kerry whose inauguration was marred somewhat by a fire in 1978 which closed the plant for eight days. Since then, installation of a new dust collector and sprinkler system have proved so efficient the firm's insurance costs have been halved.

Increasing business involved the purchase of additional property, and the firm built new drying kilns in 1964 and 1982, and doubled its office space in 1981. Despite many alterations and additions, and five serious fires in its 97-year history, the original brick building erected in 1887 is still an important part of the plant complex.

In 1983 the company opened a second plant in the local industrial park, and concentrated its new tool division there.

Sixty percent of the handle material, mainly hickory, comes from Tennessee, forty per cent from local sources – mainly white ash, maple, and some hickory which invariably show signs of sapsucker activity.

The firm has six manufacturing agents in Canada, and also sells to Britain, West Germany, Norway, New Zealand, and the United States. Some customers have dealt with the firm since the early 1900s.

The firm's 80 employees are customer oriented, emphasizing quality control, and looking forward to the challenges of the next 97 years.

Left, Clarence 'Hap' Day, president 1957-1977. Right, Kerry Day, current president. In the background is a 1948 painting of the Elgin Handles plant and sawmill by Clark McDougall.

ERECTOWELD COMPANY LIMITED

When they first met in Brandon, Manitoba, in 1958, as employees of an international engineering contractor, Francois Bollinger, Frank Walsh and Johannes Luyk had occasionally considered being in business for themselves. Deeply involved in the construction of high pressure turbine piping systems, they recognized a need in the industry for a high quality fabricator.

Oakville seemed a logical location in which to begin; in the centre of the most lucrative and rapidly expanding market in Canada. In 1963 they began business in rented premises. In 1967 the partners felt confident enough to purchase a plant in Oakville which has become the permanent home of Erectoweld.

Over the years these premises have been expanded to five times their original size and in them has been produced the fabricated piping which has given Erectoweld a reputation as a major Canadian high quality pipe fabricator. For twenty years Erectoweld has supplied many major Canadian industrial projects — the Tar Sands plants of Syncrude and Great Canadian Oil, petrochemical complexes and petroleum refineries across Canada, major steel mill expansions of Stelco and Algoma Steel, and power stations in various provinces.

Recognizing early in their business career the natural cyclicity of the pipe fabrication industry and the consequent necessity for diversification, Erectoweld acquired Coleman Machine & Tool Co. Ltd. in 1964, as a base on which to build further diversification. In 1968 Erectoweld signed a licencing agreement with an American company and established its Lift Truck Attachment Division to produce a line of lift truck attachments in Canada. Through its involvement in the material handling industry, Erectoweld recognized a potential market and in 1972, established Forged Forks Limited to manufacture forks for fork lift trucks. Forged Forks Limited now occupies its own 30,000-square-foot premises and exports the bulk of its production to the United States, where the Fork Division and the Lift Truck Attachment Division jointly market a complete line of material handling equipment to lift-truck dealers.

In 1980 Erectoweld established the Arenaquip Division to manufacture ice resurfacing equipment and supply a complete line of equipment and accessories to ice hockey arenas in Canada and the United States.

In 1982 Erectoweld acquired Altosar Corporation, a manufacturer of aquatic plant harvesting equipment, which designs and builds a line of water-management products. In recent years aquatic vegetation has become a serious world-wide problem and, in many areas of the world, bodies of water are dying from lack of oxygen. As an alternative to the use of chemcials for aquatic vegetation control, mechanical harvesting is becoming the choice of the ecologically concerned.

In 1983 Erectoweld formed an American subsidiary, Erectoweld Inc., located in Waukesha, Wisconsin, to facilitate the distribution and sales of Erectoweld's products and to acquire the assets of Aquamarine Corp., the world's largest manufacturer of plant harvesting equipment. In that same year Erectoweld purchased a 150,000 square-foot plant in Oakville to accommodate the manufacture of the aquatic plant harvesters and other water management products which are marketed by the Aquamarine Division of Erectoweld Inc. for the American market and Erectoweld Company Limited for Canadian and international markets.

Erectoweld and its various divisions and subsidiaries occupy 250,000 square feet of manufacturing space, employ over 100 people, and sell products in many parts of the world. In twenty years Erectoweld has become a highly diversified manufacturer, with a well-earned reputation for excellence which the partners recognize to be due in large measure to the enormous contribution made by their employees.

The owners of Erectoweld. Left to right, Frances Walsh, Francois Bollinger, and Johannes Luyk.

FAG BEARINGS LIMITED

Ball bearings. Without them the wheels of industry wouldn't turn. That's why FAG is proud that the skilled craftsmanship inherent in all its products can trace its ancestry as far back as 1852 when Phillip Moritz Fischer invented the world's first pedal bicycle and his son Friedrich, in 1883, founded the ball bearing industry by designing and making a revolutionary machine for automatically grinding steel balls.

The centreless grinding principles of Fischer's 'ball mill' remain even today as the basis for grinding precision steel balls to high accuracies, in large volumes.

The bearing industry founded by Fischer was successfully continued by Georg Schäfer who, in 1909, merged his own works with Fischer's. Since that time, the firm has remained under the guidance of the Schäfer family, which has transformed it into the present world enterprise known as FAG Kugelfischer Georg Schäfer KGaA with factories on four continents and 28,000 employees in fourteen plants. FAG is an abbreviation of Fischer Aktien Gesellschaft, meaning Fischer Shareholding Company. The name Kugelfischer honours the creator of the first ball mill.

FAG built its first plant outside Germany since World War II in Stratford. From this small, 32,000-square-foot plant the company has grown into its present 220,000-square-foot operation, with 660 employees, and eight sales offices and warehouses throughout Canada. With a persistent dedication to technologies improvement, and an ever broadening product line, FAG bearings keep the wheels turning on earth and into the infinite vastness of space.

FAG Stratford plant.

GEORGE HANCOCK TEXTILES LIMITED

It's only been in business since 1958 — but chances are that somewhere on your clothing you may bear a mark that came from its Cambridge, Ontario, looms.

That's because George Hancock Textiles Limited is a leading producer of woven labels, crests and specialty fabrics for the Canadian clothing industry, and its colourful "Hantex" brand labels are fast becoming a familiar standard in the U.S., U.K., and West Indies as well.

The company was incorporated in 1958 by the current president's father, but the family has been in the label business in Cambridge since 1912.

The original company, known as The Narrow Fabric Weaving & Dyeing Co., was founded by Hancock's great uncle and namesake.

Says Hancock: "He was later bought out by his younger brother, my grandfather, who after World War II sold the business to Burlington Industries. They operated it until 1958 when they closed the Cambridge mill. At that time my father purchased the label-producing equipment, one of the factories, and started George Hancock Textiles Limited."

Until 1975 it was weaving on the same equipment it used when it was founded. Then a completely new type of loom allowed it to vastly expand its production.

When George Hancock joined the firm in 1966 it was producing about 100,000 labels a day, but only weaving one type. Today, the firm produces a variety of woven products, and production has more than quintupled.

For nearly two years it has been developing techniques to manufacture specialty neckwear fabrics, and recently has begun to produce special orders for organizations, schools, clubs and companies.

George Hancock is the third generation of his family to head the expanding company, but he's not the only family member involved. His wife Nancy is secretary-treasurer.

George Hancock, president.

FAIRBANK LUMBER COMPANY LIMITED

When they rolled up the sidewalks in York Township in 1912, John T. Watson could be forgiven for being proud. After all, his firm, Fairbank Lumber and Coal Co., founded that year, supplied all the wooden planks needed for the job.

Today, John T. Watson is still remembered — there is a small park named after him in what is now the City of York — and Fairbank Lumber is still going strong. Watson's son Gordon M. Watson, has become chairman of the board. Active and fit at eighty-six, he still attends his office five days a week. The founder's grandson, John H., is secretary-treasurer.

Fairbank Lumber was founded in the distant wake of the optimism accompanying the election of Prime Minster Wilfred Laurier in 1896. All around Toronto, mothballed projects were dusted off. The Grand Trunk Railway revived plans for its Old Belt Line Railway, which would cross west Toronto to Union Station. The railroad stretched past John T. Watson's land, a 100-acre farm near what is now the Eglinton-Dufferin intersection in northwest Toronto.

Watson sold 87 of the 100 acres of his family farm to a local developer in 1909, retaining the thirteen acres that contained the home and farm buildings. (The company now owns about 3.5 acres.) In 1910 he applied to the railway for a siding.

By 1912, the immigrants who had come to take up land in that part of Toronto could purchase their coal and lumber from Watson's farm. And that year, too, Watson hired as his manager Dave Riddell, a knowledgeable lumberman. The men became partners in 1914, and formed a limited company in 1921. Both were active in community affairs in those days — Riddell served on council, and Watson was reeve of York Township in 1911-12, following five years on council.

There were five employees that first year. Today, Fairbank has ninety-two employees, a figure that rises to 100 during the busy summer season. It is also the only survivor of some fifteen family-owned lumber firms in the Toronto area during the 1930s and 40s that is still active — expanding to serve homeowners, builders and contractors.

Gordon Watson remembers that horses were kept at the stable on the family farm until 1919, when a stable was built at the yard. The firm bought its first truck that year (a flatbed Ford with solid tires), but its last horse didn't get put out to pasture until 1945.

Fairbank Lumber survived some mighty challenges — from the crushing Depression of the 1930s to two fires in adjacent companies' yards. But there were never any layoffs, not even in 1930, the only year the business lost money — a total of $500. And no needy family was ever refused coal.

Eight varieties were sold in the 1930s, ranging in price from $10.50 to $14.25 a ton. (Coal was phased out in the 40s.) It seems ridiculous now, but in 1934 Fairbank would build a client a four-room summer cottage with porch for only $295. The firm offered many other specialty services, and today it continues to cut custom mouldings and trim.

In late 1983, after nearly three quarters of a century in one place, Fairbank Lumber began construction of a second location — a combination traditional lumberyard and home-centre outlet — north of Toronto in the township of Vaughan, where it has owned a parcel of land since 1965.

"The company has always been an independent operation, and," says Watson, "always will be."

"It's been pretty tempting to join one of the big chains, and we were associated with one group of lumbermen for a while. But when they started talking about a Canadian Tire type of chain, we pulled out. They disappeared, but we're still here."

John T. Watson (1858-1945), founder of Fairbank Lumber Company Limited, and his wife Isabel, on their 50th wedding anniversary in 1941.

Gordon M. Watson, son of the founder, presently controls the company. John H. Watson, the founder's grandson, secretary-treasurer of Fairbank Lumber Company Limited.

FISHER GAUGE

Like many highly successful firms, Fisher Gauge Limited started from humble beginnings. A company that today exports more than ninety percent of its production began in the basement hobby shop of its founder, William F. Fisher.

During World War II, while working for the Ottawa Car and Aircraft Company, the Massey Harris company wanted a quotation on some gauges. Not wanting to send it to Fisher himself, and not having a company name, they addressed it to Fisher Gauge Works. The name stuck.

In 1942, Mr. Fisher started working full time from his basement shop. A partnership with himself as the sole partner was established under the name Fisher Gauge Works (the company was incorporated in 1952 and the Ltd. added). Sales that first year totalled $3,894, a figure that jumped to $20,000 just two years later.

William Fisher had two brothers who would eventually join the company: Frank in 1944 (now deceased), and Chester in 1955, now chairman of the board. All three brothers learned their skills as apprentices with CGE, a toolmaking tradition started by their father, Mr. F. Fisher, who served his apprenticeship in the U.K. before coming to Canada in 1912.

It was in 1945 that Fisher Gauge received its first major design challenge. The meter department at CGE requested it to solve a crucial design problem. This resulted in the first INJECTED METAL ASSEMBLY Machine. The design was so sound that the original machine is still in use at CGE's Quebec City plant. Other meter companies followed and today every household watt hour meter in North America uses parts assembled on these machines.

With the help of this revolutionary machine, in 1957 Fisher had total sales of $179,334 and had passed the $1 million mark from its inception.

What was to become the FISHER-CAST Division began in 1958 with the production of small zinc alloy die castings using machines designed and built in-house. These castings are used in such diverse products as cameras, computers, telephones, switches, satellites, motors and meters.

The first FIXTURBLOK System was designed and built in 1963 for use in the gas turbine industry. Essentially, the equipment casts a block of metal around a gas turbine blade so the blade can be rigidly held at just the right angle for machining.

By 1965, as a result of these technologies, Fisher Gauge's annual sales had passed the $1 million mark, and the company had seventy-two employees.

Fisher Gauge now has four plants. The 'home' plant, known as the Ashburnham Plant, is on the east side of Peterborough. It houses engineering, sales, and financial staff, as well as tool and die-making operations. The Otonabee Plant, the second in Peterborough, and the Watertown, N.Y. plant manufacture die castings for the world market. The Trent Plant, also in Peterborough and opened in 1983 is home for the equipment division, which designs and builds the die casting machines used by the FISHER-CAST Division as well as INJECTED METAL ASSEMBLY and FIXTURBLOK systems.

Fisher places great emphasis on employee relations and working conditions. This is reflected in such things as beautifully landscaped plant sites, high quality air circulation and filtration systems, and cheery plant interiors. The employees have organized their own association which is the recognized bargaining unit. An active athletic and social club offers a wide range of activities. Many key people have graduated from the company's in-plant apprenticeship and training programs.

Fisher Gauge sees its main business as problem solving through the art of injecting molten metal to accomplish a variety of unusual tasks. Its strategy, which has evolved over the years, is to develop a high degree of expertise in a particular field and use it to produce proprietary products for sale.

This is an extraordinary company made up of ordinary people with a strong social conscience, high principles, solid business ethics and faith in the free enterprise system. As stated at the entrance to every plant, they believe "The Lord giveth wisdom, knowledge and understanding." (Prov. 2:6).

Pictured in front of FIXTURBLOK Systems being tested for customers are Jack Davies (38 years) and and Graydon Hadwin (40 years) the longest service employees in the plant and office. They are shown here behind Tod Willcox, Bill Fisher, Ches Fisher, Eric Graham and Fred Jay.

F.W. FEARMAN CO. LTD.

In 1852, the first meat packing facility in the City of Hamilton was established by F.W. Fearman, a dealer in sugar-cured hams and smoked meats.

Born in Norfolk, England, in 1825, Frederick William Fearman (the family name was originally the Dutch Huguenot 'Veerman') came to Canada at the age of eight, and settled with his family in Hamilton.

Fearman opened his first business on MacNab Street, with pork packing forming its major activity — a business that was said to be the first of its kind in Canada. A quarter-of-a-century later, in 1874, Fearman opened a new slaughter operation on Rebecca Street.

By 1906, F.W. Fearman died, and the company was taken over by Frank Dingwall Fearman. He expanded operations to serve markets as distant as Ottawa, Windsor, and Northern Ontario.

In 1920, shortly after the Fearman family ceased active participation in the enterprise, the company was incorporated under its present name.

During the Second World War, Fearman purchased Mary Miles Food Products, makers of gourmet-style canned foods. Started in 1937 by three Clark sisters living in Hamilton, the Mary Miles firm grew steadily for five years until its products were established throughout Ontario, Montreal, and as far away as London, England.

War restrictions had placed limits on desperately needed expansion, however, and the sisters were forced to sell the business as a going concern. The F.W. Fearman company purchased its assets, and hired Mary (Clark) Moore to supervise the production of the fine canned goods, all of which already had an established reputation, especially its line of chili-con-carne.

F.W. Fearman underwent two changes of ownership until 1951, when it was purchased by E.R. Gunner, the present owner. This last change of ownership marked the beginning of the company's most recent era of expansion and development — an era that has led to the company's present favourable position in the Golden Horseshoe market area, of which Hamilton and Burlington are the geographical centre.

By 1960, business had grown to the point that the old Rebecca Street location was no longer sufficient to handle it. The company had purchased a new plant site on the Appleby Line in Burlington in 1955, and by 1960, construction began on a new building. The entire operation transferred there on January 15, 1962.

The new, 130,000-square-foot plant cost $2 million to build, and was originally equipped to handle 650 cattle and 6,000 hogs each week. It occupies 12 acres of the original 170 purchased, and is located alongside the main CN line, with easy access to Highways 401, 403, and the Queen Elizabeth Way.

It was the first major meat packing plant to be built in Canada in more than 20 years, and consists of general offices, abattoir and livestock barns, processing rooms, curing and canning departments, and shipping and warehousing facilities. Subsequently, there have been two major expansions, in 1975 and 1980, increasing overall plant size to 300,000 square feet.

The company markets its fresh beef and pork, processed and canned meats throughout Ontario, and Eastern Canada. It exports to New York State, Bermuda, and Britain. Thirty refrigerated trucks make local deliveries, including an occasional rare barrel of salt pork — the kind that launched the company in 1852.

F.W. Fearman's original shop on MacNab Street, Hamilton, c. 1875.

LOYAL SHE REMAINS

GORRIE ADVERTISING SERVICES

No matter what type of retail outlet you visit in Canada, chances are you will be surrounded by promotional displays and product merchandisers designed and produced by Gorrie Advertising Services.

The company which celebrated its centennial in 1982 and began by producing gilded cigar bands is now introducing programmed silicon chips and computer graphics into its promotions, signs and displays.

When George T. Gorrie founded Gorrie Advertising in 1882, at the age of twenty-four, his first products were the florid Victorian cigar bands and cigar box labels which have since become prized collector's items. Reproducing the labels was a highly specialized technique which incorporated as many as twenty colours and required skills in artwork, stone lithography and embossing. The youthful president was well prepared. The son of a Scottish cabinet maker, Gorrie had apprenticed as a printer at the Toronto Lithographing Company before starting his own firm on Adelaide Street.

The country was in the throes of a recession, and the times did not seem auspicious for the success of the young company, yet Gorrie's firm did well. Advertising was then just beginning to come into its own, as bulk sales of food products gave way to individual, brand-name packaging. Salada Tea, for example, imported in bulk, was the first to be packed in foil with a printed, embossed label by Gorrie.

Then in 1904, disaster struck. The Great Toronto Fire, which engulfed the entire downtown business area, included Gorrie's plant in its destructive path. Temporarily discouraged, Gorrie moved to California but returned to Toronto three years later. He began again under the name George T. Gorrie ADS and besides offering his former work, he also represented a group of European firms whose specialty was 'deep embossing,' a process which resulted in attractive showcards.

George's son, Harold, shared his father's ambition and enterprise. An engineering graduate, he served in World War I, following which he turned down a position offered to him by the government and entered the business. He soon bought out his father and renamed the company Gorrie Advertising Services Limited.

With the post-war economic surge, Gorrie Advertising prospered. Even the market crash of 1929 and the Depression that followed failed to stop the company's growth. In 1934, Gorrie Advertising bought a building on Birch Avenue, which was to remain its headquarters for the next twenty years.

The beginning of self-service merchandising during the 30s increased the demand for advertising displays, and the industry responded by developing new and better materials and production methods. Displays became more elaborate and permanent in form, incorporating new techniques of illumination and motion.

Yet, what counted most in enabling the company to ride out the difficult years of the 30s was the personal dynamism of Harold Gorrie who was recognized for his ingenuity and industry leadership. Gorrie invented and patented a new kind of sign he called the Repeatograph. He had discovered that backlighting a mirror, etched with a

Left: Founder George T. Gorrie.
Right: H.T. Gorrie, son of the founder

A display card, c.1901, showing H.T. Gorrie, age four, and his sister, Beatrice, age eight.

product name or logo and positioned behind a see-through mirror produced an endlessly repeating image. The 'infinity' effect fascinated the public, and Gorrie's new signs were a great hit. In fact, they were so popular in Canada and other countries that Gorrie, unable to meet the demand, licensed the technique to other companies for production abroad.

The advent of World War II brought about an upheaval in Gorrie's operations. The company lost most of its export market and licensee agreements. Display requirements dropped with the sudden conversion of manufacturing from consumer goods to military requirements. But Harold Gorrie had become prominent in the printing industry and he was asked to serve on The Wartime Prices and Trade Board. The latter dealt with the problems of material shortages and Gorrie was responsible for seeing that the limited materials made available to the printing industry were allocated fairly.

During the war, Harold Gorrie's two sons, Bruce and George, served in the Canadian armed forces. The war crystallized their thinking about their future careers, and when they returned they entered the family business as account representatives.

The post-war period was a boom time for the advertising industry, and Gorrie's business soared. In five years the company had outgrown even its expanded premises on Birch Avenue and moved to a property on Bridgeland Avenue facing Highway 401 in North York.

In the late 50s, Harold Gorrie retired as president and became chairman of the board and financial advisor. Bruce Gorrie succeeded him as president and George became vice-president.

During the 50s and 60s, self-service marketing flourished as supermarkets replaced many small, independent stores. This development created a need for better integration of media and point-of-purchase advertising and Gorrie contributed significantly to the marketing activities of Canada's leading advertisers. Gorrie's sales personnel worked hard to persuade their clients of the importance of developing overall marketing programs that incorporated the latest point-of-purchase merchandising techniques.

Celebrating the 100th anniversary at the Granite Club. Left to right: Bob, Terry Bruce, George and John Gorrie.

With Gorrie's growing expertise in display advertising came individual recognition. In 1967, Bruce Gorrie, while president of the Canadian Point-of Purchase Advertising Institute and a director of the Packaging Association of Canada, chaired POPAI's first annual members meeting held outside the United States, at Mont Gabriel, Quebec.

During the late 60s and early 70s, a fourth generation of Gorries entered the family business: Bruce's son John, and George's sons Terry and Bob. All have now assumed managerial positions and are making today's recommendations for the future growth of the company.

In 1970, Gorrie Advertising formed a partnership with Display Corporation of Milwaukee to exchange creative ideas, engineering and production techniques. George Gorrie was made vice-president of the international division of DCI/Gorrie and for two years relocated in Europe to explore the potential of that market.

George Gorrie represented Gorrie Advertising as one of the founding members of Graphics International, a world-wide association of companies in the printing and display advertising business.

In the early 70s, under the direction of George Gorrie, the Gorrie Merchandising Aids division was incorporated, offering a complete spectrum of premiums, sales aids, awards and incentive plans.

During the last decade, Gorrie Advertising's development of the international market has been an important part of its growth. A notable achievement was the design of an integrated package and display system for Timex watches which was used in Europe, South America and the Orient.

In 1978-79, Gorrie created a special line of displays for use at self-service gas stations. Manufactured by rotational molding of polyethylene, the displays are now widely used by Canadian petroleum companies.

Currently, the company is introducing its clients to the latest in shelf-management techniques and display-oriented technology such as laser holography and silicon chip programming in motion/light displays.

Having derived its past success from initiative and innovation, Gorrie Advertising has every intention of continuing this tradition in the future.

GRANT BROWN MOTORS

Grant Brown's Canadian roots go back to the 18th century on both sides of the family. His maternal ancestor, Jacob Belfry was born off the shores of Newfoundland on the ship that was bringing his mother from England.

The automobile business also runs in the family. In 1926 his father moved his wife, four sons, and two daughters to Toronto from Oro, near Barrie. An unfortunate real estate deal had left them destitute. However, things looked up when Mr. Brown walked into St. Clair-Oakwood Motors and was immediately offered a job selling cars.

Ten years later on March 17, 1936, the day he followed his father into selling at St. Clair-Oakwood Motors, Grant Brown decided that one day he would own his own business. He enjoyed his job and was very good at it. He sold a hundred or more cars a year at a commission of five percent on each new car — and that meant $20 or more on each one. The least expensive new car, a standard coupe, cost $895.

He met and married Dorothy Freeman in 1938. Dorothy fully supported Grant's ambition to own a dealership. Grant gave her his pay cheque, which she deposited, withdrawing only the bare minimum to cover living expenses.

In 1943, Grant Brown volunteered to serve in the army and became a sergeant in the intelligence corps. Three of his brothers also served overseas. Harold saw action at Dieppe and later in Africa and Sicily. Douglas, the youngest brother, was killed in action.

Grant Brown's first business opened in 1947. Len Grant Motors was a used-car dealership operating from a service station at 1385 Danforth Avenue.

Brown had been approached on more than one occasion to open a General Motors dealership, and finally, in 1956, came the opportunity he had been waiting for. Through Harry Addison he purchased Pink Motors on Weston Road, and changed its name to Grant Brown Motors.

Grant Brown has always been an individualist. A GMAC executive once said of him: "There are three ways of doing business: the right way, the wrong way, and Grant Brown's way." His approach has benefited many organizations besides General Motors.

He has served on the boards of the Canadian National Exhibition and Ontario Place as chairman, which he describes as "the Crown jewel in Ontario's Crown." He acted as chairman for the Humber Memorial Hospital drive. For many years he has been on the boards of the Ontario Motor League and the Canadian Automobile Association, and has served as president of each. The installation of emergency telephones on the Gardiner expressway was his idea, and for some time the emergency service was run by the OML before being taken over by the provincial government.

The company has acquired a number of other businesses in the automobile sales and leasing field. Grant's brother is a minority shareholder. However, size is not particularly important to Grant Brown. "Biggest never impressed me — let's be the best!" he says.

Grant Brown, founder of Grant Brown Motors.

THE HERITAGE GROUP, INC.

The Kitchener-Waterloo area of Southwestern Ontario is a fascinating blend of the old and new. Two large modern universities offer advanced computer science programs, while just a few miles away, Mennonite families live and work the same way they've done for hundreds of years.

If there's a name people outside the area connect with Kitchener, it's that of Schneider's — the popular name for J.M. Schneider Inc., a modern efficient meat processing company that clings to the tradition of making only quality products the same way it did almost a century ago.

John Metz Schneider founded the company that bears his name, in 1890. At that time he was simply a young man looking for a means to supplement his modest income from the local button factory. With his mother's recipe, J.M. began making sausages in his basement and selling it to community households.

The business grew. Three of his four sons became leaders of it. Today, his grandson, Frederick, is chairman of the board. Beginning with confidence, a strong sense of family and fairness, and a belief that consumers will always recognize quality and value, J.M. built a company that today is one of Canada's largest producers of processed meats for the retail trade.

Situated in the heartland of Ontario's rich agricultural community, Schneider's has always been an integral part of that community, drawing on it for most of its raw materials, and for its more than 2,500 employees — many of whom are descendants of those who worked beside J.M. almost 100 years ago.

But it's become much more than just a successful meat packer. Schneider's is the flagship company within the Heritage Group Inc., today, one of Canada's largest integrated food companies.

Other members of the group include Link Services Inc., a warehousing, distribution, and management information service for all Heritage companies; F.G. Bradley Inc., a pioneer in portion-controlled meat processing for the Canadian food service industry; Natco (National Consolidated Food Brands Inc.) which specializes in new products for the grocery and dairy markets, including a complete line of cheeses; and Portage Trade Development — an export company selling selected products from its sister companies abroad.

Heritage Group companies produce more than 2,500 separate food products that are sold as close at hand as the nearest convenience store; as far away as a restaurant in Japan.

With assets in excess of $120 million, annual sales in excess of $580 million, and more than 3,800 employees throughout Canada, it's possible to say that products from the Heritage Group carry the traditions and value of the Kitchener-Waterloo area not only throughout Canada, but around the world.

Corporate symbol of The Heritage Group Inc.

John Metz Schneider, the family man whose belief in quality products led directly to the creation of the Heritage Group Inc.

HUSKY INJECTION MOLDING SYSTEMS LTD.

In 1951, a 22-year-old engineering school dropout by the name of Bob Schad emigrated to Canada from Baden Baden in the Black Forest region of West Germany. Arriving with $25 to his name and not speaking much English, an expensive cab ride and a night's stay at the Royal York Hotel left him borrowing bus fare to get to his toolmaker's job.

While working fulltime during the day, the young entrepreneur sold pots and pans in the evenings to improve his English. In what was left of his spare time he designed an industrial, cargo-style snowmobile to be known as the Huskymobile.

In 1952 he quit his job and, with several partners, formed Husky Manufacturing and Tool Works.

Operating from a small garage in Willowdale, the company was to build and market the Huskymobile. As the product developed, Schad would personally test-run the strange-looking vehicle, driving it up and down Yonge Street, stopping traffic and turning heads as he went.

The snowmobile venture failed — a product ten years ahead of its time. But Schad assumed sole ownership of the company and turned to custom design and precision manufacturing. Husky received its first order for a mold for manufacturing plastic parts, and soon, capitalizing on the rapid growth of the plastics industry, the company was specializing in molds.

In 1959, sensing a further market opportunity, Husky became the Canadian agent for a line of European injection molding machines. Machines then were incapable of meeting the high-speed cycles required by molds developed by Husky for thin-walled plastic containers that had to compete against paper. Realizing the opportunity to penetrate the established injection molding machinery market, Schad developed and built in 1961 a high-speed injection molding machine to produce vending cups. It was faster than anything available, and became the basis for the company's growth.

Through the 1960s, Husky concentrated on the development of high-speed automatic equipment to produce the thin-walled plastic containers. By 1969, the Husky System had been extended to include not only molds and injection molding machines, but also automated machinery for counting, sorting, stacking and preparing plastic products for packaging with minimum labour.

During the same period, Husky developed the technology that would replace the mold-maker's craft with modern manufacturing methods. This required the development of a wide range of fully pre-engineered standard molds to fit the Husky machine, and contributed greatly to the company's subsequent success.

By this time, the company occupied six separate plants in Toronto. Still, Bob Schad managed to keep personally involved with the entire operation, walking daily from building to building to ensure that all was as it should be.

In 1969 Husky relocated to a modern new mold plant in Bolton, and in 1973 adopted the more appropriate name — Husky Injection Molding Systems Limited.

Today, Bob Schad is a fitness conscious, outdoors enthusiast who enjoys tennis, windsurfing and skiing. He spends most of his weekends on Georgian Bay, and is active in the Canadian Chapter of the World Wildlife Federation.

Schad's personal regard for quality and many of the principles in which he believes are reflected in Husky today, and are in large part responsible for the company's international reputation for excellence. His tours of the manufacturing facilities are still a daily ritual.

Husky manufactures high-technology plastics processing machinery, robotics, automated product-handling machinery and molds using the most modern manufacturing technology available in the world, including sophisticated computer-aided design and manufacturing equipment. The company employs more than 400 people world-wide, and supports hundreds of manufacturing jobs indirectly through its extensive use of subcontracting services. Bolton is home to Husky's Corporate offices, as well as its mold and machinery manufacturing divisions.

More than ninety percent of the company's sales are for export — exports of finished goods, as well as Ca-

Left: *Robert D. Schad, founder and president.*
Right: *The Huskymobile — the first single-track snowmobile ever built.*

nadian labour and ingenuity.

Husky Systems are in operation in more than thirty countries around the world. The company has subsidiaries in Los Angeles, California, Buffalo, New York, and Wiesbaden, West Germany, as well as sales agents in South America, South Africa, and Australasia.

Moreover, in an arrangement uncommon to Western countries, Husky exports technology and finished goods to Japan and Southeast Asia through Gifu-Husky — a joint venture with the Mitsui group established in 1973 to manufacture molds and to market and service Husky machines in the Far East.

Schad's strategy seems straightforward — in his own words "have the better product and the commitment." Husky's products and facilities are measured against international standards, and are second to none.

Having the better product in Husky's case means being uncompromising and meticulous when it comes to product quality. Keeping a better product in high-technology manufacturing requires a strong research and development orientation, and state-of-the-art manufacturing technology.

Having the commitment involves taking care of details. Husky adapts products to local markets.

For example, different areas have different safety regulations and electrical codes. Nameplates, brochures and manuals are in the language of the customer's country. Foreign visitors to Bolton are well taken care of and made to feel welcome. Their countries' flags are flown during their visits, and they are assigned hosts who speak their language.

Another part of Husky's export program has been its worldwide corporate identity program. Thus, the corporate image of quality and professionalism is consistently reinforced.

In 1981, the National Design Council presented Schad with the Chairman's Award for Design Management — a significant accomplishment since only two companies in the country are honoured with this award annually.

People, according to Schad, are the most important facet of any business, and maintaining a successful operation requires teamwork. This attitude is reflected in Husky's people program, which concentrates on developing skilled and motivated individuals.

Husky practices a progressive, team approach to management, encouraging promotion from within. Employees meet regularly with management to discuss and resolve various matters.

A stock-purchase and profit-sharing plan gives all employees the opportunity to share in the company's success.

At Husky, there are no time clocks, and the manufacturing facilities are bright and clean. Offices are designed to provide pleasant work areas for every individual. Each employee is free to tastefully decorate his or her own office, and may choose to designate it a no-smoking area. Employees are encouraged to further their education through a tuition rebate program, and enjoy a wide range of benefits, including a company health plan.

Now a multi-million-dollar-a-year international manufacturer of high-technology plastics-processing equipment, Husky has come a long way from the days of the Huskymobile and the Willowdale garage.

Husky's testroom equipped with ten injection molding machines. Every mold built is tested under simulated production conditions.

Husky plant at Bolton. Foreground, machinery division; background, corporate offices and mold division.

IMPERIAL FEATHER CORPORATION

Morris Mlotek and his mother came to Canada from Poland at the beginning of the 1930s and joined his father who had been here some six years working to earn the money to bring his family to their new home. This was during the Depression, and although he was going to school, Morris found part-time work at three dollars a week to help his family.

At the onset of the Second World War, Morris joined the army and served for four and a half years. On his return from overseas in 1945, he worked at his pre-war position in a clothing factory. His weekly earnings of sixty-nine dollars was a big increase from his pre-war wage of nineteen dollars.

In 1947, Morris quit his position, and with a partner, opened his feather pillow business. His venture was financed through his war re-establishment credits and the meagre savings from his previous employment. The Department of Veteran Affairs was of great assistance to him, as it was to other veterans in those early days, providing a small subsistence wage to help through the first three months. The biggest concern to a small businessman with no credit standing was the supply of wholesale raw materials, and again the D.V.A. assisted by opening accounts for him with the major suppliers. For a long time the going wasn't easy since he was buyer, manufacturer and salesman for his line of pillows, decorative cushions and baby carriage covers.

The business began on Chestnut Street, as a store front operation with only one sewing machine. This was behind what is now City Hall (The original site is now part of the Holiday Inn parking lot.)

After three years, his entrepreneurial ability and dedication resulted in greater sales and necessitated a move to larger premises on Dovercourt Road where he remained for four years before moving to Claremont Street in 1954. By this time Morris was well known in the trade and had accounts with all the major department and chain stores.

He was now in the comforter and accessory business as well as was instrumental in the introduction of the newest styles and patterns. Growth was steady and the additions of new comforter equipment eventually required taking over a second floor. At this time there were about thirty employees, although Morris was still the sole buyer and seller. With the retirement of his partner in 1967, Morris incorporated the present company and continued to aggressively expand and in 1968 he moved once more, this time to 20,000 square feet of space on Tycos Drive.

By this time Imperial was the acknowledge fashion leader in the comforter and pillow business and what is more important it had acquired a repu-

Morris Mlotek, founder and owner of Imperial Feather Corporation.
The new home of Imperial Feather Corporation on Caledonia Road, Toronto.

tation for quality, service, honesty and integrity which continues to the present day and has earned the company the highest respect from suppliers, customers and even competitors.

The 1970's and its energy consciousness, combined with a awakening of fashion awareness resulted in quite a dramatic change in the buyer habits of consumers. Thermostats were being lowered at night so warmth was necessary, but decorative value was now being considered and comforters were taking over from the old grey blanket which had served so well, for so long. This popularity of comforters with synthetic fill which provided warmth without weight was accompanied by renewal of interest in the feather and down duvet, which was so popular in Europe. This, in turn, required standards and thus drew Government attention to this area. In 1976 the Federal Department of Consumer and Corporate Affairs in Ottawa invited Morris, along with other acknowledged experts and leaders in this field, to form a Feather and Down Committee expressly to formulate acceptable standards. Morris' knowledge was of great value and his influence was a large factor in the implementation of legislation in 1980 which established the requirements for all feather and down filled products.

By 1971, the Tycos Road plant was no longer sufficient and the company moved to its present home on Calendonia Road. With 65,000 square feet at his disposal, Morris continued his expansion and eventually moved aggressively into a market which he had not previously sought to any great degree — sleeping bags. Today, Imperial is one of the major sleeping bag manufacturers in Canada and is also a supplier to leading retailers.

The present plant was enlarged in 1981 to its present 110,000 square feet and the product line was expanded at this time by the introduction of a new product to Canada — juvenile sleeping bags (called Slumber Bags) depicting licensed cartoon characters.

With the present facilities and the more recent additions of computerized quilting machines and a state-of-the-art vacuum packaging system, Imperial is maintaining its position by combining the latest in both fashion and modern technology. It is this constant search for improvement that has maintained Imperial as the country's leader in comforters, pillows and bedding accessories.

During these busy years in business, Morris found time to marry and to raise a family. In 1948 he married Helen Hacker and together they raised four children, a girl and three boys. Two boys are now Vice-Presidents in the company and perform active roles in its development; Steven, a chartered accountant, joined in 1976 and Michael, who has a Masters Degree in Business Administration, joined in 1981.

Morris' success has not affected his nature, especially his personal admiration for charitable causes. Through the company many charities have benefited from his generosity over the years and in 1983 he established the Morris Mlotek Family Foundation.

LESMITH LIMITED

Lesmith Limited was incorporated in January 1973, by Leslie M. Smith and Leo A. Ratelle, two co-workers who decided to set up their own business making quartz radio crystals.

Radio crystals? They're the critical frequency-controlling elements in communications radios. The manufacturing process for them is very exacting, and requires both precise knowledge of the crystal itself as a component, as well as the detailed requirements for the various radio models in service.

The two partners spent the first part of 1973 arranging financing for the fledgling company. Private resources raised $30,000, and the Ontario Development Corporation loaned the enterprise $50,000. The latter part of the year was spent building the first production equipment in the basement of Mr. Smith's house in Oakville. An old drill press, a South Bend lathe, and hand tools were all that were available to build it.

In late January 1974, the company moved into 3,800 square feet at 54 Shepherd Road in Oakville, and set up to produce crystals.

It shipped its first order in March – but soon a crisis arose. As the land warmed in the spring sun, the fresh north and west winds of winter were replaced by onshore breezes from Lake Ontario. This cooler air carried with it industrial pollutants that destroyed the fragile silver plating on the crystals and brought production to a halt.

In frantic haste, the process was converted to use aluminum and gold (which are unaffected by the pollutants) but a month's production was lost. The company recovered, but ended its first year with a $13,280 loss. It was close to what had been forecast, and except for that piece of bad luck the company might have reached break-even in the first year

The following year the company made a profit and has been profitable ever since.

In 1982, Mr. Smith died after a brief illness, just short of his 62nd birthday. Mr. Ratelle remains in control of the company, which presently occupies just over 6,000 square feet, and employs twenty-four people.

Lesmith ships radio crystals throughout Canada, and exports a small amount annually.

Leslie M. Smith, one of the original founders.

HOOVER CANADA INC.

"It Beats, As It Sweeps, As It Cleans." If ever an industrial slogan can be said to symbolize a 'quiet revolution' in society, this slogan of The Hoover Company, which has been part of every North American housewife's consciousness since it was coined in 1919, can be said to do so.

The advent of the Hoover, or upright vacuum cleaner, heralds the arrival of the modern age of electric labour-saving appliances. Today, a Hoover cleaner is virtually standard equipment in every North American household. Moreover, it was a woman, Susan Hoover, wife of the man whose name the company bears, who was instrumental in encouraging the revolutionary invention.

Like many inventions, it was a child of necessity. Murray Spangler, a cousin of Susan, had fallen on hard times and was forced to take a job as night janitor in an office building. Being asthmatic, he was troubled by dust which rose from the carpet everytime he tried to sweep it with the cumbersome cleaning machine assigned him.

An ingenious man, he decided to fix the machine so the dust and dirt would be swept into a pillowcase he attached to it, and in June of 1907 brought a working model of what he called his 'electric suction sweeper' to W.H. Hoover, a New Berlin, Ohio (now North Canton) leather goods manufacturer, for consideration.

For many years, Hoover cleaners were sold by door-to-door salesmen.

It was a crude machine made of tin and wood, with a broom handle and sateen dust bag, but W.H. and his son H.W. Hoover saw both an opportunity and a future in it.

In retrospect, that took unusual vision. Electricity was almost a novelty at the time and even in the cities, few homes were wired. In vast stretches of rural U.S. and Canada there was no electricity at all.

In spite of that, the Hoovers started the Electric Suction Sweeper Company in one corner of the Hoover leather-goods factory, and in 1908 began producing an improved version of the Spangler sweeper.

The company first began selling the machines through local merchants. Then H.W. Hoover himself went on the road to demonstrate and sell to potential dealers.

Hoover quickly realized, however, that this was a slow way to solve a distribution problem, and by October 1908, the company hired its first field representative to sign up dealers, and ran a national ad in the December 5, 1908, issue of *Saturday Evening Post.* This offered a 10-day free trial of the electric suction cleaner in the home, and brought inquiries from hundreds of prospective buyers. The company has never looked back.

It expanded into Canada just three years after it began operations in Canton, Ohio. The assembly plant it established in Windsor, Ontario in 1911 marked the company's first step into foreign fields, and by 1919 (the same year it adopted its famous slogan) it was breaking ground for a major new factory in Hamilton, Ontario.

This plant served Hoover well until November 1966, when the company opened a new facility for the production of its popular spin-drying washer on part of an 85-acre site at Burlington, Ontario.

Additions to the plant in 1969 more than doubled its size, and in 1972 the original Hamilton factory was closed and Burlington became the new headquarters for Hoover in Canada.

But the history of the company over the last seventy-five years is not just that of a manufacturer of home vacuum cleaners. It has become an international manufacturer and marketer of home appliances of all kinds, including irons, toasters, electric kettles and other small appliances tailored to the individual needs of dozens of countries.

The company has more than 24,000 employees throughout the world, with factories in Canada, England, Scotland, Wales, France, Australia, Mexico, Columbia and South Africa, and sales offices throughout five continents and most of the world's major cities.

It manufactures and markets in the U.S., a range of commercial floor-care appliances, and in Canada is a recognized producer of laundry appliances.

Prime export markets include the United States, the Caribbean and South America.

Housewives, though, know Hoover best for its network of carefully-trained dealers and the reliability of its products — two factors which have marked its success right from 1908.

The original Model O from 1908, and the "Concept One" from the eighties.

KILBORN ENGINEERING LTD.

After nearly twenty years of successful civil and mechanical engineering practice, in 1947 Ken Kilborn resigned as mechanical superintendent at McIntyre Porcupine Mines in Northern Ontario and embarked on the gamble of his life. He moved to Toronto and formed his own consulting business.

His first and second contracts were successful, but his third (design of a plant for a gold mine in the Cadillac area of Quebec) nearly became his undoing. When it became apparent ore reserves on the property didn't warrant a plant, Kilborn tore up the agreement for his services and the owner, to express his gratitude, offered temporary free office space at 100 Adelaide Street West.

Times were tough. The mining industry was depressed, and a move to 13 Adelaide Street didn't work out. To keep afloat, Kilborn moved his drafting offices to the basement of his Mimico home, maintaining only a small business office on Wellington Street West.

Then, in a gesture characteristic of the gambling spirit which was later to make his company one of Canada's largest engineering enterprises, Kilborn enlisted the services of Boyd Taylor to take advantage of Taylor's contacts with the provincial government. He won contracts with Ontario conservation authorities, as well as for several sewage treatment plants, including one for the Town of Weston. Taylor's brother, Hal, joined the group at this time to be responsible for field services.

By early 1950, the company won an important contract with the newly-formed Maritime Marshlands Rehabilitation Authority, which was reclaiming salt marshes along the Bay of Fundy.

Gambling again, Kilborn purchased 36 Park Lawn Road, Etobicoke and moved into a building which reflected its corporate spirit. It was a former gambling club (complete with a peephole in the door) and a gaming room which became the drafting office.

The gamble paid off. The company's fortunes improved and by early 1952 it employed thirty-five people. It won major contracts for industrial mineral, base and precious metal processing plants, for water and waste treament facilities, and for public works.

By 1954 it moved into a new building on the Etobicoke property — a building which remained its headquarters until it took possession, in 1979, of a seven-storey office overlooking Lake Ontario.

Suffering from heart trouble, Kilborn wanted to ensure his firm's continuity. Thus, in 1954, he reorganized the business into two operating companies, giving employees the opportunity to purchase shares. As a result, Kilborn Engineering today is a private, employee-owned corporation.

Ken Kilborn was stricken with a fatal heart attack in December 1959. K.M. Dewar succeeded him as president, serving until 1970 when John T. Dew was appointed.

During the 60s, Kilborn brought together a group of engineers experienced in the extraction and refining of potash, and provided engineering, procurement and construction management for a series of major potash developments in Saskatchewan. At the same time it completed several other major projects.

In the 70s, under John Dew, the current president, Kilborn initiated a program of strengthening and expanding its organization, reflecting its growing position as a major Canadian engineering firm. This program included opening offices in Vancouver, Saskatoon, Montreal, and Denver, Colorado. It also established its expertise in such process industries as oil refining, petrochemicals, and coal beneficiation and liquefaction.

By 1982, the Kilborn firm employed more than 1,500 people in eight Canadian cities as well as its Denver office, including about 900 at the head office in Toronto. Today, the firm stands as a living tribute to the spirit and diligence of a young Canadian engineer. It provides consulting, engineering, and construction management internationally.

Ken Kilborn, founder and president until his death in December 1959.

The former "gambling club" and 1950 office building of Kilborn Engineering Ltd.

LIBBEY-ST. CLAIR INC.

Wallaceburg, Ontario, the Home of Libbey-St. Clair Inc., has been producing glass since 1894, and the story behind its name of 'Glasstown' is a tribute to the industry and determination of the citizens of the town, both then and now, to succeed in the face of great difficulties.

On Wednesday, March 11, 1891, the citizens of Wallaceburg were invited to a public meeting in the Town Hall to hear a proposal for the establishment of a glass works in the town. Captain William Taylor, an English-born Great Lakes ship captain, impressed by the large sand deposits in the area, was the author of the proposal.

Wallaceburg had been a busy lumbering village, but that industry was in serious decline as the forests of the region were being depleted. Facing the loss of employment, Wallaceburg enthusiastically welcomed the establishment of the new industry. The people of the town, with their economic prosperity threatened, had little difficulty in supporting the venture with its promise of extensive and permanent employment.

Fittingly, the site chosen for the new venture was the former Patterson Saw Mill property on the banks of the Sydenham River near the Pere Marquette. The company was incorporated as the Sydenham Glass Company.

Captain Taylor returned to England to seek technical advice. Unfortunately, the samples of sand which had sparked his interest in the first place proved to have too little silica for the manufacture of glass.

Construction was halted while company officials debated the future. It must have come as a cruel blow for the financial backers. But corporate officials decided they had gone too far to back down now. The option was to locate a source of sand and continue construction. Fortunately, raw material was available in nearby Michigan.

Even with adequate sand, the venture continued to be plagued with problems. Certainly, no one in the region possessed the technical expertise required to construct the tank for the melting of glass. In fact, the design and construction of the tank proved to be a greater problem than finding suitable sand, and in the end, a highly recommended engineer was brought from Indiana to build the first one.

The fire clay for the furnace blocks was produced locally, the blocks made manually by gangs of men. Clay was formed into the required shapes and stored beside huge stoves to be thoroughly cured. As the tank was constructed, the blocks were further baked by wood fires lit at several points in the completed furnace.

On completion of the first tank, one of Wallaceburg's leading citizens climbed through an opening, and lit the fires for the first time. Several days later, to the bitter disappointment of the town, the tank collapsed.

It is a credit to the spirit of the townsfolk that they persevered in their

Top left: *Captain William Taylor, founder of the Sydenham Glass Company.*
Top right: *Glass craftsman producing glass lids for bowls.*
Bottom: *The original factory as it appeared shortly after it was built.*

The *IODE* was founded in Canada in 1900 as the Daughters of the Empire Federation during the South African war. It was to supply comfort to Canadian soldiers and to promote patriotism through service. The Queen granted her patronage to the *IODE* in 1953. The *IODE* has played a major role in citizenship, education and service, establishing the first classes in English for new Canadians, welcoming new citizens, and providing scholarships, bursaries and loans for Ontario scholars and publishing a national magazine called *Echoes.*

The John Graves Simcoe Memorial Foundation was incorporated in 1965 to honour the first Lieutenant Governor of Upper Canada. British publisher Sir Geoffrey Harmsworth, persuaded by John Graves Simcoe admirers in the early 1960s, transferred title of Wolford Chapel (the burial place of the Simcoes, in Devon, England) to the Province of Ontario. Title was accepted by the Simcoe Foundation at a ceremony held at the chapel on September 27, 1966. In addition to preservation of the chapel as an historic site, the Foundation was created to advance and disseminate knowledge of the works and life of John Graves Simcoe. In 1982 the Foundation was dissolved as an agency of the government, but its successor *John Graves Simcoe Association* was incorporated September 22, 1983 to carry out the same objectives.

The *Royal Canadian Legion* was created in 1925 from the Great War Veterans' Association and received its charter in 1926. The 'Royal' was granted by Her Majesty the Queen in 1960. The *Legion* is affiliated with the British Legion and the Commonwealth Ex-Services League. It is open to all former members of Commonwealth and allied forces, and associate membership is available to veterans' families. Organized into provincial commands and local branches, the *Legion* is active in many facets of Ontario life. It is, without question, the largest of all Loyal Societies, with more than 180,000 members in Ontario.

The *Royal Canadian Military Institute* was established in 1890 by the officers of the Toronto Garrison "to promote military art, science and literature, as well as good fellowship and *esprit de corps* among the officers of the service." In addition to providing a club for serving and retired officers, especially of the Toronto Garrison, the Institute maintains one of the most complete military libraries in North America. Not only does the *RCMI* participate in joint functions with other Loyal Societies, but its University Avenue rooms are often the scene of dinners and meetings held by those societies.

The *Royal Commonwealth Society* was established in 1868 as the Royal Colonial Society and was known as the Royal Empire Society until 1958. The Society's headquarters are in London, where residential accommodation and a library are maintained. The first Ontario branch was established in Toronto in 1950. A second branch (in Ottawa) and other Canadian branches have since been established. The Society is a Commonwealth-wide non-sectarian organization promoting the unity and welfare of the Commonwealth and holds monthly meetings.

In a province which probably has as many pipe bands as Scotland, it is not surprising that the *St. Andrew's Society of Toronto* has played a prominent role since its establishment in 1836. The Society is a charitable organization and was started originally to provide assistance to Scottish immigrants. The St. Andrew's Ball, held in conjunction with the 48th Highlanders, and other functions, provide the funds for its charitable work. Among its projects are the All Saints Community Centre and assistance to Canadian native people.

The Welsh could not fail to be represented among the Loyal Societies: The *St. David's Society of Toronto* was established in 1887 and received its charter in 1942. It is an independent organization, though in contact with other Welsh societies in the province. It exists to maintain the Welsh language and culture in Ontario and takes part in Caravan, Toronto's multicultural festival. On St. David's Day a banquet is held and a message sent to the Prince of Wales.

Any summary of Loyal Societies should mention three other groups. The *Royal Overseas League* with headquarters in London, has no branches in Ontario, but has many members who give it a presence here. It often joins in Loyal Societies' functions and is an important Commonwealth link for Ontarians. *The Heraldry Society of Canada/La Société Heraldique du Canada* is based in Ottawa with members throughout the country. It informs Canadians about correct heraldic practice. Recent years have seen a revival of interest in Ontario's military heritage and groups recreating historic units such as the *King's Royal Yorkers (KRRNY),* the *Royal Highland Emigrants,* the *78th Fraser Highlanders* and the *Queen's Rangers* (1st American Regiment) are emerging as a colourful and important part of the Loyal Societies' scene in Ontario.

The motto of Ontario is "Loyal She Began, Loyal She Remains." The Loyal Societies of Ontario have attempted to live up to that challenge by providing the framework and continuity for generation after generation of Ontarians to celebrate and demonstrate loyalty and service to their Sovereign, and the heritage left by Canadians who have gone before.

They have provided a living example of Edmund Burke's "partnership of the ages."

EARL C. MCDERMID LIMITED

Paper converters aren't usually thought of as innovative and necessary to modern business survival — when they're thought of at all, that is. But in today's high-tech environment they're as necessary as electronic technicians.

Did you ever wonder who makes the rolls of paper for your pocket calculator, or where the paper comes from that provides the receipts for your purchases from the department store or supermarket?

You'd be pardoned if you weren't sure — but the answer would be from a paper converter — and among Canadian paper converters Earl C. McDermid Limited is a force to be reckoned with.

Though only in business since 1971, the McDermid Company, because of its ability to clearly see new markets and develop new products to serve them, was instrumental in keeping a major Sault Ste. Marie paper mill in business (saving 450 jobs); developing a major export trade in paper products for computer and electonic calculating machines. The McDermid Company is currently working industriously on what it regards as a major new product that within five years, it believes, could be responsible for some twenty percent of the paper produced from Canadian mills.

McDermid, today owner of one of Canada's largest and most successful paper converters, wasn't born with a silver spoon in his mouth. Born and raised on Manitoulin Island and son of a tradesman, McDermid joined Massey Ferguson in Brantford after high school, and from a position as junior clerk worked his way up to assistant superintendent of the company's parts and shipping divison.

A bright and ambitious young man, he boldly suggested to the company that it reorganize its manufacturing and distribution system and effectively, he laughs, 'terminated my own position.'

Massey found him a new marketing position, but shortly thereafter, McDermid learned of a sales job opening up with a well established roll paper manufacturer and was invited to meet with their management.

"I was shown through the plant, and was amazed to see the potential in their product line, among it rolls for adding machines and calculators, as well as more sophisticated products.

"I remember thinking: 'I could make these products,'" says McDermid. The net result was that four years later he decided to go into his first roll paper venture and formed a partnership to undertake the manufacture of rolled paper products.

It didn't last long, however. His partner told him he felt "too old to ride on a rocket," and the business was certainly about to go into orbit. McDermid sold his interest in the company, and formed Earl C. McDermid Limited.

When he incorporated in June of 1971, he determined to engage in his own market survey before manufacturing anything. He set out to see what types of equipment were on the market — not just calculators, but business machines that required some form of paper to operate.

"To my surprise, I found that new types of computers were already on, or just entering the market, particularly in the banking and financial industries. They all used a type of paper not available in Canada, and I saw a market opportunity."

McDermid and his wife Leona both plunged into the enterprise with vigour. For the first few months the office was the recreation room of their own home in Weston. Then they did what so many entrepreneurs before them have done: they gambled heavily on the future.

They signed a lease for a large space on Weston Road without knowing if the machinery they needed would be available to manufacture the products they had decided to begin with. One needed the other, and the McDermids spent a few nervous months till everything fell into place.

That first year the business employed only three — Earl in sales, Leona in the office (and raising their family of three) and a plant manager. Earl and Leona worked without remuneration, other than for necessary expenses, until the firm's footing was financially secure. By the end of the year the business was employing fifteen, and growth prospects were excellent.

By June of 1975, the fledgling company moved to a 30,000-square-foot plant on Limestone Crescent. It also took an additional 8,000 square feet of warehouse space on Petrolia Road.

By 1980, McDermid had turned the conversion of paper into rolls for business machines and telecommunication

Earl C. McDermid, president.
Leona Krouse McDermid, secretary-treasurer.

equipment into a multi-million dollar business, and in the process introduced many 'firsts' to the Canadian market.

The company did the first professional automatic shrink-wrapping in Canada, in its industry.

It also introduced 'Autocopy,' the first Canadian-made 'self-contained carbonless' roll paper. This product allows a teletype operator to make as many as six copies (color-coded, if necessary) as required right on a telecommunications machine.

McDermid was the first Canadian company to manufacture thermal paper for computers and calculators, made only in the U.S. at the time.

More importantly, in co-operation with a U.S. mill, it produced the only existing North-American manufactured paper for facsimile machines.

The company was directly involved at its own expense in assisting the Abitibi paper mill in Sault Ste. Marie by helping it develop a new type of paper called 'Abiform' — a refined groundwood and a mix of long-fibre kraft pulp (for strength) to create a special paper for addressing the needs of a new electronic market. The resulting paper makes excellent computer forms much cheaper than traditional register bond.

"This paper has good brightness, takes ink beautifully, and enables us to manufacture a full range of roll paper at very economical prices," says McDermid.

The papermaker sold and is still selling tons of it into the U.S. Market, he says. The products his own company makes from it are called 'Electrocomp,' and are still best-sellers.

"In fact, our company has introduced new kinds of products to the Canadian market that were not even available in the U.S. — which today are extremely high volume there," he says.

"Self-contained papers are used for just about everything today. We were one of the first companies to recognize their potential."

Today, the company employs about 65 people, with sales in excess of $6 million a year, and growing. McDermid is called on as an advisor to the federal government from time to time on matters of industry, trade, and particularly on the matter of taxation and employment of young people.

The company remains in family hands with McDermid and his wife still playing a major role. Their three children, Lance, Michael, and Lori-Anne all asked to join the company on leaving school, and all are now employed there full time.

Both McDermids are quick to acknowledge the contribution received from three long-term employees. Tom Hartley, general manager, has been with the company from its early beginning. Wilf Morrison — plant manager almost as long, and Rose Pellecchia, who today heads the order department, joined when she left school ten years ago.

But McDermid believes the most exciting years of his company's expansion still lie ahead.

"We're onto a brand new product right now," he says.

In co-operation with a U.S. mill, the company has developed a new high-quality lightweight paper called ECR Ultra, which is specially for electronic cash registers and similar equipment. This unique, new, lightweight bond-quality paper can reduce the cost of paper for electronic calculating machines by twenty percent, and because it's made a new way, will also double the lifespan of the expensive special fabric ribbons used in such equipment.

But that's only the start. McDermid and his family are currently at work on the design of an ultra-lightweight paper which it believes could revolutionize paper production in Canada. He calls it Ultra II, and as far as paper is concerned it's a futuristic product. It's an airmail paper as thick as 16-pound bond, but which weighs the same as an equal-sized sheet of 10-pound tissue.

If that doesn't mean much to you, imagine being able to send an airmail letter on paper that looks and feels like ordinary bond, but which weighs only half as much. For Earl C. McDermid Limited, much of its history still remains to be written.

Top row: *Lance, Lori-Anne, and Michael McDermid.*
Bottom row: *Tom Hartley, general manager; Rose Pellecchia, order department supervisor; Wilf Morrison, plant manager.*

MISENER HOLDINGS LIMITED

The remarkable thing about this diversified holding company, whose gross revenue from operations in 1983 was more than $50 million, is that it all grew from a single vessel, and largely within the lifetime of one man — its founder Robert Scott Misener.

Misener, of United Empire Loyalist stock, was born in Brucefield, Ontario. In 1894, at the age of 14, he left his home to seek his fortune at sea. The life appealed to him and he stayed with it, becoming a first officer and marrying the daughter of his captain.

At this point he decided the time had come for him to stay ashore and settle down. With what money he had he purchased a hotel in Sault Ste. Marie, but shortly thereafter saw greater opportunities in real estate, so he sold the hotel to enter that field.

His future might well have taken a different turn had not World War I occurred. Land values collapsed, and it was clear to Misener he had better reclaim his fortune by going back to sea.

He did not, however, go back to work on one of the early timber-carrying sailing ships on which he began. This time he returned to a steam-powered vessel and within a few years he purchased his own. He named it the *Overland* — a homely old wooden-hulled steamer with a capacity of 1,000 tons, for which he had paid $25,000. The ship served him well, and two years later he was able to replace it with the *Simon Langell,* a larger, wooden-hulled vessel.

By 1919, Misener was the owner of a flourishing one-vessel steamship company, and it was from this small beginning that the company really burgeoned. He did two things that assured his company's future. First, he joined forces with a brilliant young engineer, John O. McKellar, and they became partners and lifelong friends. Then, in 1921, the pair acquired the steamer *Claremont* for $100,000, their first steel-hulled ship.

By 1928, Misener's reputation for reliability was sufficiently established to enable him to secure the financial backing of John J. Boland, of Buffalo, New York. With his assistance the partners sold the *Claremont* and purchased two new ships, constructed in England by Swan Hunter, the finest marine architects of their time. That winter, four similar ships under construction were purchased from this company.

Their business flourished even through the Depression, and during the 30s they bought three companies, bringing the Misener fleet to twenty-four vessels. During the 40s and 50s, subsequent mergers saw them expand to a fleet of thirty-four ships — all sailing under the Misener house flag.

In 1934, Misener's eldest son, Ralph, entered the business. He settled in Winnipeg where he became a vessel broker, and in 1935, opened Consolidated Shippers Limited, building a stronger bond with the important western grain trade for the Misener fleet.

By the early 50s, there were important new developments taking place among Great Lakes fleets. The small ships that used to ply the lakes were becoming antiquated because they were limited in the amount of cargo they could carry. A new line of ships called the 'supers' was developing. These were built to the maximum specifications permitted to operate through the now-sophisticated lock system of the Great Lakes. Their drawback was that they could only work the upper Great Lakes: at the time the St.

Captain Robert Scott Misener.

The ship that started Misener Transportation — the 1,000-ton wooden-hulled steamer Overland, *purchased in 1916.*

A historically-designated building, purchased and retrofitted by Misener Properties in 1979. It stands at the corner of Toronto and King streets in Toronto.

The steamer S.S. Waterton, *one of the first Misener Canallers.*

Lawrence Seaway was not yet open to vessels of such size. It was at this point, however, that Misener made the decision which was to stand him in good stead later on. He elected to change the concept of the maximum-size carrier.

Thus, when the St. Lawrence Seaway opened in 1959 to accommodate boats built to maximum specifications, the Misener line found itself in the enviable position of having almost an entire fleet of 'supers' either under construction or ready to serve the whole system. It was a competitive coup of major proportions.

In June 1963, Scott Misener died, leaving a highly organized company that he had started fifty years previously with one dilapidated old wooden steamer. He was succeeded as president by his son Ralph who had by this time left his position as head of Consolidated Shippers to head Scott Misener Steamships Limited.

At present, Misener's Great Lakes fleet consists of eight owned bulk carriers, and three managed vessels owned by Pioneer Shipping. These eleven vessels are primarily employed transporting grain for the Canadian Wheat Board, as well as for a number of other Canadian and American grain concerns; and in carrying petroleum, coke and iron ore for American and Canadian steel and aluminum companies. Also as part of this fleet are three 35,000 tonne ocean-going lakers, delivered in 1983. Their presence marked another major milestone as, for the first time ever, Misener was able to ply deep sea waters. Fixed and handled through an in-house chartering department, they traded successfully on the international front during the winter months, calling at ports in Argentina, Brazil, Cyprus, Great Britain and West Germany.

Careful forward planning and diversification have always been and remain the keys to the company's success. Today, Misener Holdings Limited, with head offices in Toronto, is a privately owned and widely diversified entity that provides management and financial resources to its various divisions and subsidiaries. These include Misener Financial Corporation, Misener Properties and Misener Shipping Limited. Misener Financial, through its Leasing, Commercial Finance and Realty Finance divisions, offers a broad spectrum of financial services to small- and medium-sized businesses throughout Ontario and British Columbia. Misener Properties owns and operates office, commercial and industrial buildings in Toronto, Montreal and other communities in Southwestern Ontario. A complete, vertically-integrated real estate holding and development company, Misener Properties offers such services as site identification and acquisition through planning and development, for both new construction and restoration, to project and construction management, marketing and lease administration.

With assets in excess of one quarter of a billion dollars, Misener Holdings Limited remains firmly in the hands of the third generation of founder Captain Scott Misener's family. His son, Ralph, is Chairman of the Board; his grandsons Scott, Paul and Peter are owners, directors and managers.

The company has never forgotten its roots, however, and believes that modern business organizations must attempt to meet an ever growing social responsibility in such areas as health services, education, medical research, cultural awareness, physical fitness and sports.

MAI CANADA, LTD.

While looking back on two centuries of growth, and the shift from a rural to an industrial society, Ontario is nevertheless at a strategic crossroad in its history again. That crossroad: the electronic revolution. Many of its pioneering companies are scarcely a decade old, yet already they have had a profound influence on our society, and chances are the pace of change will accelerate before it slows again.

One such pioneering company is MAI Canada, Ltd. Even in the computer field, which is known for its rapid growth and technological change, MAI Canada, Ltd. can only be described as a pace-setter. The company has grown hand-in-hand with the computer revolution that is exerting such a major impact on industries, the office environment, and homes. Computers have changed the way people live and work, and MAI Canada, Ltd. has been instrumental in that challenging and exciting process.

Established in 1965 as the first operation outside the United States of Management Assistance Inc., MAI Canada, Ltd. developed a reputation for reliability and quality in the purchase, leaseback and maintenance of data processing equipment.

Its first office was located on University Avenue in downtown Toronto. Seventeen employees worked from the 1,000-square-foot premises, and revenues amounted to only about $1,700 a month for its first quarter. Walter Karabin, MAI's current president, launched the Canadian operation, and remains its chief executive officer.

Within a year, however, the company had moved to a 10,000-square-foot office on Railside Road, Don Mills, and experienced rapid growth in its service contract and maintenance operations.

The company's first building was erected in 1971 on Denison Street in Markham — 35,000 square feet of space — which is currently Toronto regional headquarters.

"It was one of the first corporate buildings to go up in the area," recalls Mr. Karabin. "There was literally nothing but fields for miles around when we came."

MAI was the first of the high-technology firms to locate in Markham (itself one of the earliest-settled areas in Ontario — a magnet for pioneers since the American Revolution). Today, Markham lists high-technology companies as a major factor in its industrial development.

The move to Denison Street coincided with the introduction of the company's Basic Four® line of mini-computers. After years of research and development, MAI® began to manufacture its own product line, complimented by its full-service capability. It has built a well-deserved reputation based on product knowledge, training and complete support for its installations.

From a revenue of just over $3 million annually in 1972, MAI Canada, Ltd., reported revenue of more than $50 million in 1982. The company now employs more than 250 people in four locations throughout the Markham area.

MAI Canada, Ltd., with corporate headquarters on Amber Street in Markham, has branch operations in Vancouver, Calgary, Edmonton, Winnipeg, Toronto, Brantford, Ottawa, Montreal, Quebec City and Halifax, and with the introduction of its Basic Four micro-computer in 1971 addressed itself specifically to the needs of small businesses, an area that had been virtually ignored by other computer companies.

Based on the successful introduction of that first computer, MAI now offers a comprehensive selection of mini-computers, and has also designed and marketed a micro-computer for small business users.

MAI has been a leader in the 'information revolution,' the influence of which can be compared to that of the original industrial revolution in its lasting effects on the way people live and work.

Consider the fact, for instance, that computers did not even exist in the industrial boom created by the Second World War, yet today are being heralded as the backbone of industrial strength and growth. Industry has recognized the importance of computerization in helping it become more cost-effective, and in increasing production in a competitive world environment.

For the past twenty years, since its tentative beginnings in Ontario, MAI Canada, Ltd. has accepted its own marketing challenges and introduced computers into the work environment of thousands of Canadians. MAI does more than simply market a product — it is a vital force in the evolution of the way in which people live and work.

Proposed new MAI Canada corporate headquarters in Markham, Ontario.

MOORE CORPORATION LIMITED

In 1882, twenty-two-year-old Samuel J. Moore, general manager of the Grip Printing and Publishing Company in Toronto, began manufacturing a counter salesbook he called the 'Paragon.' This revolutionary book, which gave merchants a carbon copy of sales transactions, marked the beginning of what was to become the modern multibillion-dollar business forms industry.

Moore's deceptively simple salesbook streamlined store systems by serving several purposes 'with one writing,' fulfilling one of the principles on which the Moore worldwide business enterprise was founded.

From the beginning, Moore was ambitious and innovative. He installed the best available machinery, allowing him to compete on a national basis.

He extended his markets, first to the United States, where he set up, in Niagara Falls, the world's first plant devoted to the exclusive production of business forms.

In 1889, he assisted the Lamson Store Service Company in the founding of the Lamson Paragon Supply Company Limited in London, England, with rights to the salesbook patents and manufacturing know-how throughout Europe and Australia.

The salesbook was an immediate success, appearing at a time of spectacular expansion in business and industry. Soon, multiple-copy products were needed in manufacturing, transportation, banking and government.

Beginning with the purchase of the Kidder Press Manufacturing Company in 1889, Moore and his associates acquired nine companies over the next forty years which became known collectively as the 'Moore Group.' Operating virtually independently, these firms produced salesbooks, business forms, printing machinery and packaging, expanding Moore's capabilities to related areas. In 1929 these companies were united to form Moore Corporation Limited, whose net income in its first year as a public company exceeded $1 million.

During these formative years, Moore companies introduced a stream of new products and technical advancements, including zigzag-folded, flat-pakit forms for use in register machines, fanfold continuous forms, and an economical one-time carbon — a major breakthrough for Moore. Web-fed lithography was another important development, allowing quality high-speed mass production.

Moore's longtime policies of hiring the best people, training them well and promoting them from within continued to pay dividends in skilful management during the 1929 stock market crash. During this period, the company's U.S. organization was divided into geographic regions, allowing companies to respond more sensitively to local needs, and providing a training ground for executives.

World War II and the growth of government produced a surge in the demand for new forms. By 1945, sales of business forms other than salesbooks accounted for eighty percent of production.

The post-war era of office automation created a new, expansive business climate in which Moore played an integral role. It introduced standardized forms designed to cut costs by covering as wide a spectrum of applications as possible. Moore also instituted policies of decentralization and specialization — locating plants that produced standardized, single-product lines in small, strategically located communities — thus successfully extending service and efficiency.

In 1977, the British-based Lamson Industries merged with Moore, the ultimate step in an association begun with the introduction of the Paragon Counter Check Book to British merchants in the 1880s. From the beginning an international company, Moore has become a multinational corporation, expanding its network into thirty-eight countries, with annual sales now close to $2 billion.

The information age promises to be Moore's era of greatest expansion. The computer has made the business forms industry one of the fastest growing in North America. Moore researchers are developing a steady flow of new products and services designed to facilitate the recording, communication, retention and retrieval of computer-based information.

Moore's basic business continues to be the sale and manufacture of business forms as a medium for recording and distributing information. Technological change continues to broaden the opportunities for growth in all areas related to information processing.

Founder Samuel J. Moore, 1859-1948.

MORTON-PARKER LTD.

When E. Morton Parker, a designer and manufacturer of silverware in Trenton, Ontario, welcomed his son back from active service in 1945, they decided it was time to forge a partnership and strike out on their own. They called their new company Morton-Parker Ltd., displaying with the insertion of the hyphen a creative approach to business that would be characteristic of their future style.

Parker had begun his career in London, England, working for the silverware firm of Pringle & Sons. When he emigrated to Canada, he took a job in Trenton with Benedict-Proctor Ltd., then one of the eight companies in the country manufacturing silverplated hollow-ware. He had eventually become the company's general manager.

In the beginning, Parker and his son, E. Morton Jr., operated their new business from the family's kitchen, waiting until they could move into permanent headquarters at 99 Dufferin Street. They began production of silverware in December 1945.

The Parkers' original plan was to concentrate their energies on the export market, a direction that at first proved quite successful. But in the 50s, a revitalized European economy pushed too many competitors into that area, and the company turned its attention to the domestic market, slowly building its sales to retail stores.

Then, in the mid-60s, Morton-Parker ventured into a new area that would ultimately make the company's name in the industry: manufacturing hollow-ware for hotels and restaurants. The company's entrée into that market was made when E. Morton Sr. put in a bid for the silverware contract for Toronto's Lord Simcoe Hotel, then under construction. Competitors from several countries had already presented bids when Parker arranged a meeting with the hotel directors. "Gentlemen," he said when they were assembled, "you have a bid in your hands. We will supply you with the same items at ten percent less than that bid." Morton-Parker got the order.

Until that time, hotels in Canada had imported their hollow-ware from the United States and the United Kingdom. The Parkers were confident their company had the expertise to compete successfully in this field, and their faith was eminently justified. The company is now the major supplier of hotel hollow-ware in Canada, and it has also won many accounts abroad. Morton-Parker supplies not only all the major hotels in Canada, but all Four Seasons Hotels in the United States, the CP Hotel in Franklin Plaza, Philadelphia, the Princess Hotels in Bermuda and the Bahamas, as well as hotels in Saudi Arabia and Lebanon.

A perhaps apocryphal story has it that after a recent bombing in Beirut which destroyed the roof garden of a client's hotel, Morton-Parker received the following telex: "Silverware destroyed, send same as before, financing arranged, hope we live to use it."

The company's experience in plating with precious metals enabled it during the mid-60s, to move successfully into another lucrative and expanding market: the electronics industry. Morton-Parker has built a substantial business plating electronic components.

E. Morton Parker, president.

Over the years, Morton-Parker has expanded its physical plant, adding to the original building six times and leasing a second building. Staff has increased from the original two to more than 100. In 1982, the company purchased Benedict-Proctor, the company E. Morton Sr. had left years before to form his own. The staff acquired through the merger has given the company a strong base of expert craftsmen.

Tradesmen's methods and equipment have, of course, undergone vast improvement since 1945. The tools they used in the beginning now seem very primitive. But although modern tooling and equipment have enabled the company's silver workers to multiply production many times, they still consider their work a craft in which they take pride in exercising the highest standards of excellence.

Morton-Parker is still the family company its founder began 38 years ago. E. Morton Parker Jr. became president of the company when his father died, and his two sons, James and John, and a son-in-law, John Bryden, are senior executives.

Concerning the company's role in the community, the current president considers most important its record as a steady employer: in nearly four decades of business, Morton-Parker has had only a one-month layoff.

E. Morton Parker is also active in the community as a member of the Kiwanis Club, and member of the board of governors of Trinity College School in Port Hope, Ontario. He has previously served the Conservative Party as riding chairman, and is a former chairman of the Board of Education and alderman.

NEWPORT HOLDINGS LIMITED

Newport Holdings Limited began in 1956, the year William (Bill) Newport, then thirty-four, decided to go into business for himself. At that time he had eighteen years of varied work experience, the last ten years of which had been with James Stewart Ltd., a respected local manufacturer of residential central heating equipment in Woodstock.

Bill Newport's entry into the world of free enterprise was not entirely of his own choosing. After almost a century of family ownership, James Stewart Ltd. was bought by another company and it soon became apparent that Newport's future career did not lie with the new owners.

It was a time when major changes were taking place in the commercial and residential central-heating industry. Wood and coal were rapidly losing ground to oil. It was a change that particularly affected homeowners and tenants in rural and semi-rural areas. So with the furnace-conversion market booming, Bill Newport went into business and William Newport Heating Ltd. was born.

Using a converted backyard garage as his home base, and a $365 bank loan (underwritten by his father) as his operating capital, Bill Newport made his early, difficult start. Shortages of money were chronic, made more difficult by a growing family.

Nevertheless, the company prospered, and by 1964 expanded its operations into recreational marine sales and service. To accommodate and support his expansion program, Bill Newport secured the backing necessary to build and equip a modest manufacturing plant in Woodstock. To more accurately reflect his expanded operations, he changed his corporate name to Newport Heating and Marine Ltd.

The decade from 1964 to 1974 was a good one for the company. During this time of accelerated progress, various structural extensions were added to the original building, and although they permitted a tripling of the company's manufacturing capability, were soon insufficient for the demands made on them.

In 1975 it was necessary to expand once again. By now, the firm was known as Newport Custom Steel Fabricators Corp., and it was recognized as a leader in its industry.

At about this same time, the international price of crude oil began to rise steeply, and the federal governments of Canada and the United States began urging consumers to return to the use of renewable fuel for central heating purposes. It was a perfect opportunity for the company to capitalize on two complementary areas of its expertise — custom steel fabricating and heating.

Bill Newport restructured his operations. He located a new, 50,000-square-foot manufacturing plant in Eastern Canada, named it Newmac Manufacturing Inc., and began to manufacture a new type of furnace.

At the same time, he relocated his steel fabricating operation, in Woodstock. It, too, had 50,000 square feet of space, and had facilities to back up the manufacturing capabilities of the Newmac operation.

To protect his interests, and to administer both these investments, Bill Newport formed a third company, William Newport Holdings Limited.

Unfortunately, the success that followed his first entry into business was not to follow on the second. The company was caught up in the economic recession that struck Canada in 1980, then battered by two more endless years of business conditions as difficult as those experienced in the Great Depression. Newport was eventually forced to liquidate the custom fabrication operation in 1981.

It was a severe blow to the stability of the entire company, and a period of intense re-examination and self-evaluation (specifically designed to prevent a 'domino effect' from obliterating the whole company) followed. Difficult though it was, the strategic evaluation succeeded, and by the end of 1982 the company appeared to have weathered the worst of its losses.

It may be too early to write an epilogue to the Newport Holdings story, but Bill Newport, can be said to have the last word on it.

"To destroy a dream, you must first kill the dreamer," he says. At sixty-one years of age, Bill Newport is as durable as his Canadian heritage — and his dream remains intact.

The finished and functional Newport Custom Steel plant, Woodstock, July 1978.

O. E. INC. (OFFICE EQUIPMENT COMPANY OF CANADA)

The Office Equipment Company of Canada Limited has led a chequered career marked by steady growth since its establishment in Montreal in 1902 to sell desks, chairs, filing cabinets and safes.

It was originally established by William Hayman who was joined by Percy N. Jacobson in 1906, and ultimately federally incorporated in 1924.

That year, the company moved to a famous Montreal address — Beaver Hall Hill — at the corner of Lagauchetière Street. Two years later, the company purchased the Beaver Hall Hill site and the five-storey, red-brick building on it.

It must have been a satisfactory move, because the company remained there until the mid-1970s. Following the Second World War, John H. Lowbeer, owner of Granby Aviation Ltd. (a manufacturer of aircraft propellors, moulded airplane parts, and furniture), joined the company, and when Percy Jacobson died in 1952, assumed the post of president. A year later Granby Aviation acquired control.

Granby, today located in Toronto, has long since ceased to manufacture wooden aircraft parts, but remains Office Equipment's parent company.

In 1956 OE began to move into modern office machinery products, a role in which it is well known today. It formed a photocopy division for national distribution of the 'Lumoprint' machine — a piece of West German equipment for making blueprints.

In 1958 it formed a Philips dictating machine division, and a calculator division, the latter to handle the 'Totalia' line of calculators manufactured in Italy.

Still expanding, in 1961 it formed Office Equipment Systems Ltd. to handle all new and existing machine products. In addition to West German, Dutch, and Italian equipment, these included 'Ormig' spirit duplicators, 'Remington' and 'Olympia' typewriters, and 'Rex-Rotary' adding machines.

By 1964 it had acquired national distribution rights for 'Saxon' photocopiers, 'Cimatron' calculators and adding machines, and acquired the franchise to distribute 'Canon' electronic calculating equipment in the Province of Quebec. It also decided that a separate company for machine distribution was not a good idea, and dissolved Office Equipment Systems Ltd., bringing all distribution and sales back within the parent company.

By 1968 business had expanded so greatly the company decided to open an office in Toronto on Leslie Street, Don Mills, but confined its activities at that time to the sale of photocopying equipment and supplies.

The year 1969 was a banner year for the company. To broaden its Ontario base further, OE acquired Mitchell Houghton, an established office furniture dealer with offices in both Montreal and Toronto. It acquired the Canon franchise from Manitoba, east to the Maritimes, and it formed the Toronto calculator division, housed in the same premises at 82-84 Richmond Street as its office-furniture showrooms.

In 1972 it expanded again in Quebec, with the purchase of Gérard Poulin Inc., a Quebec City office equipment dealer. This company became known as the Gérard Poulin division of Office Equipment Company of Canada Ltd.

In 1973 it acquired Office Appliances Ltd., an Ottawa office equipment dealer, and renamed the company as the Office Appliances division. That same year it relinquished distribution for the Saxon photocopier line, but became distributor for Canon in both Ontario and Quebec.

Continued Ontario expansion led, in 1974, to the relocation of all Office Equipment's Ontario services. Its photocopy, furniture, and calculator divisions, moved into a facility under one roof on Denison Street in Markham, a suburb north of Toronto. That same

President John Lowbeer at his desk with a photo of the company's founder, Percy Jacobson.

year it sold its Lagauchetière Street premises in Montreal to Bell Canada, but leased the building back from Bell on completion of the sale.

Continued rapid growth, however, forced the company to move its head office and Montreal branch from the downtown location to new premises on Côte de Lièsse Road in the Town of Mount Royal, maintaining only a showroom downtown.

In 1978 OE acquired the Philips dictating machine franchise for Toronto from 'Facit-Addo' and established a dictating machine division in that branch.

By 1979 the company had relocated its downtown Montreal showroom to 1055 Beaver Hall Hill. That same year saw the whole Lagauchetière block demolished to make way for a new office complex to house Bell Canada and Provincial Bank employees.

The decade of the 80s saw still further growth for the dynamic company. It entered a joint venture with a group headed by Steven Dmytrow to open an office in Burlington, Ontario, to distribute photocopying equipment and supplies. It also relocated its Quebec city offices to larger premises.

By 1981 it acquired and became sole distributor in eastern Canada for the 'Silver-Reed' typewriter, made in Japan, and formed a Toronto based wholesale distribution network.

At a shareholders' meeting that year it changed its corporate name to OE Inc. That year it also entered another joint venture — this time with a local group in Sarnia, Ontario, for the distribution of office equipment and supplies. The company is known as Office Equipment of Sarnia Ltd.

Office Equipment Co. of Canada Ltd. in Markham, Ontario.

Still growing, OE Inc. has developed a 'one-stop shop' concept for office equipment and supplies, a boon to companies who have to establish themselves quickly, or who want to deal with a single supplier for all office material.

It has also involved itself in community and charitable activities wherever it locates. In Toronto, for instance, the opening of a new downtown retail store, in 1983, was marked by donating the first day's sales receipts to charity. It also compiled a portfolio of important Toronto sites, colour-copied them, and sent them to every Ontario tourism office in the world, to help sell the city as a good place to live and work.

ONTARIO HYDRO

"Power For The People" isn't the new slogan of some radical revolutionary regime. It's been the constant theme of Ontario Hydro ever since 1906 when the public utility was first established, with Adam Beck former mayor of London, Ontario, its first chairman.

In the nearly eight decades since its creation, Ontario Hydro has become one of the world's largest electric utilities. Moreover, a comparison of its rates with those of other major utilities in North America shows it has more than lived up to its public mandate.

It began far from the seats of power in Kitchener, Ontario, in 1902 when a group of 25 small businessmen and municipal representatives held a luncheon meeting at the famous Walper House Hotel to see if they could capture the force of electricity from its private owners and make it serve the common man.

"Socialism!" proclaimed its private-enterprise detractors. "Power to the People," was the reply — and indeed, on October 11, 1910, when Adam Beck pushed the button to bring electric power to Kitchener where it had all begun, bulbs in the street outside spelled out: "For The People."

By 1914 Hydro built its first generating station, and was producing its own power for 104 municipal systems.

With the Great War came an enormously increased demand for electricity, and demand for power from Niagara tripled in four years. It was then that the utility decided to build a generating station at Queenston, now known as Sir Adam Beck — Niagara GS No. 1, at the time the largest power project in the world. The first unit began producing in 1921.

In the 1930s the Depression brought a temporary halt to Hydro expansion but by 1936 Hydro was again expanding northward. Power from Niagara via long-distance transmission lines reached the mines at Copper Cliff and Red Lake, and just when the utility thought it had things neatly in order, World War II began, and again a new scramble for kilowatts began.

It didn't end when peace came in 1945, either. Hydro launched eight major hydro-electric developments in Southern, Eastern and Northern Ontario, and converted its entire system from 25 to 60-cycle power — an enormous undertaking.

By 1950, the 25th anniversary of Sir Adam's death, work had begun on Sir Adam Beck No. 2 at Queenston, and by 1954 on the St. Lawrence Power Project.

Barely two years later the utility, without major hydraulic sites to develop, was turning back to steam produced from coal, and looking ahead to the age of nuclear power. It had 65 hydro stations and two coal-fired stations — and construction was beginning on a nuclear demonstration plant at Rolphton on the Ottawa River. The nuclear age was about to begin.

Today, Hydro, now a Crown corporation, draws nearly a third of its power from nuclear generating stations at Rolphton, Douglas Point, Bruce and Pickering, another third from its thermal power stations, and the balance from hydro generation.

One of the most rapid rates of industrialization in the world has been served and facilitated and Ontario residents have been provided with electricity at very low rates compared with other provinces and the United States ... At the same time, Ontario Hydro has achieved a reputation among its peers as a world leader.

Today, things are changing again. Conservation, inflation, and higher energy prices are having an effect on consumption patterns. But the utility continues to reflect the determination of the 25 men who met in the Walper House in 1902: public power to serve the common man.

Left: Toronto Niagara Power Company crew erects poles for a 12,000-volt line in 1907.
Below: Aerial view of Pickering Nuclear Generating Station, 1983, looking east.

ONTARIO RENDERING COMPANY

We tend to think of recycling as a relatively new industrial process. In fact, it's an age-old business, and rendering one of its most basic forms. What is rendering? It's the business of reprocessing discarded animal material (fat, bones, poultry feathers, hide, offal) into highly-beneficial products for further use in other forms.

The Falco family has a background in farming, cheese-making and butchering — the latter of which supplies renderers their raw materials. Thus, when James V. Falco sold a slaughterhouse in 1947, it was natural for him and his brother, Steve, to consider investing the profits in a rendering business.

Jim and Steve went to Cornwall, where they put their money and imagination together to build a small rendering plant from salvaged wartime equipment. Their decision was a good one. The company they started, St. Lawrence Rendering, is still in operation today.

In 1951, the Falco family operation truly got under way. The four brothers, Jim, Steve, Lou, Joe, and their brother-in-law, Murray Tonello, purchased a site north of Dundas, Ontario. The plant they built there is still part of the Ontario Rendering Company (Orenco) complex. It was equipped with one hand-fired coal HRT boiler and one cooker. Restaurants, slaughterhouses, and butcher shops in the surrounding area provided bone, fat, and meat scraps, which were collected by Orenco's fleet of three trucks. Only two were actually needed to handle the routes; the third was always available to ensure uninterrupted service to suppliers.

Orenco's first major customer was Procter & Gamble, which bought fancy tallow to make soap products. Shur-Gain Feeds, a division of Canada Packers, bought meatmeal, which is used in animal feeds for its high-protein quality.

Orenco soon grew to be one of the largest independent renderers in Ontario. By the early 1980s, it had also developed a significant export market for its tallows.

The growth of the restaurant industry in the 1960s and 70s has meant that used cooking fats and oils have also become a significant source of raw materials. Today, the company has a large fleet of trucks helping many Ontario restaurateurs keep their premises clean by removing waste grease, bones, and fat. The company employs more than 100 people.

In 1958 the Falcos formed another venture, Dundas Valley Food Products Limited. They built a plant on land adjacent to the Orenco site to produce edible oils and related products, such as shortenings, salad oils, and margarine oils. The company was soon competing with industry giants such as Canada Packers, Monarch Foods, Procter & Gamble, and Lever Brothers. By the late 1970s, the company held sixteen percent of the commercial and institutional market in Ontario.

Orenco and Dundas Valley Food Products have long played a significant role in the recycling and food processing industries. In 1979, the Falcos were approached by one of their vegetable oil suppliers, CSP Foods of Saskatoon, to sell the edible oils facility. CSP, which is jointly owned by the Saskatchewan and Manitoba Wheat Pools, is a large producer of crude and refined vegetable oils. It wished to enter the Eastern Canadian market, and the Dundas Valley plant seemed ideal for its purposes. The owners felt the CSP offer was attractive, and so, in January 1980, sold Dundas Valley Food Products.

In January 1982, Canada Packers Inc., having a need for Orenco's facility, acquired the company from the Falcos. However, the company continues to operate with the same people, style and philosophy. Right from the beginning, the Falcos recognized that people were the key to success and this philosophy still holds true today and is recognized as being the 'Orenco Advantage.'

Left to right: *James V. Falco, Stephen Falco, A. Morris Tonello, Joseph Falco, Louis Falco.*

O-PEE-CHEE COMPANY LIMITED

In 1911, the first package of Gipsy Gum rolled off the assembly line at the O-Pee-Chee Gum Company, a new London, Ontario, firm that today is probably one of the largest independent, privately-owned confectionery manufacturers in Canada.

The owners were the McDermid brothers, John McKinnon and Duncan Hugh. The name they chose for their company, O-Pee-Chee, was an Indian word for robin – and, perhaps, a reference to a bit of slang then current, 'Oh! Peachy!'

The McDermids had been in the confectionery business since 1897, the year they joined the C.R. Sommerville Company, a manufacturer of boxes, popcorn, candy novelties and chewing gum. When the owner became ill later that year, they had taken over management of the company and in 1910 had purchased the box division, Somerville Paper Box Limited. The McDermids operated Sommerville until 1944, when they sold it to Garfield Weston.

In its first year of operation, the O-Pee-Chee Gum Company made a handsome profit – $1,850.90.

A decade later, O-Pee-Chee's profits had quadrupled, and its staff had increased to 30. Besides gum, the company made mints and several kinds of popcorn, the most popular of which was Krackley Nut. In 1921, the firm incorporated as O-Pee-Chee Company Limited, a public company with five shareholders and four directors, all members of the McDermid family.

As business grew, the company began exporting to Britain. By 1928 it was necessary to build a new factory mainly to supply the export trade. That plant, at 430 Adelaide Street, London, still operates today.

The company weathered the Depression by securing a licensing agreement with a Buffalo firm to manufacture, market and export a line of paraffin chewing gum and novelties. Then World War II, with its sugar rationing, dealt a further blow to gum and candy manufacturers: O-Pee-Chee survived, mainly on the strength of war contracts to supply dried egg powder to Europe. Employees of the company recall a time during the war when a boat carrying a shipment of egg powder was sunk in the St. Lawrence by a German submarine. The shipment was retrieved, sent back to London, and repacked.

The McDermid brothers died in the early 40s. At the end of the war, O-Pee-Chee reverted to private ownership, and in 1946 John Gordon McDermid, John McKinnon's son, became president and ran the company until his death in 1953.

Frank P. Leahy, who had joined the company during the 30s, became the new president. In the late 50s, he arranged licensing agreements with two firms, one in Brooklyn and one in St. Louis, to manufacture and market their products in Canada. The new arrangement dramatically increased the firm's future potential by boosting sales volume and thus allowing more efficient manufacturing and marketing of all O-Pee-Chee products. Leahy bought the company in 1961.

In the 60s two phenomena – gum-card collecting and Beatlemania – merged happily for O-Pee-Chee, which obtained the rights to make and sell Beatle Bubble Gum Cards in Canada. The product mushroomed into a long and successful line of picture-card gums, from Batman to E.T., as well as the ever-popular hockey and baseball versions.

At Leahy's death in 1980, his son-in-law, Gary E. Koreen, became president and owner of the business. Today, O-Pee-Chee is a thriving company with several plants in London housing some of the most modern gum and candy making equipment available. Thrills, Bazooka, SweeTARTS and Fun Dip are names well known to young customers throughout the country who have given the O-Pee-Chee Company cause to describe its products as "Young Canada's Favourite."

Gary Koreen, president of O-Pee-Chee Company Limited, holds an original vending machine from the 1920s.

PARK PROPERTY MANAGEMENT, INC.

Real estate ownership is not a passive affair. Investors must constantly attend their properties lest they lose value. It was this concern that drew a group of investors in the ever-growing Metropolitan Toronto area together in 1975. They suspected values might be deteriorating as a result of a short-term view that concerned itself with return on investment only, without considering the elements of aesthetics and structural integrity that are essential for long-term investment security. The advent of rent control had only increased the challenge to those who planned to remain in this important industry.

Their solution was the formation of Park Property Management, Inc., a group of highly experienced people. Initially, Park was incorporated in February 1975, to manage fourteen residential, three industrial, and four commercial properties, most of which had been acquired by investors from Europe during the 1960s. These were conservative people, with an interest in long-term investment in a politically stable environment. It's this type of client, those with a genuine interest in the future, that Park prefers to serve.

The early days were hectic. Park's offices on Martin Grove Road in Rexdale, buzzed with activity as company philosophies were being established. Training programs were set up; a communication network was established; a quality control system introduced. A Central Maintenance Department was established to provide the buildings with services not readily available, and a public relations program quickly established quality relationships with suppliers of goods and services, enabling Park to work with expert tradespeople in an environment of mutual comfort and trust.

Park Property acquired an additional 2,142 units, more than doubling its initial responsibilities of 1,137 units, and by 1984, various additional transactions saw more than 5,700 apartments in their residential portfolio.

The key to Park's organizational structure is the on-site property manager. Each manager is responsible for several buildings. The staff in each building includes a superintendent (usually a husband-and-wife team) and other support people. Most larger complexes have a person on staff to deal with minor mechanical matters. Other staff members are concerned with security, housekeeping and building maintenance. Specialized areas, such as recreational facilities, including swimming pools and tennis courts, are managed and maintained by specialists on a contract basis.

Building superintendents attend monthly seminars, where topics such as housekeeping, public relations, mechanical and electrical maintenance are discussed, and this operating structure has been adapted to suit Park Property's industrial and commercial portfolio as well.

Flexibility is a key word at Park. The company always tries to make the best use of each employee's capabilities, whether they fit the standard job description or not. Park has also been quick to take advantage of modern technology. For example, data processing techniques have fostered the efficient use of energy, and heating and ventilating equipment has been computer controlled since 1981.

Park also offers a complete financial package of management services including budgeting, accounting, cash management and computerized reporting.

The company's growth has been selective and carefully planned. It relies solely on referrals and word-of-mouth recommendations consistent with their management philosophy. As summarized by President Herb Lavine: "We manage them as though we own them."

Modern, well-maintained apartment buildings purchased in 1979 provide desirable accommodation.

PARR'S PRINT & LITHO LTD.

If you are a record collector, chances are your Canadian-made disc would be enclosed in a colourful dust jacket made by Parr's Print & Litho of Markham, Ontario. It's hard to believe today that only a relatively few years ago record jackets were virtually unknown — but in its 30 short years of life, Parr's has not only participated, but also often been the leader in this burgeoning special graphic arts field.

After apprenticing at age 16 in London, Ontario, then serving with the Royal Canadian Navy overseas in World War II, Victor Parr started his company on the ground floor of 625 Yonge Street at the corner of Yonge and Isabella, right in the heart of Toronto.

That was in 1954. During those early days, Parr operated as a salesman by day and pressman by night, constantly looking for new clients and more business. He found the work alright, including the printing of back liners for record jackets at a time when jackets were either imported whole, or made in Canada from imported fronts and backs.

With his knowledge of the printing industry, he recognized an opportunity when he saw one. His business steadily expanded, as did that of the music industry which was among his best clients. By 1958 his company was incorporated.

In order to maintain a steady production flow, he formed a commercial sales department and in that same year, added senior management and production staff to guide him in setting up departments for creative art, film, camera and plate-making.

In the years preceding the company's move to Nantucket Boulevard in Scarborough (1971), the Canadian music industry experienced a sudden period of intensive growth. Album sales soared. Eight-track tapes and cassettes were becoming more popular every day — and they all needed graphics.

The move to Scarborough involved a major expansion for the company — the construction of a combination office and plant on one and one-half acres designed to house Parr's total operation, with emphasis on efficiency, productivity, and ability to expand.

In one of the many developments over the years, Victor Parr, in conjunction with a major paper manufacturer, designed a paper stock which would enable record labels to withstand the tremendous heat and pressure involved in record manufacturing. The special paper that resulted is called P.P.L.X., and Parr's maintains exclusive rights.

Within a decade business had doubled at the Scarborough site, and with future growth assured, Parr's purchased a building of 46,000 square feet on Ferrier Street in Markham, Ontario. In 1981, the business moved to this location.

Today, Parr's continues to build on its solid reputation for innovation and reliability. With its state-of-the-art equipment, it's able to supply record jackets or cassette cards and labels from film to finished product in only three days — an incredible turnaround time for any printed product.

The company has grown from a small, one-colour operation to a modern, high-speed, four-colour printing facility, with all the necessary ancillary equipment to provide complete service to all its clients. The company emphasizes computerized techniques, including estimating and typesetting, right down to computerized cutting equipment in its bindery.

Victor Parr has always believed the people he employs are the most important ingredient in his company's success. That's why the company has honoured its long-term employees at celebration dinners with ten, fifteen, and twenty-year commemorative gifts.

Community involvement is also a part of the company's policy, with sponsorship and participation in local amateur athletic sports groups and associations.

Tomorrow, with its ever-expanding technology, will require the retention of experienced hands and time-tested methods, while giving due consideration to the energy of youth and their new ideas. Parr's has a history, is part of the present, and looks to the future with confidence.

Victor W. Parr, founder of Parr's Print & Litho Ltd.

PATHEX (CANADA) LIMITED

Pathex is a Canadian company manufacturing hydraulic presses and systems for the rubber, aluminum, decorative laminate, and composite wood industries. It had its beginnings in the spring of 1952 when Hungarian immigrant Charles Kosa and his family arrived in Toronto and established a business to sell industrial machines. At this time, the company involved its founder, his wife, and a secretary whose duties included English-language instruction to her co-workers. The total sales for the first year in business amounted to a modest $23,000.

After four years of selling machines and tools, an event took place some 3,000 miles from Pathex's office that triggered a major change in its operation. The 1956 Revolution in Mr. Kosa's homeland provided a flood of highly qualified immigrants to Canada. Combining a personal desire to help his countrymen, with the opportunism of an entrepreneur, Kosa altered his company from a dealership to a machine shop. He hired tool and diemakers, and machinists to provide items for the highly competitive and growing Canadian aircraft parts industry, with the multi-million dollar fighter aircraft the Avro Arrow as a major client.

The cancellation of the Arrow project came as a blow, and marked another critical phase in the life of Pathex. The manufacture of aircraft parts had provided eighty percent of the company's business, and virtually overnight all those contracts had been cancelled. Pathex was just one of countless companies with no work for its employees.

Realizing that survival depended on separating the company from all the other idle tool and die shops, Pathex took the bold and innovative decision to manufacture complete machines.

But changing an entire company from a tool and die shop to designing and building industrial machines is a monumental task. Pathex hired designers, and geared its staff and plant for the new venture. Lack of orders during the transition period created severe financial problems for the company, but Charles Kosa did not look back. He created a proposal for the expansion of the company, including relocating the plant and office facilities to a new site in Don Mills. The bank approved the plans, and financing was made available for a new headquarters.

In 1972, the death of Pathex's founder placed the future of the company and its thirty employees in jeopardy again. Mrs. Hedvig Kosa, until now involved only in bookkeeping and finance, took up the challenge of running the entire business — against the counsel of many advisors. They needn't have worried. One of the keys to her success is paying attention to costs and obligations, while sales policies and targets are planned in detail. Every month the company measures actual results against the target. Each aspect of the company's operations is similarly monitored. Since Pathex builds heavy equipment, in particular hydraulic presses, one large project could mean $500,000. "On projects of this size there is no room for error," says Mrs. Kosa.

The history of Pathex is one of accomplishment and growth. Its aim is to manufacture the best quality equipment within the projected cost and time-frame of the contract, to the full satisfaction of its clients. The company's present facilities in Don Mills have grown from 15,000 square feet in 1959 to today's 50,000 square feet.

The expertise Pathex has acquired has allowed the company to enter world markets. Of 1982 sales, which totalled $8 million, some seventy percent involved export contracts. Pathex machinery and systems are operational in Argentina, Brazil, Denmark, England, France, Holland, India, Mexico, Nicaragua, the United States, Russia, and Venezuela.

From a dealer, to a tool and diemaker, to a machine-tool builder, to an integrated supplier of complete plants, Pathex has demonstrated the ability to respond quickly to the needs of its markets, and looks forward to continuing this successful tradition.

"Tough times never last, but tough people do," says Mrs. Kosa.

Hedvig Kosa, president of Pathex, displays a tire tread produced on one of the machines her company makes.

PAYNE METAL ENTERPRISES LTD.

Harold Payne, in his own words, is a man not easily daunted.

"I like to achieve, and my personal motto all my life has been 'achieve one goal every day,'" he says. He's walking proof of his own theory.

Payne has parlayed a basement jewellery-making enterprise into a company that now produces satellite dishes and computer parts for such high-tech giants as Xerox and IBM. He's known and respected throughout the industry as an inventive, innovative, hard-driving supplier who's not afraid to tackle tasks others think are almost impossible.

Born in Bishop's Falls, Newfoundland, Payne came to Ontario with his parents in 1923. He left school early and went to work for the Russell Motor Car Company in Toronto, which ultimately became Canadian Acme Screw and Gear.

By the time the Second World War came along, that company became involved in making automobile parts and other products important to the war effort, and Payne's talents were rapidly recognized. By the time the war ended he had been offered the position of superintendent, a job that would have made him the youngest and highest paid such officer in the company.

But Payne had other ideas. His jewellery-making hobby had captured the imagination of a friend, who saw in it the seeds of profit. His interest fired Payne's own entrepreneurial spirit, and Payne decided to turn down the promotion to go into business for himself.

Within a year the enterprise moved into a building on King and Jarvis Streets. A year later, the company relocated to still-larger quarters on Front Street, hired a staff of ten, and began producing a line of souvenirs.

By 1948 Payne's business had expanded and moved again, this time to the present site, an 800-square-foot building on Bering Avenue surrounded by acres of market garden. At that time there was only one road into the plant, and employees had to park on Islington Avenue and walk along a mud road to get to work. Extended at least five times, most recently in 1970, the factory now occupies 50,000 square feet on two and a half acres.

The souvenir line grew into a giftware line, and then into parts for office equipment. Payne's first customer for these products was IBM, a client it has retained for thirty-five years.

Never a company to stand still, Payne moved on to making parts for the undercarriages of CF-100 and CF-105 aircraft for Dowty Equipment, a sub-contractor of Avro Aircraft. This contract gave him entry into Avro Aircraft and Orenda Engines, and won the company an award of excellence for high-quality workmanship. Payne also manufactured the outer shell for the first Canadian satellite "Allouette One."

The age of telecommunications provided Payne with new markets, and an opportunity to develop new areas of expertise. The company made the parabolic dishes for the DEW Line and Pinetree Line radar early warning systems, jobs that led to a number of similar contracts. It produced all the solid dishes for the Andrew Antenna Corporation for the trans-Canada telecommunications system, six dishes for the CN Tower, and the dish for the National Research Council's satellite tracking station.

Always an inventive man, Payne devised (and his company built) a new type of metal spinning machine for parabolic reflectors that was capable of manufacturing 'dishes' up to thirty-two feet in diameter.

"We never actually made one that large," says Payne. "We would have had to cut a hole in the roof and lift it out by helicopter. We did, however, make dishes up to twenty-seven feet in diameter — the largest ever produced in North America."

The company's current efforts are toward high-tech growth industries, and is expanding into the international market. Recently it won a contract to produce a large range of office equipment components for Xerox Corporation's multinational network.

A good corporate citizen, Payne has sponsored numerous scholarships over the years at various colleges and uni-

Harold Payne, founder of Payne Metals Enterprises.

Two Newfoundlanders, Smallwood and Payne.

versities, has sponsored junior teams in various sports, and pursues various other community activities.

Harold Payne's personal interests are as diverse as those of his company's. He is well known as an antique collector, and the corporate boardroom of the company is graced by fine furniture and paintings that would not be out of place in the manorial hall of an English castle.

He is an inventor, with a number of recognized patents to his credit.

He believes in keeping fit, but he does it by dancing.

"I've been doing it all my life," he says. "I just decided that instead of setting aside space for a gym at home, I'd build a dance floor." So a dance floor he built — twenty by thirty-seven feet.

He is an ardent supporter of the Metropolitan Toronto Board of Trade, and is past chairman of the Board of Trade Club within that organization.

He is a life member of the Masonic Order, a family tradition, active in fund-raising for various charitable organizations, and involves himself in politics at the behind-the-scenes level.

Of this latter activity Payne says: "I'm known by my friends as a staunch Conservative, but I'll support a good man wherever I find him, regardless of party. I'm a Canadian first and foremost. I have a deep love of my country, and always try to do what's best for Canada in the long run."

Boardroom at Payne Metal is decorated with antiques, the result of Harold Payne's antique-collecting hobby.

This metal-spinning machine, designed and built by Payne, turned out the largest telecommunications dishes ever made in North America.

Payne Metal Enterprises plant on Bering Avenue, Islington.

SHELL CANADA LIMITED

The history of Shell Canada in this country has been one of steady and systematic development; it is a history that began in 1911 and continues today. Shell Canada is now a corporation with assets that exceed $5.2 billion; in 1983, it reported earnings of $102 million.

The Shell Company of Canada Limited, as it was known in the early days, began its operations with a bunkering plant which opened in Montreal in 1911. During the 1920s, the company began direct marketing operations, gradually establishing a network of distribution plants and dealer outlets in Eastern Canada and British Columbia.

In 1930, Eastern Canada's head office moved from Montreal to Toronto, and the following year the company's name was changed to Shell Oil Company of Canada, Limited.

The Sarnia refinery, built in 1952 by the Canadian Oil Companies, Limited, became part of Shell Canada's operations in 1963. It is located along the St. Clair River in Moore Township, south of Sarnia; that is, in the heart of 'Chemical Valley' where virtually half of Canada's petrochemical manufacturing is concentrated. The refinery manufactures a wide range of products, including feedstocks for the adjacent petrochemical manufacturing facility.

In 1952, the Trans-Northern products pipeline from Montreal to Hamilton was completed, a project in which Shell had a one-third interest. Eleven years later the refinery at Oakville, Ontario, came on stream, and the flow of Trans-Northern pipeline was reversed to move products to Kingston, in keeping with the National Oil Policy. At this time the company became Shell Canada Limited.

In 1967, the company's data processing centre was completed at Don Mills, Ontario. This was one of Canada's largest computing and data processing centres at that time.

Three years later, Shell built a Research Centre at Oakville, Ontario, a strikingly modern building that covers 70,000 square feet, and built at a cost of $3.5 million. The building allowed consolidation and expansion of research that had previously been carried out at Montreal and Sarnia.

Further developments in Ontario included a new polymer laboratory at the Oakville Research Centre in 1977; an aromatics plant expansion at Sarnia in 1978; and in 1979, completion of construction in Sarnia of world-class isopropyl alcohol and polypropylene plants.

The Sarnia refinery as it appeared in 1961, nine years after construction began.

In 1980, prompted by the widespread public interest in the development of alternative fuels, the company constructed a BioShell plant at Hearst, Ontario, to convert wood waste to fuel pellets. A second BioShell plant was built two years later at Iroquois Falls, Ontario, producing up to 100,000 metric tonnes of pellets a year — equivalent to 47 million litres of domestic fuel oil.

By 1983, a $22 million lubricants re-refinery was completed in Toronto. The plant is capable of producing nearly 25 million litres a year of high-quality base oils from used lubricating oil collected in several provinces. The re-refinery, largest of its kind in the world, not only conserves a valuable resource, but helps overcome an environmental waste disposal problem.

In the same year, major expansion of hydrocarbon solvents facilities was also completed at the Sarnia Manufacturing Centre.

The company opened Ontario's first outlet (in Toronto) for retailing compressed natural gas as an automotive fuel. Diesel, propane and other compressed natural gas outlets are being added to the retail network as markets develop for these fuels.

On the broader national scene, Shell's thrust is towards the exploration for and development of oil and gas, in both the conventional producing areas of Western Canada and the frontier area off the east coast, as well as in the creative marketing of its petroleum and petrochemical products.

By 1950, Shell had become established in Canada's petroleum refining and marketing sector after a period of rapid expansion in service stations, tank trucks, tank cars and marine terminals. During the 1950s, it participated in construction of the Trans Mountain Pipeline to carry products from Alberta oil fields to Vancouver. It also became the first Canadian oil company to manufacture chemicals from petroleum.

The 1960s was another decade of major expansion as a fully integrated oil company. Large land holdings were acquired through Western Canada, on the east coast in the vicinity of Sable Island and off the west coast. It was during this period that the company pioneered its first self-serve gasoline retail outlets.

In the 1970s, Shell moved into exploration of more remote regions of Canada; introduced non-leaded gasoline; expanded its Montreal East refinery; explored the Arctic mainland; discovered oil and gas in the Mackenzie Delta; and made further gas discoveries in Alberta. Vigorous efforts were undertaken, alone and with others, to find new sources of Canadian oil and gas.

By 1980, Shell's capital and exploration expenditures amounted to $518 million, and within two years, had reached more than $1 billion. Also in 1980 Shell Canada Chemical Company was formed as a division responsible for all chemical activities.

Reflecting its determination to be a competitive and profitable participant in the oil and petrochemicals products sector of the industry, Shell Canada, in 1984, will open its new $1.4 billion refinery and petrochemical complex at Scotford, near Edmonton. Up to 3,000 people have been employed on this project, the largest single capital expenditure in the company's history.

The company accepts responsibility to assist in the social and cultural development of Canada, contributing some $2.3 million to a variety of social, educational and cultural organizations in 1983. In Ontario, funding has been provided to many universities, including Toronto, Trent, McMaster and Waterloo. Hospitals such as the new Ontario Regional Burn Centre at the Wellesley Hospital and the cardiac unit at Toronto General Hospital have also received support.

Shell, in conjunction with The Toronto Symphony, sponsors high school concerts at Roy Thomson Hall which enable students each year to develop an appreciation of classical music.

Shell's new re-refining plant.
Research at the Oakville lab.
Shell services *the Blue Angels* at Toronto, 1961.

SOUTHAM MURRAY PRINTING

Southam Murray Printing, today the largest printer under one roof in Canada, is the result of a merger between two outstanding printing companies, each of which traces its origin to late 19th century Toronto.

At a time of great growth and expansion for the graphic arts industry in general, James Murray and Co., printers and bookbinders, opened its doors at 26-28 Front Street West in 1884. By 1893, the firm had moved to 31-33 Melinda Street, and changed its name to the Murray Printing Co.

Murray specialized in the printing of railway timetables and folders, and printing for theatres — everything from posters, to shredded paper for snow scenes on stage. James Murray was joined in the business by his son John, and on John's retirement, by brothers Douglas and Joseph. Douglas eventually became president. After his death in 1945, Joseph served as president until 1957, when his own son, John D. Murray, became president.

By 1932, Murray Printing Co. had purchased Canadian Gravure Limited, whose gravure equipment was added to Murray's existing letterpresses. The company name changed to Murray Printing and Gravure Ltd.

By 1952, Murray was printing forty percent of Eaton's catalogues, using its gravure presses. A year later it began producing them all, and took over three Eaton printing plants. Some 700 employees moved in 1954 to new facilities in Weston (at that time the most modern printing plant in Canada) to handle one of Canada's largest printing contracts.

Southam's Toronto business, meanwhile, had started in 1880 when William Southam, founder of the vast communications empire that today bears his name, purchased a printing firm and moved it into two floors of the *Toronto Mail* building.

Southam had barely got his own start by that time: in 1877 he and a partner, William Carey, had purchased the financially troubled Hamilton *Spectator*. However, he was quick to realize that a printing company could be a profitable complement to his newspaper, and for years the printing business made more money than the papers.

By 1909 the Mail Job Department, as Southam's firm was known, changed its name to the Mail Job Printing Co., and then to Southam Press Limited. The firm moved into a five-storey building on Duncan Street where, on land it bought from Upper Canada College, it built the first reinforced concrete industrial plant in Toronto — designed to accommodate its enormous presses. For years, when all the presses were running, the Duncan Street building had a noticeable sway.

In 1913 Southam secured a contract to print the colour pages of the Robert Simpson Company Limited Fall and Winter Catalogue. The following year, and until 1930 (when Simpson's started its own rotogravure plant) the entire catalogue was printed by Southam.

The company established a group insurance plan for employees in 1920, the first printing company in Canada to do so. In 1940, it established a contributory pension plan, and in 1945 a Quarter Century Club.

Murray Printing also formed a long-service group, and in keeping with the family atmosphere the president's mother served tea to shareholders prior to annual meetings.

By the time the companies finally joined forces, roughly eighty-five years after their separate foundings, their merger seemed natural. Both were family-oriented organizations that had carved niches for themselves by specializing in high-speed, long-run printing contracts — especially for department store catalogues. Both had a commitment to reinvesting a large proportion of their profits in capital expansion.

Thus, in 1961, about a third of the shares in Murray Printing were sold to the Southam Company. Three years later Southam purchased the remaining shares, enlarged the Weston plant, and in 1966 moved its operation, including its offset lithography equipment, to the Murray plant which is still home to the company's printing facility and head office. The merged companies became known as Southam Murray Printing.

James Murray established his printing company, much later to become part of Southam Murray, in Toronto in 1884.
William Southam, founder of the newspaper empire Southam Inc., took over a printing business in Toronto in 1880.

Printing has come a long way since the days of William Southam and James Murray, as reflected in the company's new high-speed, web-offset presses.

For a decade things went well. The years between 1966 and 1976 were years of great growth in the graphic arts industry. Then, in 1976, Southam Murray's largest client, the T. Eaton Co., closed the cover on an era. That year Eaton's annual catalogues, mainstay of winter reading for generations of Canadians, rolled off the presses for the last time. At a stroke, it virtually halved the company's business. Other firms might have gone under from the shock: not Southam Murray.

It took the bitter measures necessary to offset the loss of business — including halving its staff from 1,200 in halcyon days, to 600 people — took a hard look at itself, and emerged stronger than ever.

Today, the firm has a new, leaner look, designed to meet the challenges of staying at the forefront of printing technology. It remains the largest printer under one roof in Canada, with its 342,000-square-foot plant in northwest Toronto.

It still specializes its printing services, printing numerous merchandise catalogues and special-interest magazines, annual reports, newspaper flyers, and inserts. It also offers a full range of personalized printing services, including creative design, phototypesetting and composition, pre-press camera work and platemaking, as well as a complete bindery and mailing service. Most of the work is done on high-speed, web-offset presses, although Southam Murray still operates letterpress and gravure equipment.

It expects that presses of the future will mostly use web-offset technology, and since 1979 has purchased seven large high-speed web presses, the last of which cost $4.3 million for total installation.

Computer technology is also important to the modern printer and here, too, Southam Murray is adapting the new technology to traditional printing services to improve speed, efficiency and costs.

Southam Murray Printing is a division of Southam Printing Limited, one of several autonomous companies that compose the communications giant, Southam Inc. A completely unionized operation, it has traditionally enjoyed good labour relations, and is proud of its highly skilled, often long-term employees. With the crunch of 1976 now behind it, officials at Southam Murray predict the future will hold plenty of good news that's fit to print — in sufficiently long press runs, of course, to keep the new presses warm.

SUNCOR INC.

In 1919, a young salesman, John W. Fourney III, was sent to Montreal by Sun Company of Philadelphia to investigate the potential for Canadian sales and expansion. Sun U.S. had sold Sunoco lubricants to Montreal factories during World War I and prospects looked promising.

His instinct to invest in the future of Canada led Sun U.S. to open a Montreal office to sell lubricating oils and greases.

In 1923, Sun Oil Company Limited was incorporated in Canada, a Toronto branch was opened, and by 1925, the first Sunoco service station began serving the needs of Toronto drivers. Expansion in Ontario and Quebec proceeded throughout the decade, and by 1930, Sun Oil Company Limited had established its Canadian head office in Toronto. The following year it built the first company-owned Sunoco service station on the corner of Queen Street East and Berkshire Avenue in Toronto.

In 1944, spurred by the vast energy consumption during World War II, Sun U.S. drilled its first well in Amherst, Nova Scotia.

In 1949, Sun U.S. set up a Canadian production division in Calgary. The company's first successful oil well was two years later near the town of Wetaskiwin, Alberta, in 1951.

The 1950s brought a burgeoning of the company's activities. In 1953, Sun Oil Company's Sarnia refinery came on stream and the company became the majority owner of a new 320-kilometre products pipeline which linked the refinery to terminals in London, Hamilton and Toronto. It cost $5.4 million, and was completed in a record 132 days.

In 1954, the company introduced Sunoco premium gas at regular prices, and four years later, installed new custom blending motor fuel pumps at all its stations. Instead of the standard two-grade system, motorists could now choose from seven gasoline grades at a single pump.

Although Great Canadian Oil Sands was incorporated in 1953, it wasn't until the early 1960s that Sun U.S. took a financial interest in the venture. A $200 million investment led to the construction of a mining-extraction-upgrading plant just north of Fort McMurray, Alberta, the first plant in the world to tap the enormous resources of the oil sands on a commercial basis. The plant was officially opened by Alberta's Premier Manning on September 30, 1967 with a daily production capacity of approximately 7.15 km^3 (45,000) barrels a day.

Also in 1967, a $6 million gas plant and alkylation unit was added to the Sarnia refinery. Three years later the company led the industry by introducing low-lead gasoline.

During the 1970s, the company again expanded the refinery to a daily capacity of some 14 300 m^3 (90,000) barrels a day.

On August 22, 1979, the amalgamation of Great Canadian Oil Sands Limited and Sun Oil Company Limited, Toronto, took place. A new name — Suncor Inc. — was adopted. The merger made the new company one of Canada's largest petroleum companies.

In December 1981, Suncor Inc.'s major shareholder, Sun Company, Inc. of Radnor, Pennsylvania, sold twenty-five percent of Suncor's common shares to Ontario Energy Resources Ltd., a subsidiary of Ontario Energy Corporation.

In 1982, Suncor announced a total spending program of more than $700 million to: upgrade the Sarnia refinery to make it one of Canada's most flexible and efficient; add additional oil sands reserves and improve operational reliability of the oil sands plant; and develop significant new sources of oil, including an expansion of the in-situ heavy oil project and a concentrated search for conventional crude in Canada's western provinces.

Today, Suncor operates both mining and steam stimulation projects recovering hydrocarbons from the oil sands of Alberta. The company explores for, and produces, conventional crude oil and natural gas in Canada's western provinces and participates in the search for oil and gas in the frontier areas of the Arctic Islands, the Beaufort Sea, the Mackenzie Delta and Offshore Labrador. It is also assessing opportunities for coal and other minerals.

Suncor manufactures, distributes and markets transportation fuels, petrochemicals, home heating oil, heavy fuel oil, lubricants and specialty products under the Sunoco and Sunchem names. The company has about 850 service stations in Ontario and Quebec. Suncor employs about 5,200 people in Canada, with approximately 2,500 in Ontario.

An early Sunoco station in Ontario, easily recognized by its markings.

TELE-DIRECT (PUBLICATIONS) INC.

Incorporated on July 1, 1971, Tele-Direct (Publications) Inc. has built upon a strong tradition of quality and value in 'Yellow Pages' directory advertising. Although the company is young, its past thirteen years of growth are solidly based upon more than a century of experience.

It was, in fact, in June 1879, just one year after the world's first commercial telephone exchange opened in New Haven, Connecticut, that a compilation of names of what was eventually to become a household phrase appeared in the form of a 'List of Subscribers to the Toronto Telephone Despatch Limited.' This 'telephone directory' listed all of 56 entries, 39 more than Hamilton's (which also appeared in 1880, and beat the Toronto directory to the distinction of being the 'First Classified Telephone Directory in Canada') Most of the Toronto listings were business or professional names. But the directory contained listings for two Fathers of Confederation — George Brown, founder of the *Globe,* and Sir Oliver Mowat — as residential subscribers. No advertisements appeared in this four-page directory — none, that is, except for those of the printer of the directory — Bingham & Taylor. The printer decorated the cover and every page with various solicitations, such as: "We can safely assert Our Work Cannot Be Surpassed — Send for Samples." If the 'Yellow Pages' had not exactly arrived, they had been anticipated, and it wasn't long before other advertisements began to appear which heralded the beginning of classified directory advertising as an integral part of the telephone directory service.

By 1909, the directory format was altered to provide a separate classified section, along with the alphabetical section, and by 1910 the familiar yellow paper was introduced to highlight the two distinct sections. This marked the dawning of 'Yellow Pages' directory advertising in Ontario, a practice which had been started in the United States before the turn of the century.

In 1920, the Bell Telephone Company of Canada formed a directory department to address the advertising needs of the business community. The first Toronto sales office was located at 76 Adelaide Street and consisted of seven salesmen (no saleswomen) and a small management and clerical staff. When Paul Carroll started working as a salesman for 'Yellow Pages' in advertising in 1936, he worked on straight commission with a $200 draw account.

He recalls that things were strict then. Commuting trips to Oshawa and Hamilton, for instance, could not be done in one day. The salesmen were not permitted to drive home the same day: they were booked two to a room — no single occupancy allowed. Today, there are about 730 employees for the Ontario 'Yellow Pages' business operating out of six offices. About eighty percent of them are female.

Although the basic structure of the telephone directory has remained unchanged, many alterations have been made to meet the growing demands of the business and residential community. Today, the telephone directories of Ontario contain 3,724,134 white pages listings (including Thunder Bay and Ottawa/Hull, but excluding the government 'blue' pages) and 162,333 directory advertisers. Over nine billion pages are produced each year to meet the demands of Ontario's citizens. This is the equivalent of thirty white and yellow-page directories.

With the increased use of computers, 'Electronic Yellow Pages,' although not replacing the conventional book, will become a reality. Such a service offers advantages not available through traditional advertising. For instance, it allows advertisers the luxury of updating advertising text, and even graphic designs, with great frequency, thus permitting greater flexibility. Whether these changes take place tomorrow, next month, or several years from now, one thing is certain: the 'Yellow Pages' can only continue to grow more important as an indispensible guide to the goods and services available within our society.

('Yellow Pages' and 'Electronic Yellow Pages' are registered trademarks of Tele-Direct (Publications) Inc.)

T.J. Bourke, President and Chief Operating Officer, Tele-Direct (Publications) Inc.
F.E. Allen, President and Chief Executive Officer, Tele-Direct (Canada) Inc

TECK CORPORATION

Today, Teck Corporation is a Vancouver-based organization with assets in excess of $430 million, and interests in mining, oil, and natural gas. It is constantly breaking new ground in mine development, and its gold mine in the Hemlo area of Ontario, currently under construction, will be its seventh new mine brought into production in a span of ten years.

But the company bears an Ontario heritage from the day in 1912 when James A. Hughes and Sandy McIntyre staked their first claim three quarters of a mile west of Kirkland Lake. Incorporation took place the following year as The Teck-Hughes Gold Mines Ltd. In 1919, David L. Forbes was appointed managing engineer of Teck-Hughes, and astutely directed the mine's operations for the next thirty years. The initial fifty tons per day operation was increased to a high of 1,300 tons in the early 1930s. During the depression, gold mining in this area was by far the most valuable source of income for Ontario. From 1927 to 1930 the cost of production was reduced from $8.41 to $5.78 a ton without any increase in mill capacity — a world record for the lowest cost per-ounce gold output. By 1941 Teck-Hughes was in difficulty, and its production dropped that year to $3,645,000. The next ten years saw an average yearly output of only $1,250,000.

Although the closure of the mine was predicted as early as 1930, it continued to produce until 1968. 'Old Faithful,' as the mine was dubbed, during its lifetime produced gold valued at more than $105 million — more than ten times that value at current prices. The Teck-Hughes Gold Mine became the flagship for the huge and diversified Teck Corporation of today.

The success of Teck Corporation today can be traced to the genius of one man, Dr. Norman Keevil, former professor at Harvard and MIT and later, the first Canadian professor of the new field of geophysics at the University of Toronto. He left teaching in 1946 to begin his second career as a consulting geophysicist, introducing the concept of airborne magnetic surveys to geological mapping and mining exploration.

Nine years later, using the airborne magnetic survey methods he had championed, he was able to locate a number of high-grade copper orebodies on Temagami Island in Northern Ontario. The deposit was so rich he had a tombstone company polish the ore surface until it shone — a gesture that impressed potential investors in his newly-formed Temagami Mining Company. The discovery of this bonanza was even more gratifying since Dr. Keevil's geophysical research had found the extremely rich deposits on the same land previously under option to a major United States mining company, which had recently abandoned the area.

In a move that surprised the financial community in 1959, Dr. Keevil used his new financial clout to purchase the The Teck-Hughes Gold Mines, the Lamaque Mining Company and Consolidated Howey Gold Mines. By 1961, Teck-Hughes also found itself in the oil business. Gulf Oil (then BA) made a take-over bid to purchase Canadian Devonian Petroleum and was twice outbid by Teck-Hughes. Explained Dr. Keevil Jr.: "Frankly, we fully expected Gulf to go up one more time, but they didn't. We had ourselves an oil company."

In 1963, Dr. Keevil consolidated his various holdings into Teck Corporation, the same year that his son Dr. Norman Keevil, Jr., holder of a Ph.D. in geophysics came aboard as vice-president/exploration (now president and chief executive officer). Since 1932, Teck had its main office in Toronto, but it moved to Vancouver in 1972, a change reflecting the changing focus of its resource activities. Yet Teck maintains a highly visible presence in Toronto, with spectacular modern offices occupying the 70th floor of First Canadian Place which were designed by Vancouver architect, Arthur Erickson.

The Drs. Keevil and their team of associates have, in recent years, been among Canada's most active developers of new mines throughout the country — from a Newfoundland zinc mine through the Niobec niobium mine in Quebec, to the Afton and Highmont copper mines in British Columbia and a placer gold mine in the Yukon's Klondike District. In addition, Teck has under its umbrella, gold, silver, coal, molybdenum, gas and oil proper-

The Drs. Keevil with the Afton stockpile in the background.

ties, and its operations cover seven of Canada's provinces as well as the Yukon Territory.

Teck's imaginative search for new ventures is not limited to Canada. The search for minerals, working with its own airborne electro-magnetic survey system, through its subsidiary DIGHEM Ltd., is being carried out in New Zealand and Australia.

Teck's most ambitious new venture to date is the Bullmoose coking coal mine in northeastern British Columbia. Teck has signed a contract with Japanese steel producers to supply 1.7 million tons of metallurgical coal annually for fifteen years, extendible to twenty years. Bullmoose is part of a $2.5 billion mega-project involving two new mines, new rail lines, a town and port facilities.

The Bullmoose mine is a joint venture managed by Teck Corporation, with a fifty-one percent interest, Lornex Mining Corporation with a thirty-nine percent interest, and Nissho-Iwai Canada Ltd., ten percent interest.

Although the capital cost was budgeted at $312 million, the mine was recently completed, successfully, at a cost of $275 million, or $37 million under budget. Teck's share of the construction cost was financed by a consortium of Canadian, German and Japanese banks, led by the Bank of Montreal.

"I think there is a tendency for some people to think of Teck as a company that takes fairly high risks," says Dr. Keevil Jr. "But, if you look at them, they have a fairly good financial structure underpinning them."

During the last decade, because of weak metal prices and a shifting tax climate, some of the nation's mining companies simply 'pulled in their horns,' braced themselves to ride out the slump, and hoped for better times. Not so Teck Corporation. The Drs. Keevil, with their robust and bullish management team, carried on a visionary expansion programme which may be unequalled in Canadian history for a resource company its size.

In a sense, the company is coming full circle back to its gold-mining roots in Northern Ontario. The 1980s successor to the Teck-Hughes mine lies in the Hemlo district, 200 miles east of Thunder Bay, Ontario, where Teck owns a fifty-five percent interest in the promising Teck-Corona gold property. Expectations are that Hemlo will be the site of the next big gold-mining boom — and Teck Corporation will be a part of it all.

Dr. Keevil Jr. sums up Teck's philosophy: 'We're proud of what we've built, partly because we've usually managed to do the things we said we were going to do, but we're not about to rest here. The interesting thing about this business is that it's future-oriented, whether in exploration or in development, and for every mine we build we've got a team of keen geologists and engineers out there looking for the next one." Such an attitude bodes well not only for Ontario's future, but for Canada's.

Aerial view of the Bullmoose Coal Plant, with the mine in the background.
Core shack at the Teck-Corona gold project near Hemlo, Ontario.
The abandoned Teck-Hughes mine in Kirkland Lake.

WAGNER SIGNS INC.

Corporate history is often made by men who least expect to, who are often more concerned with 'doing a good job,' or 'grasping an opportunity,' or 'making the most of things' than making a record. And corporate history isn't often the stuff of epics (although it should be), and it's frequently, as Henry Ford used to say, "next door" and hard to see because it's so close.

The story of Wagner Signs Inc. is a bit like that — hard to see because it's so close to us, and because its affairs are still so much a part of our current society we haven't 'historicalized' them yet. But that's just the time to take a closer look, because nearby history has a habit of becoming 'forgotten' history if we pay it no attention, and firms like Wagner are worth remembering.

The company began at the least auspicious time possible — in the depths of the Great Depression (1936) — when it was formed by sign-painter/artist Herbert W. Wagner, who would much rather have devoted his time to the landscape painting for which he was already becoming well known.

It was a difficult time for artists, and it must have taken great courage to launch out in such a career, but Herbert W. handed his one-man Star Signs Studio (as it was then known) to son George Herbert, and went on to international fame in his chosen field.

George renamed the company Wagner Signs, and hoped that one day he could make his business as successful as that of a contemporary competitor — Cunningham Signs — a modest enough objective to anyone looking back, but at the time a major goal.

In the early days, Wagner was the proverbial 'one-man-band.' He was sign-painter, salesman, collector, office manager — everything — but his business began to grow. First he hired one sign painter, then another — all to produce hand-painted signs.

The original employees of Wagner Signs worked for $38 to $40 a week, the equivalent of .75 to .80 an hour — a sum that seems incredible now, but which represented a 'living wage' in those distant days. Wagner himself pegged his own salary at $18 a week for the first eight years he ran the business, and put any surplus back into the company to help it expand.

The Depression gave way to World War II, and still the business prospered. World War II ended, and two years later, in 1947, George Wagner learned Cunningham Signs was for sale.

He quickly made an offer, and for a total of $8,000 (a $1,000 down-payment and a promissory note for the balance) took over his rival.

It was a shrewd move at just the right time. The receivables acquired in the purchase paid for the business, allowing him to pay off his loan quickly.

And still the company grew. With the takeover of Cunningham it now operated from two locations. By 1949 it boasted a complete carpenter shop, woodworking, silk screen and spray equipment. It employed fourteen people, and was large enough to incorporate under the name of Wagner Signs Limited.

That same year several other major developments took place. The company departmentalized, spreading its work among three groups — the Commercial Sign Division, the Spray Division, and the Silk Screen Division. It also acquired the equipment to do direct labelling on glass and plastic containers for the cosmetic industry, and began the Container Decorating Division.

George H. Wagner is still active after 45 years as president

Consolidating its business under one roof, Wagner moved into a building on Weston Road, which it renovated to suit its purposes. But even this did not provide enough space for expansion.

It rented a second building, a former theatre, again in the west central Toronto area, and again began operating from two locations.

"In those days I recall having to run back and forth between the locations," says George Wagner.

"I no sooner solved a problem at one place than I would be rushing off to the other. The problems never seemed to cease. We felt the answer was again to consolidate the business, so land was purchased on Milford Avenue, off Keele Street — which in those days was a two-lane gravel road."

"I remember my friends and relatives feeling very concerned that I had moved so far from the business centre of Toronto," laughs Wagner.

"They felt that though, up to this point, I had shown good business judgement, the move to such a 'remote' area would make it impossible for my business to progress."

They had reckoned without the explosion of suburban development that turned Toronto from a small city into a sprawling megalopolis that would ultimately expand miles beyond the Milford Avenue location.

As the city grew, Wagner Signs grew with it. In 1955 the company added a carpenter shop, then in 1956, a metal shop. Larger offices became necessary, so a second floor went on in 1959. In 1963 the sign shop and shipping area were opened, and in 1964 the company started a whole new department — the Art, Creative and Engineering Division.

In January of 1973, the reorganized Wagner Signs Inc. emerged — testimony to the vastly different range of products and services the new company offers.

In the course of its growth, Wagner Signs Inc. has become one of Canada's largest and most complete national sign service, whose diversification al-

Wagner Signs plant in northwest Toronto

lows the company to service accounts from coast to coast and into the United States.

The Sign Division manufactures illuminated fluorescent and neon signs, as well as non-illuminated painted signs for various purposes.

Indeed, almost any material can be used to make a sign — aluminum, stainless steel, galvanized metal, crezon, plywood, masonite, arborite, plastic, reflective materials and tapes. They can be flat, cut-out, cast, molded — their variety is virtually endless. The company's national sign services include installation and removal, rental and maintenance, a complete art and design service, baked enamelling, and various metal products.

The Silk Screen Division specializes in printing on aluminum and metal with a baked-enamel finish, on plastic paper, card, as well as crezon, plywood and stainless steel.

The Commercial Division provides sign lettering on trucks, windows, walls and bulletin boards — even gold-leaf lettering on glass.

Signs are designed by Wagner's Art and Design Department, which provides a coloured sketch to clients to show exactly how their sign will appear. And from this rough sketch the art department can provide the production department with blueprint and construction drawings, together with patterns and finished artwork.

But it's the company's Container Decorating and Direct Labelling Division, in 16,000 square feet of space, that has taken the company into the high-technology world of the 20th century — a far cry from the one-man sign-painting studio that began in 1936 at Toronto Junction.

It has made the company Canada's largest independent container decorator. Chances are if you buy cosmetics, pharmaceuticals, automobiles, liquor or wine — somewhere along the line you're looking at a 'Wagner Sign' direct labelling application.

In a semi-automatic operation (which makes full use of 38 decorating and silk screen machines), Wagner can direct-label on glass and plastic containers. It can also ceramically spray-frost, or spray-colour glass bottles of any shape or size, then fire them in either of two of Canada's largest decorating lehrs (ovens), that fuse the inks to the containers so they become an integral part of the glass.

Building a business from a one-man shop into a corporation is usually enough work to encompass anyone's lifetime, but in the process of building his, George Wagner did not ignore the community around him.

He has been active as president of the Etobicoke Kingsway Lions Club; as deputy district governor, Lions International, District A, Zone 7; past president of The Business Club of Metropolitan Toronto; one of the founders and past president of The Canadian Sign Manufacturers Association and past president of the Sign Association of Canada; a past president of the International Sign Association; past director of the National Electric Sign Association; and chairman of the Recreational Committee for Swimming Pools in the Township of Etobicoke.

George Wagner chaired fund-raising committees of the United Way for a dozen consecutive years, and served on the Training Committee for Loaned Executives to the United Way. He is also an Honorary Big Brother for the Big Brothers of Metropolitan Toronto.

His vice-president, general manager, and close associate C. Elvin Nash, has also served the community well as a member of the Kiwanis Club of West Toronto, first as chairman of numerous committees, as a director for 10 years, and vice-president for four. He is a director of the Sign Association of Canada; has served on the board of directors of the Canadian Cosmetic, Toiletry and Fragrance Association for eight years; has acted as president of the Canadian Figure Skating Association of North York, and the Canadian Swimming Association of North York; as well as being on the advisory board of his church for many years.

Wagner Signs Inc. has a corporate history that does not yet stretch quite through a half-century — but it is still 'history in the making' — worth recording now for what it represents for the future.

THE WAR AMPUTATIONS OF CANADA

Have you lost your keys recently? Chances are they'll come back to you if you have a War Amps Key Tag. Each day at 140 Merton Street in Toronto, more than a hundred sets of keys and other items arrive in the mail. To each is attached a miniature key tag. The amputees and other disabled employees of The War Amps Key Tag Service check the numbers on the tag and refer to their records to find the owner. Soon each item is on its way home. Since the service started in 1947, The War Amps Key Tag Service has become internationally known.

Service to its members and to others has been among the aims of The War Amps since the association was formed in 1920 under the name of The Amputations' Association of The Great War. Its first president was Lt. Col. Sidney Lambert, an army padre who had lost his left leg in action in France. During his rehabilitation in Toronto's old College Street Veteran's Hospital, he conceived the idea of a national association to help solve the problems of 'all men and women who have lost a limb or limbs or complete eyesight whilst giving their services to Canada, the British Empire, and the Allies in the Great War.'

During the Second World War, new amputees began to return from the war zone. The name of the association was changed to The War Amputations of Canada, and the friendship and help of the older veterans was extended to the younger members. Today, membership in the association is still confined to those who have lost a limb or limbs or complete eyesight while serving in one of the two world wars or in Korea.

War Amps Key Tags, and since 1971, return address labels, are valuable services for all Canadians. These services are also invaluable to the disabled Canadians who have found careers in them at wage levels equal to or even greater than those in the private sector, and to the many more who have taken courses in computer technology and gained experience at the Key Tag Service's Training Centre. Without opportunities like these, disabled persons find employment extremely elusive.

The concept of 'amputees helping amputees' led to the Civilian Liaison Program. Members offer counselling and hospital visits to Canadians who have lost limbs through causes other than war, and the association provides artificial limbs (to the limit of its resources) wherever they are not provided by government or private health plans.

Information for both civilian and war amputees on ways of coping with physical disabilities, advances in prosthetic devices, research projects both in Canada and abroad, and other matters of interest is provided through the association's library of print, film, and video materials, and through the association magazine *The Fragment.*

The War Amps, today, direct two major programs to children. Child amputees face all the problems adult amputees do, but they must also deal with a completely different set related to growth, both physical and psychological. The Child Amputee (or CHAMP) Program provides special prostheses, education, and counselling to help child amputees cope with their disabilities. Former Canadian Football League all-star Karl Hilzinger acts as physical education consultant to the CHAMP program, teaching his young friends to swim, ski, ride bicycles, and even play golf.

Out of the CHAMP program came the PLAYSAFE Child Safety Program. PLAYSAFE produces school safety films featuring child amputees who recount how they lost their limbs in accidents so that other children will be aware of the dangers they face in today's environment. CHAMPs also appear on floats in nationally televised parades and visit schools and libraries to deliver the safety message firsthand.

There will come a time when the war amputees will no longer be able to run the affairs of the association. According to the constitution a new organization, The Canadian Amputees Foundation, will continue its work. For many years to come, however, The War Amps will continue to provide many valuable services to its members, to other disabled persons, and to the Canadian public.

Out of the trenches and from the battlefields of World War I and World War II came The War Amputations of Canada — still a thriving charity in Canada and Ontario, now dedicated to improving the quality of life for all amputees.

GEORGE WESTON LIMITED

In 1882, at the age of sixteen, George Weston bought two bread routes from his employer, Mr. G.H. Bowen. Shortly thereafter he started his first bakery on Sullivan Street in Toronto, and in 1897 built a new bakery at the corner of Soho and Peter Streets. This Model Bakery was considered one of the finest plants in Toronto, employing forty people and fourteen horsedrawn vans at a time when Toronto's population was only 90,000. From its inception, George Weston Limited established a Canadian tradition of quality and excellence, one which its 60,000 employees carry on today.

Many of the companies which today form the basis of George Weston Limited began in those early years. E.B. Eddy was established at Hull in 1851; Connors Bros. began in 1893 in Black's Harbour, N.B. William Neilson operated a small ice-cream plant on the site of today's modern Toronto facility, and the canning industry in British Columbia, the forerunner of B.C. Packers, began.

The company grew steadily and in 1924, following the death of his father, Garfield Weston assumed responsibility for the business. Shortly thereafter, the company offered shares to the public for the first time and continued its steady growth.

William Patterson, a Brantford biscuit and confectionery manufacturer since 1863, joined the operation. Sweet biscuits became popular under the name 'Vanilla Wafers' and the manufacture of plain and fancy biscuits became part of the company under the McCormick's and Paulin's labels. In the late 1930s, operations expanded to include Western Canada. 'Canadian Made English Quality Biscuits' received wide recognition, and carried the 'Weston' trademark into virtually every store in the country. Biscuit operations expanded into the United States, and became the cornerstone of today's U.S. biscuit operations.

The 1940s and 50s were years of great growth and development for Weston. Such familiar names as Southern Biscuit, Westfair, William Neilson, and Famous Foods of Virginia (FFV) became associated with the company. Weston also expanded into forest products (E.B. Eddy), into fisheries (B.C. Packers and Connors Bros.), and later into food distribution.

By 1960, two out of three Canadians lived in metropolitan areas. Shopping centres and plazas sprang up, and the growth of Weston's food distribution group — Loblaw Companies Limited and its subsidiaries — was immense. A period of consolidation and reorganization culminated in the mid-70s with the restructuring of the group.

George Weston.

Today, George Weston Limited is a broadly based company conducting food processing, food distribution, and resource operations in North America, with sales of more than $7 billion in 1983. The company operates in a highly decentralized manner, with corporate headquarters in Toronto, and subsidiary companies throughout Canada and the United States.

Today, with a century of success behind it, Weston's is one of Canada's major public companies, with ninety-eight percent of its shareholders Canadian residents. New ideas and technology ensure that it will continue to provide the best products at the lowest prices, and retain the market position it has built over the years.

The pulp and lumber mills in Espanola and Nairn Centre, Ontario, have been expanded and modernized. A new dairy is in operation at Halton Hills, Ontario. Other developments include the addition and upgrading of Weston's food distribution stores and warehouses, and continued emphasis by the Weston Research Centre on quality control systems, new product development and improvement — both permanent expressions of Weston's ongoing concern with quality and efficiency.

While the company has changed dramatically over the years, the elements of its success remain the same: competent, loyal employees; the quest for quality, efficiency and service to the public; and an enduring enthusiasm for the future.

The Model Bakery, 1897.

WELDO PLASTICS LIMITED

It's a long way from running a small family leather business in South Africa to becoming the 'loose-leaf binder king' of the world, but Lew Cohen of Weldo Plastics can claim that distinction.

In the late 1940s, Cohen, a recent graduate in mechanical engineering, was asked by his father to run the family's leather goods operation when the father developed eye problems and required surgery overseas.

Cohen found himself distressed at the state of the business. Since artificial leather vinyls were then just coming into general use, he proposed the firm look carefully at the new leather substitutes, seek new markets (especially in the luggage trade), and look for equipment to 'weld' plastic to permit this growth.

His father agreed, and Cohen was assigned to do the research and development work. By 1951, he was seeking equipment to weld plastic sheeting, and discovered it at the Festival of Britain. The development of high frequency heat-sealing equipment was then in its infancy, but the young entrepreneur soon had a machine installed in South Africa, and was busy experimenting with it.

Shortly after its installation, he read a report in a South African newspaper that a major government contract for plastic wallets had been let to a West German supplier. As chairman of the footwear and leather manufacturing association of South Africa he quickly sought an opportunity for South African manufacturers to bid on the contract, entered a bid himself, and with his new equipment, won.

That contract marked the birth of Weldo Plastics Limited. Cohen developed other vinyl products, but it wasn't until 1954 that he began to experiment with the product that was to make his reputation throughout the world — loose-leaf binders.

Then, most binders were made of leather, and manufactured in costly, time-consuming stages. Cohen first developed an appliqué process which enabled him to achieve vinyl coverings with a sculptured, three-dimensional effect, then applied it to loose-leaf binders. The result was an innovative product which made his company one of the leaders in the South African market, and saw it awarded the first gold medal for plastic products in 1960.

Uneasy at increasingly oppressive conditions in South Africa, Cohen emigrated, in 1961, with his wife Sonia, mother Hilda, daughters Rochelle, Vivienne and Babette, and brother Norman. His brother-in-law, Elly Gotz (married to Lew's sister, Esme), wound up the family's affairs in South Africa, then joined the Cohens in Canada later.

By 1962, Norman and Lew were in business here, but orders were slow in coming. Everyone in the Canadian stationery trade (a major market in South Africa) agreed their samples were excellent, but no orders were forthcoming. Cohen was determined, however.

In what proved a lucky gamble, he rented 7,500 square feet of factory space on Davenport Road, installed one machine, and started looking for orders.

"The place was like a football field," he laughs today. "The kids used it as a playground."

At the end of its first year the company had earned only $3,700 — not even equal to its hydro bill. Then Cohen shifted his sales tactics.

Instead of trying to break into the old-line stationery business, he went after commercial and industrial accounts on a direct basis. He convinced companies they could improve their images by using quality loose-leaf binders to advertise their products. Once companies saw his binders, they agreed. By the end of the second year, his gross was $80,000.

The company outgrew the Davenport facility, then moved to a building of its own on MacPherson Avenue. That lasted for several years, but, in 1970, Weldo bought land on Bridgeland Avenue and erected a 72,000-square-foot plant. By 1980 it was ready to move again, this time into a renovated warehouse on Oak Street.

Meanwhile, in 1968, Weldo had entered the U.S. market. It gained some good accounts, but soon ran into difficulties from U.S. customers whose unions objected to their companies selling products marked 'Made in Canada.' To overcome this, Weldo opened an assembly and finishing plant in Hornell, New York, but shortly relocated in Buffalo.

Then, in 1974, it purchased a Chicago company in an allied field which was having financial difficulties. With-

Lew Cohen and daughter Vivienne (in Lew's office).

in three months, Weldo had restructured it, introduced Weldo methods and techniques, and placed it in a break-even position.

Known in the U.S. as Durand Manufacturing Company, and selling products under the Weldo and Cardinal names, the business grew from less than $1 million sales in 1974, to $13 million in 1979. In the process, it created a very high-profile image in a highly competitive field, and received a purchase offer from a large U.S. manufacturer in the school and college trade which was looking to diversify. Weldo sold Durand to the Jostens Company in 1980.

During the decade, parallel developments had been taking place in Canada. In 1970, The Nelson Burns Company, a marketer of vinyl advertising specialties, was acquired by the wives of Lew, Norman, and Elly. Using technology available to it through Weldo, Nelson Burns began to grow rapidly. Sales quadrupled in three years.

It made another stab at selling to the stationery trade, and this time it succeeded. It formed a new division, Cardinal Products, to provide a 'package' of quality stationery products that were not only better than anything their competitors were offering, but also bore an identifiable product name.

Weldo, in fact, revolutionized the binder industry in North America by introducing first the D-ring binder, then, just when its competitors had started to copy it, the Slant D-ring binder. Both were revolutionary binder products.

The D-ring moved the ring metal from the binder spine to the back cover. It eliminated paper movement in the sheets. It wouldn't jam. It increased binder contents life, and added additional binder strength.

As demand for D-rings grew, competitors began to copy the innovation. Weldo and Cardinal were ready. Weldo had developed the Slant D-ring, which removed the page-turning problems associated with the D-ring. It also enabled customers to gain twenty-five percent more capacity in every binder, and because of its angled format allowed index tabs to be clearly visible.

Weldo, the developer of these binder innovations, went far beyond its competitors to make better products. It developed special reinforced seals for the edge of binder covers where the vinyl is heat-sealed around the backing board. It developed a new type of 'island' hinge which it originally thought would improve binder lasting quality by fifty percent.

To justify its advertising claims, the company bought a stress-tester to open and close both conventional and Cardinal binders to see which would last longest.

"I'm ashamed to say that we still don't know how long a binder with an island hinge will last," says Cohen. "The binder with the conventional hinge started to crack at 33,000 cycles. The binder with the island hinge still hadn't cracked at 900,000 cycles, when the stress tester broke down."

Today, both Weldo and Nelson Burns remain in family hands. Lew bought his brother's and brother-in-law's interests in Weldo, in 1981. His wife still owns Nelson Burns now a division of Cardinal Business Products. His daughter Rochelle, currently vice-president of corporate affairs, is being groomed as president of Cardinal.

Other family members still take a keen interest in the business, too. Says Cohen: "My mother Hilda, who was active in the business with my father since she married him, is 78 years old. She is still enthusiastic about working, and opens the factory every day."

The company has its own designers and art department, and not only makes a binder but also typesets, prints and assembles its contents, packages and mails it. It employs between 160 and 250 people on a seasonally-adjusted basis.

Says Cohen: "Today we can't claim to be the sole users of the technology (much of which we developed), but the company has dominated industry awards in its category for the past dozen years. The constant stream of awards indicates that we still 'do it better.' '

Rochelle Blaier in Weldo's showroom with some of the award-winning products.

Lew and Carl Millard in front of some of the more than forty awards presented to the company for product design and excellence.

W.C. WOOD CO. LTD.

When Wilbert Copeland (Bert) Wood was born on December 6, 1896, Ontarians, like his Grandfather John and Uncle Charles were still clearing land for farming. In fact, it was on just such a family farm that Wood spent his early years, later, again like many Ontarians, trekking to Saskatchewan where the family took up a homestead eight miles north of Davidson.

Bert was a good student, and gained a degree in agricultural engineering from the University of Saskatchewan following service in the First World War. He continued at the deparment of agricultural engineering there until he accepted a position as field research engineer with Massey-Harris in Toronto.

However, in 1930, like thousands of other Canadians, he suddenly found himself without a job and decided to strike out on his own.

The electrification of rural Ontario was in full swing at the time, which prompted Wood to design an electric feed grinder. At this time, farmers were taking their grain to the local mill, having it ground, then trucking it back to the farm to feed livestock. He had patterns and castings made and tooled, in a local machine shop. He assembled the parts on the back porch of his landlady's house, constructing his first grinder. He sold it to a local farmer in the Brampton area for $150. With this capital, Mr. Wood decided to go into business.

He rented an empty candy store on Howard Park Avenue in Toronto. It had less than 384 square feet of space. He bought a lathe, and machined his own castings for his electric grinder. His first employee was a sixteen-year-old boy whose mother brought him to the shop saying: "I will feed and house him if you will teach him a trade." From this modest beginning, the company, over the next half-century, progressed to become one of Canada's major appliance manufacturers.

By 1934, W.C. Wood Company was settled in its third location on Dundas Street north of Bloor in Toronto, in a factory of 2,500 square feet. The company now also manufactured an oat roller, and a farm milk cooler to keep milk 'sweet.' At the same time, Wood purchased a car with a large trailer as a travelling display room — the best possible way in the 30s to show farm machinery products at rural fairs.

In 1941 the company moved to Guelph, where its products now included grain grinders, oat rollers, milk coolers, farm freezers, electric fences and milking machines, all of which, after the war, were exported to the United States, South America and Europe, and later, to the Caribbean, the Middle East, and Japan.

Things weren't always easy for the fledgling company. During the early years, money was a constant problem. One morning when Mrs. Wood was looking after things (W.C. was ill with the flu), her bookkeeper reported the bank refused to honour the company's payroll. Mrs. Wood borrowed $500 from a relative, and the company kept going. Even in the early years in Guelph the company's banker, on at least one occasion, suggested the only solution to the company's problems was to declare bankrupty. They hadn't reckoned with the determination of the Woods, nor with the strength of the company's employees.

Key to the success of the W.C. Wood Company has been its people. It is a non-union company with 500 employees who have their own labour-management committee. During the 1981-82 recession, no employees with more than a year's service were laid off. To keep the staff fully employed, the company, in 1982, acquired Elec-

The family farm in Luther Township on which Bert Wood was born in 1896.
W.C. (Bert) Wood, company founder.

J.F. Wood, president and general manager.

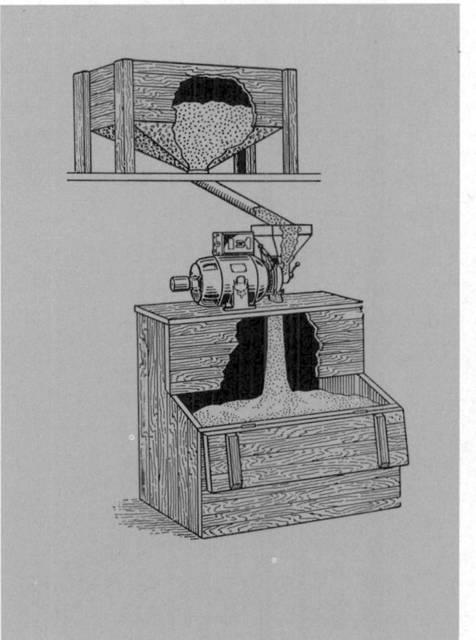

trohome's line of humidifiers, dehumidifiers and electronic air cleaners, and Miami-Carey's line of range hoods, bath cabinets and accessories.

In 1955, C.D. Howe presented the company with a National Industrial Design Council Award for its combination freezer-refrigerator for the best design in practicality, eye-appeal, and consumer acceptance. By 1977, a million freezers had rolled off the company's production lines and six years later, another million had gone into service. In 1980, the Ontario Ministry of Industry and Tourism presented the company with its 'A for Achievement' award for making an outstanding contribution to Ontario's economy.

W.C. Wood Company's success can be attributed to the goal that at the end of each year, its suppliers, customers, employees and shareholders are all better off. The company is pledged to continue to stress the importance of quality and productivity for the benefit of everyone who shares in the operation.

***Top right:** Taking W.C. Wood products to rural fairs involved this trailer display.*
***Middle left:** The W.C. Wood grain grinder — the product that started it all.*
***Middle right:** The oat roller was also an early farm appliance.*
***Bottom:** Showing the line at the Royal Winter Fair in 1932.*

ZENITH RADIO CANADA LTD.

In 1983, Zenith, a household name in consumer electronics products, marked the 25th anniversary of its Canadian division. That's not long in terms of years, but neither is the history of electronics.

Zenith got its start in Canada selling hearing aids from a small sales and distribution office it opened in Windsor in 1946. It was not until 1958, however, that the company made a major move into the Canadian market with the opening of a sales and distribution office on the Queensway, in Toronto, to distribute consumer electronics products.

By 1966 it had moved to a much larger building to accommodate the added distribution of colour and black and white television sets, radios and stereo sets.

It moved into its present premises in 1976. From this facility it still markets a wide range of consumer electronics products, but also manufactures cable-TV equipment for the Canadian cable television industry — and the company is still growing.

Zenith has entered the rapidly expanding market for microcomputers and related products, and has distributor locations in British Columbia, Ontario and Quebec.

The company's Heath Division, headquartered in Toronto, is responsible for the sale of Heathkit products, and through its mail-order business and retail stores is well known to Canadian kit-building enthusiasts.

Zenith Data Systems Division, also based in Toronto, provides sales and software support for Zenith Data Systems Corporation products sold in Canada by the company's Consumer and Data Products Division.

As an international, Chicago-based company, Zenith is truly one of the electronic era's pioneering enterprises. In its 66-year history, the company has grown from a kitchen-table workshop manned by two young radio amateurs to leadership in the manufacture of colour and black-and-white television sets, stereophonic high-fidelity systems, and in radio.

The company had its beginnings in 1918, at the end of World War I, when two youthful radio 'hams,' Karl E. Hassel and R.H. G. Mathews, set up their 'factory' on a kitchen table and began making radio equipment for other amateurs. The trademark 'Zenith,' meaning 'the highest point,' was derived from the call letters of the amateur radio station 9ZN, which Hassel operated.

In 1921, Hassel and Mathews were joined by the late Commander Eugene F. McDonald, Jr., who saw a great future in radio. In 1928, Hugh Robertson joined the company as treasurer.

The way it is — Zenith's wide-screen sets are a far cry from earlier models. The way it was — one of Zenith's early model TV sets with a round viewing screen.

Zenith Radio Corporation was first formed in 1923 as the exclusive sales and marketing organization for the Chicago Radio Laboratory, which built the radio equipment. The assets of the latter company were later acquired by Zenith, which became a manufacturer in its own name.

In that same year, Zenith persuaded a U.S. Arctic expedition led by Admiral D.B. MacMillan to take the world's first portable radio with it, and the transmissions of the expedition proved to be a landmark demonstration of the efficiency of shortwave.

Among Zenith's early electronic 'firsts' in the 1920s were the world's first portable radio (1924), the first home receiver that operated directly from regular AC electric current (1926), and automatic pushbutton tuning (1927).

The stock market crash in 1929 threw the radio industry into chaos, Zenith along with it. But the company recovered and by 1936 was doing well again. During the 30s it concentrated on the sale of smaller, low-priced receivers, and became famous for its 'big black dial' for radios. The large clock-style dial featured figures so distinct they could be read without glasses.

By the end of the decade, Zenith was pioneering in television and FM broadcasting. In 1939, Zenith's W9XZV, the first all-electronic television station in the U.S., went on the air, followed by W9XEN, the second or third FM station in the U.S.

The stereo standards for FM broadcasting, in fact, were based on the stereo FM system pioneered and developed by Zenith. (Their adoption in the U.S. by the Federal Communications Commission, with only minor modifications, ushered in a new era in the enjoyment of FM radio listening.)

Using its electronic know-how in another field, Zenith also produced the first low-cost hearing aid in 1943.

With the advent of World War II, Zenith converted to wartime production, which included the manufacture of radar and communications equipment.

It began marketing its first line of

Top: *Current Zenith Radio Canada Ltd. facility is located on Islington Avenue in Etobicoke.*
Middle: *Cable television de-coders, essential to today's TV viewing, are assembled on Zenith's Canadian manufacturing line.*
Bottom: *Zenith television sets, among the best in the world, in a showroom for dealers.*

black-and-white television receivers in 1948, two years after the resumption of civilian production, and introduced its consumer electronics products to Canada in 1958.

Though Zenith had demonstrated colour television as early as 1953, it did not introduce its first sets to the market until 1961, when it believed it had solved maintenance and repair problems associated with early television receivers. Its late entry into the then-burgeoning market did not prevent it moving rapidly to a position of leadership in the field.

The explosive growth of colour TV made it necessary for the company to expand its production facilities in Chicago, and in 1967 it opened a new plant in Springfield, Missouri (where, by 1982, it had consolidated all colour television final assembly).

Continuing Zenith research and development resulted in the commercial introduction in 1969 of the Chromacolor picture tube, described by Zenith engineers as the most important advance in the display of colour pictures on large screens since the introduction of the colour TV. The new tube design provided a picture that was brighter and had greater contrast than any previous colour reproduction.

In 1978, Zenith introduced its System 3 colour TV which incorporated a new modular chassis, a new picture tube, and automatic colour control.

In 1980, Zenith researchers combined telephone and television technology to produce what it calls Space Phone. The device allows TV viewers to place and receive telephone calls through the TV receiver.

In 1981 it introduced a new line of home entertainment products — Video Hi-Tech — including a unique 45-inch diagonal television projection system, new colour TV receiver/monitors, video cassette recorders, and other video products. It also announced plans to phase out its radio and stereo business to place greater emphasis on video, computers, cable television and other new high-technology business areas.

Zenith's Video Hi-Tech products proved so successful the company again expanded the line in 1982 with a component video system, which makes it possible to custom-build a home video system in much the same way as a stereo system.

For 1984, the company introduced an advanced System 3 line called 'Smart Sets,' as well as adding again to its Video Hi-Tech products.

Zenith believes it is well positioned to serve an expanding Canadian market with a series of quality high-technology consumer and business products, and that its business, headquartered in Ontario, will continue to grow with the country.

It places great importance on its loyal and experienced dealer network, as well as on the fact that Canadians who have experienced Zenith's quality electronic products continue to express strong 'pride of ownership' in them.

ACKNOWLEDGEMENTS

When Ontarians, during the summer of 1982, were invited by the provincial government to celebrate the 1984 bicentennial birthday party, The U.E.L. Association of Canada responded by announcing its intentions to publish *Loyal She Remains*. In less than eighteen months, this first ever comprehensive history of Ontario was born, a testimony to teamwork rarely matched anywhere and to the total dedication and immense energy of William Koene, Publication Co-ordinator, whose devotion to the project was a constant inspiration to those associated with this bicentennial production.

To The Right Honourable Roland Michener and The Honourable Eugene Forsey, distinguished Canadians who kindly volunteered to write the Foreword and the Preface respectively, the editors express wholehearted thanks for their generous support.

Additionally, to the more than twenty authors who have submitted chapters, the editors recognize that without their commitment, this historical volume would not have been possible.

Over the last year, the editors have attempted to compile a comprehensive list of those who have assisted in this project. Two alphabetical lists have been compiled – one recognizing individuals, the other institutions. Hopefully, no one has gone unrecognized. To all of them, the editors are grateful!

Alexandra Adams, John Coldwell Adams, Tony Adamson, Jack Allen, Robert S. Allen, Ed Anderson, Mr. James Anderson, Bill Angley, Mr. and Mrs. Wilf Anthony, Robert L. Armstrong, Bob Atkinson, Gil Baker, Barbara Bartley, Ted Bartram, Fern Bayer, Norman Best, The Honourable Margaret Birch, M.P.P., Dr. Michael Bird, Mrs. Elizabeth Blair, Mrs. Judith Bohnen, Walter Borosa, Robert Bowes, Gerald E. Boyce, Lydia Boyko, Dr. Fred Branscombe, Heather Broadbent, Don Brown (C.B.C.), Ken Brown, Dr. Mavis Burke, Ruth Burritt, C. Lorne Butler, Mrs. Loveday Cadenhead, Lou Cahill, Susan Campbell, C.A. John Cappelli, Dr. J.M.S. Careless, Dr. Adrian Ten Cate, Sir Arthur Chetwynd, Mrs. Jean Murray Cole, Lyn Cole, Lt. Col. A. Frank Cooper, Russell Cooper, Mrs. Katrin Cooper, Les Corbin, Gerald M. Craig. Michael Crawford, John Crosthwaite, Paul Crouch, Sam Cureatz, M.P.P., Jill Cuthbertson, Jo Daly, Marguerite R. Dow, Wendy Doy, Mr. and Mrs. Everett Drake, Dennis Duffy, Dorothy Duncan, Rev. Stewart East, Al Emerson, Jean L'Esperance, Wendy Evans, David Faux, Ina Ferguson, Mr. and Mrs. Robert Fleming, Celia Franca, John Foster, Kathy Garside, Arthur Gelber, Naomi Goldie, Chris Graham, Kelly Green, John Grimshaw, Paula Groenberg, Donna Guglielmin, Pamela Hancock, David Hannah, Mr. and Mrs. John Harbinson, Mrs. Hilton Macdonald Hassell, Ida Hewett, R. Melville Hill, Mary Howarth, Major The Rev. Donald Howson, Suzanne Hughes, Dr. and Mrs. Charles M. Humber, Gayle Humber, Karyn Anna Humber, George Hunter, F.E. Ibey, Bea Johnson, George and Mary Ann Kamphuis, Calvin Katz, Fiona Keith, Martha Kidd, Grace Koene, Piet Koene, Simon and Bep Kort, Robert Lansdale, Eula Lapp, Lorrie Leblanc, Julien Lebourdais, Nick Ledwidge, Dr. and Mrs. Gordon Leggett, John Lunau, Thomas McCabe, Peter McGarvey, Kathy McKay (Frederick Varley Estate), Jocelyn M. McKillop (Hudson's Bay House, Winnipeg), The Lord Maclean, Gerry McMartin, Kenneth McNaught, Bill McNeil (C.B.C.), Hugh MacMillan, Nelson and Dorrine Macnab, Ken Macpherson, Earl and Countess of Malmesbury (Basingstoke, Hants., England), Mr. and Mrs. Arnold Matthews, Jim Matthews, Mr. and Mrs. Louis Mayzel, Cecelia Merkley, Steve Miller (New York), Mr. and Mrs. John Mitchele, Mr. and Mrs. John Mitchell, Professor Desmond Morton, Dr. Vernon Mould, R. Robert G. Mutrie III, Pauline Newman, Michael Norton, Jennifer O'Rourke, Steve Otto, Marion Parker, Graham Patterson, George Pearce, Lillian Petroff, John Phillips, Kristina Potapezyk, Bernard Pothier, Terry Poulos, Arlene Powderly, Joan and John Powell, Joanne Powell, Elizabeth Price, Lorna Proctor, Dan Proctor, Martha-Anne Rankine, Roberts family (Westport), Donald A. Roberts, Sheila Robertson, Pat Rogal, Major General Richard Rohmer, Gerald Rogers (Montreal), Mrs. Anna Rolen (Miami), Professor and Mrs. H.U. Ross, Mr. and Mrs. Henry N. Ruttan, Lorne Ste. Croix, Tom Scanlon, Judy Schwartz, Dr. Ben Shek, Carol Wilton Siegel, Jean Simonton, John Smele, Felicity Nowell-Smith, Robert Snetsinger, Michael Stevenson, Col. and Mrs. David Macdonald Stewart (Montreal), Vic Suthren, Maia-Mari Sutnik, Len Swatridge, Second Baron Thomson of Fleet, Carl Thorpe, Katherine Tyrrell, Bob and Joyce Vander Velde, Bill Vankoughnett, M.P., John Whebell, The Hon. John White, Betty Ann Van Wijk, Dr. J. Tuzo Wilson, Bill Yeager.

Academy of Medicine (Toronto), Archives of Ontario, Art Gallery of Hamilton, Art Gallery of Ontario, Borealis Press (Ottawa), Brockville District Historical Society, Canada Post Corporation, Canadian Opera Company, Christian Reformed Denominational Offices (Burlington), Confederation Life, Continental Public Relations, Dundurn Press, The Federation of Women Teachers' Association of Ontario, *The Globe and Mail,* Gooderham and Worts, Government of Ontario Art Collection, Governor Simcoe Branch, U.E.L., Harold Innis Foundation, Holy Blossom Temple, Imperial Oil Collection, Independent Order of Foresters, James Shaver Woodsworth Homestead Foundation, John Graves Simcoe Association, Jordan Museum of the Twenty, Law Society of Upper Canada, *London Free Press,* Macdonald-Stewart Foundation (Montreal), McClelland and Stewart Ltd., Masterfile, Metropolitan Toronto Library, Metropolitan Toronto and Region Conservation Authority, Miller Services Ltd., Monarchist League of Canada, Multicultural History Society of Ontario, Museum of Applied Military History, The National Ballet of Canada, National Gallery of Canada, National Museums of Canada, New York State Parks Commission, Niagara District Historical Society, Norfolk Historical Society Collection, Ontario Black History Society, Ontario Editorial Bureau, Ontario Heritage Foundation, Ontario Historical Society, Ontario Ministry of Citizenship and Culture, Ontario Ministry of Industry and Tourism, Ontario Ministry of Natural Resources, Ontario Ministry of Transportation and Communication, Ontario Secondary School Teachers' Federation, Ontario Track and Field Association, Osgoode Hall Archives, Parks Canada, The Parkwood Estate, Perth County Archives, Peterborough Centennial Museum, Public Archives of Canada, Queen's York Rangers, Roman Catholic Archdiocese of Toronto, Royal Canadian Air Force, Royal Canadian Military Institute, Royal Canadian Yacht Club, Royal Ontario Museum, Canadiana Department, Ryerson Polytechnical Institute, Toronto Board of Education, *The Toronto Star,* United States National Parks Service (Philadelphia), University of Toronto (Hart House), Women's Canadian Historical Society, Women's College Hospital.

PHOTO CREDITS

Chapter 1

2 OVL Simon and Robert Kort
4 Simon and Robert Kort
5 York University Department of Geography
6 National Gallery of Canada
7 Masterfile BM 5559 – Hans Blohm
8 Masterfile B 8532 – Bill Brooks
9 RT Metropolitan Toronto Library; RB Ontario Archives
10 LT John Powell; FLB Joan Powell; LB John Powell
11 Joan Powell
12 Charles J. Humber Collection
13 Ed Bartram
14 LT G.R.D. Fryer; FLB John Powell; LB Simon and Robert Kort
15 from Gourlay's *Statistical Account for Upper Canada*
16 York University Department of Geography
17 John Powell
18 L Joan Powell; FLB G.R.D. Fryer; LB G.R.D. Fryer
20 Masterfile – Mike Dobel
21 RT from Thad. Leavitt's *History of Leeds and Grenville* RB Joan Powell; FRB Simon and Robert Kort
22 L Ontario Heritage Foundation; FLB Charles J. Humber Collection; LB Charles J. Humber Collection
23 Charles J. Humber Collection
24 Ontario Ministry of Natural Resources
25 Ontario Ministry of Natural Resources

Chapter 2

26 OVL William Armstrong from *Canadian Illustrated News* – Charles J. Humber Collection
28 R. Melville Hill
29 RT Masterfile F2212 – John Foster; RB A.G. Ten Cate; RBC after Leechman; FRB after Leechman
30 Ontario Archives
31 RT Caroline Hayward, Charles J. Humber Collection; RB Ontario Archives; FRB Charles J. Humber Collection
32 LT Masterfile DL 1679 – Mike Dobel; FLB Charles J. Humber Collection; LB Charles J. Humber Collection
33 Charles J. Humber Collection
34 LT Charles J. Humber Collection; LC Charles J. Humber Collection; LB Charles J. Humber Collection
35 Independent Order of Foresters
36 Ontario Archives
37 John Powell
38 FLT Charles J. Humber Collection; FLB Charles J. Humber Collection
39 LT Public Archives of Canada – Phillip John Bainbridge; LB Charles J. Humber Collection

Chapter 3

40 OVL Masterfile – D4903 – Freeman Patterson
43 RT Royal Ontario Museum; FRB Metropolitan Toronto Library; RB Metropolitan Toronto Library
44 Paul Crouch
46 Charles J. Humber Collection
47 Brockville & District Historical Society
48 Metropolitan Toronto Library
49 Public Archives of Canada C-1664
51 J.D. Kelly, Charles J. Humber Collection
53 RT Humme; RB C.W. Jeffreys; FRB Public Archives of Canada C-1843
54 Metropolitan Toronto Library
55 Charles J. Humber Collection
56 Charles J. Humber Collection
57 RT Hudson's Bay Co. Archives, Winnipeg; RB Public Archives of Canada; FRB Public Archives of Canada C-5198
58 Public Archives of Canada
59 G.R.D. Fryer
60 Paul Crouch
61 Metropolitan Toronto Library

Chapter 4

62 OVL Masterfile B-15307 – Bill Brooks
64 Public Archives of Canada
65 Metropolitan Toronto Library
66 L Charles J. Humber Collection; LB Mary B. Fryer
67 Mary B. Fryer
68 Public Archives of Canada C-117699
69 The Macdonald-Stewart Foundation (Montreal)
70 LT Metropolitan Toronto Library; LB Metropolitan Toronto Library

Chapter 5

72 OVL Mary B. Fryer
74 FLT Metropolitan Toronto Library; LT Metropolitan Toronto Library; LB Charles J. Humber Collection
75 United States National Parks Service (Philadelphia)
76 The Lord Maclean
77 RT Mary B. Fryer; RB Charles J. Humber Collection, FRB Metropolitan Toronto Library
78 R. Melville Hill
79 Public Archives of Canada
80 LT Mary B. Fryer; LB Charles J. Humber Collection
81 Mary B. Fryer
82 Mary B. Fryer
83 Public Archives of Canada
84 Niagara District Historical Society
85 Public Archives of Canada
86 Public Archives of Canada
87 Metropolitan Toronto Library
89 R Robert Girard Carroon (Litchfield, Connecticut) and C. Lorne Butler; FRT Mary B. Fryer; FRB Charles J. Humber Collection; R Mary B. Fryer
90 Public Archives of Canada
91 Mary B. Fryer
92 Museum of Applied Military History
93 Niagara District Historical Society

Chapter 6

96 OVL Metropolitan Toronto Library
98 Charles J. Humber Collection
99 RT Confederation Life Collection – Rex Wood; RB Metropolitan Toronto Library
100 LT Public Archives of Canada; LB Public Archives of Canada
101 Mary B. Fryer
103 FRT Dundurn Press; RT Charles J. Humber Collection; RB Metropolitan Toronto Library
104 LT Charles J. Humber Collection; LB John Graves Simcoe Assoc.; FLB Metropolitan Toronto Library
105 Ontario Archives
106 Mary B. Fryer
107 RT Metropolitan Toronto Library; FRB Charles J. Humber Collection; FRB Confederation Life Collection – J.D. Kelly; RB Metropolitan Toronto Library
108 LT Charles J. Humber Collection; FLB The U.E.L. Association of Canada; LB Mary B. Fryer
109 Metropolitan Toronto Library
111 RT Confederation Life Collection – J.D. Kelly; FRB Charles J. Humber Collection; RB Metropolitan Toronto Library
112 LT Charles J. Humber Collection; LB Ontario Archives RB Ontario Plaque Inscription
114 LT Ontario Archives; LB Ontario Archives
117 RT Metropolitan Toronto Library; RB Ontario Archives
118 LT Charles J. Humber Collection; LB Charles J. Humber Collection
119 The U.E.L. Association of Canada
120 Metropolitan Toronto Library
121 Charles J. Humber Collection – C.W. Jeffreys
122 G.R.D. Fryer
123 Mrs. Elizabeth Blair
124 Ontario Heritage Fondation
125 G.R.D. Fryer
126 Mary B. Fryer
127 RT Mary B. Fryer; FRT Mary B. Fryer; RB Metropolitan Toronto Library; FRB Reproduced Courtesy Canada Post Corporation

Chapter 7

131 Canadiana Gallery – Royal Ontario Museum
133 Courtesy of the Earl & Countess of Malmesbury, Basingstoke, Hampshire, England
135 Courtesy of New York State Parks Commission
137 John Ross Robertson Collection, Metropolitan Toronto Library
139 National Museums of Canada – Canadian War Museum

Chapter 8

140 OVL Metropolitan Toronto Library
143 RT Women's Canadian Historical Society; RB Metropolitan Toronto Library; FRB G.R.D. Fryer
144 Public Archives of Canada
145 Charles J. Humber Collection
147 RT Metropolitan Toronto Library; FRT Metropolitan Toronto Library; RB The U.E.L. Association of Canada
148 LT Metropolitan Toronto Library; LB Ontario Archives
149 Metropolitan Toronto Library
150 Charles J. Humber Collection
151 RT Charles J. Humber Collection; FRT Mary B. Fryer; FRC Metropolitan Toronto Library; FRB Metropolitan Toronto Library; RB Metropolitan Toronto Library
152 Metropolitan Toronto Library
153 Metropolitan Toronto Library
154 Charles J. Humber Collection
155 RT Metropolitan Toronto Library; RTC Metropolitan Toronto Library; FRT Charles J. Humber Collection; RB Metropolitan Toronto Library
156 LT Charles J. Humber Collection; LB Lossing's *Field Book of The War 1812*
157 Ontario Archives
158 Charles J. Humber Collection
159 Metropolitan Toronto Library
160 LT Metropolitan Toronto Library; LB Ontario Archives
161 Women's Canadian Historical Society
162 Charles J. Humber Collection
163 Metropolitan Toronto Library
164 Charles J. Humber Collection

Chapter 9

168 OVL Masterfile – Janet Foster
170 The United Empire Loyalists' Association of Canada
171 RT Ontario Archives; RB Metropolitan Toronto Library
172 LT Public Archives of Canada; FL Metropolitan Toronto Library; ML Charles J. Humber Collection; LL Public Archives of Canada
173 Metropolitan Toronto Library
174 Metropolitan Toronto Library
175 RB Metropolitan Toronto Library
176 LT Ontario Archives; FLM Charles J. Humber Collection; LM Charles J. Humber Collection
177 Parks Canada
179 RT A.G. Ten Cate; RM Charles J. Humber Collection; FRM Bill Angley; RB A.G. Ten Cate; FRB Charles J. Humber Collection
180 Charles J. Humber Collection
181 Charles J. Humber Collection
182 Charles J. Humber Collection
183 RT Metropolitan Toronto Library; RM Charles J. Humber Collection; RB Royal Ontario Museum
184 Metropolitan Toronto Library
185 Metropolitan Toronto Library
187 RT Charles J. Humber Collection; RB A.G. Ten Cate
188 LT Ontario Ministry of Industry & Tourism; LM Charles J. Humber Collection; LB G.R.D. Fryer

Chapter 10

190 OVL Royal Ontario Museum – Canadiana Gallery
193 RT Royal Ontario Museum – Canadiana Gallery; FRT Markham District Historical Museum – John Lunau; RM Charles J. Humber Collection; FRM Charles J. Humber Collec-

527 RT Art Gallery of Ontario; RB University of Toronto, Hart House, Courtesy Frederick Varley Estate
528 FLT Canadian Women's Historical Society; LT G.R.D. Fryer; FLB Charles J. Humber Collection; LB Charles J. Humber Collection
529 RT G.R.D. Fryer, RB Masterfile V 2870–John de Visser
530 Professor and Mrs. H.R. Ross
531 R Art Gallery of Ontario; RB Charles J. Humber Collection
532 FLT Miller Services–Notman Studio; LB Charles J. Humber Collection; LT Women's Canadian Historical Society
533 RT Celia Franca; RB National Ballet Company of Canada, FRT Canadian Opera Company

Chapter 30

534 OVL National Gallery of Canada (Ottawa)
536 L and RB R. Melville Hill, courtesy Public Archives of Canada
537 RT R. Melville Hill, courtesy Public Archives of Canada
538 L and RT The United Empire Loyalists' Association of Canada; L and RB Courtesy Confederation Life
540 The Monarchist League of Canada
541 RT G.R.D. Fryer, RB Monarchist League of Canada
542 Jim Matthews
543 RT Charles J. Humber Collection; RB Charles J. Humber Collection
544 Mary B. Fryer
545 Public Archives of Canada
546 Loveday Cadenhead, courtesy The Canada Post Corporation
549 RT Public Archives of Canada; FRT Upper Canada College Archives; RB Christensen, *The Globe and Mail*
550 LT Ken Woolley, Monarchist League of Canada; RT Monarchist League of Canada–courtesy Hart House, University of Toronto Archives; LB Sara Joan Aggiss; RB G.R.D. Fryer
551 T Milne N. Hassell courtesy Monarchist League of Canada; LB Garry Toffoli, Monarchist League of Canada

Chapter 31

552 OVL Ontario Heritage Foundation
554 G.R.D. Fryer
555 RT James Shaver Woodsworth Homestead Foundation; RM Masterfile V 10177–John de Visser; FRM Masterfile DL 7708–Mike Dobel; RB Courtesy The Canada Post Corporation; FRB Charles J. Humber Collection
556 FLT Charles J. Humber Collection; LT Ontario Black History Society; FLB Ontario Ministry of Tourism and Recreation; LB G.R.D. Fryer
557 RT Canadian Women's Historical Society; FRT Charles J. Humber Collection; FRB Charles J. Humber Collection

INDEX

A

B

C

D

E

F

J

K

L

M

N

O

P

T

U

V

W

Y

Z